STEELHEAD
FLY FISHING

A steelhead so fresh from the sea I can see my hand through its fins. *Photo by Don Roberts.*

STEELHEAD
FLY FISHING

Trey Combs

ILLUSTRATIONS BY

LOREN SMITH

THE LYONS PRESS
Guilford, Connecticut
An imprint of The Globe Pequot Press

Black-and-white photography by B. J. Meiggs and Trey Combs

The Lyons Press is an imprint of The Globe Pequot Press.

First Lyons Press paperback edition—1999

Printed in the United States of America

10 9 8 7 6 5 4 3 2

Library of Congress has cataloged
the hardcover edition as follows:

Combs, Trey.
Steelhead fly fishing / Trey Combs : illustrations by Loren Smith.
p.   cm.
Includes bibliographical references and index.
ISBN 1-55821-119-5 (cl)
1. Steelhead fishing. 2. Fly fishing. I. Title.
SH687.7.C65 1991
799.1'755—dc20   91-23638
CIP

ISBN 1-55821-903-X (pb)

Color fly plate photography by Paul Boyer

Typesetting by Fisher Composition, Inc.

T O

VINCE AND BUNNY COMBS

CONTENTS

Acknowledgments xi

PART I ❏ TACKLE AND TECHNIQUES

1 STEELHEAD 3

2 TACKLE NOTES 11

3 EQUIPMENT NOTES 35

4 FLY DRESSING NOTES 43

5 HOLDING WATER 51

6 PRESENTATION 56

PART II ❏ THE GREAT RIVERS

7 KLAMATH RIVER 81

8 ROGUE RIVER 91

9 NORTH UMPQUA RIVER 109

10 DESCHUTES RIVER 130

11 CLEARWATER RIVER 145

12 NORTH FORK STILLAGUAMISH RIVER 169

13 SKYKOMISH RIVER 181

14 SKAGIT RIVER 191

15 STAMP RIVER 209

16 THOMPSON RIVER 219

17 DEAN RIVER 229

18 BULKLEY RIVER 245

19 KISPIOX RIVER 259

20 BABINE RIVER 267

21 SUSTUT RIVER 279

PART III ❑ THE ANGLERS AND THEIR FLY PATTERNS

22 FRANK AMATO 293

23 JIM GARRETT 295

24 ALEC JACKSON 305

25 LES JOHNSON 311

26 WALT JOHNSON 315

27 RANDALL KAUFMANN 321

28 HARRY LEMIRE 327

29 MIKE MAXWELL 335

30 BILL McMILLAN 339

31 DAVE McNEESE 345

32 GARY MILTENBERGER 355

33 BILL SCHAADT 359

34 COLLIN SCHADRECH 369

35 JIM TEENY 371

36 LANI WALLER 375

37 BOB YORK 379

38 NEW STEELHEAD FLY PATTERNS 385

39 TRADITIONAL STEELHEAD FLY PATTERNS 473

Bibliography 482

Index 485

COLOR SECTION FOLLOWS PAGE 462.

ACKNOWLEDGMENTS

U P O N completing *Steelhead Fly Fishing and Flies* nearly fifteen years ago, I expected never to write another book on steelhead. This was not because I thought that work represented the last word on the subject—I had simply exhausted all I wished to say and felt that the book would prove sufficient to bring some definition to a sport that had only a modest following. Knowledgeable anglers and fine writers could fill in the details.

Book sales documented for me the steady growth of steelhead fly fishing. Some American and Canadian rivers became as well known internationally as the rivers of Atlantic salmon fame. New lodges sprang up on wilderness rivers and guiding businesses devoted exclusively to steelhead fly fishing were established on both summer and winter rivers. I saw the emergence of talented young fly tyers who put me and most of my generation to shame. Scottish spey flies, accurate in every historical detail, were fished for steelhead. Rods to cast them grew longer and lighter. A re-evaluation of hatchery programs and the preservation of native races of steelhead—particularly in British Columbia—were nurtured by these angling attentions.

As the sport matured, our finest rivers became institutions of specialization, each with an angling history, optimal seasons for native runs, trusted techniques, favored steelhead patterns, and local experts who gave it a distinct flavor. Steelhead fly fishers appreciated the differences and became connoisseurs of particular rivers and their steelhead.

The sport had grown multifaceted, and, in my mind, a new kind of book began to take shape. I wanted to tell about steelhead and how they are often attracted to the fly, and to do so through the cultural ambiance of our great rivers. As a practical matter, the story could only be told with the cooperation of our finest steelhead fly fishers, many of whom I knew personally, but whom I also knew to be guarded, if not outright secretive. I wanted to create a photographic record of the project. Ralph Wahl's *Come Wade the River* would become my inspiration and, literally, the focus for BJ Meiggs. The number of rivers would have to be very limited in order to avoid the book becoming a travel guide and thus exploiting the very rivers I was seeking to protect. Because of the finite dynamics of conservation issues, I wanted to complete the book in four years. This would require leaves from my job so that I could be on the rivers and writing at least two hundred days each year.

The anglers proved enormously cooperative. Each was patient with my endless requests for his fishing time, flies, custom lines, and methods of presentation. They were my companions during these years and they provided my best memories of the project. Those who became the subject of a book chapter and to whom I am especially indebted are: Frank Amato, Jim Garrett, Alec Jackson, Les Johnson, Walt Johnson, Randall Kaufmann, Harry Lemire, Mike and Denise Maxwell, Bill McMillan, Dave McNeese, Gary Miltenberger, Bill Schaadt, Collin Schadrech, Jim and Donna Teeny, Lani Waller, and Bob York.

Many other talented fly fishers inspired in me a special appreciation for their rivers and their skills at the vise: Bob Aid, Bill Alspach, Bob Arnold, Walt Balek, Ron Beitelspacher, Dennis Black, Dick Blewett, Wally and Carol Booth, Bob Borden, Steve Brocco, Mike Brooks, Mark Canfield, Clay Carter, Bob Clay, Doc Crawford, Mike Craig, Glenn Cruickshank, Bobby Cunningham, Fay Davis, Albert De-Bernardi, Raelene DeBernardi, Dick Van Demark, Danny Diaz, Brian Douglas, Ken Driedger, Doug Fagerness, Dennis Farnworth, John Farrar, Sean Gallagher, Steve Gobin, Rusty Gore, Jorge Graziozi, Jimmy Green, Tim Grenvik, Loren Grey, Dawn Grytness, Dave Hall, Merle Hargis, Don Hathaway,

Lani Waller casts a Waller Waker on British Columbia's Skeena River.

John Harder, John Hazel, Daryl Hodson, Roland Holmberg, Joe and Bonnie Howell, Cliff Hunter, LeRoy Hyatt, Bob Hull, Jimmy Hunnicutt, Brad Jackson, Joan Kennady, Mike Kinney, Mel Krieger, Craig Lannigan, Jimmy LeMert, Arthur J. Lingren, Lynn "Radar" Miller, Mel Leven, John Mathews, Richie Montella, Frank Moore, John Mintz, Gordon Nash, Bob Nauheim, Rick Nelson, Mark Noble, Scott Noble, Billy Pate, Gene Parmeter, Tom Pero, Bob Pierce, Mark Pinch, Dan Reiff, Don Roberts, Salty Saltzman, Joe Saracione, Tony Sarp, David Shoff, Carl J. Sieracki, Mark Spence, Randy Stetzer, Keith Stonebreaker, Jim Vincent, Ralph Wahl, Bob Wagoner, Olga Walker, Stew Wallace, Jerry Wells, Paul Weyland, Judd Wickwire, Jimmy Wright, Jim and Sharon Van Loan, Bob Veverka, and Stan Young.

Fishery biologists from state and provincial agencies provided the wealth of information, including unpublished studies, that I needed in order to document the races of steelhead. I am especially indebted to the following people for their invaluable assistance: James S. Hopelain, California Department of Fish and Game; Tom Satterthwaite, Mick Jennings, Brian Johanson, and Eric Olson, Oregon Department of Fish and Wildlife; Keith Kiler, Steve Petit, and Bert Bowlin, Idaho Department of Fish and Game; Curt Kraemer and Bob Forbes, Washington Department of Game; Eric Beamer, Skagit System Cooperative; Dr. David W. Narver, Steve Cox Rogers, Bob Hooton, Jack Leggett, Dennis Wilders, Gerhardt Trolitsch, John Cartwright, Ian McGregor, Brian Chan, and Al Caverly, Fishery Branch, Ministry of Environment, British Columbia.

My thanks to George Cook of Sage and to Bruce Richards of Scientific Anglers for much needed technical advice. Tom Rosenbauer of Orvis and Les Johnson, editor of *Canoe* magazine, provided wise counsel at critical times in the course of my writing. Bill Keep, Western Washington University, and Dale Edmonds, Portland Community College, read drafts, made corrections, offered suggestions, and reminded me how far this fly fisher had wandered from the English language.

I was fortunate to work with Paul Boyer, a Port Townsend, Washington, photographer with a well-deserved national reputation. His expertise is evident in the fly plates, both color and black-and-white, that illustrate this book. Niki Thane retouched photographs and kept a careful record of negatives. Linda Townsend brought out from the black-and-white negatives their fullest potential.

Ralph Wahl searched his marvelous photographic record to make available photographs of many legendary Washington steelhead fly fishers.

Additional photographs of historical value were provided to me by the following: Alanna Fisher, Curator at The American Museum of Fly Fishing; Theresa Cowen, Editorial Assistant at *Field & Stream;* and Vin Sparano, Editor of *Outdoor Life.* Bob Arnold, Dan Reiff, and Mary Randlett are Washington friends whose rare photographs filled gaps in my story.

I found in Loren Smith's graphite illustrations the perfect transition from photograph to printed page. His work filled a year, each drawing the product of discussion and planning, each commissioned separately, each a portrait from life.

My special thanks to BJ Meiggs, whose editing brought order to my writing and who spent years wandering river bars in search of many of the photographs that illustrate this book.

My final acknowledgment must be for Nick Lyons, my editor and publisher, who patiently listened to my wishes and concerns. Far from growing fainthearted, he encouraged me to write and assemble the book I imagined. He can never fully appreciate what that meant to me.

STEELHEAD
FLY FISHING

Harry Lemire presents a Golden Edge Orange on Washington's Skagit River.

PART ONE

TACKLE
AND
TECHNIQUES

For several generations, steelhead fly fishers cast silk lines with cane rods and generally left the winter rivers to baitcasters. Thus the steelhead celebrated in fly-fishing literature were summer fish. Discoveries of their rivers began with the Eel in the 1890s and continued north until forty years ago, when a handful of anglers began sampling the wonders of the Skeena, Nass, Stikine, and Taku watersheds, deep in the wilderness of British Columbia and Alaska.

The introduction of lead-core shooting heads during the 1950s had anglers taking a second look at winter rivers. Led by Myron Gregory, Bill Schaadt, and Grant King, Californians made the Russian and Gualala famous fly waters.

Winter steelhead fly fishing grew in popularity throughout the Northwest. As anglers cultivated a taste for two-handed rods, developments in sinking lines expanded angling opportunities, winter and summer, and made new rivers of old favorites.

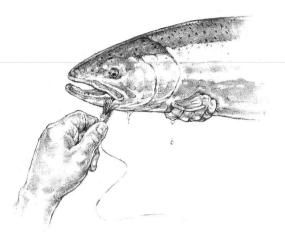

STEELHEAD

       I hold the steelhead as firmly as I dare, a hand around the wrist of her tail, while my fingers, stiff with cold, free the Winter Orange of its hold. Thickly silvered gill plates rise and fall as she gasps and flushes the faint currents. Plainly, she is stressed, but shock does not cloud her brilliance. I judge that in a minute her recovery will be complete, and her focus will turn to escape. To restrain her then would be a threat to her survival. I must hurry about my business.

  "Where have you been?" I ask, curiosity mixed with wonderment. What collaboration of instincts, what fusion of natural forces sends a hundred smolts to sea and returns to me this single adult? Beyond her own good fortune, what special traits for survival has she brought back for the next generation? Her ocean world is alien to me, and she carries few messages hinting of her past. But these have grown into the small understandings that fill me with admiration for her spirit and wandering ways—characteristics at the core of my romance with this gamefish, and why I am jubilant on this dreary winter day.

  She is in magnificent condition. But what else? I spread my arms. A tape measure isn't necessary to know that they span at least twelve pounds. Hatchery steelhead have clipped adipose fins, but hers is pristine and documents her wild origins. Her robust size strongly suggests three years of ocean growth beginning with a first summer moving ever farther north and west from the coast of Washington and into the Gulf of Alaska. Late the following spring, she migrated north to the Aleutians and at least as far west as the Hawaiian Islands, 160° west longitude. But how much farther? Across the International Date Line, 180°? To the very shores of Russia's Kamchatka Peninsula, 165° east longitude? Other American steelhead have traveled this far. In 1983, at 42°51' north latitude, 167°32' east longitude, a Japanese research vessel caught a hatchery steelhead, in its second high seas summer, that had been reared at Dworshak, on Idaho's Clearwater River, and released as a smolt below Bonneville Dam.

The ocean cooled in the fall and drove my steelhead south, until by winter she was feeding hundreds of miles off the Oregon coast. She passed most of her third winter beyond the continental shelf before leaving the ocean for the Strait of Juan de Fuca and Puget Sound. Then, amid conflicting smells from dozens of rivers and Washington's industrial sweat, she found the Skykomish, the river of her birth.

Though she is now sixty miles from salt water, her fins still possess the clear translucence of an ocean steelhead. A slight blush to her silver-grey flanks and an opaque darkening to the ventral edge of her tail testify to advancing sexual maturity. For ten days during early March, almost no measurable rain has fallen, and the few warm days did not raise the river with snowmelt. I think she held in various downriver lies for several weeks, moving along a few miles each day, perhaps five miles on an overcast morning. I look closely at her mouth, and the slight tear from my fly is the only mark. I note a thin, barely perceptible scarring forward of her dorsal fin. I turn her over and find the line continuing on the other side. Taiwanese high seas squid net? Possibly. Ocean steelhead have been found in water ranging in temperature from thirty-eight degrees to sixty degrees Fahrenheit, but rarely do they frequent ocean currents warmer than fifty-three degrees—water too cold to support squid. In recent years there has been disturbing evidence that some squid fleets are not even targeting squid but are running north to pirate the far more valuable stocks of salmon and steelhead. What of the Japanese mother-ship salmon fishery? According to catch records compiled by the North Pacific Fisheries Commission, nine thousand North American steelhead perished in their nets in 1989. Tens of thousands were caught in Canadian seine nets and gill nets the same year. Alaska and Washington fishermen find steelhead in their nets, too, though the law prevents them from admitting that fact. Perhaps on her maiden spawning run, she escaped from one of the Tulalip Indian gill nets set at tidewater on the lower river, the Snohomish. A scale sample would tell if she had ever spawned before, but that would not necessarily explain this old wound. I know that she is an international traveler whose survival at sea becomes less certain each year.

The flank now turned to me reveals a pectoral fin slightly nubbed. A bite from an estuary sculpin when she was a smolt? A more recent attack from a seal? When I carefully turn her over, both pectoral fins row about for equilibrium, a sure sign that she is ready to be upright and on her way. Her eyes roll up, roll down, and look back at me. She remains docile, but she has collected herself. She seems to say, "Get on with it!" I have a few seconds left.

This steelhead and I met when she rose to my fly from a soft lie below me. She took my line and a hundred feet of backing to the far side of the river, jumped twice, and then turned downriver with the heavy currents that swept below the blackberry-covered bank. I panted along behind, letting her have her head, palming the reel only hard enough to prevent an overrun, and when she stopped I began moving her across the river with the two-handed rod. She came easily at first, but turned and moved well out into the river each time I tried to bring her into the shallows. When she could no longer maintain her balance, I eased her in until her flanks barely brushed the submerged gravel bar and then ran to her side while stripping line from the reel.

We met because she crossed thousands of ocean miles to negotiate this narrow corridor of freshwater currents. In four to six weeks she would spawn, but the odds of any three-year ocean steelhead returning to spawn a second time are remote. These few minutes become our first and only meeting, and I always find in that bittersweet fact the ultimate wildness of these remarkable creatures. Once you have caught a steelhead you can't go back to the river and say, "This is where my steelhead lives," for the fish of your memory may be ten miles upstream or thousands of miles offshore, near lands you'll never know. That she can live out her life in the ocean so tugs at my imagination that I could never consciously be an impediment to it. I turn her out into the river and open my hands. She swims off easily, holds for a moment to get her bearings, and then steadily blends with the stream bottom. I am still straining to make her out when I realize she is gone and the mystery of her whereabouts has been resumed.

To make polite conversation, acquaintances who know of my interest in steelhead fly fishing sometimes ask me, "What exactly is a steelhead?" To help them conceptualize the basic elements of the fish's life, I give a dishonest answer. I explain that a steelhead is a rainbow trout that goes to sea, but that it comes back to the river of its birth to spawn. This usually satisfies, because only a goldfish is better known to the public than a "rainbow trout." I have occasionally tried to be more truthful and said that a rainbow trout is actually a resident steelhead, but this explanation can't stand on its own. I must go on to explain that the steelhead is more or less marine, and that resident rainbows will not migrate to sea even if they have the access to do so. They are the same species, but different forms of that same species. I cite examples until my listener can no longer make sense of it.

Trying to "make sense of it," trying to group the earth's plants and animals by associated characteristics is a science called taxonomy, while the rules that decide what a life is to be named are embodied in the international code of zoological nomenclature. Each species of animal and plant known to science has a genus and species name, a system of binomial nomenclature always expressed in Latin. Humans, for example, are *Homo sapiens*.

When I was memorizing classification in college, kingdom to species, my biology professor explained that taxonomists could be divided into two groups, the "splitters," who found in the most insignificant differences reasons to name new species, and the "lumpers," who often supplanted several species names with a single name. A former species might become a subspecies, or be dropped altogether, and a subspecies might be elevated to species status. Because the discoverer of a new species could attach his own name as the species, and thus gain some degree of scientific immortality, no little professional jealousy attended the wars between the two groups.

When I began reading about trout and salmon, I realized that the late nineteenth century was the Golden Age of splitters, for a new species of trout was thought to inhabit nearly every major watershed and more than a few lakes. In David Starr Jordan and Barton Warren Evermann's *American Food and Game Fishes* (Doubleday, Page and Company, 1923), thirty-three species of trout are described under "The Trout of Western America." A few of these were remarkably esoteric. The "spotted trout of Lake Southerland," (*Salmo jordani*), the "salmon trout of Lake Southerland," (*Salmo declivifrons*), and the "speckled trout of Crescent Lake," (*Salmo crescentis*) are three examples from Lake Sutherland and Lake Crescent in Washington's Olympic Peninsula. I have caught all three "species." The "spotted trout" is a race of cutthroat, while the other two are rainbow trout, locally called blueback trout and Beardsley trout, and look very much like steelhead.

These three trout illustrate the confusion that resulted when numerous local names became part of the angler's lexicon. "Spotted," "speckled," "blueback," "brook," and "silver" were indiscriminately applied to several species of trout and char.

Insofar as the steelhead trout is concerned, the taxonomists were on shaky ground from the very beginning. Sir John Richardson described for science the first new species of trout in western North America. This discovery was based on a premigrant steelhead sent to him in 1833 by Dr. Gairdner, a physician with the Hudsons Bay Company at Fort Vancouver, on the Columbia River. When Richardson published *Fauna Boreali Americana* in 1836, he placed the trout in the genus *Salmo* and honored its discoverer by naming the species *gairdneri*, giving it the common name, Gairdner's salmon. In 1855, Dr. William P. Gibbons, founder of the California Academy of Sciences, identified a "new" species of trout, based on premigrant steelhead secured from San Leandro Creek. These trout were given the scientific name *Salmo iridea* (later *irideus*), literally "rainbow trout." Many other species of rainbow trout followed, most notably those trout of the Shasta River (*Salmo shasta*), and trout in the lakes tributary to the Fraser and upper Columbia rivers, the Kamloops trout (*Salmo kamloops*).

The lumpers soon weighed in against this proliferation of trout species. Early on, they understood that Dr. Gairdner and Dr. Gibbons had described the same species. One of the rules of nomenclature is the rule of priority, in which whoever adequately describes the species first will be granted the only scientifically valid name. Because Dr. Gairdner's discovery preceded Dr. Gibbons's by nineteen years, the steelhead became known as *Salmo gairdneri*.

The residential races of rainbow proved more troublesome. Because of their physical appearance and residential habits, they were easily separated from steelhead. Furthermore, many lived in reproductive isolation, not spawning with steelhead, even when the two fish occupied the same river. But the reduction of species generally increased the range of *Salmo irideus*, the rainbow trout, again because of the rule of priority. What began as a pecking away at less-than-earth-shattering discoveries of new species of trout and a cleaning up of obvious ambiguities, ended more than a generation ago with the elimination of all species of rainbow trout except one, *Salmo gairdneri* (some populations were granted subspecies status). Two common names survived and pretty much meant the same thing to fly fishermen. "Steelhead" referred to anadromous populations, and "rainbow" to resident populations, whether residing in lakes or streams. Anglers said they were fishing for Kamloops rainbows, Shasta rainbows, Deschutes redside rainbows, and so forth, and never strayed far from the scientific nomenclature.

Concurrently, stricter guidelines were applied to "species" of brown and cutthroat trout. The members of *Salmo* with full species citizenship suddenly decreased in number, most notably from the standpoint of North American anglers, the Atlantic salmon, and the brown, cutthroat, rainbow, and golden trout.

About this time, steelhead and salmon stocks from the Pacific Coast were successfully transplanted to rivers tributary to the Great Lakes. The forage-rich lakes became the fish's ocean, and their spawning runs up Michigan, New York, and Canadian rivers became heralded events. Anglers adopted West Coast steelheading customs and jargon with equal zeal. Suddenly, "steelhead" were everywhere. The question, "What is a steelhead?" now had different implications.

I have no experience with Great Lakes steelhead. I've caught lake-run rainbows from rivers tributary to Alaska's Lake Iliamna and from the waters of Chile's Lake District. To my eye, the trout were very similar to ocean steelhead. I have no quarrel with calling these, or any other lake-dwelling rainbow trout, steelhead. For me, a steelhead will always be a creature of the ocean that returns to its natal rivers to spawn. If "steelhead" is to be applied to steelhead stocks that have only a freshwater life history, then "land-locked steelhead" would, I feel, be more appropriate.

However its individual membership has been made known, *Salmo* was salmon and trout in sea-run and landlocked forms, Old World and New, gamefish and habitat of variety sufficient to satisfy every angling passion. It had given birth to a wealth of literature that grounded my fly fishing and civilized it with a measure of rules. Arthur Wood, George Kelson, Roderick Haig-Brown, and a hundred others are in my tackle, in the pattern I knot on, in the very tempo of my fishing. Without this tradition, my steelhead fly fishing would be little more than exercise without recreation, a sport without mystique.

My belief that we all worshipped at the same altar, *Salmo*, was knocked asunder in 1989, when I read an announcement by the American Fisheries Society's Committee on Names of Fishes. The trout species naturally indigenous to western North America and the northern Pacific Ocean drainages, the rainbow, cutthroat, golden, Apache, Mexican golden, and Gila would no longer have the generic name of *Salmo*. Henceforth, these species would be classed as *Oncorhynchus*, the genera of Pacific salmon. The Atlantic salmon and brown trout remained *Salmo*. My steelhead, *Salmo gairdneri*, a name fixed in Northwest history, became the incomprehensible and largely unpronounceable *Oncorhynchus mykiss*.

I greeted this with disbelief and consternation. Pacific salmon died after spawning. The United States and British Columbia managed salmon as a food fish. A steelhead and an Atlantic salmon were closely related in literature. I saw them as cousins, a romantic notion doubtless imbued by the crosspollination of fly dressings and methods of presentation invited by the two gamefish. My favorite resident trout, rainbow and brown, lived together in angling harmony in rivers far from their native origins. To link a golden trout with a chinook salmon seemed hopelessly misguided. Of course, none of this mattered to the taxonomists.

They based their decision on a more complete discovery and interpretation of fossil records. The common ancestor of today's trout and salmon lived some 20 million years ago. A major branching split this family into a North Atlantic population that led directly to the Atlantic salmon and the brown trout, and a Pacific population. The Pacific group split again about 10 million years ago, one group becoming western trout, the other Pacific salmon. Because taxonomists seek evolutionary relationships upon which to base their classifications, the decision to place western trout with Pacific salmon was logical. Other lines of comparative scientific investigation such as chromosome counts, DNA, and electrophoretic analysis of proteins support the findings of the paleoichthyologists. Outward habits and general appearance aside, the trout of western North America and eastern Russia have more physical characteristics in common with Pacific salmon than with Atlantic trout and salmon.

In 1792, Johann Walbaum described five species of North Pacific salmon, the Dolly Varden char, and the rainbow trout found in Russia's Kamchatka Peninsula. He named the rainbow *Salmo mykiss* the species a transliteration of the Russian. Investigators have now clearly established that *S. mykiss* and *S. gairdneri* are identical. When the generic name was changed to *Oncorhynchus*, the species name *mykiss* was retained because it predated *gairdneri* and thus had priority.

If nothing else, the tempest in this nomenclatorial teapot has focused attention on the eastern coast of Russia's Kamchatka Peninsula, where steelhead are locally abundant from the Penzhina to the Bol'shaya rivers. (Steelhead are also known to ascend rivers on the west coast of the Kamchatka, south of the Ozernaya River, and a few continental rivers that enter the Okhotsk Sea.) I am not alone in hoping to visit the area and cast a fly to these Asian steelhead. The Russians know about their steelhead, though not as a gamefish. That is sure to change. Sophisticated studies contrast the physical differences of steelhead in the various watersheds. Steelhead are known to reach a length of at least ninety centimeters, or about thirty-five and a half inches. In the next decade, rivers such as the Kamchatka, the Yuka, and the Bol'shaya may become as well known as the Dean and the Babine, while the clan of steelhead fly fishers will include members who extol the virtues of the Purple Peril and Green-Butt Skunk with a Slavic accent. Thoughts of waking a "Bol'shaya Bomber" down a Kamchatka river makes *Oncorhynchus* seem much more fraternal—and the loss of *Salmo* a little more palatable!

The steelhead of western North America ascend cold water rivers from Cook Inlet off Anchorage, Alaska, to the Big Sur coast south of San Francisco. Their range once extended south to rivers in Baja California del Norte. Loss of Mexican and southern California steelhead was due to the partial-to-complete loss of their spawning rivers to myriad urban and rural uses.

This range contains hundreds of rivers and thousands of spawning tributaries, the steelhead dividing into two seasonal populations. The summer-run return from March until November and do not spawn until the following winter, while the more common winter-run steelhead ascend rivers from November and December, when they are still quite immature sexually, to April and May, when they are ready to spawn almost immediately. An overlap of the two seasonal races on the same river is uncommon, but does occur. An example is Washington's North Fork of the Stillaguamish, where each May a few fresh winter steelhead join a strong run of summer fish with Skamania hatchery origins. The majority of rivers have only summer-run or only winter-run, but many have both, while a very few rivers, such as Washington's Kalama and Oregon's Siletz, have fresh steelhead ascending every month of the year.

In California, newly hatched steelhead fry remain stream residents for at least a year, sometimes two years. In the northern reaches of the steelhead's spawning range, the rivers are colder and less fertile, and growth rates are slower. Young steelhead, the parr, typically occupy a stream for three, four, and even five years before smolting and migrating to sea.

Adult steelhead remain at sea for one to five years before returning to the rivers of their birth to spawn for the first time. The exception is the so called half-pounders of northern California and southern Oregon that smolt in the spring, migrate to sea, and return that fall—but not to spawn. On successive spawning migrations to their rivers, these little steelhead will have remained at sea for only a few months. They are more nearly residential than any other steelhead and contrast sharply with Washington's spring-run winter steelhead, which are almost entirely marine.

Where steelhead go while at sea has been the subject of increasing concern by state and federal agencies, the little information available compiled by the International North Pacific Fisheries Commission for member nations: Japan, the United States, Canada, and the Soviet Union.

Kate Meyers is the Project Leader of the High Seas Salmon Study that was funded by the National Marine Fisheries Service. Two published studies have resulted from this research: *High Seas Distribution of North American Steelhead as Evidenced by Recoveries of Marked or Tagged Fish*, Jeffrey T. Light, Susan Fowler, and Michael L. Dahlberg, September, 1988; and *Ocean Distribution and Migration of Steelhead*, Jeffrey T. Light, Colin K. Harris, and Robert L. Burgner, September, 1989. These studies had been submitted to the International North Pacific Fisheries Commission when I spoke with Kate Meyers in July, 1990. Information gathered on the distribution of steelhead stocks on the high seas was based on the recovery of coded plastic tags from steelhead tagged on the high seas and later caught in inland waters, and from smolts fin-clipped or carrying a microscopic coded wire tag in their heads. Investigators determined that U.S. and Canadian steelhead stocks mix as far west as 165° east longitude, waters on the Soviet doorstep. No steelhead tagged on the high seas were recovered in a Kamchatka River. No conclusions were drawn from this information, but investigators thought that Asian steelhead may not be so wide ranging as their North American counterparts. Neither have high seas research vessels recovered any steelhead known to possess a half-pounder cycle. Kate Meyers felt that in North America, these steelhead must remain on continental shelf waters during those few months they are marine fish. At least, three months is inadequate for them to enter into the north-south, east-west migratory cycle that would take them to the Aleutians and back to the coasts of California and Oregon. Even less is known of the Asian half-pounder. It is now thought that their ocean migration is localized, very much on the order of sea-run cutthroat, and probably similar to American half-pounders. I asked Meyers whether she had noted any separation of migratory habits based on watershed origins. Specifically, do the huge steelhead of the Skeena watershed migrate to a particular forage-rich part of the ocean that promotes rapid growth? She thought not. "We have looked at it from all sorts of angles, and there just seems to be a general mixing from all rivers."

Over the millennia, rivers generate environmental stresses sufficiently severe to produce "races" or populations of steelhead with physical characteristics easily as contrasting as the many resident races of rainbow trout. Whether this process of natural selection is ongoing or reflects conditions that existed long ago remains, of course, speculation. But anyone who has looked into the Fraser River canyon or the great falls on the lower Dean knows why the steelhead that ascend these barriers are so extraordinarily strong.

Most physical characteristics are less celebrated but equally sublime. Klamath half-pounders number in the tens of thousands and may be little more than a foot long. A few miles north, steelhead of twenty pounds are caught each season in the Smith. Kispiox steelhead are famous for their mass and weight; males average nearly twenty pounds. Morice River steelhead occupy the same watershed and are quite average in size. Oregon's Rogue steelhead spend most of their lives migrating up and down the river. Some of Washington's Skagit steelhead are gone for five years before returning to spawn but once. Winter steelhead ascending in late spring may immediately spawn just above tidewater. Salmon River steelhead migrate over eight dams and though great mountain ranges, climb six thousand feet, and travel nine hundred miles to reach their Idaho spawning grounds, an odyssey that takes months.

Thus the question, "What is a steelhead?" has many answers. A taxonomist would answer one way, a fishery biologist another. To a fly fisherman, the answer would reflect a certain time of year on a favorite river with a race of steelhead that for reasons of personal prejudice are presented a fly in a specific manner. As often as not, the dressing will be unique, a creation divined by the angler himself, and when a steelhead rises to the offering, the fly takes on a life and a reputation. This is such a spiritual bonding that a river's steelhead cannot long be discussed without describing the fly that attracted them.

I have fished for steelhead on the Navarro, a valley cathedral in the California redwoods, and picked out my lies through blazing shafts of light. I have cast my flies into the gloom of an early morning rain forest deep in the Olympic Peninsula. I have seen steelhead race for my low-water Night Dancer on Oregon's Deschutes when the desert shimmered in hundred-degree heat and the water temperature was sixty-eight degrees. I have taken comfort in my neoprenes during a Skykomish winter when ice rimed the shore, the water temperature dipped to thirty-seven degrees, and a steelhead came hard to my Admiral Spey. I have flown into the Dean and the Sustut by helicopter and fought great Thompson steelhead just below the exhaust level of passing cars and trucks. I have reached favorite pools by bush plane, rubber raft, jet boat, McKenzie boat, and on foot. My companions have been bighorn sheep, black and grizzly bears, moose, elk, and deer. I've shared many pools with osprey and eagles. I tell friends that I've never seen a steelhead river that wasn't beautiful, and I've never seen two that were alike. I make the same claim for their steelhead, and take pains to appreciate the distinctions and share my understandings.

My friends may see steelhead differently. Some are dry-fly specialists who refuse any other approach. A few will not fish a fly with a hook beyond a certain size. Others refuse to deal with any fly line that does not float. An increasing number of friends only fish two-handed rods. Seeing who can fish the shortest sink tip in the winter is a game that appeals to some. Trying to fish the smallest possible fly—and usually a dry at that—commands the attention of a handful of anglers. I have friends who will not fish tippets above a certain fine diameter. Other friends successfully fish little spring creek rods, but disdain light tippets. A half-dozen friends communicate in hushed tones about the glories of their cane rods, and they will tell you that steelhead deserve nothing less. They are related to steelheading's master tyers, who present extraordinarily crafted flies to steelhead, their fishing but a fine excuse to tie.

I do not argue with the opinions and methods of these fly fishers, because they do not necessarily represent something better so much as something different. When they make a rule for themselves and raise a steelhead because of it or in spite of it, I want them to settle in with the pleasure. I like to hear about the joy of their fishing life, not about the rightness of their discoveries.

Among the hundreds of steelhead rivers, a few are famous as fly-fishing rivers. Rarely is an entire river suitable for the fly. The riffles and glides we most cherish are usually but a few miles in length and often below a major spawning tributary. Most are summer rivers. More each year are winter rivers. Many depend upon hatchery steelhead to maintain their angling reputations. Too many have endured a century of heedless exploitation.

My friends, who see steelhead in so many different ways, join together for the right to continue to do so. They are the court cases and public hearings, the fight against streamside clear-cuts, erosion into spawning beds, upcountry dewatering, and the insidious nature of mining tailings. They are the ad hoc organizations, the "friends of" a river with a dam that shouldn't be relicensed, a fishway that doesn't function, or an irrigation canal that hasn't been screened. They are Oregon Trout, Cal Trout, and Washington Trout. They are Trout Unlimited, the Federation of Fly Fishers, the Association of Northwest Steelheaders, and The Steelhead Society of British Columbia. They are a Bill McMillan who works to save the few remaining native steelhead in the Washougal, a Frank Amato who has the lower Deschutes set aside for the public good, an Alec Jackson who works tirelessly so that one day we will see the North Fork of the Stillaguamish again fill with Deer Creek steelhead, an Olga Walker, Gary Miltenberger and a Bob Clay who become outspoken critics of British Columbia's commercial fishing industry and its devastating impact on steelhead stocks.

These fly fishers, and hundreds like them, create the stories of the great rivers and their steelhead.

This summer-run buck rose to a spey fly I presented with a two-handed rod and custom sink-tip line.

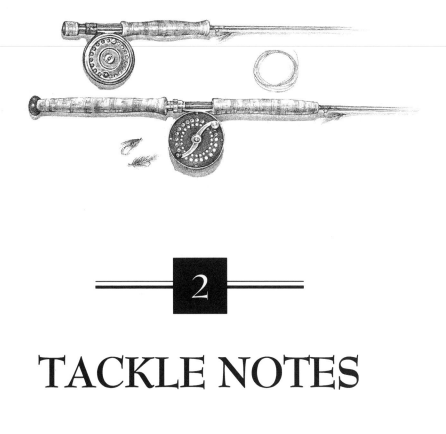

TACKLE NOTES

2

SINGLE-HANDED RODS

Experienced steelhead fly fishers talk of "gearing up" or "gearing down" depending on the character of the river, its race of steelhead, the time of year, and water conditions. Their steelhead may be half-pounders averaging fourteen inches, summer-runs weighing six or seven pounds, or Canadian stocks averaging fifteen pounds. Their rivers may be floating-line August waters with temperatures in the sixties, or December Deep Water Express rivers with surface currents holding in the high thirties. Light-wire low-water flies and marabou spiders on 4/0 irons may both find ten-pound steelhead, but only one of the dressings can be cast satisfactorily with a 6-weight rod.

During the past several years, I have fished for steelhead with rods from 2-weight to 10-weight, in lengths from eight and a half to sixteen feet. These were as many different rods as I could afford to purchase, rods I field-tested for tackle companies, and rods borrowed from friends—at least thirty-five different models divided unequally among nine manufacturers: Sage, Orvis, Winston, Thomas and Thomas, G. Loomis, Lamiglas, Fenwick, Fisher, and Scott. Steelhead fly fishing hardly requires such wealth, but I was able to compare models and to decide what advantages various lengths and actions provided. I also found it possible, for example, to first fish through a run with a 6-weight, and then, using the same flies, repeat the casts and mends with a 4-weight of the same length and action by the same manufacturer. No two steelhead are alike, but a half-dozen with each rod made for interesting comparisons and had me rethinking long-held convictions.

A friend who watched me rig up several rods for a day's fishing once described me as a "tackle whore." He casts a single rod for his steelheading, an "Old Betsy" nine-foot 8-weight, and he limits his fishing to a couple of rivers during the summer and fall. I thought he would be better served with a nine-and-a-half-foot 6-weight, given the very average-sized steelhead typical of his rivers. However, I had no real quarrel with his choice. I understood that an angler can get used to anything, if anything is his only choice.

My first "steelhead" rod, a nine-foot three-piece 7-weight cane rod, was made in Japan. With a box of cheap trout flies thrown in, the rod sold for a couple of dollars. I told companions it possessed a "wet-fly action" or a "slow action," because it bent to the corks and cast like a noodle. The tip section bore off to the right, but the action of the rod was so awful the defect wasn't noticeable. This was all I had, and ultimately I hooked some fifty steelhead on it before purchasing a fiberglass rod. At one point along the way, I really liked that rod.

When the subject of rod action and length comes up and opinions are flying about, I like to know how many rods my companion fishes. If the answer is one, I am charitable, even if I have fished the rod myself and don't care for it. When a companion sings the praises of a rod with which I'm not familiar—and this happens often as new rods suitable for steelhead appear—I again ask that his opinions be put in a frame of reference. I am far more interested in his prejudices when they are contrasted against other rods. In this context, words like "fast" or "stiff" become relative and have meaning.

Before giving my opinion of various steelhead rods and their actions, let me first say that "action" is how a rod resists bending. A "slow" or "soft" rod takes a bend right to its butt end. A "fast" or "stiff" rod takes most of the bend in the tip section. These rods are said to have a "butt action" and a "tip action." Between the two extremes is a "progressive action," in which the bend continues all the way to the butt as the load increases. From a practical standpoint, all steelhead rods today have a progressive action, the amount of load necessary to achieve this determining whether a rod is "fast" or "moderate." These terms are applied most generally.

Thirty years ago, rods were sometimes described as having a "dry-fly action." This meant fast, presumably an advantage for quick pick-up and mending of a floating line. They were short by today's standards, seven and a half to eight feet, and would cast a weight 6 line. I recall a famous fishing writer of the period stating that there was no excuse for any rod to be more than eight feet long! Short fast-action rods were in. Lee Wulff and Walt Johnson were touting the virtues of Orvis's six-foot cane rods for Atlantic salmon and steelhead. Fly rods longer than eight feet—dinosaurs of the era—were heavy and usually very soft. With the development of fiberglass rods in the 1950s, and Fenwick's introduction of graphite rods in the mid-1970s, fly rods became stronger and lighter than cane. Unfortunately, some manufacturers sought to duplicate the soft-butt action of their cane rods in graphite. Presumably, this somehow bridged the gap between traditional cane and graphite. I'm reminded of a story about Sir Francis Herrshoff, a nineteenth century marine architect. He designed some of the most beautiful wood yachts ever to sail, and he lived long enough to see a fiberglass boat. When asked what he thought of this new material, he allegedly said, "It reminds me of congealed snot." A lot of fly fishers who loved the aesthetics of their cane rods first thought the same about glass and graphite rods.

Lighter and stronger meant a lower "swing weight." Longer rods, always desirable among steelheaders, became less fatiguing. Steelhead fly rods began growing in length even when their actions were less than wonderful. By 1980, graphite was fast replacing fiberglass as the material of choice in fly-rod construction, with each "new generation" of graphite "lighter and stronger" than its predecessors.

Graphite rod blanks are made on a tapered metal form called a *mandrel*. In a general sense, the mandrel determines the taper of the rod, while the layers of graphite material—the wall thickness—determine the stiffness of the rod. The graphite fibers run the length of the rod in one direction. "Scrim" fibers are wrapped around at right angles to the graphite fibers. The scrim provides hoop strength and prevents the rod from becoming oval and collapsing when under compression. These cloth layers are rolled around the mandrel under high pressure, bound together with an epoxy resin, and held in place with shrink tape while the entire assembly is cured in an oven. When the curing process is completed, the shrink tape is removed, leaving slight grooves in the finish. Some companies leave the tape marks. Others sand this down and give the rod a polymer finish. In either case, rod strength is not affected.

The scrim was traditionally made of fiberglass, but in the late 1980s a number of American companies began using an aerospace graphite scrim that produced much lighter rod blanks, because fewer of the strong graphite fibers went into each rod. These rods were often described in "modulus," a coefficient of graphite stiffness in pounds per square inch, or psi. Fiberglass rates 6 million psi, and traditional graphite of 33 million psi is considered "low modulus." The G. Loomis IMX (46 to 48 million psi) and Orvis HLS–19 (42 million psi) rate as "medium modulus," while Sage's Graphite III, at 50 million psi, rates as "high modulus."

These new rods have become wonderful assets to steelhead fly fishers. They may be as much as two feet longer than previous rods of the same weight, a startling reduction in swing weight. The result is greater line speed for the same length rod, and better control of mends and higher backcasts because of the longer lines anglers can bring into play using the same amount of exertion. "Damping," the rod's recovering from the oscillation that occurs on the casting stroke, is improved. These rods also track better, the rod tip better able to stay in a single plane during the cast. This results in casts that are longer and more accurate.

My choice for single-hand graphite rods is fast action, *regardless of rod length, whether I'm fishing a deep running shooting head or a dry fly with a floating line.* My reasons are several. Mending line is accomplished with far greater precision. I find that when rod length goes beyond nine feet, mending becomes very laborious, unless the butt section is stiff enough to resist deflection. A stiff butt makes for a more powerful rod, one that drives a line with tighter loops. This faster action requires better timing and may initially be a problem for a weak caster. But the alternative is a rod that collapses to the handle when under load, a characteristic I find extremely aggravating whether casting, mending, or fighting steelhead. A stiff rod also has lifting power, necessary on the strike when I'm trying to remove slack quickly from a deep-running sinking line, and helpful when fighting a powerful fish.

The rod that is soft in the butt section loads early and casts well at shorter distances. A stiff tip-action rod may cast poorly at short distances because it is so underloaded. In order for the rod to flex beyond the tip—and thus become "progressive"—a fly line one or two sizes heavier than the manufacturer's designation may be necessary, particularly if small water is likely to keep casts short. Typically, when fishing my Sage III ten-foot 7-weight rod on big water, I cast a weight 8 forward-taper sink-tip line, a weight 8 or 9 shooting taper, a weight 7 floating long-belly line or weight 7 double-taper line. The only sure way to properly line a rod is to actually cast it with the desired line. The manufacturer's recommendation should be accepted only in a general sense.

I have read that rods with butts on the stiff side tear out flies and break off light tippets. This is nonsense. First of all, light tippets don't match up with powerful rods and big flies. And if the rod is too stiff for the size of the fly, leader, and fish being caught, the angler needs only to drop down in rod weight while continuing to fish a rod that casts well.

Once I am satisfied that the rod's action will meet my steelhead fly-fishing needs, I look for other attributes. I much prefer an uplocking reel-seat system in which the forward end of the reel's foot fits up into the cork handle. Depending on the diameter of the reel, this allows at least a small part of the reel seat, i.e. the butt end of the rod, to extend beyond the reel. I find this arrangement convenient on several counts. I can stand my fly rod up against a tree, rock wall, or jet-boat rod rack without the reel touching the ground and collecting dirt and sand between the spool and the housing. I also like it that when fighting a steelhead, I can put the butt against my neoprene waders without interfering with the reel's rim control. On steelhead rods to 6-weight, an extension butt is unnecessary, and on heavier rods it can be kept short and permanently fixed.

Except for two cane rods, I no longer own any rods with down-locking reel seats, an arrangement in which the reel is beyond the end of the rod.

I detest removable extension butts. When I'm fighting a steelhead, all my attention is given to getting the fish on the beach. I don't have time to remove the butt cap, place it somewhere, get the extension butt, and place it in the rod. If I take a removable extension butt and fix it permanently to the rod, the rod will no longer fit in its storage tube.

If the extension butt is permanently fixed, it need be no more than an inch long and should contain some sort of rubber button to protect the cork. Solid cork or wood extension butts become so chewed up they detract from the beauty of the rod.

Though I have only average-size hands, I find the cork grips on many steelhead rods too narrow in diameter. I like a cork handle to be a good inch in diameter directly beneath the place my palm naturally grips the rod. That requirement leaves no room for handles with long and fine front tapers. These grips cramp the hand, cause unnecessary fatigue, and reduce the power of the cast. My strongest steelhead rods have full wells grips, while the midrange rods have full wells or half wells grips. Some of my light rods have cigar-shaped handles with a fine front taper. These grips are still comfortable, as long as the diameter is sufficiently large.

2- and 3-weight rods: eight to nine feet

For years, I've used an eight-and-a-half-foot Orvis Western Series 2-weight for both resident trout and steelhead. I've caught brown trout of twenty inches, rainbows to twenty-three inches, and steelhead to four pounds with the rod.

A 2-weight is ideal for half-pounder steelhead and easily manages the occasional adult steelhead of fifteen to twenty-five inches, as long as it is sufficiently powerful in the butt section. A full flexing action designed to protect gossamer tippets and to make short casts should be avoided. I expect the rod to have enough backbone to reach sixty feet without working at it, and to allow for crisp mends at this distance. Because the belly of the forward-taper line is more nearly the mass of the running line, the entire working part of the fly line should be cleaned and dressed several times a day to achieve maximum casting distance. I go up one line weight so that the rod loads early. The extra belly weight in proportion to the running line also helps to reduce my casting labors. Typically, the tippet tests four to six pounds, and I present thinly dressed low-water flies up to #6. The rod brings a new dimension to my fishing when an eighteen-inch steelhead has taken me into my backing and survives the experience with a minimum of harm.

This 22-inch Klamath River Steelhead is a remarkable gamefish on a 2-weight outfit.

Some anglers scoff at the notion of such light rods for even half-pounder steelhead. They claim that nothing less than a 7-weight is suitable, yet they never press such rods to their maximum unless they find themselves playing a hot steelhead in the teens. When watching fly fishers playing steelhead, I am often astonished by the lack of pressure they can safely bring to bear. The rods are hardly bent at all as they tentatively play the steelhead off their reels. Lighter rods take a much deeper set, better absorb the shock against tippet and tissue, and tire the steelhead more quickly. Along the way, lighter rods are far more pleasant to cast.

But 2- and 3-weights have their limitations. They won't cast in wind, and they limit the size of the fly and the distance it can be cast. Only floating lines are available for them, usually in forward taper, but then these rods weren't designed to cast weighted flies or sink tip lines.

4- and 5-weight rods: nine to nine and a half feet

Rods in this category are my first choice for northern California and southern Oregon rivers where steelhead populations possess large half-pounder components, and anywhere on summer rivers where one-year ocean steelhead predominate. (Oregon's Deschutes and Idaho's Salmon are examples.) In fact, I wouldn't hesitate to fish for steelhead under ten pounds with these rods. They cast circles around the 2-weight rods, and are a special joy to fish with low-water flies.

Besides the forward-taper floating lines normally used, various sink-tip lines are available from the major line manufacturers, including Scientific Anglers and Cortland. The factors that limit the use of such rods are wind, the distance to be cast, and the weight or wind resistance of the fly. They easily handle light-wire hooks to #2, and #4 heavy-wire hooks. Heavily weighted Ugly Bugs are not for these rods. Neither do I choose them for winter work, for I like more powerful rods to fish sinking lines.

6-weight rods: nine to ten feet

These are the lightest steelhead rods that I describe as all purpose. Nearly every important line taper and sinking line used in steelhead fly fishing is available for 6-weight rods. They penetrate wind, and an average caster can obtain as much distance with them as he can with any outfit. When using a weight 7 shooting taper, flies as large as 1/0 can be cast. However, one must be aware that the sink rate for a weight 6 or 7 line is little more than half the sink rate for a weight 12 line: 3.75 inches per second compared to approximately 6 inches per second. Six-weights are a disadvantage only in discolored winter water where large marabou spiders with big hooks must be quickly carried down. I don't think the size of the steelhead is much of a factor until fish in the teens are anticipated. The Kispiox and Thompson come to mind.

7-weight rods: nine to ten feet

Today's 7-weight rods of nine and a half and ten feet are light, powerful, and more nearly all purpose than any other rod in steelheading. I have caught summer steelhead of twenty pounds from three different rivers while using a 7-weight, and I never felt compromised. I can control large, silhouette-type summer patterns dressed on 2/0 heavy-wire hooks on my longest casts. Wind-resistant deer-hair dries and waking damp flies can be cast as far as they can be worked. For many anglers, these rods are the most powerful they can cast for hours each day.

Fast-sinking shooting tapers—weight 8s and 9s—can be driven into the teeth of anything but a gale. The weight of the fly is the only factor that limits the use of 7-weight rods.

An 8-weight was used to cast the large Marabou spider that attracted this 12-pound winter-run steelhead.

8-weight rods: nine to ten feet

A ten-foot 8-weight is the most powerful single-hand rod I can cast all day, winter or summer, wet or dry, without excessive fatigue. If I use rods stiffer than this, I must come down in length, because the leverage becomes more than I can handle physically. (A ten-foot 9- or 10-weight is my ticket to the physical therapist.)

This rod is a logical first choice for many anglers bound for British Columbia's Babine, Kispiox, and Dean rivers. It is the only rod I have fished on the Thompson. The weight 8 forward-taper long-belly line I use puts a lot of grains in the air, and it carries heavily weighted marabou and rabbit leech patterns to distant lies. Long mends are easily made, whether fishing wets hitched to wake or big wind-resistant dries.

9- and 10-weight rods: nine to ten feet

Joe Howell on the North Umpqua and Dave McNeese on the Santiam use ten-foot 9-weight rods for their summer angling. Each man can pick up more fly line than the average angler can cast and then cover lies a hundred feet away with 4/0 silhouette patterns. But the typical steelheader is more likely to choose a 9-weight or 10-weight in the less demanding length of nine to nine and a half feet.

I use these rods exclusively for winter fishing to cast sink tip lines, either hybrid lines I have constructed myself, a Teeny 300, or lines by Scientific Anglers, Cortland, and Orvis. I believe these hinging lines are better cast with the shock absorbing quality of more progressive, slightly slower actions.

Large heavy winter flies such as Bob Aid's Marabou Spiders, Les Johnson's Steelhead Bunnies, or any of the rabbit leech patterns size 1/0 or larger are best cast with 9-weight or 10-weight rods. A length of nine to nine and a half feet turns the flies over, controls any sink-tip system while the line is swinging well below the angler, and has the backbone to move a lot of deep running line when the steelhead strikes.

SINGLE-HAND RODS: FLY LINES

In recent years, manufacturers have developed fly lines specifically for steelhead. Add to these the general purpose lines that have application in steelheading and the hybrid lines concocted by anglers who feel that commercially made lines don't meet their special needs, and you have a variety of fly lines probably unequaled in any other area of fly fishing.

At the heart of these needs is a gamefish that leaves the ocean to ascend some river every month of the year. Finding a way to reach a steelhead with a fly under varying water conditions is the impetus for the continuing development of steelhead lines. Gearing up or down for the various races of steelhead can multiply basic line needs by a factor of three. For example, the same forward taper floating line is necessary in several sizes to match 4-weight, 7-weight, and 9-weight outfits.

The weight in grains of the first thirty feet of fly line determines its number, one to fifteen, lightest to heaviest, a standard established by the American Fishing Tackle Manufacturers Association.

AFTMA Fly Line Standards

Weight	Grains	Range
1	60	54–66
2	80	74–86
3	100	94–106
4	120	114–126
5	140	134–146
6	160	152–168
7	185	177–193
8	210	202–218
9	240	230–250
10	280	270–290
11	330	318–342
12	380	368–392

For each weight heavier than weight 12, add 50 grains to the previous weight.

Every fly line except those with a constant diameter—level lines—has a tip, about one foot of level line that attaches to the leader, and a front taper that leads to a heavy belly section. In forward-taper lines, the belly is followed by a rear taper that leads to a narrow-diameter running line. The "head" of the forward-taper line describes the forward taper, belly, and back taper. A double-taper line has an identical front and back taper separated by a long belly section. A shooting taper has only a forward taper and level belly section. This head is attached to a running line, either narrow-diameter or monofilament. These three general types of lines, with slight variations in their tapers, describe all the lines used in fly fishing.

In theory, a 7-weight rod would take a weight 7 line, regardless of the line's taper or sink rate. In practice, the match-up is unlikely to be so precise. What is a 7-weight rod? is somewhat subjective, and not constant from one manufacturer to another. An individual's casting skills, the distance likely to be cast, and what weight line he finds most comfortable for the rod he is fishing become additional considerations. For example, when I take my little 2-weight to Montana for hopper floats, I purposely overline the rod. I know that casts will be short, and I want the rod to load early, so I fish it with a weight 3 or 4 forward-taper line. But even lines of the same size will load a rod quite differently. A shooting taper, or head, is traditionally thirty feet long. A forward-taper line, including the tip, front taper, belly, and rear taper above the narrow running line is about forty feet long, while a taper, including tapers and level belly, measures sixty-five feet. All three lines may be assigned the same number, based on the weight in grains of the first thirty feet, yet the weight of the line be   nd the rod tip—and forward of the running line—prior to shooting, will vary significantly. To illu   e, the following are the weights of the head sections—both tapers and belly—of three weight 7 lines by Scientific Anglers: shooting taper (thirty feet) 185 grains; forward taper (forty feet) 238 grains; steelhead taper (sixty-five feet) 350 grains. This is not a problem as long as the angler understands that if his rod loads properly with a standard forward taper line, he will want to go up a line size when purchasing a shooting taper (210 grains), or perhaps use an 8-weight rod when casting a steelhead   r.

How a fly line concentrates its weight also has a bearing on how stiff a rod must be in order to cast the line. For example: A rod designed to cast a forty-foot forward-taper line of 238 grains will be underlined if the 238 grains are incorporated into sixty feet of forward taper, assuming the heads are both beyond the rod tip prior to shooting, and it will be overlined if the 238 grains are concentrated into twenty feet. Thus, the weight of the long steelhead taper may not overload the rod nearly as much as would be suggested by the weight of its sixty-five-foot head section—350 grains. The only way to determine this with certainty is to cast the line on the rod for which it is intended.

The following fly lines are useful with a single-hand rod.

Double Taper (Floating). These traditional lines have a fine, relatively long front taper at each end, which allows the line to be reversed when one end becomes worn. They shoot poorly and are best fished short to medium distances—fifty to sixty feet—with relatively small flies. Because heavy line is tapering to lighter line, their principal advantage is superb line control, especially where across or upstream casts are mended in greased line and some dry-fly presentations. No other line can be so effectively roll-cast or spey-cast for distance. I particularly value these lines when fishing low-water, damp, and riffle-hitched patterns on thin summer water.

Today's reel manufacturers often base the backing capacity of their reels on a forward-taper line, half of which consists of a thin running line. A double-taper line with its long heavy belly fills a reel much faster and dramatically reduces the reel's capacity to hold backing. I choose a 6-weight or 7-weight rod of nine and a half or ten feet to use with these lines. If big water requires longer casts with larger flies and maximum line control, I switch to a 9-weight double-handed rod.

Note in the figures below how the belly length decreases a foot and taper length increases six inches at each end for each line weight increase. The heavier lines have a thicker belly and require a longer taper to delay the turnover and to dissipate the line's energy to the fly for a smooth delivery. Because properly swimming the fly, rather than a delicate presentation, is the primary goal in steelhead fly fishing, all level line forward of the taper, the tip, should be cut off. And for punching out large wind-resistant dries with a 7-weight, it may be useful to cut an additional six to twelve inches off the tapered end.

Line Weight	Tip	Taper Length	Belly Length	Taper Length	Tip
2	1'	2.5'	77.5'	2.5'	1'
4	1'	4.0'	74.5'	4.0'	1'
6	1'	5.0'	72.5'	5.0'	1'
8	1'	6.0'	70.5'	6.0'	1'
10	1'	7.0'	68.5'	7.0'	1'

Forward Taper (Floating). The front taper of a standard forward-taper line is identical to the front taper of a double-taper line, and it allows anglers to make short, delicate presentations. However, belly length is reduced and leads to a very short rear taper and narrow diameter running line. The angler is able to clear the entire head—about forty feet, including front taper, belly, and rear taper—and shoot the line long distances. Even an average fly fisher can come close to casting an entire twenty-five-meter line. This versatility has made the forward taper the most used line in steelhead fly fishing.

When making a standard across-and-down wet-fly presentation, the rod tip is raised to lift the running line, the tension mending the fly line and keeping the line straight to the fly. The angler cannot depend upon the light running line to transfer sufficient energy to the heavy belly to mend the line. Thus, to make distant line corrections, the head of the fly line must be below the angler and coming under tension. For this reason, mending to reduce drag is better accomplished with either a double-taper line or a forward-taper long-belly line.

Forward Taper (Slow Sinking). I used one of these slow sinking "Intermediate" lines and found it to be almost worthless for presenting a fly on summer steelhead waters. When dressed, it would not float, and because the running line would also sink, mending was next to impossible.

Forward Taper (Full Sinking). Some very capable anglers fish these lines, but I find them aggravating. Because the whole line sinks, they tangle in rocks lying between the fly and the angler, and big loops of line left in the water stop a cast like an anchor. On the swing, however, if the line is straight to the fly, there is not the slack one finds in a floating-line/sink-tip arrangement, and a hookup can be very positive.

Forward Taper (Triangle Taper). I have limited experience with the Triangle Taper lines introduced by Lee Wulff in the mid-1980s. The "triangle" is achieved by continuously tapering the belly to the fine tip, the forty-foot taper connecting to the running line with a short rear taper. The continuous taper—as opposed to a level belly section and a relatively abrupt front taper typical of a conventional forward-taper line—generates a continuous transfer of line energy with a minimum of disturbance on the water. This really doesn't matter in steelhead fly fishing, but the line does turn over low-water flies well, is a marvelous roll-casting line, and shoots like a rocket.

Forward Taper (Long Belly). Floating long belly forward taper lines, in one taper configuration or another, have the greatest general application in steelheading. With today's longer, more powerful rods, these long heads can be aerialized and cast greater distances. More important, mending can be accomplished at distances well beyond what is possible with conventional forward taper lines. And once a tight loop is formed, the line drives big wets and bushy dries with ease.

For the past two years, using two ten-foot rods, a 7-weight and an 8-weight, I cast Scientific Anglers's 105-foot Steelhead Taper lines on British Columbia's Thompson and Dean rivers. The lines are unusual for their long back taper. This allows for mends at distances up to seventy feet. They roll-cast and spey-cast better than any steelhead lines I've used, an advantage I appreciated in the North Umpqua's canyon water. I prefer these lines for working greased-line flies on big waters. They come in two finishes, one soft and pliable, the other a stiff, pebbly monocore. I've used both and prefer the stiffer line for the longer distance it can be cast and the remarkable ease with which it can be mended. On cold mornings, however, the line has a memory and comes off the reel in coils. Then it is necessary to pull off whatever length you can cast and stretch out the line.

Steelhead Taper lines are available in only four sizes. Their tapers are as follows:

Line Weight	Tip Length	Front Taper	Belly	Rear Taper	Running Line
7	1'	7'	33'	25'	40'
8	1'	8'	32'	25'	40'
9	1'	9'	31'	25'	40'
10	1'	10'	30'	25'	40'

Forward Taper (Sink Tip). Forward-taper lines with a permanently attached sink tip of ten to twenty-four feet in sink rates of II (medium sinking) to V (very fast sinking) are available from a number of manufacturers, including Scientific Anglers, Cortland, Orvis, and the Teeny Nymph Company. Unfortunately, most of the weight of these lines is in the sink-tip portion and is the weight that determines what size fly line you're casting. The rest of the head is usually a belly so thin as to be a running line. The result is a forward-taper line that hinges when cast, the weight and specific gravity of the sink-tip portion barely under control.

When the many tip-section lengths are multiplied by the sink rates available, the potential number of lines is staggering. At one time or another all are useful, but by no means are all of them necessary. I first decide what is to be my primary rod. For most anglers, this is likely to be either a 6-, 7-, or 8- weight, depending on the river fished and whether the fishing will include winter-run steelhead. My own choice is a 7-weight, but a two-handed rod is my primary winter rod, and I can afford to go light for my all purpose rod. For this 7-weight rod I'll have a complete assortment of lines, spare spools, even a spare reel, and I can handle virtually any situation during any season. My first line would be a floater in a forward taper long belly, specifically a Steelhead Taper by Scientific Anglers. Then I would shop for sink tips. I don't generally use sink tips with a sink rate of II (1.50 to 2.00 inches per second) in my fishing. They are handy when trying to keep a fly below the surface on the swing, but I can pretty much obtain the same results by switching to a fly dressed on a heavy-wire hook. Sink tips rated III (3.00 to 3.75 inches per second) have their place—discolored summer water, especially soft winter lies, or keeping a fly down on the swing through especially fast lies—but I can often achieve a satisfactory sink by carefully manipulating a floating line or quartering, well below me, a sink tip rated IV (4.00 inches per second for a weight 7). This leaves a sink tip with a sink rate of V (5.50 inches per second for a weight 7). I carry both a IV and a V for my 7-weight outfit, normally in lengths of twelve to fifteen feet, though I wouldn't hesitate to use a twenty-foot tip on broad winter drifts. In addition, I carry a Teeny Nymph T-200, with a long twenty-four-foot sink tip rated V (5.50 feet per second). This line has a sink tip of Deep Water Express, and for a given diameter sinks nearly as fast as lead core.

The following are a few of the sink-tip lines available in 1991. I have used all these lines in one weight category or another. (I have used the T-400 and T-500 only in salt water.) They will fill any need, regardless of the river and the time of year.

Manufacturer	Tip	Length	Sink Rate	Size
Cortland	444SL Extra Fast Type 3	10'	3.5–4.0 ft/sec	5–10
	444SL Super Fast Type 6	20'	6.25–7.0 ft/sec	5–10
Orvis	Hy-Flote Sink Tip (25 meters)	15'	3.5–5.5 ft/sec	5–12
	Easy Mend Sink Tip (33 meters)	15'	3.5–5.5 ft/sec	5–12
Scientific Anglers	Supreme Wet Tip II	10'	1.50–2.00	4–10
	Supreme Wet Tip III	10'	2.50–4.00	5–10
	Supreme Wet Tip III	20' (Hi-D)	2.50–4.00	6–10
	Supreme Wet Tip III	30' (Hi-D)	2.50–4.00	6–10
	Steelhead Sink Tip III	13'	3.00–3.75	7–10
	Steelhad Sink Tip IV	13'	4.00–4.75	7–10
	Steelhead Sink Tip V	13'	5.50–6.50	7–10

Forward Taper Hybrid Sink Tip Lines. Steelhead fly fishers have a long history of creating their own fly lines. Myron Gregory is credited with introducing the shooting head. He and fellow members of the Golden Gate Angling and Casting Club were, I believe, the first to use lead core shooting heads on steelhead rivers. Washington's winter steelhead fly fishers have been splicing together their own lines for decades. While many of these lines of yore cast poorly, they did provide sink rates unavailable commercially. And though sinking lines are now available in almost endless variety, custom lines are still preferred among the majority of experts. On occasion, I have found that not one of the half-dozen fly fishers sharing a winter drift is fishing a commercially manufactured line.

What's the appeal? Why go through all the aggravation of building a sinking line when fly fishing shops have boxcar loads in every description imaginable? Steelheaders generally are better-than-average casters who quickly find fault with the severe hinging characteristic of commercially manufactured sink-tip lines. They can build custom lines that turn over without this problem. *The key to their lines is a belly section that has more grains per linear foot than the sink-tip section.* With this, the transfer energy passing down the floating section will be sufficient to move the sink tip, whether casting or mending. The physics is simple: The sink tip becomes the taper. As an example, a fifteen-foot sink tip would be constructed as follows: fifteen feet of lead from a weight 9 High-Speed Hi-D shooting taper spliced or looped to fifteen to eighteen feet of level weight 11. This head is then spliced or looped to a narrow diameter running line. A simple shortcut makes good use of one of the less expensive double-taper lines. A weight 11 double taper has a front and rear taper of seven or eight feet, less a foot or so of level tip. Cut off the level tip. Measure up twenty-two feet—seven feet of taper and fifteen feet of level belly—and cut. Do this at both ends. Attach the fine-diameter end to the running line. The taper of the line now becomes the rear taper of your sink-tip line. The sink tip will be attached to the heavy-diameter end of the belly. The result is a thirty-seven-foot forward-taper sink-tip line that casts without hinging for an 8- or 9-weight rod. (You will still have about forty feet of level belly left, enough to make at least two more belly sections, if you don't care to have a built-in rear taper.)

This basic approach can be achieved in a variety of sink-tip weights and lengths. Just remember to keep the belly section a weight or two above the sink-tip portion, and *never try to taper the belly section to the sink tip.* This creates an unforgiving hinge. I rarely use sink tips shorter than twelve feet or longer than eighteen feet. The difference—six feet—isn't enough grains to change belly sections or change rods. Graphite rods are far more forgiving than that. If a seventeen- or eighteen-foot sink tip section is used, I find it better to cast a head with a belly/rear taper total of seventeen to twenty-two feet—ten to fifteen feet of level belly and seven feet of taper. This is not critical and can be adjusted to suit rod weights, casting skills, fly depth sought, and so forth.

A final note: The sink-tip portion cannot pull down a heavy belly section so well as a light belly section. This means that although the line can be more properly mended, the sink tip will not fish as deep. Don't worry, the trade-off is worth the loss of a little depth.

For additional specifics on hybrid lines, see Chapter 37.

Shooting Taper (30 to 40 feet). Twenty-five years ago, the shooting head was the nuts and bolts of steelhead fly fishing, summer or winter. Tremendous distances could be cast, particularly when the head—customarily thirty feet long and often cut from a double-taper line—led to monofilament running line. Huge loops of mono were gathered and held in the angler's mouth while his two arms cast and double-hauled. Heads could be quickly changed for the few sink rates available. Lead-core shooting heads plummeted to the bottom for angling opportunities until then unimagined. Almost overnight, chinook salmon, winter-run steelhead, and numerous saltwater bottom fish became fly-rod gamefish.

Perhaps because I was overly impressed with the distances I could cast, I stuck with heads longer than most of my Washington companions did. The head was, I reluctantly realized, a highly specialized fly line, a thirty-foot lure, a "chuck and duck" lead-core missile that severely limited the angler's options once the line was cast. Mending, spey casting, and roll casting—the manipulation of a fly line that gives fly fishing such grace and charm—were lost. Far more pragmatically, an inexperienced angler never appreciated that the fly line dredging the bottom was passing downstream with the *belly of the line leading the way.* The fly raced along behind, passing downstream too fast to attract a fish before beginning a crack-the-whip swing. Not until the line was almost dead below the angler was the fly fishing properly. Of course, the experts of the day knew all this. They kept their casts quartering down, discovered which pools helped to mend their lines, raised their rods to square around the butt end of the head and make sure the fly was passing downriver first, and then fed line into the drift. But as hybrid sink-tip lines grew in sophistication, and anglers discovered that flies did not have to be flat on the bottom to attract, shooting heads began declining in popularity.

Well-designed sink-tip lines will cast nearly as far, can easily be changed to fish different depths, and can be mended to fish more effectively. But no sink tip will fish as deep as an entire head of the same sink rate, and heads are still preferred when a deep sink is necessary, when extra distances must be reached, and when currents are so light or nonexistent that careful manipulation of the line is not needed. On California's estuary pools, for example, action is imparted to the fly by stripping back—and shooting tapers remain highly valued.

I still carry shooting tapers and fish them each season, but I only carry those that have a sink rate of at least IV. Because a single reel spool filled with backing and running line will serve any number of shooting heads, I use my largest click-drag reel. It holds 150 yards of thirty-pound backing and can be used to cast a weight 10 head for chinook salmon.

TWO-HANDED RODS

The largest steelhead of each sex that I caught during the past year, an eighteen-pound winter-run hen and a twenty-four-pound summer-run buck, came while I was fishing a two-handed rod. During those twelve months, I fly-fished 115 days, usually for steelhead, and at least half of that time I was swinging one of my double-handed rods.

Four years ago, I purchased my first two-handed rod, a thirteen-and-a-half-foot model by Orvis, and discovered that it stubbornly refused to function as I thought it should. My difficulties were not entirely of my own making, though my casting skills were dreadfully wanting. I intended to use the rod for winter steelheading, but no suitable lines were commercially available, and I worked at developing my own by splicing together sections of various existing lines. These largely unsuccessful experiments led me in two directions. I contacted Bruce Richards at 3M's Scientific Anglers and Tom Rosenbauer at Orvis. They provided me with lines to cut up, and my experiments became more systematic. Then I visited Mike Maxwell at Gold-N-West Flyfishers, the shop he and his wife, Denise, operate in Vancouver, British Columbia.

Mike is the foremost expert on two-handed rods in North America, and he has schooled many anglers in their use. When we drove to a nearby casting pond and assembled a half-dozen double-handed rods, I was not surprised when he took up the rod I'd been fighting and spey-cast a double-taper line nearly a hundred feet. Mike instructed, cajoled, and berated. By the end of the day, I could make a single and a double spey cast. We talked of lines, casting styles, and his approach to using the rods. After purchasing Mike's videotape and instruction manual on the subject, I returned home to savor his wisdom and to practice casting.

Mike Maxwell always begins his instruction by contrasting spey casting with overhead casting, and how the design of two-handed rods differs depending on which kind of cast is to be executed. Make no mistake, Mike spey-casts, double and single, and the fly line never travels behind him; it is a balletic series of moves at once elegant and purposeful. Without backcasts to compromise presentation strategies, "unfishable" lies are routinely searched. Great rod length permits mends that control the line with astonishing precision. By leading a sink-tip line, for example, a constant fly depth can be maintained. Because no shooting of line is necessary to make even hundred-foot casts, one can wear gloves, a boon during frigid weather. I believe that, more than any other single factor, the double-handed rod has contributed to the rise in popularity of winter steelhead fly fishing.

Spey casts are more favorably executed when the rod's energy is released in even doses, and a full-flexing rod with a thick, powerful tip section is preferred. A rod with a powerful butt and fast tip is better suited for overhead casting, and likely will be a weak-casting spey rod, the thin tip collapsing under the high energy load that takes place near the end of a spey cast.

Though stupendous distances are obtainable using overhand casts and either forward-taper or shooting-taper lines, Mike disdains the practice as unnecessary and, well, cross-cultural, something like hitting a golf ball with a baseball bat. I fished the Bulkley with Mike, and even when he had a mile of backcast room he would not throw his line behind him. I realized why after watching him control a fly's drift from 100 feet away.

I have arbitrarily divided two-handed rods into three categories: light, medium, and heavy. The actions of individual rods determine whether they are designed for overhead casting, spey casting, or suitable for both. How an angler uses his rod becomes a matter of personal interpretation, regardless of the manufacturer's recommendations. A few manufacturers specify between the two types, overhead and spey. An example is the Thomas and Thomas fourteen-foot Gaula, an overhead rod, and their fourteen-foot Spey model. Both are designed to cast identical double-taper weight 11 lines.

The names of these rods reflect the history of two-handed rods. Spey casting originated on Scotland's Spey River, where trees border so closely that fishermen developed casting techniques that would permit them to cover lies without backcasts. Conversely, Norwegians like stiff rods to overhead-cast fast-sinking shooting tapers. On their famous Gaula River, they sometimes rely upon "heads" of Deep Water Express to take six-inch tube flies down on huge runoff-filled pools.

While the weight of single-hand rods is based on which thirty-foot length of line, on the AFTMA fly-line standard, will load the rod, the double-handed rod must be expected to either spey-cast or aerialize two or three times that amount of line. To accomplish this, a 9-weight two-handed rod must have considerably more power than a 9-weight single-hand rod. I have watched anglers cast a weight 9 shooting taper with a two-handed rod and almost have a stroke trying to get the rod to load with only 240 grains of line in the air. Keeping in mind that the 240 grains includes the front seven-foot taper, a spey cast of ninety feet with a double-taper weight 9 line involves moving at least 850 grains of line through the air! This doesn't mean that one should fish an 850 grain shooting taper line on a two-handed rod. The thirty-foot head section would so concentrate the 850 grains that the rod would be badly overloaded. It does mean that a somewhat different standard is used when applying a "weight" to a double-handed rod.

Light: Twelve to Thirteen Feet; Line: Weight 6 to 9

I am not aware of any genuine two-handed rods of less than twelve feet marketed currently, and I question the value of dropping below twelve feet. Lightness in double-handed rods doesn't translate to shortness. Any trend toward shortness reduces command of the water, which is the entire point of fishing such rods.

Sage now markets a powerful 8/9-weight eleven-foot three-inch rod (GFL 8113–3), which is listed as a two-handed rod, but is really more a single-hand rod that can be cast two-handed. In November 1990, Don Green, the president of Sage, showed me a prototype 7/8-weight fourteen-foot two-handed rod. This rod should be spectacular for-dry fly and greased-line fishing on the larger steelhead rivers.

Mike Maxwell, under his Gold-N-West label, markets a twelve-foot six-inch rod for weight 8/9 line. Bruce and Walker offers the Grilse, twelve-foot for weight 5 to 7 lines, and the Bruce, twelve-foot for weight 7 to 9 lines.

Medium: Thirteen to Fifteen Feet; Line: Weight 8 to 10

Most steelhead fly fishermen will find two-handed rods in this category to be the most useful, regardless of the season fished. More than a dozen models are available from a number of manufacturers and businesses: Hardy Brothers, Thomas and Thomas, Bruce and Walker, Sage, Orvis, and Gold-N-West. I have cast and can recommend three of these. Mike Maxwell's fifteen-foot 10-weight is a superb spey rod, and will perform well overhead, too. Orvis's thirteen-foot six-inch 10-weight Salmon model is very popular with steelheaders. I believe that Sage's fourteen foot for a weight 9 line is the best of the medium-weight overhead rods, and though light in the tip for spey casting, is more than adequate for this purpose.

I have found that medium-weight two-handed rods under thirteen feet—and often under 14 feet—have too quick a taper to be useful spey rods. However, they can be *very useful* overhand rods. Fly fishers who are weak casters are encouraged to try such rods, especially when fishing a deeply sunk fly. Last winter, I sometimes fished a Sage twelve-foot six-inch 9-weight rod with a custom built weight 10 long-belly sink-tip line. It was a not altogether agreeable spey rod, but a delight for overhead casting. Two arms working on a rod weighing only 7⅝ ounces is a revelation. Great line speed can be generated and considerable distances reached. I introduced two friends to the rod. One was a rank beginner, the other an experienced fly caster. Both were soon booming out casts. Their delight reminded me of Collin Schadrech's comments regarding the merits of two-handed rods. He said they were so forgiving that the elderly, the inexperienced, even the handicapped can, with proper instruction, take pleasure in their use. I appreciate his assessment, for an injured elbow left me casting a single-hand rod with such pain that, for a year, a two-handed rod became my salvation.

Heavy: Fourteen to Sixteen Feet; Line: Weight 10 to 12

When I am winter fishing with Jimmy Hunnicutt, I keep track of my friend by the sound of his sixteen-foot rod ripping through the air, a wind sound replete with the energy of a mini tornado as 800 grains of fly line are sent flying over nearby trees on the backcast, and then driven 120 feet out to a distant lie. Sixteen feet is too much rod for me to use all day, especially with overhead casting tapers. The raw weight of the huge rod is likely to be twelve ounces or more, and the reel needed to hold a long-belly double-taper weight 11 line and a reasonable amount of backing must necessarily be the largest built for freshwater angling. Even when holding the rod at its balance point just above its forward cork grip, one feels the leverage. Yet no other rod in steelheading so commands big water. The largest marabou flies soar through the air like nothing. Stupendous mends are routine. Most important, the heaviest—and fastest sinking—sink tips can be used. To illustrate this point: Scientific Anglers' High Speed Hi-D has a sink rate of 3.75 to 6.25 inches per second in weights 6 to 13. Fifteen feet of weight 12 or 13 sink tip will sink at a rate thirty to forty percent faster than the same material in weight 8 or 9. Sink tips can also be longer; twenty feet is not a problem if the belly section is heavy enough to control it.

A number of manufacturers market these rods in actions for both spey and overhead casting: Thomas and Thomas's Gaula and Spey rods; Sage's fourteen-foot for a weight 10 and sixteen-foot for a weight 10; Gold-N-West's sixteen-foot Spey rod for a weight 10/11; Orvis's Spey for a weight 11; Bruce and Walker's Salmon models at sixteen feet six inches and seventeen feet six inches, and their Expert models at sixteen, seventeen, and eighteen feet for weight 10 to 12; Hardy's sixteen-foot Favourite Salmon for a weight 11 and their fifteen-foot four-inch Deluxe Salmon for a weight 10.

TWO-HANDED RODS: FLY LINES

Double Taper (25 meters). These lines, approximately eighty-two feet long, have a front taper of six to seven feet, which means that about seventy-five feet of fly line can be beyond the rod tip. Counting leader length and rod length, an angler can make casts of at least ninety feet—certainly adequate for most low water and dry-fly needs, when using light to medium two-handed rods. But because of rod length, he would be left holding backing in his hand. This problem is eliminated by splicing ten to twenty feet of running line to the end of the rear taper. When the front taper becomes worn and it is time to reverse the line, this lead can be cut off and spliced to the other end.

Why go to so much trouble if double-taper long-belly lines of 105 feet or 120 feet are available? Extremely large reels are needed to house all that belly, an additional purchase and likely an expensive one. By using a conventional line, any large steelhead fly reel suitable for single-hand rods—reels 3¾ inches in diameter, for example—can be used on the lighter line models of two-handed rods. This is true even if a sink tip is added to the leader.

Double Taper Long Belly (105 and 120 feet). A long belly line often becomes necessary because of the longer distances cast while using medium and heavy double-handed rods. Tapers are otherwise identical with the double taper lines associated with single-hand rods, about the weight of the line in feet. The only drawback to their use is finding a reel large enough to hold this length of large-diameter line.

Double Taper Sink Tip (Scientific Anglers). Scientific Anglers manufactures a very small number of double-taper sink-tip lines called the Air Cel Supreme Wet Tip that come with a ten-foot Wet Cel II (two to three inches per second) sink tip at each end. Because there is almost no call for such lines in western North America—indeed, few anglers are even aware of them—they are made essentially for export to Great Britain. This is a pity. The line can be fished almost as a full-floater, but with a large fly and fairly long leader, a strong back-mend will get the fly to a good depth. I have used the line, a weight 10, for summer steelhead, and have found it useful when I want to hold a big marabou or General Practitioner dressing down through heavy runs but keep it from fouling in soft, boulder-filled tailouts. Surely, as the popularity of two-handed rods grows, additional double-taper sink-tip lines in a variety of sink rates will become available.

The primary disadvantage I find with these lines is in their fixed sink tip length. I prefer the latitude of a sink tip system in which a basic lead of belly section becomes the terminal for any number of sink tip lengths in any number of sink rates.

Double Taper Sink Tip System (Mike Maxwell). Cutting off some part of the front taper of a floating fly line and splicing in a length of sink tip, whether permanent or looped, can have disastrous results if the grains per foot of the floating line at the junction is much less than the grains per foot of the sink-tip section. The energy being transferred down the line is dissipated through a taper designed for a delicate delivery, and no energy is left to move around twelve or fifteen feet of sink tip. The result of this flat spot is severe hinging on the cast and almost nonexistent mending qualities. The entire matter is made more troublesome because shooting tapers—the raw material for sink tips—have a front taper. This feature makes determining the grains per foot of its butt end—the end that will attach to the floating line—only guesswork. Knowing this, let's proceed with Mike Maxwell's approach to a sink-tip system.

Mike begins by cutting off the level lead, about one foot, then measuring up two feet of taper and cutting off the line. To the end of the line he attaches a monocore loop. (See Chapter 2.) He then takes a thirty-foot shooting taper *at least one weight less* than the double-taper line and, by measuring from the level butt end, cuts the line first at five feet and then again ten feet up from this first cut. The result is three pieces, five, ten, and fifteen feet long, the latter carrying whatever taper has been incorporated into the leader end of the shooting taper, but likely six to eight feet. Braided monocore loops are attached to both ends of each piece. This allows sink tips to be used singly or daisy-chained, with these lengths: five feet, ten feet, fifteen feet, twenty feet, twenty-five feet, and thirty feet.

Mike recommends that this series of sink tips be carried in at least two sink rates. To keep them separated, he employs a color coding system based on the color of thread used in whip finishing the butt end monocore loops to the fly line.

Mike also has integrated a floating head into this line system. He chooses a double-taper floating line two weights less than his basic double-taper floater. He multiplies the basic line size by 1.5 to determine the length of the additional floating tip. This tip is often a different color.

Line Weight	Line Weight of Taper	Length of Modified Taper
9	7	13'6"
10	8	15'0"
11	9	16'6"

Mike has found that in spite of the nearly complete taper remaining in the base line, an excess of energy remains at the completion of a single or double spey cast. He can explain this in engineering terms, but essentially the large-diameter line permits a longer, more efficient taper than is provided by the manufacturers in the base line. His addition of a taper from a second line two lines sizes below the one being cast produces a long single taper. Though not continuous—the butt section of the additional taper is larger than the tip of the original taper—the overall length is still twenty to twenty-five feet.

I have watched Mike cast this combination of tapers. On a spey cast, the first line rolls out and appears to be nearly finished when suddenly, at the very end of its turn-over, a quick final kick of energy rolls out the second taper just above the water. This sequence is quite unlike any other I have witnessed in fly casting.

Forward Taper. A conventional forward-taper line with a front taper, belly, and rear taper totaling about forty feet is, in my opinion, a poor line for use with two-handed rods. The head is too short to use in spey casting, and the overall length, about eighty-two feet, is too short for overhead casting. Only a thin running line connects the rod to the head, and positive mends are impossible to make. Finally, the weight of the line is too concentrated in forty feet for fluid casting with rods typically fourteen to sixteen feet long. However, if a conventional forward-taper line is used, it should be two sizes larger than the manufacturer's recommendation, for example, a weight 11 line for a 9-weight rod.

Forward Taper Long Belly Sink Tip System (Trey Combs). A saltwater long-belly line has a front taper either the same or slightly longer than the front taper on a double-taper line. Belly length is approximately forty feet—about ten feet longer than a conventional forward-taper line—and is followed by a short rear taper that leads to the narrow-diameter running line. The entire line is usually 105 feet (thirty-three meters).

Line Weight	Tip Length	Front Taper	Belly	Rear Taper	Running Line
9	1'	7.5'	40.7'	3.7'	53.8'
10	1'	8.0'	40.0'	4.0'	53.8'
11	1'	8.5'	39.2'	4.2'	53.8'
12	1'	9.0'	38.5'	4.5'	53.8'

I begin my sink tip system by removing the one foot of level tip. I then measure the front taper, tip to level belly, and *cut off at least three-fourths of the taper.* For example, I begin with a line one or two weights heavier than the manufacturer's recommendation, usually a weight 11, which has a front taper of 8.5 feet. After removing the single foot of level lead, I cut off six or seven feet of taper and attach a braided monocore loop. All sink tips and floating tips are looped to this line.

The first thirty feet (less the foot of level tip) of my weight 11 line weighs about 330 grains, or an average of 11 grains per foot, while the entire head weighs 570 grains. This weight includes the front taper, which drops well below 11 grains per foot, and the belly, which is 12.6 grains per foot. (At 12.6 grains per foot, a thirty-foot length weighs 378 grains, a weight 12 line.) *By removing seven feet of the taper, I have cut away all line that weighs less than 11 grains per foot, or line that is less than weight 11 line.* Actually, because the taper represents twenty-five to thirty percent of the first thirty feet, the first thirty feet of the "new" line, including the now very short front taper, is a weight 12 line.

Because I have cut the taper back so severely, I do not have to loop to sink-tip sections less than weight 11, and can go to weight 12 sink tips without difficulty. In effect, I have a line that tapers to a weight 11 sink tip. This is an advantage because of the higher sink rates inherent in these heavier tips. The basic line has so much turn-over energy that sink tips of twenty feet can be spey-cast without difficulty and *without hinging.* My preference is for sink-tip sections of continuous level line, that is, line without any taper. If that is not possible, and a shooting taper is cut up, I make sure that the front taper of the head is not reversed.

I prefer sink tips of twelve, fifteen, and eighteen feet, and I obtain them by cutting up two thirty-foot High-Speed Hi-D shooting tapers. I get two fifteen-foot sink tips from this approach, one with a slight taper and one without a taper. This is convenient, because I find fifteen feet to be my most used length in winter. When I cut for the twelve- and eighteen-foot sections, I make sure the eighteen-foot section has the front taper. If additional lengths are desired, I cut a shooting taper for lengths of ten and twenty feet. I often use a sink tip of twenty feet; I infrequently use one of ten feet, and I never use a sink tip of less than ten feet for winter fishing. For this particular double-handed rod sink-tip system, a tip of five feet is poor. It casts badly and meets no fishing need that is not better served by a longer sink tip with a slower sink rate.

Most of my winter fishing is satisfied with four sink tips of High-Speed Hi-D with a sink rate of 6 to 6.5 feet per second, depending on what weight tips I'm using, 11, 12, or 13. Because my purpose is to get the fly down to various depths, I don't need to duplicate the entire series of lines in a slower sink rate. A twelve- to fifteen-foot sink tip with a sink rate of IV is consistent with the casting qualities of my other sink tips. In addition, I carry a single ten- to twelve-foot tip with a sink rate of III. This line is for use when first-light steelhead are right on the beach, holding in water almost without current.

When six or seven feet of taper is removed from the basic weight 11 line and is replaced with fifteen feet of sink tip, the new head section grows by 9 feet, to a total length of 60.9 feet (section by section: 15 feet + 2.5 feet + 39.2 feet + 4.2 feet). Add rod and leader length, and I have a working distance of seventy-five to eighty feet. I also have more than sufficient belly weight to launch the most vigorous single and double spey casts. Either shoots considerable additional distance, the sixty-foot head easily carrying out the narrow-diameter running line. If I'm making an overhead cast, I strip in line until the back taper of the head has reached my stripping hand, roll out the sink tip, pick up the line, and after a single backcast, shoot the head on the forward cast. In this way, I easily make casts of 100 feet.

Scientific Anglers's Steelhead Taper is an alternative starting point. Using the weight 10 monocore line, in grey or orange, cut eight feet from the front taper and loop-connect to a fifteen-foot sink tip of weight 9 or 10 High Speed Hi-D. This produces a head length of seventy-two feet. The breakdown is: fifteen feet sink tip, two feet taper, thirty feet belly, twenty-five feet back taper.

I will like this approach even more when Scientific Anglers markets their Steelhead Taper in weight 11 and 12.

Forward Taper (Custom). Sometimes the line color or finish desired is available only in a forward-taper line of conventional length. In that case, two lines can be purchased and spliced together to produce either a forward-taper long-belly or a double-taper line.

To make a forward-taper long-belly, cut the entire front taper and up to ten feet of belly from one line. Cut the second line at the transition of the rear taper and the belly. Splice the two lines belly to belly. (To be effective, the splice must have the core of both lines overlapping. If this does not happen, the lines will hinge so badly as to be worthless.) The resulting line will have a front taper of seven to ten feet, a sixty-foot belly, a rear taper of four to five feet, and forty feet or so of running line, a total of about a hundred and ten feet. Since one of these lines could have a factory-built sink tip, this splicing approach allows the use of many manufactured sink tip lines with two-handed rods.

Shooting Taper. A shooting taper can be cast out of sight with a two-handed rod. I have heard some wonderful stories of anglers taking shooting heads with monofilament running line and casting across the river and so far into the woods that the heads are still there. But rarely is such a distance desirable, even on the largest rivers. Other forward-taper lines can be cast nearly as far. Casting a line a hundred feet is one thing; maintaining control of the deep running fly and properly setting the hook at that distance is quite another.

If some combination of extreme distance and depth is needed, I still don't use a thirty-foot shooting taper. My preference is to purchase a full-sinking forward-taper line with a sink rate of V. (Example: Weight 10 Wet Cel V Ultra Fast Sinking forward taper line with a sink rate of 6 inches per second.) By cutting off all the running line, I create a forty-foot head. This can be looped to a conventional floating running line or to a monofilament running line.

REELS

In the mid-1960s I sold a mismatched set of golf clubs and used the proceeds to purchase two new Pflueger Medalist reels. They were, at the time, a symbol of serious angling, an "expert's" reel that came complete with a drag system. I knew of the British reels by Hardy Brothers, but years went by before I began to lust for one. Beyond that, I couldn't find much to choose from.

My American reels were remarkably durable, even when I took them to salt water to pursue sea-run cutthroat and forgot to wash them afterwards. I know now that they were stamped out, and they had tolerances shameful by today's standards. They didn't have rim control or counterbalanced spools, but neither did any other reels. Looking back, a lot of features were absent from the old Medalists. They didn't have handles that fell off. Their reel spools wouldn't override or go into freespool on the strike. A slight jar to their side wouldn't forever bind the spool to the frame. Microscopic springs and pawls did not routinely migrate about their insides.

Before I gave up my Medalists, a few anglers were taking the largest model, a warhorse called the 1498, and chasing after huge saltwater denizens, including billfish. Nevertheless, the reel's popularity waned, particularly in steelhead fly-fishing circles. It remained inexpensive and durable, problems it never overcame in an increasingly upscale fly-fishing market.

Today's angler may select from dozens of reels that are miracles of metallurgy and engineering. The best are machined from solid aluminum bar stock to extremely fine tolerances. Some are designed to evoke memories of a bygone era, others are space age in appearance as well as technology. All are satisfyingly expensive, some lavishly so, most needlessly so. In the general absence of cane, reels have become fly fishing's lone bastion of genuine status, elegant symbols of wealth and aesthetic perfection.

Amid all these high-tech masterpieces, the steelhead fly fisher's needs remain remarkably basic, a rim-control reel with a good click system that will help to prevent an overrun. Many reels have an adjustable click that, by and large, is worthless. Indeed, "adjustable click" is something of an oxymoron. The click keeps clicking, regardless. Adjusting the click hardly changes the resistance enough to matter. In all my years of fly fishing, I have yet to see someone adjusting the click while fighting a fish. Like me, most anglers don't know—or don't care—which way the adjustment wheel is even supposed to turn. For steelhead fly fishing, I simply want a click with some resistance to it, just a little overrun insurance when I'm not leaning on the steelhead with rim control.

I avoid small reels that gain line capacity with an extra wide spool. Once into the backing, the rate of retrieve may be based on a spool scarcely more than an inch in diameter, about three inches of line for each turn of the spool. Generally, for midweight outfits, I like reels 3½ or 3¾ inches in diameter with arbors an inch or less. Even when fishing a 4-weight, I choose a reel with a diameter of at least 3¼ inches.

Incredibly, some reels, even expensive ones, are manufactured with interior parts that rust. Steelheaders spend a lot of time wading to their armpits, and their reels are frequently submerged. I don't want to bother with drying out and oiling my reel at the end of each day's fishing. One cleanup at the end of a week-long trip should be sufficient.

Additional considerations are mostly cosmetic and personal. A very hard anodized finish is desirable. When traveling by boat I protect my reels with neoprene reel covers. (A boat's nonskid surface will turn a new reel into a very old reel in a single afternoon.) I want to be able to change reel spools quickly, without using any tools except my fingers. I don't care for reels that are silent when line goes out. A click tells me a lot, often telegraphing a steelhead's desperation before I am visually aware of it. A racing click is still music to my ears, a sound I associate with my happiest moments.

I have used only a few reels for steelhead fly fishing. Those without a substantial drag mechanism that I can recommend include the following: Sage 508 and 509, Orvis CFO IV, Hardy Marquis 10, and Hardy Perfect. That's a very short list, and I'm sure that many other reels are acceptable.

A sound argument can be made for a reliable drag system, but not for the reasons one might expect. A drag is not needed to wear down a steelhead so much as to prevent overrides on the strike. Some friends think I make too much of this, but I have had the sudden load of the strike impact so severely on the click pawl that it was knocked out of alignment and the reel was sent into freespool. Once this happened on the Deschutes with a nine-pound hen that put together an incredible run. I could barely watch her attempt at returning to the ocean; palming a freespooling reel requires intense concentration.

Reels with powerful drag systems often represent considerable increases in price and weight, especially when they were designed for use in saltwater. For the most part, their cork, Teflon, or Rulon disk-drag systems are overkill for steelhead fly fishing. I have used an Orvis SSS 9/10 (now discontinued) on Canadian rivers for both steelhead and salmon. I set a light drag for steelhead, and then turned up the drag when a chinook salmon had settled down and only heavy pressure could wear it out. The reel is lightweight, strong, and has done well for me in salt water, too.

The Abel 3N at 7.8 ounces is powerful yet light. So, too, is the Pate Salmon by Juracsik Tool & Die. A cut below these reels in price is Scientific Anglers's System Two, models 78 (7.2 ounces) and 89 (8.5 ounces); and Orvis's D-XR 7/8 (6½ ounces), and D-XR 9/10 (7½ ounces). The Orvis reels are a recent introduction, the D-XR performing very well for me on the Dean. Both the System Two and the D-XR have a drag lever on the side plate, opposite the reel handle, which permits anglers to adjust the drag while a fish is running.

The magnificently crafted reels built by Stan Bogdan, Ted Godfrey, and Joe Saracione have dependable drag systems, yet were built to be used on rivers. To my eye, they are the most beautiful reels in angling, each possessing a classic look I find irresistible. Invariably, they are back-ordered; anglers wait years to get a Bogdan. I've fished only the Saracione reels and own two models, the largest for use with a double-handed rod. All these reels are expensive.

The number of single-action reels large enough to accommodate one hundred to two hundred yards of backing and more than a hundred feet of double-taper line is limited. Hardy's Marquis Salmon No. 2, the Orvis CFO VI and SSS 11/12 (discontinued), Sage's 722, and the Saracione Classic American in the four-inch diameter are the models I use on my two-handed rods.

The Marquis Salmon is also available in the No. 1, a larger model that will hold a weight 12 double-taper line and sufficient backing, and a No. 3 model, which is slightly smaller. They are an excellent value, but need to be carefully maintained. The CFO IV was the first quality reel I purchased, and I happily fished it for fifteen years. The CFO VI is the giant in this series. (Before fishing it, remove the spool and make sure that both click pawls are engaged. If only one is engaged, the reel is subject to overrides.) The Sage 711, with a 4¾ inch diameter and rim control, is the largest model in the 700 series. These reels are characterized by a large hole in the center. Three pairs of rollers turn on stainless bearings and support a large inside rim, the hole. The drag operates in both directions; whatever drag I set I must reel against. This is not a problem, because I set the drag up only enough to prevent an override. The reel's principal advantage is light weight, 8.25 ounces, and a very rapid rate of retrieve regardless of how much backing is out. The 711 spool empty of line measures 2¾ inches in diameter, or 8.635 inches per turn of the reel handle.

KNOTS AND SPLICES

Backing

I prefer thirty- to twenty-pound test braided Dacron backing. I like the heavier line because it is much stronger than anything in front of it, even if nicked or slightly abraded. This line may or may not be less prone to tangling or to burying itself in the spool when under a heavy load. Because I insist on at least 100 yards of backing on even my smallest reels, I often use twenty-pound test when connecting to lines weight 6 and under, and the thirty-pound backing on lines weight 7 and up.

One hundred yards of twenty-pound test backing is a very small diameter and a correspondingly low rate of retrieve. I prefer to use larger reels and fill them with 150 to 175 yards of thirty-pound backing.

The backing is secured to the reel by making an overhand knot at the end of the line (the tag end), and drawing it tight. The tag end is taken around the spool and secured to the line (standing line) with a second overhand knot. When the standing line is drawn tight, the two overhand knots snug against each other against the hub of the reel spool.

Several approaches can be used to attach the braided Dacron backing to the fly line. I always begin with a six- to seven-inch loop at the end of my backing. A loop of this size is absolutely necessary for changing lines quickly, for it must pass around a factory spool of fly line. If I have chosen thirty-pound test, I use a bobbin threader to draw the tag end of the line four to five inches into the standing line. When under tension, the braid acts like a Chinese finger puzzle and constricts on the line in its center.

The procedure is simple and quick. Measure twenty-four inches back from the tag end and, with the bobbin threader pointing toward the tag end, insert it in the line and run it four or five inches up its core. Push the threader out and insert the very tip of the tag end into the threader. Then withdraw the threader from the line, which pulls the tag end up into the standing line. To disengage the threader, pull the tag end out from the standing line, at which time the threader can be freed. By lightly pulling on the tag end side of the loop, the tag end can be drawn back into the line. The resulting loop is knotless and passes smoothly through the guides. As long as the line of pull is direct, the tag end cannot come free. However, the loop can easily be removed by grasping two sides and pulling them apart. Almost no pressure is necessary to draw the tag end free. Because I open the loop when passing it over the spool of fly line, I use Aquaseal to saturate the first and last half-inch of tag end within the core.

Twenty-pound test backing cannot be drawn into itself, and I knot the loop in place. Either a perfection loop, double surgeon, or Bimini twist will make this loop. A surgeon's knot creates too large a knot, while the Bimini twist produces a twisted loop with securing hitches that do not pass easily through the guides even when coated with Aquaseal or Pliobond. My strong preference is for the perfection loop. To help the loop's small knot pass easily through the guides, I cut the tag end to within one-eighth inch of the knot, and then I apply a tiny drop of Superglue (or equivalent cyanoacrylate glue) to this end. Capillary action draws the glue into the knot. When the glue has dried, I use clippers to trim the tag end flush with the knot. Then I apply a small drop of Aquaseal above and below this tiny knot and give it twenty-four hours to dry.

Braided mono loops

All loops from my fly line that loop to backing, running line, or sink tips are made with braided mono. I purchase the loops from Orvis or make my own from fifty-foot spools manufactured by Cort-

Using 10 pound monofilament,
a nail knot below the frayed-out part
of the loop completes the connection.

land. The procedure described earlier for making a backing loop is repeated in miniature with braided mono, the loop being no more than one-half inch long, with one to two inches drawn up into the core and two to three inches left to work over the fly line until it butts against the core from the loop. After working the loop in place, I put a drop of Superglue at each end to prevent any part from slipping. Finally, I tie a nail knot over the butt end of the braided mono and trim off the ragged ends that extend beyond the nail knot. Except for the loop, I coat the entire splice with Aquaseal. Only the backing loop must pass through this loop, and I like it small—a quarter inch or so.

These braided mono loops slip over shooting tapers and running line, but they are not large enough to slip over the heavy belly sections of fly lines. The following is what I do when putting together a sink-tip system built on a cut-back long-belly floating line: I strip the coating from the last 1 to 1½ inches of the floating line and put a drop of Superglue on the last 1/4 inch of braided core. After it has dried, the tip of the core is stiff enough to be worked up the center of a braided mono loop. I continue to do this until the frayed-out butt end of the loop is beyond the coated fly line. (I find it helpful to hold the loop in place with a drop of Superglue.) Then I secure the frayed-out portion of the loop to the coated fly line with a nail knot. I usually use twelve-pound Mason for this purpose. As added insurance, a second nail knot follows just below the first to secure the loop to the core. I then use Aquaseal to coat that part of the braided mono loop covering the core of the fly line. This gives the loop the same flexibility as the fly line. *Note*: If the frayed-out butt end of the braided loop does not overlap the coated section of fly line, the braided loop will hinge at the transition of coated line to core.

When I put together a sink-tip system, I like the loops to be extra small to reduce any possibility of hinging. As a result, I am unable to pass a fly through the loop; the fly must be removed to change sink tips.

Changing Fly Lines

First, I carefully separate the two halves of the plastic fly-line spool, place a drop of Superglue on the inside rim, and rejoin the two parts. This prevents the spool from falling apart while I am winding on line. After running my backing loop through the loop attached to the butt end of my fly line, I pass the backing loop over the entire spool and draw it snug. This loop to loop connection takes the configuration of a square knot. After placing a pencil through the spool, I wind on the fly line. Every fly line spool has two holes, one beside the other. To remove a fly line from a reel, wind it on a spare spool by putting one pencil through the center and a second pencil through the second hole. Using this primitive crank, I can wind off an entire line in just a few minutes.

By winding straight from one spool to another, I insure that no twists are placed in the line. The entire process is quick, so purchasing a number of expensive spare reel spools isn't necessary. Also, the loops won't bind up, which is not the case when backing is looped either to the core of the fly line or to Dacron loops spliced in place.

I never use the core of any fly line to form a loop connection. Years ago, I would strip the outer covering of my fly lines and whip-finish a loop using the braided core. I did this to connect shooting heads to running line, and fly lines to backing. The shooting-head connection wore badly because it passed so frequently through the last few guides, the result of rolling the head out on the water before picking it up to cast. I can remember fouling a head far out in the river and after a few sharp tugs breaking it off at the loop. Also, the loop to loop connections would bind up so tightly that changing heads involved picking away at the knot with whatever sharp pointed object I could find.

Dacron Loops

A loop can be formed by whip-finishing sixty-pound test braided Dacron to the core of fly line and coating the result with Pliobond or Aquaseal. This is time-consuming and messy, and the result is inferior to a braided mono loop.

Leader to Fly Line

The traditional approach to connecting the leader to the fly line involved cutting off most or all of the foot of level-tip section of fly line and securing the leader to the tag end with a nail knot. If a long leader was used, it became necessary to coat the nail knot with some sort of contact cement so that the knot passed smoothly through the guides. In time the leader had to be replaced. This involved cutting it off the fly line and nail-knotting on a new leader. I found that a butt section of six to twelve inches nail-knotted to the fly line and ending in a perfection loop was a good semipermanent solution. After placing a perfection loop in the butt end of a new leader, a loop-to-loop connection was easily made. Learning to tie the perfection loops as small as possible became important, because I used this approach even on far and fine dry-fly streams.

The nail knot can actually strip the outer coating from the fly line if the leader comes under long and heavy pressure from a steelhead. To prevent this, I double the end of the fly line and nail-knot to this, drawing the knot tight almost to the end of the tiny loop. Under pressure from the knot, a small bump of line forms and prevents the nail knot from ever slipping off. A second approach is to pull the butt end of the leader into the core of the fly line a quarter inch or so and run it out the side. A nail knot is then made above the exit hole. To make this needle nail knot, the leader must first be carefully tapered with a razor blade. The very thin monofilament is passed through the eye of a fine-diameter needle and the needle passed up the core and out the side of the line. Some anglers feel this knot is an advantage, because the leader flows from the center of the fly line and does not come off from one side as it does in a conventional nail knot. A third approach involves securing a braided mono loop to the end of the fly line and looping the leader to this section. This bulks up the tip of the fly line more than I like, and it is often hard to get the loops to form a proper square knot. However, the braided loop is the most satisfactory method of attaching a leader's braided mono butt sections to the fly line.

Leaders

Monofilament leaders consist of three sections: butt, taper, and level tip. How these sections are proportioned, the diameter of monofilament in the proportions, and the degree of stiffness in that monofilament determines the casting and fishing characteristics of the leader.

Steelhead fly fishermen need a leader that will turn large flies over and possess high abrasion strength; a hard, stiff leader that will not become weak at the fly knot after a hundred casts; that won't curl or pigtail when an improved clinch or blood knot is drawn tight. These requirements eliminate soft, limp monofilament, and should eliminate most super-strong, super-fine-diameter monofilament.

On occasion, I have watched a companion cast for hours with a fine-diameter twelve-pound test tippet and then lose the only steelhead hooked all day. What a shame! Steelhead are not leader-shy. The toughness of the monofilament, not its breaking strength for a given diameter, is the primary consideration.

In general, I use Maxima for all parts of my leader, butt, taper, and tippet. I never tie in a tippet of limp monofilament. Sometimes I use Mason, a spillover from making up saltwater leaders. These are very tough leaders, not at all strong for their diameter, but enormously strong in any fishing situation.

I tie up my own leaders, following a general 60/20/20 proportion of butt/taper/tippet. A typical nine-to ten-foot leader of Maxima would consist of five to six feet of twenty-five-pound (.020), twelve inches of twenty-pound (.020), twelve to eighteen inches of fifteen-pound (.015), and eighteen inches of twelve-pound (.013). A perfection loop is tied in at the butt so the leader can be looped to the short butt section previously nail-knotted to the fly line. The individual sections of leader are connected with blood knots.

Depending on water conditions, fly size, and the anticipated size of the steelhead, my tippets will run from fifteen-pound (.015), to twelve-pound (.013), ten-pound (.012), eight-pound (.010), or six-pound (.008). In winter, I fish a tippet of twelve-pound, and in summer one of eight- to ten-pound. I only go to six-pound Maxima when using a 2-weight or 3-weight outfit. If I don't use Maxima, I follow these diameters. For example, for winter fishing I may use Umpqua's .015-diameter leader, which tests twenty-pound.

I don't like to fuss with blood knots in the field, especially in poor light. When it becomes necessary to attach a new tippet, I use a double surgeon's knot. It's not nearly so smooth as a blood knot, but it *is* stronger, and I can tie it blindfolded. Because I may attach a new tippet a couple of times a day, I consider the length of monofilament directly above the tippet to be sacrificial, and I tie it in with this in mind. Replacing a tippet with a double surgeon's knot is so quick that I don't bother to remove tightly drawn wind knots.

The short leaders used with shooting tapers and sink tips are easily made, consisting principally of a butt section, a sacrificial taper, and a tippet. The following is typical of a four- to five-foot winter steelhead leader looped to six to twelve inches of fixed butt testing twenty-five-pound breaking strength: two to three feet of twenty-pound, twelve to fifteen inches of fifteen-pound, fifteen to eighteen inches of twelve-pound.

When I'm at a fishing camp and not breaking my rod down at day's end, I replace the entire leader each night. After tying on a new fly and securing it in the crossbar of my reel, I wind the leader on the reel and put it under tension. The next morning I'm fishing with a new leader that is absolutely straight.

Knots to the Fly

One needs knowledge of several knots to secure the tippet to the fly. I usually tie my flies on hooks with upturned eyes, and I want the knot to come straight from the shank of the hook, not from the top of the eye. An improved turle knot or a double turle knot are both loop knots that pass around the fly and cinch up behind the eye.

The double turle is simple: Run the end of the leader through the eye of the hook and pass the tag end twice around the standing end before running the tag end through the knot. Draw the knot up, but do not completely tighten it. Pass the loop over the fly and draw the knot up against the eye of the hook. Now, pull the tag end tight.

Some years ago, I spent a week on the Sustut River at Steelhead Valhalla Lodge fishing with Dennis Farnworth for chinook salmon. Each time I fouled my fly on the bottom and had to break it off, the break occurred at the blood knot connecting the tippet to the tapered section of the leader. Replacing the fly required that I also replace the tippet. When I changed from a double turle knot to a clinch knot, the break occurred at the clinch knot. I subsequently discovered that if I tied on the tippet with a double surgeon's knot, the break would occur at the fly, regardless of what knot I used. All this is very unscientific, but knot strength in the field, from strongest to weakest, is: double surgeon's, double turle, blood, clinch.

An improved clinch knot is stronger for light tippets, but they are rare in steelheading. I use a clinch or improved clinch when tying on dry flies that have been dressed on a ring-eyed hook, or when I am fishing in almost total darkness and can't confidently make a double turle knot.

Recently in the Northwest, a handful of anglers have been cutting off the return wire of a turned up eye hook, tapering the single wire with a file, and lashing down a loop of braided Dacron or braided monofilament with tying thread to the end. (If the fly is a "show fly," the loop is made by twisting three strands of silkworm gut.) To secure this fly to the leader, a nail knot (the same type of knot salmon anglers use when tying a herring loop) is tied in behind the loop. To make the knot, it is necessary to first secure the tippet to the fly, then attach the tippet to the leader. The loop itself is not used to hold the knot. This arrangement allows the dressing to ride much more positively and the currents to impart more "life" into the fly.

3

EQUIPMENT NOTES

SEVERAL winters ago on the Skagit River I asked John Farrar, a Washington steelhead guide, what tackle or equipment purchase he had made in recent years had advanced his fly fishing more than any other. He didn't think long on the matter. "My five mil boot-foot waders," he said. "I ran out and got the first pair that was available."

Though I might have hunted elsewhere for an answer—latest line? high modulus rod?—I realized his choice was logical, and I agreed with it. We were, in fact, both wearing the waders he described. The insulated boot and the heavy neoprene body that extended to our armpits had kept us warm in January currents that held in the mid-thirties. Not once that winter had our legs and feet been cold—or wet. What at first seemed a wonderful luxury was by now a necessity; we could not imagine winter steelheading without them.

These waders, which have become synonymous with fall-to-spring fishing, are indestructible, comfortable, and very functional, attributes often missing in fly-fishing equipment. I can't speak for fly fishers in other areas, but based on the depressing number of equipment failures I have observed, I am convinced that the Pacific Northwest is a tough proving ground for wading equipment—waders, vests, and rain gear—and that much of this merchandise is improperly designed, poorly made, and even just plain silly. Looking glamorous in your local pro shop isn't the same as standing to your waist in an ice-cold river for ten hours while gusts of wind drive sleety rain up your nose.

I've had more than a few fishing days when misery is all that lingers in my memory. Several years ago at a fly-in wilderness camp I walked out into the river wearing a new, right-out-of-the-box pair of

35

Tom Pero and Don Roberts demonstrate some advantages of stream cleats and wading staffs for the North Umpqua's ledge rock pools.

wading shoes. As I followed the swing of my fly on the first cast, I noticed a white object floating downriver. This proved to be the heel from my wading shoe. The second heel soon followed it. I once exposed my "breathable" and very expensive rain jacket to a day-long rain on the Hoh River. By late afternoon I was soaked to the skin, shaking with cold, and dimly aware, in my hypothermia, of why Alaskans call this type of jacket "Gore-Leak." I've owned so many leaky waders that for years I thought the best waders were those that leaked least. Then there was the manufacturer who boasted that his mesh vest had waterproof pockets. When they filled with water—as they did every time I waded to my waist—the water stayed *in* the pockets. No drain holes. Each time I exited the river, I had to either stand on my head or remove the vest to dump off two full pints of water. I stowed my flies in an upper row of pockets designed to hold small gadgets rather than aluminum fly boxes. The vest became one of the many I used to own. During these moments of travail, I think hell for manufacturers is where they are forced to use their own equipment.

What follows is what has worked for me in steelhead fly fishing and why. My comments are not product reviews, and no company is paying me to say nice things about its products. Consider them only in a generic sense—a few words of guidance that might prove helpful.

WADERS

I prefer neoprene waders to any other type. The material, first used in making wet suits, is remarkably durable, provides wonderful insulation against the cold, remains cool when wet, and is completely waterproof *if the seams are properly bonded*. Models come in thicknesses of three, four, and five millimeters. (Some Scandinavian models are made in a thickness of seven millimeters.) Undergarments can make up for some differences in thickness; I normally depend on a single layer of light, medium, or heavy weight long johns in Capilene or polypropylene. I use my "3 mil" waders for summer fishing where water temperatures do not drop below the high forties. Four millimeter is an all-purpose summer and winter thickness. My five-millimeter waders are an ideal choice in winter. Early models of neoprene waders were plagued with seam leaks. If this occurred in the heal of the stocking foot, the leg could be blown up, cinched at the knee, and put in a bathtub. A trickle of bubbles revealed the leak. (I did this so many times with one pair of waders that the entire foot became a patch.) But tiny "sweat leaks" above the knee, especially in the crotch area, are almost impossible to locate. I carry a couple of patch kits and several tubes of Aquaseal, and I'm prepared for the worst.

Steelhead fly fishers choose either stocking-foot waders with wading shoes, or boot-foot. I wear both and find advantages and disadvantages to each.

Boot-foot waders are easy to slip on and off, a convenience I value when I break my fishing day into several sessions. The insulated boots keep my feet far warmer than any stocking-foot type. They cannot, however, be turned inside out, and they are exceedingly difficult to dry, particularly when I have taken a dunking and the boot lining is soaked. Commercial boot-foot wader driers are available, but they are too large to be portable. If wader dampness is only the result of sweat, I turn down the waders to the waist and hang them over the back of a straight-back chair. Usually, this will do the trick overnight. As insurance, I always pack at least one extra pair of waders.

Putting on stocking-foot waders involves a lot of rigamarole, what with socks, wading shoes, gravel guards, and so forth. The feet of these waders also lose some of their insulation when compressed by wading shoes, even when the foot, the sole, or both are an extra mil thick. For this reason alone I prefer boot-foot waders for winter steelheading. For many anglers, the downside of stocking-foot waders is offset by these advantages: They pack and travel well and can be turned completely inside out and dried quickly, no matter how severe the soaking. Also, walking is more comfortable in neoprene-lined wading shoes than in insulated rubber boots.

Some manufacturers have recently introduced five millimeter stocking-foot waders of sufficient thickness that, when combined with good wool-and-polyester socks and properly fitting wading shoes, make comfortable wading in waters into the low forties. Gary Miltenberger, a Canadian guide, cuts the stocking feet off these waders and glues the uppers to snowmobile boots. Roland Holmberg, an Atlantic salmon guide from Stockholm, Sweden, buys new insulated rubber boots every season or so, cuts the old feet free from his waders, and glues on the replacements. He gets a lot of mileage from a single pair of neoprenes! This conversion takes courage and absolute confidence in the deceptively simple technique of stretching the two parts over a large coffee can, giving the edges plenty of overlap, and applying the glue. The result is a boot foot wader at considerable savings. It is also a great way to get additional use out of waders when the stocking feet are beyond repair.

The soles of waders should be felt, glued to the boot foot, stitched to the wading shoe. If this does not provide sufficient traction, and it won't on the North Umpqua, the Thompson, or the Salmon, stream cleats should be worn. My favorite brand has soft aluminum cleats secured to felt soles bonded to rubber slippers. I wouldn't be without them for much of my fishing. Caution: When the cleats are new, they are very sharp. If you step on your fly line you'll cut it in two.

I own a pair of three millimeter boot-foot waders which has felts containing built-in carbide-tipped steel studs. These do not grip as well as stream cleats, cannot be removed, can easily puncture a rubber raft, badly mar the deck of a boat, and must be removed before entering your cabin or motel, an inconvenience when it is raining. I intend to replace them with standard felts, and rely upon removable stream cleats for additional traction.

Some fly fishermen swear by Seal Dri stocking-foot waders. These are made of pure latex rubber, contain no seams, and possess "give" that permits great freedom of movement. In addition, they pack well and are easily repaired. Their downside is twofold: Insulation from the cold is almost nonexistent, and they are easily punctured. Harry Lemire overcomes these drawbacks by wearing heavy pile undergarments and putting rain pants over the waders. Other anglers cut off the stocking feet and glue the uppers to inexpensive rubber boots. Either way, steelheaders should purchase the extra thick Seal Dri #100's.

Boot foot waders with rubberized nylon uppers are appropriate for summer use if worn with medium- or heavy-weight undergarments. Lightweight nylon stocking-foot waders should be considered only as a backup.

Hip boots of any type are not appropriate for any serious steelhead fly fishing.

UNDERGARMENTS

The first items I reach for when packing for a trip are the polypropylene long johns I'll wear under my neoprene waders. Polypropylene wicks moisture away from the body and provides warmth. They are an absolute necessity, winter or summer.

Polypropylene takes on the combination smell of sweat and neoprene, an unpleasant odor after only a day. After a week, it becomes an invitation to dine alone, even when camping. For this reason, I always have two sets and can change daily, for they dry in a few minutes. A couple of years ago I switched to Patagonia's Capilene. It doesn't take on body odors or pill from wear as readily as polypropylene does, and is smoother on the skin.

Winter fly fishing can be very sedentary. One stands in ice water, makes a cast, and waits for a steelhead while rain and sleet fall. On these cold days I wear "Expedition Weight" over "Light Weight," both long-john bottoms and long-sleeve tops, beneath my five-millimeter neoprene boot-foot waders. For late winter and fall fishing I rely upon medium weight, while lightweight is ideal when currents top the mid-fifties in temperature and I'm wearing three-millimeter neoprenes. (Lightweight can also be purchased in T-shirts so that the layers do not bunch up at the cuffs.) The three weights are available in different colors for those who like to be organized.

VESTS

Lee Wulff is credited with developing the modern fly-fishing vest in 1931. Originally called the Tak-L-Pak, it had a single large pocket on each side of the front for fly boxes. Above this pocket were two smaller pockets and above these a single small pocket, with three exterior pockets on each side: six in all. A single large pocket across the back for a rain jacket or spare reel and a few interior pockets provided additional storage. By the early 1950s, no self-respecting fly fisher would dare be caught afield without one. All of today's fly-fishing vests are variations on this theme.

What began as a great idea was soon improved, a constant proliferation of pockets upon pockets that became ridiculous. What is a steelhead fly fisher supposed to stow in twenty-five or thirty pockets? For years, I pretty much gave up on vests. I placed a spool of tippet material, a fly box, and clippers in the front pocket of my waders. That still left my two shirt pockets to fill!

Not many steelheaders are such minimalists, but neither are they matching the hatch and carrying all the flies attendant to resident trout. Our sea trout needs are simple, straightforward, and *critical*. First, the vest must be short. It should have, on each side, one—and only one—large pocket that will hold a typical aluminum (or plastic) wet-fly box measuring approximately 3½ by 6 inches. Above each of these pockets, the vest should have a single pocket five or six inches deep and wide enough to take a plastic box holding dry flies. Any extra pockets stitched to the outside of these pockets—and there can be several—should house three-inch-diameter tippet spools. The bottom wet-fly pockets should close with a zipper. Upper pockets set high should close with Velcro tabs; I don't want to fool with a zipper I can't see without taking off the vest. A single large back pocket is useful for stowing a lightweight waterproof jacket. A single, flat inside pocket is nice to stow a fishing license. (I put all my fishing licenses in a reclosable plastic bag. I'm legal as long as I'm wearing my vest.) When I am wading particularly treacherous water, I stow my big swing-leaf aluminum fly box in a reclosable plastic bag. If I slip and go in, I won't have to dry out a hundred flies. The bag is worth the bother. The plastic boxes holding my dry flies keep water out during a short dunking.

I like all pockets to be constructed of a waterproof material with drain holes sewn into the lower row of pockets. I dislike wearing my rain gear over my vest. Why, in a sport synonymous with rain, should a vest only function properly in fair weather? I much prefer to wear a short rain parka under my vest. (This makes pockets on the rain parka useless, unless it is designed to hold fly-fishing paraphernalia and to replace the fishing vest altogether.) If the vest offers some protection from the rain, it is possible to put the rain parka inside your neoprene waders. I often do this when wearing my Patagonia shorty vest. The arrangement works well except in heavy rain.

VEST CONTENTS

What goes into the vest depends on individual needs and the area and season fished. My all-season essentials begin with a small waterproof flashlight (Splash-Lite by Tekna) carried on an Orvis Zinger. This is necessary for picking out a trail, changing flies, finding items in my boat bag, and so forth, before first light and long after sunset. Other contents are routine: Nippers (or small pair of scissors), a tube of sunscreen and insect repellent (summer), thin polypropylene gloves (winter), Chapstick, forceps for removing flies from a deeply hooked fish, plastic measuring tape, 2X half-glasses, thermometer, hook sharpener, small smooth-jawed scissor-pliers for mashing barbs down or crimping lead split shot (where it's legal), a folded up handkerchief with which to clean my sunglasses, and small tin of Advil or equivalent ibuprofen-base medication for muscle and joint soreness. During the summer when I am dry-fly fishing I throw in a silicone spray, even though I treat the flies before I go fishing. I also carry "Mono Slick," a plastic box containing a foam pad that I fill with a silicone line dresssing. After the box is closed around the line just above the reel, the line is cleaned and lubricated by stripping it twice through the box.

TACKLE BAG

A tough nylon bag made stiff with a styrene liner serves so many needs that I now find mine indispensable. When filled with my vest's contents, and fly reels, camera, tape recorder, glasses, and so on, it becomes my carry-on luggage. As a boat bag, it keeps dry all the items I don't carry in my vest. When I return home, I stow the bag on a shelf, its pockets keeping myriad items neatly separated. I currently own two: a Wood River Classic boat bag, and an Orvis Fly Fisherman's Kit Bag.

RAIN GEAR

Three basic types of rain gear are currently marketed: rubber or PVC-coated nylon; breathable synthetics supposedly impervious to rain but permeable to water vapor; and waxed cotton, which has characteristics of both and the advantages of neither.

My comments earlier in this chapter illustrate my prejudice against breathable fabrics. I have sailed thousands of miles offshore on ocean-racing sailboats and have spent many years fly fishing in cold-weather rains, and for waterproof protection, I depend on coated nylon with welded seams. Everything else has leaked.

I believe the advantages of breathable fabrics when it is actually raining are oversold, being mostly those of comfort and tailoring. My undergarments wick away moisture from within my neoprenes. Unless I am heated up from a hike, an open zipper at the throat and a vented back keep me reasonably sweat-free. The level of exertion is certainly a factor when weighing the advantages of breathable fabrics, but every guide who ever rowed me down a winter river was wearing a rubberized nylon slicker.

Most breathable rain gear doesn't start off leaking. It gets that way from repeated washings, from campfire smoke, from dirt, grime, and sweat, from not getting sprayed with this or getting seams sealed with that. In heavy rain, the jacket soaks up water on the outside, then rain gets through the seams and spreads. I've been assured by manufacturers that vast improvements have been made since the days of yore. I purchased my first breathable rain jacket in the late 1970s, and my last in 1985. Both were very handsome windbreakers and equally worthless as rain gear.

The first treatment of a fabric that would keep rain from getting in while dissipating sweat vapor was an expanded Teflon that Bob Gore developed around 1970. Patented as Gore-Tex, it has remained the leader in the field ever since. Today, a number of other manufacturers have introduced breathable rain gear specifically for fishermen. Columbia, StreamLine, and Simms use Ultrex coated nylon. Patagonia nylon is treated with "H2NO-Storm coating," while Loomis uses a tightly woven cotton material coated with a "hydrophilic film." They all work, are lined, have built-in hoods, and are expensive. No one is yet claiming that these breathable rain jackets offer the kind of protection provided by rubber-coated garments, but based on my recent use of two models under less than downpour conditions, they're getting close. That may be enough to justify their continued use if the protection they provide can be maintained over several seasons.

Regardless of whether the fabric is breathable or rubberized, I look for certain construction details in jacket design. I want it cut high, no more than an inch or so longer than a "shorty" model fishing vest. It should not have slash pockets; they just fill up with water. A pocket on each side set high with a Velcro flap is fine, but it must be able to hold a conventional fly box. I avoid jackets with deep pockets. Fly fishers spend a lot of time with a hand pointed skyward, and without a good fit at the cuffs, rain will run down the arm. I like sleeves that close with Velcro. The StreamLine jacket goes one step further, with Velcro cuffs lined with neoprene to provide a nearly watertight fit. No jacket should be without a built-in hood, and it should be designed so that it will not drape over the face when a stocking cap is worn. On bitter winter days I don't want to wear a baseball cap just to keep the hood off my face. Also, the hood must employ a simple, foolproof drawstring system that will snug the hood down around the face. I like a plastic zipper with a storm flap, and an elastic drawstring at the bottom of the jacket. Some jackets offer Velcro-closed reach-through slots set beside the front zipper so that (theoretically) the vest can be searched for an item when the rain gear is fully closed. I find this of very limited use.

FLY BOXES

I use two styles of Wheatley boxes to stow my wet flies. Both measure 6 by 3½ inches, are crafted of polished aluminum, and secure the flies with metal clips. My all-purpose box has twenty large clips on one side (1/0 and 2/0 flies), thirty-five small clips on the other (6's, 4's, and 2's), and is one inch deep. My winter box has a swing-leaf that has thirty-five small clips on each side, and twenty large clips on each side of the box. The swing-leaf is secured with a pin. Harry Lemire showed me that the pin can be knocked out and the swing leaf removed. This leaves a box, with twenty large clips on each side, that is 1⅛ inch thick, a perfect size to house my marabou spiders and largest spey flies.

When I am flush with wet flies, I like to fill the swing leaf model, 110 clips in all, with a thoughtful assortment of everything wet and damp, bright and somber, high water and low. This one box lets me fish for steelhead anywhere.

The large marabou spiders blow around and tangle in other flies. Bob Arnold cuts up a large-diameter soda straw into short sections, notches one end, and runs the notched end over the marabou fly until the notch comes up against the bend of the hook. The straws are stowed in a plastic box.

Some anglers prefer to stow their wet flies in plastic boxes. They tell me that damp hooks will rust and stain aluminum boxes. When this begins to bother me I'll remove the stains with metal polish.

Wheatley markets boxes with black-rubber bars, each bar containing slits into which runs the point of the fly. This works as long as you have both good close-up vision and good light. I often have neither and no longer use these boxes in my steelheading.

Sheepskin fly books are very romantic and handsome. I once filled these with marabou flies, big overdressed 2/0s, but the flies either were hard to remove or fell out on their own. In a short time, the whole thing was a mess. I only use sheepskin fly books to hold 4/0 or 5/0 flies that are difficult to stow any other way.

I stow my tube flies in an Allumite fly box manufactured in Sweden. Instead of clips, it has rows of metal prongs that secure the tube flies. The boxes are hard to obtain in Sweden and not available in the Canada or the U.S. This unhappy circumstance will likely change as tube flies grow in popularity for use both on rivers and in salt water.

I stow all dry flies loose in plastic boxes. Dividers separate the dressings by category (Bombers, Wakers, hairwings, and so on). The boxes have tight-fitting lids that prevent their contents from getting wet during the occasional unplanned plunge.

POLARIZED SUNGLASSES

Polarized sunglasses protect the eyes from overexposure to ultraviolet light. I know that native fishing guides who work tropical waters without glasses tend to suffer early blindness from cataracts. Like most trout fishermen, I wear glasses to protect my eyes from an errant backcast, and to cut the glare on the water so that I can spot fish.

Cutting the glare means removing blue from the light spectrum. This increases the contrast between objects, a steelhead from surrounding rocks, for example. Grey lenses, the most popular all-purpose choice, are neutral-density filters, serving to remove light from across the entire color spectrum equally, blue light as well as red light, so colors look natural. An overcast day filters out long-wavelength reds and lets the short-wavelength blues and violets through. These scatter when they hit moisture, such as clouds, which gives distant objects a hazy look. Yellow or amber lenses remove more of this blue than do grey lenses, as much as ninety-five to ninety-eight percent. (Eliminating one hundred percent of blue light—the color blue—is neither necessary nor desirable.) Color is distorted, but contrasts are greater.

I carry two sets of polarized sunglasses, one with grey lenses and one with amber. I rely on grey lenses for general wear and when fishing under very bright conditions. I wear the amber glasses under all other conditions.

TRANSPORTING RODS

Three- and four-piece single-hand travel rods, with actions the equal of two-piece rods, are now available for steelhead fly fishers in 4- to 9-weights and in lengths from nine to nine and a half feet. These rods are carry-on luggage on destination trips, whether by plane, train, or bus. If you arrive, they arrive. The convenience is obvious.

Travel rods may be transported either in PVC-lined, nylon-covered carrying cases capable of holding three or four rods, or in nylon bags that hold four rods in their aluminum cases. In the first example, a second carry-on bag is necessary to transport the angler's reels and fly boxes. However, on crowded flights, airlines sometimes restrict passengers to a single piece of carry-on luggage. In the latter example, the rod bag has outside pockets that hold reels and fly boxes, eliminating the need for a second bag. Most overhead baggage compartments on planes are thirty-six inches long. Three-piece nine-foot rods are longer than this, but they will fit and can be carried aboard.

Many of the finest steelhead rods must, because of their length, be checked as baggage. When you arrive at your destination, you go to baggage claim and pray that your rods arrived. This frequently involves waiting impatiently at the freight elevator long after all your other bags have been picked up. (I once stood with seventy other anglers before an open freight elevator filled to the top with PVC rod tubes. Those of us with tight connections nearly had heart attacks.) Taking the rods out of their aluminum tubes and stowing them in a PVC tube is one solution, though I once had a rod tip broken when the PVC tube was thrown like a javelin. If a couple of these rods are removed from the tube and taken to a boat for a day's float, they have no protection. Carrying the entire PVC tube in a small raft can be inconvenient at best. A second strategy involves carrying the aluminum tubes in a canvas bag that disguises its contents. If you're lucky, the tubes will only get dented. My best solution is to tape together my two or three favorite rods in their five-foot aluminum tubes, have the airline place a large "fragile" tag on them, and sign the disclaimer. If the rods come through looking like they've been recycled, it's my fault. In six recent flights to Canada, the rod tubes haven't even been scratched.

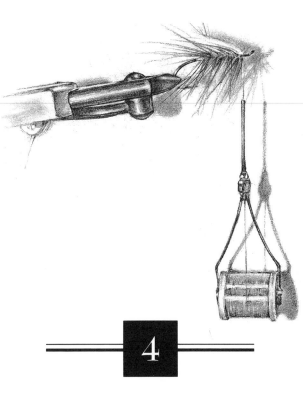

4

FLY DRESSING NOTES

Salmon Hooks

The hook is fundamental to fly fishing. Its design and construction, along with the style of the dressing, determine how a dry fly floats and how a wet fly swims. Too frequently, however, steelhead fly fishers choose hooks on the basis of tradition and marry their choice to a style of fly they find aesthetically pleasing. This lack of pragmatism can be costly. Flies, even expensive custom flies, often do not fish properly, the hook being too light, too heavy, or too long to efficiently carry the dressing in the water fished.

Over the past twenty years, steelhead fly fishermen have adopted the Atlantic salmon hook for much of their fishing. This classic design with a turned-up looped eye and japanned black finish has become an elegant standard, one integral to the art form of tying steelhead flies. But considerable variation in style and quality exists among these hooks.

The wire diameter of a hook is given an "X" designation followed by "fine" or "stout." A hook that is said to be 2X Stout has a wire diameter typical of a hook two sizes larger. The opposite can be said of a hook 2X Fine. The length of a hook is also given an X designation, but followed by "long" or "short." A hook 3X Long has a shank length as long as a regular hook three sizes larger. Conversely, a 3X Short has a shank length of a hook three hook sizes smaller. This X business is a loose standard applied most generally by manufacturers, and often in conjunction with the type of bend given the

Left column top to bottom:
TMC 7999 2/0, 1/0, 2, 4; Partridge M 2/0, 2, 4, 8; Partridge Wilson, Partridge Bartleet.

Center column top to bottom:
Bob Johns "Winter Run," Partridge streamer type with turned-down looped eye; TMC 700 1/0, 2, 4, 6; TMC 800 B, TMC 8089.

Right column, top to bottom:
Veniard low-water light wire salmon; Alec Jackson Spey, 5/0, 1, 3, finished in nickel, Japanned black, gold, silver, and bronze

hook (i.e., Model Perfect, Limerick, Carlisle) and whether the hook at the bend is straight, or offset for fishing bait. In this manner, the general configuration of the hook is quickly communicated.

The system of describing hook diameter and shank length with X designations is rarely applied to salmon hooks. Diameter is sometimes said to be "light," or "light wire," which can be taken as a dry-fly designation, or "low water," which has a fine diameter and a shank as much as 6X long for thinly dressed wet flies, and "stout" or "heavy," for standard wet-fly work. Such designations obviously have meaning only in a very general sense. For example, Partridge in 1991 describes its M style as 2X heavy, "traditional" length; its N style as 1X heavy and 2X long, a low-water hook; and its dry-fly hook simply as the Wilson. A fourth Partridge hook, known as the Bartleet Salmon, has the sweeping shank length of a streamer hook and the proportional wire diameter of a low-water or dry-fly hook. The Partridge hooks M and N compare to Tiemco's 7999 heavy wire, and 7989 light wire, and to Daiichi's 2441 and 2421 low water. Comparisons are made no better when including the Alec Jackson Spey hook (formerly by Partridge, now by Daiichi); the Bob Johns series of straight-loop-eye hooks, including the Winter Run and Short Shanked Bartleet, by Daiichi; or other models of salmon hooks by Mustad or Eagle Claw.

The turned-up-loop eye, in which the wire is bent back along the hook shank, has no exposed edge for the leader knot to abrade against. For this reason alone I prefer the looped eye—whether it is turned up, turned down, or straight. There are secondary advantages as well. The looped eye, turned up or down, permits me to tie a turle knot behind it and to achieve a very direct line of pull. (I never use a clinch knot with a turned-up-loop eye.) When tying the fly, I leave a small space between the end of the head and the eye of the loop to accommodate this knot.

The return wire alongside the shank provides a good base for tying in the hairwing. Again, I must leave myself sufficient room to make my leader knot. If I crowd the head, I also have trouble trimming the wing butts, for they work down between the two wires.

The doubled wire is also a flat skid, helpful when riffle hitching the fly. In the smallest sizes for steelhead, eight to sixteen, wet or dry, the turned-up eye maintains a more open gap than a turned-down eye. In larger sizes, however, this is not a consideration.

When I shop for salmon hooks, I look for certain attributes. The return wire at the loop should be tapered. If it is stubbed off, tying a clean body becomes difficult and, also, the tying thread snags on the rough edges. I like hooks with small, thin barbs that can be flattened or easily broken off without weakening the hook. The point of the hook should be tapered evenly, a reasonably long "needle point." In some cases, the point is "chemically sharpened," that is, the point is ground by hand and then put in an acid bath to remove the microscopic grooves caused by the grinding process. This produces an extraordinarily sharp point, sharper than most anglers can obtain using a stone or file.

Though steelhead are not known for their hard mouths, large males have very tough skin that makes penetration difficult. A hook with a short spear point and a large barb is an especially poor choice with these fish, the hook either sliding off or taking such a shallow hold that it easily comes away. Of course, once such a hook has fully penetrated, the hold is very secure, but the trade-off is not remotely worth the aggravation. Partridge, the legendary firm in Redditch, England, makes many fine hooks, but for all the above reasons, I do not think their famous Model M salmon hook is one of them.

While salmon hooks are marketed in three basic weights, from heavy wet fly to dry fly, all serve important wet-fly functions. In most cases, the heavy-wire hooks are expected to take a fly down with no additional weight. The size of the hook can add considerably to the sink rate of the fly, and not just when fishing a floating line. For example, if I am fishing with a fifteen-foot sink tip, I know there is a considerable difference among the sink rates of three hooks commonly used for winter fishing: the Partridge Bartleet in #1, and Tiemco's 7999 in size #1/0 and #2/0. The three have similar overall dimensions and can accommodate nearly identical spey dressings. Their weights, in grams, are as follows: Partridge Bartleet 1, .335; Tiemco 79991/0, .508; Tiemco 79992/0, .670. Note that the Tiemco 2/0 is exactly twice as heavy as the Bartleet. If I find I am hanging up while using a 2/0 fly, I can change to the 1/0 size. This is often sufficient to keep my fly out of the rocks. If I am leading my fly through lies with still lighter currents, I'll pick the fly tied on the Bartleet. At any time, I can change to a fly style that will sink faster, such as a dressing in my Winter Series, or sink slower, such as any Marabou Spider or fully dressed General Practitioner. When the sink rate of the fly is combined with sink tips of various lengths and sink rates, the parameters become endless.

Fly fishers sometimes point out to me that the sinking line—not the fly—takes a fly down. They choose a light-wire hook for easy penetration, and use a short leader. Consider first that the sink tip is usually tapered, the sink rate at the fine end of the line less than the sink rate of the belly section. The fly—like the line—has lift when under tension. A heavy hook helps offset this, especially when the angler leads the fly. When tied to a leader of six feet or more, a heavy 2/0 hook sinks faster than the sink tip if the line is strongly back-mended and the fly and sink tip are given time to sink. And finally, a heavily dressed light wire hook does not swim properly when it comes under strong tension. Lift will not only bring the fly off the bottom, it will roll the fly on its side.

The heavy hook is excellent for summer's low waters when surface currents are so swift that a light-wire hook will not pass through a hard swing without rolling over or skidding across the top. For this reason, I carry wet flies on heavy- and light-wire hooks, including a few very sparsely dressed low-water flies tied on dry-fly hooks.

If currents are not so severe, I to go to the lighter hook, particularly the Alec Jackson Spey. Less tension is needed to set the hook, an advantage when greased line fishing. Light currents generate considerable action, or wobble, from the fly. And in very soft currents, the fly can be led through the swing without any danger of it becoming lifeless and sinking.

Salmon hooks are offered in lengths from "regular" to at least 4X long. The longer the hook shank is in proportion to the gap, the less stable it becomes. A 4X to 6X long hook is extremely unstable, likely to swim on its side under strong tension. The most unstable steelhead hook is Partridge's Bartleet, the shank sweeping up so severely that the hook wants to ride upside down like a keel hook.

Any weight added to the shank of the hook makes the fly less stable. Lead wire wrapped around a hook shank can cause a fly to ride upside down. Some heavily weighted nymph and shrimp dressings roll around nearly weedless, and will pass through their swings on their sides or upside down. Heavy lead barbell "eyes," will also flip a fly over and turn it into a jig. Some anglers anticipate this and tie in a long marabou wing at the throat.

Hackle or fur tied under the wing make a fly less stable. For this reason I reduce the hackle on low-water flies, but retain a modicum of wing material. The result is an enticing silhouette that maintains its balance through the swing, even in heavy currents. The classic low-water flies of English salmon tradition had just a touch of throat hackle, and though tied on light-wire hooks, remained reasonably stable during a well-led swing.

In the absence of any tail and almost all current, a fly sinks bend-first, a very unnatural attitude. Several types of dressings, including the General Practitioner, marabou spiders, and spey patterns, swim without this problem. I like these flies for winter fishing because I can lead the fly through very slow currents right to the beach and have it swim properly the entire way.

Because of its classic lines, the spey fly has attracted an enthusiastic following, both in a summer and winter dressing. Surprisingly, few anglers appreciate that the dressing's tiny wing and considerable hackle below make it the least stable of all salmon and steelhead flies. When this characteristic is combined with the sweeping, long shanked salmon hook typified by the light-wire Bartleet, you have a lovely pattern that fishes poorly except when penetrating very light currents. If the classic lines of the Bartleet are preferred, I tie on the Alec Jackson Spey hook, strip the fibers from one side of the hackle before palmering the body, and use a large hook in proportion to the fly.

My choices of general-purpose steelhead hooks are the Tiemco 7999 and 7989. They are approximately 2X long with a slight Limerick bend, a good practical and aesthetic balance. The return wire of the loop is nicely tapered. The length enables me to tie in the tag, tip, butt, and so forth, in a graceful manner, without compromising the fly's stability. The hook point is extremely sharp, the barb small and brittle. When I have not removed the barb, I often find it missing after releasing a large steelhead. I also fish the Alec Jackson Spey by Daiichi, and the Partridge Wilson.

An attractive salmon hook can be created by straightening out the severe bend of an English bait hook. The hooks are available through Cabela's in a number of sizes, including 3/0 to 5/0, sizes otherwise expensive and difficult to obtain.

A couple of years ago I began tying my dry flies on the Tiemco 8089, a straight-eye bass "stinger" hook. The light-wire construction and sharpness of the hook point made it excellent for greased-line work in #6 and #10. Mike Maxwell swears by it for his Telkwa Stone.

When tying leech patterns with lead barbell eyes, I like a short-shanked heavy-wire hook with a straight eye. The Tiemco 800B is an excellent choice.

The traditional heavy-wire hook with a turned-down eye is used to tie Comets (including the Boss), nymph patterns such as the Ugly Bug, and occasional bucktails. As a high-quality hook with a loop eye and Limerick bend, it is superb for steelhead, though it possesses neither the graceful line nor the mystique of the traditional salmon hook. The desire of many steelheaders to tie flies along Atlantic salmon lines has probably doomed this style of hook to infrequent use.

WORKING FLIES

Single strand floss is my choice of fly-tying thread in nearly all steelhead flies, wet or dry. I begin each wet fly by securing my tying thread near the back of the looped eye. If the body of my fly is either floss or dubbing in any bright color—anything but black—I use my thread to secure tinsel at this point, wind the tinsel evenly until above the point of the hook, and wind it forward two or three turns to form a tag before letting it hang by securing hackle pliers to the end. I wind evenly over the tinsel to the tag with my tying thread and secure the tail of the fly. If a body is to be dubbed, I form a dubbing loop, twist it moderately, and after coating the underbody with cement, wind it forward and tie it off. The tinsel is wound forward four or five turns to rib the body, and should be wound in the opposite direction from the dubbing. (When the tinsel rib is wound in the same direction as the dubbing or chenille, it slips unevenly into the seams.) Don't pick out the dubbing until the cement has dried thoroughly. If I choose a floss body instead, I simply wind the floss back and forth several times, each turn throwing a twist in the thread. I don't object to this until I want to complete the final two layers of floss. I then spin the bobbin to open up the floss so that it lies flat on the body. This finish produces a very even professional-looking body. The hackle is then wound on, the wing tied in place, and often a second hackle is tied in as a collar. If I want the head to be a different color from that I've used to construct the body, I change bobbins after the hackle is tied.

When a floss-bodied fly is completed, I run a bead of cement down the dorsal part of the body and on the ventral part of the tinsel tag, being careful not to touch the cement until it has thoroughly dried. This is how I construct the floss bodies in my Winter Series. (See Chapter 38.) Without the tinsel underbody, the body of dubbing or floss has a dark core when wet.

I often wind the hackle on last as a collar so that it covers the wing butts. A fly finished in this manner can have an extremely small head, just a turn or two of thread. The collar blends attractively with colors incorporated into the wing.

A number of tyers tie the wing in first. The wing tips extend out over the eye, the butts run down the body, seemingly backwards from convention. The body construction, and later the hackle, hide the wing butts. Only then is the wing pulled back and thread secured in front of it to force the wing tips in a conventional direction. The resulting head is small and neat. The approach has advantages. The wing is very well secured, and it rides high to provide plenty of action on the swing. However, I like very slender flies for low water, and I prefer the lower set the wing takes when tied conventionally.

A second wing-first approach involves slipping the wing butts between the hook shank and the return wire of the looped eye. The loop is closed with tying thread, the wing is trimmed from below, and the base of the wing is tied down to sweep toward the rear at the completion of the fly. This, too, permits a very small, neat head.

I use French metal tinsel. It is very strong, and considerable pressure can be applied when binding down a freshly dubbed body. The tinsel then helps to hold the body together.

If a floss tag is called for, I secure my tying thread and my flat silver tinsel two-thirds of the way down the hook. The tinsel is wound to the bend of the hook and back to the thread. The thread—single strand floss of whatever color the tag is to be—is wound back and forth over the tinsel. To prevent it from becoming frayed out, the tag needs a drop of head cement along its top. The tag remains natural looking if it is not touched before thoroughly drying.

The choice of body materials affects the overall size of the fly and its sink rate. I like a thin body of floss or dubbing for low water flies because of the fine silhouette produced. A floss body develops a fuzzy patina that no other body material can match. I cherish my old greased-line dressings! I tie my Winter Series with a floss body because I want the flies to sink well and the hook to act as a keel for the considerable marabou above it, a factor that keeps the flies swimming properly under substantial tension. My heavily dubbed summer flies give me the kind of silhouette I want at first and last light, or the "shrimpy" look I find desirable when tying deep-winter spey flies or the General Practitioner.

No dubbing material for steelhead flies is the equal of seal fur. This coarse, translucent fur is first bleached so that it can take any color of dye; it is dazzling in red, orange, and purple. Seal fur can no longer be imported to the United States, but the ban does not prevent the sale of existing stocks. However, the material is very expensive and alternative materials are routinely used. Angora goat, Australian opossum, Seal Clone (Hareline Dubbin), and polar bear dubbing are good substitutes.

No body material is so cheap and simply applied as chenille. It comes in many regular, variegated, and fluorescent colors, provides quick bulk and a dense silhouette, and makes the loss of a fly less painful. In the past several years this material has been marketed in exotic metallic and hot plastic finishes that steelheaders find especially useful.

I resisted putting Flashabou and Krystal Flash in my steelhead flies. The materials lacked tradition and seemed overly gaudy. I found myself missing out on a lot of creative fun, and eventually I was slipping in a bit here and there and was delighted with my cleverness! Pearl Flashabou proved fascinating, able to take on any color it happened to be mixed with, including black. My General Practitioner soon sported orange Krystal Flash "feelers," my Night Dancer reflected strange colors from the black Krystal Flash in its wing. Even the drab Purple Peril did not escape these attentions. Steelhead liked my more fashionable flies. They liked the old flies, too. When used sparingly, the new materials probably made a difference.

Marabou, the fine, stiff, "blood plume" section, is the most useful winging material today. It is cheap, comes in endless colors, and ties neatly for small heads. In the hands of a skilled tyer, it can be spun to produce lovely spey flies. Dyed grey, it becomes a passable substitute for blue heron. Though it cannot be stacked like most furs, marabou can be removed from the center stem in even bunches. I even use it this way to wing my finest winter spey flies. It lacks the durability of furs, but it possesses far greater action, which is a fair trade-off in winter when deep running flies do not long survive. Adding in a few strands of Krystal Flash gives a little extra sparkle and remains even if the marabou gets thin from wear.

If I use fur to wing my steelhead flies, my first choice is polar bear mask, the short fine fur around the face. Most other polar bear hair is too coarse. This material is extremely expensive, available when a fly shop is able to purchase an entire skin (often a bear skin rug) and sell it by the square inch. Because half my summer-run steelhead flies have black wings, my second choice is natural black squirrel tail. My third choice is bucktail. I often wing with natural brown, preferring it to fox squirrel for the Purple Peril, and I'll hunt through a bin of bucktails to find one with the finest textured fur on the top of the tail.

Occasionally I use bucktails, calf tails, and grey squirrel tails dyed hot fluorescent colors for winter fishing. Duck and teal flank, grizzly saddles, even entire golden pheasant and ring-neck pheasant skins are now marketed in fluorescent colors.

Bob Wagoner tells me that calf tail hair can be made absolutely straight with commercial hair straightener.

I usually prefer to use saddle hackle to hackle my wet flies. It has a finer stem, and the feathers possess more body than neck hackles. But body and web can be overdone, resulting in hackle fibers that mat. When tying my Winter Series patterns, I often wind on a final collar of stiff neck hackle to give the fly additional body.

Almost any summer pattern, and many winter patterns as well, can be made more attractive by winding a turn or two of teal or duck flank over the wing butts. I do this with many summer patterns, remembering to draw most of the flank up into the wing as I tie the head. This gives the wing a finely barred appearance while preventing too much throat hackle from interfering with the fly's balance when under tension.

Syd Glasso once explained to me how he used hackle tips to wing his reduced spey flies. My source for this material is white saddle hackles too fine to use as saltwater flies. I like to use six or eight tips, split evenly and tented so that they set low over the hook. They do not extend beyond the hook point. Since only the stems are tied, the resulting head can be extremely small. The individual tips are not so likely to turn under the pressure of tying thread if the stems are gathered together and crushed flat. Needle-nose pliers, or your teeth if you're not fussy, do the job.

Whether spinning deer, caribou, elk, or moose for dry flies, cut the tips off first. Additional wraps of single-strand floss can be taken below and above the initial flare point without matting down the hair. Antelope has no tips, but should still be cut down. Some tyers tie this hair only on top of the hook and do not bother spinning it. This saves time and material, for they don't have to trim away at the undersides of their Bombers. Such flies are not so attractive, but they are equally functional.

Anglers are discovering that by coating the lower half of the dry fly's wings with Goop or an equivalent cement, the wings aid in planing the dragging fly over the surface. Lani Waller's Waller Wakers for 1991 have this feature. To seat any spun-fur body, mix one part Duco cement with one part acetone. Apply as you would head cement. This glue will hold the body in place like nothing else.

Worm hooks popular with bass fishermen are useful steelhead hooks. Their keel causes a steelhead fly to ride upside down, an advantage when fishing rock gardens housing steelhead in their fly-grabbing grottos.

5

HOLDING WATER

S T E E L H E A D do not give up their lives of wandering when they seek out a river to ascend. Waters foreign to their homing instincts can exercise a strong influence on their behavior. Each fall, thousands of Idaho steelhead travel as far as 100 miles up Oregon's Deschutes. Nicola River steelhead often winter over in the Thompson River, fifty miles above the confluence of the two rivers. When Washington's Toutle River was devastated by the explosion of Mount St. Helens, its steelhead still at sea adopted other rivers for spawning. Kalama and Washougal steelhead are known to pass up the fishways of the Columbia River's Bonneville and The Dalles dams to breathe in the smells of a dozen rivers before returning to their natal waters. By late September, steelhead hold in forty miles of the Methow River, but when snow fills the Methow Valley, they migrate downriver to pass back over Wells Dam and winter in the warmer Columbia.

Pondering this, I ascribe the movements to water temperature, imperfect hatchery imprinting, and strong survival instincts. But outside my reasoned explanations is a fish that may travel downstream as well as upstream, or up tributary creeks and back, doing so with no apparent reason other than curiosity. That, however, does not obscure the overriding fact that steelhead finesse, rather than confront, their rivers, their route being the less strenuous travel lanes along the edges of the central currents, those "creases" that fly fishermen look for. They maintain their bearings by keeping in touch with the shore, resting along quiet beaches for a night, sometimes for days, before continuing on in the safety of summer's early morning and late evening shadows. Winter fish may hold until the sun

LeRoy Hyatt's line
← leads his rod to keep
the dry fly waking over the lie.

51

has been directly on the water and warmed surface currents. The steelhead stop for weeks, and they stop for nothing, storming through miles of river and a dozen long pools in a single day. Loners at sea, they travel the rivers singly and they travel in pairs. They enter an estuary otherwise empty of steelhead and stop in pools filled with steelhead, a group of individuals passing for a school. When they break out of a pool and porpoise past, I stop fishing to watch them for the enjoyment they provide, no longer bothered by the lack of attention they give to my fly.

Rain, or the lack of it, can speed them on their journeys or delay their upstream movements. A river low and clear with every freestone pebble exposed to the unremitting glare of eighteen-hour days finds steelhead retreating to the cool safety of deep pools. Enough rain to raise the river, a touch of frost in the night air, and cold fog that lies heavy on the water can all energize steelhead and pull them into the oxygen-rich turbulence of shallow lies where greased-line flies will attract them.

When none of these conditions prevails, there is first light, those few minutes no longer night and not nearly day, when surface currents are at their coolest. Then, even under very low water conditions, steelhead ease out of deep water to move furtively into the thin riffles at the very top end of pools. At such times I have observed them in less than a foot of water with their noses literally beneath the froth. They are hair-trigger nervous, and to raise them to a fly requires a careful approach from well upstream.

Unfishable rivers, "out" with muddy water, do not discourage migrating steelhead. The fish slowly pick their way along whatever new shore is available, even when this takes them through stands of shoreline willows. A river remaining in this condition for days becomes choked with steelhead, a bonanza for fly fishermen when pools first drop and clear. The steelhead's instinct to move on is temporarily suppressed, but they are fresh, very in touch with their surroundings, and aggressive.

A river "going out" from rain, a river "coming in," clearing and dropping from the lack of rain and high-country snowmelt, is an afternoon last week or a morning next week, a few hours when steelhead are fresh fish that have never seen a fly. The most successful steelhead fly fishers I know live for these moments, bend their work schedules accordingly, and know where to find these fish.

Some pools are classic, accessible, and famous; others are difficult to reach, troublesome to fish, and known to a small brotherhood of anglers who cordially share their ways. These are the public and private waters of steelhead fly fishing, the pools introduced to beginners and those held in secret by experts.

Friends who share with me the tying recipes for their favorite flies or the formulas of their most exotic hybrid lines become vague when the subject of their holding water comes up. I try to be circumspect, for I don't want to give the appearance of panhandling for this information, and I don't expect it to be given. Their knowledge is too hard won, the result of years, and seasons, and many fishless days. If they are experts on the rivers they fish, it is not because they can cast farther or wade deeper, but because of their knowledge of holding water. They do not prospect. They go where they know steelhead were, and where they will be again. Their holding water is the reason they can average a winter steelhead a day on a fly. To give away this knowledge is tantamount to inviting the public to their private fishing hole, for as surely as there'll be a fish in the lie, there'll be a fisherman, a stranger who is your friend's friend. These strangers will ask, "How did *you* find out about this spot?"

A few years ago, on a float down a winter river, I drifted quietly around a bend and came upon two well-known Northwest fly fishermen spey-casting along a bank slot of holding water. I had passed this obscure piece of water many times, obviously failing to appreciate its potential, for I had never cared to fish it. It soon became evident the anglers had seen me first, for they were hotfooting through the woods long before I reached their water. I laughed at this before realizing I had come upon one of their secret pieces of holding water. Later that day, I visited the pair at their campsite, and we talked of many things, but this incident was not one of them. They knew I could act upon what I had seen, if I could make sense of the water and fish it properly, and that a day might come when they would have to share this pool with me. They would not begrudge me that opportunity, for I gained my knowledge fairly, and possibly this observant pair of fishermen happened upon this water in the same manner.

Because steelhead are given to frequent and sometimes erratic movements, finding them suggests a methodical approach. You start at the top end of a pool and systematically work through, making a cast, taking a half-step when the flow is turgid, a small step in winter, or two large steps in summer, and casting again. When the pool has been covered, you move to another pool and repeat the process. Custom and streamside also dictate this courtesy. Like golf, it's considered bad form to dawdle while others wait to get on with their sport. You take your turn, work through the pool, and get out. This is neither a good nor a terribly wrong way to fish a pool; it is often the only one possible, given what little is known of the water.

But steelhead do not distribute themselves in a pool—much less a river—in any orderly fashion. A beginner watching experts learns that the water being fished isn't being covered methodically. Parts of the pool are fished through rapidly, other parts quite carefully. Casts vary in length, flies are changed to achieve various sink rates, sink tips are changed to reach specific parts of the pool: the head; the edges of runs; the clearly defined gut, bucket, or honey hole that so often holds a steelhead; and the broad tailout. How do the steelhead pass through this particular pool? Where do they hold just before exiting the pool? How do they distribute themselves when they rest? The answers are far more complicated than we imagine.

Years ago, I realized that some lies typically harbored large male steelhead. Or that large steelhead were often found in lies that demanded the least exertion of them. If this were true, I wondered if some sort of pecking order existed, and if it did, whether size, or sex, or both, established it. I knew this sort of thing existed where chinook salmon and steelhead occupied the same pool, the salmon holding where they pleased, the steelhead warily holding below them. Whenever possible, I discussed this with steelhead guides, for they repeatedly fished the same water and presumably would note such a pattern. These discussions were interesting but often inconclusive, because the guides noted holding

High water scallops the long gravel bar into small parcels of holding water. I walk along, stopping to fish the soft winter lies below each point.

water on many pools, but they rarely bothered with any comparative analysis of what kind of steelhead came from the lies. That fact doesn't call into question their powers of observation. On some rivers the steelhead are essentially one size and one age group; aggressiveness, not size, may be the factor deciding which fish takes which lie. During very hot weather, when stream temperatures reach nearly seventy degrees, a large pool well upriver becomes a cool oasis for dozens of steelhead. They collect here to survive, and it would be nearly impossible to know, in such a confined area and unnatural setting, if there were any pattern to their distribution.

When I first fished for steelhead with Roland Holmberg, an Atlantic salmon guide on Norway's Gaula and Aa rivers, I brought up this line of speculation. We were camped on a Canadian river, and I wished to see if he found my views had application on the camp pool we would be fishing, or whether his experiences with Atlantic salmon would challenge my convictions. Roland didn't find me sophisticated in the least, something of a disappointment. He explained that in Norway, a guide is responsible for a short length of river, a beat that may be no more than 200 meters long. The fortunes of his clients often depend upon his understanding a single pool, for they do not have the luxury of moving on if they cannot find fish or are unable to get the salmon in view to take a fly. "Everything a salmon does means something," said Roland. "When a large salmon comes up and slaps the water with its tail, it isn't doing that for nothing. It's telling other salmon that this is his pool."

Do the largest salmon in the pool have a certain lie, one that ultimately is filled by another big salmon? Roland was certain of it, and he described how a cock fish will drive off smaller males that run the risk of being killed if they are not hasty in their retreat.

"Some seasons a pool will fish extremely well. Other seasons there are no salmon in the pool. When salmon come in the river, they won't stop in pools that are empty of salmon. Salmon trickle from a pool as others fill it, and in this manner the water holds salmon all season. But if the first salmon to enter the river passes up a certain pool, it may not hold fish for weeks, and it will be poor the whole season."

Much of Roland's guiding took place on pools close to the sea, the movements of these salmon doubtless more dramatic than if they had been filling the miles of holding water farther inland. Nevertheless, his observations confirmed my own thoughts about steelhead and their holding water.

I believe that large pools often have primary and secondary lies, and that how these lies are filled is often the result of which steelhead is the largest. Large male steelhead are more likely to take up the deep lies within the gut of a pool, and smaller hen steelhead more frequently hold at the top and bottom of the pool where currents are stronger. I explained this to Roland and described to him a memorable summer-run lie, a small narrow slot just off a large boulder that was a third of the way down a pool a full quarter of a mile long. The lie never held more than a single steelhead, always a large buck, sometimes twenty pounds. Other parts of the pool below this lie held many steelhead, but rarely a male fish of this size.

Roland and I fished our long camp pool several times each day, usually dividing the water between us and not following each other through. All this took one to two hours, rarely more, until rain discolored the river and reduced visibility to a foot. We rose approximately forty steelhead in five days and noted the size and sex of each fish whenever possible. After two days, we had searched all the nooks and crannies we could reach with our flies. Six major lies emerged. (We suspected an additional lie but couldn't wade deep enough to fish it properly.) Just below the top end, a part I sometimes call the throat, the water was swift but with consistent hydraulics, and a fly fished well. Though this was a fairly large area, it was never good for more than a single fish, always a hen, and usually during morning light. We thought the bucks were exiting the pool in a different manner, probably along the far shore, which we could not reach. Farther down the pool were two nearly opposite lies, one off our shore and the other flat against the sheer rock wall of the opposite bank. Each of these gave up steelhead of both sexes, hens to fourteen pounds and bucks to perhaps twelve pounds except for a very hot sixteen-pound buck Roland took from against the opposite bank. Nearly halfway through the long pool, and dead in the middle of the river, was a narrow lie we discovered only because we caught steelhead there. The river possessed hardly any current, and nothing on the surface served to distinguish the lie from the acre of water around it. This small lie held only large bucks of sixteen to over twenty pounds. For a few days it was so dependable that I called it Hog Heaven and shook when my fly began the first swing though. Well below this lie, and just above the tailout, was a much larger, but equally soft, piece of water. Roland waded to his armpits and found only hen steelhead, ten pounds or so, and one evening he beached four. I rowed across the pool to fish the other side of the tailout. I knew that many steelhead were caught here, but now there were only spawning salmon, huge chinook so territorial that steelhead dare not take up the lie. Though I fair-hooked a twenty-pound male chinook, I didn't raise a single steelhead.

As the days passed, Roland and I could predict where the fish would take, conforming so completely to our expectations that we could "see" the steelhead in the pool. What emerged was not only a keen understanding of this holding water, but an appreciation of arrivals and departures, of fresh fish and residents of some weeks, and learning how each was determining our angling fortunes.

A pool so remarkably blessed is rare, but I find smaller pools no less challenging. Although the travel lanes may be narrower and the holding slots shorter, the dynamics are the same. Steelhead move in, pass through, and exit the pool, the more condensed nature of the water making it harder to read and, once read, placing a greater premium on proper placement of the fly.

Several years ago I watched a fly fisher take one or two winter steelhead a day from the very top end of a pool. He did this in an hour before going to work, hooking his fish after other anglers had pounded the pool with their flies. What made his success curious was his choice of water. Whenever possible, he fished the very top of the run—fast, relatively shallow currents. Halfway down the pool the river slowed for thirty feet before picking up speed again. Like most anglers, I was always anxious to work down and swing my fly through this gut; on a hundred trips through the pool, most of my steelhead had been hooked here.

One day I had the opportunity to stand at the head of the pool and watch closely as the angler began down with his spey rod. His casts were far shorter than mine, the small black marabou fly he fished coming under such light tension as to be nearly dead-drifted. I realized he had discovered how the steelhead were leaving the pool, and was sliding a fly right down this lane. Other anglers, myself included, overcast the water and entirely missed the lie. This was a mistake I wouldn't repeat. Two days later I hooked my first steelhead from the top end of the pool.

On this same water, well into the tailout, I saw a steelhead roll 100 feet from where I cast. After this happened several times, I reached the spot with my double-handed rod, and in a week I rose five steelhead. When a friend rowed me to the lie, I discovered a sizable ledge. Evidently steelhead would come up into the pool and for a time hang just off this ledge. I was delighted with my discovery and swore my friend to secrecy. "Private water on a public pool," I said, and wondered how many other secrets were mine to discover.

6

PRESENTATION

Wet Fly—Greased Line

My standard wet-fly presentation is intended to keep the fly swimming just below the surface. To make the necessary mends, I use either a double-taper or a forward-taper long-belly line. I begin by casting across and slightly downstream. I then mend upstream strongly enough to work the mend down the line and turn the fly so that it is facing upstream. This initial mend accomplishes several things at once. The fly line immediately above the fly is pointing upstream. A small amount of slack has been created. As the current takes out the slack, the line will not belly. I keep my rod pointing across and slightly upstream to bring the fly under tension as soon as possible.

Tension, the force of the current against the fly, is what gives it action, whether the fly is surface or subsurface and fished waking, damp, wet, or hitched. By keeping my rod pointed behind the swinging fly, mending as necessary to keep a straight line to the fly, the fly will be under maximum tension as soon as the slack is gone from the initial mend. *When the fly is under tension, it is working.* However, if I make the initial mend and then point my rod at the fly, that is, drop my rod tip downstream, I create additional slack that delays tension on the line. The fly passing downstream nearly drag free is not working effectively until it again comes under tension. The top part of the swing, often over the very lie holding a steelhead, is wasted and less water is covered effectively. For this reason, my habit when fishing a wet fly barely subsurface is to keep my rod pointed above the swing of the fly. I do

56

A summer steelhead taken using the classic greased line presentation and a low water Purple Peril.

not normally lead the fly with the rod. By having the line lead the rod, I reduce the speed of the fly as it crosses the river and passes through the swing, but I increase the tension on the fly and thus increase the action of the fly. The mends I make are normally designed only to maintain that tension on a straight line.

Greased-line fishing, sometimes generally applied to the above method of presentation, takes its name from the book, *Greased Line Fishing for Salmon: Compiled from the Fishing Papers of the late A. H. E. Wood, of Glassel,* by Jock Scott. The book was first published in 1935 by Seely, Service, and Co. Ltd., in London. Many editions followed, the most recent by Frank Amato Publications in 1982, containing an introduction by Bill McMillan.

Donald G. Rudd, writing under the pseudonym of Jock Scott, described a method of presenting a fly that Arthur H. E. Wood developed on his lower River Dee beat at Cairnton in Scotland during the early years of this century. Wood had been writing a book on the subject but died before it could be completed. His papers passed to his son, Captain E. G. Wood, who made them available to Rudd.

Whenever possible, Rudd used Wood's own words, including offhand remarks made at streamside. Rudd supported these with his own commentary, an unfortunate mix. Rudd's imperfect knowledge of salmon fishing resulted in semantic ambiguities that plagued the book from the day of its publication. Many expert anglers, salmon and steelhead fly fishers alike, have dithered over passages that defy literal translation.

In Wood's time, the accepted method of presenting a wet fly to salmon was to quarter a cast well downstream and simply hold the rod as the fly completed its swing. The silk lines sank slowly and could not be mended. Currents swept a belly into the line, a fact of life that forced anglers to swim their flies through very conservative arcs. Salmon typically took the fly almost diretly below the angler,

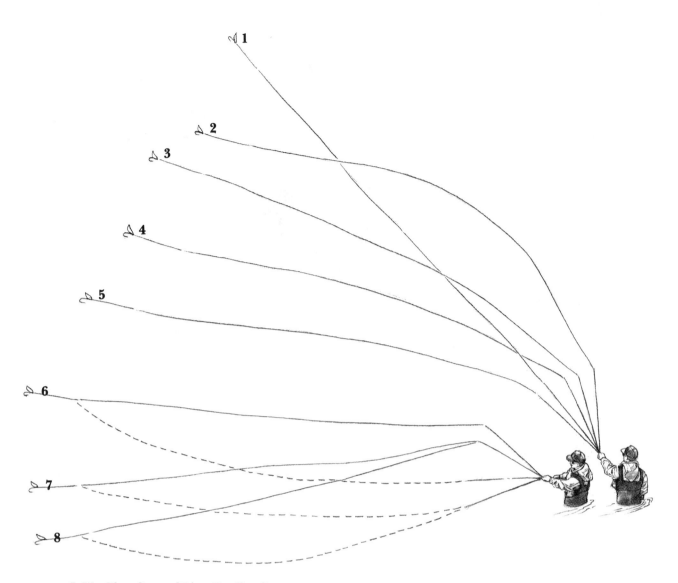

I. Wet Fly—Greased Line (Steelhead)

1-2 Following the initial presentation, an upstream mend is typically made. By keeping the rod pointing upstream, the mend works out quickly and the fly comes under tension.

3-6 The line leads the rod and the fly is kept under maximum tension while additional mends reduce the speed of the fly across the stream.

6-8 If current speed becomes too light, the fly can be led (dotted line in 6, 7, and 8) or a *downstream* mend made and the rod tip pointed as in 7. Either example will increase the swimming speed of the fly across the stream. I often find necessary to use this traditional greased line approach when my wet, damp, or waking dry has reached quiet holding water below my casting station.

and in setting the hook, the fly was often either pulled free or took such a light hold at the end of the salmon's mouth that it soon came free.

Arthur Wood kept his line floating by greasing it with animal fat. This enabled him to mend and to maintain control of the swing by removing any belly that currents might set in his line. This simple act permitted him to fish a greater part of the river's salmon lies while keeping his fly barely submerged, a working level Wood felt to be far more effective than the mid-depth fished in a conventional wet fly approach. More importantly, Wood led a thinly dressed fly so that it was somewhat broadside to the salmon, and then he fed slack into the rise. In this manner, the line would drag the fly into the corner of the salmon's mouth and the hinge of its jaw, where the hook penetrated for a most secure hold.

I won't belabor the controversial aspects of *Greased Line Fishing*, but some elements of this must be addressed to provide a satisfactory understanding of how Wood actually fished and to see how this integrates into current steelhead fly fishing.

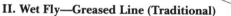

II. Wet Fly—Greased Line (Traditional)

1. The cast is made across and slightly downstream.

2. An initial mend is made so that current between the fly and the angler does not cause excessive drag on the fly. This upstream mend may be repeated, but should not be made so forcefully that the fly and leader are left pointing upstream. If the fly is in strong currents on this presentation, it may be necessary to drop the rod tip to keep the fly swimming across the currents. This, of course, eliminates the need for an initial mend.

3. As the fly line straightens, the fly is on a dead drift.

4. As the fly comes under tension, the rod begins to lead the fly. *This action reduces, but does not eliminate, tension on the fly.* If drag, i.e., tension on the fly, becomes excessive, the angler works to lead the fly rather than make additional upstream mends.

5. As the angler leads the fly into the lighter currents near shore, the rod tip continues to lead the fly to increase the speed of the fly across the currents.

6-8 As the currents become weaker, the angler can increasingly lead the fly until his rod tip is pointing at the beach, some 150 degrees from the initial cast. If leading the fly does not bring sufficient swimming action to the fly—and it may not, especially with hard waking dries—downstream mends can be initiated to bring additional belly to the line and drag on the fly. Also, once belly has formed, additional tension to generate across stream speed can be produced by pointing the rod tip farther upstream, moving the rod from 7 to 6, for example.

Jock Scott writes:

He [Wood] often told me that he liked the fly to float down like a dead leaf. What he regarded as fatal was any pull on it by the action of the stream on the line. When the cast is made and mended, and line floating delightfully without drag, you should lead it around by keeping the rod point in advance of it. This is another matter of importance. You must lead the line, without pulling it, keeping just enough touch on it to feel it, and manoeuvering it so that there is at no point what Wood called a "knuckle," that is a small acute curve caused by the stream. Sometimes when standing by me, he has called out, "You can't get rid of that knuckle by mending; lead the line instead," and it will be realized that such a bend is best put right by moving the top of the rod towards the fishermen's bank, thereby straightening the line.

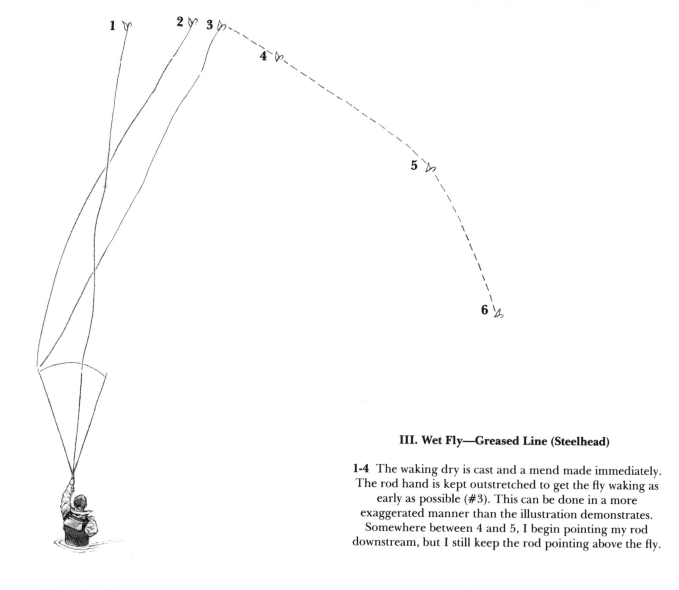

III. Wet Fly—Greased Line (Steelhead)

1-4 The waking dry is cast and a mend made immediately. The rod hand is kept outstretched to get the fly waking as early as possible (#3). This can be done in a more exaggerated manner than the illustration demonstrates. Somewhere between 4 and 5, I begin pointing my rod downstream, but I still keep the rod pointing above the fly.

"Drag" refers to a belly in the line that will, literally, drag the fly around. "Pull on the line" also referred to a belly. The word "drag" as applied by Wood did not refer to drag in any dry-fly sense. Obviously, you can't "lead a fly around" from one side of the river to the other without drag. Neither can you float a wet fly downstream free of drag without feeding additional line into the mend, something Wood did not practice as part of his presentation. Furthermore, a wet fly fished absolutely drag-free will sink. Greasing the line won't change that. In fact, Wood greased all of his thirty-five-yard line except the last yard so that the grease would not inadvertently get on the "cast" (the leader) and keep the leader and the fly on the surface.

Wrote Wood:

The lifting over of a line is done to correct a fault, namely, to take the downstream belly out of the line and thus relieve the pull or pressure of the current on the line, which is communicated to the fly *and exhibits itself as drag.* (Italics added.)

Then what to make of floating a fly "like a dead leaf?" Wood's presentation began that way because he mended and then led the fly. This initial move created sufficient slack to send a wet fly downstream a short distance without any tension (drag) on the line. Anglers have taken this one reference and assumed that Wood was fishing wet flies entirely drag free. That's as ridiculous as it is ineffective.

Some anglers try to fish a wet fly completely drag free near the surface and then pick up the line before the fly comes under tension during the swing. That may be an interesting way to fly-fish for steelhead, but it is not greased-line fishing as practiced by Arthur Wood.

I am astonished by how much some anglers and writers have made of this drag-free business while never mentioning Wood's technique of leading the fly. That and mending are the crux of his method. If that is not understood, *Greased Line Fishing* makes no sense, for one cannot lead a fly drag-free through the swing.

In Wood's own words:

A word about this "leading" the fly. I find in practice that it is a great point to lead the line with the rod as soon as you can and not follow it. By moving the rod in advance of the line—but not of course dragging it—you help the fly swim more downstream than across.

There is a tremendous lot in this leading; it serves several useful purposes. If the rod were held steady, the fly would come round in more or less a true circle; but when leading, the rod-point is going downstream in advance of the line, leading and coaxing it down as well as across.

I should like to say again how very important this leading is, because whenever you can do it—and of course in some waters you cannot—invariably the hook has a firm hold in the back of the fish's mouth. You can hardly help hooking it there!

When I first read *Greased Line Fishing* and I tried to present a fly broadside to the fish under drag-free conditions, nothing happened as I thought it should. The fly sank and passed downstream under a variety of attitudes. When under tension, the fly was not broadside to the fish. Once the line was swinging, it was anything but drag-free. Even when I understood that "drag" meant "belly," Wood's descriptions did not translate well in the field. Not until I strongly led my fly did I come to appreciate what Wood's descriptions were about.

Leading the fly increases its speed across the stream while it reduces current speed—tension—on the fly because the rod tip is passing downstream with the fly. Some action is given up for cross-current speed—speed through the swing. *This lead gives a salmon (or steelhead) more or less a broadside view of the fly. And this lead swings the fly into the salmon's mouth.*

Arthur Wood fished several different single-hand cane rods, all of which were twelve feet long. Anglers who have never worked with rods of this length, who have never fished two-handed rods two to four feet longer, cannot appreciate how much "leading" is possible. Following the initial mend, Wood could move his rod tip at least fifteen feet downstream before a line coming under maximum tension. That means that as the fly began to swing through an arc, current speed on the fly was reduced (but certainly not eliminated) as the rod point moved downstream with the swing of the fly. At the same time, current velocity decreased as the fly neared the shore. In this manner, tension on the fly was fairly constant.

Wood was no more hidebound about leading a fly than steelhead fly fishers are about keeping the rod behind the line. We do both depending on the strength of the flow and what we are trying to accomplish with the fly.

Wood did likewise. An example:

As soon as the fly gets round to your side, it may pay to keep the rod point *behind* the line instead of in front of it and gradually raise the point; this prevents a sudden snatch that sometimes occurs when a fish lying below you takes the fly when the line is taut.

What does all this mean to a steelhead fly fisher? Depending on how the rod is manipulated, the fly's swing can be dramatically slowed or speeded up, darting across open water to wobble tantalizingly over a particular lie before dashing off again for another likely spot. Steelhead lies are often under swift currents and along narrow creases. If one leads his fly through such water strongly enough to give the steelhead anything like a broadside view of the fly, the fly will pass through the lie so abruptly that the steelhead hardly has time to react. At such times, I slow the fly by keeping the rod point behind the swing of the line. If a current is so strong that the fly cannot swim properly, I immediately lead the fly away from the turbulence by dropping the point of the rod. Soft tailouts may have currents that move so slowly that the fly must be led strongly to prevent it from sinking. It may even be necessary to throw a downstream mend so that the speed of the fly through the water increases.

Knowing of Wood's propensity for leading his fly, I wonder if the differing emphasis salmon and steelhead fly fishers place on line manipulation is not due in large measure to the speed of the current above the lies. Summer steelhead take up temporary holding stations in currents far too swift to lead as strongly as Wood's presentation would suggest. I think that slowing the fly near the end of its swing is especially important, because a following steelhead is most likely to take at that time.

I am less than enthralled with this business of getting a fly broadside to the steelhead. I believe that the advantage of presenting a steelhead with a broadside view of the fly has little to do with the fish finding the fly. Regardless of whether or not you lead the fly, it swings into a steelhead lie to give the fish a side view. And whether it is presented somewhat broadside or not, steelhead take the fly from behind. They do not take the fly crosswise like a dog with a bone. However, when we strongly lead the fly, we generate considerable cross-stream speed, even a little downstream belly, that will carry the line past the fly when the fish rises to it. This momentum is sufficient to set the fine-wire hook, if the fish either remains stationary or turns away from the direction of the pull.

By contrast, when the rod is pointed behind the fly and the line is mended to slow its swing, the steelhead takes the fly without the momentum of the line swinging across the currents. If, on the rise, we then drop line, we do so without this momentum. I prefer to drop my rod and give the steelhead a moment to turn and to begin a return to its original station. I don't use slack line to set the hook (an approach I believe has limited application in steelhead fly fishing), but rather to give the fish enough slack so that when it turns, the fly doesn't pull out or take a light hold in the skin at the end of the fish's mouth. Hen steelhead, in particular, often take the fly so rapidly that dropping line to set the hook becomes ludicrous. In a blink, the fish just grabs the fly and races downstream. When Roland Holmberg first fished with me, he couldn't believe how much faster than Atlantic Salmon steelhead accelerated away after the rise.

Regardless of how quick the rise, doing nothing more than letting the steelhead take the rod down will give it time to turn and drag the fly to the corner of its mouth. Female steelhead do this more dependably than males, and for this reason I have always found them easier to hook than large male fish. A buck often comes up directly behind the fly, takes it in its mouth, and settles back into the river without turning. As the line comes under tension, the fly may either slip out or take a light hold at the end of the fish's nose. I don't offer a solution to this problem. Sometimes extreme patience on my part has been sufficient to work a fly deeply into the side of the jaw. If fishing a large heavy-wire hook, dropping line and letting the current set the hook is almost certain to be ineffective.

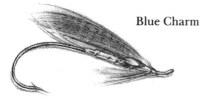

Blue Charm

Low Water Flies

The overdressed steelhead bucktail patterns that proliferated from the 1930s to the 1960s were the starting point for a reduction in dress that continues to this day. A shorter wing and less abundant hackle produced a fly with superior swimming qualities, a necessity with anglers searching surface currents with floating lines. Canada's Maritimes offered a wealth of Atlantic salmon flies sleekly tied with squirrel tail and fox, materials we adopted so readily that "bucktail" soon had only generic application. When our sport embraced Jock's Scott's *Greased Line Fishing for Salmon*, anglers found, to their satisfaction, that the thinly reduced patterns Hardy Brothers had been selling for years as "Wood Low Water Flies" were incomparably beautiful and highly functional when dressed on the heavier hooks often required by our more turbulent waters.

Jock Scott lists ten favorites, but quotes Wood as follows:

As regards pattern, I do not believe that this matters at all. Blue Charm and Silver Blue are my stock,. simply on the principle that one is more or less black, and the other white and so give *me* a choice. I once fished through the whole season with a March Brown only, and got my share, and more, of the fish caught.

This crosscultural melding birthed a steelhead fly more functional and certainly more pleasing to the eye, but a style I think fly fishers too generously describe as "low water."

Arthur Wood's dressing preferences through the season illustrate how very specific are the characteristics of a low water fly.

In February and March I generally use No. 1 hook with ordinary dressing; as the water gets warmer and clearer I use smaller sizes down to No. 6. As weather and water become still warmer I use smaller flies, No. 6 to No. 12; but as long as the fish will take a No. 6 I do not go any lower. I only reduce the size of the fly as the fish become shy of the larger sizes of small hooks.

In May, and sometimes in April, these flies and hooks are too heavy in iron and dressing for clear water: I then use summer flies tied for me with an extremely sparse dressing, no part of it going beyond the point of the hook. *The hooks are made of fine oval wire and have a long shank; they swim well, and, in a stream, do not hold the water.* (Italics added.)

Arthur Wood describes an unstable fly. The light wire gave the fly a light keel in proportion both to the dressing and to the hook shank. When dressed on these hooks, even severely reduced dressings would barely sink, but this combination met his needs. When he led the fly and reduced the drag on it, the unstable fly wobbled about and came alive in a manner impossible to achieve with a heavy-wire hook. When a salmon rose to the fly, slack line successfully swept the extremely fine point of the hook into the back corner of the salmon's mouth for a secure hold.

Many years ago, a friend in England sent me some 3X long light-wire Veniard hooks. They were on the order of those used by Wood, and I anxiously tied a number of thin hairwing dressings with them, fishing the flies on low August waters. I found steelhead hooked in the corner of the jaw, but sometimes with the fly set upside down. Occasionally, a steelhead took the fly with a very visible rush and then would not be hooked. This prompted me to have a companion wade out into the riffle I was fishing and watch carefully as my fly passed through its swing. I found that very little tension was needed to set the fly in motion, but when it was swinging hard downstream and under maximum tension, the fly would roll on its side. I assumed that some of the missed rises and unusual holds were due to this, and I realized that when my line was leading the rod in strong currents, the light-wire hooks were merely a fashion statement.

For greased-line summer fishing, I carry flies on heavy-wire and medium-wire hooks in a length of about 2X, and in sizes from 8 to 2/0. My standard tie is somewhat low-water, the wing extending no farther than the bend of the hook and often just to the base of the tail. I reduce the fly still more if bright midday conditions warrant; I won't drop below #8 unless fishing for half-pounders.

Fishing "small" flies for steelhead is only relative to a given area and largely meaningless if only the hook size is described. An overdressed #8 hook can be sizable, a reduced #4 quite small.

The need for a fly of a particular size is governed by the time of day, temperature of the water, and whether the steelhead have pooled up and grown stale. As late afternoon begins creating pockets of deep shade, I fish larger dressings, dark silhouette patterns that will not pass unnoticed. Many anglers choose thinly dressed small flies for their aesthetic appeal and then fish them right through the day. For all their beauty, they lack both size and density and are less likely to trigger a rise. The opposite is true when lies are sun-drenched and their steelhead unresponsive. I then like thin hair-wings, truly reduced greased-line flies that wobble and glint in the bright sun when tied on medium-weight hooks. A fine alternative to these flies is thinly dressed spiders, but only if the currents are not especially strong, for they cannot support themselves upright in the kind of water my other low-water flies can swim through.

This is the same approach I use on stale steelhead if I've chosen to stay in the surface film, though I am then far more likely to supplement the presentation by fishing the fly with a riffle hitch.

I think a good deal of arcane nonsense is made of how anglers manipulate their rods to give flies additional action. Twitching the fly, if rhythmical and conservative, probably doesn't hurt. I know from experience that when a steelhead is about to take the fly, any sudden erratic movement of the fly can send the fish fleeing in panic. A strong mend at the wrong time can put it down to stay. I'll take my chances with the currents bringing the fly to life. Supplementing the river's tension by bobbing the rod tip up and down when fishing long, thin flies; twitching the rod tip; stripping the line back in short retrieves; and stripping line in and immediately letting it back out are methods infrequently practiced by fly fishers.

Purple Peril

Pattern Selection

Unlike Arthur Wood, I most definitely believe that low-water fly-pattern selection matters, often greatly. I have watched steelhead remain unmoved by the enticements of a particular fly and then rise to the fly that replaced it. As a general rule, I favor somewhat somber flies for most summer fishing, switching over to bright dressings incorporating traditional steelhead colors when waters become discolored. My list of favorite standards is short: Ken McLeod's Purple Peril, Frank Amato's Night Dancer, Bob Arnold's Spade, and Randall Kaufmann's Ferry Canyon and Signal Light. I don't tie the Spade larger than #2, but routinely fish the other patterns up to 2/0, often tying in a few strands of Krystal Flash in these larger sizes. I like a 1/0 or 2/0 fly in the evening and early morning, particularly on rivers such as the Thompson or Kispiox. I don't usually dress any of these flies on hooks smaller than a #4, but I will reduce the dressing, often tying the leaner result on a Tiemco 7989 or the Alec Jackson Spey.

No doubt purple is a wonderful greased-line color, either used boldly as in the Purple Peril and Ferry Canyon, or mixed subtly as in the Night Dancer. I add it to many other patterns as well, including a Spade with a facing hackle of teal dyed purple.

The Purple Peril fishes better for me when winged with brown bucktail than with fox squirrel tail, often the winging fur of choice with this pattern. It is an old standby, more than a half-century old, but no dressing has produced more crushing strikes for me when a river has a faint tinge of color to it.

I suspect that many dark patterns will satisfy when the day is bright and the water clear, but the Night Dancer has proven so remarkably reliable under these conditions that I dress it on hooks from #8 to 2/0 in a variety of styles, from low water to rather full, even a modified spey, in which the forward half of the body is palmered. As a hairwing I use black squirrel.

To this list I add the Lady Caroline, the Blue Charm, Orange Charm, Black Bear, Coal Car (with a black squirrel-tail wing), Muddler (and its many variations), and the Grey Rat. The bright flies I fish greased line include the Green-Butt Skunk, Skunk, Macks Canyon, and Brad's Brat.

Many patterns approximate this color range, and describing them here serves as a general theme.

Some anglers consider the Skunk a dark fly because it has a black body. The dressing also has a red tail and a white wing. I call such flies bright. Dark flies are primarily brown, grey, wine, purple, black, and so on. They do not have white wings.

The Lady Caroline, a somewhat drab fly, possesses such special powers over difficult fish that I always carry a few in #4. A fly shop blends the olive and brown dubbing of angora goat for me in quantities sufficient to tie them by the gross. I do not dress the pattern with blue heron hackle, a material impossible to obtain commercially. I omit this or substitute grey schlappen or blue-eared pheasant before adding several turns of red golden pheasant, the tail material. Then I tie in a small clump of brown bucktail for the wing and overwrap the wing butts with finely barred pintail, gadwall, or hooded merganser flank. Flat gold tinsel provides both a tip and a rib. I believe the substitutions blend to approximate the original (see below) and create a durable tie. Steelhead seem to find these differences unremarkable and take the fly as faithfully as they do the original.

LADY CAROLINE (Arthur Wood)

Tail Point of golden pheasant breast feather
Body Reddish brown olive seal fur
Rib Flat silver tinsel flanked with silver thread and gold thread

Throat One turn of golden pheasant breast feather
Wing Bronze mallard, set low on the body

The Blue Charm wound with rich blue hackle is most attractive to steelhead—and parr. Several times I have hooked parr while removing a wind knot from the leader, the little steelhead throwing themselves at the fly as it washed against my waders. Their attentions often become so bothersome that another pattern must be fished. If not overdone in orange hackle (not fluorescent orange), the Orange Charm produces many rises from steelhead and is not so murderous to parr.

The Muddler Minnow, possibly the most widely used fly pattern in North America, has inspired numerous improved steelhead versions (see Chapter 38). When tied commercially, it is usually so over-dressed as to be useless for steelhead. It should be dressed on a 2X or 3X long hook with the head spun loosely and the collar cut away severely to give the fly a better streamer-type action.

The Skunk and the Green-Butt Skunk stand together as the two most popular steelhead flies over the past twenty-five years. The flash of white is extremely visible and may draw steelhead from a considerable distance; the black-and-white combination is one of the most reliable in fly fishing (the Black Ghost and Coachman come to mind). Their early reputation was based primarily on their quali-ties as deeply sunk flies. Today, they are more frequently fished greased-line, which has, if anything, increased their standing. They are arguably the finest white-winged greased-line patterns for steelhead, and on that basis alone the two dressings will likely remain synonymous with the sport. However, where I once used the patterns as the basis for much of my fishing, I now rely on them more as change-of-pace flies to be alternated with more subdued, natural-appearing dressings.

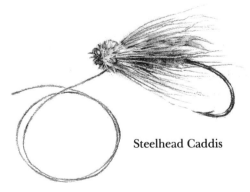

Steelhead Caddis

Riffling Hitch

The hitched fly allegedly evolved on Newfoundland's Portland Creek more than a century ago. According to Lee Wulff in *The Atlantic Salmon* (A. S. Barnes and Company, 1958), British warships anchored off the river so that their officers could come ashore to fish. Salmon flies of the period had gut loops, and when these showed signs of wear, the flies were given to the grateful locals. Not trusting the gut loops, the Portland Creek fishermen tied on the fly and then passed two overhand knots behind the head of the fly so that the leader came off beneath the eye. In the process of safeguarding against the loss of their flies, these fishermen inadvertently—and dramatically—changed how the flies fished.

When a properly dressed wet fly with a turned up eye has been hitched and brought under sufficient tension, the head pulls up until it breaks through the surface to create a V wake. All the movements of a greased line fly that largely pass unnoticed are now dramatically evident. The conflicting currents impact on the fly's progress, sending it on erratic and unpredictable turns, a life magically transformed as it tears a furrow through the undulating ceiling of the steelhead's world.

What this represents is not clear, for nothing in nature really duplicates it. Mayflies, stoneflies, and caddisflies have moments during their lives when they struggle in the surface film and are no longer aquatic but not yet terrestrial. An injured parr may swim heedlessly at the surface. Reptiles and amphibians swim across rivers with their heads up, too. Dave McNeese told me of finding voles, mouselike rodents, in the stomachs of spring-run Alaskan steelhead caught more than a mile above tidewater.

I once spent an afternoon on a Canadian river watching a fresh-run summer steelhead of fifteen pounds that had taken up a station beneath the overhanging limbs of a huge alder. A fall southerly was pushing through a storm, and with each gust of wind, bits of tree would shake loose and rake the currents below. The fish crashed these, a series of violent rises that continued for hours. Perhaps this was a fish simply territorial and full of itself; I doubt that it thought the dragging bits of flotsam were food. Regardless, its antics were the kind of hair-trigger response I associate with flies fished with a riffling hitch.

Bill Bakke, long the guiding spirit of Oregon Trout and currently its Executive Director, introduced me to the riffling hitch in the late 1960s, when we were fishing the Wind and Kalama rivers in southwestern Washington. He was a keen and resourceful angler whose October Caddis was the first pattern I tied specifically to be fished with a riffling hitch.

OCTOBER CADDIS

Tail   Golden pheasant crest
Wings Brown squirrel tail, sparse, set well forward and divided (wing butts will be covered by the body)
Body   Orange dubbing (I prefer burnt orange)
Hackle Brown, two turns; leave a small space between the hackle and the wings to set the hitch

Where the leader comes off the October Caddis is a pivot point, the fly swinging under tension, wobbling and vibrating from the influence of the currents. The farther back a hitch is made, the more radical the action. But if too much material is forward of the hitch, the fly will be dragged along on its side. If the hook is at least 2X long and the wings are sparse, the loops of the riffling hitch may be set between the wing and the hackle.

Setting the hitch directly behind the head of a conventional wet fly may flatten carefully arranged feathers or hair. To avoid this, the head can be tied longer than usual with a low point in the middle so that the hitch doesn't slip forward.

Wet flies, or dry flies with large heads of spun deer hair or large flared clumps of deer hair, usually cannot be hitched between the collar/wing and the head. Once the fly has absorbed some water, it ends up being dragged sideways. If the head is small enough, however, these flies can be hitched in this manner, particularly if the hook is 2X long or longer. A sparsely dressed Muddler, or McMillan's Steelhead Caddis, sends out considerable wakes when hitched.

I prefer a somewhat sparse and drab wet fly to hitch, one that entices rather than startles. The Lady Caroline—and various alternatives on this color theme—is a favorite. But almost any conservatively dressed fly will work if it doesn't have an overly long wing or an abundance of throat hackle that might keep it from riding true.

The amount of current necessary to set a fly waking depends on the design of the dressing. If an angler leads his fly through a presentation on moderate currents, it can pass through all but the end of its swing before waking. Just as with wet flies fished greased-line, to obtain the proper action from the fly over distant lies, it is necessary to bring the fly under hard tension as quickly as possible. After making my initial mend, I often extend my rod arm and keep it pointing upstream. I make sure I don't start following the swing of the fly with the rod tip until the fly has started waking. In this regard, the waking fly is a good teacher, reminding me, when I am fishing a greased line wet without a hitch, that if I'm not paying attention, the fly is likely under insufficient tension.

The erratic action of the waking wet makes the steelhead's rise less sure, its lunges corrective measures employed to nail the fly. Amid this sudden commotion, a strike on the part of the angler becomes involuntary, a tensing that pulls the fly away from a steelhead that does not yet have the fly in its mouth. I fish the fly as I would a waking dry, my rod tip pointed up at a forty-five- to sixty-degree angle, a couple feet of loose line held in my hand. The fish either has the fly or it doesn't, and a sudden splash may not telegraph the truth. To then drop the rod and dump all the line immediately kills the action of the fly. I let the steelhead tense the line for me by taking my rod tip down and pulling my coiled line through my fingers. When the steelhead has run out this slack, it will have turned so that the hook point is pulled into the side of its jaw and not into the end of its mouth.

DRY FLIES—GREASED LINE

I have cast directly upstream with a dry and hooked steelhead of over ten pounds. I have presented a wet in an identical manner and had steelhead take the fly the instant it touched the water. I believe these incidents are more often responses from steelhead, fresh from the ocean, that have not yet been set upon by fishermen or grown stale from long holds in pools. I am also certain that the least effective dry-fly presentation for steelhead is one made upstream and drag-free.

I initiate a drag-free float by making a conservative cast across or slightly down and across, and feed line into the drift with a series of mends. Each mend transfers to the fly and causes it to come alive with a touch of drag. A steelhead may take the fly at any time, but the vast majority of the rises occur just after the fly has come under drag. Since the rise so often occurs just as the fly begins dragging, my conclusion is that the steelhead sees the fly coming for a considerable distance and moves to it decisively only when the fly drags.

Mike Maxwell's method of presentation with a two-handed rod involves a long drag-free float followed by a swing that Mike controls precisely with the long rod. He keeps a careful record of where in the swing the rise occurs. Mike anticipates a steelhead first seeing the dry fly (his own Telkwa Stone), on the drag-free part of the float, but rising to it only after the fly has come under tension. Rises are rare when the fly is entirely free of drag.

I think the best design for a drag-free steelhead dry fly is a hairwing with the wings divided and set well forward and a sparse amount of hackle. A long tail will prevent the fly from tipping over; a body of dubbing, or better yet, of spun deer hair, provides additional flotation. Many patterns satisfy this general description, none more so than Roderick Haig-Brown's Steelhead Bee, the prototypical dry for Northwest steelhead waters. I also like the Royal Wulff or Royal Humpy for their visibility and floating qualities if they're not too generously hackled. I want the fly to ride low if I am fishing it drag-free, for the steelhead is then less likely to push it away with the commotion of its rise.

This is not, however, the best dry-fly design to fish waking, even if it is given a hitch to help keep it up. Under tension, these classic hairwings will drown in riffles, sometimes spinning on their wings or working streamer fashion with the wings folded back. Only a slack line and their natural inclination to float will get them back on top. Even then, picking the fly up and shaking it out on a backcast is

The Kispiox hen took my Black Bomber when it had nearly completed its swing below.

usually necessary to get it floating properly again. For this reason, I don't use low riding hairwing dries unless I am going to fish drag-free, or unless I'm on tailouts and flats so free of surface riffles that turbulence will not drown the dragging fly.

As a fly for steelhead, these dries are often fished in sizes 10 to 6, a searching fly presented drag-free or selectively waked. An increasingly popular approach is to use them heavily hackled, in 10s and 12s, as a follow-up "eating" fly skated seductively over steelhead that have been successfully raised but have refused every subsequent offering.

Harry Lemire's Fall Caddis

Skating, Waking, and Damp Flies

Among steelhead fly fishermen, "skating," "waking," and "damp" are relative terms describing how a dry fly drags on the water and whether it rides on the water and "skates," drags through the surface film and "wakes," or swims "damp" in the surface film, both wet and dry. The terms are usually applied loosely, the fresh dry often more a skater, the same fly waking after several dozen floats.

The damp fly describes dry flies that naturally ride very low in the water and, under tension, may go wet unless tied with a riffling hitch. Going wet is not considered a failure, but an expected part of the damp fly sequence, for unlike skaters or wakers, the damp fly fishes wet most effectively. Examples of this type of fly include Harry Lemire's Fall Caddis, Thompson River Caddis, and Grease Liner; Bill McMillan's Steelhead Caddis; and the Muddler Minnow.

Bob Wagoner recently introduced the Steelhead Skater, a hairwing dry with the wings inverted so that the fly rides on wing tips and tail. Other pure skaters include all-hackle dries like the Atlantic salmon Bottlewasher, small heavily hackled Wulffs and Humpies, full-palmered Bombers, and Scott Noble's Steelhead Dry and Autumn Sedge.

I haven't used all-hackle locater flies like the Bottlewasher in years. They float marvelously well, but only for a cast or two before drowning and no longer skating, regardless of the false casting. So many better locater flies are available today that I would bother with them only in smaller sizes, as a one-time shot over a difficult fish.

Randy Stetzer's Fluttering Termite.

The second generation of steelhead dries includes the leaner Bomber without hackle, the Bulkley Mouse, Mark Pinch's Riffle Dancer, the new Waller Waker, Brian Douglas's Steelhead Bee, and Randy Stetzer's Fluttering Termite, flies that naturally float like corks, with designs that promote their surface activity. For example, Brian Douglas's Bee is tied with wings of moose, the short wings are divided and set forward so that, under tension, the fly wants to climb up on the water and surf. Lani Waller uses the same principle with calf-tail wings stiffened along the lower third with Goop. Mark Pinch bends the forward third of the hook up, gives this a bubble of spun deer hair, and, as added insurance, ties in a small clump of moose on top.

Even without a hitch, a moment of slack is normally all that is necessary to get these flies popping back onto the surface. If a hitch is used, the flies may still go down in turbulent water, but they will be dragged back on top by their design and the hitch. On a hard swing over productive lies, knowing these dry flies won't fold up and stay wet is reassuring!

The "third generation" in the evolution of steelhead dry flies involves waking patterns designed to stay on top as long as they are under tension. Examples are Lani Waller's Waller Waker with a short stubble of calf-tail for a wing; Mark Noble's Fall Caddis and Fall Hopper, both with "bubbleheads"; Judd Wickwire's Riffle Express; John Mintz's Bulkley Moose; and the original Bubblehead. These flies have a flared face of hair stiffened with fly dope or Goop that forces the fly up on the surface as long as it is under tension. For this reason they are nearly unsinkable.

The typical presentation for all of these flies begins with a cast made across and slightly down. But all do not begin working properly under equal amounts of tension. The skaters, riffle-hitched Bombers, the full-hackled little hairwing drys require very little tension to set them skating and waking. If the river's currents are smooth enough to encourage their use, these flies work the largest possible arc. For example, if fishing a Bomber as a general locater fly, I have a hitch behind the wing as I cast slightly downstream and across. After making an initial mend, I hold my rod with my arm fully extended and point it quartering upstream. I even change hands, if necessary, to accomplish this. In this way, I quickly bring the Bomber under tension and start it waking when it is well out in the river. The fly wakes and skates through a huge arc. I don't drop my arm and follow—or lead—the fly through the swing until the fly is fully waking. The ease with which I accomplish this is the primary reason I prefer the Bomber to many other dressings, and why it remains a favorite locater pattern for broad, even-mannered flats.

Bill Bakke's Dragon Fly is a strong rock-and-roll waker, but the wings that give the fly such remarkable action are too much resistance in strong currents. I prefer to fish it down and across on relatively flat runs.

Flies that wake by plowing through water while rocking back and forth, or by pushing up on top of the water, do so only when the current is sufficient to set them in motion and the fly is well into the hard part of its swing. These flies work a smaller arc and are better suited for more turbulent flows.

Some dry flies, such as the best-designed Bombers, the Riffle Dancer, and many damp dressings can be fished in all current flows—flat tailouts as well as boulder-laced riffles. Understanding what conditions bring out the best in the dry fly's design is basic to presenting the fly.

Appreciating the amount of current needed to start a dry fly working helps me to properly fish my greased-line wets. Because the wet fly's action is not nearly so visible, I find it easy to overlead the fly through its swing, reduce the tension, and take away from its action. On occasion, I have tied on a hard-waking dry just to see when the waking occurs and to determine if I am fishing the wet fly under sufficient tension. Sometimes I am dismayed to discover that in my lackadaisical approach I have been swinging a wet fly on entirely too much slack, and it has passed through its swing possessing very little life.

The rise from a "player," a steelhead that fully intends to eat the waking fly, is dramatically matter-of-fact. The steelhead comes up behind the fly, fins itself up until its nose is out of the water, and takes in the fly. If the steelhead misses, the next cast brings it back, or perhaps the cast after that. Changing fly patterns and strategies on a player may or may not be helpful. My approach is to stay with the fly until the steelhead's interest obviously wanes, or it refuses the fly altogether. Then I rest the fish, and try again with the same pattern. If this fails, I switch patterns. I make this change earlier rather than later, if the dry that drew the intitial rise was large, a #4 or #2 Waller Waker or a #4 Bomber. Many anglers fish these large drys as one part of a two-fly approach, a much smaller dry becoming the follow-up "eating" fly.

Unlike Atlantic salmon that can be cast over again and again before they finally take, a steelhead's interest tends to decline with each rise. I believe that repeatedly casting over an unresponsive steelhead intimidates it. This approach reduces one's chances for bringing the steelhead back with alternate patterns and strategies.

Steelhead often follow a wet fly and swirl around it without the angler's knowledge. I've had companions take a vantage, such as a hillside or railroad bridge, and describe for me how this was happening. Their excitement and cries of alarm were hardly matched by the uneventful swing of my fly! But when a steelhead exhibits this same interest in the swing of my waking dry, it is far easier to detect. Perhaps only a dimple in the water or an odd confusion of currents around the fly signals its presence, but the rise more commonly experienced is an explosion of water that never fails to leaves me a little stunned. The general impression is that someone dropped a clear plastic bowling ball in the water, for the splash seems to have nothing in it.

When I was at the Silver Hilton, Judd Wickwire shot video footage of a Babine steelhead rising explosively to his Riffle Express. He played this back in slow motion, revealing a steelhead slashing over on its side from behind and coming down with its mouth open over the top of the fly, an odd angle, and one I would never have suspected. The fish was not hooked, and Judd's Riffle Express bobbed out from the end of the cascade of water like a surfer running before a collapsing wave. I think many rises are of this slashing nature, the erratic behavior of the fly promoting lunges that miss. Other abrupt rises that produce a lot of surface disturbance seem be made more by the fish's tail as it returns to its station, the fly never intentionally taken into the fish's mouth.

My experience has been that the violent type of rise is often a one-time affair. Because these rises are so common, many strategies have been developed to bring the steelhead back. All of them work from time to time. None of them works all the time. But after resting the fish for a few minutes, I think the most effective follow-up fly for this type of rise is a wet spider or thin-hackle fly fished on a dead drift and tensed as it begins swinging through the steelhead's lie. If I intend to stay on top, I try a small well-hackled dry and skate it over the lie. One of LeRoy Hyatt's clipped deer-hair versions of Bob Wagoner's Steelhead Skater is an excellent choice. Another alternative is to fish either a small low-water wet or damp fly with a riffling hitch. Jerry Cebula of Golden, Colorado, told me how he moves below the steelhead located by his Steelhead Bomber so that he can present the fly again, but drag-free. This worked for me the first time I tried it, though I gave the dry a twitch or two.

Pure skaters are also used as locaters, with a smaller low-riding waker as a follow-up. My only problem with this approach is that even great skaters don't skate like thistledown for long, while most waking flies will perform well for hours. Very soon with this approach, the alternative to a large waker is a smaller waker.

Two arguments are commonly used for not fishing dry flies. The first—and most generally accepted—is that below a certain temperature steelhead will not rise to a fly. This is true only if that temperature is thirty-two degrees, the freezing point of water. Many examples support this view. Bob Clay told me of raising a Bulkley River hen steelhead on a dry in the dead of winter, when the water temperature was thirty-three degrees. (Astonishingly, she had one complete gill cover ripped off.) Lani Waller and I fished dries when the Kispiox was a chilly thirty-seven degrees, and neither of us experienced problems raising steelhead to our flies. In fact, the high thirties are considered only slightly marginal by Canadian standards. No one makes a fuss over summer steelhead taking drys during the harshest days of winter any longer. For a handful of dry-fly addicts, keeping guides free of ice is a far greater concern.

We should, however, recognize certain considerations in this aspect of steelhead fly fishing. As the water temperature drops, steelhead become less active and are less prone to move to any type of fly. The swing of the dry fly must be slowed down, the more the better, by repeated mending. Sometimes it is possible to hold the rod out and keep the waking fly almost stationary over the suspected lie. I have kept a fly waking in place for a full minute before the steelhead came up for it. Lies should be chosen for their optimum depth, three to five feet, and for the reduced speed of their flow. Late-season steelhead are moving less and will often hold the same stations for days. They won't select lies that require exertion, and I don't look for them at the top of a run, water I fished with such anticipation in September.

I am convinced that low temperature is less a factor among northern races of summer steelhead than in U.S. rivers where surface currents in the thirties pretty much keep the fish tied to the bottom. My dry-fly experiences on domestic rivers have only been productive when temperatures were in the high forties. My experiences are hardly quantitative, but my hunch is that the difference between Skeena steelhead and Puget Sound or Snake River or coastal Oregon summer-runs rising to a dry fly is at least five degrees, and may be as much as ten degrees.

The second argument against the use of dry flies is that they limit the size of the steelhead. I think this claim has an element of truth to it, because the largest steelhead are the less-active males, and these fish take up the deeper, least-strenuous lies, factors multiplied by frigid late-season water. Earlier in the season, when the steelhead are more active and holding in shallow lies, the very largest steelhead can be brought to a dry, particularly if the swing is slowed down. Two enormous steelhead come to mind—and help the rest of us maintain the faith. Bubba Wood of Dallas, Texas, took a forty-two-inch by twenty-two-inch male from the Bulkley River using a Bulkley Mouse. Ed Exum of Denver, Colorado, also using a Mouse, beached a 44½-inch by 23½-inch Kispiox steelhead in September, 1987. This carefully measured fish, estimated at between thirty-three and a half and thirty-four pounds, is probably the largest steelhead ever caught on a dry.

If I could choose one method of presentation to securely hook a steelhead, I would choose a wet fly fished greased-line. If I want to employ the most certain way to locate a steelhead, I would put a riffling hitch on a dry and wake it greased-line.

WET FLY—FLOATING LINE

The quickest way to get a large fly or a weighted fly deep is to quarter a cast across and upstream with a floating line and long leader, a strong upstream mend giving the fly time to sink on the slack. Additional mends are made to remove belly from the line while the rod point leads the fly and reduces tension on the fly during the swing. The fly passes downstream on a dead drift, probably riding butt-end down. The fish may take the fly any time during this sequence, but very modest tension on the line while still leading the fly imparts some swimming life into it. I find that steelhead most often take the fly early into the swing, as it comes under tension.

I use this method often when casting weighted leech patterns of marabou or rabbit on a leader of twelve to fourteen feet. These are not much fun to cast, but with barbell lead eyes, the fly rides upside

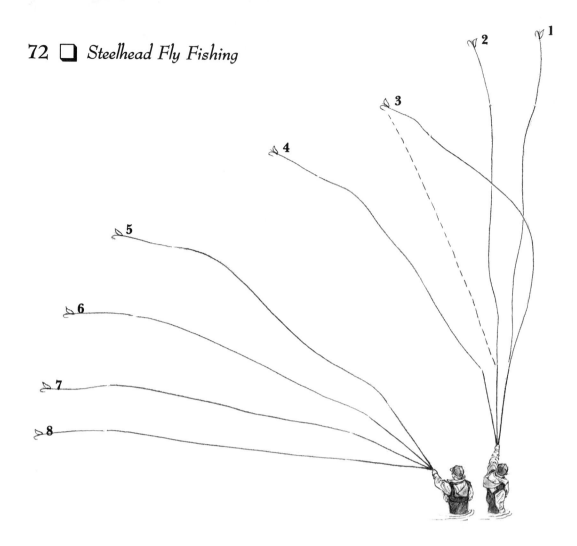

IV. Wet Fly—Floating Line (Dead Drift)

This floating line presentation (1) has three parts: sinking the fly on a slack line (2-4), the "dead drift" (4-5) and the swing (6-8) when the fly is strongly led to reduce tension.

"Dead Drift" literally means the deeply sunk wet fly is passing downstream without any drag. Realistically, there is nothing entirely "dead" about this presentation except the initial sink. I want to stay in touch with the fly by means of very subtle but definite tension and I work to avoid having the fly line overrun the fly.

1. The initial presentation can be quartered more upstream than the illustration indicates when currents are progressively stronger toward the center of the river. If that is the case, I do not immediately mend, but wait a moment for the fly to sink before mending my line to the leader.

2. The fly and leader are sinking.

3. The initial mend is made. This can be subtle or dramatic depending on the speed of the current and the depth sought. It will, however, draw in the fly. Knowing this in advance, I will over-cast the lie I wish to cover.

4. The fly is sinking and comes under tension at 4. I can minimize this tension by leading my fly. With a single-hand rod of 10 feet, I can pass my rod tip through a very considerable arc to accomplish this lead.

4-5 If the fly has not reached the desired depth, a second mend can be made, and *additional line fed into the mend*. This mend can extend the "dead drift" portion of the presentation. If that is the purpose of a second or third mend, some tension on the fly should first be experienced so that the floating line is not running over the fly.

5. I will lead my fly and reduce drag to a minimum as the fly begins to swing. I often experience a take just as the fly starts its swing. Also, at 5 I will take my step or two downstream to extend the "dead drift" portion of the presentation that is coming under tension.

6-8 I continue to lead my fly through the swing. This may leave me with my rod pointed at the beach rather than, as shown, my rod parallel to the currents.

down and is nearly weedless, the dead drift getting the fly down, rolling it along the bottom, and bringing it to life with a minimum of tension. Steelhead pick up the fly so confidently that they do not bolt away on the take, and the hook must be set. The angler must concentrate, for the take may be very soft.

Sometimes summer waters get quite discolored, and sinking a fly closer to holding steelhead is desirable. Rather than go to a sink-tip line, one can lengthen the leader and tie on a larger fly that will sink quickly and then be led to swim through holding water. (I have no illusions regarding the difference between my looking down into the water and a steelhead picking up my fly against the backdrop of the surface.) Nevertheless, getting my fly down a couple of feet has proven effective.

Arthur Wood said, "I therefore aim at keeping the fly at the surface, or sink it right down to the stones; and I have entirely forsaken the ordinary practice, which causes the fly to swim at mid-water." Other anglers give this same advice, but I don't agree. Steelhead usually hold a station a foot or more above the stones, not flat on the bottom. If I am casting to water five feet deep with visibility reduced to two feet, and I'm able to swim my fly a foot or more below the surface, my chances have improved.

Bill McMillan has written eloquently about the virtues of a double-taper floating line, ten-foot leader, and flies up to 6/0 for winter steelhead. An upstream cast followed by back-mends gets the fly down. The dead drift becomes a slow, controlled swing, the fly led to reduce tension, the considerable weight of the large hook helping to swim the fly deep.

Bill admits that hooking steelhead on the dead-drift part of the presentation takes great concentration. I could add that salmon hooks in sizes larger than 2/0 or 3/0 are very hard to find, and when barbless, their penetration of a midsize steelhead may be life-threatening. Also, they require a heavier line than I routinely like to cast with a single-hand rod. Nevertheless, working the big irons through holds with a floating line is a classic achievement.

I prefer casting the large flies with a two-handed rod and hybrid sink-tip line, either double-taper or long belly. For me, this fishing is immensely satisfying. Only hitching dries and low-water wets on the greased line is equal to it.

WET FLY—SINK TIP

Other than floating lines, I find sink tips the most versatile of all steelhead fly lines, regardless of the season. They are the basis for my winter fishing, having eliminated my former reliance on shooting tapers. The reason is line control, particularly when the belly section has sufficient mass when mended to move around the sink tip.

If casting either commercially manufacturered or custom-made sink-tip lines in a forward taper of forty feet or so, the line is mended only by raising the rod tip and lifting the running line when the line is quartering downstream. In this manner belly is removed and the sink tip squared around so that the fly passes downstream first. If a very short cast is made, an outside mend is made with the belly section to provide enough slack so the sink tip has a chance to sink. To manage a long-range deep sink, additional running line must be fed into the swing as the rod gently leads the fly. Slipping additional line also helps to reduce tension on the fly any time during the swing.

The sink rate and length of the sink tip are not the only criteria determining the depth the fly can reach for a given current. Many commercially manufacturered lines have a very modest floating belly section behind the sinking tip. The line hinges on the cast and is carried down by the sink tip on the dead drift. Assuming a short cast, an additional stack cast, in which additional line is cast into the mend, allows the sink tip to pull additional running line into the drift. Custom lines usually cast better and are more easily mended because of their much heavier belly sections, but all that flotation is not so easily carried down, and although the fly can be fished more positively, for the same length of sink tip it doesn't run as deep.

Either my custom sink tip long belly lines, or Mike Maxwell's double-taper sink-tip lines are the

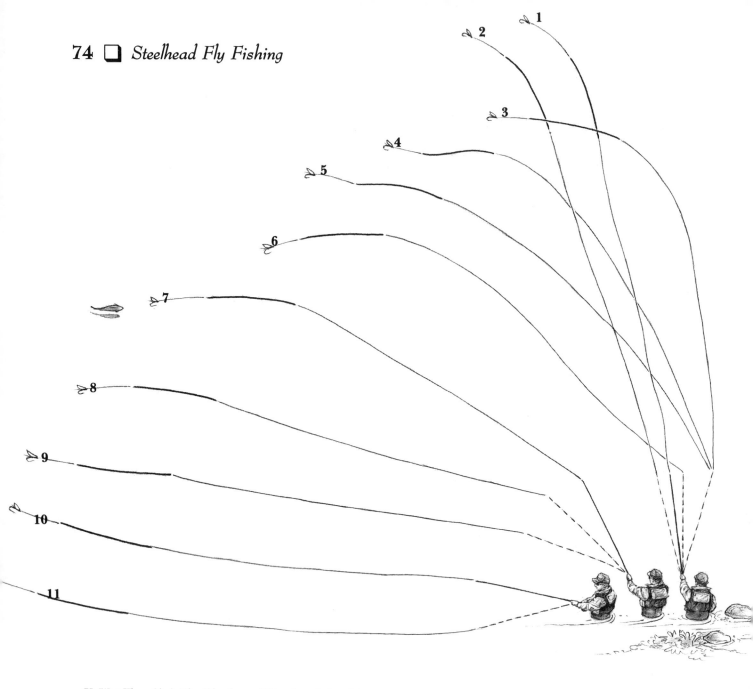

V. Wet Fly—Sink Tip (Single and Two-handed rods)

1-2 The cast is made across and slightly downstream, the fly sinking immediately.

3. A very strong upstream mend is executed. The greater the depth of the lie and the speed of the current, the greater the mend. If using a two-handed rod, this mend can shorten the distance cast by at least the length of the sink tip.

4-5 At the completion of the mend, the rod is still pointed upstream. Ideally, the rod can be kept pointed in this direction until the fly has sunk to the desired level and come under tension. Sometimes it becomes necessary to cast line into a second mend and extend the dead drift to reach the desired level. The rod should not be pointed downstream when the fly first comes under tension for then there is little "leading" left that can reduce tension on the fly and prevent it from swimming toward the surface.

6 The rod leads the fly to reduce tension on the fly and prevent it from swimming toward the surface.

7-9 The fly is continuously led through the swing.

10-11 If currents are light, i.e., "soft" I may find it necessary to lead the fly by pointing the rod at the beach, a greased-line lead. Winter lies, in particular, may require this approach, starting as early as 8.

ultimate wet-fly line when fished with two-handed rods. They can be cast without hinging and possess ample mass in the floating section both to spey cast and to mend at long distances. But it is how the lines can be manipulated after completing the cast that makes the pairing of line and rod so ideal.

Upon making my cast across and slightly down, I execute a very strong outside mend, which straightens out the sink tip and drives a belly of line upstream so that the line hooks. This shortens up the cast and sets the depth of the line. The greater the initial mend, the greater the depth, and the longer my sink tip. The considerable slack is gone when the fly has reached fishing depth. During this time my rod is still pointed quartering upstream. If I do not change the position of the rod, the line will come under maximum tension and the fly will begin moving toward the surface. I concentrate to feel for the slight pull signaling that all slack is out and the fly is working. I wait a second or two before moving the rod point downstream, continuing to do so until I am leading the fly. The rod tip continues to move before the fly to reduce current tension, to keep the fly swinging, and to prevent the fly from rising toward the surface. Some experimentation is necessary to get a feel for this, but I have remarkable control, given that the rod's length is a radius of fifteen feet and a diameter of twice that. The rod will never be pointed straight upstream after the initial mend, but it definitely will end up pointing straight downstream or even toward shore at the completion of the swing. At this point the rod tip has described an arc of at least twenty feet. Thus, a cast of ninety feet that would end with the fly ninety feet below the rod tip if the rod were not moved in the slightest (thus describing a perfect quarter of a circle) sees the fly move ninety feet downstream and across while my rod tip is simultaneously moving twenty feet downstream.

This series of rod and line manipulations is imperfect greased-line, but a practical application of Wood's methods because of the soft lies holding winter steelhead. I find the quiet water near shore, the broad tailouts, the guts below the central sweep of the river ideal water on which to practice this approach. Were the lies in faster currents, they would be fished with much greater difficulty, for strongly leading the fly to reduce tension would send it across the river too quickly to catch the interest of winter steelhead. To slow the swing enough to attract the steelhead would so increase tension that the fly would no longer run deep. Winter steelhead lies, long rods, and those special sink-tip lines are fly fishing at its classic best.

With the floating line at an angle to the sink tip, some slack in the swing is certain. This line is also penetrating a variety of current speeds, which subjects the sink-tip portion of the line to additional and less obvious belly. For these reasons, it is necessary to tighten early when the steelhead takes the fly. That may be all that is necessary when the hot fish turns and races away, but many steelhead simply stop the fly, and it becomes necessary to strike forcefully. This is not a case of driving the hook in so much as removing slack from a deep running line quickly enough to set the hook.

WET FLY—SHOOTING TAPER

In the hands of experienced fly fishers, fast-sinking shooting tapers— "heads"—are very useful extensions of the fly-line assortment. Long distances can be cast and the greatest possible depth reached, especially when monofilament is used as a running line. But these anglers do not simply fish the river for steelhead, they evaluate each pool in terms of their shooting head, and they know almost instinctively how to apply the line's few attributes.

Immediately after the line is cast quartering down and across, the head is mended by raising the rod tip and swinging the butt end of the head around so that, as it passes below the angler, it is pointing upstream and on a reasonably straight track to the fly. This mend takes something out of the distance cast, but failure to set the line in this attitude results in a head that fishes out of control, often coming down with the heavier diameter and faster sinking butt section leading the way. The line then tenses and whips around the head, a presentation largely worthless and unseen.

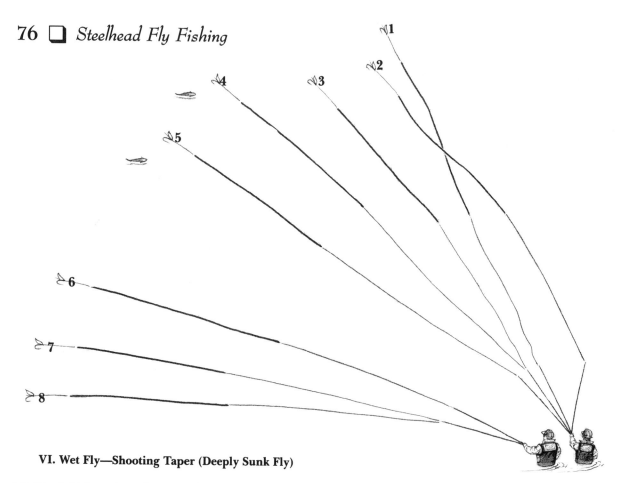

VI. Wet Fly—Shooting Taper (Deeply Sunk Fly)

1-2 The initial cast is made quartering downstream. As the fly begins to sink, the rod is brought forcefully upstream to pull around the butt end of the head and point it upstream.

2-3 The fly line, leader, and fly are without tension and are sinking.

4. Additional sink is provided by slipping running line into the presentation. In the example illustrated, 15 or 20 feet is fed into the drift. As this is done, I like to point my rod at a right angle to the current. As the fly comes under tension, I will prevent the fly from working toward the surface by moving my rod tip downstream.

5. I lead my fly into the swing. If this does not sufficiently reduce tension on the fly to prevent it from working toward the surface, I will take a step or two downstream and possibly slip some additional line.

6-7 I continue to lead my fly through the swing. If the current is too strong below me to permit this swing without the fly working to the surface, the pool is, at best, only marginally fishable if a deeply sunk fly is necessary.

If the line is sinking properly, reducing tension on it is achieved by slipping additional line into the drift and modestly leading the fly.

If water is discolored, the swing must be slowed down as much as possible so that the steelhead has a moment to respond to the fly. This, of course, increases tension on the line, the currents forcing the fly toward the surface. Casts are then shortened considerably, the fly led with the rod, the angler more sensitive to how the fly is behaving during the swing. At such times, the thirty feet of sinking line is a disadvantage; anglers are better served with a sink-tip line. But again, the head may be the only line capable of reaching lies near the bottoms of deep pools.

As with any sinking lines, if the steelhead takes the fly during the dead drift part of the presentation or early in the swing, it must be struck. I always hold my rod in one hand and line in the other, my line hand able to remove additional slack from the line on the strike. If the line is straight to the steelhead and passing through a hard swing, the fish will be felt immediately, and tightening of the line may be all that is necessary to set the hook.

MANAGING HOOKED STEELHEAD

I may fish for days to hook a steelhead. When I finally succeed in doing so, I want to manage the fish in a manner that efficiently brings it to hand without injury. To accomplish this, I must keep my head when the steelhead panics.

Although I will strip in a half-pounder or a parr to expedite its release, I always play an adult steelhead from the reel. Usually, as the steelhead takes the fly down, I raise my rod and let slip the slack I normally maintain (whether the fish is taking line directly from the reel or holding a position in the pool). Occasionally, a steelhead will follow a fly as it is being stripped back and then unexpectedly take the fly with a rush. I fished a Canadian river where this happened, sometimes with the striking steelhead only twenty feet away. With fifty or sixty feet of line coiled up, there was an immediate danger of a huge tangle and a lost fish. I found the easiest solution was dumping the line off onto the water and keeping careful track of *it*, not the fish. If the fish runs, it will take line dragging in the river. If it doesn't, a minimum amount of tension to the fish will give me a moment to reel line through the rod hand and back onto the reel.

For all the stories of incredibly long runs by out-of-control steelhead, the vast majority of these fish don't leave the pool, particularly the males. They run downstream, often for a considerable distance, but they usually stop before exiting the tailout. Even when the rise occurs right at the tailout and the downstream run immediately takes the steelhead into heavy water below, I still look for pauses between dashes. I've had steelhead exit a pool by leaping into a torrent of white water and suddenly stop in some faint pocket in the middle of it all. They hold this position until jogged again into flight by tension from my upstream position. But these pauses are a clear invitation for me *not* to press the steelhead, so that I can work down to its new hold where control can be more easily maintained. Dropping below the fish may then be possible, the slight tension from the rod and the current quickly taxing it. The fish will try to swim away from the resistance and move upstream. After a few minutes of this, the steelhead is exhausted.

The steelhead's downstream flight from the initial hookup, complete with jumps and cartwheels, exhausts it more than any rod pressure I can bring to bear. I only want to stay connected, to prevent overruns of my reel, to drop my rod each time the steelhead jumps so that it will not fall on a taut leader. When the steelhead stops to catch its breath, I will regain control and press my advantage. I don't want the steelhead to recover from its runs and jumps. I do want the hookup to interfere with its breathing, for the pressure to cause additional stress. I don't want a sulking fish and a ragged struggle.

Hot steelhead often race down a pool, jump several times, run again, and stop almost in a faint. I have been able to put my rod over my shoulder and march up the pool, the steelhead obediently following along. If, however, I am near the steelhead at the end of such a run, I can beach it almost immediately. That is rarely the case, and more than anything else, it is why bringing a steelhead to the beach takes time—"a minute to the pound," says the oldtime rule of thumb, often a much too generous assessment.

Anglers are either unable or unwilling to react boldly to pauses in the steelhead's frantic oxygen-burning efforts to rid itself of the fly. Too often I have observed anglers applying light tension on a steelhead that has settled into recovering from its exertions. They never take control, but hang on until the steelhead has regained its strength sufficiently to jump again. The process is repeated several times until the steelhead becomes so feeble its recovery is threatened. Some inexperienced fly fishers don't even stop then. Once, I watched the sad spectacle of a Deschutes fly fisherman playing a seven-pound steelhead until it died. Then he beached it. My advice fell on deaf ears—as it usually does at such times.

The dash of most hens and many spirited bucks provides the kind of action that makes steelhead such wonderful gamefish. These fish explode into my consciousness with predictable violence, and they carry the burden of the struggle. I rely upon finesse and timing, picking my openings, pressing my advantage. In several minutes, I've had large steelhead on their sides in the shallows. I don't make a race of this, but if I hurry to reach them and slip out the hook without ever touching them I'm enormously pleased with myself. This rush of exhilaration, a reaction from a quick and violent encounter, leaves the steelhead none the worse and gives me much to dwell upon.

The large male steelhead that does not jump gives me my worst moments. They are often lightly hooked, which I sometimes see on the greased line rise when it does not turn after taking the fly. They shake their heads, make short runs, turn and twist, conserving their energy and prolonging the struggle. A hook that has only caught the skin of the mouth will soon tear free. But not to press them results in a messy, almost interminable struggle.

Some anglers hold their rods parallel to the water with the rod first to one side and then to the other side of the steelhead. This is a saltwater technique designed to keep the fish off-balance and moving, but it must be used with discrimination. A river, unlike the open ocean, has currents that can be used to advantage or disadvantage, and I don't want to find myself pressuring a steelhead by pulling it upstream. Also, saltwater hooks are usually short-shanked, fished with barbs, and are more likely to hold regardless of the fish's position. This is not the same as a long-shanked barbless hook. Pressuring a steelhead when the barbless hook is on the far side of the fish is a fine way to make an early release. Some anglers welcome this. I'm not one of them, at least not yet.

I've had steelhead make a run out into the main current nearly to the tailout before rolling on their sides nearly unconscious, their pectoral fins waving in the air. If the fish is exceptionally large—in the high teens or more—and well below the angler, it becomes very difficult or impossible to pull to the safety of a quiet eddy. The force exerted by the current on such a disabled steelhead is considerable, nearly impossible to deal with if it has washed out of the tailout. I try desperately to keep the steelhead under some sort of tension while racing to get slightly below it. This chase after a nearly dead fish is not an altogether glorious enterprise. With luck, however, I eventually draw my trophy from the heavy current for its release.

PART TWO

THE
GREAT
RIVERS

Anglers measure the greatness of steelhead rivers in many ways. The size of the run, the ultimate size of individual steelhead, and how much of the river is good for the fly have long been fundamental considerations. Whether the river speaks to us historically or possesses a fly-fishing-only section or a catch-and-release season are additional factors that influence the choices. These criteria promote a handful of rivers, the classic waters that give our sport its dimension and much of its mystique.

Years ago I began to understand that among our finest steelhead fly fishers, a single pool can stand for a river, and a single river can stand for the sport. Roderick Haig-Brown spent much of his life learning the ways of a short length of the Campbell River. General Noel Money fished a Stamp River pool so often that it came to define his fly fishing. Al Knudson devoted entire winters to one relatively obscure drift on the Skagit. Ralph Wahl's Steelhead Shangri-la was little more than a backwater eddy. Ted Trueblood could be found each fall on a few hundred yards of the Grande Ronde.

I can often remember the name of a pool, every detail of its geography, and how it revealed its secrets before I can recall the river that holds it. Great fishing rivers are collections of great pools, and even the least noteworthy river has one pool that holds a few steelhead, and is truly great, when I know where to look and how to search.

7

KLAMATH RIVER

B E F O R E the Kispiox or the Thompson, the Clearwater or the Skagit anchored our yearnings to fish a fly for steelhead, the Klamath River flowed with unlimited virtue. Its annual runs of steelhead, hundreds of thousands of sea-bright trout representing many discrete races, sought dozens of spawning tributaries. Some fish were as small as ten inches, others as large as ten pounds, rarely more, though their ultimate size was no barrier to legend. When anglers cast flies and hooked steelhead they could not hold, they said the fish were fifteen pounds or twenty pounds, and their friends did not believe them, but they were telling the truth.

The Klamath remains faithful to that memory. The reputation of its steelhead survives in a much greater context, and I think that has changed our perception of it, but it is a great river still, unspoiled and bountiful.

The river's fame came to us principally along two lines, the first being its steelhead, trout that typically smolt, migrate to sea, and return several months later only slightly larger than when they left. Though they join older, sexually mature steelhead that are on a spawning migration, the little half-pounder steelhead are sexually immature, and they will not spawn. They migrate as far as 100 miles upriver, remaining throughout the fall and often well into winter before making their return to the ocean. When they ascend the Klamath again the next fall, they are mature steelhead of eighteen or nineteen inches, far more modest in size than steelhead of comparable age on almost all other rivers. Their small size is directly attributable to their considerable time in fresh water and their lack of

81

foraging time, of rapid growth time, in salt water. Given this life history, "large" steelhead of six or seven pounds have either survived many spawning migrations, are atypical steelhead that remained at sea for a full year after a half-pounder migration, or made an initial ocean migration of one or two years before returning to spawn the first time.

The steelhead of the upper Klamath River share these life history traits with several other races of steelhead in northern California and southern Oregon, most notably those of the Rogue River.

Unusually small steelhead would hardly make for a great sport fishery were it not for their incredible numbers. Whereas a single steelhead per day must be considered excellent fly fishing on the very best of our rivers, twenty or even thirty steelhead in a day on the Klamath was once routine, and still happens today. On no other river in North America can one catch such numbers of rainbow trout, whether sea-run or residential, that are so large, for Klamath steelhead commonly exceed twenty inches in length.

Down through Cade Canyon with my 2-weight.

The second reason for the Klamath's fame is how much of its water lends itself to the fly. I have always felt that the river's reputation was based as much on how its waters could be fished as on what its waters contained.

The Klamath drainage is two large rivers, the Klamath and the Trinity; several major tributaries, the Shasta, Scott, and Salmon rivers; and numerous small tributaries that drain an area of more than twenty-five thousand square miles in northern California and southern Oregon. This volume represents more than one-third of the runoff for the entire state of California. While the sum of the parts is most impressive, it is the parts that are fished; and the pools above where the Klamath and Trinity rivers join at Weitchpec can be long and shallow, and as gracious to steelhead fly fishermen as any in angling.

The Klamath never belonged solely to fly fishing, though for three generations its steelhead have been most frequently extolled in that light. Claude Krieder waxed euphoric in chapter after chapter

A mature, first-spawning Klamath River Steelhead.

of *Steelhead* (G. P. Putnam's Sons, l948). His writings about his time on the Klamath are easily the best documentation we have about the river and its steelhead a half-century ago.

All winter we talk or dream of those divine conditions on our river when the big bruisers simply wore us out, charging up and down the riffles. That particularly deep, foaming run where it took a long cast of ninety feet to reach *the* spot and where I lost that certain fifteen pounder. You bet I'm going back! And I'll use a heavier leader there this year. Why, that might have been a record steelhead.

Krieder and his longtime friend, Roy Donnelly, fished "Shangri-La" water, and "Indian Frank's Secret Riffle," and they called the Klamath a "Steelhead Paradise." Donnelly's best from Shangri-La was nearly fourteen pounds, Krieder's a couple of pounds less, wonderful steelhead on any river. Their fly patterns were longtime favorites even then, the Jock Scott, Royal Coachman, Carson, and Thor, all in #4s and #6s.

Peter Schwab found in the Klamath the very essence of steelhead fly fishing. The famous outdoor writer's wire-bodied bucktail patterns were developed for this, his favorite river, and the Queen Bess, Paint Brush, Brass Hat, Bobbie Dunn, and Bellamy remained popular steelhead dressings for years. Late in his angling life, often ill and depressed, he saw the Klamath moved off center stage as increasing attention was paid to the new steelhead rivers being discovered in Washington, Idaho, and British Columbia. He seemed to take the rejection personally. In a letter to Ralph Wahl, he said:

What was that about a thirty-pound steelhead? Taken on a fly? Does the guy know the difference between a nice fresh-run silver or chinook and a steelhead? I'm not skeptical, of course. I was called a liar, screwball, horsethief, wife beater, everything for having once estimated a steelhead dragged out of the lower Klamath by an Injun to have weighed a good 25 pounds—steelhead, not the Injun.

Many steelhead patterns have Klamath origins, and some are still in frequent use: Silver Hilton, Orleans Barber, Weitchpec Witch, Trinity, Brindle Bug (and Mossback, its alternate), Burlap, Green Drake, Brown Drake, and the Chappie.

The list of anglers who fished these dressings and frequented the Klamath in more recent years would be a long one. A few who should be mentioned specifically: Outdoor Franklin and Lloyd Silvius who gave us, in turn, the Chappie and the Brindle Bug; Bill Schaadt, a chinook salmon fly fisherman of international renown; Walton Powell, of rod-making fame; outdoor writers Ted Trueblood, Larry Green, and Jim Freeman.

When I set out to visit the Klamath after an absence of many years, I had decided I would fish the river in the classic greased line manner with tackle in keeping with its steelhead. I would avoid the lower river, which could only be adequately covered by 7- or 8-weight rods, and concentrate on the more intimate confines upriver, where a long 2-weight outfit would put most, if not all, of the water within my reach. A 3-weight forward-taper line quickly loaded my Orvis eight-and-a-half-foot rod and easily carried the burden of wet flies in sizes 8, 10, and 12. Just for the fun of it, I would fish traditional British patterns, sometimes on double hooks if the little flies could not penetrate currents without laying over. In this way I traveled to the Klamath confident that I would be discovering a new river. I needed only a mentor and companion.

Tim Grenvik was my good fortune. The pleasant young man was a fishing guide in Happy Camp, a tiny logging community 100 Klamath River miles from the Pacific. He certainly knew something about the steelhead runs, how they might proceed, and where individual fish were likely to hold. His clients usually did not fly fish, and Tim would pull plugs. This was not a special pleasure for him, but neither was it an indignity to be suffered. He sometimes provided the same service for fly fishermen, working their flies through canyon water that could be fished in no other way, and through easily waded riffles that ran beside long gravel bars.

Of course, the occasional fly fisherman who disdained this approach would wade for his fish and cast from an anchored boat on exceptionally difficult water. Tim did not find these clients especially liberating. He liked to row, and his personal interest in fly fishing was as yet without hubris. The fly outfit he cached in his boat was an 8-weight with a full-sinking forward-taper line, and he never fished it unless a client invited him to do so.

Like so many young guides today, he was knowledgeable about the social and environmental issues that affected his region. Gold mining and Indian fishing, senate bills and house bills, dams and irrigation projects became alternate topics of discussion. During the off season he bossed a three-man helicopter crew that fought forest fires, surveyed timber reserves, and kept track of peregrine falcon aeries.

That Tim found the companionship of his clients important and the angling methods they employed unimportant seemed curious to me at first. This wasn't a case of his business sense ruling his heart. His lack of prejudice was genuine. He enjoyed fly fishing, but he had recently written an article on fishing spinners. He fished plugs, and he also fished bait. I had no sense that he considered one method more refined than the other. I knew he was not fully aware of the richness of the steelhead fly-fishing traditions born on the Klamath, but I thought that was symptomatic of the area. As if to reinforce that opinion, I encountered just one other fly fisherman during my days at Happy Camp. He, like Tim, cast a full sinking line on a powerful rod.

Cliff Hunter, a friend of mine from Aloha, Oregon, shared the river with me. The first of our days together began with Tim downshifting his truck through the tight turns on the dirt road that led to Cade Canyon. Over the din of the engine and the aluminum drift boat clanging behind, he called our attention to the natural history of the area. Cliff and I were eager students, ready with a new question for every answer.

"Alaska yellow cedar is little more than a big shrub here—we're at the southern end of its range. We also have one of the northernmost stands of coastal redwoods."

"But these are *oaks*," I hastened to point out.

"Yes, tan and black. We'll see others on the float. And lots of pines."

Tim explained that the area can be as moist as mixed stands of Port Orford cedar and Brewer's spruce, and as arid as live oaks. We would see it all from one bend of the river to another.

The Klamath still carried the light somnolent buzzings of deep summer on this first week of fall. Tailout currents were muffled, bird songs desultory and infrequent by midmorning. Bright green algae were abundant on the rocks, and as we wrestled with the boat I was thankful for the metal studs set in my felts. Tendrils of free-floating algae made soup of the currents. At times this would prove troublesome by fouling my double hook flies. "We need a big rain to get rid of the algae," Tim said. "That would scour out the river."

I asked about the foam that had collected to form drift-lines along the grassy shores and completely fill the quiet eddies. "Photosynthesis," he said, and gave the McKenzie boat a final push into the river. Algae was again the culprit. Wading would be especially difficult with the bottom completely obscured.

Tim's advice on the best riffles started with a deadly serious admonition. "See that mound of gravel out in the river? That was caused by a gold-mining dredge. We'll see a number of the contraptions before the day is out. The dredge sucks gravel off the river bottom, sends it through a sluice, and dumps the gravel back into the river. Just upstream of that mound is a hell of a hole. Sometimes they're hard to see, and sometimes they're impossible to see. Beware the dreaded dredge holes!"

Thus oriented and warned, we set off to find steelhead with the lightest of fly tackle and English flies. Only occasionally would Tim have us fish from the boat, and then to cast to pocket water that, from his plug-pulling experiences, he knew held steelhead. When we beached the boat and Cliff and I began wading through the first run, it was late morning, and the river sparkled by without so much as a touch of shade. Cliff started below me, and in a flash he was gone with scarcely a ripple. I noticed nine feet of 4-weight rod and a hand working downstream.

"The dredge hole!" I exclaimed, as Cliff came sputtering up from the depths.

"He located it for us," said Tim.

"What a guy! Our dredge hole detector!" I called downriver. Cliff staggered to shore, bent over to ship a few gallons from his waders, and came back to the boat.

As my friend stripped down, I began fishing a #10 Blue Charm sparsely tied on a double hook so sticky sharp that even the lightest take would be the steelhead's undoing. I was worrying about a salmon or steelhead parr throwing itself at the fly, or a steelhead taking it deeply, when a bright half-pounder struck the fly sharply and shot into the air. The rod managed the foot-long trout in delightful fashion, and the release was completed without undue damage.

Cliff sat naked in the front seat of the boat, his clothes draped over the gunwale and drying in the warm sun. Perhaps the shock of his sudden dip had tired him, for he was fast asleep. Tim walked down to join me. "My logging friends are going to think I go to San Francisco for my clients!"

As the afternoon wore on, seven more of the immature steelhead caught the Blue Charm and left me wondering where the adults might be. When Cliff returned to swimming a #8 Spade through the best riffles, he too found only half-pounders. I knew they came in waves, but we were near the up-stream range of these immature steelhead. The season was well advanced, and mature steelhead should be about.

I first guessed that Cock Rock Run honored the drumming site of a love-starved ruffed grouse. Tim dashed these romantic notions, and directed my attention to the end of the run where an enormous stone phallus stood. "Rock hard and erect," he said. Casting before this imposing monolith would provide us with memorable fishing in the days to come. A hint of this occurred when Tim rose a fine steelhead that pushed up a rooster tail of spray as it came down off the top end of the run. The fly soon came away, but we were encouraged.

We came upon our first gold dredge, a Rube Goldberg affair atop a raft that was anchored to one side of the river. Two men in neoprene suits gave Tim a wave of recognition. The sound of machinery turning the stream bottom upside down made polite conversation impossible.

"Modern day gold rush! Started about three, four years ago!" yelled Tim.

"You'd think the gold would be long gone!" I called back.

"Oh no. A man can make a thousand dollars a day doing this!" We drifted by and around a bend.

"Doesn't this absolutely ruin the river bottom for spawning fish?" I asked.

Tim smiled. "Well, they get their permits from our Department of Fish and Game!"

We pulled out for afternoon coffee beneath a shale hillside of olive green live oak. This was a startling contrast to the neighboring slopes of pine. Tim noticed my gaze. "Rude ground. Always reminds me of Mordor."

"That forest of twisted, gnarled trees belongs in Tolkien's netherworld," I replied to his reference to *The Hobbit*. "It's easy to imagine brave little Bilbo leading his friends safely through its dangers."

Tim showed me that it was the south-facing slopes that held the ponderosa and sugar pines. The north-facing slopes were dressed with Douglas firs and, at four thousand feet, red cedars. White pine and jeffrey pine and knobcone pine were there also, each with its own special requirements in this land of microclimates.

Late in the day, we anchored in the Allen Ranch water, a big run with a reputation for producing some of the largest steelhead found in the upper river. Cliff and I, right- and left-handed, cast from opposite ends of the boat and rose a steelhead each before a buck of nearly five pounds solidly took his Spade fished greased-line in the surface film.

When we pulled anchor, we drifted down to the cliff that looms above the tailout of the run. I have been fascinated with raptors all my life and the cliff face prompted me to ask Tim if he had ever found peregrine falcons nesting here. He answered my question with a story.

"I received a notice from the U.S. Forest Service that our helicopter was to fly no closer than a thousand feet from nesting peregrine falcons. I wrote back and asked how we were to do this without knowing where the nest sites were located. They finally gave me a map showing the locations. I found two additional nest sites and added them to the map." Tim went on to explain that the bird's rarity and extraordinary black market value require that these locations remain closely guarded secrets.

As we came through the bottom of the run, an adult peregrine falcon was perched on a bleached snag. "Did you arrange this?" I asked.

"Certainly!" With a look of smug delight he held the boat in the current, while Cliff got off a series of telephoto shots.

Just above our take-out at Gordon's Ferry, Tim shipped the oars and made the following bronze-plaque statement: "Here Tim Grenvik caught a twelve-and-a-half-pound steelhead!" This was a plug-caught winter-run male, he explained, so remarkable for the Klamath that he killed the fish and sent it to a taxidermist. He knew of another steelhead of fifteen pounds. Rumors of steelhead still larger persisted, including one of nineteen pounds. Tim speculated that such fish may be part of a "ghost run," a little understood February run of exceptionally large winter steelhead that spawn somewhere in the vast watershed.

Cliff and I came to know Cade Canyon well. We delighted in our new knowledge and savored our time on familiar water with ever-increasing pleasure. A heron rookery, osprey, and a family of eight otters that raised unbelievable hell with the crayfish stitched together our days. We fished the English patterns I had promised myself, and gradually integrated a #10 Green Butt Skunk, and then, late one day, a #8 Night Dancer on a single light-wire hook for an hour of grand fishing.

I had worked down Cock Rock Run until I could go no farther. The long glide below reminded me of winter steelhead water where a dead-slow swing matched chilled metabolisms. To get the necessary distance with the 2-weight, I had been cleaning and dressing my line several times a day. Now I also dressed the leader in order to keep the fly riding in the surface film. Careful not to overcast, I laid out forty feet of line on the downstream quarter. The fly broke through the surface film once or twice as it came alive on the swing. I tensed as a large bulge cleaved the water just below it. An instant later, the steelhead was racing downriver, jumping in panic from the drag of the line. I palmed the reel and held the fish with fifty feet of backing on the water. The rod flexed into the cork handle, yet I was free of worry that the fly would tear out. The steelhead, a twenty-three-inch male, was soon cradled in my hand.

So great had been the commotion that I did not expect a second steelhead from this water. On progressively longer casts, however, a second, third, and fourth steelhead charged up to take the Night Dancer. All were nearly identical in size and spirit.

Several weeks after I returned home, Tim wrote to tell about Dan Hynes, a client who caught an eight-pound hen on a #10 Woolly Worm. The steelhead was the largest Hynes had taken from the Klamath in twenty-five years of fishing, and the largest ever caught from Tim's boat on the fly. This exciting news—the ostensible reason for the letter—had a proud epilogue. After congratulations all around, the once-in-a-lifetime steelhead was carefully revived and released.

NOTES

Klamath steelhead are "trouty" by nature, a free rising race that may actively feed both as half-pounders and as adults of all ages. Dry flies can be skated or waked, traditional wet flies presented greased-line, or dark stonefly nymphs, Ugly Bugs, and Woolly Worms fished weighted or unweighted on floating or sinking lines.

I think the effectiveness of the low-water Night Dancer and Spade was due to their very nymphlike character when given a dubbed, picked-out body.

A straight 2-weight outfit is not completely suitable for the Klamath. It severely limits the weight of flies and the distance they can be cast. The rare large steelhead might be troublesome, though I would value that consideration least of all. One cannot obtain a full complement of fly lines in weights 2 or 3, and many anglers would find this a disadvantage.

I found the eight-and-a-half-foot 2-weight rod quite up to handling a 4-weight forward-taper line. This was important to me, because I could fish a ten-foot sink-tip line—the lightest manufactured—and get a small weighted nymph down quite deep. However, if a longer sink tip had been desirable, or a fast-sinking shooting taper needed to put the fly flat on the bottom, a nine- or nine-and-a-half-foot 4- or 5-weight rod would have been a better choice.

LIFE HISTORY

No dams or weirs block the Klamath or Trinity rivers below their headwaters. Steelhead spawn below Iron Gate Dam on the Klamath and Lewiston Dam on the Trinity, principally in streams tributary to the main stems. The lack of collection points in this vast system of rivers has made life-history information difficult to obtain and mostly piecemeal in nature. Escapement figures have been only general estimates based on sport-fishing success or on the commercial gill-net harvest of winter steelhead stocks on the Hoopa Valley Indian Reservation.

The reliable information that is currently available is contained almost entirely in James S. Hopelain's study for the California Department of Fish and Game, *Age, Growth, and Life History of Klamath River Basin Steelhead (Salmo gairdnerii) As Determined From Scale Analysis.* (The preliminary data was assembled in 1987, but was still unpublished in 1989.) Scale samples were obtained by electrofishing and angling, from steelhead trapped at the Iron Gate Hatchery, and from winter-run steelhead caught in Indian gill nets.

Three distinct seasonal runs of steelhead were identified. The winter run, including a small half-pounder component, was thought to vary from ten thousand to thirty thousand. The spring run, also containing a half-pounder component, only numbered five hundred to three thousand. The fall run of steelhead contained 55,000 to 75,000 adults and 150,000 to 225,000 nonspawning half-pounders.

The Klamath and Trinity rivers proved to support somewhat dissimilar steelhead stocks. Main-stem Klamath River tributaries (Shasta, Scott, and Salmon rivers) had an average half-pounder incidence of 95.2 percent, that is, approximately nineteen of every twenty steelhead migrated to sea and returned several months later as sexually immature steelhead. The average incidence of half-pounders dropped to 54.4 percent for Trinity River summer-runs, 22.2 percent for North Fork Trinity spring-runs, and 23.2 percent for the Klamath River's winter run.

Freshwater ages, the period of premigrant residency, was consistent throughout the Klamath-Trinity system: one-year 4.5 percent, two-year 90.8 percent, three-year 4.6 percent.

Average lengths for maiden fall-run spawners were 19.5 inches (upper Klamath) and 21.6 (Trinity River). Average length increased to 23.2 inches for maiden spring-run steelhead (North Fork Trinity), and 25.5 inches for the lower Klamath's maiden winter run.

The destination of the Klamath's winter run is unknown. This is the so-called ghost run Tim Grenvik described. These steelhead are remarkably similar to the North Fork Trinity's spring run in half-pounder occurrence, incidence of second-time spawners (30.8 percent), and lengths at various life-history stages.

A comparison of ocean-life-history categories of six different Klamath-Trinity races illustrates considerable variation and is worth noting and briefly commenting upon.

Stream	1(1s)	2(1s)	2(h-1s)	2(2s)	3(1s)	3(2s)	3(h-1s)	3(h-2s)	3(3s)	4(h-2s)	4(h-3s)
Shasta River (Klamath)		0.8	51.7	0.8			24.6	24.6			20.3
Bogus Creek (Klamath)			82.4	8.8				8.8			
Willow Creek (Trinity River)	1.9		66.7	20.4				9.3	1.9		
N.F. Trinity		38.5	11.5	11.5	3.8	7.7	3.8	19.2	3.8		
S.F. Trinity	11.8	20.6	17.6	2.9	8.8	14.7	2.9	11.8	5.9	2.9	
Klamath River (winter run)	2.3	47.7	2.3	4.5	11.4	15.9	6.8	9.1			

Note: h = half-pounder run during first ocean year
1s = sample taken during first spawning run
2s = sample taken during second spawning run
3s = sample taken during third spawning run

Almost all steelhead in the Klamath's Shasta River have a half-pounder component in their life histories (98.3 percent). This is fairly typical of all steelhead in streams tributary to the upper Klamath. The average adult steelhead measured 21.7 inches and ranged from 16.9 to 27.6 inches.

Bogus Creek and Shasta River stocks are essentially the same. Bogus Creek steelhead have a higher mortality rate. They uncommonly survive to spawn a second time, while no steelhead were evident in the sampling (sixty-eight) returning to spawn a third time. They averaged 19.7 inches and ranged from 16.1 to 26 inches.

The North Fork Trinity steelhead is atypical within the Klamath-Trinity system, but has life histories consistent with steelhead stocks in many other California and Oregon rivers. The most common life history exhibited, 38.5 percent, was a two-year ocean steelhead spawning for the first time. This would suggest considerable size, but the steelhead ranged from approximately 19⅝ to 26 inches.

The forty-three winter-run steelhead removed from Indian gill nets in the lower Klamath during February and March ranged from approximately 21⅝ to 32⅝ inches. Nearly half of these steelhead were spawning for the first time after spending two years at sea. Repeat spawners comprised 30.2 percent of the sample; no steelhead survived to spawn more than twice in the sampling.

Where in these samplings are the great steelhead Claude Krieder described in *Steelhead*? The number of steelhead in the Hopelain study was very small compared to the total escapement of the Klamath-Trinity drainage. Certainly fall-run steelhead that are larger than any found in the sampling are caught each year. According to Larry Simpson, a fly-fishing guide on the Klamath and Trinity, the largest steelhead taken by fly fishermen are likely to be in the eight- to nine-pound class. But Norman Ploss took a perfectly proportioned fifteen-pound buck in October 1988 near the Tectah Riffle. And Gary Tucker reportedly caught late fall-run steelhead of 18 and 20½ pounds on the lower Klamath near the mouth of Blue Creek.

There is still much to learn about the many races of steelhead we collectively call "Klamath" steelhead. Searching through the escapements and sorting out the mysteries during all the seasons is an exciting prospect for the next generation of steelhead fly fishermen.

At Winkle Bar I examine one of the boats Zane Grey used to run the lower Rogue. *Photo Credit: Rick Nelson*

8

ROGUE RIVER

THE elderly man approaching our McKenzie boat was an onlooker drawn by the activity that surrounded the Rogue River's Grave Creek launch. Rick Nelson and I waited our turn in what passed for a line, while ahead of us a flotilla of whitewater rafts stood by in various stages of readiness. Young guides in broad-brimmed Stetsons hastily pumped and provisioned as their clients laughed nervously and tried to help.

"Nice boat!" He ran his hand along the white ash gunwale that delineated the walnut-stained plywood hull.

Rick nodded thanks. He encourages these compliments by taking meticulous care of his boat, even waxing the sides from time to time, and I liked to tease him about that.

"Are you going to take this down the river?" The man was sincere, his rhetorical question holding only an edge of incredulity. We smiled and he shook his head.

"Look at the bottom," I said. "That sheet of plastic covering the plywood is very much like Teflon, and it's just about bulletproof." He checked the underside, and gave us a "whatever-you-say" shrug.

"Well, good luck!" He waved and wandered toward the pandemonium of the launch. If we haven't convinced *him*, at least we've convinced *ourselves*, I thought. I felt no lack of faith in Rick's ability on the oars, and I trusted the boat. I had a nearly identical boat, and the two of us had covered many river miles together.

When our turn came at the launch, we quickly floated the boat clear of the trailer and beached it to one side. Thus cleared, we could load the boat, taking care to tie everything down. After weeks of planning, we set about the task with enthusiasm.

Grave Creek is at the end of the road. Rick had arranged for a shuttle, and my truck would be waiting downriver for us at Foster Bar.

This forty miles of Rogue River we were about to float entertains many passions. Rafting is a mania, and with good reason. On this one section are forty named rapids and falls. Many waters are Class III or Class IV on the American Canoe Association's rating scale of I to VI. While a Class I is hardly a riffle, a VI is impassable, run only in barrels by individuals harboring death wishes. A Class V is a

The canyon waters of the Rogue.

tremendous threat to life, a Class IV offers the possibility of severe injury, and a Class III is, at least, dangerous. The numbers don't necessarily signify the violence of the rapids, but rather the degree of difficulty in negotiating them safely. Connoisseurs of whitewater challenges look for high numbers to test their skills. The same numbers give advance warning to those less sure of themselves, or to those not exotically equipped and seeking only safe passage down a river. Whether the rapids are the main attraction or not, the Rogue from Grave Creek to Foster Bar is more popular than any other comparable water in Oregon.

The Wild and Scenic Rivers Act was passed by Congress in 1968. It provided for the lasting preservation of rivers under three classifications—Wild, Scenic, and Recreational. An eighty-four-mile segment of the Rogue, from Applegate Creek near Grants Pass to Lobster Creek near Gold Beach on the coast, is designated under this act. The forty miles from Grave Creek to Foster Bar has been given a Wild River classification. This means the river must be free of impoundments, generally inaccessible, and protected in a primitive state. Backpackers gain access to the entire Wild section on the Rogue River Hikers' Trail, which begins at Grave Creek. Otherwise, access is only by boat. Either way, visiting this wild canyon water that cuts its way through the Coast Range is a wilderness experience, and many individuals need no other reason for making the visit.

There are, of course, the famous Rogue steelhead. The river and this gamefish are so nearly synonymous, so easily define each other, that the blending of mystiques has produced an image more powerful here than on any other American river. This is perhaps less true today than it was two or three generations ago, but for much of the public, steelhead first means *Rogue steelhead*. To a remarkable degree, that fact is the legacy of Zane Grey.

Steelhead fly fishing was in its infancy when the famous novelist first fished the Rogue in 1919. He returned to the river nearly every year, and in 1925 organized an expedition that successfully floated the river in wood skiffs through what is today the Wild and Scenic River section, Galice to Gold Beach. This adventure was described in *Tales of Fresh Water Fishing* (Harper and Brothers, 1928).

Today's sophisticated angler can hardly appreciate the impact this book had on the angling public. An international following made Grey the highest-paid writer of his time. If his many world records for saltwater gamefish—and no one had more—can be considered a measure of greatness, then he was our foremost angler. He wrote volumes about his fishing adventures. One of his popular novels could be completed in a month, and many were made into movies. He was a charismatic blend of Hollywood and the Wild West, as handsome as any leading man, one of his own noble nineteenth-century characters come to life. The breast-beating hyperbole of his writing may seem embarrassingly macho today, but it captivated its generation. Grey, more than any other writer, planted steelhead in the American consciousness, and the connection between that and the Rogue River is forever fixed. His spirit lives on here with such vitality that, while visiting his old haunts, I found his presence palpable.

Our use of a wood drift boat to float the Rogue was admittedly a sentimental concession to this history. Rick knew the water well by whitewater raft, but that would not do. The wood boat demanded considerations not granted a raft. It would not ricochet easily off canyon walls. It would be nearly helpless if filled with water. Its thin plywood sides could easily admit holes.

We could not hope to copy Zane Grey's float in historically accurate detail, and that was not our goal. We could camp and fly-fish in the same places, see the autumn river much as he saw it, and hunt for steelhead with the same sense of adventure. If that engendered a certain comaraderie with his legend, then so be it.

During the winter of 1925, Zane Grey fished in the South Pacific on his motor sailing yacht and found himself thinking fondly of his time the previous year on the Rogue. Between bouts with billfish and tuna, he dreamed of a return that would include yet another adventure. This time he wanted to float the Rogue through its remote canyon waters. Grey thought no angler had ever done this before, and he was probably right. He returned to his home in Altadena, California, and spent July and August trolling for swordfish off Catalina Island. There the memory of "cool green forests, the dark shade, the thundering rapids, and the wonderful steelhead trout of the Rogue" became a sanctuary from the intense glare of the sea. He decided to make the trip.

Grey's always considerable entourage—friends, servants, and relatives—gathered, and a mountain of gear was assembled. Although Grey was an excellent photographer himself—it was one of his many hobbies—he brought along a photographer to document the trip. He called Joe Wharton, an old friend in Grants Pass, and ordered four eighteen-foot rowboats built.

Wharton had opened the first fishing tackle store in Grants Pass, on H Street, in 1907, and it soon became a gathering place for visiting anglers. He came to write an angling column for the *Rogue River*

Courier, sometimes published articles in *Forest and Stream,* and eventually gave fishing reports on the radio. He may deserve credit for attracting English and Scottish anglers to the Rogue. Certainly their use of the rod and reel was a sophisticated departure from the local custom of a long pole, a short length of line, and a fly or spinner. At Grey's urging, Wharton stocked fine quality English fishing tackle. By the 1920s, this self-styled "Sage of the Rogue," had become the most notable spokesman for the Rogue's steelhead fly fishing.

The same year Zane Grey published *Tales of Fresh Water Fishing,* 1928, Wharton published "Game Fish of Rogue River" in *Forest and Stream* in June. He wasn't bashful about the Rogue's summer-run steelhead:

This is the run that furnishes the grandest fly fishing the angler has ever known. This is conceded to be a fact by experienced anglers who have fished all the well known trout water of the world.

As in all fish stories, the biggest always gets away, sometimes taking part of the tackle with him. Individuals of the summer-run will weigh up to fifteen pounds with average around six- or six-and-a-half.

(These weights are unbelievable. See "Life History," at the conclusion of this chapter.)

Zane Grey reached Grants Pass on September 3, 1925, and finished equipping his expedition at Wharton's store. He wrote: "Wharton had secured the services of a guide and market fisherman,

Joe Wharton pictured himself on the fly envelopes from his shop. The flies were tied by Wharton: No. 1 Special, Turkey and Red (hairwing), and Golden Demon.

Claude Bardon, who was born on the Rogue and depended upon it for his livelihood. Bardon said he had obtained four of the Rogue River boats, and that he did not think much of the eighteen-foot skiffs Wharton had built for me."

In fact, Bardon bluntly told Grey that the boats would never survive the trip. They were rowing skiffs, possessing squared-off transoms, and able to track well, advantages on lakes. However, they would be hard to maneuver on the Rogue, and they would come down the river stern-first, *backwards*, in effect. (Because river boats float downstream, with the sharp end and the rower facing downstream, they are maneuvered by rowing against the current. In this manner, they proceed downriver more slowly than the currents carrying them.) But Grey was fortunate. Wharton had found Grey's original recommendations completely unsatisfactory. The changes he had made were so complete that Grey hardly recognized the boats as those he had ordered.

Bardon arranged for four additional boats to be put at Grey's disposal. "The four boats Bardon had secured for me were of a type new to me, and certainly unique. They were about twenty-three feet long, sharp fore and aft, rising out of the water, very wide and deep, with gunwales having a marked flare, twelve inches to the foot. They looked heavy and clumsy to me, but upon trying one I found to my amaze [sic], that, empty, it rowed remarkably easy, *turned round as on a pivot*, and altogether delighted me." (Italics added.)

Zane Grey had taken a turn in what was the forerunner of the modern McKenzie boat.

The boats had what designers call "rocker," the fore and aft curvature of the bottom much like the two curving pieces of wood on which a cradle rocks. This curvature prevents the bow and stern from digging into the water. Also, the flat bottom had no keel, so the boats could be pivoted. This complete lack of directional stability permitted them to float comfortably downstream in any attitude, even sideways.

These craft were work boats in the coastal salmon trade. Robert Hume, the "Salmon King of Oregon," owned the lower twelve miles of the Rogue and had built the company towns of Wedderburn and Gold Beach. The Hume Company's enormous seine nets set at tidewater brought in thousands of chinook salmon. Fishermen picked out the salmon, loaded them into their two-man "Rogue River" boats, and quickly rowed the catch to the cannery at Gold Beach. With their considerable length and flared sides, the boats carried tremendous loads, easily moved when both rowing stations were employed.

The design principles of the modern McKenzie boat are identical. When these early Rogue boats were used on Oregon's McKenzie River, the upstream sharp end was squared off so that an engine could be mounted on the transom. This made it possible to motor upstream to a launch after floating downstream to fish. Today, a McKenzie boat with pointed fore and aft ends is said to have a "Rogue style."

As Rick and I began our float, he explained that Grave Creek Rapids was immediately below the launch, and that no more than a minute later we would pass over Lower Grave Creek Falls. Each was a Class III rapids.

I looked down the river, and saw that it was split by an island. "Which side do we take?" I asked.

"As soon as we launch, I'll pull hard for the left side. There isn't enough water to take the right side."

We shoved off and rowed for the south side. The rapids that had looked so inconspicuous from upstream quickly grew larger in size and sound. We were swept to the edge, where Rick held us with quick, short oar strokes. We could look down through the entire run and trace our safe route through. There was a midstream rock to avoid, and a sucking eddy before the wall at the end, where the river turned to the right in a boil of foamy rapids. When Rick was satisfied, he gave the oars a forward stroke, then feathered back lightly with little strokes for control as we raced through. We had no time for congratulations, because there was a needle to be threaded at Lower Grave Creek. Rick again carefully lined us up and eased us over the four-foot vertical drop. With a resounding splash we were past our first obstacles.

Final preparations for Zane Grey's float down the Rogue took place at the Lewis Ranch just below Galice, and approximately seven miles above Grave Creek. Bardon and his assistant, "Debb" Van Dorn, trucked the boats down from Grants Pass to complete final provisioning. Camp was set up on the banks of the Rogue, and old friends were received: Fred Burnham, Joe Wharton, Lone Angler Wiborn, and the Lewises. The roster of those making the run was filled: the two boatmen, Bardon and Debb; Romer, Grey's son; Ken and Ed, assistants from California who were now driving a truck and Grey's Lincoln to Gold Beach, which was the takeout; Captain Mitchell, a dear friend from Nova Scotia, a world-class fly caster and an experienced Atlantic salmon angler; George Takahashi, Grey's Japanese cook, a man of great good humor and astonishing resolve. Romer Grey shared a boat with Takahashi, and for the next month they would argue over rowing duties. Otherwise, each man rowed his own boat.

When the drive-around had been completed, the party of eight commanded seven boats (apparently one skiff wasn't needed), with Grey running the largest and best of the lot, a Rogue boat named 76. Though the boat was loaded without regard to weight, he was amazed to find that it drew only six inches of water. They shoved off on a misty September morning amid cheers and waves from well-wishers.

The first easy rapids, and then Chair Riffle, were passed without incident. Grey grew confident and followed Bardon and Mitchell through a more dangerous set of rapids. The other four boats were lined through. Alameda Rapids was next, and it was at the end of the road. To Grey's consternation, onlookers with cameras at the ready had gathered on both sides of the river to watch his party shoot the narrow gap of rapids.

Grey was anxious to row his own boat, but he remained prudent. At the next set of rapids he let Bardon take his heavily loaded boat through, while Captain Mitchell managed his own lighter skiff successfully. The procedure was repeated at Argo Mine Rapids, but this time Mitchell ran the skiff head-on into a cliff, badly smashing the bow. The chastened group lined the other boats down.

They continued downriver to "Rapid Number 8," an easy piece of water with a sharp turn at the bottom. Grey, managing his own craft, lost control, and the boat smashed up on a rock and remained perched there. It was leaking, and the efforts of four of the party were required to dislodge it.

"I was considerably taken aback and discomfitted, and viewed with dismay the leak in my boat."

Grey says that, now "We had smooth river and easy going for a long distance." In fact, his boat was nearly wrecked only two miles above Grave Creek Rapids. Minutes later at Grave Creek: "Soon a sullen roar greeted my ears. That sound recalled the roar of a jungle river I had once navigated from mountain plateau to the jungle level. My hair stiffened on my head, as it had many times on that wild trip."

Bardon had beached his boat to hike below and scout the rapids. The party pulled their boats to the shore and waited. He returned and ordered the boats lined through, a tedious, tense, and potentially dangerous process. It was midafternoon before the last boat was through.

Immediately below them was lower Grave Creek, "a chute that was almost a sheer drop," according to Grey. The three best boatmen, Bardon, Debb, and Mitchell, would run all the boats through, while Grey and the rest of the party hiked below to get some pictures. Three boats were brought over without a hitch, and they returned upstream for a repeat, but this time Bardon struck a midchannel rock that ripped open the bottom of the boat as it went over. By the time he reached shore, the boat was nearly swamped. They switched its contents to other boats, and it was abandoned. The party resumed the float, its destination Rainie Falls, a Class VI rapids less than two miles from Grave Creek.

The Rogue River Canyon is volcanic, a creation of lava flows 140 million years ago. A greenish-black rock called serpentine extruded from deep within the earth through fault zones to become the hard and shiny bedrock channels of the Rogue. Nowhere is this more evident than at Rainie Falls.

The river is forced into a short, very narrow chute, a vertical drop of twelve feet with such dangerous hydraulics and big-water turbulence that no one dares to risk passage through unless they are in the largest raft that will fit the channel. However, on the far right side is a small side channel, a natural fish ladder, cauldron pockets strung on a stairstep no more than eight feet wide. The area immediately flanking its passage is serpentine, worn glass-smooth and slick as ice.

Rick and I brought our McKenzie to the ladder side and scouted its abrupt descent. There were no trees at the head to line from. The upstream man could only take the line around a boulder while his companion guided the boat down, pushing and pulling it here and there, hoping to avoid the worst of the rapids. We followed this plan, with me slipping and falling on the unforgiving rocks while Rick muscled out the line. There is a severe drop near the end, and we were forced to let the line run and hope for the best. The boat splashed into the quiet pool below without a scratch, more than I could say for either of us. I was glad we didn't have to repeat the process.

Grey's party landed here with six heavily loaded boats. Lining them all through proved to be a stupendous and painful labor. Several forest rangers gave them a hand, but when Grey began lining his own boat down he was on his own, holding the line directly without purchase. He badly misjudged the physics of the operation: "When my heavy boat turned into that pitway it shot down like a flash. I could not hold the rope. My feet were jerked from under me and went aloft, while the back of my neck, my shoulder and right elbow crashed down on the rock. I was almost knocked out. Fortunately, the boat lodged below, and soon the men got to it."

The boat had not suffered further damage. When the exhausted party finally made camp at Whiskey Creek, Grey summed up the prevailing attitude. "What a terrible day!" he exclaimed.

The origins of the Rogue River are found on the west-facing slopes of the Cascade Mountains, and for much of its 215-mile length it is a desert river of sagebrush and pine until it is deep within the lee of the Coast Range. Here, in fascinating transition, the lush vegetation of the foggy coast is stippled in, plant by plant, as the Rogue beats its way through the mountains. Grave Creek is still the interior, with hillsides of canyon live oak, white oak, tan oak, and manzanita, all mixed with ponderosa pine. Firs and cedars are here, too, the slopes and ridges playing favorites, holding brief stands of first one, and then the other. More often the evergreen is tucked away, the single odd neighbor in a community democratically given to many species.

As we floated downriver, I noticed how one slope was less thickly forested than another. I immediately suspected the culprit was past timber cutting practices, but Rick told me that this is a natural phenomenon. The mountain slopes on the south side of the Rogue get less direct sunshine, but they are windward slopes, receive more rain, and are forested more luxuriously. The coastal moisture-loving trees, the Douglas fir and western hemlock, make their appearance early on at these locations. Rick pointed out that some broadleaf trees actually had larger leaves on one side of the river than on the other. We discovered that far down the Rogue River Canyon the oaks remained until they were but remnant groves surviving on the little parcels of more arid ground that lay below the rain-swept mountains.

Rick pointed to shrubs growing precariously more than fifty feet up the nearly vertical canyon walls and called my attention to river debris woven into their twisted branches. "How do you think that stuff got up there?" he asked.

"The river doesn't get that high! Does it?"

"How would you account for it, then?"

I couldn't, but then I couldn't imagine a Rogue running many, many times stronger than the often violent river that was carrying us so swiftly downstream. The matter was not settled to my satisfaction until I received information from the Oregon State Game Commission and read that the river is subject to remarkable changes in level, a condition emphasized in the narrow canyons. Peak stream flows occur in January, and to a lesser degree in May, corresponding to periods of peak rainfall and melting snowpack. Extremes recorded range from 45,000 cubic feet per second (cfs) in late January 1970, to 663 cfs in late September 1963, a ratio of nearly sixty-eight to one! These remarkable differences are due to the large area drained, approximately 5,000 square miles, a basin measuring 110 miles long and 50 miles wide that includes California's Siskiyou Mountains, the headwaters of the Rogue's Applegate and Illinois rivers.

Canyon water is often poor fly water for the angler who prefers the intimacy of wading while finding his steelhead. This is particularly true of the Rogue's canyon, where much of the fishing is done from McKenzie boats. Anglers port and starboard strip line from their reels until the flies are working well below the boat. The guide backrows, slowing the boat down and working the flies through the lies, in effect doing the fishing.

"Hotshotting" flies is not a practice without appeal here. Elderly people, wives who would otherwise not fish, rank beginners, and children enjoy grand sport amid spectacular scenery. The flies are small, traditionally with a split wing for additional disturbance in the surface film, and often tied on double hooks to assure an even keel run in riffles. Experienced anglers could, of course, cast from boats in this water, but few do. Most wait for the convenience of the few open bars to do their wading.

Lodges exist along the Wild river, too, beginning with Black Bear Lodge at mile 8.8 from Grave Creek and ending with Peyton Place Lodge at mile 31, a half-dozen in all. Guided parties can travel from lodge to lodge, a convenience we did not seek, and a luxury not available to Zane Grey's party in 1925.

Tyee Rapids, Class IV, is the first serious piece of white water that Rick and I encountered. It gained its rating for the considerable maneuvering required to avoid a midchannel rock in the throat of the run, a demonic suckhole just left of center, and a rock ledge waiting at the end to dismantle your craft. "SCOUTING MANDATORY!" say the guidebooks. We were only too happy to oblige.

Rick studied the passage until he had memorized a "distance divided by strokes equals time" formula. Confident of where he would be and what he would be doing through Tyee's entire length, Rick nudged the boat back into the currents and picked his way down the rapids. I wanted to hold up a card with a "10" on it, so perfect was his performance.

Zane Grey camped at Whiskey Creek for several days. He hiked down to Tyee Bar and caught his first steelhead of 1925, "one about two pounds and the other around four." He had fished all the standard fly patterns without success; both trout were caught on a spinner. Bardon and Debb shot two blacktail bucks and satisfied the camp's need for fresh meat. They also hiked back upriver to Grave Creek and were able to repair and bring down the abandoned boat. Early on a cold September morning with the promise of rain in the air they shoved off, Grey again at the oars of 76.

"We ran two rapids, one a short dip, and the second a long shallow curve full of rocks, before we came to Tyee Bar Rapid. This was a zigzag aberration of the river, and not even Bardon had a notion of running it. We shoved, waded, pulled, and lined the boats over Tyee, with the amount of labor that gave us a foretaste of the day ahead."

Slim Pickens, Class III, was named by early miners for the extreme narrowness of the chute between a house-sized boulder that sits well right of center, and a rock outcropping on the right side of the river. The wisdom gained from a casual glance would send any sane boatman fleeing from this gap. It is so narrow that oars must be shipped, and it looks narrower still from an upstream vantage point. Water left of the midstream monolith is most inviting, but rocks are lurking there just beneath the cascade of foam. Those miners—no fools they—dynamited this chute out to its present claustrophobic dimensions. When Rick called my attention to it, I was dismayed.

"You're not going to try running through that, are you?"

"That's what the book says to do."

Rick often went left with his large whitewater raft, not caring to squeeze its bulk into the narrow chute. My question caused Rick a moment of indecision. He was pushing hard on the oars, driving us to the left, going with his instincts, when a powerful current grabbed the boat and shoved us hard to the right. Rick was no longer slowing us down by rowing upstream, no longer pointing at what he didn't want to hit, and the McKenzie, with crack-the-whip suddenness, smashed into the huge rock. We glanced off, and he laughed, the second of terror not really registering.

"Are we okay?" he asked, confident that we were. I looked along the inside chine, and then stood up, leaned over, and checked the hull.

"No, Rick, there's a hole in the boat, and water is coming in."

"No! You're kidding!"

"No, I'm not. See for yourself."

I moved aside and he peered over the seat.

"No! No! NO!" He was sitting down now, head bent low, and he was moaning his despair. Self-loathing is a by-product of such mistakes. I told him there was no immediate danger of us sinking. I assured him that the boat could be repaired, that the disgrace would be reduced to a cosmetic blemish. But he was deaf to my reassurances. In the end, a new set of rapids, and the concentration they required, prevented Rick from blaming himself to death.

Zane Grey makes no mention of Slim Pickens, and we encountered no difficulty with Horseshoe Bend Rapids. This is a series of two Class II rapids, followed at the end by a Class III, the higher rating due to an abrupt left turn the river makes, leaving one flying toward a rock wall guarded by a barely submerged boulder. My guidebook warns of this hazard. "This is a dangerous boulder and has taken several lives and many boats!"

One of those boats was part of Zane Grey's party.

Bardon's custom when he arrived at water that required scouting was to pull ashore and warn those who followed by waving a red handkerchief. This he did above what is innocently described in the guidebooks as "Rapids Number 3." The group decided that Captain Mitchell, Debb, and, of course, Bardon, should run the boats through. Eventually, six boats were safely below the rapids. Debb returned upriver to bring down the last and most heavily laden boat. The boat struck the rock in the gut of the run and flipped, spilling its contents into the river, filling with water, and wedging itself among rocks along the tailout only ten feet from shore. When Grey ran upstream he found Ken running downstream trying to rescue dozens of lemons dotting the current. Shoes, loaves of bread, cans, and assorted boxes were chased, and most of the cargo was recovered.

The boat was another matter. Bardon ordered, instructed, and coached. Logs, poles, and all the rope they could find in the remaining boats were used to lever and pry. Bit by bit, they pulled the boat apart. The stern seat was ripped out, the ring-bolt in the bow pulled out, the seams opened up, the ribs broken out. When they finished, what was left of the boat was still jammed in the rocks.

Four miles later, they camped across the river from Battle Bar, the site of a "battle" between the U.S. Cavalry and a resident band of Indians in 1856.

Colonel Kelsely's command of 545 men attacked an encampment of 200 Indians, mostly woman and children, on Battle Bar, from his north-side position. He had collapsible boats but dared not use them. Each side was reduced to shooting across the river at the other. The Indians reportedly lost twenty to thirty of their group; one soldier died. This event was the last chapter in an extraordinarily dreary relationship between Rogue River Indians and whites.

Whites first explored the Rogue River area for the Hudson Bay Company in 1825. Apparently, the Indians were hostile from this first meeting, for French trappers referred to them as *Les Coquins*, "the Rogues," and the river as *LaRiviere aux Coquins*, "The River of the Rogues." Jedediah Smith led a party of seventeen men into their lands in 1828, a decision he soon regretted. Only Smith and three companions escaped from an attack.

The Indians were pretty much left alone until the early 1850s, when the discovery of gold started a general invasion of their lands, first at Josephine Creek on the Illinois River, the major tributary of the lower Rogue, and then at Galice Creek on the Rogue itself. Skirmishes led to hostilities and vigilante justice by "volunteers," local citizens organized into a murderous ragtag militia. More than once, the army was called in to protect Indians from white citizens. On September 10, 1853, both sides signed a treaty giving to the United States the entire Rogue River Valley and to the Indians a reservation at

Table Rock. This should have been the end of it, but a "volunteer" group, organized in a saloon, attacked an encampment of Indians at Little Butte Creek, killing eighteen women and children and twelve old men. Thus began the Rogue River Indian War of 1855–56. The Indians made life hell for valley settlers and paid dearly for their outrage. Faced with the prospect of combat with a thousand soldiers, Chief John and his thirty-five warriors surrendered on June 29, 1856. His revolt was the last.

About a mile below Battle Bar, the valley abruptly opens up on the north to a sloping sward of green that holds a grove of white oak. Along the beach, the river is a smooth glide, perfect steelhead water for at least a quarter of a mile, and any reasonably skilled fly fisherman can cover it all. The slopes above the river to the south are steep and blanketed with evergreens. Early in the afternoon they throw long steeples of shadow across the run as the oaks remain toasting in the bright heat of the day. Above the top end of the run, Hewitt Creek enters. Steelhead know this and may linger below the confluence to enjoy the smells. These are lovely parts, and the whole is perfection, doubly so when one is so dramatically liberated from the confining ways and tense nature of the canyon waters.

In 1925, a gold prospector owned this bar and the neighboring hillsides. He called his mining claim Winkle Bar.

Grey's party stayed for days at Battle Bar, fishing mainly camp water, but striking out occasionally to explore other riffles. No one was faring well in their collective hunt for steelhead, and Grey, in particular, was beginning to chafe over his poor luck. And now, intermittent rain and overcast added to his personal gloom.

One day, George Takahashi arrived back at camp with a three-pound steelhead and a broken rod. The little cook, without guile or vanity, tells a fishing story that is a perfect blend of fortitude and awe. If there is a patron saint of the big one that got away, this man is it.

My rod bent down to water. Then big steelhead come up, crack! He jump way up high. More bigges' steelhead I ever see. He jump and jump. He tuzzle like dog shakin' water off. Oh, awful big fish! He weigh twelve or fourteen pounds. He go down an' run up rapids. Make my line whistle in water. He jump out of white water, six feet up. Awful pretty! But I scared I no get him. Then he run downriver an' I run too. He jump more times. I count fourteen jumps. But he go faster down run than me. He take the line. I fall down. Break my tip. But steelhead still on. I get some line back. Lots big rock. Deep water. Me have to go slow. Steelhead make more faster run an' tear out hook. Then I feel awful sick.

Grey knew enough to believe the story and set out immediately in the rain for the very water Takahashi had left. He "tried George's way of casting as well as my own." Not a touch.

"I trudged campward through the wet willows and under the dripping alders to end my seventh unsuccessful day of fly fishing."

The next morning, a forest ranger appeared at their camp. He told the party that the big run of steelhead wasn't in yet, and that the best fishing water was actually below them at Winkle Bar, only a mile down the trail.

A couple of days later, Grey hiked up to the ridge line, picked up the trail, and walked downstream for Winkle Bar. The storm had passed through, and brilliant sunshine cheered him.

"And then up and down Winkle Bar, I fished all of one of the briefest and happiest days I ever had."

A day later, Ed returned to Winkle Bar and killed a magnificent steelhead of 8½ pounds. The day after that, Takahashi brought in one of nearly six pounds. The irrigation dam above Grants Pass was opened, and the lower river was badly muddied. Grey railed against the unwelcome appearance of miners, prospectors, "half-breed Indians," and a few whites who were destroying his solitude. Also, he could not find a steelhead. While he remained unfailingly gracious about his lack of "luck," it must have been wearing on his sense of pride. As the party left for the "long dreaded encounter with Mule Creek Canyon," he nurtured a single thought: "I was sorry to see the last of Winkle Bar, and resolved to get possession of that particular strip of sand and rock if such were possible."

It was. The next summer, he purchased Winkle Bar. Charles Pettinger was hired to pack a massive amount of gear to the site, using the north-side trail. The task required sixteen mules, and eight saddle horses brought in the gang from the previous year. Bardon, his father, and Debb had already been at Winkle Bar for a month, constructing a flume that would bring water down to Grey's future cabin. R. C., Grey's brother, and Loren Grey, the author's nine-year-old son, joined the group.

In the grove of oaks, they constructed a cabin that was large enough to house the immediate family. Cabins, open on one side, really tiny shacks, were built to accommodate the many guests that Grey's adventures attracted. There would be a woodshed, an outhouse, running water, and a New England style stone wall to border the little complex. Though it looked little better than a hobo camp, Winkle Bar became the most celebrated steelhead camp of its time.

Rick and I arrived at Winkle Bar late on a radiant morning, floating out of the canyon shadows to be carried unexpectedly back in time. The cabin and outbuildings looked as though they had been left by Grey the day before. Squirrels busied themselves about the stone walls, and I waited for little "Lorie" Grey to chase them for their cheeky ways. A large shed housed one of the Rogue River boats that Bardon had secured for Grey. It has fallen into disrepair, but its lapstrake lines were remarkably pleasing to the eye, the two rowing stations evident, the construction details of interest to this boat-builder. The sides just above the chine were doubled, early "rocker" panels that gave extra protection against obstructions. The log cabin was about twenty feet on a side, the roof extending over the front door and stoop. Several bunks and a woodstove appeared spartan and cheerless in the faint light. I stared inside until I grew tired of listening for voices. I sat on the stoop and looked down on the Rogue. Soon Winkle Bar would be in shade, its steelhead liberated from the bright exposure while the cabin faced into the last light of day. I could sit with Grey and watch Captain Mitchell, Romer, and George Takahashi work their flies through the sweep of Winkle Bar.

When the past had seeped into my every pore, I returned to the McKenzie boat, slipped into my waders, and gathered up my fly tackle. We had brought our boat in behind a tiny hook of the gravel bar about a third of the way down the run. So perfect was this accommodation that I wondered if it had been dug out with boats in mind. I studied the little bight of water, computed that a half-dozen of Grey's Rogue River boats would fit into it nicely, and then headed for the top end of Winkle Bar, entering the river well above the holding water.

The steelhead came to my fly, a half-pounder that jumped mightily and wrestled unequally with the force of my 5-weight rod. Another half-pounder followed the first, and another after that, as I came off the top end of the run. No steelhead was more than fourteen inches. They recklessly charged after the low-water Skunk, and so long as I didn't think that larger steelhead should be about, I was satisfied. My success gradually generated a sense of unease. I was finding only half-pounders in my sampling of Rogue River steelhead. Where were the fall fish of Rogue legend—those big steelhead that, as Joe Wharton put it, leave and "take part of the tackle?" Could my fishing in some way be selective for these smaller steelhead? Was I fishing the wrong kinds of water? Was I too early in the run? Too late? Other questions occurred, more fundamental and troubling. Was this a different Rogue from the river of Zane Grey's time? Or had the author indulged his fantasies with some artistic license? These thoughts were emotional checkpoints as I took my pleasure with the spirited little trout. I didn't regret that they weren't larger, only that my tackle wasn't lighter. A 2-weight outfit would have been ideal.

Winkle Bar is at only mile 14.9 in the forty-mile Wild section of the Rogue River. At mile 20.8 the river plunges through an extremely narrow gorge with such severe upwellings that a boat is suddenly beyond the control of the most skilled oarsman. Rick and I spun our way through Mule Creek Canyon with my hands on the gunwale and my feet on the canyon walls, our cries of alarm blending with the roar of the rapids. Zane Grey's party passed this way in a similarly graceless fashion and was equally undamaged.

Less than two miles below Mule Creek Canyon, Class IV, is Blossom Bar Rapids, Class IV, the most difficult piece of water on the Rogue. Bardon announced the rapids in this manner: "'Blossom Bar!'

he yelled to us. 'An' she's a wolf—she's a bear cub! It'll take all day tomorrow to drag an' line an' skid the boats round here.'"

Bardon's apprehension was well placed. Blossom Bar, named for the wild azaleas dotting its flanks, is a snaggle-toothed cauldron of foam and trailer-sized boulders. There is no direct line through it. In fact, one must pull from one side to the other while passing around the obstacles like some sort of fear-crazed pinball.

Rick pulled out above the rapids, and we walked to a vantage point where we could discuss the run. "Over there a raft got caught crosswise, pinned right against the big rock," he stated.

More descriptions of agony and travail followed, a rite of purification I could have done without. Then Rick fell into contemplative silence and studied the run while I walked back to check on the boat. When he returned, we ran Blossom Bar without hesitation. I was thankful that this dangerous water had been civilized a bit since Grey's time. Otherwise we, like Bardon, would have faced the dispiriting task of lining our boat through. But we did not, and that night we drank a quiet toast to Glen Woolridge, the "Grand Old Man" of Rogue River folklore.

Grandfather Woolridge had settled a mining claim on Foots Creek of the Rogue in the late 1850s, and Woolridge was born here. He was nineteen years old in 1915, when he constructed a crude boat, and with a fellow gill-netter named Cal Allen floated from Whiskey Creek to the coast in five days, almost certainly the first people ever to make the entire trip. During the next half-century he repeated the trip hundreds, if not thousands, of times. It became his habit to clear parts of the river by placing dynamite in a sack of rocks, lighting the fuse, and lowering the sack down to the base of the rock that needed moving. Then he quickly removed himself from the scene to view the results. Rock by rock, difficult portages became challenging runs. Nowhere is his success more celebrated, and his artistry with dynamite more evident, than at Blossom Bar.

Zane Grey knew Woolridge, knew his reputation, and several times hired him to guide. When Grey stated that he was the first *angler* to float the Rogue to the sea, he was mindful of Woolridge's far-less-celebrated Huck Finn journey.

Once the exhausting work of lining their boats through Blossom Bar was completed, Grey's party floated on to Solitude Riffle, mile 26.8, and camped on the long bar of sand and gravel running beneath wooded benches. Ivin Billings, a "native," informed the party that he had taken five steelhead from Solitude the night before, the largest going seven pounds. The prospect of fishing the long-awaited run seemed all but certain, and the anglers were greatly encouraged. On the third day, Romer caught a four-pound steelhead on a two-and-a-half-ounce Leonard, a contest accompanied by considerable merriment, because he was soon floundering with the steelhead in the river. Captain Mitchell found nine steelhead to three pounds with a small double-hook Dusty Miller. Grey's "persistent bad luck," lasted only through this day. "On the thirteenth day of my protracted spell of unrewarded fishing, late in the afternoon, I caught my first steelhead on a fly."

The fly used to bring about the change was a Golden Grouse, one of a number of English patterns the party generally fished with Hardy Brothers rods and reels. (Grey's little U.S.-built Leonard rod being a lovely exception.) Two more steelhead came to Grey's fly. All were killed, and that night's entrée was fresh steelhead.

George Takahashi called to Grey across the campfire, "My goodnish! Now you be in good humor!"

Ivin Billings returned to their camp to tell them that the salmon cannery at Gold Beach would shut down on October first, and the market fishermen would then be pulling their nets from the river. He predicted the big steelhead would arrive at Solitude by October 4.

Grey writes: "On October 5, steelhead began to arrive in considerable numbers, and after that the run increased. On another fine cloudy day we caught twenty-two steelhead, seventeen of which fell to Captain Mitchell, Romer, and me. Captain beached a six-pounder, and Romer one over five. These fish were extraordinary fighters."

Solitude was the high point of the float, a realization of expectations, a time of carefree byplay among friends. Grey was finding steelhead almost at will, usually when fishing a Professor with jungle

A page from General Money's gamebook following his stay at Weasku Inn. Note entry for October 9.

cock wings. There was some deer hunting among the tan oak groves. The party noted the sudden cerise of the fall vine maple, the golden tones of the big leaf maple along the river corridor. Now there was frost in the morning. The big fall southerly that traditionally marked the passing of summer was overdue, and when it came the Rogue would be out for days.

The decision to leave was made for them when the Rogue grew discolored, the result of an irrigation dam above Grants Pass. A couple of days later the party heard the "low distant pounding of the surf" at Gold Beach.

Rick and I would not follow Zane Grey to Gold Beach. When we reached Foster Bar, our take-out, the Rogue was flowing to the ocean rather than tumbling from the Coast Range. For the next thirty-five miles only a few Class II rapids required more than casual consideration. Grey's adventures were over at Foster Bar, too. Nevertheless, as we pulled our boat free of the river one last time, I was sad to be leaving his party. I would meet Grey, Romer, Takahashi, Bardon, and Captain Mitchell again on another float down from Grave Creek, a happy reunion with old friends, but one I knew to be several years away.

Grey's *Tales of Freshwater Fishing* focused national attention on the Rogue, and for the vast majority of anglers who had never seen the river or its steelhead, the Rogue could be only as Grey described it. When they sought to experience the Rogue firsthand, lodges and resorts were built from Grants Pass to deep within the wilderness.

Rainbow and Peggie Gibson sold their lodge in Big Bear, California, and purchased Weasku Inn on the Rogue in 1927. It soon attracted a celebrity crowd from the motion picture industry that included Clark Gable, Carole Lombard, Ann Sothern, Robert Sterling, David Niven, Jackie Cooper, and famous Hollywood directors and producers.

Glenn Woolridge guided President Herbert Hoover and Ginger Rogers, and both became Rogue regulars. The actress eventually bought her own ranch on the river. A famous photograph shows Rogers standing with Woolridge and holding a 6¾-pound steelhead, the largest caught that year on a fly from the Rogue. President Hoover once hired Woolridge to repeat Zane Grey's trip, and the two floated all the way to Gold Beach.

Novelist Jack London and heavyweight boxing champion Jim Jeffries came to fish the Rogue. Al Knudson of Washington steelhead fly-fishing fame moved to the Rogue in 1929 and tied flies commercially. No less a figure than the much-venerated General Noel Money of Qualicum Beach, British Columbia, made a trip to the Rogue the first week of October 1936, and stayed at Weasku Inn.

Not all anglers who came to the Rogue did so for its steelhead. Chinook salmon were a special attraction. They were an unusually robust race, were commonly found in fresh runs from spring until fall, and often exceeded thirty pounds.

At Rainbow Gibson's Weasku Inn, piers and floating salmon boards were built, and eighteen boats kept in operation for guests, who *averaged ninety salmon a day*. During the peak run, the boats were anchored so close together in famous Pierce Riffle that one could cross the river by walking from boat to boat.

These chinook salmon were the source of great commercial enterprise and intense disagreement between commercial factions. A famous brawl near the mouth of the Rogue between Claude Bardon, a gill-netter, or "market fisherman" as they were then known, and George Macleay, who headed up a group of seine-netters, became the basis for Zane Grey's novel, *Rogue River Feud*.

What was at first a conflict between seine-netters at the mouth and gill-netters in the Grants Pass area ended when commercial netting was outlawed in 1910. This law was compromised in 1913, when gill nets were again allowed. But in 1935 all commercial nets were outlawed, and the Rogue remains free of nets to this day.

No other river in the West can claim such glittering alumni as the Rogue. Today its fame rests most solidly on its extraordinary recreational value, and to a degree, this has always been so. But during the early years of steelhead fly fishing, this wild and beautiful river was the essence of our sport.

ROGUE RIVER FLY PATTERNS

Rogue anglers divided their river into three sections, the canyon waters of the Coast Range, a middle section through Oregon's interior valley, and an upper section with headwaters in the Cascade Mountains. By the 1950s they had come to associate small split-wing flies tied on double hooks with the lower Rogue. Guides would backrow their McKenzie boats and fish their clients' flies through the most desirable riffles. These double hooks were, of course, a British tradition, especially useful when a small hook was expected to hold a large salmon. But their value among Rogue anglers was due to the manner in which the fly fished, the double hook hardly necessary to hold trout rarely exceeding four pounds. The split wing supplied a lot of action, whether the fly was swimming subsurface or waking in the surface film, but without a double hook it was likely to lie over on one of the wings, its action spoiled. Colors were generally bright for the fresh runs of ascending steelhead. Some examples used down through the years in #8 and #10 have included the Juicy Bug, Red Ant, Old Mare, Rogue River Special, Golden Demon, and Curt Special.

Double hooks have never been popular on the middle and upper Rogue. (Today, "upper" is likely to be from Gold Ray Dam, Mile 125, to Mile 160; "middle" is still somewhat vague, but generally between the start of the canyon water, Mile 68, and the dam.) Some patterns are common to both ends of the river, but flies for the upper Rogue in #6 and #8 tend to be more somber for the temporarily residential steelhead. The single wing is tied long and reaches to the end of a long tail, a style every bit as characteristic as the compact little double-hook dressings of the lower Rogue.

Bob Pierce, a Rogue regular and former fly-shop owner from Talent, Oregon, feels the Juicy Bug, Red Ant, and Golden Demon are the most popular patterns on the lower Rogue, while the drab and

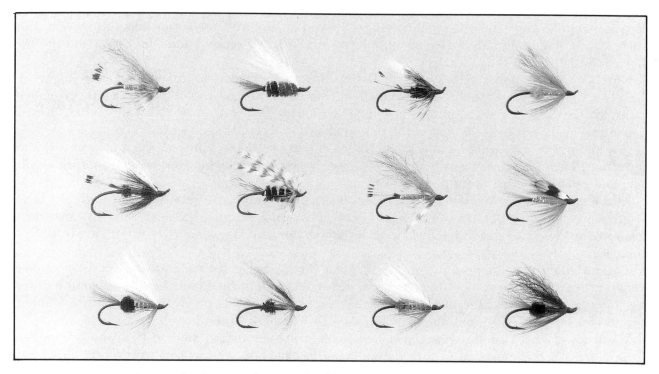

Row 1 Blue Rogue, Juicy Bug (chenille variation), Rusty Rat, Curt Special
Row 2 Royal Coachman, Silver Hilton, Chevaney, Golden Demon
Row 3 Juicy Bug, Red Ant, Old Mare, Black Ant
Note: The Rusty Rat is relatively new to the Rogue but has become very popular and is generally tied as pictured. Tail:
Golden pheasant tippet. Butt: Red floss. Body: Peacock herl. Hackle: Grizzly. Wing: Gray squirrel tail
Flies tied by John Mathews

deadly Chevaney, Green-Butt Skunk, and Silver Hilton are favorites on middle and upper sections. The Girdle Bug in a variety of colors, Irish Hilton (identical to the Silver Hilton save for a tail of peacock sword fibers), Brindle Bug, and the Tiger Paw, a Joe Howell dressing recently brought down from the North Umpqua, are also much in evidence on the Rogue from Grants Pass to above Gold Ray Dam.

LIFE HISTORY

The Rogue steelhead divides into two discrete races, summer-run fish that enter the river from May until November, and winter-run steelhead that begin to enter the river in November. For years, anglers assumed the summer run was further divided into three subraces. There was an early "springer" run in May, June, and July, with a high proportion of adult fish weighing two to eight pounds; an enormous August run of mostly half-pounders averaging less than a pound: and a fall run that began in August and lasted until well into October that again held a high proportion of adult fish from two to eight pounds. By midwinter these three groups had all moved well upstream to mix with winter-run stocks. The adult steelhead would spawn from January to June, depending on their time of entry and racial origin.

The Oregon State Game Commission conducted an extensive study to determine the exact nature of these runs so that they could be more properly managed. *Ecology and Management of Summer Steelhead in the Rogue River*, Fishery Report Number 7, revealed that repeat-spawning adults are often casual in their run timing, a "June" steelhead becoming July or August steelhead the next year. In one sampling, 432 maiden wild steelhead were netted from the Rogue estuary in 1969, with 103 fish from the early run (June, July) and 329 from later runs (August, September). For all practical purposes, the life histories for the two periods were identical.

JUNE-JULY

Age	Number	Percentage	Average length (inches)
1/+	6	5.8	11.8
2/+	71	68.9	13.2
3/+	23	22.3	14.1
2/1	1	1.0	18.5
3/1	1	1.0	20.9
2/2	1	1.0	29.1

AUGUST-SEPTEMBER

Age	Number	Percentage	Average length (inches)
1/+	32	9.7	12.5
2/+	251	76.3	13.6
3/+	34	10.3	13.7
4/+	1	0.3	15.5

A total of seven life-history categories were represented. The steelhead's freshwater residency before smolting and making an initial migration to sea was typically two or three years. One year was uncommon and four years extremely rare for a single fish. The percentages of half-pounders in each sampling was remarkably similar, 97 percent and 96.6 percent respectively. The balance of fifteen steelhead from the sampling of 432 maiden steelhead consisted of fourteen with one complete year of ocean residency, and a single two-year ocean steelhead. The sampling illustrated that nearly all Rogue steelhead pass through a half-pounder stage of development.

The size of the fourteen one-year ocean steelhead ranged from 18.5 inches to 22.3 inches, the larger steelhead in this age-class generally having had a three year premigrant residency.

The single 2/2 steelhead is representative of an extremely rare age category. (At 29.1 inches it weighed approximately nine pounds.) The very largest Rogue summer-run steelhead will have this life history, for three-year ocean steelhead are unknown. The single fish makes it impossible to determine average or maximum size, but based on angling literature available on the subject, twelve pounds would be a most extraordinary Rogue summer-run steelhead, a fish rarer than a thirty-pound Kispiox steelhead. (Just before driving to Grave Creek, Rick Nelson and I visited Jim Matney, a guide who lives on the Rogue near Galice. I asked him about any trophy steelhead caught that fall. "The largest I've heard about was twenty-five inches," he said.)

In a second sampling, wild steelhead were tagged on their initial upstream migration and 154 recaptured on a second run. The half-pounders averaged 14 inches on their first run, and 19.2 inches on their second, an average growth of 5.2 inches with a range of 2.5 to 8.5 inches. This is typical of all steelhead in the ocean for a similar period—two to four months. The difference, of course, is that most other races do not return to their natal rivers so prematurely.

Steelhead recaptured on their third, fourth, and fifth spawning migrations averaged 22, 25.3, and 27 inches, respectively.

The length frequencies for all samplings combined (1969 and 1970), showed that approximately sixty-five percent of the Rogue's steelhead were less than sixteen inches long. The balance (thirty-five percent) was dominated by first-spawning steelhead under twenty-two inches. Steelhead over twenty-two inches for all age groups comprised less than five percent of the entire run, and most of these fish were between twenty-two and twenty-four inches. Steelhead more than twenty-four inches made up less than one percent of the total.

The speed of the steelhead's upstream migration was directly related to their time of entry and spawning destination. Adults tagged in the estuary in June and later recaptured at Gold Ray Dam covered the 125 miles at an average daily rate of 4.5 miles. One adult reached the dam in nineteen days, an average of 6.5 miles a day. The maximum observed rate of travel was thirty-two miles in four days. Adults tagged in July, August, and September averaged about one mile per day. These later arriving steelhead also tended to spawn lower in the system. Approximately five percent of the steelhead spawned between mile 65 to 95, eighty to eighty-five percent spawned between mile 95 to 125, and twelve percent above mile 125.

The half-pounder population, over 100,000 steelhead with a male-to-female ratio of one to one, remain almost entirely in the lower fifty miles of river. The exception is a small percentage of sexually precocious males, perhaps as many as six thousand, that migrate above mile 68 to spawn with adult steelhead. An underwater census by divers suggests that immature half-pounders may begin returning to the ocean as early as November. It is suspected that the half-pounders' nonspawning migratory cycle is shorter than that of the adult steelhead.

The Rogue steelhead's annual spawning migrations take eight to nine months, leaving only three to four months at sea each year. This very short growth period is the reason why even old Rogue steelhead, the survivors of many spawning migrations, do not obtain the size other steelhead races reach for the same age.

The Rogue River of a half-century ago that inspired such high-blown praise for its large steelhead is recognized today for its abundance of steelhead that are the world's smallest. While the past and present do seem to describe two different races of steelhead, we are probably viewing the same race from opposite ends of the life-history spectrum. Zane Grey and Joe Wharton wrote in bigger-than-life terms, and their embellishments were not easily confronted in the 1920s. (The reader searches in vain for stories of days with the little half-pounders.) Perhaps more important, the river was its own unique frame of reference, and it did not suffer from the demystifying scrutiny that scientific investigations can bring to legendary reputations. Conversely, because of today's heavier angling pressure, the Rogue steelhead is less likely to survive four or five spawning migrations and reach five, six, or seven pounds. As always, the quality of our sport is a direct result of how we manage the resource.

NORTH UMPQUA RIVER

ON a fog-grey high-tide dawn in early April, the first of the North Umpqua's spring-run steelhead come in from the ocean. As they pass between North Spit, the cape of great white sand dunes, and the lighthouse that signals the south entrance of Winchester Bay, their travel is unhurried, still somewhat random. Unless feeding, they cover a mile in an hour while swimming a meter below the surface.

The shoreline becomes a new and constant bearing. Brackish estuary channels, skeins of smells vaguely familiar to the steelhead, appear and disappear under the opposing forces of gravitational action, the tides of the sea, and the gradient of the river. Some few molecules of river, imprinted on their subconscious years before, fix their attention and hold them during the ebbing tide. Several steelhead, nervous and tentative, break from the group and ghost in on the evening's flood tide. They begin tracking their origins, deliberation becoming a compulsion that carries them past the bridge at Reedsport and almost beyond the reach of the tides. By nightfall they have taken up stations near the beach. They rock almost imperceptibly with the faint currents and pass their first night as adult steelhead in the Umpqua River.

Movement upriver is sporadic and highly individual. Three miles per day is a good average, the greater part taken in the afternoon, when the sun has raised the river's temperature a few degrees. The steelhead are frequently seduced by the strange smells of tributary creeks, and a single fish may stop to breathe in their heady turbulence for days.

Clarence Gordon at his fly tying bench at Steamboat Inn.
Photo courtesy of Jim and Sharon Van Loan.

The steelhead are so immature sexually that they will not spawn for ten months. About three of every four fish have spent two years in the ocean, one in four but a single year. As a race, they average seven pounds. The rare steelhead—two or three in every hundred—has stayed out for three years. These are usually males, and they have been known to reach twenty pounds.

The temperature of the Umpqua rises each week, ten degrees in a single month, twenty degrees by late spring, thirty degrees by summer, and the steelhead of May and June are more businesslike in their drive for spawning headwaters. The river is at its coolest in the early morning, and migration is best resumed then. The creeks can still be refreshing layovers, but steelhead tarrying too long in August will be trapped, the water above and below them reaching eighty degrees. Ultimately the creeks, too, will become lethally warm, and the steelhead will perish.

Halfway through their journey, the river splits. Unerringly, the steelhead choose the branch that leads north, and two days later they reach Winchester Dam on the North Umpqua. Six weeks have passed since they crossed the tidal bar at Winchester Bay.

At the dam is a fish ladder, the first serious impediment to their upstream progress, and a temporary source of intimidation. Once they enter, however, they transit the ladder quickly.

An Oregon Department of Fish and Wildlife employee sits in a viewing chamber and peers into the fish ladder through a plexiglas window. He works a single eight-hour shift, usually from four in the morning until noon, and he records each steelhead that passes. The afternoon-to-evening shift, only occasionally completed, provides a necessary frame of reference. All information is fed into a computer. Few, if any, steelhead pass up the ladder at night, and some extrapolation is necessary, for not every fish has been observed, but the overall count is accurate.

As the count proceeds, the steelhead are easily divided into three groups. At least three of every four are fin-clipped hatchery stock, the fleshy little adipose, the fin behind the dorsal fin, having been completely removed by hatchery personnel just before their release. Most, if not all, of the remaining steelhead are wild-born, native North Umpqua stock. Several winter-run steelhead may appear. These are dark, highly colored, and ready to spawn.

Within a week, the steelhead have entered the bedrock canyon water, for which the North Umpqua is famous, and reached Rock Creek, the first of several major spawning tributaries.

Several hundred feet above the mouth of Rock Creek is the Rock Creek Hatchery, where both wild and hatchery stocks are temporarily blocked by a weir. Only wild steelhead are used for brood stock. They are purposely not selected for any particular size or age, the goal being a hatchery plant as much like the wild strain as possible. Furthermore, to assure the broadest possible run timing, brood stock are secured throughout the many weeks covering the main body of the run.

As the wild steelhead arrive, they are held in a concrete pen to grow to sexual maturity until they are ready to be spawned in December or January. The 300,000 eggs gathered will result, one year later, in a plant of approximately 170,000 smolts, five or six to the pound, each about eight inches long. Mortality is extremely high—only five percent or fewer survive to return as adults. In the meantime, hundreds of native steelhead proceed up Rock Creek to spawn naturally.

The steelhead that have continued up the North Umpqua—and this includes many steelhead born and reared in the Rock Creek Hatchery—have already entered the thirty-four-mile-long fly-fishing-only section. Most are nearing their final destination, Steamboat Creek, eighteen river miles above Rock Creek, the most important spawning tributary for native steelhead in the entire North Umpqua system. It has taken them two months to travel the 125 miles from the coast. They remain chrome-bright and magnificently strong. The steelhead will not immediately enter their home stream, preferring instead to concentrate in the holding water immediately below the confluence.

These are the pools of North Umpqua legend, a series of ledge-rock channels, rapids, riffles, and glides, each with a name, a special character, and a history. They are the most celebrated waters in all of steelhead fly fishing.

THE OLD ROAD

Merle Hargis was a service packer. In l930 he owned a saddle, a horse, six mules, and a six-shooter. His little pack train transported everything from kegs of whiskey to human companionship for the gold camps, hunting and fishing camps, geologic survey crews, and Forest Service lookout stations that were tucked into remote corners of the Cascade Mountains above Steamboat. In a good month he made $125.

Sixty years later, he still reminds himself of the handsome frontiersman he was in his youth. Carefully manicured grounds surround his home that overlooks the North Umpqua, but animal traps are cagily placed in the shrubbery, and the toll on neighborhood cats has been high. His trusty six-shooter, a pearl-handled Colt revolver, is kept oiled and loaded in its holster at his bedside. When we last visited, on a warm July afternoon, he shook a handful of cartridges like castanets, and recalled his adventures when the forest above Steamboat was still uncharted wilderness.

"Oh, it was good then!" he said.

The gold camps, those remote outposts of hopeful labor and nefarious scheming, indirectly christened Steamboat Creek. If a mine or a creek was represented as having gold but did not, the unlucky prospector was said to have been "steamboated." The term did not distinguish whether salting a played-out claim or blind bad luck preceded this grim reality.

The twisting road that paralleled the North Umpqua upriver from Idleyld Park to Steamboat Creek was completed in 1927. The old pack train trail was widened for one-lane traffic with coolie labor and given a gravel surface. When Merle made the trip in his Ford roadster, he passed through virgin stands of fir and hemlock, gave his terrified passengers glimpses of the North Umpqua five hundred feet below, and with a hoot of his horn swooped down on the Forest Service Guard Station at Steamboat where his brother, Eldon, worked as a trail foreman.

Eldon already knew about steelhead. Good holding water was directly below the Guard Station on the north side of the river. A two-foot wide plank led from shore to a rock about thirty feet out. This was a fishing convenience—no waders necessary—as well as a place to gather water and to wash dishes. Eldon would cast a fly from the plank, and one day Merle watched him catch a steelhead.

"This was the first time I can remember anything about steelhead," he said. "That was about 1929."

As a practical matter, however, Merle was a trout fisherman. He had a bamboo rod, a three-dollar reel, and an enameled line that rarely lasted more than one season. The outfit was easily packed on his saddle. Native trout, highly colored little rainbows and cutthroat, were abundant then, and Merle fished for food. Steelhead, "large rainbows," couldn't be handled on his tackle and left abruptly with his few precious flies. He always bought the same three, Royal Coachman, Grey Hackle, and Queen of the Waters.·

"I caught lots of steelhead. 'Course I snagged 'um. Had a big treble hook and some line. Got all I wanted."

But steelhead fly fishing was coming with a rush to the North Umpqua.

John Ewell, who operated a motel in Roseburg, had recently built a few rustic cabins where Canton Creek joins Steamboat Creek. Major Jordan Lawrence Mott visited in 1929. Though Mott was an experienced steelhead fly fisherman—he had fished the Rogue the previous summer—this was his first trip to the North Umpqua. Captain Frank Winch, who represented *Forest and Stream* magazine, accompanied him. Mott was so taken with the fishing that he obtained a permit from the Forest Service and immediately began setting up a fly-fishing camp that overlooked the pools below Steamboat Creek on the south side of the river. Wood platforms were constructed and tents set up. Zeke Allen, a local guide, became Mott's "bull cook" and general man-about-camp. They were in business that first summer, and the camp flourished. In the fall, Zeke broke camp, and Mott returned to his home on Santa Catalina Island in southern California, and wrote "Umpqua Steelheads," an article published in *Forest and Stream* in July 1930.

Mott was born in 1881, heir to the J. L. Mott Iron Works fortune. After graduating from Harvard, he married and became a newspaper reporter in New York City. In 1912 he sailed for Europe with another man's wife. His father promptly disinherited him. During World War I, he was commissioned a major in the U.S. Army Signal Corps. Ultimately, he divorced his wife and married "Mrs. Bowne," in 1928. Somewhere along the line, all may have been forgiven. That probably didn't matter. Mott, a man of considerable charm and talent, could pay his own way. He reportedly wrote novels and had worked in early radio. By all local accounts, he was remarkably decent and generous.

Major Jordon Lawrence Mott poses with a morning's catch before one of his tent "cabins."

Fred Asam, the District Ranger at Steamboat, was Mott's closest friend on the North Umpqua. Each spring Asam arrived with his four children—David, Dorothy, Jeanette, and Alvina (who would later marry Merle Hargis)—and spent the summer. When Mott discovered he had incurable cancer, he gave much of his tackle away to Asam's children. David received a Hardy Brothers rod and reel and a Wheatley fly box, Alvina got his salmon rod, and so on. Today, Mott memorabilia can be found throughout the valley of the North Umpqua.

Mott insisted on the dignity of spending his last days at his own camp, and he returned to Steamboat early in 1931. He died that spring, having spent only two full seasons on the river. Merle Hargis remembers with sadness driving in and meeting the hearse containing Mott's remains on its way to Roseburg.

A bronze plaque beside the bridge built across the Umpqua in 1937, just above Steamboat, reminds visitors that they are crossing Mott Bridge. The pathway leading to the many pools below Steamboat Creek is called Mott Trail. The most famous water on the North Umpqua is divided into three pools: Upper, Middle, and Lower Mott. Kitchen Pool was named because it could be seen from the camp's kitchen tent. Zeke Allen ferried visitors across Boat Pool in a rowboat after they signaled their arrival by ringing a bell. The pools are collectively called Camp Water.

Bill and Muriel Hopkins owned the Circle H Ranch, a dude ranch operation that had been catering to anglers for years. It was located on Susan Creek just above Idleyld Park, where the road ended before 1927. One of their guests was Fred Burnham, an extraordinary fly fisher and a close friend of Zane Grey. The two men had fished for steelhead together on the Rogue, and almost certainly Burnham first regaled Grey with stories of the North Umpqua.

Grey journeyed north to Campbell River late each spring to fish for chinook salmon, and in 1932 he planned a detour to the North Umpqua. He arranged to stay for a month or so at John Ewell's cabins on Canton Creek. Grey and his family and friends would drive to the end of the road at Steamboat and then find a way to move their belongings up to the cabins.

When the famous writer arrived, he sought out Fred Asam to see if a Forest Service packer could be hired for the day to pack their gear the four hundred yards to the cabins. Merle Hargis was in camp that day. The event is still fresh in his memory.

He had his son and that Japanese cook and a whole flock of girls, secretaries, or whatever. There were several of them. They had quite a bunch of stuff, and armloads of fishing rod cases, you know, footlockers, boxes, and tents. So anyway, he saw the ranger—it was on Sunday—and he says, "I wonder if you would let us have your packer to pack us up to John Ewell's cabins." Boy, that set me on fire because I figured on a twenty spot there, see, a tip. I wasn't to get paid 'cause I was gettin' paid anyhow. So I went up with the pack train, six mules and I had that strawberry roan, a dandy horse and I put on quite a show, smartin' all the girls there. I could touch her spurs and tighten up a little and she'd walk on her hind legs. Had a lot of fun! Anyway I packed this stuff up there. I knew my stuff at packin', throw a hitch quick, and they sit back a'watchin, you know, and try to help. I put in a pretty good day. Three trips, eighteen loads. After the last trip up as I was a'gettin' ready to come back and Zane Grey come up to me and put his arm on my shoulder, shook me a little, and said, 'God bless you my boy, you did a good job Here!' And I stuck out my hand. Four half-dollar pieces! I said, 'Oh, you don't owe me anything, I was glad to do this.' Ha, for two lousy dollars!

The Grey entourage was even larger than Merle imagined. Romer Grey, the author's oldest son, owned the Romer Grey Motion Picture Corporation. He wanted to make a movie of this adventure, and his cameramen and technicians joined the party. Grey was a working writer whose daily output in longhand was often prodigious. Secretaries—the "whole flock of girls" Hargis described—were in camp to edit, rewrite, and type manuscripts. Romer's wife was there, as was Grey's close friend, Dr. J. A. Wiborn, often referred to by the incurably romantic author as "Lone Angler." And, as always, there was George Takahashi, the Japanese cook Grey called "The Great Takahashi—the inimitable, the irrepressible, the indefatigable."

Joe DeBernardi was hired to guide the party. He and his brothers, Albert and Horace, worked with their father, Goliah, on the family's thirteen-hundred-acre ranch near Glide, on the North Umpqua. They were Swiss of Italian extraction, immigrants who first settled in Crescent City, California, before packing their belongings on horse-drawn wagons and moving to Oregon. They grew vegetables, caught salmon and steelhead, and shot deer for the table. Cattle and their turkey farm provided an income. They were not poor, but the Depression was a hard time, and Joe guided to augment the family income. For three summers, starting in 1922, he had guided U.S. Coast and Geodetic Survey crews into the Umpqua National Forest. By the time Zane Grey came to the river, Joe DeBernardi was well known locally as a dependable guide for hunting and fishing parties. They soon became fast friends.

Zane and Romer Grey came to the river extremely well equipped. Their Granger and Leonard rods were matched to Hardy Brothers reels. Silk lines by Ashaway and leaders by Hardy Brothers completed their outfits. They purchased their flies from Joe Wharton in Grants Pass, Oregon, and from Hardy Brothers in England. Over the years, they gradually weaned themselves from most English flies, particularly as they began to devise their own steelhead patterns. Joe DeBernardi was not born to the sport, but he learned to cast and to tie his own steelhead flies, a skill Grey came to appreciate. They especially favored the hairwing Coachman and Parmachene Belle, and followed these choices with the Turkey and Red and the Turkey and Gold. Grey had Wharton add a brown bucktail wing to an orange demon-type fly he had first fished in New Zealand, and the Golden Demon filled out their short list.

Joe's first summer with Grey was nearly his last.

Romer scripted an adventure for his movie company to film. A couple of wood Rogue River boats, of the type being built in Grants Pass by Glen Woolridge, would be used in an attempt to run the North Umpqua from Steamboat Creek to Rock Creek. Romer would crouch in the bow and star in his own film; Joe would run the boat through the rapids. The boat was smashed, swamped, and flipped, the impact sending an oarlock through Joe's side. His daughter, Joan, told me, "Dad had a big dent in his side until the day he died."

Romer filmed comic relief, too. Little Takahashi would climb a tree and fly fish from a branch. As

Zane Grey with a brace of North Umpqua steelhead.→

Joe DeBernardi, longtime guide for Zane Grey.

a technician, out of view of the camera, pulled violently on the line, Takahashi, a look of astonishment on his face, would come flying out of the tree and into the river. Presumably this was hysterical to everyone except the star.

Umpqua steelhead weren't *that* strong, but their size and strength were an impressive departure from the Rogue. Grey's allegiance changed that first summer. He later wrote: "It ought to be a guarantee that I am honest and sincere about this noble river, practically unknown to the world, when I confess that I have given up the Rogue, and the fishing lodges I own at Winkle Bar, on the most beautiful and isolated stretch, to camp and fish and dream and rest beside the green-rushing, singing Umpqua."

Loren Grey, who joined his father on the North Umpqua in later years, told me that the sudden release of water above Grants Pass raised the level of the Rogue, discolored the water with algae, and drove his father wild. This, more than any other factor, caused his father's disenchantment with the Rogue. Regardless. "The North Umpqua was my father's favorite river," Loren Grey said.

Zane Grey returned each year to stay nearly the entire summer. In the spring, Joe and Albert DeBernardi would drive to Steamboat and set up a camp that, once in place, was comfortable and somewhat permanent. The tents had wooden floors, cots, and chairs. A pole was erected in the center of camp, and a flag, bearing the initials ZG, was run up. Joe stayed on to guide, and often brought with him his young daughters, Joan and Raelene, to stay in camp. Joan recalled for me how her dad would organize wading safety drills. "Grey's boys would cinch a belt around their waders and jump in the river. Everyone ended up splashing each other!" Sometimes on weekends Loren and Romer would stay at the DeBernardi place in Glide and go on into Roseburg for a movie and a night on the town.

A valley story that has circulated for years claims that the famous Umpqua Special pattern was inspired by Joe DeBernardi and Zane Grey as a hairwing cross between the Parmachene Belle and Parmachene Beau. I know that the Belle was a favorite of Grey's. Joe's daughter, Joan, has pictures of her dad tying flies at his house. The story sounds plausible enough; longtime locals can provide no other explanation.

Romer Grey

The only magazine article Zane Grey ever wrote about the North Umpqua appeared in the September 1935 issue of *Sports Afield,* and was based on his experiences during the summer of 1934. It was vintage Grey.

"Deer and bear and cougar, wolves and coyotes are abundant," he wrote. There was a steelhead forty inches long and ten deep that "made my reel smoke as no Newfoundland salmon had done" during a battle that lasted two and a half hours and took Grey a half-mile downriver. Grey caught 64 steelhead that season, his son Loren an even 100. Readers could not help but be enthralled.

Grey assembled in camp a crude deep sea fighting chair fitted with a large bamboo pole and weights. Training on this for thirty minutes each day maintained his fighting shape for battles with billfish. He otherwise fished in the morning, napped, wrote furiously, and fished in the evening. He named Upper Mott the "ZG Pool," and may have named Ledge Pool. He had the trees behind Takahashi Pool cut down to make room for his backcast, and he occasionally had Joe DeBernardi stand guard over the best pools. He often seemed aloof and lost in thought, "kind of a funny duck," according to Merle Hargis. Except for Joe DeBernardi, locals didn't know him and never really knew what to make of him. As the fame of the Umpqua spread and the pools at Steamboat became crowded, Grey moved his camp to Williams Creek. The present highway would not be completed for twenty years. There was then only the old road far above the river, and the site satisfied his desire for wilderness isolation.

Zane Grey's last season on the river was in 1937. The valley was scorching hot, and after a morning of fishing he fell asleep in a lounge chair. There, in the bright sun, he suffered what Loren Grey described to me as a "heat stroke." Grey was carried to his car by Romer and Joe DeBernardi and was driven to the hospital in Roseburg. An ambulance returned the partially paralyzed Grey to his home in southern California. Despite intense physical therapy, the author never fully recovered. He died two years later.

Clarence Gordon, too, is found in nearly every seam of North Umpqua lore. He was managing the Smoke Tree Ranch, a resort in Palm Springs, California, when he first stayed at John Ewell's cabins on Canton Creek, in 1929. He returned each year, and in 1931 camped above Steamboat with his wife, Delia. Mott had just died, and his camp cook, Zeke Allen, now maintained the camp. Gordon imagined a real lodge on the old Mott site, and in 1934 he obtained a lease from the Forest Service. At first he took over the old Mott site and hired Allen to run a simple tent resort. This soon changed—as did the clientele.

By the late 1930s, North Umpqua Lodge was a permanent structure and a prominent destination in American angling circles. Gordon, the consummate fly fisher, acted as host, guide, and fly tyer. Guests arrived from all over the world. No other river at the time so strongly defined steelhead fly fishing.

At Gordon's invitation, Ray Bergman, the fishing editor of *Outdoor Life,* came to Steamboat and wrote about his experiences in *Trout* (Knopf, 1938). The chapter "Steelhead of the Umpqua" became my introduction to the sport. I thought the chapter far and away the most interesting part of a book otherwise informative but tedious.

Clark C. Van Fleet frequently visited the river, and in his book, *Steelhead to a Fly* (Atlantic, Little Brown, 1951), he said, "You will find in Clarence Gordon an expert on the ways of the fish in these waters, casting a beautiful fly himself and fully acquainted with all the hot spots."

Claude Krieder found the North Umpqua a very tough proposition, and wrote in *Steelhead* (G. P. Putnam's Sons, 1948), "I sought the famous Mott Pool and the Kitchen Pool, waters in which many tremendous steelhead had been taken over the years by the great among the Umpqua specialists. And none of them yielded a single strike."

Clarence Gordon developed three steelhead patterns for the North Umpqua. The Black Gordon remains a local favorite and is one of a handful of standard steelhead dressings. The other two, the Grey Gordon and the Orange Gordon, are elegant and effective, but less well known.

GREY GORDON

Tail Lady Amherst tippet
Body Black dubbing with a silver tinsel rib

Hackle Guinea
Wing Grey squirrel

ORANGE GORDON

Tail Bronze mallard
Body Orange wool with a gold tinsel rib
Hackle Brown

Wing Bronze mallard (brown bucktail was later substituted)

Two species of caddis of the genus *Dicosmoecus* are found on the North Umpqua. The grey sedge is commonly seen in late spring and summer; the orange-colored fall caddis, the famous "October Caddis," is found in late summer and fall. Each is about two inches long. It is hard not to believe that Gordon was inspired by the two caddis when he developed these patterns, so closely do their colors resemble the adult insects.

In 1952, the Oregon State Game Commission passed a resolution to maintain the North Umpqua from Rock Creek to Soda Springs as "fly only" water, the third summer steelhead river so designated. This decision was accomplished only at the urging of Clarence Gordon and the Roseburg Rod and Gun Club.

It is a sad irony that these promising changes should have paralleled developments that brought about the end of the North Umpqua Lodge.

Construction of a hydroelectric dam upriver at Toketee so silted the river that fishing was impossible. The dam was built in conjunction with a new river-level highway that would ultimately connect Roseburg with Diamond Lake. The road bed was blasted out of the basaltic palisades that created the turbulent corridor of river from Idleyld Park to well past Steamboat, and it opened many new miles of river to anglers when it was completed in 1957.

Gordon closed the lodge to guests from 1952 through 1955 and leased the building to a construction company to house their personnel working on the new highway. The North Umpqua Lodge was later sold to the Forest Service and became the Steamboat Ranger Station. Today, hardly a trace of these enterprises remains.

The Circle H Ranch, its ownership having passed to Mildred Young, was forced to close its doors in 1954. It never reopened.

During this period on the north side of the river, the enterprising Gordon opened up a small lunch counter and grocery, the Steamboat Store, to cater to the construction crews. When his business prospered, he was inspired to move the entire store downriver to a point overlooking the great string of pools below Steamboat Creek. The dining facilities were enlarged and a kitchen added. Then, in early 1957, Clarence and Delia Gordon sold the Steamboat Store to Frank and Jeanne Moore and retired to Seal Beach, California.

Frank Moore was a Roseburg restaurateur (Moore's Cafe), who had learned the difficult ways of the North Umpqua so well that he often shared guiding duties with Joe DeBernardi. Jeanne was experienced at simultaneously running a kitchen and raising children. "I had it easy by comparison," says Frank. They had new cabins built below the dining room and changed the name of their business to Steamboat Inn. The new highway was nearly completed as far as Steamboat, and the river again ran crystal clear with the completion of Toketee Dam. Former guests, often well-to-do Californians whom Frank had guided for Gordon in the late 1940s, were contacted and invited back. Frank was there to welcome them and to guide them once again.

Steamboat Inn captured the ambience of the old days. A young guide and a logger had once teamed up for Clarence Gordon and hewed from a single enormous sugar pine log a table top of Bunyanesque proportions. This was a fixture in the old North Umpqua Lodge and integral to Gordon's celebrated

Frank Moore

"Fishermen's Dinners." The Moores maintained the tradition on the same great table, though in deference to their fly-fishing guests, dinner was not served until thirty minutes after last light. Photographs of Major Mott, Zane Grey, and Clarence Gordon lined the walls, interspersed with more contemporary angling photography by Dan Callaghan. Steelhead fly fishing history was literally below on the river and above on the walls. Steamboat Inn had soon so replaced the old North Umpqua Lodge in the affections of visiting fly fishermen that it became synonymous with the North Umpqua and her wonderful spring-run steelhead.

The regular guests became close personal friends: Jim and Laddie Hayden, Stan and Yvonne Knouse, Dan and Mary Kay Callaghan, Loren Grey, Don Haines, and Ken Anderson, to name but a few. It was Anderson's idea to form a special interest group of fly fishermen who would work to protect their magnificent river. Stan Knouse offered "Steamboaters" as an appropriate name for the group, and Anderson designed the club's logo. Clarence Gordon and Roderick Haig-Brown were made charter members. Initially limited to 100 members, the Steamboaters eventually grew to three times that number.

I believe that, were it not for the Steamboaters, the fly fishing-only section of river would have been lost long ago, logging would have destroyed the few fine spawning tributaries, and the native run of North Umpqua summer steelhead would be but a fine memory.

The old road doesn't go all the way to Steamboat anymore. Frank and Jeanne Moore live near the end of it, far enough above the logging trucks to assure a sense of peaceful solitude. He did most of the construction work on their large log cabin home, skinning the logs and notching them with an ax. When I last visited him there, he reminded me of when I had gone around Steamboat Inn photographing his photographs for *Steelhead Fly Fishing and Flies.* That had been nearly twenty years before, about five years before he and Jeanne sold their business to Jim and Sharon Van Loan.

In 1989, Frank was still youthful, still moved easily on difficult wades while casting a lovely line. Romer Grey had sent him his father's leather wading shoes, which now hung on the wall in the living room. There were steelhead flies in display frames, huge photographs of friends, Major Mott's tackle, conservation awards, and, next to the grand piano, a fly-tying bench filled to overflowing.

Frank grew up in Oregon and has always been a fly fisher. "My dad used to make his own bamboo rods and his own lines back in the 1920s," he recalled. We chuckled over the controversy involving the origins of the Skunk pattern. "Mildred Krogel was from Roseburg. She first tied the pattern for her husband, Lawrence, and her kids. It was in the late 1930s and 1940s that she was tying it. They used to come up here and stay at Canton Creek Campground the entire summer. They would have a race each morning to see who would get the 'pool of the year.' Sometimes this was Station, other times Kitchen, and so on." The Skunk remains Frank's favorite fly pattern for the North Umpqua, and he usually fishes no other.

Claude Batault, the recently retired French ambassador to Italy, was a houseguest. I was surprised to find that he had been fly-fishing the Dean and Babine rivers since 1966. Frank and Claude would be fishing the Pigeon Springs area of the Kalama the next week; a month later, possibly a chalkstream in Auvergne or Derbyshire.

Frank and I walked across his backyard to meet his trout. He had bulldozed out the little lake with forest on one side and lawn on the other. A pump recycles water, and Frank has built two screened-over spawning channels. A dozen perfectly conditioned rainbow trout to seven or eight pounds darted about as Frank tossed out tiny pellets of food. He assured me that the trout were for the entertainment of his grandchildren. A pair of screech owls were nesting in a wood-duck box. Swallows darted about for insects.

"Mayflies?" I asked.

"Yes," he replied. "They began taking over the pond when the water was only a few inches deep."

JOE HOWELL

"What size flies did you bring?" Joe asked.

"Twos and fours, mostly," I answered, already anticipating his approval. I had worked for weeks to fill a couple of Wheatley boxes. Joe's brow was knitting up.

"Do you have anything larger?"

"A few 1/0s," I said. He nodded and gave a little "we'll do the best we can" kind of shrug.

"How big do you go?" I asked.

"One summer I decided to see how large a fly could be used for summer steelhead on the North Umpqua. I fished them as large as 6/0 and they took steelhead as long as the sun wasn't on the water. Even low light was okay."

I whistled softly over the first of many new slants I would get from Joe on his steelhead fly fishing.

Joe and Bonnie Howell own the Blue Heron Fly Shop in Idleyld Park. They have been in business only since the early 1980s, but the shop has become a local institution, and Joe is widely known as a guide with an intuitive understanding of the North Umpqua and its steelhead. For a couple of weeks, when his busy schedule permitted, we would fish together, spend hours talking about these steelhead, and discuss his fly-pattern preferences.

I remember the first dawn when I met Joe and learned the importance of knowing which rock to stand on, for this knowledge is pertinent on the North Umpqua as nowhere else. Many parts of the river cannot be waded. There are braiding runs, and each channel demands a special approach, the

Joe Howell

fly often presented from a single wading station, the proverbial rock. Sometimes it is exposed, but more often it is submerged and not evident beneath the metallic surface currents of early morning. For this reason I got in the habit of scouting and fishing new water in the middle of the day. I would make careful note of how the run should best be fished and return to fish it again in the evening. Even so, I occasionally managed to wade out beyond the top of my waders.

Some sections of river are little frequented by anglers because they provide no room for a backcast. Roll casting or spey casting is necessary, as is slipping line on the swing to enable the fly to cover additional water. My ten-foot rod and long belly-forward taper line were often an advantage.

Of course, not all the fly fishing requires hopping from rock to rock. Some fine traditional cast-and-step glides flow over freestone bottoms. But, until late summer, the river can run with such speed that the fly is forced immediately to the surface and sent skidding through the surface film on the controlled swing. To remedy this, Joe and I fished with sink-tip lines, casting and mending them exactly as we would a full floating line, the sink-tip portion helping to keep the fly working just below the surface. In these strong currents we also found it necessary to use flies without a lot of throat hackle or long body hackle, because this caused the fly to lay over on the swing.

One morning, halfway down a small run, I rose a steelhead on a Ferry Canyon. When the steelhead would not come back, Joe suggested I work the softer water against the far bank. This would require a very long cast with an immediate back-mend to avoid pulling the fly from the lie. I couldn't make this cast from anywhere without catching a tree, and in truth probably couldn't have made the cast regardless of where I stood. I invited Joe to give it a whirl. His rod is kind of the Babe Ruth bat of steelhead fly fishing, a stiff ten-and-a-half-foot 9-weight that I called the "Thunderstick." But Joe is a big man with remarkable coordination, and he immediately set to work. Standing on a rock to get maximum height, he fired a backcast over the low trees and sent the Muddler out more than a hundred feet. A ten-foot leader and some quick line work enabled him to dead drift the Muddler through most of the lie. When the current began to drag on the fly, he mended his line through a very long controlled swing. When no steelhead showed after twenty casts, he reeled in and changed to a full-dressed 4/0 Skunk with a bucktail wing, chenille body, and plenty of hackle. I had never before seen a fly of this size cast over summer fish. I stopped fishing to watch as he explained.

"I call this a 'heavy silhouette' fly." Joe made a prodigious cast to the water already covered thoroughly with a Muddler. "You want to mend only once with a fly this large. I have watched steelhead start to come to the fly and then turn away when it suddenly darts from a mend."

"But what happens when the fly begins to drag?" I asked.

"You just let it go. Don't mend it. The steelhead will move for these large flies." As if to demonstrate, his Skunk was now dragging, and he brought the fly through the swing with his rod tip, but after the initial mend, he left the presentation alone.

On the dead drift part of the presentation, a steelhead rose to the 4/0 Skunk. The fly came away almost immediately, but I could not have been more impressed.

Joe's opinion was that you often must "hit a steelhead on the head" with a small fly to get it to take. At the same time, repeated mends while using a small fly are much less likely to put a steelhead off. Because the large silhouette pattern is certain to cause some sort of response from a steelhead, (i.e., it will be moved one way or the other), Joe leaves this approach for last.

When Joe and I played the game "If you only had three patterns," I found that his third choice of steelhead flies to go with the Muddler and the Skunk was the Black Gordon, an oldtime favorite on the river. But, of course, he could not leave it at that. For soft water, dead drifts, late summer season, and the steelhead of winter he had developed four beautiful spey-type flies: the Orange Heron 1, Orange Heron 2, Silver Streak, and Gold Streak.

One morning, Joe and I fished Famous Pool, a punch-bowl of ledge rock with steelhead holding in brilliantly clear water of very moderate current. On this and similarly placid water he fishes dry flies, casting upstream for drag-free floats. He looks for virgin fish (steelhead that have not been cast over that day), and he favors the cooler waters of late summer and fall. He uses three patterns, the Muddler, Royal Wulff, and the high floating MacIntosh, the latter better known as an Atlantic salmon dry.

When skating dries, Joe fishes two patterns of his own design, the Golden Stone and the Orange Scooter. Both are variations of the Muddler. In that context, he calls his "standard" Muddler a Coon Muddler. Because of the difficulty and expense in obtaining oak turkey when he ties commercially for his shop, he has taken to substituting matching slips of white-tipped wood duck for the underwing and raccoon for the overwing. He feels this variation is at least as effective as the original, and he regularly fishes both.

For June and much of July, the steelhead moving up the North Umpqua are plainly in a hurry. I have watched them, an hour after first light, move into, through, and out of a pool in a few minutes, oblivious to any fly offered. They become more responsive when they near their destinations and take up holding stations for longer periods of time.

The North Umpqua at Steamboat that is fifty degrees the first of June will top sixty degrees by the end of July, as the main stem downriver reaches eighty degrees. The river warms up at ever higher elevations, and by late August the river can be sixty degrees at Steamboat. Some combination of time in the river and water at least twenty degrees warmer than when they entered makes the fish dour and hard to move from deep lies. Except for first and last light, casting over steelhead using a greased-line method is frustrating.

Several approaches, all involving going down to the fish, can then be used. The heavily weighted flies generally fall into two categories, black leeches and dark nymphs—as complicated as Kaufmann's Stone or as simple as the Montana Nymph—and any black Girdle-Bug-type rubber-leg nymph.

"Black Leech" is more generic than specific. Any fly with black marabou tied on a heavily weighted hook qualifies. Joe alternately calls the fly Ugly Bug, Thump Bug, and Beaded Wonder. Everyone seems to apologize for its use; no one questions its effectiveness. The following is a typical example.

BLACK LEECH

Tail	Black marabou, short	**Hackle**	Black, long and webby
Body	Black chenille ribbed with silver tinsel; palmer with webby black hackle	**Head**	Flame single stand floss

Many pools are little more than very narrow channels between ledge rock. To cover the water, one does not swing a fly through so much as run a fly down on a dead drift. To properly accomplish this, Joe had me lengthen my leader to between twelve and fourteen feet and include a thirty-inch tippet of .010 leader. Depending on the brand, this can run from twelve-pound test (Umpqua River Feather Merchants), to eight-pound (Maxima). The heavily weighted fly is "cast" across stream and immediately back-mended to give it slack to reach the bottom. At more than moderate distances, a long-belly forward-taper line is helpful in accomplishing this big initial mend. The fly is then "rolled" along the bottom, the rod tip following the fly until it comes under tension. At this point, either additional line can be slipped into the drift or the swing completed to end the drift. A steelhead may take at any part of the presentation, from the beginning of the dead drift to the end of the swing. I have had no trouble detecting the take during the dead drift, though constant vigilance is necessary to keep the fly free of drag.

When bearing an underbody of lead wire, these heavily weighted leech flies often ride upside down. If they don't, they will immediately foul the bottom. The easiest way to make sure the fly is "weedless" is to secure a lead barbell or bead chain eyes at the head on the top of the hook. If the hook is small—size 4, 6, or 8—the fly will ride hook-up regardless of how the marabou wing is tied.

Two local variations of the black leech, essentially the Roelof's Leech, use only a long piece of black marabou tied in at the head. The hook may be a #6 short-shank, "bait" style, or two hooks, the second hook trailing the first by an inch and connected with Dacron line. The first hook is cut off at the bend. Presumably, this prevents short strikes. In both examples, the fly is weighted at the head with lead barbells (1/16 ounce) or medium- to large-size bead chain. The flies are amazingly snag-free, often extremely effective, and take only seconds to tie.

Nymphs are usually the most effective way to fish the North Umpqua when the summer steelhead are sated and being particularly difficult. A very small weighted nymph, a #8 or smaller, can be effectively cast upstream on a 12-foot leader and fished on a dead drift using a strike indicator.

Joe told me about a variation on this method that involves fishing two nymphs, a heavily weighted medium-size nymph as the point fly, and a very small weighted nymph as the dropper. The point fly is cut off at the bend and is used solely to take the small nymph down. Anglers allegedly do this to get around the rule prohibiting the use of any weight (i.e., split shot), other than that tied directly on the single fly.

Joe is so intensely busy guiding anglers through the summer that it is rarely possible for him to fish at his leisure until fall and winter. Fortunately, a few fresh steelhead arrive each day right through October, while the doldrum steelhead that have summered over are revitalized by the cooler fall water.

The North Umpqua is open all year, with November and May the low points in fresh escapements. A small sprinkling of fresh summer and winter steelhead appears in November, but the river is essentially fallow, and even the diehard angler is likely to wait a few weeks for the main run of winter steelhead.

The North Umpqua's winter-run steelhead number approximately eight thousand native fish that average about eight pounds. Hatchery steelhead have never been introduced into the river. That fact alone may make the race unique in Oregon, where winter-runs are invariably supplemented with hatchery plants. A three-salt male can easily top twenty pounds, and individuals weighing nearly thirty pounds have been recorded. Joe describes the winter steelhead as being more robust and heavier for their length than the steelhead of summer.

The winter river temperature is typically forty-two to forty-eight degrees. Joe recalls once taking a steelhead when the water registered a frigid thirty-seven degrees, and he feels that these steelhead are nearly dormant at that temperature. His line of choice is a fast-sinking shooting head with a four-foot leader, and his fly list begins with a 2/0 Muddler, "an excellent winter steelhead fly. I swing it on a shooting head and not necessarily very deep. The fly may be down only a couple of feet." Of his second choice, a 4/0 Skunk, he says, "I began using this size fly when I saw the driftboat guys doing so well with hot shots. When you're swinging a large fly, it's not much different from a hot shot, except, of course, it doesn't have the wobble to it."

When fishing dingy water, Joe will go to a big Polar Shrimp, General Practitioner, or the simple Silver Orange, a silver-bodied fly with fluorescent orange hackle and white bucktail wing. He prefers to fish his elegant spey flies whenever conditions permit. The difficulty in obtaining genuine blue heron spey hackle prevents their being more commonplace.

Joe and I sought the shaded runs in summer, and we always cared how and when the sun played on the water. The opposite is true for his winter angling. He searches for the pools with sun hard on the water, the rays of warmth raising the surface temperature and charging up the sluggish steelhead.

STATION TO BOAT

Tom Pero, Don Roberts, and I had been fishing the last pools below Steamboat that could be reached either by the Mott Trail or by the highway. We would drive to the water and they would drop down into the canyon, cross a shallows below Ledges, and work upriver to fish Ledges, Knouse's, and Takahashi's pools. I would pick my way down the jumble of rocks and very carefully ease my way into the water to begin fishing opposite my companions. At about eight o'clock, the sun crested the ridge line above Steamboat Creek and flooded the runs with light. On some mornings, however, the air would be cold and so thick with fog that the sun wouldn't burn it off until midmorning. This granted us an extra couple of hours to fish.

Much has been written about the difficulty of wading the North Umpqua. The ledge rock has been polished ice-smooth from the fine grit of countless springs, and it is annually slimed with algae. Zane Grey described the rocks as "slipperier than slippery-elm," and they are. The rocks along these famous pools bear tiny deposits of aluminum that glint in the sun. These are the spoor of stream-cleated anglers who have presumably defied gravity to fish another day. (Anglers not familiar with the river could do no better than to follow this trail.) The old literature never mentions the piles of rock that line much of the north side. They were deposited in the 1950s, when the highway was dynamited from the rock walls, the basalt cleaving along predictable angles and falling into the river to land atop the ledge rock. The North Umpqua is unusually free of decent spawning gravel, a factor that limits the natural spawning of its steelhead and prevents these rock piles from filling up with sediment and becoming monolithic reefs. Unlike other rivers, the rock piles here remain sharp-edged, interstitial, and all but impossible to wade.

As I rooted through the rock pile, I would alternately wade to my knees and to my armpits. My waders go that far, but occasionally an icy trickle would become a breathtaking flood after I crossed my fingers and tiptoed off a rock. I would shortly find myself ignominiously crawling up another rock face like a beached seal, swearing that this would be my last time through the water. Ever. Later, when I had dried off, I would remember that the water was always open, and that no one else wanted this wretched little orphan pool. But mostly I would remember that earlier in the week, a thirty-inch hen had come to a Ferry Canyon fished on a greased line, twice crossed the river, and given me fits as I flailed and staggered around in the rock pile. When I finally released the steelhead, I apologized to the pool for having called her so many horrible names. But this truce lasted for only a few minutes.

My friends returned to their homes in Bend, Oregon, and I stayed to fish the pool a dozen times, usually each morning, sometimes in the evening, and the pool unfailingly dashed my hopes. I was fishing other waters as well and meeting with Joe Howell for lunch to discuss the river and determine how his clients had fared. I was looking for some equally miserable company and sometimes finding it. The weather was perfect for going to the beach, and I told Joe the greased-line fly was getting me

Jorge Graziozi quarters a cast on the Mott Pool.

only halfhearted responses. Even the little parr were in a funk. He said that wasn't a good sign. The last few days hadn't been a lot of fun for him, either.

"I'm going back to getting up at four and fishing Upper Mott or Kitchen at first light," I announced.

"Then I'd fish Station," he said, "it always holds a few steelhead."

He reached into his vest and dropped a small, very heavily weighted black leech pattern with a flame head and an articulated body. "If all else fails," he added.

The next morning, I crossed Mott Bridge in the dark, parked my truck, and took the Mott Trail down to the river. I went directly to Upper Mott, and, at first light, discovered an angler standing in the water but not yet fishing. As I was wondering whether to go in at Kitchen, another angler silently slipped into the water and began casting, his white strike indicator describing a lobbing arc above the black currents. I walked back up the trail, took a side path, and began pushing across the river for Station before it, too, was filled.

Station Pool is just below the confluence of Steamboat Creek. It got its name more than sixty years ago from the Forest Service Guard Station that once overlooked the pool from the end of the old road.

I recalled Merle Hargis's story about watching his brother take a steelhead while fishing from the plank that then extended from the shore to a large rock some thirty feet out.

Walt Johnson, of Stillaguamish River fame, told me he once fished Station, just after World War II. As he was making his way out on the plank early one morning, a water ouzel momentarily distracted him, and he walked off into the river. An elderly man came to his aid, admonished him for not paying better attention, and identified himself as "Umpqua Vic" O'Byrne, a legendary recluse who lived in a cabin above Steamboat.

The ledge rock opposite me once supported that plank. Steelhead hold directly beneath it, or directly beneath the long piece of ledge rock I was standing on. They won't hold in the tongue of water between, and a swinging fly doesn't properly cover the far lie.

Below Station is a violent rapids with a falls here and there. A less-dangerous side channel creates a scrubby little island that ends when the river comes together and roars into the quiet of Boat Pool. The distance from Station to Boat was well over a hundred yards. As I began casting, the end of a short recollection by Zane Grey kept running through my head: " . . . he [Romer] would get up at daylight and try to beat everybody to the Ranger Station Pool at Steamboat. Half the time he beat the fishermen who were camped right on the bank. And did he snake steelhead out of that strange and wonderful hold! Twenty-seven he caught there, and lost twice that many. *But when the fish start down, it's time to weep.*"

Joe had told me that it was best to fish my side of the ledge channel first before back-mending and sliding a fly down the opposite wall, dead-drift propositions his leech pattern would make more precise.

The steelhead took halfway down, ran out of the pool without hesitation, and jumped in the first piece of heavy water. She then caught the full force of the rapids and raced downriver past the top end of Boat, where an angler stood casting. The line hung up a bit on a midchannel rock. That, and the long run the steelhead had put on, made me certain she was gone. I couldn't feel anything. I had, as the locals say, been cleaned. After picking my way downriver, I hopped from rock to rock to midchannel and was just able to free my line. To my astonishment, the fish was still on. When I finally arrived at Boat, the angler courteously backed out and called over to me, "I was standing on that rock and this silver streak came right across my boot tops trailing an entire fly line!"

"I've never seen such a non-stop run! Not even a pause!" I said.

In a few minutes, she was beached, a Steamboat Creek native only twenty-seven inches long with a faint trail of pink down her silver side. After she was sent on her way, I saw that Station was still open, and I hastily returned to the pool. A second steelhead immediately took the fly and held for a minute in the pool. As I was thrashing about to get below the lie, the fish catapulted out of the run and streaked for Boat. Again a steelhead trailing a fly line came rocketing past my neighbor, and again the steelhead, a male of identical length, was successfully beached and released. Station was vacant no longer, and I hoped the couple now alternating casts would be equally fortunate.

I looked downriver, and I could see the curl of smoke from Steamboat Inn and smell the coffee, the bacon, and the pancakes to be filled with sour cream and strawberries. I was soaked, a combination of sweat and river, and famished. Jorge Graziosi, an Argentine who leads fishing expeditions in Patagonia, was sometimes my breakfast companion, and this morning I would be especially glad to visit with him.

I told Jorge about the steelhead. I said I thought these breakaway natives were the very essence of this river, that my morning was a classic North Umpqua experience. He had chased a big buck down a couple pools the previous week before releasing it, and he recalled this, his first steelhead. He reminded me that there had been days when he almost stopped believing in steelhead, and then when he hooked two, he lost them both. "You know," he said, "this is a very difficult river."

"Yes," I replied, "and a great one."

Billy Pate casts a fly on the more traditional pools below Steamboat. →

10

DESCHUTES RIVER

M Y steelhead fly-fishing education began when I first visited the Deschutes River nearly twenty-five years ago with Frank Amato and Bill Bakke. I had caught steelhead on a few other rivers, but the encounters had always surprised me as much as they'd startled the steelhead. I had certainly been able to draw little from these experiences. I did learn that if I spent enough time casting a sinking shooting head and dredging out runs with bright, often fluorescent flies, a steelhead would come my way. Months or an entire winter could pass between fish, but I found this a heady quest where suffering and success went hand in glove.

It was easy to be a disciple of Enos Bradner, Ken and George McLeod, Tommy Brayshaw, Al Knudson, Syd Glasso, Ralph Wahl, Walt Johnson, Wes Drain, and, of course, Roderick Haig-Brown. As these anglers were sorting out new rivers in terms of the fly, they were pulling me away from the strong steelhead fly-fishing traditions of southern Oregon and northern California and giving my sport a Northwest bias that still exists today. They demonstrated that the Skagit's great winter steelhead were a springtime celebration, that the "springers" of the Wind and Kalama rivers were the most potent of all the summer-runs, and that when very large steelhead came to a dry fly the event was no accident. They traveled north into the Skeena drainage and, for a time, rewrote the record books with summer-run steelhead that proved to be the largest on earth.

Hard on their successes came a second wave of anglers who gathered from them the raw material to continue refining techniques and to show how well steelhead could be caught. Bill Bakke, Bill McMillan and Harry Lemire began preaching a gospel that told of floating lines, sparsely tied low-water wets, Portland hitches, and deer-hair drys fished across and down, a cross-pollination of Atlantic salmon techniques and Northwest rivers. I became a passionate proselytizer of this new faith, totally convinced of its practical and aesthetic rightness.

When Frank and I began fishing, he offered me a fly. I would have preferred one of my own had this dressing not been so attractive. It was a Skunk, a bread-and-butter pattern for all steelheaders, but now tied on a low water salmon hook with a thin body and a bucktail wing set low, short, and sleek. The proportions were better than I had ever conceived, and were in contrast to my own clunky, early California style of steelhead flies.

"Did you tie this?" I asked. I did not know Frank to be a tyer in any classic sense.

"No, Randall Kaufmann tied these several months ago. This is the first chance I've had to fish them," he said, holding the box out for inspection. We both knew the talented young tyer who, with his brother, Lance, operated a tiny shop in Tigard, Oregon.

I was soon casting Randall's fly and praying against its loss. If I back-mended my line, the fly would sink quickly and then on the swing come up from the depths to scintillate in the surface film. Before long, a six-pound buck dashed from the bottom, took the fly, and turned toward its holding station. All this happened so nearby that the entire rise was plainly visible. What I saw made my brain go numb, and my response to the rise correct. I did nothing. A few minutes later, I was releasing my first Deschutes steelhead.

The fly had survived the ordeal. I washed it and continued fishing, but when the next fish turned out to be a jack salmon, I so feared for the safety of the fly that I cut it off and saved it for when I was certain it would only attract steelhead.

Bill Bakke had a new fly that possessed none of the low water qualities I so admired. It had a plump orange body. The squirrel-tail wing was tied upright, divided, and set so far forward as to leave room *behind* the wing to riffle-hitch the fly. He called the pattern an October Caddis, and at the time I could only guess at what it might suggest. The next evening, I fished Bill's creation, and while admiring the surface-film commotion created by this wet fly or dry fly—I knew not which—a hen steelhead of just over thirty inches confidently rose to it. To this day I've never seen a prettier trout. I cradled her in the water, the twilight giving her pink-and-white flank a dazzling brilliance. When she swam off, I knew that the way I tied my steelhead flies and the manner in which I fished them were changed forever.

The Deschutes had been a fortunate choice. Unlike other rivers in my experience, it had thousands of summer-run steelhead ascending in a single month, August. It was a desert river with water temperatures that frequently topped sixty degrees, and its steelhead drew from this warmth a remarkable vitality. Fly drifts were languorously long in the summer heat, the always-clear-running currents giving plenty of play to the flies I was soon tying on low water Veniard hooks.

A year later, Frank Amato and I floated the twenty five miles from Macks Canyon to the Columbia River in his little wood McKenzie boat, braving the four great rapids that guard the lower Deschutes: Gordon Ridge, Colorado, Rattlesnake, and Moody. We took an island campsite, its grass still green in early August and browsed short by cattle. There was an outhouse nearby, a picnic table in the center of the lawn, and a fire pit off to one side. A quarter-mile fly drift fronted the camp. It was paradise.

We sat on the grass and began setting up our rods. As we talked, I glanced over Frank's shoulder and noticed a rattlesnake coiled scarcely a foot from his behind. I was momentarily speechless, afraid to say anything, and afraid not to.

"Frank," I said in a chatty, friendly sort of way, "look to your left."

"Well, well, I'll be!" He took the tip section of his fly rod and goosed the snake. It made a buzzing sound. Frank poked it again and began herding it into the bright sun. He relocated the rattlesnake in the shade of the picnic table.

"It will be okay here," he said.

"The *rattlesnake* will be okay? What about us? Where are we supposed to eat? Frank, we don't have

Frank Amato swings a fly through the great canyon waters of the Deschutes. →

My 4-weight outfit and a mint-bright Deschutes Steelhead

a tent. Good God! Where in hell are we supposed to sleep?"

"Oh, he won't bother us," said Frank. He tied on a fly and studied the river, the snake all but forgotten. After he waded in and began working out line, I returned to the picnic table and stared at my adversary. It stared back.

I walked upstream and started casting. Two hours passed without either of us raising a steelhead. I was finding it hard to concentrate on fishing. While the light was still decent, I wanted to find the rattlesnake and plot its murder. It could easily be dispatched. I was still hatching my scheme when I looked down into the inch or two of water and discovered that I was standing on a huge rattlesnake. The scream I emitted was primal hysteria accompanied by body levitation. Frank looked up, noted my remarkable exit from the river, and resumed fishing.

I was now in a frenzy, and I began a long-range artillery salvo with derby-size rocks. The snake didn't move, because it was already dead, the victim of some other angler's terror and prejudice. I was shaking all over as I made my way to the picnic table.

The rattlesnake was gone.

Frank returned to camp. I tried to look casual perched atop the picnic table. He was either too kind or too tired to take notice and shortly began scouring the area for wood to burn. I took heart and joined him beside the fire for dinner. We rested in our sleeping bags and looked into the desert's night sky, this planet's best view of infinity, and as our talk turned to steelhead, my thoughts were of snakes. When Frank fell asleep, I searched the grass through the flickering shadows of the rapidly dying fire. If I encountered the rattlesnake, it would be at his level. The image made sleep impossible. Soon it was dark, and a few minutes later I heard a rustle of activity in our little compound.

"Frank! Listen!" I whispered. He searched the duffle beneath his head and pulled out a powerful flashlight, the beam of light swinging across the camp from boat to food boxes to fishing vests. Skunks were everywhere, eight or nine in all, and they were rummaging through and dragging around everything but the boat. I offered to bounce a rock off one of the enterprising vagrants. Frank discouraged the idea.

"Oh no, that could make a terrible mess of things."

"I hope we can recover all our gear," I said glumly. We lay back in our bags as the skunks boldly tore around the camp. Could they also be policing the area against a rattlesnake invasion? I brightened at the thought and fell into a deep sleep.

In the morning I shook a scorpion out of my boot and checked the outhouse pit for black widow spiders, then I gathered water from the river for coffee. The strong winds I associated with late afternoon were already blowing up the canyon, sending sand flying through our campsite. Fishing was out of the question. Without shelter, we turned our backs to the wind, and eventually I simply stretched out on the ground and put my head in my sleeping bag for protection against the storm. The hours passed slowly. By late afternoon the wind eased up, and the temperature topped a hundred degrees. We returned to our fishing, and that evening Frank beached a steelhead, a native fish of seven pounds, which he would not kill; only fin-clipped hatchery fish would be sacrificed for roasting over sagebrush roots for dinner. No other steelhead came to our flies, and that night we dined on one of Frank's favorite meals, canned chili topped with chunks of raw onion. For the occasion, he heated it.

I've made other trips to the Deschutes, so I'm pretty blasé about rattlesnakes today, though I still hate to be buzzed by one. When the subject comes up, I say, "Oh, I've done rattlesnakes," and I think of this wonderful river and its steelhead. But if a toast is to be offered, I make it to skunks—regular, Green-Butt, and the four-legged variety.

EARLY HISTORY

By nine o'clock on Tuesday morning, October 22, 1805, Meriwether Lewis and Captain William Clark had broken camp on the Columbia River about four miles east of the John Day River. Their party of thirty continued downriver in the five dugouts they had fashioned from ponderosa pine logs on Idaho's Clearwater. Apparently they were delighted when Yakima Indians traded forty dogs to the party for "beeds, bells & thimbles." It was probably Clark who had finagled firewood from the Nez Perce Indians the previous evening, enabling them to roast a few of these dogs for dinner.

The party was doubtless weary of a salmon diet only occasionally supplemented with camass root, grouse, coyote, and even crow. As the most famous expedition in American history continued to the Pacific, their dugouts filled with dogs to be eaten, thousands of Indians were engaged in the most ambitious commercial food gathering enterprise known to have existed in North America.

Salmon glutted every waterway. They were split, dried, pounded into pemmican for nearly indefinite storage, packaged in salmon skins, and stowed in large reed baskets. The baskets assured a food supply in lean times, or were traded in a thriving east-west commerce that extended all the way to the Great Plains. At no place on the Columbia River was this activity more intense than at Celilo Falls, where dozens of tribes collected each year to snag and net chinook salmon.

Clark noted in his diary an island with a number of Indian lodges, drying racks, and pounded fish, and "several Indians killing fish with gigs." Opposite the island they discovered the mouth of a very large river that they estimated was fully one-fourth the volume of the Columbia. It was known to the Indians as *Towornehiooks*. Lewis and Clark ordered the party to the west side of the river mouth so that they could investigate. The viewing must have been cursory, for they shortly resumed their trip, continuing on to Celilo Falls, the Narrows of the Columbia River, which has rested beneath the placid waters behind The Dalles Dam since the 1950s.

When Lewis and Clark began their return trip, they named the river for Clark. (Lewis granted himself a similar distinction on the north side of the Columbia.) The name tidied up some cartographic loose ends, but otherwise didn't survive. Twenty years later the ubiquitous French fur trappers of the Hudson Bay Company came to call the water the *Riviere Des Chutes*, literally River of the Falls, presumably for its location by Celilo Falls.

These early explorers hardly made note of this river, no doubt because of the magnitude of the Columbia and the dramatic nature of Celilo Falls. However, even against such comparisons, and on the grand scale by which we measure our western rivers, the Deschutes is a colossus. It is 250 miles long, drains an area of 10,000 square miles, and in March may have a volume of over ten thousand cubic feet per second. The lower 100 miles rushes along at an average speed of four miles per hour, propelled by a gradient approximately the same as the Colorado's, thriteen feet per mile. Its rapids are legendary.

Saying where a river actually begins is rarely possible. For the sake of convenience, a sign or a map may claim that beyond a certain point there is a river, but practically speaking, the spring tenure of some nameless trickle with origins in a soggy meadow often marks the uppermost headwater.

The Deschutes bears no such burden. Little Lava Lake springs to life on an eastern slope in central Oregon's Cascades, and the outlet at its southwestern shore marks the beginning of the Deschutes River. From this tranquil start, a continued low gradient maintains the river in a bucolic state for many miles. Then the impassable rowdiness of Pringle Falls, Benham Falls, and Lava Island Falls marks a dramatic character change, and the river becomes a serious gatherer of other rivers, ultimately coming together with the Crooked River and then with the colder Metolius. The Deschutes plunges on to cut ever deeper through ancient lava flows, the history of its prehistoric past written on towering canyon walls.

The entire drainage has extremely porous volcanic substrata that store excess rainfall and snowmelt and release the absorbed water during drier months through springs. No other river of comparable size has such a remarkably even flow, its maximum but 4.5 times its minimum. As a consequence, steelhead lies are usually dependable from year to year, and the angler need only learn once how a water is best fished.

DESCHUTES STEELHEAD

For a hundred years after the Lewis and Clark Expedition, steelhead entered the Deschutes and sought their ancestral spawning grounds well up the Crooked River, into the lower Metolius, and up the Deschutes main stem probably as far as Lava Island Falls. There is no documentation for the size of this run, and any good estimate is, at best, guesswork, but it was certainly in the tens of thousands.

The Deschutes system remained free-flowing until this century. The Federal Reclamation Act for Power and Irrigation of 1902 led to the construction of two dams and two trout-rich reservoirs, Crane Prairie and Wickiup. Their location was so far upriver that it is extremely doubtful either dam blocked runs of summer-run steelhead or spring and fall chinook.

On December 21, 1951, the Federal Power Commission granted a license to Portland General Electric to construct a dam approximately 100 miles up the Deschutes. Pelton Dam was the result. Rising 204 feet above bedrock and spanning 965 feet, it was completed in 1958, at a cost of $21 million. A much smaller regulating dam was built a couple of miles downstream of Pelton to help maintain the river's natural flow and to prevent sudden fluctuations in water level. To enable steelhead to pass over Pelton Dam, a three-mile-long fish ladder was constructed between the Pelton Regulating Dam and Pelton Dam.

The success of the fish ladder had hardly been determined when the Federal Power Commission granted Portland General Electric (PGE) a second license in 1960 to construct an enormous rock-filled dam just upstream of Pelton Dam. Called Round Butte, it would rise 440 feet above bedrock, span 1,380 feet, and measure 1,570 feet across at the base. A cable tramway was constructed to transport adult steelhead and salmon over the dam. At both Pelton and Round Butte, artificial outlets were constructed for emigrating smolts. On paper it was a grand success. In practice, the entire effort was pretty much a failure, and runs of steelhead declined rapidly during the 1960s. Engineers had not taken into account the lack of flow in Lake Billy Chinook, the reservoir behind Round Butte, and smolts were unable to locate the artificial outlet in order to successfully complete their downstream journey. To mitigate against this loss, Portland General Electric began financing hatchery operations in 1969, and constructed the Round Butte Hatchery in 1971. This facility, owned by PGE and operated by the Oregon Department of Fish and Wildlife, reportedly releases l60,000 steelhead and 240,000 spring chinook smolts each year. Approximately two-thirds of these smolts are trucked downstream to various release sites. Adult hatchery steelhead will delay their return by lingering at these areas of release, making them available to sports fishermen for longer periods.

The total escapement of summer-run steelhead in the Deschutes is not known, because no collecting point or counting station provides reliable numbers below the fish trap at Pelton Dam. Here steelhead, mostly of hatchery origin, are captured and trucked farther upstream to Round Butte, where they are used for brood stock. Those steelhead not needed for hatchery operations are donated to the Confederated Tribes of the Warm Springs Reservation. About five thousand Round Butte hatchery steelhead are trapped at Pelton each year. They first arrive in September, their numbers fluctuating dramatically due to increased stream flows caused by winter rains and snowmelt. The peak periods normally are December and January, but they continue to enter the trap through April. Most are close to spawning when they arrive.

As many as four thousand steelhead from the Round Butte hatchery may spawn in the main stem of the Deschutes. The vast majority will spawn between Sherars Falls, mile 45, and Pelton Dam, mile l00 from the Columbia River.

About ten thousand steelhead are harvested from the Deschutes each year, approximately seventy-five percent from the intensive sport fishery and twenty-five percent from an Indian subsistence fishery using traditional dip nets at Sherars Falls. All the sport-caught fish are of hatchery origin; wild fish must be released. Hatchery fish outnumber wild fish about two to one in the Indian dip net fishery. When the thousand or so wild fish are subtracted from the above total, it leaves nine thousand hatchery steelhead killed annually. These numbers add up to an escapement of eighteen to nineteen thousand hatchery steelhead.

In recent years, the escapement of wild steelhead has ranged from five thousand to nine thousand. Most spawn above Sherars Falls in eastside tributaries, or in the main stem of the Deschutes. Hundreds find their way to the Pelton Dam and make up about fifteen percent of the total captured at the fish trap. This is probably not an instinctive longing for ancestral spawning grounds, but a natural wandering inherent to these steelhead.

By means of electrofishing, the Oregon Department of Fish and Wildlife has demonstrated that wild steelhead hold in the lower forty-three miles of river longer than hatchery steelhead. Their numbers do not decline until February, when they pass upstream to search out spawning tributaries. The wild fish characteristically spawn farther down in the system, and late in the fall they dominate the lower river. This is true even though hatchery smolts are taken to release sites on the lower river to reduce the propensity of returning adults to hurry through the system so quickly that their recreational value is reduced.

My experience on the lower river suggests that although wild steelhead are a smaller percentage of the total escapement, they are far more in evidence when I am fly fishing. I have discussed this at length with Oregon fishery biologists familiar with Deschutes steelhead. They view the increased runs of Deschutes steelhead with some satisfaction, and are understandably reluctant to doubt the value of hatchery steelhead in the overall scheme of things. However, numbers of steelhead are not as important as the recreational value of the fish. It doesn't really matter if the waters are filled with steelhead if the hatchery process has programmed them to race upriver with such speed and single-minded determination that they no longer respond well to the fly.

A Deschutes stream-born premigrant normally smolts after two years in fresh water and then, whether wild or hatchery-reared, spends one or two years in salt water before returning as an adult. The one-year ocean steelhead typically weighs four to six pounds, the two year six to nine pounds. Native Deschutes steelhead spending three or more years in the ocean are unknown. But other Deschutes steelhead with this life history, giant fish of twenty pounds or more, are not.

In l946, Morley Griswold, the governor of Nevada, was fishing the Deschutes just above the mouth when he landed a twenty-eight-pound steelhead on a fly. The fish was then an all-tackle world's record, and today it is still an Oregon record for the fly. What makes the record an interesting one is that Griswold's great fish was what Oregon biologists prosaically call a "stray," a steelhead that wanders into the Deschutes for a time before resuming its migration. Remarkably enough, an intelligent guess can be made as to this fish's origins.

For many years we have known that a few of Idaho's famous "B" steelhead, North Fork of the Clearwater and Middle Fork of the Salmon stocks with individuals exceeding twenty pounds, migrated up the Deschutes, encountered an angler here and there, and sparked some legendary angling tales. The lower river is large and open, the currents strong, perfect water for immensely strong, fresh-from-the ocean steelhead to test an angler's skills.

Several years ago, Randy Stetzer and I began reminiscing about our days on the Deschutes. Randy is an extraordinary talent with a fly rod, and he has caught many large steelhead. Only twice have steelead taken out all of his backing and broken him off. Both experiences came on the Deschutes. "I want to go back in the fall, maybe October, and have a reel with a good drag system," he told me.

The presence of these fish has been attributed to differences in water temperatures between the Deschutes and the Columbia. I've heard the explanation both ways, that is, one river or the other being either too cold or too warm, and possibly there is something to this. Also, a theory is commonly held that these aberrant migrations occur only on the lower river, that large steelhead above Sherars Falls are only Deschutes stock.

Fishery biologists for the Oregon Department of Fish and Wildlife recently began tagging steelhead at Sherars Falls to help determine the migratory habits and ultimate whereabouts of these "Deschutes" steelhead. The tagged fish showed up on the John Day, Salmon, Clearwater, Imnaha, Snake, Wallowa, Icicle, Kalama, Washougal, Klickitat, Grande Ronde, and Yakima rivers! To get to the Washougal and Kalama rivers, the steelhead had to reverse themselves and pass down the Dalles and Bonneville dams to relocate their rivers. Futhermore, it was known for certain that many of these steelhead *never* returned to their rivers of origin. During l981 through l988, 7.4 percent to 33.4 percent of all the steelhead found in the Pelton fish trap were strays. The latter figure represents l,550 steelhead checked during the winter of l986–87. The average for the period was 24 percent, nearly one in four. This means that hundreds of steelhead, born in other rivers, will migrate l00 miles up the Deschutes and enter the Pelton fish trap. I discussed these stray steelhead with Brian Johanson and Eric Olson, biologists at The Dalles office of Oregon's Department of Fish and Wildlife.

"Many of these stray steelhead must be spawning in the Deschutes," I said to Brian.

"Oh, yes, I'm sure they do!"

"If they spawn with wild Deschutes fish, aren't they changing the genetic makeup of the native stock?"

"We're not sure there *is* a native Deschutes steelhead," he replied with a laugh.

I asked Brian what might account for such strange behavior. And had these races of Columbia River steelhead always been so haphazard in their freshwater migratory habits, or was this a recent development? How about the trucking of smolts around dams? Has this contributed to a deterioration of natal imprinting? Or have investigative tools simply uncovered long standing habits? These are not trivial questions, but Brian as yet had no definitive answers. It should be remembered that the Pelton fish trap captures only a fraction of the total steelhead population, perhaps 20 percent. Hundreds, perhaps thousands, of stray steelhead may thus enter the Deschutes and spawn, or leave as they came, their ultimate destination unknown, but likely east. The true magnitude of this phenomenon, and how it enriches our fly fishing, is one of the most fascinating enigmas in all of steelheading.

I recall a story Frank Amato once told me. He was fishing an obscure riffle known only to a few of his friends as Confrontation. In two days he landed sixteen steelhead that averaged ten pounds, with one weighing sixteen and another fifteen pounds. Never in his many years on the Deschutes had he experienced anything like this fishing. Frank thought these were native Deschutes steelhead, and they could have been. But I think this is unlikely. In light of what we know currently of the many races that ascend this river, and the modest size of steelhead we know to be typical of Deschutes stock, it is hard not to believe he encountered a group of alien steelhead with Idaho origins.

FRANK AMATO

Frank Amato has returned to the Deschutes each August for over twenty years, usually finding ways to stay nearly the entire month. He has witnessed the enormous increase in angling pressure, and in recent years this has kept him working at his publishing business on weekends and driving for the Deschutes with his jet sled in tow on Sunday afternoons. He'll stay at least three nights, sometimes four, if the fishing is particularly good. He has become an outspoken guardian of this river, and the fishing magazines he publishes are at the vanguard of the many conservation battles waged in its behalf. I don't think the Deschutes has ever had a better friend—or a more observant student—for Frank catches and releases more than a hundred of its steelhead annually.

When we fished the Deschutes in 1987, Frank told me that he had been using a 4-weight outfit for steelhead. I was dubious, for however suitable the gear was for half-pounders, the typical Deschutes steelhead was another matter. I asked if sufficient pressure could be applied to make businesslike work of the contest. Or was the point to cast tiny flies and protect gossamer tippets, a need I had never encountered? Was the rod a straight 4, or a 4 that cast like a 6, a 4 in name only? As my reservations came spilling out, Frank told me that he had caught many steelhead to sixteen pounds on an eight-foot, four-weight rod, casting flies as large as #4 on tippets as heavy as 12-pound test. He thought there was nothing light about it. The rod was a delight to cast, and the flight of the steelhead seemed to come right from his finger tips.

Frank's approach, so pragmatic and understated, bored into my consciousness all winter. Thus it happened that when BJ Meiggs and I joined him on the Deschutes the following summer, I had two 4-weight outfits, one that was identical to Frank's, and a second that was a foot longer.

We motored upriver from the Heritage Boat Ramp in Frank's jet sled, bursting through the rapids while winding our way beneath great basaltic walls, and in less than an hour we had arrived at our favorite campsite in a little grove of white alder. It was late afternoon, and Frank urged me to fish the camp water, Boulder Pool, for if one of us failed to hold it, other anglers would soon be upon it, and the water would be lost to us until the next day.

The canyon waters of the Deschutes are fished in accordance with how the sun plays on the lies, and Boulder Pool is typical. Early in the morning during the first week of August, the pool is in deep shade. This changes at precisely seven o'clock, when the sun crests an eastern ridge and shines directly into the eyes of holding steelhead. At this time, the pool goes totally dead, and no one well acquainted with the river bothers to fish it. But by early afternoon, the sun has passed behind the steelhead and they can often be enticed into striking. At about six in the evening, the sun drops below a downriver canyon wall, and Boulder Pool is again in shade.

In late afternoon, heavy winds howled up the canyon. Frank left me at Boulder Pool and motored away to search other water. We were both fishing 6-weights to cut the wind, and I was soon making casts between gusts and trying to hold a low-water Night Dancer down in the surface film. Halfway through the run, a steelhead took solidly and raced for the end of the pool. I was certain this fish would pause, and I was slow to clear the water. To my astonishment, the steelhead never hesitated, flashing its broad flank for only a second as it surged away from the shallow tailout and disappeared into the main channel of heavy currents. I frantically palmed the reel, but control was already lost, the whirling spool measuring out the run until the fly came away a hundred yards below.

I returned to the head of the pool and was still collecting myself, still trying to settle an involuntary shaking of my knees, when a second steelhead took. The outcome was never in doubt, and while the hen did eventually manage to leave the pool, she was easily beached directly below camp. She was petite and graceful, a native fish just over six pounds, but, I thought, not half the size of her male companion. I held her briefly while BJ's motor drive whirred through a dozen shots.

When we gathered for a late dinner, I discovered that Frank's experiences had paralleled mine, one runaway and one release, and we felt this presaged days of angling plenty. We cooked by lantern light, blending garlic, onions, and a bit of cooked pork sausage in olive oil and pouring it over fresh pasta. Enough garlic, I told Frank, to ward off the most Transylvanian of spirits. Red wine, nectar of the gods, was an antidote never known to fail, he promised me. Across the canyon ran the railroad tracks, the Great Northern going one way, the Union Pacific the other, and in the darkness we could see the lights and hear the sounds of two trains passing each other. A bat flitted through camp, the cool evening still alive with caddis flies that swarmed into the light.

"There is a rattlesnake in a little depression right below the rock I tied the boat to," warned Frank.

"I was buzzed as I came down from the tent," added BJ.

"You must have nearly stepped on it!" I exclaimed.

"Oh, if we leave them alone, we'll be okay," said Frank.

"This is a story on myself," I said, "but it begins with Frank nearly sitting on a rattlesnake!" We had a grand time with the tale, one of my best memories of the river. BJ's confidence grew with the telling, and the subject, far from being loathsome, was the source of giggles in the days that followed.

Frank woke me after a few hours of sleep. From past experience I knew exactly the time, fifteen minutes before four, an hour before first light, and at most an hour before upriver guide camps would begin spotting their clients by jet boat. The rule of first come, first served, was respected by all, but our camp water was up for grabs if we were still in our sleeping bags. At such an ungodly hour there wasn't enough light to take pictures, and for the moment I envied our photographer, still blissfully asleep.

Frank had often said, "Give me the river and a crust of bread and I'm happy." I'm not that Spartan by half. Gourmet coffee is my reward for lost sleep, and I began my morning with freshly ground French roast, filters, and a glass cup, the latter a ridiculous eccentricity I can't live without. Two cups later I was struggling into my neoprenes and listening for the whine of jet boats heading downriver on their appointed rounds. A small underwater flashlight was secured to my vest. I turned it on as I waded into the very top end of Boulder. Below me, Frank's jet engine coughed to life. Our day had begun.

I waited only five minutes before the first jet boat roared into view, the sound and running lights marking its passage. When it was throttled down, I could hear the voice of the driver and muttered curses from one or two of the eight anglers aboard when they noticed my little light. Their inconvenience wasn't belabored, and they roared off as quickly as they had come. I still had ten more minutes to wait before first light.

The morning was without wind—no difficulty covering all the water with the 4-weight, the sleek little Night Dancer working through lies sixty feet out. This was the only day Boulder failed me, and when Frank returned two hours later, neither of us had turned a fish. We changed locations throughout the day, breaking only for a short nap. In the afternoon, I sat on a rock and waited for a lengthening canyon shadow to cover the pool below camp. Just as the sun dropped below the canyon rim, I began casting a Patriot, and exactly where Frank told me I might find a fish, a steelhead came out and ran right over the fly. Repeated casts with the yellow-bodied pattern wouldn't bring it back. Rarely do I bother changing flies, and if I do, it is usually to change from one size to another. On this occasion, however, I returned to the very dark Night Dancer that had started my day, and the steelhead took the fly with a rush on the first cast.

I quickly found that the time needed to bring this steelhead to the beach was hardly different from what it would have been with my 6-weight. The rod took a deeper set, and there was more cushion in it, but I thought this was a good thing. I did not hesitate to "put the rod" to the fish, for fear the thin-wire hook would tear out. The entire rod was flexing deeply and absorbing the shock of a tired fish laboring violently in the shallows. I was impressed but not surprised when, after five minutes, the six-pound steelhead lay nearly motionless in the shallows. I felt that rougher treatment than this for these midsize steelhead would have been pointless.

The third morning dawned overcast and cool, and we enjoyed the best fishing of the trip. I took two steelhead from Boulder Pool before breakfast, resting the pool between fish. This probably wasn't necessary. Frank once made nine straight passes through the pool before failing to hook and beach a steelhead.

BJ had brought her cameras down to the river just as the second steelhead hit and took me to the end of the pool on a dead run. Suddenly, I heard a strange coughing sound. When the fish surfaced perhaps thirty feet from shore, a bright-eyed head appeared beside it.

"Look, an otter!" I cried.

It paused over this temporary distraction while BJ tried to focus on the little pirate. I threw a stone which caused the otter to sound and the steelhead to leave the pool and flee downriver. BJ laughed.

"You've lost a step or two in your old age!" she called.

It was just seven o'clock, the sun cresting the ridge and illuminating the pool with dazzling suddenness. The fish was still on and could now be moved easily toward the shore. My messy performance was forgotten as BJ bent to the task of getting a steelhead portrait.

We were congratulating ourselves when Frank drifted down and invited us to join him for a run upriver. How far up, he couldn't say; a lot of traffic was on the water. The miles slipped away quickly, and we soon came upon a row of tents dominated by a large mess area covered by a huge canopy. A man in a baseball cap and shorts stepped out and waved us over. Frank leaned over the console. "Steve Koler's camp," he said. I nodded, and we idled into Dead Cow Run, Koler's superb camp water.

"Frank! Good to see you! How've you been? Say, the boys took off this morning without fishing here. You should give it a try. First, come check out my kitchen." We followed him to an assortment of large plywood boxes holding two complete propane ranges, four burners each, ovens, the works. He showed us shower tents and a dining area, too. By law, camps must be relocated every week, though guides are not above trading locations with one another. Steve hates moving his camp, because it is a terrible labor. But "Fish Cops" patrol the river, note campsites, and levy fines, so he has no choice.

We walked along the shore between the tents and the rods in sand spikes. Bells were attached to the rods while a well-anchored diver kept a lure working in the river. A bucket of soapy water suddenly came flying out of a tent. Wash water. Children were crawling around the tents. There was a dog. Add a gambler and a few painted ladies and this could be a gold camp, circa 1850.

"Frank, let me show you my baby." He gathered the child from its young mother and held him up. Marriage and fatherhood had come late to this guide's gypsy life. "Our boys got a dozen fish, but they really had to work for them. We've been getting some nice redsides here, too, sixteen, eighteen inches. Got one yesterday that took me down the pool. Thought it was a steelhead until I beached it."

Steve's comments served as a reminder that on the Deschutes one casts for steelhead while watching the famous resident "redside" rainbow rise to caddisflies. To experience such a choice is extravagant, and I sometimes feel silly ignoring this remarkable trout fishing in the hope that somewhere out in the currents lurks a steelhead. No other river in North America has the same species of trout so equally anadromous and residential, and regarded with such equal fervor. "World class" is a cliché. However devalued the superlative, nothing else quite describes this remarkable fishery.

"How do you want to work this?" I asked Frank as we walked along the river toward the upper end of the run. He was fishless this morning, and the choice was his.

"I'll start at the very top," he said. "You can start here."

I began stripping line off the reel and after a false cast or two sent a dark fly seventy feet out. The fly lit and was smashed so hard the impact knocked the reel's click pawl out of alignment. As the steelhead streaked away downriver, jumping twice and falling over itself, I concentrated on palming the free-running spool. When the fish stopped at the tailout, I gave the reel a whack, and the pawl clicked back into place.

"I hooked one yesterday on the first cast, too!" Steve called. As the steelhead tired and was moved into the shallows, a youngster squatted beside me.

"It's a buck! Colored up, too. Some steelhead are firecrackers, and some are duds," I said, repeating an oft-used homily of Frank's. "I would have thought hen for sure."

"Is it a keeper?" asked the boy.

"It's a wild fish," I replied. He understood, and there was no further discussion on the matter. Steve bent over the revived fish to ask what fly it had come to. "Night Dancer," I replied, holding up the fly.

"I got mine on a Del Cooper."

Frank was carefully working a Patriot above me, still covering new water. I borrowed one of BJ's cameras and waded out into the river to shoot Frank. Just as I depressed the shutter, his little rod bent right down into the handle. He palmed hard on his reel and brought the taking steelhead back to the surface before it made the first of a series of runs that ended in a silver splash opposite me. At first, I did not think the steelhead exceptional, but he said it was a good fish, and I knew Frank badly wanted to release this one himself. His three previous steelhead had all rid themselves of the fly on their own, and although this did not necessarily displease him, sooner or later he felt compelled actually to touch one, a brief intimacy that always restores him.

The steelhead was well downstream, the reel nearly empty of backing, when Frank grimly clamped down on the spool and stopped the fish. He gained line a few inches at a time as rod pressure continued to tire the steelhead. Frank would not beach the fish, choosing instead to bring it into knee-deep shallows and cradle it there for my photograph. I thought the buck could weigh twelve pounds, easily the best steelhead of our trip.

Steve's guides would be back soon enough, and Frank thanked our host for the opportunity to fish his camp water. As we loaded into the sled, Steve brought out a fly rod to show us. "Snagged this from the river this morning. If you run into anyone who's lost a rod . . . ? Expensive!" And good for tarpon, I thought. The powerful 9-weight, with an extension butt and a huge reel, could not have been in greater contrast to Frank's petite 4-weight.

The next morning at dawn the overcast turned to rain, a rare event and a shock when one is sleeping under an August desert sky. The driest shelter was our waders. As we scrambled to put soggy gear into dry bags, the coffee water was heating, and we were soon plotting a strategy that no longer factored in the sun's intimidating glare.

Frank again left me at Boulder Pool and motored upriver, quickly disappearing into the swirling mists that had reduced the grand vistas of this desert canyon to the camp water before me. Halfway down the run, a steelhead boiled beside the fly, a commotion all out of proportion to the light pluck I felt. This was so uncharacteristic of these steelhead that I thought perhaps the fly was lying over on its side, the rise coming on its dorsal side. The rise was repeated on the next cast, but the steelhead would not come back after that, and I continued through the pool. The next time through I fished the same Night Dancer pattern, but on a #1 heavy-wire hook. The fly looked huge, but the steelhead dashed to it, again boiled beside it, somehow touched it, and returned to its station. I was in no danger of losing the water to another angler, and I wanted to think on the matter, so I pulled out of the pool and returned to camp. Halfway through a cup of coffee, I remembered the low-water Night Dancer I had retired the day before after raising eight and beaching four steelhead on it. The fly was in tatters, parts of the floss body streaming out in pieces, the ribbing only a memory. Maybe, I thought, this dilapidated—but buggy—fly would be good for one last fish. When I again waded into Boulder, I was midway down, and in a cast or two I was over the lie. The hen struck so violently that the entire fly passed through the side of her jaw, penetrating the inside of her mouth on the opposite side. Had I not seen this for myself, I would have sworn such a hookup was impossible. She was massive for her length and weighed over seven pounds, a grand steelhead on the 9-foot 4-weight. The only blemish in her otherwise splendid coloration was a fresh gill net scrape received a few days earlier in the Columbia River Native commercial fishery. After cutting the tippet, I removed the fly and released her, a native fish, as were three of every four we hooked on this trip.

Frank returned and could claim two more steelhead. I pressed him for details.

"About six and eight pounds," said Frank. "The larger fish was a hen. Oh, it fought hard! The first run was so long! I thought it would never end. When I was finally able to stop her, I had about this much line left on the reel." Frank formed a dime-sized hole with his thumb and forefinger. "When I beached her I discovered she was a hatchery fish. I was going to kill her, but she was a beautiful fish and she fought so well, I released her."

The conversation prompted us to count up the steelhead we had hooked during the three-and-a-half days, and we could remember twenty-six. Frank thought about this for a moment and gave the trip a C+. (He has described for me his rare A trips, and they are not of this world.)

Our mood was expansive, and I told him what marvelous low-water instruments the 4-weights would be. I could see Atlantic salmon patterns, Black Bears, Blue Charms, and Orange Charms mostly, and they were swimming on light tippets through clear tailouts. Frank nodded and smiled at the convert before him, but he did not join me in my reverie. "You know," he said, "I'd like to try a 2-weight on these steelhead."

"A 2-weight? Are you serious?" I said. He shrugged at my rhetorical question, his eyes twinkling. It was time to leave, and we broke our rods down and gathered up our gear. I probably wouldn't be back again until next year, plenty of time to think about serious fishing matters during the winter months, and to see if yet another spell had been cast over me.

Ted Trueblood holds a Clearwater steelhead. *Photograph courtesy of Field & Stream, permission by Daniel J. Trueblood.*

11

CLEARWATER RIVER

COLUMBIA RIVER

More than 150 tributaries, each large enough to be called a river, are the branches of this giant twisted trunk. They reach into an area the size of Texas from seven states and British Columbia, and give the Columbia a volume exceeding the total of all the other rivers that meet the Pacific Ocean between Canada and Mexico.

The journey is precipitous. The Columbia's tributaries draw from thousands of wildly coursing streams and creeks, the snowmelt, glacial runoff, and rains that tear away at the continent's grandest mountains. Rising in the Selkirks, some twelve hundred miles from the ocean, the Columbia gathers its primary volume from Montana's and Wyoming's Rocky Mountains, drains Idaho's Sawtooth, Salmon, and Bitterroots, draws mightily from Washington's and Oregon's Cascades, and receives a final boost from the Coast Range.

This high-gradient drainage possesses more horsepower than any other river on earth, one-third of all the water power in North America, more than sufficient to spin turbines in fifty dams that are the largest structures ever built by man. The Columbia system is also the world's largest and finest cold-water drainage, thousands of miles of oxygen-rich spawning gravel that once supported Pacific salmon runs totaling fifteen and twenty million fish. Unfortunately, these remarkable resources, fish and hydropower, were never thoughtfully hoarded. As with the forests, the wealth proved too staggering to be exploited rationally, and each resource came into serious conflict with the other.

The Lewis and Clark Expedition, 1803–1806, reached the Columbia by way of the Clearwater and Snake rivers in 1805. The journals of William Clark and Meriwether Lewis provide a detailed record of how the Indians harvested salmon for both subsistence and commercial trade. A number of tribes, often linguistically divergent, communicated in Chinook, first of all the language of a family of tribes along the Washington side of the lower Columbia, but also a trading jargon containing words from Indian dialects and white traders who were English, Russian, and French. The Chinook Indians were so closely identified with the runs of Columbia River salmon that early settlers applied their name to the largest of the salmon.

The geographic scope of the Indians' commercial and subsistence fishery is well documented; the size of the salmon harvest is not. Numbers are general: Thousands of Indians, a million salmon. More important than knowing the exact numbers, however, is appreciating that no matter how many salmon were removed, they were replenished each year. The perpetual nature of this harvest, like the Indians' cultural dependence upon salmon, was to change in a remarkably short time.

The first salmon cannery along the lower Columbia River began operation in the late 1860s. Led by William Hume, the "King of the Canneries," the number of canneries increased each year until 1883, when the Columbia's runs of salmon required thirty-nine canneries and their Chinese workers to process a pack that totaled 630,000 cases, more than 30 million one-pound cans. That was the peak year, with something like ten million Columbia River salmon and steelhead canned or sold fresh. During the next decade, Finns, Swedes, and Norwegians put to sea from Astoria, Oregon, and swelled commercial landings with ocean-caught salmon. The pack of 1895 was the equal of 1883, but from that year forward, the decline was continuous, always the result of too many fishermen and too few fish.

The chinook, whether gathered by gill nets or by fish wheels, was the mainstay of this commercial industry. Averaging twenty-two pounds and sometimes weighing several times that, the "Royal Chinook" of can labels divided into three distinct seasonal races beginning with the spring-run, sexually immature fish that entered the Columbia in late winter for spawning areas as far as a thousand river miles away. Summer chinook more typically spawned farther down in the Columbia River Basin, while the fall run were mostly concentrated in the lower river.

Coho salmon were far less numerous, but common each fall in the Methow, Wenatchee, Yakima, and Grand Ronde rivers, and usually abundant in tributaries of the lower Columbia.

The sockeye, locally called "bluebacks," entered the Columbia in June for the Okanogan system of rivers and lakes in British Columbia, Idaho's lakes that headed the Salmon River, such as Redfish, Alturas, and Stanley, and Washington's lake-headed Wenatchee. They were small salmon, averaging five pounds or so, but with flesh that kept its red color so well when canned that it held premium market value. For its rich and oily flesh, the Indians, too, valued the sockeye above all other salmon.

Before Oregon classified the steelhead as a gamefish in 1935, the Columbia River pack often exceeded two million pounds, with another million pounds sold frozen, both winter-run and summer-run. East of the Cascades, the steelhead was strictly a summer-run, known to travel hundreds of miles up the Salmon River to Stanley Basin, a mile above sea level; up the spectacular North Fork of the Clearwater and into the Clearwater Mountains; up the main stem of the Columbia to Kettle Falls and into British Columbia; up the Snake River to dozens of spawning tributaries in Idaho and Oregon. Only the Snake River's Shoshone Falls prevented steelhead from reaching into Wyoming, though Salmon Falls Creek led them discreetly into Nevada.

During the 1930s, the Army Corps of Engineers surveyed all American rivers for potential dam sites. Rivers were reduced to hydroelectric power, flood control, irrigation, and navigation when dams were engineered with lock systems. Their completed study, called "308 Reports," included many recommendations for the Columbia River and its tributaries. The first of these federally built hydroelectric dams on the Columbia would be named for Captain Benjamin Eulalie de Bonneville, first commandant of the Vancouver Barracks in Washington Territory.

Bonneville Dam was sited just below the Cascade Falls, some 145 miles from the ocean. Construction began in 1933. When completed in 1938, Bonneville's locks allowed ocean ships to reach into the wheat country of Washington's interior. The dam also incorporated a system of fish ladders and counting stations so that adult salmon and steelhead could pass unimpeded upstream. For the first time on a large western river, accurate escapement totals, species by species, could be determined.

In the spring, downstream migrating smolts passed over the spillway, and through the turbines, or they were conducted through four bypasses. The annual average number of adult salmonids passing up the fish ladders during the next ten years was as follows: 359,054 chinook; 127,431 steelhead; 72,834 sockeye; 9,437 coho; and 1,600 chum.

Bonneville was not the first dam on the Columbia. Rock Island Dam, completed by Puget Sound Power and Light in 1931, was constructed just below the Wenatchee River confluence. Like Bonneville, it had a fish ladder and operates to this day.

Grand Coulee, at a site nearly six hundred miles from the ocean, was the third Columbia River dam. Salmon and steelhead had once passed hundreds of miles above this point, above Kettle Falls, where each fall for centuries Indians had netted thousands of salmon, and above the confluence of the Clark Fork and the Kootenay rivers in British Columbia. Yet when the dam was completed in 1942—the most massive structure ever built by man—it contained no fish ladders. Runs above the dam were simply terminated. The reason was first a practical one. The reservoir created was 151 miles long, and no fish ladder could help salmon find their way in such a vast reach of still water. The second reason was legal.

In 1911, a sawmill in Port Angeles, Washington, began construction of a small hydropower dam near the mouth of the Elwha River. No fish ladders were built, and when the dam was completed in 1913, the largest strain of chinook salmon known to inhabit the contiguous United States was blocked from spawning. Washington, like other states, recognized its obligation to protect its runs of salmon and took the company to court. Years passed while the two parties litigated. Ultimately, the run was lost, but a settlement was eventually consummated: If the company funded a hatchery to compensate for the loss, the dam could remain without a ladder. This arrangement became an important legal precedent, one that gave tremendous impetus to hatchery programs, and one that delighted politicians. Farmers could get ample water for irrigation, the cities could purchase cheap and abundant power from state and federal governments, and the fishermen could depend on their rivers filling with salmon and steelhead. "Go forth and multiply," said the government to the Army Corps of Engineers. "Mitigation" and "hatcheries," said the Army Corps of Engineers to the State, the mantra repeated over and over, dam after dam.

Mitigation for the loss of salmon and steelhead above Grand Coulee began by trapping fish at the Rock Island fishways and transporting them to four tributaries below the dam, the Wenatchee, Entiat, Methow, and Okanogan rivers. The fish were ripened in holding ponds, and the fertilized eggs were hatched at salmon and steelhead hatcheries sited on the rivers. Increasing production of salmonids *below* the dam became mitigation for the loss of salmonids *above* the dam.

More dams followed, each with a fish-passage facility, each with locks, each with an enormous reservoir behind it, each a monument to our industry and engineering skills. The Dalles, John Day, McNary, Priest Rapids, Wanapum, Rocky Reach, Wells, and Chief Joseph dams hobbled the Columbia's free flow. Ice Harbor, Lower Monumental, Little Goose, and Lower Granite dams reduced the lower Snake to barely measurable currents. To reach Idaho's Clearwater, Salmon, and Snake rivers and Washington and Oregon's Grande Ronde, steelhead would now have to cross over eight dams. They did, by the thousands, and hatcheries worked furiously to keep them coming.

All is not well, however. Smolts pass over spillways during the May runoff and suffer from nitrogen supersaturation, a condition that leads to deformities and even death. They suffer additional mortalities passing through the turbines. The reservoirs become huge predator sinks, with thousands of squawfish, smallmouth bass, walleye, and channel catfish feeding greedily on the smolts. Ring-billed gulls line up below spill gates and account for the loss of many additional smolts, possibly as many as two percent of the total. Each dam results in a loss of ten to fifteen percent of the fish; the loss through eight dams is staggering. A partial solution at upriver dams involves installing diversion screens that lead smolts though a complicated series of conveyances to a collection facility. They are loaded into trucks or put on barges and taken downriver though each dam's lock system to be released below Bonneville Dam. Though the overall benefit is substantial, the procedure stresses the smolts and causes additional losses.

In addition, when all, or nearly all, brood stock has hatchery origins, the juvenile populations are so isolated that bacterial and viral diseases can devastate annual populations. On occasion, millions of eggs and adult brood stocks must be destroyed in an effort to eradicate diseases such as infectious hematopoietic necrosis virus (IHNV), and infectious pancreatic necrosis virus (IPNV). Biologists are so concerned about the possibility of hatchery plants infecting wild stocks that they refuse to plant juvenile salmon and steelhead in areas where natural spawning is producing wild, disease-free juveniles. Yet releasing juveniles only from hatchery points results in a glut of adult fish at hatchery weirs and a hog line of anglers immediately below this point.

No one more appreciates the problems of getting healthy juvenile salmon and steelhead safely to the ocean than Steve Pettit. Anglers know him for his steelhead fly-fishing skills and his remarkable knowledge of the Clearwater River. But Steve, a fisheries staff biologist with Idaho's Department of Fish and Game, is the State's Fish Passage Specialist and Chairman of the Fish Transportation Oversight Team, a multiagency crew that runs the juvenile transportation program. The team receives input from federal, state, and tribal agencies, and negotiates a plan that becomes the guideline for individual operators at Lower Granite, Little Goose, and McNary, the "collector dams," with screens that gather smolting juveniles released upstream.

When I spoke with Steve in Lewiston, Idaho, in September 1990, he first explained that the diversion screens were not 100 percent effective. "Approximately fifty to sixty percent of the juvenile chinook are diverted, and up to eighty to eighty-five percent of the steelhead."

"What of the other dams?" I asked.

"Congress has ordered the Army Corps of Engineers to complete bypass systems on the remaining unprotected dams between here and the ocean by 1994." Steve paused, and then added, "As money becomes available."

"Would this solve your greatest problem?"

"The main problem is short and sweet. No longer is there adequate flow to get the juveniles downstream in a timely and safe manner. What we're learning now as we get into this impounded river system—if you can call the Columbia a river—is that the delay associated with having eight reservoirs instead of a free-flowing river probably has as significantly a high mortality as the physical mortality experienced when they pass through the dams. The delay challenges the fish to reach the ocean in that physiological window when they are transforming from freshwater organisms to saltwater organisms. The longer you delay the fish down these impoundments, the greater the likelihood of having them arrive at Astoria already reverting back to parr instead of being smolts."

We discussed what the future is likely to be for the declining runs of Columbia River salmonids. I found the losses especially chilling when viewed against a time line of only two generations. Some forty-five hundred river miles have been lost to spawning. Runs once totaling 15 to 20 million fish are down to 2 million. From a high of 10 million, the commercial take is down to a million. The runs of sockeye salmon have been reduced by ninety-eight percent. During 1990, a single male sockeye made it to its ancestral spawning area in Idaho's Redfish Lake. Idaho's sockeye, as an anadromous species, is now unofficially considered extinct. Coho salmon, reduced by ninety-two to ninety-six percent, have been extinct in Idaho's Snake River since 1984. The great runs of chinook salmon above Bonneville Dam have been devastated. The Snake River's fall chinook decreased from 27,700 in 1962, to 600 in 1989. The loss of the river's summer chinook is equally depressing, 30,900 to 4,200 for the same period. Though supported by a vast system of hatcheries, the combined escapement of all races of the Columbia River Basin's chinook salmon remains but seventeen to thirty-three percent of previous size. Nearly the same can be said for steelhead, where the overall run size represents sixteen to twenty-seven percent of predevelopment size. As with chinook salmon, most of these steelhead have hatchery origins; only four to seven percent of the Basin's steelhead now spawn naturally.

Steve's life is fish and fly fishing, and he has worked tirelessly to save the remnant runs of salmon and steelhead. His tone was pessimistic.

"Since I've been working in this field, it's been a steadily deteriorating situation. The rivers are tweaked more and more for hydropower. We've gone from a surplus state in hydropower to a position now where we're barely meeting the requirements of the Northwest. Because we're not in a surplus situation anymore, the Bonneville Power Administration and private PUD's are trying to maximize the water that is left in the main stem to produce power. The fish are the losers."

Idaho's State Senator Ron Beitelspacher shares that view with Pettit. As Chairman of the Pacific Fisheries Legislative Task Force, he deals with an often intractable federal bureaucracy. We met in 1990, at the Kelly Creek Fly Fishers' annual fall fair in Clarkston, Washington. For a politician, he is re-freshingly blunt. "The law calls for fifty percent of the Columbia's flow for fish and fifty percent for power. The BPA and the Army Corps of Engineers have not recognized what the law says." He explains how power from BPA is sold throughout the West, even to Los Angeles, and describes this as "helping to balance the federal budget." He charges that "The BPA moves the water through the dams when they can get the most for the power, not when it is most beneficial for the fish. They take money from here and ship it to there. That's billions of dollars going the wrong direction. The BPA isn't responsible to anyone."

Perhaps that will change. In April 1990, Idaho's Shoshone-Bannock Tribes petitioned the National Marine Fisheries Service for endangered-species status for Idaho's nearly extinct Columbia River sock-eye. Two months later Oregon Trout petitioned on behalf of Snake River spring, summer, and fall chinook, and lower Columbia coho salmon. The agency must make its determination within one year. If the ruling is favorable to these runs, the Service must submit a plan one year later detailing how the "threatened and endangered" races can be saved. Everyone knows what the principal answer will be. More water.

As Steve Pettit prepares to join the battle to save Idaho's salmon and steelhead, he says, "The utilities and the power people are screaming bloody murder. This will make the spotted owl controversy look like kindergarten."

Clearwater River

Approximately 325 miles above its mouth is the Columbia River's confluence with the Snake, a join-ing of the two main branches that form the vast interior drainage of the great river. Another 138 miles upriver, the Snake enters Idaho at Lewiston and meets the Clearwater, forty miles of desert river running between mountains narrowly terraced by a century of browsing cattle. Its branches are the North Fork; the Middle Fork, which becomes the Selway and Lochsa rivers ("smooth water" and "rough water" in Nez Perce); and the South Fork. Steelhead entering the North Fork will have trav-eled almost exactly five hundred river miles.

The North Fork's origins are in the Bitterroot Mountains, its spawning gravel the valleys of the Clearwater Mountains, a geography unremarkable among north Idaho's steelhead rivers. At least no terrible rapids nor nearly impassable falls can be identified as factors in the natural selection process that produces a population of summer steelhead that are larger than any others in the United States. But that is the overriding fact of this race, giants known to weigh over thirty pounds, the legendary steelhead of the Clearwater and all the rivers to which it flows: the Snake, the Columbia, and the mouths of a dozen tributaries.

These are remarkably fast-growing two-salt fish, rarely three- or four-salt, whereas nearly all other steelhead native to the forty rivers that feed into the Snake River are typically one-salt fish. Biologists call the North Fork strain "B" fish to distinguish them from the more common "A" fish found in other branches of the Clearwater, the Lochsa and Selway, the many tributaries of the Snake and Salmon

Doug Fagerness on the Clearwater River. →

rivers, the Grande Ronde, even the Deschutes. Of course, the respective size of different ocean ages easily distinguishes the differences, but even when the A's and B's are the same ocean age, both one-salt or both two-salt, morphological differences are evident. North Fork steelhead are noticeably larger and more robust, a true giant race, typically weighing twelve to fifteen pounds.

The A fish peak at Bonneville in July, the run dropping off dramatically in late August, with early September historically the low point in the Idaho escapement. From then until the run peaks again at the end of October, the steelhead are counted as B fish.

Steelhead reach the main stem of the Clearwater in July, and by August those A fish destined to spawn in the Middle Fork, the Selway, Lochsa, and South Fork, can be found in satisfying numbers in the Clearwater. September and October are peak angling months, the great B steelhead arriving and joining the A steelhead that delayed pushing on to their spawning tributaries with the onset of winter. They pull out of the thin water to hold in the deeper pools, or drop down into the warmer Snake until late winter warms the surface currents and sends them racing for their spawning tributaries.

Early Clearwater anglers mostly fished bait—usually roe—but shrimp, crawfish tails, and worms had their place. A few spin fishermen cast spoons, red-and-white or hammered brass. By the 1950s, locals got the hang of backtrolling with a Flatfish-like lure that had a metallic finish. Jet drives weren't yet available, but the careful operator could keep his propeller off the rocks even when the river ran at its fall low of eleven thousand cubic feet per second, big water not yet cut down to size by fly fishermen.

Local fly fishing focused on resident trout: the exquisite native cutthroat, the famous rainbows of Silver Creek and Henry's Fork of the Snake. Here flourished the science of matching hatches and the attendant tying skills that made joining this spectacle possible. New dams added to the resident trout water each year, and not a few anglers found satisfaction in that trade-off. Lakes had always been a bountiful source of quality fly fishing, so much so that special fly-fishing-only restrictions were never considered. The largest lakes, like Pend Oreille, housed Kamloop rainbows that sometimes topped thirty pounds, always a gear-fishing proposition. Except for Ted Trueblood and a handful of his closest friends, Clearwater steelhead were related to in much the same manner—something to be muscled up from the depths, dragged into the boat, and hit on the head.

Ted Trueblood lived in Nampa, Idaho, fly-fished for Clearwater steelhead, shot big game, and hunted the wealth of upland gamebirds that grew fat on cheatgrass along the rimrock benches. During the late 1950s, this Renaissance outdoorsman worked as Associate Editor of *Field & Stream*. Fellow columnists included Corey Ford, Robert Ruark, and Kip Farrington, a grand tour of Carolina quail hunts, African safaris, and Peruvian black marlin. For my rural generation, Ted Trueblood epitomized the rugged individualist, very much the West still wild, a man with an impossibly perfect surname.

Twenty years ago, I wrote to Trueblood and asked about fly patterns for Idaho's steelhead. He wrote back to say that in Idaho the Clearwater was "just about the only stream of importance." He did not tell me about his favorite steelhead river, which he truly kept secret, the mile or two of Washington's Grande Ronde just above its confluence with the Snake that could be reached only by dirt road from Lewiston, Idaho.

When Trueblood fly-fished the Clearwater for steelhead, he shared his discovery with Ed Ward, the husband of Jane Wyatt, star of TV's "Father Knows Best." Ward, a professional tennis player, related his Clearwater experiences in confidence to other Hollywood fly fishermen. This soon included two executives at Disney Studio: Ken Anderson, the studio's Art Director, and Milt Kahl, an animator. Ken Peterson and Duke Parkening soon joined the group. Like Trueblood, all had previously made annual trips to California's Klamath River for its three- and four-pound steelhead.

After his first trip to the Clearwater, Anderson showed Mel Leven a snapshot of two eighteen-pound steelhead. Mel, a songwriter and lyricist at Disney, recalled thirty years later, "At first Ken wouldn't reveal where the steelhead came from. Later in the day he told me. Idaho. 'Idaho?' I said. 'Ah, cut the crap!' But he drew out a map for me, showed me where the pools were, and I knew exactly where to go."

Mel Leven, now seventy-five, and one of the world's most knowledgeable fly fishermen (Mexican sailfish? Welsh sea trout? freshwater dorado?) is probably the most entertaining. He has been the voice in TV commercials and Sesame Street tunes, the writer of Academy Award winning songs, and cartoon voices for the late Mel Blanc. His peripatetic schedule of destination trips would easily defeat a man half his age. He talks of where he's going, not of where he's been, and I must press him about the early days of angling for the Clearwater's fabled steelhead. He says, "Oh, God! So big you couldn't hold them!" He and Terry Gilkyson, a songwriter, first visited the river together in 1960, often in the company of Duke Parkening. They fished shooting heads, he explains, homemade at first, but Wet Cel heads as soon as they became available, and ran them to 20-pound monofilament.

Mel was sure that the first Clearwater fly patterns were brought in by the Disney people from the Klamath River: the Golden Demon, Silver Hilton, and the orange-and-black Woolly Worm, for example. "We only had the Skunk, no such thing as the Green-Butt." Mel modified the original by dropping the wing, winding white hackle at the head, and tying in bead-chain eyes, kind of a short, compact Comet. "Eventually they were sold that way in Lewiston." He also fished a hot-spectrum hackle fly of red, orange, and yellow, called the Orange Bastard. Mel remembered the Cole's Comet, some of Jim Pray's optics, and the Juicy Bug. Ken McLeod's two Washington classics, the Purple Peril and Skykomish Sunrise, filled out his list.

Ed Ward fished a Princeton Tiger (orange wing and tail, black body) sometimes on a keel hook to prevent the deep running fly from fouling the bottom. (I had never heard of this approach until Lani Waller showed me the Krystal Flash Boss tied in this manner.) He liked his own Ward's Wasp. Mel still carried a few originals tied by Ward in his tightly packed and multilayered fly book. They had obviously been fished, for the hooks were points sharpened until the bare metal shone.

WARD'S WASP

Tail	Golden pheasant tippet fibers	**Hackle**	Yellow
Butt	Yellow chenille	**Wing**	Dark brown or black fur
Body	Black chenille ribbed with flat silver tinsel		

The Disney people hardly passed unnoticed, and fly fishing quickly became an accepted method of angling on the Clearwater. Then, in the early 1960s, a Seattle musician named Dub Price began fishing the nearby Grande Ronde with a sparsely dressed #8 or #10 Muddler on a floating line. He and Bob Weddell, a local from Orofino, enjoyed tremendous success, sometimes hooking forty steelhead in a day. Word of this fishing reached Keith Stonebreaker, a young Lewiston insurance agent long aware of the Disney people and their doings.

Keith had come across Lee Wulff's *The Atlantic Salmon*, and discovered the author's account of how Portland Creek anglers in Newfoundland used the "Portland Hitch," a riffling hitch, to secure salmon flies discarded by British officers because the gut leader was worn and no longer reliable. Of course, today's steelheaders are familiar with this method of pulling the fly up into the surface film so that it wakes when swinging under tension. But twenty-five years ago, the approach was revolutionary for steelhead. Keith began waking the Muddler Minnow introduced by Dub Price, and for the first time he raised Clearwater steelhead to a damp surface fly.

At the time, Idaho's two powerful U.S. Senators, Henry Dworshak and Frank Church, had gained federal approval for the construction of an enormous dam across the mouth of the North Fork of the Clearwater at Orofino. This dam, six hundred feet high, would produce a reservoir so vast that the river itself would be eliminated, and with it, the spawning grounds of the North Fork steelhead.

Arguments for its construction began with flood control, its proponents reminding citizens that on May 29, 1948, the Clearwater had flooded the valley at a rate of 177,000 cfs. This new dam, it was claimed, would protect cities as far away as Portland, Oregon. The dam had a six-turbine capacity but would operate with three and still provide for local power needs. Naturally, a huge hatchery complex would be mitigation for the loss of the North Fork's unique run of steelhead. In fact, claimed its supporters, the size of the historical run would increase because of the hatchery. The reservoir would be stocked with Kamloops trout and bass, the resulting recreation area a wonderful asset to the area. Finally, a dam on the North Fork would render a dam on the Selway unnecessary; with this dam, the Selway would be spared.

Dworshak Dam was also a pork barrel, the federal payroll a boost to the Orofino economy that would filter through the region for years to come.

Idaho's timber companies, which had grown rich by high-grading old-growth ponderosa and white pine, began running out of virgin forests to cut. One of these companies was the politically powerful Potlatch Corporation. Originally Maine-based, it had moved to northern Idaho in 1903 and purchased vast tracts of forest lands in the Clearwater watershed to supply the lumber mill and wood processing plant it was constructing in Lewiston. During spring runoff, the North Fork and the main stem of the Clearwater were used to transport logs to the mill. Potlatch owned logged-over land that would be flooded by Dworshak Reservoir and it, too, became a vocal supporter of the dam.

Dworshak was not the first dam on the Clearwater. The Washington Water Power Company had constructed a dam across the Clearwater in 1927. This generated power for the city of Lewiston and provided a log pond for the Potlatch Corporation. As a perfunctory obligation to the runs of salmon and steelhead, the company built a fishway. Its poor design allowed neither coho nor spring chinook upstream, and both runs were lost. The steelhead survived, but the run was considerably reduced. With the completion of Dworshak at hand, the dam was removed in 1973.

The coho salmon was never replaced in the Clearwater. From 1947 until 1953, small hatchery plants of chinook salmon from the Salmon River reestablished the spring chinook salmon in the Clearwater drainage.

Dworshak National Fish Hatchery currently (1990) releases about one million chinook salmon smolts and two million steelhead smolts into the Clearwater system each year. In a typical year, these plants return twenty thousand adult steelhead, half of which are caught by sport fishermen. Perhaps another fifteen hundred are netted by the Indian tribes, and at least several thousand pass upriver of Dworshak to the Middle Fork. This leaves five thousand or so steelhead surviving to return to the hatchery.

This hatchery program is no longer concerned only with returning numbers of adult steelhead to the parent "river." A danger exists that endlessly recycled hatchery stocks will inexorably reduce the genetic diversity within the race, and thus its racial distinctiveness and vitality. With all the race's eggs, literally, in one basket, viral diseases can so devastate annual hatchery production that it ultimately represents a threat to the race itself. Run timing becomes more condensed, the hatchery fish moving rapidly though the lower river to reach the hatchery. Even as hatchery production increases, the recreational value of the resource decreases.

On the Columbia River, Indians are allowed to commercially harvest thirty-three percent of the steelhead and salmon. Net mesh size is often eight inches, designed to target chinook salmon, but the largest steelhead are also caught. When no mesh-size restrictions exist, the smallest steelhead are still those most likely to pass safely through the nets. Keith Kiler, a biologist and game enforcement officer for Idaho's Department of Fish and Game, is concerned over the long-term effects of this netting. He said in 1990, "The downstream nets tend to select the larger fish in the harvest. Even when there are net mesh restrictions, our really big Clearwater fish seem to be on the decline. The net fishery is taking our three- and four-salt fish. We may eventually lose those big Clearwater steelhead."

Some of Dworshak's production has been earmarked for an experimental effort to increase the production of steelhead in the South Fork between Orofino and Kooskia. Using this area for release sites might produce a fall run where none currently exists. If successful, these steelhead would take some of the pressure off the Clearwater.

I discussed the hatchery program and my concern for the few wild stocks with Bert Bowlin, a biologist with Idaho's Department of Fish and Game. In Idaho, all wild steelhead must be released. "How many remain?" I asked. "What is their future?"

"We have two drainages in Idaho in which we're not going to release any hatchery steelhead. One is the Selway, the other is the Middle Fork of the Salmon. Also, the Lochsa is on hold for any hatchery production."

"What is their importance?"

"Nearly all the wild steelhead that arrive at Lewiston in the Clearwater are Selway stock, two thousand to five thousand fish. They come in the fall, and winter over in the Middle Fork of the Clearweater or the lower Selway. The traditional sport fishing site was Selway Falls. It was used heavily in the springtime. Now there's a fishway around the falls. The Selway supports the best steelhead habitat. It is still mostly wilderness."

"And the Lochsa?"

"The Lochsa was never much of a steelhead sport fishery. What there is comes from Fish Creek. We've termed Fish Creek the Sistine Chapel of steelhead production in the Lochsa. We're only talking about several hundred adult steelhead. But if you have wild stocks you had better hang on to them and not dilute them at all with hatchery fish."

Bert Bowlin's description of the Clearwater's tributaries underscored the importance of the North Fork, and how painful has been its loss.

"Even back in the 1970s, this dam would never have been authorized. We lost a world-renowned, naturally producing steelhead population, 'B'-run fish that had the capacity to produce fish over twenty pounds."

As Dworshak was being completed, Alan Johnson, a distance-casting champion from Chicago, came to Lewiston and fished the first Bomber on the Clearwater. He was an Atlantic salmon fisherman, a regular on New Brunswick's Miramichi River, where Bombers were being waked to entice salmon to the surface. The discouraging decline of the Canadian fishery found him investigating the North Fork for its giant steelhead. Idaho became Johnson's second home.

Keith Stonebreaker discovered the natural deer-hair Bomber through Alan Johnson, and was soon tying the original without hackle and calling it a Cigar Butt. The low-riding, slick-bodied fly with a white calf-tail wing and tail did not skate so much as wake, and it possessed a rocking motion like a little boat plowing though a sea. Best of all, it was simple to tie and enticing to steelhead. He also married the Purple Peril and Green-Butt Skunk, calling the hybrid offspring a Purple Skunk. He did not extol its effectiveness and needn't have. That Keith used it was reason enough for others to fish it. These two patterns became the first popular steelhead flies with Idaho origins.

PURPLE SKUNK

Tail	Grey squirrel tail, sparse	**Hackle**	Purple
Butt	Fluorescent green chenille	**Wing**	Grey squirrel tail, sparse
Body	Purple chenille ribbed with silver tinsel		

When I last visited the Clearwater, in late September 1990, I intended to stay two or three weeks, ample time to find a few steelhead before the catch and release season ended on October 15. That does not necessarily end the fly fishing, but locals feel the change in regulations erodes the civilized nature of their sport. This is, they remark, the start of their "combat fishing," when hundreds of jet boats, the "aluminum hatch," roar up and down the river and jockey for room before settling down to back-trolling plugs. The steelhead that hold inside the currents along the shore, those lies that make fly fishing possible on the truly big steelhead rivers, now become rare, the constant angling pressure driving them into deeper water. Boatloads of anglers with six, or even eight, rods working plugs can now reach those steelhead, and they do so with a vengeance. These gear fishermen have waited impatiently for weeks while the fly fishers mucked around with their long rods. The Clearwater is full of steelhead by mid-October, surplus stock Dworshak can't possibly handle. Fall is harvest time. It's in the air, like the smell of windfall apples and backyard smokers filled with venison sausage.

Keith Stonebreaker

The "catch-and-kill" season continues through December, less a time of competition between gear and fly fishermen than of gear fishermen with themselves. Nuthouse Pool near Orofino has been the scene of some locally famous battles. "That's one of the pools where the baseball bats and guns come out," an angler told me.

Much of the Clearwater is a tailwater river, a flow sedate and dependable, the modest changes in water level determined more by power needs at Dworshak than by seasonal rains. This robotic state should be perfect for fly fishing. The river usually comes to Lewiston at fifty-six degrees, a fact changed little by the lingering desert summer. This fall, the Snake flowed at a tepid seventy-two degrees, nearly lethal to migrating steelhead, and created a situation the Army Corps of Engineers calls a "thermal barrier."

A thermal barrier occurs when the Snake runs so warm that steelhead won't move on the water. The Clearwater, running at 12,000 cfs in late September, should mix with the Snake and improve this situation below their confluence, but that does not happen. Instead, the Clearwater slides under the much warmer Snake, a substratum of cold water leading from the base of Lower Granite Dam to the Snake and the Clearwater. The steelhead that brave the Snake River in the fishway have little encouragement to continue their journey to either of the drainages. Those that do are often schizophrenic, temporarily ignoring their Snake River origins for the Clearwater and its more tolerable temperatures. I hear about two steelhead that are caught in the Clearwater in two weeks. Both are "A" hatchery fish, possibly with Middle Fork origins, but probably not. The "B" steelhead are still a dam or two away and showing no signs of homing in on the water spilling over Dworshak. Only cold weather would cause that. I thought of what Roland Holmberg, an Atlantic salmon guide, once said: "When I get up in the morning and the sun is shining, I want to cry." He was flying from Sweden to fish with me and would arrive the next week. I began praying for lousy weather.

Thermal barriers make bad public relations. The engineers at Dworshak release extra water to get the steelhead moving. They announce this as if the act were a benevolent sacrifice. Locals greet the news cynically. They call this "ramping up the river." The Corps is required by law to provide adequate flow for the escapement of the Clearwater's steelhead and salmon, but more cold water under warm water doesn't move the fish. Fly fishers know that raising the Clearwater only obscures many of the best steelhead lies, making them difficult or impossible to fish properly.

I stayed in Lewiston with Bob and Toni Wagoner, fishing the Clearwater each day with friends, while Bob tended to his business, the Fly Den, a commercial fly-tying operation that supplies companies from Alaska to Vermont with flies for every imaginable gamefish.

I have found that the typical Clearwater fly fisher can give you *Greased Line Fishing*, chapter and verse. He is committed to skating and waking dries, and swimming the most sparsely dressed wets of any steelhead river, #6's and #8's with only a few strands of hair for a wing. The dressings are unique, a low-water style strongly influenced by Mike Arhutick's Green Ant, the most popular of the Clearwater dressings.

GREEN ANT

Tail	Golden pheasant tippet, very short, and tied well forward of the bend	**Hackle**	Black
		Wing	Grey squirrel tail, very sparse
Butt	Peacock herl		
Body	Fluorescent green floss		

Other Clearwater dressings often take this form. For example, Marty Sherman's The Stewart has the tail of tippet fibers shortened up, and the black body with gold rib is thinned out while the wing of black calf-tail topped with a few strands of orange calf-tail becomes a few hairs of grey squirrel tail dyed orange. The black hackle is no more than two turns—a very different-looking The Stewart.

Besides Stonebreaker's Purple Skunk and a few other Ants (the traditional Red, for example), is Jimmy Green's Green-Butt Skunk. Never mind that the pattern looks very similar to the Black Bear, the popular Atlantic-salmon fly. Anglers on the Clearwater and neighboring Snake and Grande Ronde rivers care as much for the dressing as they do for Jimmy, a revered folk hero in these parts. He and his wife, Carol, live in a splendid mountaintop home overlooking Ted Trueblood's old Grand Ronde beat. Jimmy designs rods for Don Green at Sage, and the long-retired tournament caster still lays out a line with wonderful grace. Visiting them is an homage, and one I would not fail to make.

When I fished with Bill Alspach and Glenn Cruickshank, two highly regarded local experts, they cast Bombers while I swam low-water wets. I wasn't sure that so small a wet fly was necessary, and I raised two steelhead to a #1 Purple Peril. These were both "A" steelhead, no more than five pounds, but one came from the main current to run the fly down right to the beach. Was the fish's miss due to the size of the fly? I think not. Glenn raised a steelhead to his dry, and we found no other fish. We worked miles of river, including Coyote's Fish Net, and Ant and Yellow Jacket, two pools with names from Nez Perce folklore.

"You can see these figures on the hillside if you have enough hallucinogenic drugs," said Glenn. He pointed across the river to the birthmark of black basalt stark against the pale grasses and sagebrush.

"It's no secret where to find the best pools," I said. A highway borders the Clearwater for forty miles—eighty miles of shoreline not counting the braids. I have arrived at these highway pools before first light only to find anglers standing at the ready in the dark. The first person through will almost certainly raise a steelhead, a good reason to be on the road at four in the morning when steelhead are in the river. In their own way, fly fishers are just as competitive as gear fishermen for time on the right water.

We floated the river in Glenn's McKenzie boat and worked both banks to fish the many secondary pools, obscure lies the visiting angler is not likely to discover and even less likely to be told about. Where the Clearwater braids, we pulled the boat out and fished the island runs. The many creases and flats were the Clearwater in miniature, and each of us become lost in his own water.

When Bill Alspach tires of the Bomber, he ties on a very large Bloody Muddler on a dropper with a small wet fly secured at the end of the leader. The Bloody Muddler, a local tie by LeRoy Hyatt, has

Bill Alspach and Roland Holmberg on the Snake River.

all but replaced the original in Idaho's steelhead circles. Bill fishes it greased-line, a big locator fly plowing surface currents and moving steelhead from long distances. When steelhead rise to investigate the commotion, they are seduced by the petite offering bringing up the rear. On no other river have I seen this arrangement employed so frequently.

We didn't see any more steelhead, and our flies couldn't locate the hidden fish. This discouraged me. Steelhead are telltale animals. If an angler does not blunder about, he can often observe them

holding in various lies. Moving fish frequently roll while passing up a pool. A steelhead will crash the surface for no apparent reason. A large boil on the fly is almost certainly a steelhead. Nothing of this sort happened in the afternoon, and I became certain the river was empty of fish other than the schools of squawfish that darted away from the shadow of our boat.

I fished with Keith Stonebreaker on his favorite piece of water. Keith, Jack Hemingway, and Will Godfrey had served on Idaho's Game Commission together, and had been instrumental in setting aside twelve hundred miles of river to be managed as catch and release water. Keith had a clear understanding of the big picture in all its bureaucratic glory, and he knew how to present a certain fly on a specific slot of holding water. He could not, however, find a steelhead where none existed.

One day Craig Lannigan ran Bill Alspach and me from pool to pool on *Sushi*, his nineteen-foot boat. "Last year at this time we had forty thousand steelhead over the Lower Granite Dam. This year it's five thousand," said Craig. In case I didn't appreciate the arithmetic, he added, "That's one-eighth as many."

"That's plenty! If only they would come on up!" I answered.

Craig once took a wild Clearwater buck that was forty-four inches long. His dad, Darrell, caught a hen that weighed twenty-four pounds, fourteen ounces. Both were late-season fish. I found Craig to be one of the few local anglers who pushed his fly fishing well into winter. "When the water temperature drops below forty degrees, I fish my December Gold," he said. The beautiful dressing—often tied on a double hook—was somewhat like Haig-Brown's Golden Girl.

DECEMBER GOLD

Tail Large golden pheasant crest
Body Hot orange dubbing palmered with orange saddle

Wing Matching golden pheasant tippet feathers, set low and extending to the tail

At the end of the week, Danny Diaz and I went twenty miles upstream to the town of Lenore to begin a long float with his high-speed raft. My friend knows all the upcountry ravines and the white-tailed deer that hide in their deep cover. Each year he hikes a thousand miles to learn the habits of trophy bucks, and he is known nationally for his hunting success. He steelheads with equal enthusiasm, and he located several fish, which we could not raise.

The valley of the Clearwater is less arid here, hillsides of ponderosa pine contributing to a setting as beautiful as any in steelhead fly fishing. Yellow daisies and blue asters carpeted the river bars, while blue-winged olives filled the air above the long pool. An occasional October caddis sent me hunting through my fly box for a burnt orange dressing. I counted these blessings, looked at the hillside far above my head, and gave a shudder.

In the mid-1970s, the Army Corps of Engineers announced plans to install a fourth turbine in Dworshak Dam and to build a regulating dam on the Clearwater at Lenore to moderate the extra flow. As a formality, public hearings would be held in Lewiston. Fishermen still like to remind one another about what happened. Five hundred outraged Idahoans showed up, each sick to death of the Army Corps of Engineers and its dams. While the Association of Northwest Steelheaders spearheaded the opposition, it was LeRoy Seth, a spokesperson for the Nez Perce, who best summed up local feeling for the dam. "It's about time for the cowboys and Indians to get together and fight the cavalry!" he shouted.

The dam was never built, a fact Danny and I appreciated as we floated through the canyon.

I joined LeRoy Hyatt for two days on the Grande Ronde, water ten to twenty miles above the mouth of the Snake. This is wildly spectacular country where the ancient river has cut away mountain slopes to make stupendous cliffs of their basaltic cores. Hackberry, the "forest" climax tree, grows twisted and desiccated by canyon winds until the groves look prehistoric. Sumac, oddly lush on the harsh talus

← LeRoy Hyatt leads a Bloody Muddler through the Grande Ronde's Hole in the Wall.

slopes, gives sparse cover to the coveys of chukar that call down from rock outcroppings. We saw cock pheasant around patches of poison ivy that had turned fall crimson. Just before Hole-in-the-Wall, a pool named for the old stagecoach tunnel it borders, LeRoy herded twenty-five wild turkeys along with his pickup. Golden eagles, prairie falcons, and bighorn sheep kept me squinting skyward all day.

Almost with the first cast I saw a four-pound steelhead hurrying through Hole-in-the-Wall, a traveling fish searching for cooler water upstream. Our river was sixty-six degrees—tepid, but not dangerous for steelhead. LeRoy and I each raised a fish, the tiny vanguard of what was to arrive when the weather turned cold. The next day, LeRoy caught several smallmouth bass with his Bloody Muddler.

"If you're finding bass, you won't find steelhead," went the local adage, and it was true.

I returned to Lewiston, waited for Roland Holmberg, and for the Snake to cool. Most of all, I waited for the steelhead. On the day Roland arrived from Sweden, Indian summer still hung in the valley of the Clearwater, a prolonged plague of clear skies. Bob Wagoner proudly explained to my Viking friend that Lewiston was in a banana belt. Roland caught my look of dismay. "The problem isn't *stale* fish," I said. "The problem is *no* fish."

We haunted the rivers, visited old friends, and talked of fly fishing. Roland had guided Jack Hemingway on Norway's Aa in July. I hadn't seen Jack since we roomed together two years before at Far West Lodges on the Bulkley River. I knew him to be a fine fly fisher who enjoyed putting his rod down to chase after grouse. Now he was building a cabin above the Grande Ronde for his wife and their bird dogs. He and Keith Stonebreaker, his old pal on the Game Commission, joined us for an evening of steelhead gossip.

Bob Wagoner took Roland and me to fish the Snake below its confluence with the Grande Ronde. Jimmy Green was there with Mel Leven and later with Bob Stroebel, harbingers of the season's houseguests. We drove up to his new house and visted his fly-tying room. "Jimmy," I said, "let me describe a rod you should design."

"I've discovered a new kind of cast." he answered.

I showed Roland the gravel points that reach out into the Snake to create holding water for steelhead. Only a few anglers were about, and most of those cast two-handed rods. Long casts really weren't necessary, but when standing up to a river so vast that human sounds are lost, the big rods help one to maintain a sense of proportion. Roland's salmon rod sliced at the air to send a shooting head far out into the river, the fly swinging through a gigantic arc. His expectations were not yet dulled, and his excitement rekindled my own enthusiasm.

The Snake River drainage once produced more steelhead than any other in the world. No more. Three dams, Brownlee, Oxbow, and Hells Canyon effectively eliminated all runs of salmon and steelhead from the upper Snake River, a vast drainage with dozens of rivers covering most of southern Idaho. When completed in 1959, Brownlee proved too high for a fish ladder. Idaho Power trucked the steelhead and salmon around. A net was placed to capture downstream smolts, but they passed through the mesh and into the turbines. Two years later, the effort was scrapped, and the steelhead runs to the Weiser (a favorite with Ted Trueblood), Payette, Boise, and dozens of other rivers were lost.

Oxbow and Hells Canyon Dams added to a power-generating complex capable of producing a million kilowatts per hour. Mitigation for the loss of salmon and steelhead—a requirement by the Federal Regulatory Commission before a license can be issued—consisted of a steelhead egg-taking station on the Pahsimeroi River and a steelhead hatchery at Niagara Springs.

Due to water-level fluctuations, the sixty miles *below Brownlee* were also lost as spawning habitat. For that, there was no mitigation.

Lynn "Radar" Miller invited Roland and me to float the Salmon River from Rice Creek to the Snake confluence, about forty miles, and then twenty miles of the Snake to Heller's Bar, the point just below the mouth of the Grande Ronde. Guidebooks claim this "River of No Return" is the longest river entirely in one state in the country. Radar promised a wilderness trip with dangerous rapids and a

Rusty Gore and Roland Holmberg on Idaho's Salmon River,
the legendary "River of No Return."

remarkable assortment of gamefish, everything from sturgeon to smallmouth bass and Kamloops trout. He said that some of the river's "A" steelhead had already slipped up the river, and that its Middle Fork held a native run of "B" steelhead that reached twenty pounds and more. The sun still blazed down on Idaho's rivers, and nothing yet was really stirring from the lower Snake's deep pools. Should the steelhead start moving, they would reach the Salmon as quickly as the Clearwater.

The nickname "Radar" relates to the X-ray vision he depended on for years when running huge commercial jet boats into the Hells Canyon of the Snake and always avoiding barely submerged rocks. Now he owns his own business, the Lower Salmon Express, and enjoys an epicurean approach to river rafting. "I only have four cans of food on board," he told me proudly. He also had four coolers filled with salmon fillets, beef steaks, fresh vegetables, fine wines, and sinfully fattening desserts. Rusty Gore, his partner on our float, is a fellow outfitter from Salmon, Idaho, who has guided anglers for steelhead in the far upper reaches of the Salmon River for twenty years. On this trip, he would run the McKenzie boat while Radar operated the nineteen-foot commissary raft cum garbage scow. "*Everything* we bring in is brought out," he said, and pointed to the raft. Lashed down atop the mountain of gear was a spotlessly clean portable toilet.

Rusty calls his beloved fish "Mile High Steelhead," because they are caught a mile above sea level, in the Stanley Basin, more than eight hundred miles from the ocean. He thought that with dams having exterminated so many interior races, these steelhead now migrate farther than any other. I asked whether some of the steelhead we hoped to find on the lower river would eventually spawn in the Stanley Basin area.

"This is a spring fishery, March and April," he said. "The hatchery fish are brick red, especially the males. We call them 'factory fish.' They enter the lower Salmon in the summer and fall. But the native Stanley steelhead, 'A' fish twenty-three to twenty-seven inches, come in bright. They winter over in the Hanford Reach, the part of the Columbia River below Priest Rapids Dam, and then race up to Stanley Basin in the spring. But I don't think anyone is sure exactly when they come in from the ocean."

"Why do they hold in the Columbia?" I asked. "Why not in the Snake or the lower Salmon?"

Rusty wasn't sure. "Ranchers are dewatering, and the drop in water level leaves the Salmon warmer in summer and colder in winter."

"But the steelhead wouldn't know that from Hanford Reach," I said. Many interior races drop down out of spawning rivers for deep pools in larger rivers with the onset of winter. But these Stanley steelhead come in and park. It almost seemed like a genetic trait.

Rusty wondered if an absolutely pure strain of wild Stanley steelhead now existed. They mix with "natural steelhead," hatchery fish allowed to spawn above the hatchery projects. He was sure that Stanley fish were different genetically. Were they slowly being lost to hatchery plants?

During the drought of early fall, the Salmon is a small turbulent river flowing at 3,000 cfs, a "pool and drop" river falling an average of ten feet per mile. The carefree rafting water of summer becomes rapids fanged with exposed boulders, nasty little runs that sent Radar and Rusty scouting ahead to time the currents and work out strategy. Both are experienced watermen, and we made our way down the whitewater chutes with no mishaps.

The river was sixty-two degrees, down from seventy degrees in early September, still warm enough to keep smallmouth bass and enormous squawfish chasing after our Woolly Buggers. Where the river broke into glides, Roland and I found planted Kamloops rainbows to sixteen inches with our steelhead flies. This fishing kept us from despairing over the whereabouts of the steelhead. We passed four anglers who had been pulling plugs for a week and had yet to land a steelhead. "Hooked one yesterday and lost it," they called to us They were like men who had run a hundred quarters through a slot machine. Their luck—and ours—was about to change. The odds promised nothing less.

We camped on white-sand beaches, set up the kitchen shelter, and baited up the sturgeon rod. Roland and I filled the firebox with dense limbs of curled leaf mahogany and settled in for campfire stories. Radar told about white sturgeon, how they were once anadromous and how they are now

An Idaho "A" steelhead and a Night Dancer.

entirely landlocked because of the dams. Like wild steelhead, all sturgeon must be released. They proved safe from our casual attentions, however, and the big rod remained a conversation piece.

The second night, the wind blew so hard we dared not leave our free-standing tents for fear of losing them and their contents. This was the first big southerly of fall, the collapse of the high pressure system that had caused Idaho's long Indian summer. The rain that followed was not much of a show, a few midday sprinkles between sun-breaks, but hourly the day grew colder, and the next morning we awoke to find water in the kitchen pail frozen solid. The river and the air temperature felt frigid, the surface currents only fifty-six degrees in early afternoon.

As the outfitters busied themselves with lunch, I worked a thin low-water Night Dancer through the run that ended a short distance above the Snake. A steelhead immediately rose to the fly and turned to dash downstream, a perfect take that took the point of the hook to the corner of its jaw. This hatchery steelhead, a bright and spirited hen weighing five to six pounds, took me fifty yards into my backing on the first run. She was in all ways a wonderful fish, an "A" steelhead five hundred miles, eight dams, and eight fishways from the ocean, running downriver so hard that my heart was pounding in my ears.

I released her to continue her journey. I was sure—albeit wishfully so—that she would reach those distant headwaters to spawn. I was equally certain that in a life almost impossibly circuitous, she would never return to spawn a second time. Historically, several steelhead from each hundred managed a second spawning. Dams reduced those odds. One in a thousand is hardly an expectation; more a statistical degree of error than a contribution to the future of a run.

I was finally in the thick of the fishing, and a week remained before the catch-and-release season ended. This was my window of opportunity, less this year than perhaps ever before. No matter. These free rising summer steelhead of the Snake River's tributaries give classic definition to my sport as on no other waters in the United States.

Al Knudson takes home a Deer Creek native he rose to a dry fly, July 18, 1955. *Photo Credit: Ralph Wahl*

12

NORTH FORK STILLAGUAMISH RIVER

W H E N Walt Johnson paused on our wade up the long tailout, I could hear him over the sounds of the Stillaguamish. "The cabin I owned is in that grove of trees. See, to the left of the red cabin? That one belonged to Frank Headrick. Now his son owns it. Just downstream from my place was Wes Drain's."

"Didn't Al Knudson have a cabin here, too?" I asked.

"Not really. Kind of a shelter, you know, four posts and a roof. There was a picnic table and an outhouse. Al kept one of those big commercial soft drink coolers out front. Had his property next to Drain's place. Some people had lots just off the highway for trailer sites. Ralph Wahl had a trailer here for a while."

"And Enos Bradner?" I said.

"Oh, Brad and Sandy Bacon owned a place upstream of Headrick's. You can't see it from here. And there was Ken and George McLeod. They had a concrete cabin just up from here on the Flats, just below the Deer Creek Riffle."

The little colony on the North Fork of the Stillaguamish River marks the birthplace of steelhead fly fishing in Washington, its many famous anglers now revered as the sport's founding fathers. Walt settled here in 1943, and he was the first. He and his friends built their summer cabins just above where the Stillaguamish makes an extremely sharp bend, the water called Elbow Hole. He told me the run had fished well in the early days. Two generations of spring freshets had cut away at the gravel

169

bank, the sweeping bend gradually becoming a deep, hooking millrace. No one bothers to fish it today, though the lower end remains classic water.

"You can't believe how the river has changed. Most good holding water lasts five, maybe six years. Then the bottom fills up, the river changes course, something happens to make it different," said Walt. This was no complaint, and there was no hint of regret. I found him as keen as ever to understand the ways of his river.

Mike Kinney and Trey Combs on the Elbow Hole.

"You still don't have far to walk for your fishing," I said. A couple hundred yards of dirt road connected Walt's house to his daughter's and the short path to his home pool. He had fished this water thousands of times in forty years, and he would fish it again this morning.

"No, but even after I retired and had built my new place on the south side of the river, I kept the cabin. Gosh! I hated to sell the place. After a few years, I did," he said, and we continued our wade up the center of the river for the top end of Pocket Water.

Walt's friends also sold out. During the 1970s, the summer homes along the river were routinely burglarized. Even stoves were stolen. At the same time, some of the most elderly anglers could no longer regularly work a fly through the river's pools. They were free with stories of their river and could recount better times, claiming they had enjoyed the North Fork and her steelhead when both were at their best. This was no curmudgeonly view of the river they were leaving. For nearly two generations, they had sampled their fly water from early June until fall, and as they found the runs declining, a foreboding sense grew that their beloved Stillaguamish and her steelhead were also being burglarized. Although there was no shortage of opinions as to the reason, they knew for certain that they had always owed their fishing to Deer Creek, the principal spawning tributary for North Fork steelhead. Most suspected that logging had caused the erosion that silted in the creek and buried its spawning habitat. If true, most of the eggs and fry in the gravel were suffocating. As always, hatchery fish could mitigate the shortfall. The old-timers said, in effect, that two wrongs won't make Deer Creek right. Discouraged and disillusioned, they quit the river, until only Walt Johnson remained to cast his fly each day.

We waded to Pocket Water, where jagged midchannel boulders once could house a dozen Deer Creek steelhead. Sediment has so filled the valleys that today their peaks barely break through the river bottom, and the upper part of the pool is no longer reliable. However, the bottom remains the "pocket," a depot of shade and faint currents where steelhead collect before picking up the line of traveling water and continuing their journey.

Walt started through the pool with a delicate 4-weight, his favorite rod for summer work. He cast a Deep Purple Spey on tight loops, the fly dropping with scarcely a ripple into the gut of the pool. A sink-tip line was a concession on this June day to early-returning fish and to water still cold with spring. He did not like this approach, but he would not argue with reason. Walt said there might be time, come evening, to exercise his memory with a dry fly down Pocket. In the meantime, the years fell away as the river boiled against his waders, and each cast traced a strong arc over the cabins below.

The history of fly fishing for steelhead on the Stillaguamish River in large measure begins and ends with the history of Deer Creek, for the summer-run steelhead of this tributary were what brought fame to the river and created such folk heroes of its anglers. The reason was uncomplicated. Before disappearing into inaccessible canyon pools to wait out sexual maturation, steelhead would hold for weeks in the North Fork immediately below the Deer Creek confluence. Almost no summer-run steelhead spawned above Deer Creek, either in the main stem or its tributaries.

The Deer Creek summer-run steelhead is a highly specialized race. Curt Kraemer, a regional fish biologist for Washington's Department of Wildlife Region Four, determined from scale samples that ninety-five percent of the steelhead were three years old, having spent one year in the ocean after a premigrant residency in Deer Creek of two years (2/1). At this age they were small, four to five pounds and twenty-four to twenty-five inches. Size extremes found were nineteen and twenty-nine and a half inches, *but all were still one-year ocean steelhead.* The remaining five percent consisted almost entirely of premigrants that had spent three years in Deer Creek (3/1), and repeat spawning steelhead (2/1S1). The largest steelhead he examined was thirty inches and approximately ten pounds. Kraemer told me that among the native Deer Creek steelhead, "two-salt fish are extremely rare."

This small, one-year ocean race was typical of native summer-run steelhead in the short, steep gradient rivers of Puget Sound. They ascended to the extreme headwaters to spawn, periodically fed in fresh water, and rose freely to a fly.

Two aspects of this race's life history make it vulnerable to loss. Its spawning environment is fragile, the headwater trickles especially sensitive to any loss of streamside cover and to erosion. The Deer Creek steelhead is, for all practical purposes, a three-generation race in which the entire spawning generation enters the river at one time. (On other steelhead rivers there may be as many as a dozen or more life histories covering many different ages from a single generation.) Any loss of spawning habitat will immediately have a devastating effect on a large percentage of the entire race.

Trey Combs wakes a dry above the Deer Creek confluence. →

These free-rising steelhead and their relationship with Deer Creek were well known locally when Zane Grey first visited the Stillaguamish in 1919, a trip he described in *Tales of Freshwater Fishing*. He was making his annual sojourn to Vancouver Island's Campbell River for tyee salmon when a Seattle stopover left him time to pursue the area's summer-run steelhead. Local fishing tackle dealers suggested Deer Creek, as did two Seattle anglers, "Hiller and Van Tassel." Accessibility, the two men promised, would be a problem. An alternate plan they encouraged involved fishing a pool at the mouth of the creek, and, yes, they would guide Grey and his party.

Grey noted that both men were bait fishermen who employed fly rods and fly reels with enameled lines, stowing the lines in canvas baskets strapped to their waists. A flip of the rod sent the sinker and a small hook baited with salmon eggs out across the pool. None of the party caught any steelhead, and Grey pressed on, more determined than ever. He hired a guide from Lake McMurray, who would take them all the way in to Deer Creek. After a harrowing trip by logging train and an arduous overnight hike, they reached their destination, "the most beautiful trout water I had ever seen," wrote Grey. Here on this remote tributary of the North Fork of the Stillaguamish, Grey hooked his first steelhead, "savage and beautiful, fight in every line of his curved body."

Nine years later, in 1927, Roderick Haig-Brown traveled from his native England to the Northwest to work in the lumber camps. This led to his first experience with steelhead, an introduction told with wry good humor in his marvelous classic, *A River Never Sleeps*.

It was January when I came with a rod to my first river in North America—the Pilchuck near Snohomish in Washington. My good friend Ed Dunn took me there, and we caught nothing, at least partly because neither of us knew very much about the fish we were after; but I cannot forget the day, because it was the first day and it started me thinking of steelhead—a habit I haven't grown out of yet. Two or three days later we went to the Stillaguamish, and I remember that day too, though the river was roaring down in tawny flood and I suppose we hadn't a chance to fish even if we had known all there was to know . . . Soon after that I went up to work at a logging camp near Mount Vernon in Washington, first as a scaler and then as a member of the survey crew.

Bunkhouse stories were of "cougar and bear and steelhead," often told solely to impress the young immigrant.

. . . the steelhead talk was distant; the fish ran in June and July, which was six months away, to Deer Creek, a good many miles through the woods . . . Ed Phipps told me he had gone into Deer Creek the previous July, hooked a steelhead and lost rod, reel, and line before he had time to think of moving.

Haig-Brown's first opportunity to fish Deer Creek occurred early the following June when his survey team was camped only four miles from the fabled water. Using a nine-foot casting rod and a silex reel, he fished spoons and Devon minnows and caught Dolly Varden trout to four pounds. He doubted these fish were steelhead, and he hoped they were not, for their size and spirit were a disappointment. Late on the second day, however, while working a Devon minnow through a deep pool: "There was no question of striking; he was away before I had the rod point up, taking line with a speed that made the ratchet of the reel echo back from the timber. Then he jumped three times, going away, and the sunset was gold on his side each time."

This first steelhead was free shortly after the third jump, and it set things right for him, properly fitting what he had been led to believe about steelhead. He does not elaborate on how he came to return to Deer Creek, but several weeks later he caught his first steelhead, "a fish of seven pounds."

That two of the most notable angling writers of this century both fished an obscure creek in Washington for their introduction to steelhead is a wonderful coincidence, but it was not overly significant. As Zane Grey's experiences illustrate, the "secret" of Deer Creek and the North Fork below their confluence was general knowledge among Seattle anglers by 1919. At the time, these waters didn't provide Puget Sound anglers with the *best* summer-run steelhead fishing, but with nearly the *only* such fishing. There was simply nothing else with which to compare it.

Years after Grey's and Haig-Brown's departures, when Washington fly fishermen were diligently mining other steelhead runs, Deer Creek summer steelhead still numbered in the thousands, far more than in any other of the many rivers entering Puget Sound. That makes the North Fork's conversion to a fly-only river all the more remarkable.

In 1934, the Snohomish County Sportsmen's Association proposed to the State Game Commission that one mile of the North Fork below the Deer Creek confluence, and Deer Creek in its entirety, be administered as fly-fishing only water. The proposal was accepted, followed immediately by objections from gear fishermen and valley residents. Rather than take a firm stand on the issue, the Game Commission backed down, reversed their decision, and hid behind the bureacratic convenience of closing the river to all fishing. A few fly fishermen from the Steelhead Trout Club of Seattle urged their membership to take up the cause. When more devisiveness resulted from the discussions, they broke with their club and formed the Washington Fly Fishing Club. This new organization, with Enos Bradner as its first president, immediately set in motion a series of fly-fishing-only proposals that would forever change the face of Northwest angling. After a club resolution embodying their proposals was approved by a county sports council, it was submitted to the State Game Commission and passed into law in January, 1941. The North Fork of the Stillaguamish was to be exclusively fly-only during the summer-run season, the first steelhead river ever to be so designated.

Bradner was an obscure figure who had moved from the Midwest in 1929, opened a bookstore on Capital Hill in Seattle, and developed a passion for steelhead on a fly. Other charter members in the new organization included Letcher Lambuth, an inventive bamboo rod builder, Dawn Holbrook, a professional fly tyer who would pass his skills on to many a "Stilly" regular, and Ken McLeod, the outdoor editor of the Seattle *Post-Intelligencer*. Against an opposition often voicing outrage—elitist and discriminatory, they said—the fledgling fly club campaigned tirelessly for continued support of the new regulation by the State Sportsmen's Council and the outdoor clubs it represented. The Washington Fly Fishing Club's victory remained tenuous for months, but this time the Game Commission remained steadfast in its support, and opposition to the ruling was gradually beaten back.

According to Steve Raymond in his book *The Year of the Angler*, Bradner was the first to take a steelhead from the North Fork under the new fly-only regulation, a divinely wrought ending to an often bitter struggle.

Washington Fly Fishing Club members, confident that their more enlightened sport fishing ideals would protect this unique race of summer steelhead, now set about enjoying the fruits of their labor. As Walt Johnson had pointed out to me, two principals in the struggle, Bradner and McLeod, soon had cabins on the North Fork and were his neighbors for many summers to come.

Bradner, at age fifty, became outdoor editor of the Seattle *Times*, a position he held until well into his seventies. He authored *Northwest Angling*, the bible for Washington fly fishermen, and a book I nearly memorized before my copy fell apart. When I first wrote to him in the late 1960s, he was an institution—I was in awe of the man. He carefully answered every question I posed, banging out the letters on an old typewriter. I loved him for that. His Brad's Brat is still one of the most popular of all steelhead patterns, and if I tie it sparse with red and burnt orange angora wool (or seal fur), wind the webby brown hackle as a collar, and use orange tying thread throughout, I think it is a good October Caddis dressing.

Ken McLeod is now remembered for the record-size steelhead he and his son, George, caught from the Kispiox, and for three of the most effective and enduring fly patterns in steelheading, the McLeod Ugly, the Purple Peril, and the Skykomish Sunrise. The McLeod Ugly is "ugly" only when in the company of classic low-water dressings and fly choices are being made on the basis of aesthetics rather than effectiveness. Steelhead find the dressing so attractive that hardcore steelhead fly fishers wouldn't be without a few. The Purple Peril, the original purple steelhead dressing, is now about a half-century old, and one of the ten or so patterns I always have in a variety of sizes and styles. The Skykomish Sunrise is simply the most popular steelhead fly pattern in the history of the sport, and it is often the first dressing the neophyte ties and fishes.

Walt's fly now worked through the deep holding water that marked the end of Pocket Water. No steelhead moved to the fly, and he repeated the cast again and again. When this final effort had exhausted his patience, he called up to me. "I don't know where they are anymore! The steelhead just boom through now!"

"Hatchery fish are like that!" I called back. That was true enough, an imprinting flaw too often possessed by "designer" steelhead, and these fish, bound for the Whitehorse Rearing Ponds, were typical. This particular state of affairs was something of a paradox. Walt was both an outspoken advocate of wild steelhead and the man who assisted in the first successful rearing and planting of summer-run steelhead. That occurred forty years ago, when pioneering hatchery operations for salmonids were already seen as a cheap alternative to preserving runs naturally.

By the mid-1940s, North Fork anglers had grown concerned that summer-run steelhead escapements were down. In an effort to address the problem, the Washington Fly Fishing Club formed the Summer-run Steelhead Committee and named Walt Johnson as its chairman. Two schools of thought prevailed on how the situation might be improved, and both involved artificial propagation. The first called for plants in Deer Creek. The second approach—more daring and controversial—involved planting smolts well above the Deer Creek confluence in hopes that a strong, self-supporting run of summer-run steelhead could be established there. If successful, the new run would spread out angling pressure while increasing the total escapement.

Ken and George McLeod and Enos Bradner approached Don Clark, Director of the Washington Department of Game, and proposed securing brood stock in winter with rod and reel from Deer Creek. The plan was approved and, fortunately, the steelhead failed to cooperate. Only then did it occur to the Committee that winter-run stock were also in Deer Creek, and there was no way to distinguish between the two seasonal runs. At the time, no one was even certain whether the summer-run steelhead was a genetic strain that would breed true, or if other factors caused spawning returns at various seasons. Taking no chances, Lew Garlick, the fishery biologist in charge of the project, set a weir at the mouth of Deer Creek in the summer of 1945 and trapped seventy-two adult steelhead. These were trucked to the hatchery at Arlington and placed in a holding pond until they fully matured. The fish proved to be extremely temperamental, and mortality was high. Only thirty-two survived, the eleven females producing 35,340 fertilized eggs. More than two years later, in April 1948, 22,628 young steelhead were ready for release. After dividing them into three groups for the three different release sites selected, each fish was fin-clipped and injected with a tiny celluloid tag, a code that would identify these sites. On April 10, 1948, Sandy Bacon, Enos Bradner, Wes Drain, Frank Headrick, and Walt Johnson released 4,950 steelhead smolts in Deer Creek at miles 10 and 15 from the mouth. Game Department biologists made additional releases at the mouth of Squire Creek, *above the Deer Creek confluence* (4,655), and at Brown's Creek, a tributary of Squire Creek (11,764). (Seven hundred nine smolts bearing no marks of any kind were released; five hundred fifty marked Deer Creek smolts were released in Minter Creek near Tacoma, Washington, and two of these steelhead returned one year later.)

Returns were very disappointing. Anglers caught six, or perhaps seven, hatchery steelhead below the Deer Creek confluence. (Frank Headrick caught one.) These fish were either Deer Creek or Squire Creek plants, and all proved to be one-year ocean fish that averaged four to five pounds. Apparently no angling recovery was made from the nearly twelve thousand smolts planted in Brown's Creek. Surely other steelhead survived to maturity, but no angling record exists. No two-year ocean steelhead from the plants was fly-caught the next year, 1950, and no steelhead from these plants was ever caught above the confluence.

These cooperative efforts by Washington's Game Department and Seattle's Washington Fly Fishing Club did prove that the progeny of summer steelhead, raised in hatcheries and planted in rivers for life in the ocean, would return as sexually mature adults. From this standpoint, the experiment was a success, and as such, it set the tone for Washington's steelhead hatchery programs, which soon followed on the Washougal and Skagit rivers.

Walt was reeling in when Bob Arnold called to us from the far bank. We were delighted to have his company, and waded over to join him. Bob has a cabin above Deer Creek and lives there for much of each summer. He is a collector of North Fork lore, a fine writer, and the former editor of *The Osprey*, a newsletter published by the Steelhead Committee of the Federation of Fly Fishers. Whenever I see him on the North Fork, or the Sauk, or the Skagit, he is about to catch a steelhead, or has just caught one, his head always filled with currents by the cfs, water temperature by the season, and stream-bottom silt by the thousands of tons. This kind of bedrock thinking serves him well as he deftly threads his way through the convoluted politics of watershed management. He knows every tier in the bureacracy—federal, state, and local.

"We're going over to visit the cabins," I said. "Come join us."

We followed the river down to Drain's place and worked upstream past Knudson's property to Walt's beautifully finished log cabin, then to Headrick's cabin, and on to Bradner's, which bears the sign, "Trespassers Will Be Eaten." A short walk has covered it all. Bob knows this history because he knew the anglers. I knew most of them, too. We traded anecdotes with Walt and talked of the fly patterns they gave to the sport. I noted that these few anglers who summered on the North Fork below Deer Creek developed just about all the popular steelhead patterns for Washington. Besides the dressings by Bradner and the McLeods, I could name more than a dozen from memory, another six or eight when I included Ralph Wahl. I asked Walt what flies they liked before he and his friends developed their own "Stilly" patterns. He could recall the Orange Shrimp, Thor, and Royal Coachman. Jim Pray and his Eel River patterns guided their selections back in the early 1940s, though his optics never played well here.

Historically, the North Fork's run of Deer Creek steelhead peaked about mid-July, the odd fish appearing as early as late May, and the river holding steelhead well until September. Not very long after the river's fly-fishing-only restriction went into effect, a few stubborn souls began to press their fishing on into winter.

"Oh, Bradner thought I was crazy," said Walt. "He said, 'Why do you want to do that?'" Walt chuckled with satisfaction. "He never did fish a fly for winter steelhead." Before long, Walt, Ralph Wahl, Al Knudson, and others were also fishing the Skagit. Some great fish fell to their flies.

"There's a pool near Cicero I want to show you," said Bob.

Trustworthy pools below Deer Creek were being erased by a meandering river too often filled with silt. It was worth hunting for new water, walking the long gravel bars, casting a fly, and perhaps finding a steelhead where no angler had found one before. We joined Bob and fished away the afternoon until dark clouds blew up the valley from Puget Sound, and it started to rain. The tailout fished especially well, and I thought Walt and I had done it justice. We quit the river and left Bob to battle with a gusting wind that was dapping his General Practitioner across the surface. He must not have lingered, for in less than an hour he had landed a sixteen-pound hatchery steelhead from the Deer Creek Riffle just upstream from Walt's house.

DEER CREEK

During the winter steelhead season in 1984, Bob Arnold thought the North Fork below Deer Creek would never clear. The river ran so grey with silt that fishing was out of the question. Favored mainstem runs were actually filling up with the tons of sediment running out of Deer Creek. Disgust soon turned to concern, the loss of his fishing secondary to the calamity he imagined taking place somewhere in the Deer Creek watershed. Bob made calls to those state and federal agencies administering Deer Creek lands, an investigation that led to Al Zander, a hydrologist for the U.S. Forest Service with the Mount Baker Ranger District. The two men met in Oso and together visited Deer Creek. Zander was shocked by what he saw and set off to explore the headwaters and find the source of the massive siltation that would, he knew, be catastrophic to steelhead and salmon stocks. He discovered an enormous slide in a logged-off area at the mouth of DeForest Creek, an important tributary of Deer Creek, and land under the administration of Washington's Department of Natural Resources.

Bob Arnold sent out hundreds of flyers announcing a public meeting in Oso, and asking "What's Killing Deer Creek?" and containing the follow-up question: "Can Anything Be Done About It?" Jim Doyle, a biologist with the U.S. Forest Service, would help chair the meeting and present a slide show of the area under discussion.

The year before, Doyle had begun a comprehensive evaluation of logging's impact on the Deer Creek watershed. During the course of his survey, he discovered that the loss of streamside cover and resulting erosion had so reduced stream depth that water temperatures in summer could reach seventy-five degrees from top to bottom, lethal for some young steelhead and coho salmon. As a result of slash burns, entire hillsides remained sterilized and denuded during years of erosion. Slash-choked runoff creeks and washed out logging roads caused additional erosion. Almost all the spawning habitat had disappeared under tons of silt. Where there had once been thousands of steelhead, there were now approximately two hundred. Documentation was skimpy, the watershed far more vast than the name "creek" would suggest.

Doyle recorded this devastating picture of mismanagement and neglect with a thirty-five-millimeter camera, and at the public meeting in Oso put on a slide show that outraged his audience.

The Department of Natural Resources took initial responsibility for the DeForest slide, though in truth, damage to the watershed had occurred for half a century or more on lands held privately and corporately and under numerous state and federal administrations. Work began the next summer to clear the slide, using both volunteer and convict labor. When this effort proved futile, heavy earth-moving equipment was contracted, and the slide area was regraded in 1985. Rains that fall and winter eroded this work, the slide continuing to dump tons of silt into the creek *each day*.

The magnitude of the task and the gravity of Deer Creek's condition led to the formation of the Deer Creek Policy Group, a coalition of state and federal agencies, timber companies, private landowners, environmental groups, Trout Unlimited, the Federation of Fly Fishers, the Tulalip and Stillaguamish Indian tribes, and the two counties containing the watershed.

The interagency cooperation that developed out of the Policy Group led the U.S. Forest Service to declare a moratorium on all their Deer Creek logging operations and the initiation of a comprehensive rehabilitation of the watershed. Trucks brought in enormous rock-filled wire cribs called gabion baskets to hold back erosion along the creeks. Helicopters flew in concrete "Jersey barriers" (often used as temporary freeway dividers) to retard erosion in less-accessible areas. Sediment fences and settling ponds were installed, old logging roads stabilized, and bare hillsides planted with trees. It was a start.

Alec Jackson and Bob Arnold represent, respectively, the Federation of Fly Fishers and property owners on the Board of Directors of the Deer Creek Policy Group. They have established the Deer Creek Restoration Fund for private contributions to help finance the massive rehabilitation of the Deer Creek watershed. Because of the coordinated efforts of the Policy Group, all manner of funding, and the very different special interests these monies represent, have a common goal. Steelhead are but one facet of this environmental disaster.

Deer Creek has been a steelhead spawning sanctuary for half a century, and since 1983, a thirty-inch size limit has effectively excluded them from the creel limit. Even with this protection, however, their numbers have declined as less and less spawning habitat remains viable. During the summer of 1989, I discussed the prospects for survival of the native Deer Creek steelhead with Curt Kraemer. He had conducted the pioneering life-history study on this race and knew the watershed well. "Oh, there might be two hundred adult fish in the system," he told me. I thought this figure as good as any, the same one that comes up each year. Kraemer cares deeply for these steelhead; "two hundred" contains more promise than "almost extinct."

Bob Arnold fishes the Deer Creek Riffle on a regular basis, a sampling as unscientific as any other. Several years ago, he thought the estimate of two hundred steelhead to be low. He caught twenty-five Deer Creek steelhead that summer and a like number the next year. Bob could not believe this would be possible if the overall population were so down, though this race has always concentrated in a few good pools below the confluence. When I last spoke with him about Deer Creek, it was mid-July 1989, traditionally the peak of the summer run. "I'm worried," he told me. "So far this year, no one has caught a single Deer Creek steelhead."

Walt Johnson and I were in touch all that summer, and I knew hardly a day passed without him hiking to the river and passing a couple of hours on his home pool. Early in August he called me. "I finally got one!" he exclaimed.

"Wonderful!" I said. "A hatchery steelhead?"

"No, a native Deer Creek fish. It wasn't fin-clipped. About five pounds."

We talked about his fish. I wanted to know every detail. I asked whether he had heard of any other Deer Creek steelhead. He hadn't. Neither of us wanted to discuss the terrible irony playing itself out, the last of this race being caught by the last of the North Fork's venerated regulars. I reminded Walt that my first steelhead on a fly, a Deer Creek hen, had come on the North Fork. Between my first and his last we could call into account only twenty-five years.

That September, Bob Arnold called to confirm that Walt's steelhead was the only Deer Creek native caught in the North Fork during the summer of 1989. (Several Deer Creek steelhead were caught in 1990.)

SKAMANIA STEELHEAD

The Skamania Hatchery is on the North Fork of the Washougal River, a southwest Washington tributary of the Columbia River. Construction of the hatchery began as mitigation for the decline of steelhead runs above the Columbia River dams. Plants of Washougal summer-run steelhead smolts were made soon after its completion in 1956, and the first returns of adult steelhead were realized in 1960.

The native Washougal steelhead is unusually robust and thick shouldered, typically a one- or two-salt fish, though a three-salt life history is not rare. Historically, the earliest returns occurred in late winter—the much heralded "springers," fish so sea-fresh and sexually immature that they possessed great strength and dash.

As the Skamania hatchery program grew, more and more Washington rivers received hatchery plants to supplement native runs, and by the mid-1960s some twenty major rivers possessed runs of Washougal steelhead. One of these rivers was the North Fork of the Stillaguamish River.

In about 1970, Skamania hatchery personnel began selecting brood stock from returning steelhead that were, in the main, three-salt fish, females of at least thirty inches, and males of at least thirty-four inches long. On paper, at least, the concept was brilliant. Selectively breeding steelhead would, in a relatively short number of generations, produce a "super race" predisposed to spend an extra year at sea and averaging nearly twice the size of their native counterparts. The program showed such promise, and initial results seemed to be so spectacular, that Skamania steelhead became the darling of Washington's fish culturists.

However, discriminating only for size produced some undesirable side effects. For reasons of economy, brood stock were gathered over a period of a few weeks and presumably reached sexual maturity at the same time. In similar fashion, the young steelhead reached smolting age at about the same time and were released over a period of only a few weeks. Whether or not all this cultivation was inadvertently tapping into a genetically distinctive subrace is not clear. But the result of selecting steelhead from one narrow period of the year did produce a dramatic change in the overall breadth of run timing, the hatchery escapement soon becoming far more condensed than that of the native steelhead. The hatchery fish also traveled more rapidly up the river to reach the hatchery weir or the security of a few good pools below the weir. In an effort to slow the hatchery steelhead and spread their numbers more evenly through the river, biologists released smolts at staggered times and at points well below the hatchery, but this was only marginally successful. Fly fishers found that these older, larger fish favored the very deepest pools for weeks at a time, and were not easily distracted from their nearly comatose state by even the deeply sunk fly. The shallow riffles less frequently held two-salt steelhead because these smaller steelhead were being selected out of the gene pool. In fact, the one-salt steelhead, the very kind of steelhead that brought such fame to the North Fork, was genetically eliminated from the Skamania race of summer-run steelhead, a loss deeply regretted by greased-line fly fishermen.

So the Skamania steelhead, with its ponderous size and character flaws, has gradually replaced the slim, small, quick-rising Deer Creek steelhead. They are both atypical races, marvelous creatures, but only one a national treasure.

During his fifty years on the North Fork, Walt Johnson never caught a Deer Creek steelhead that made twelve pounds. Yet, he says, "They were the most graceful steelhead I've ever seen. Sometimes they came upriver so quickly they arrived at Elbow with sea lice still hanging on them. Then they stayed here for weeks."

Walt fished his delicate midge rods then, bamboo wands of less than two ounces, 3-weights with 5X leaders for small dry flies, and he cast upstream for drag-free floats. The stories of his days with Deer Creek steelhead stir the memory and prick the conscience like nothing else in fly fishing.

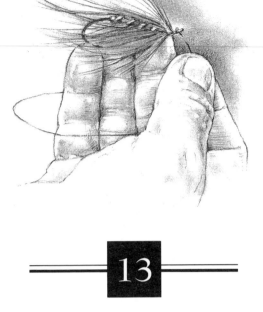

13

SKYKOMISH RIVER

I F I could design and build a winter-steelhead fly-fishing river to suit my every fancy, I would use the eight miles of the Skykomish between Sultan and Monroe as a model. The braiding currents upriver are better left for summer steelhead and the floating line, while below flow the deep, featureless drifts so dear to gear fishermen. Between the two towns, however, is a succession of classic pools surely created for the long rod and fly. Their flats and tailouts hold shallow lies easily penetrated with sink tip lines. The footing along their edges remains so sure that presenting the fly and wading become pleasures that commingle between rises. Their steelhead are among the largest of all winter races, three-salt bucks known to have weighed more than twenty-five pounds, and yard-long hens that can run off a hundred yards of backing in a single burst.

Some less-desirable traits help me appreciate these finer ones. Challenging lies invite especially long casts, while strong currents make deep wades tentative. Gear fishermen parade in drift boats, skillfully pulling plugs through the best fly drifts. Bitter winter weather dampens the keenest enthusiasm. When the river is in flood, steelhead hold in the trees, and during periods of drought they skulk about in pools too deep for my flies. I am never completely satisfied with my lot, yet on no other river can I fish a deeply sunk fly so well, a fact that always contributes to my satisfaction, whether or not I find a steelhead.

This Skykomish River that borders valley farms and the foothills of the Cascades is a small part of one great tributary of the Snohomish River. The Snoqualmie is the sister river, a wonderful winter river also, but with fly water less abundant, and the best of it less-storied.

Along the lower Snohomish River, the Tulalip Indians set their nets for the watershed's run of winter steelhead. This commercial fishery may account for fifty percent of the total harvest, as many as ten thousand steelhead, but only a few hundred will be wild stock. Most are December- and January-run hatchery steelhead weighing six or seven pounds. One in five will have spent an extra year at sea, sufficient time to grow to twice these weights. With the current practice of promoting hatchery stocks to sustain the commercial fishery, these early-returning steelhead become vitally important to sport fishermen. Less than five percent of the creel limits during the early season contain native-born steelhead.

As the first steelhead arrive, the chum salmon are spawning and dying. Their remains attract bald eagles, which congregate along the river corridor to feed, and in December one might count forty of the birds during an afternoon of fishing. Unless a flood carries away their food, the eagles remain through January, about when the first hatchery steelhead spawn and the first solid flush of native steelhead arrives. By mid-February, the chums are bleached-out pieces of cartilage shining up from the bottom of eddies, and the adult eagles have departed. The few remaining juveniles will leave shortly, most to scavenge along the coast where spring tides are exposing the rich bounty of intertidal shorelines.

During the earliest years of Washington's sport fishing, little was understood about steelhead, a steelhead "salmon" in the minds of most anglers, while "rainbow trout," the juvenile steelhead, populated every stream and were synonymous with the sport of fly fishing. Initially, winter steelhead seasons were not even set. Spring was the traditional opening of the trout season, and sometimes spawning steelhead, huge "rainbow trout," were found, first by chance but soon by design, with spoons and spinners, never by choice with flies. Our most esteemed taxonomists supported the misconceptions. In David Starr Jordan and Barton Warren Evermann's *American Food and Game Fishes*, anadromous steelhead trout and resident rainbow trout were listed as separate species, *Salmo gairdneri* and *Salmo irideus*. Based on this scientific knowledge, anglers were catching steelhead in winter and rainbow trout in spring. The Skykomish River became famous for producing record fish of both species.

A grain of truth did attend these perceptions, however. The Skykomish, like the Skagit and other large river systems in Washington, maintained small resident trout populations that lived in reproductive isolation. That is, the rainbow trout and the steelhead normally maintained separate genetic identities, one population never reproducing with the other. But as a practical matter, "rainbow trout" were steelhead parr and late spring smolts of six, seven, even eight inches, and a skilled wet fly angler could be expected to take his daily limit of fifty with satisfying regularity.

No history identifies the first Skykomish River angler to take a winter steelhead on a fly. The event was almost certainly an accident, like being hit by a bolt of lightning, and did not reflect the angler's genius for harnessing raw energy for his recreation. A handful of anglers, however, gave such colorful definition to the sport that finding a steelhead with a fly on a certain river became a tradition eternally bound up in their experiences. Examples of this heritage would include Jim Pray and the Eel, Bill Schaadt and the Russian, Zane Grey and the Rogue, Clarence Gordon and the North Umpqua, General Noel Money and the Stamp, and Roderick Haig-Brown at "Above Tide" on the Campbell.

To this group of associations must be added Ken McLeod and the Skykomish River. The man was a giant in our sport, often remembered as the main character in steelhead fly fishing's most romantic tale. Ken and his son, George, were driving east to the Skykomish River one January morning in 1936. The sun was coming up over the snowcapped Cascades, a splendor of red, yellow, and white. "Tie me a fly with those colors in it," Ken told his son. That evening, George used red tying thread to secure a mix of red and yellow hackle, a red wool body, and a white polar bear wing. The completed fly was named the Skykomish Sunrise. George christened the pattern with three winter steelhead from a single pool near Monroe. The day included a seventeen-pounder. The new fly became a sensation.

I knew about the Skykomish Sunrise even before I knew about the river, and many years before I actually fished there. I am certain it is the best known steelhead fly wrought from this area, so much

Ken McLeod *Photo credit: Bob Arnold*

so that it is often used as a logo for the sport, very much analogous to the Royal Coachman and trout fishing.

The story of the Skykomish Sunrise was first told to me without dates, and this was the story I repeated to friends. Soon fact became legend, a little tale out of historical context but comforting in its charming simplicity. A half-century later, the original Sunrise remains the consummate winter fly, and continues to inspire anglers to new flights of aesthetic fancy. I tie the original with fluorescent floss and marabou, add a few strands of Krystal Flash, and still believe in its magic.

To fully appreciate the McLeod collaboration, it should be noted that in 1936, fly fishing for summer-run steelhead in Washington was in its infancy, and almost no one was fly fishing for winter fish.

That year Jim Pray in Eureka, California, tied a fly for Walter Thoresen, calling it "Thor" when Thoresen won the *Field & Stream* fishing contest with an eighteen-pound Eel River steelhead caught on Christmas Day. The steelhead was remembered as much for its great size as for the time of year it was caught, the longest December of low water and benign weather anyone could remember. When Claude Krieder wrote *Steelhead*, a fly-fishing classic, he included a chapter called "Winter-Steelhead Tackle and Methods," a detailed account of bait-casting rods, casting reels, and salmon roe. This was his tackle of choice when he fished the Eel in winter. He does not mention fly fishing for winter steelhead anywhere in the book, regardless of the river. The same must be said of Clark C. Van Fleet's *Steelhead to a Fly*. When Roderick Haig-Brown wrote the original two-volume *The Western Angler* in 1939, he commented upon how difficult it was to take a winter steelhead on a fly. When the book was revised and published as a single-volume edition in 1947, his opinion had changed: "During the winter of 1938–39 I began to use the fly at least as frequently as the minnow and found myself doing not too badly with it. Since then I have used the fly exclusively and, as nearly as I can judge, its effectiveness is at least seventy percent that of the minnow." (Note: "Minnow" is a Devon minnow, a lure popular in England for Atlantic salmon.)

The story of the Skykomish Sunrise shows that Ken McLeod and his son George were already taking winter steelhead on flies in 1936. As far back as the mid-1920s, Ken was fly fishing with a stripping basket in order to achieve the long distances sometimes necessary to attract steelhead. He soaked braided line in melted paraffin and wiped off the excess before laying it out to dry. The result was a stiff running line that permitted long friction-free casts from his stripping basket. Of course, a running line so fine meant that some sort of radical forward taper, a shooting head, was being cast. Ken McLeod used such lines to cast wet flies and to make long drag-free floats with dry flies.

This Washington native was the outdoor editor for the *Seattle Post-Intelligencer* from 1930 to 1950, and a founding member of both the Washington Fly Fishing Club and the Steelhead Trout Club. He assisted in the writing of salmon legislation, helped to negotiate the United States/Canada treaty for the allocation of Fraser River sockeye stocks, and for half a century joined numerous preservation efforts on behalf of steelhead. In 1983, he was commended by the Washington State Legislature for his many contributions to the state's salmon and steelhead resources.

During the early 1950s, Ken and George assisted in the development of the original Wet Cel lines with Leon Martuch of Scientific Anglers. While fishing these lines, they placed steelhead in the annual *Field & Stream* fishing contest. For seven years, George held the unofficial world record for the fly, a Kispiox buck of twenty-nine pounds, two ounces caught on October 6, 1955. The fly he fished was the Skykomish Sunrise.

Until Ken McLeod's death in 1989 at age eighty-nine, he and George fished for steelhead each summer below their cabin on the North Fork of the Stillaguamish. I'm told by his friends that it was here, nearly a half-century ago, that he first cast his Purple Peril, sometimes adding extra deer hair to the wing and fishing it as a waking dry. He leaves a remarkable legacy.

MARCH

Winter fly fishermen know in their bones that spring begins on the first day of March. The Skykomish goes to catch-and-release, an opening day for many of these anglers, and the end of the season for others, who will not bother to fish solely for the pleasure of it. Regardless of how one fishes, it is impossible not to take satisfaction in the reduced river traffic. The "new season" is two months long, spring days that alternate between winter and summer but begin with the certainty that the river is wrung dry of hatchery steelhead. Fishermen now search for fewer steelhead, but they are wild winter-run fish possessing such beauty and strength that annual vacations are devoted to finding them with a fly.

On the first day of March 1989, snow began to fall before first light, and by midmorning the storm had built to a full-blown blizzard. During the time it took me to swim a fly through a single broad

Opening of the catch and release season, March 1, 1989. →

swing, my spey rod grew a peak of snow along its entire length. Surface currents became slush. When my thermometer read thirty-two degrees, a foot of snow ran to the water's edge. No fish were moved, none were expected, and no practical reason for fishing remained, except that the river was a continuous shiver of excitement in its new surroundings. As I worked down the long pool, a line from Robert Service's *The Cremation of Sam McGee* kept me company. "There wasn't a breath in that land of death," I whispered, and was startled witless when the gravel bar at my feet exploded into twenty killdeer, their flight a din of mournful calls that I could still hear long after they had disappeared into the

Russ Miller at the top of Two Bit.

snowfall. "You must think you migrated in the wrong direction!" I called after them. They signaled spring. This snow, the heaviest in thirty years, wouldn't last.

One year later, the temperature reached almost seventy degrees, and I was shedding garments all afternoon. The river was low, clear, and ideal for fly fishing, except the steelhead were nowhere to be found. March browns were coming off the river in spiraling updrafts that four species of newly arrived swallows swept through, an aerial steeplechase that entertained me for hours. Far above their activity, swifts twinkled against the blue sky. I have seen these species drawn together many times while I was anchored in one pool or another, and I can now tell the swallows apart—the barn, violet-green, rough-winged, and the tree, by the rate of their wing beats and the adroitness of their movements. (Once, on Oregon's Molalla River, cliff swallows joined this group.) I am not an expert at such things, but one sees a lot and learns a good deal when quietly standing on the seam of two universes. On this day larger mayflies were about, grey drakes, I thought, and a scattering of small stoneflies. (The huge *Pteronarcys* stoneflies of "salmon fly" fame are uncommon on the Skykomish and do not hatch until early May.) The surface currents were now forty degrees, not yet warm enough to lift the parr out of their dormancy to chase after the struggling emergers or peck at my big spey flies swimming toward the beach. Late in the afternoon, I felt my first pull of the new season. "God, a steelhead!" I said

A pull is the bittersweet signal that somewhere among the currents there is life, certainly a steelhead, never a parr or a Dolly Varden or a sucker. The pull can be as simple as a pluck, as strong as a hard yank, and it may even have weight to it. It is not a hookup, however, and the whole affair is usually over in an instant. If this occurs after several fishless, pull-less days, the initial reaction is stunned disbelief, followed by disgust, evaluation, recrimination, more evaluation, and then, blissfully, the rationale that the fly and the presentation were right.

Fireman's, Thunderbird, IRS, Two-Bit, Taylor's Flat, Ben Howard, and Buck Island name the better-known waters downriver from Sultan that stitch together a full-day float for gear fishermen who cast lures, fish roe, or pull plugs. Each of these pools and most of the connecting water are systematically and thoroughly searched. No water is too shallow or too deep or too wide. The totality of the approach is not unlike the summer fly fisherman searching acres of surface currents with a floating line for a steelhead. Admittedly, in winter the lure is pretty much taken to the steelhead, and in summer the steelhead move to the lure, but the ability to cover a lot of the river is an ingredient common to both.

Winter fly fishing bears little resemblance to either approach. Most parts of the river are simply not productive for the fly. The angler floating in a boat to the few pools that fish well with a fly will spend the greater part of the day rowing past steelhead that are either on their upriver journey or are parked in lies beyond the capability of the fastest sinking lines. A better method is what Bob Arnold calls "spot fishing," and what I call the single-pool approach. In either case, it involves finding a pool that is known to hold steelhead, one that can be covered properly with a fly, ideally from bank to bank, and then fishing the water again and again until its lies are understood for water level, clarity, and time of day. As the angler learns the geography of the unseen bottom, he will understand what length and sink rate is required of his sink-tip line, and the pool will be fished more and more effectively. I believe that if only a single pool is known this well, but fished hard for the hours of first and last light, the opportunity for hooking a steelhead is considerably greater than if one is taking a day-long float and fishing hard the entire day. If several such pools are known, and can be reached by car, the chances for success are even greater, for the angler will be fishing in prime water almost constantly.

An eight-mile float on the Skykomish by anglers pulling plugs is a very, very long day. This same eight-mile float by fly fishermen is a delight, and fortunately filled with all kinds of recreational value only marginally related to getting a steelhead on the beach.

Floating a river by raft or McKenzie boat can give fly fishermen access to water they could reach in no other way. Some of the finest winter anglers I know—Harry Lemire and Jimmy Hunnicutt, for example—carry one-man rafts ("two-man" rafts in a pinch) solely to reach specific pieces of water. When that water has been fished, the raft is either broken down or thrown on top of their car, and they drive to a new piece of water. To save time, they use electric pumps that operate off the car battery.

I like a two-handed rod for this winter fishing, more so each year, and during the 1990 season I did not cast a single-hand rod even once through two months of almost constant fishing—March and April. Command of the water is the primary reason, but reduced fatigue becomes an increasingly important secondary consideration.

Les Johnson opened the season with me. He likes his Steelhead Bunnies, and normally he fishes them to the exclusion of all other patterns right through the spring months. When neither of us could find a steelhead at the top end of Two Bit (twenty-five cents is charged by the kind farmer for access to the pool), Les changed to a dark summer dressing as we started down into the soft gut of the run. He cast below me, and I told him that he was almost to where I had hooked an eleven-pound buck that could have just come over the tidal bar.

"The steelhead took directly below you!" I called. "The fly will barely complete its swing without sinking to the bottom. Don't be too anxious to strip it back." His cast was right, and the fly dead below him when the steelhead took. This is always the most difficult angle at which to securely hook a steelhead. No swing is left, and no angle is left to bring the fly naturally to one side of the mouth. Dropping a short loop can be helpful, because it gives the fish a few seconds of slack. If the steelhead does not immediately turn—and lethargic bucks often do not—the fly is at the end of its mouth. Tightening on the fly will often simply pull the fly free.

Les's steelhead had his rod bent to the cork. Just as I was sure the hold was secure, the fish was free, a loss that set our course for the days ahead. We found steelhead, and they found ways to avoid an in-the-hand release. I ran off a string of six or seven before I was able to lead one to quiet water. The frustration included a large buck hooked one Sunday evening at the bottom end of the Ben Howard Pool.

Jimmy Hunnicutt tells me that once these spring-run steelhead are driven from their shallow lies, they are not nearly so responsive to the fly. He wants to find virgin water at first light. Failing that advantage, Jimmy searches lies he suspects have not been fished for several hours. When we're together he sometimes must wave me back from standing in the very lies we are fishing. I know better, for I have hooked winter fish that were holding in little more than a foot of water, but like most anglers, I expect to wade at least to my knees when I'm fishing. Jimmy has convinced me of the importance of these very shallow lies, and now I often fish first-light water twice, once through with a shallow running tip, a twelve-foot III for fish nearly on the beach, and again with a deeper running tip, a fifteen-foot IV. Naturally, the amount of back-mend sets the running depth for either of these lines. On especially thin, slow-moving water, a floating line is useful, and I carry floating tips, too, but I rarely use them, preferring to fish the slow-sinking tips. I use this two-tip approach even if a friend is leading through first, for I do not want to risk disturbing the water by fouling the bottom or wading too deep and moving fish off that he may have missed. Jimmy and I will fish through the lie in the same manner. If I wish to give the fish a choice, I choose a fly pattern different from his, a bright fly playing to his dark fly, for example.

"The big one," says Ralph Wahl of the 20 pound 8 ounce buck he took from his Skagit "Shangri-La" on March 3, 1967. *Photo Credit: Ralph Wahl*

14

SKAGIT RIVER

FOR as long as any living angler can remember, the Skagit has been the flagship of Washington's winter steelhead sport fishery and a river repeatedly dammed for the electricity it could generate for the city of Seattle. These resources seem never to have been in dire conflict and, in fact, have enjoyed a remarkably harmonious relationship compared to other dams and other runs of steelhead.

Gorge Dam was completed in 1924. Sited in the Cascade Mountains at the base of a long, exceedingly narrow and violent run of canyon water, it rises 300 feet, spans 670 feet, and creates a lake four miles long. Two miles below the dam, and connected by a twenty-foot-wide tunnel, is Gorge Powerhouse. Here at the tailwater is a river less subject to the seasonal forays of drought and flood, to severe temperature changes, and to discoloration through snowmelt, for the lake helps to settle out the opaque runoff.

The long, shallow glides of clear currents below the Powerhouse were as far up as winter steelhead ever spawned, the canyon creating a natural barrier that a few summer steelhead may have ascended. But the myriad headwaters that threaded together alpine lakes and glacier-filled cirques were for resident trout and char, not for salmon and steelhead.

More dams followed immediately upstream of Gorge. Diablo was the tallest arch-type dam in the world when completed in 1930, nearly a hundred feet higher and twice as wide as Gorge, but picayune compared to Ross Dam. Rising 540 feet above bedrock, and a quarter-mile across, Ross backed up

191

the Skagit a mile or so into British Columbia when it was completed twenty years ago. These two dams generated many more kilowatts for Seattle City Light, and helped to safeguard the farms, eighty miles downriver, that crosshatched the flood plain of the Skagit Valley.

In a decent year, fishermen expected a run of at least twenty-five thousand steelhead, a trickle in November and May, but bright fish right through winter and spring until the season closed in April. When the Skagit reopened in June for the statewide trout season, winter steelhead were still spawning, and many kelts were making their way to the sea. A few bright winter steelhead still ascended the river, joined by early-returning summer steelhead bound for the Skagit's Cascade River.

The native December and January steelhead were remarkably immature sexually, fish analogous to the springers of summer-run fame. These sea-bright fish moved quickly into the system, then stayed all winter, and often well into spring, before joining later arrivals and spawning in May. They were, everyone agreed, great biters. Mortality was high. So, too, were their numbers. Thousands filled the lower river in just a few weeks.

February steelhead mixed with the December and January fish still holding main-stem lies, and this was often the peak angling month. Truly huge male steelhead that had been grazing in the ocean's fastness for three, four, even five straight years were now found in the lower river, March bucks that in the less-forgiving upriver currents left bait-casters swearing to their deathbeds that the one that got away was four feet long.

March steelhead entered as other steelhead left the Skagit for tributary rivers and for stations on those broad tailouts suitable for spawning, often shallow lies two to four feet deep. Selecting spawning gravel and digging redds spread steelhead throughout the system, and by mid-May, fish were spawning from Newhalem, Seattle City Light's company town below the Gorge Powerhouse, to near tidewater in those lower two channels of the Skagit that deliver the river to the ocean, a hundred river miles in all.

March rains only infrequently brought snow to headwaters. When this marine weather pattern was followed by a strong high pressure system, spring became summer and tributary rivers churned out glacial grit, snowmelt, and mud torn from clay banks along the elbow holes. Steelhead traveled on these flushes of turbidity, and the confluence points became way stations filling and emptying almost hourly.

Of these suddenly unruly rivers, none was so elementary yin to the Skagit's yang as the Sauk, a truly great steelhead river in its own right, the parent river's largest tributary, and a spring river breathtakingly beautiful, mercurial, and cranky. Anglers claim that its steelhead were like that, too, short-fused native stock with such big shoulders that they could be easily distinguished from the more gently streamlined Skagit fish.

The Sauk reached west and south eighty miles for many lesser Cascade streams, the Suiattle chief among them, before joining the Skagit at Rockport, one of three hardscrabble settlements, including Marblemount just upriver and Concrete close below. In spring, plunkers with roe, gear fishermen casting spoons, and guides with their clients still confidently searched the Skagit below the confluence for Sauk steelhead.

"Most of the steelhead come up and hang a right," said the old Skagit hands.

APRIL

Howard K. Miller Steelhead Park, a fairway of green campsites with a boat launch, lies between the Skagit River and the block of houses, two bars, one restaurant, and a gas station that make up Rockport. In early spring, the park is full on weekends and only a little less so on weekdays. Most of the campers are fly fishermen, old friends whose happy reunions are annual vacations timed so that they might find an April steelhead with their carefully crafted flies. If this results in a fish in the hand, it is truly an epiphany for those whose faith has remained unshakeable. Talk is of little else the entire month.

The object of this devotion is the most marine of all steelhead. Their spawning run may be completed in as little as a month, and when encountered, they are so full of the ocean, so silver-grey and white, that one searches in vain for even a hint of rainbow on their flanks. They enter the river when summer is on the water and surface currents are in the midforties. With metabolisms at cruising speed, they move well to the fly, as tentative or as crushing on the take as any summer-run. No steelhead are stronger. No steelhead are more beautiful. Never are they commonplace. "Run" is much too generous. Thousands in winter become hundreds in spring, and late in the month a flush of steelhead counts a dozen. The single fish racing for your fly must fulfill a day. To expect more of the river, to demand more of yourself, becomes passion without joy.

When I launched my McKenzie boat at the Park one morning in early April, I intended to stay until the season closed at the end of the month. My boat was new, an aluminum replacement for the wood McKenzie I'd wrecked on the Hoh. Ash oars with yard-long blades would keep me moving discreetly downriver. A small jet engine mounted on the transom would allow me to run back upriver, a noisy concession to the inconvenience of hitchhiking around for my car when fishing alone. A pair of two-handed rods lay along the gunwale. My boat bag was full of gear and my Wheatley boxes full of flies. I didn't want for anything.

Huge alders shade the park's water. Only the careful wader who can spey-cast his double-handed rod will cover these lies, water so deep that few anglers even try. At the bottom end, a fly fisherman was silhouetted in the glare. As I watched him, he swept his long rod upstream, executed a delicate figure S, and then drove the line eighty feet out. Only one angler in the world did a double-spey exactly that way. I kept the boat tight to the bank and drifted down. His back was to me when I called out softly, "Harry?"

Harry Lemire turned and began reeling in.

"I heard you were coming this week," he said.

"How's the fishing been?"

"Awful!"

"Tell me about it! I was here for four days last week with Bob Arnold and hooked one steelhead, a five-pound hen. A native, I think. The Game Department says the two-salt steelhead are unusually small this year."

"I had one good day last week," said Harry. "On a pool below Concrete, I rose three fish and hooked two. The steelhead I got to the beach was thirty-seven inches. A buck."

"What was the fly?"

He held out his rod. A large Golden Edge Orange was secured to the crossbar of his Hardy reel. This is a classic pattern of bronze mallard and golden pheasant crest with jungle cock cheeks, not the kind of dressing I associate with winter steelhead. Harry calls my box of bright marabou spiders, "damn Buck Rogers stuff," or "pillows."

"Do you want to go for a boat ride? I have enough sandwich makings for both of us. Coffee and pop, too."

"Sure! Let me get my stuff."

Harry returned from his truck with a bag of gear, a jacket, and Penny, his seventy-pound Collie, a fly fisherman's dog that would move along the beach just ahead of her companion. Neither of us had to worry about our backcasts.

We drifted downriver until we came opposite the Sauk. The past couple of days had been warm, and this day would reach into the seventies. It takes at least eight hours for any snowmelt to reach this confluence. Not until late that afternoon would we know if the Sauk was going out. For the time being the river was clear, but, typically, not as clear as the Skagit. For more than a mile the two rivers run side by side until forced together in a deep pool with hydraulics so severe that it is called the Mixmaster.

The Skagit River below the Sauk is paradise. To the east lies North Cascades National Park, and this morning its pale blue glaciers sparkled in the sunlight. The other cardinal points have lesser mountains that still carried snow well below their ridge lines. Only the Dean River below Moose Rapids and the Skeena below the Kispiox offer such a spectacular backdrop.

At Harry's suggestion, we started at Island Pool, split the water between us, and began swimming our flies through on fifteen-foot sink-tip lines, each with a sink rate of IV. This is a good average. I had sink tips I could change to from twelve to nineteen feet with sink rates of III, to V (Deep Water Express). Getting the fly down was not nearly so important as slowing the fly on the swing. Neither did we want to hang up. When that happened, it was usually on a waterlogged branch or a piece of driftwood. Often our flies were three or four feet above the bottom, sufficient unless the water temperature dropped precipitously or the river filled with turgid runoff.

Some pools are known to fish best in high water, others in low. A few pools hold steelhead regardless of the water level, but individual lies will change depending on the volume of flow. Skagit anglers soon learn that when the river rises and falls a foot at a time, extra water is being let out of the dams. This happens early in the morning, the river then dropping throughout the day. The Sauk is not dammed and provides an additional set of parameters as its runoff and turbidity is factored into Skagit pools below the Mixmaster.

Of course, no pool is entirely static. Each water changes a bit from year to year, dredged out here, filled in there, and the lies change accordingly. Some pools are lost altogether. Harry is always searching for new lies, especially the subtle, often overlooked pocket that will produce a single steelhead when anglers up and down the river are glumly finding the well-known pools completely empty.

We did not turn a steelhead in Lake Pool, nor in two pools just below the Sauk, nor in the Mixer, the famous Skagit drift just above the Mixmaster, known locally as Sauk River Bar. After ten hours of fishing we returned to Rockport and planned a full-day float from Marblemount to Rockport the next day.

The Skagit River below Marblemount is better known for the hundreds of bald eagles that winter there than for its steelhead. They are drawn by the huge schools of spawning salmon. The chums that follow the pinks do not finish spawning until the second week of December, and their carcasses are an important food source into early February. By March, the adult eagles have left. To safeguard river frontage for these feeding and roosting eagles—the largest such concentration in the United States outside of Alaska—the Nature Conservancy purchased over nine hundred acres along seven miles of river below Marblemount. Private and commercial eagle-watching floats take place, gear fishermen in drift boats make their daily rounds, and early-morning fly fishermen sometimes find themselves competing with eagles for places on the gravel bars.

Even without the eagles, the upper Skagit is a magnificent float. Frequent braids take the river away from the nearby highway, and wildlife boldly come into view at every turn. Beaver, otter, mink, and deer are everyday sightings, and black bear and mountain lions roam the foothills outside the clear-cuts.

Biologists disagree as to what percentage of Skagit/Sauk steelhead are main-stem spawners above Rockport, that is, above the Sauk River. I don't think nearly as many April steelhead continue on past the confluence as pass up the Sauk, an opinion no doubt fostered by my poor showing on the upper Skagit. It is a higher-gradient river than just below the Sauk, and many lies in high water are only marginally fishable. Plug pullers speak of five-fish days, mostly sea-bright "chromers," caught in four to eight feet of water. Their desirable water and mine barely overlap. Yet the ten-mile float contains a half-dozen pools that so promote my fly fishing that success is pretty much up to my persistence. John Farrar, a friend of mine who has for years guided fly fishermen on the Skagit, told me that around the middle of April the upper river gets a fresh push of fish. John knows of what he speaks and can find these steelhead when I cannot.

Harry and I fished the familiar lies, sometimes with difficulty due to the high water, and turned a single fish, perhaps a steelhead, but more likely a Dolly Varden. These char were shaking off winter by chasing after the newly hatched chum-salmon fry, often foraging their way to tidewater before returning weeks or months later with a patina of silver over their handsome colors. As stream residents they'll consume the spawn of other salmonids, and anglers often kill them for this reason. Most fly fishermen malign them simply because they aren't steelhead.

We found no steelhead that day, nor on the day after, nor on the day after that. This was the longest period without hooking a steelhead that I could remember. For Harry, the bad run was incomprehensible. After a run downriver one morning, we came back to the launch and retired to Mom's Cafe for breakfast.

"I don't think I'll ever see another steelhead again!" he said over coffee. His tone was rueful, but Harry Lemire, the complete steelhead fly fisherman, never despairs.

"Years ago I read an article by Ted Trueblood about fishing for winter steelhead in the Olympic Peninsula," I said. "There was a photograph of Trueblood, and the caption went something like, 'After a slow week, Ted got this bright sixteen-pound steelhead.' That's when I learned what *slow* means in angling. Harry, we're just having a slow week!"

He needed no reminding that you don't beat up on yourself during a slow week. Our fishing wouldn't change a pool empty of steelhead. Empty is merely a temporary condition capable of changing on the next cast. We cast our flies with the conviction that a steelhead is out there, and although it does not gladden my heart when they fail to materialize, I really do believe that a day or two of empty pools can still be recreational. Jimmy Hunnicutt, a frequent fishing companion, says this is "getting into the flow of the river," and I agree. It is the river, not the steelhead, that I must come to understand. But regardless of how philosophically we drone on about the joys of rushing water and the long rod, four or five days of nothing is not recreational. By then the fly patterns look awful, their magic completely in tatters. I stray from the dressings that enticed steelhead in the past—and thus provided confidence—for the one-off, experimental tie that might catch lightning in a bottle. When backing this longshot doesn't work, I return to recycling the standards. I remain as hopeful as any gambler, convinced that the next cast will be *the* cast, the start of a three-fish day. Soon, however, the lively rhythm of working the fly becomes a labor as fatigue, monotony, and disappointment set in. I look through my fly boxes and ask, "What don't I want to raise a steelhead on now?"

The long run of lovely weather finally broke, replaced by a cold and determined overcast that drifted over the surrounding foothills and locked the valleys in a drizzly fog. Harry and I thought the dark day could entice steelhead from the deeper pools and nurture them in shallow lies. We drifted past the familiar riffles of holding water with renewed expectations and found the Mixer in a state of virgin grace. I could not imagine what we had done to deserve such a remarkable stroke of good fortune. Three hours later I had my answer. The gods had granted us only one wish. Our second wish—that the pool hold steelhead—had been ignored.

Farther downstream we split two small pools between us. On the lower water, I was twenty casts into the run with an Admiral Spey when a steelhead took the fly almost directly downstream. I held fast to the fish and was determined to make it turn and take the rod down to properly drive in the hook. Negotiating this takes a second or two of mind-numbing patience. As I was thinking that this was going well and my double-handed rod was taking a deep set, the steelhead simply and violently left with the fly. Breaking off a winter steelhead on the strike after a slow week is a journey to the brink of insanity. I did not tie on another fly, but stood and tried to remember the last time such a thing had happened. I couldn't.

The lost opportunity marked a change in our fortunes. The rains came that night, and in the morning persistent showers sent fresh steelhead up through the pools. I found a hen of twelve pounds with a Deep Purple Spey, while Harry landed a hen several pounds heavier with his Golden Edge Orange. A day could hardly pass now without a steelhead touching our flies.

When Bob Arnold and I fished Island Pool in late March, he had observed, "Twenty-pound winter steelhead are caught on flies each year, now. I don't think there are more big steelhead than in the past. There are a lot more fly fishermen, and they are better equipped."

Bob has written often and well of Washington's early masters of steelhead fly fishing: Ken and

Jimmy Green on the Sauk River.

A 35-inch April Buck. *Photo credit: Dan Reiff*

George McLeod, Al Knudson, Ralph Wahl, Walt Johnson, and Wes Drain, for example, regulars on the Stillaguamish River's North Fork during the 1940s. These men and their Stilly friends were also fishing winter pools for Skagit steelhead that could easily be several times larger than the North Fork's Deer Creek fish. This was not so much a matriculation as a quantum leap. The river was imposing, the winter-run steelhead holding in more challenging lies and in water ten to twenty degrees colder. Anglers tried to make the best of it with old silk lines dressed with everything from graphite to red lead paint; the steelhead could be incredibly difficult to take.

Ralph Wahl looked to Jim Pray and Peter Schwaab for inspiration at the tying vise, and his early winter patterns, the Lord Hamilton and Lady Hamilton (1940), and Painted Lady (1945), were compact and optic-like. Al Knudson sometimes used 5/0 to 7/0 Carlisle streamer hooks to take his marabou flies down. Wes Drain, the finest tyer in the lot, took a twenty-pound, seven-ounce Skagit steelhead in 1947 on a fly he came to call Drain's 20. No one claimed a larger fly-caught steelhead in Washington

for twenty years. When that finally happened, it was Ralph Wahl who settled the matter with a Skagit steelhead of twenty pounds, eight ounces. Between these two great bucks were many fine steelhead caught on flies by a handful of pioneer anglers.

When Wes Drain caught his unofficial state record in 1947, the *Field & Stream* fishing contest allowed "rainbow trout" entries if caught during the traditional trout season, April to October. Steelhead could be counted as rainbow trout, but not if caught during Washington's winter steelhead season, December 1 to April 15, on the Skagit. As a result, the Skagit received little national recognition as a trophy river and source of fly-fishing records.

Ralph Wahl managed Wahl's Department Store, a family business in Bellingham, the Puget Sound city just north of the Skagit. Once, while on a buying trip to New York, he dropped in to the *Field & Stream* office to argue for a needed change in the regulations. Shortly thereafter, a steelhead caught anytime during the year was eligible to be a "rainbow trout" in the magazine's fishing contest. Winter steelhead from both California and Washington were soon included. Ralph and his longtime fishing companion, Judge R. O. Olson, and Al Knudson and Russ Willis all placed Skagit steelhead in the contest.

Among Washington's hardy breed of winter fly fishermen, only the Skykomish River and the Skagit's own Sauk have seriously divided affections in the years since.

After a long day on the Skagit, my custom was to join friends at the Fish In for a pitcher of Red Hook, a Seattle brew that exorcises despair and liberates the tongue. John Farrar, his guiding day over, would *skol* with clients and then head for the tavern. BJ Meiggs was photographing winter steelhead, while Bob Arnold, Dale Edmonds, and Harry Lemire were looking to catch one, and they

Jim Vincent on a Skagit pool above Rockport.

liked Red Hook, too. By the second pitcher, inhibitions were sufficiently suppressed to promote steelhead gossip with the locals, referred to hereabouts as "tarheels," but generically, like redneck or cracker, and not as a reference to family origins. Outsiders sometimes liked to think of them as hunchbacks in bib overalls. "They live so far in the woods they have their sunshine piped in," said one angler-anthropologist. The tarheels, in turn, believe that "yuppie" is a curse, both an expletive and descriptive of such a complete fall from grace that one's soul has been blighted beyond redemption. They often precede the word with a series of vigorously perverted adjectives, a creative outlet that has become a local craft, like quilting.

This cultural gamesmanship has deeper roots than the uneasy relationship between city mice and

country mice, but it is rarely at mean-spirited loggerheads unless the conversation turns to the management of steelhead stocks. Then the gloves come off. The relative perceptions between some local gear fishermen and visiting fly fishermen could not be more different.

Fly fishermen see the gear fishermen's need for more hatchery steelhead to be insatiable because "quality" and "sport" are interchangeable with "limit." Catch-and-kill is an exalted way of life, and "maximum sustainable harvest" the buzzword for properly managing native stocks. The gear fishermen sarcastically counter by claiming that selective fishery regulations—such as the Skagit's April-long catch-and-release season—are laws made for fly fishermen so that they can fish over spawning redds. They also believe that the worst defeat America ever suffered occurred in the courts, in the "Boldt Decision," in which Native Americans with treaty rights were given the right to take half the annual run of steelhead on Washington rivers.

"Indian" is another curse heard in these parts.

Indian fishing has been a bone of contention, the state and federal governments historically on opposite sides of the fence, the matter litigated in federal court, the decisions handed down invariably in favor of the treaty Indians. Nevertheless, "Indian fishing," the harvesting of steelhead with gill nets, either drift or set, and the commercial sale of those steelhead, must be coordinated with Washington's need to manage stocks at sustainable levels. This is not law so much as necessity, the reasons not always penetrating the sportsmen's bitter resentment. First, the Indians have a court-ordered right to fifty percent of the total run, *whatever that might be*. Both user groups, sport and commercial, suffer if either one exploits stocks to the detriment of the run. Secondly, the value of the Skagit steelhead fishery, particularly insofar as the Indian take is concerned, depends heavily on hatchery plants. Though Skagit Indians have their own fishery biologists, hatcheries, and stocking programs, they still depend on state hatchery plants in the Skagit to obtain their fifty percent of the run. Just as important, hatchery-reared steelhead smolts return as adults early in the run, mostly December and January. This predictability makes their commercial harvest more timely and efficient, while simultaneously taking pressure off native stocks. The native stocks remain the genetic depository for the race's size and spirit.

Three tribes net steelhead and salmon from the Skagit River. The Swinomish Indian Reservation is on Fidalgo Island at the mouth of the Skagit. Traditionally, the tribe nets from tidewater to the city of Mount Vernon. The Upper Skagit Indian reservation is near Sedro Wooley, its nets set between Mount Vernon and the mouth of the Baker River.

The Sauk-Suiattle Indians have ancestral fishing grounds on late season spawning waters along the upper Sauk, but they limit their commercial netting to the lower Skagit, doing so by invitation from the other two tribes.

I discussed this netting with Eric Beamer, a Swinomish Indian and the Managing Biologist for the Skagit System Cooperative. He explained that the tribes own and manage the Red Creek Hatchery. Fry are transported to rearing ponds at Lake Shannon. Approximately fifteen thousand to twenty thousand smolts are released a year later. This is not a trivial number, but it remains small compared to the State's hatchery plants in the Skagit that typically run from two hundred thousand to three hundred thousand. The tribal fishery takes place in December and January, and sometimes for a few days in February. Over the past twelve years, the Indian steelhead catch has totaled two thousand to five thousand, with three thousand to four thousand a typical season. By late in December the run size is updated, the Cooperative able to establish fishing days, hours of netting, and so forth.

Following is a breakdown of the 1988–89 annual run of Skagit steelhead:

	Run Size	Sport	Indian	Escapement
Wild steelhead	14,422	1,892	676	11,854
Hatchery steelhead	4,912	1,177	2,964	771
Total	19,334	3,069	3,640	12,625

Hatchery stocks are exploited at a much higher rate than wild stocks. Although the Skagit's state hatchery program is funded by the sale of licenses and punch cards to gear fishermen and fly fishermen, it is the Indian net fishery that actually takes most of these hatchery steelhead, more than seventy percent of the total, though the tribes provide less than ten percent of the hatchery smolts. Yet I would not have it otherwise. To net native stocks commercially—the Indians account for only 676 steelhead from a run of 19,334—would be an unforgivable waste. It can be said that sportsmen fund Indian netting in order to protect the native Skagit steelhead.

Our dependence upon hatcheries to sustain the early-returning winter-run steelhead is accomplished by nearly eliminating the native, December-run steelhead, for they make up less than ten percent of the December run. This trade-off troubled me, and I discussed it with Curt Kraemer. He explained that some progeny of February and March native steelhead would always be predisposed toward returning early in the run, that in effect, the Skagit's winter run will naturally continue to reseed for the extremely high mortality suffered by early-returning fish.

Following the Boldt decision in 1974, the "minimum sustainable harvest" numbers determined by the state were challenged by tribal biologists and then mostly ignored. The tribes and Washington's Department of Game (now Wildlife) had their own agendas, and the Skagit's native run of steelhead went into swift decline until, by the late 1970s, it had reached a low of about four thousand fish. It was evident that the tribes would ultimately need to depend on hatchery stocks, make peace with the Department of Wildlife, and co-manage the resource more intelligently. An outgrowth of this cooperation has been a division of hatchery stocks and a spring catch-and-release season.

I believe that a catch-and-release season is nothing more complicated than a way of making a world-class and critically finite resource go farther. That's it. According to Kraemer, the law was not put into effect to build native stocks. "If numbers were depressed, I'd shut down the river," he said. Neither does catch and release have anything in common with minimum sustainable harvest. The concept that a river's run of native, wild steelhead can be enjoyed at historically high escapement levels is for me the ultimate experience. I do not care to have this fishery gutted by a handful of anglers catching and killing these steelhead for their annual thirty-fish limit and then the river shut down because the minimum sustainable harvest has been reached.

The relative positions held by fly fishermen and gear fishermen as to what constitutes the sport of steelheading and how the Skagit's steelhead stocks should be managed are predictable and unlikely to change soon. But both groups are deeply committed guardians of the river, and that fact makes our differences less significant. And while we drink beer at the Fish In, our differences are forgotten when talk turns to the river's great winter-run bucks, valley gossip that is sure to heat up the imagination and keep the Red Hook flowing. In April of 1990, the question was more intriguing than in any other spring in memory.

Jerry Wintle's giant steelhead was the reason.

I had heard his story and seen it in print, all reported third-hand, and I didn't believe it. The facts were sketchy: On the last day of the previous season, April 30, 1989, Jerry caught a Skagit steelhead forty-eight inches long, and had, of course, released it.

I knew Jerry, and no one so understated his angling. This retired Canadian fished a cane rod with an old, battered English reel. Though he might be gracefully losing a step or two, he remained athletic, a good wader who cast a pretty line. No one read water better—or kept shorter fishing hours. Ehor Boyanowsky, a Canadian who is very knowledgeable in the ways of steelhead, once told me: "Jerry Wintle is the best steelhead fly fisherman in British Columbia—and he makes it look so easy. He goes out, makes a few casts, and before you know it he's caught a couple of steelhead!"

Last fall, when I met Jerry on the Thompson River's Graveyard Pool, I wasted little time getting around to his Skagit steelhead. He said that a couple of times he just about decided to break the fish off, for he became worried that the rod wouldn't hold up.

"You mean you hooked the fish on your little cane rod?"

"Oh yes," he said. "I had a hard time getting the fish in. It was so long I couldn't even hold it up."

"I understand you measured the fish with your rod?"

"Yes. I carefully measured its length. When I got back to camp I found my tape and measured the rod. No one would have believed it, so I knocked a couple of inches off."

"And that's how you got 48 inches?" I asked. Jerry nodded. He showed me, head to tail, rod butt to nearly halfway down the rod, the length of the steelhead.

"Just its head came to here," he added, and pointed to a place above the grip in the butt section.

"Such a steelhead would weigh over thirty pounds, could weigh over forty pounds. That's easily the longest steelhead I've ever heard of!" I paused to catch my breath and visualize it all. "What fly did he take?" Jerry doesn't tie and often fishes whatever is available in a friend's fly box.

"Oh, one of those orange things, you know, a shrimp fly."

"A General Practitioner?"

"Yes, that's the fly," he said. "Bob Aid had just given me one to try out."

John Farrar was in camp that day when Jerry came back. He recalled, "Jerry called out to Jean, 'Where's my tape?' and climbed into the cab of his pickup. Things began firing out of the back as he tore the truck apart. I couldn't imagine what had happened. No one had ever seen Jerry in such a state!"

Jean Wintle often goes fishing with her husband, and in recent years has videotaped some of his catches. Unfortunately, she had stayed in camp on this last morning of the season.

John and I retold our stories in the Fish In. We both believed Jerry, but neither of us could quite believe in such a steelhead, an odd dichotomy that I thought would only be settled when we had thoroughly exhausted a discussion of our mutual faith. One evening, when Bob Arnold had joined us and the topic had again turned to this fish, a local on the next bar stool explained that he was a Wildcatter, a member of a local steelhead club that had spearheaded many good works and possessed considerable political clout. When these credentials had sunk in, he leaned over and confided, "The Indians have caught steelhead of fifty pounds in their nets!"

I wondered if he believed his own story, whether this chapter in valley mythology was for the long-rod rubes swathed in pile and polypropylene. Years ago I heard this exact tale about the Kispiox River, but many angling experiences supported it. The Skagit was another matter. After all, an entire generation had passed between two fly-caught twenty-pound steelhead. Nevertheless, my friends and I greeted this news with courteous solemnity.

Shortly thereafter, I met Bob Forbes, a Washington Department of Wildlife enforcement officer. A couple months earlier he had checked in a forty-seven-inch steelhead that a gear fisherman caught from the lower Skagit in the Mount Vernon area. "The fish was a snake," said Forbes. "It weighed only twenty-nine pounds."

By his account, the buck was in good shape, somewhat colored, and certainly had lost a little weight. Given its slim build, its ocean weight would likely have been unremarkable, but certainly over thirty pounds. Other than Jerry Wintle's extraordinary fish, this was the longest steelhead (by nearly two inches) I knew of that had been reliably measured.

When I asked Curt Kraemer how real he thought these steelhead could be, whether the Skagit winter-run possesses the genetic potential for length beyond that of any other race of steelhead, I expected some sobersided debunking. Fish biologists are not by nature given to romantic speculation—no dreams of elephant graveyards in their carefully documented world. Besides, one fish—or even two—doesn't make a race. But Curt had a story to relate.

"Years ago, a dairy farmer on the lower Skagit caught a huge steelhead, which the Department of Wildlife heard about. When a biologist was sent out to investigate the catch, all that remained of the fish was a number of enormous steaks. The farmer, however, reported that the steelhead had weighed thirty-six pounds on his milk scales."

"Are there more recent records you can draw from?" I asked.

Jerry Wintle. *Photo credit: Don Roberts*

"Each year we have steelhead entering the Skagit that measure forty-four to forty-six inches," he said. "Potentially they could weigh thirty-five pounds plus. You've heard of the 48-inch steelhead caught by a fly fishermen?"

"Yes," I said, "Jerry Wintle. I know him. He wouldn't make up such a story." Curt then told me about the 47-inch steelhead that Bob Forbes had checked in.

Had Kraemer ever aged such a steelhead? Not these fish, he said, but he told me that he has used bait-fishing gear to secure brood stock for the hatchery operation at Chambers Creek, and one day he had caught steelhead of 16½, 22, and 31½ pounds. Scale samples determined the ages of the three fish, all remembered for their remarkable life histories. The 16½-pound female was spawning for the third time, while the 22-pound male was spawning for the second. The 31½ pound male was 43½ inches long and had spent two years as a premigrant in the Sauk, and then more than five complete years in the ocean, a 2/5 life history, and a first-spawning steelhead in the eighth year of life.

Five straight years of rapid ocean growth, a very rare component in any race's life history, represents a size potential of awesome proportions, a steelhead four feet long, for example. Two fly-caught Skagit steelhead of nearly this size, bucks of twenty-five to thirty pounds, were caught by Bob York and Dan Reiff. Twenty-five Pounder Hole now celebrates Bob's fish, a steelhead he had to chase for more than a half-mile before beaching it for a safe release.

Kraemer brought our discussion back to less-celebrated steelhead, and explained that although approximately fifty percent of the first-spawning native fish spent two years in the ocean, *fifty percent spent three, four, and five years in the ocean.* This breakdown was strongly at variance with hatchery steelhead, of which eighty-five percent spent two years in the ocean and fifteen percent spent three years. The rare one-salt steelhead, with either native or hatchery origins, were invariably "jacks," sexually mature males only sixteen or seventeen inches long. (A sampling of three hundred steelhead contained a single one-salt male.)

What all this means to the angler invites generalizations. Most December and January steelhead will be hatchery stock smaller than later-arriving native fish. Eric Beamer, Managing Biologist for the Skagit System Cooperative, claims that twenty-pound steelhead are a very uncommon catch in their nets.

That fully half the native fish spend three years or more in the ocean helps to explain why these spring-run steelhead typically weigh over ten pounds. Anyone claiming the Sauk and Skagit races to be the largest of all winter steelhead would soon hear arguments on behalf of the Skykomish, or perhaps for Olympic Peninsula Indian rivers less well known to fly fishermen, the Quinault or the Queets. Regardless, the list of Skagit-class winter rivers is very short. And I would begin that list with the Skagit itself.

Late in April, Don Roberts flew up from Bend, Oregon, to join me for a week on the Skagit. He would not even pick up a rod, so that he could give his full concentration to completing a magazine pictorial on winter steelhead fly fishing. We both knew this sport to be ever so slow, in the worst possible light and weather. However, some reading material and a large umbrella would enable him to pass the time while I tried to find a pretty steelhead for his cameras. There was enough rain to encourage the steelhead to move, and we found a ten-pound buck at last light on the very first day. That night, rain fell in a driving deluge that blew out all the waters from just below the Cascade snow pack to Puget Sound. The feeder creeks, the larger streams that supported angling reputations, and the Sauk were all so roiled that they were taking out even the Skagit. When we launched the boat the next morning, the Skagit was up more than two feet, and I couldn't make out my boot tops while standing knee deep in the river and the rain.

We found the Mixer deserted, a rare event for any April morning, but a natural expectation this day. The river flooded the gravel bar and was tearing away at the newly leafed willows, which only the day before had caught my lazy backcasts. Entire cottonwoods, alders, and evergreens floated by and served as awful reminders of the hell breaking loose on the Skagit's tributaries. A raven perched in a passing tree and croaked out a greeting.

"He must be looking for his mate," I said. "All the animals, two by two." Don shook his head and happily set up housekeeping beneath the umbrella.

I worked through the long pool, confident that I would find a steelhead near where I had been wading the previous day, all but certain that the fish would prefer the new lies close to shore, water now three to four feet deep. This did not happen, and on the second pass through I reached out somewhat farther, to water at least six feet deep. The fly I chose for this was my marabou version of Bill McMillan's Winter's Hope, a high-visibility dressing that could, I thought, pull a fish from the deeper holds to track the fly into the shallows and take it hard on the swing. When my second time through was no more successful, I returned to the boat to complain to Don and to note that even the gear fishermen were not about.

I wondered aloud if perhaps the steelhead were still holding their old lies, water really too deep for the fly, but at a distance I could reach with my two-handed rod. Don has little experience with winter steelhead, but he is a shrewd judge of rivers and of people. I told him I had deeper-running sink tips, and he urged me to start at the head again with a nineteen-foot sink tip I had made by cutting off the lead from a Teeny 300 line.

Each cast made slightly upstream and across was followed by a strong back-mend and a dead drift that gave the line time to work the fly down deep. I was above the softest water in the long drift with the fly just beginning to swing when a steelhead took the fly solidly, made a single jump, and raced for the middle of the river.

"There he is!" I called. The big salmon reel's ratchet changed to a higher octave as the backing knot disappeared into the river. Don came down the shore with cameras flying, a one-man production company with exclusive film rights to the unfolding drama. I prayed the hook would hold. It did, and with the brilliant buck of twelve or thirteen pounds panting in the shallows, Don the director, the passionate artist, went about his business.

"Work with me!" he cried. With the fish's panic not yet rekindled, Don was in macro heaven. Shoot at water level and underwater, switch cameras, shoot in color, more in black-and-white. Give the fish sips of oxygen. I was watching for a change in the steelhead's complexion, a telltale blotching that would signal serious stress and shock. Nothing of the sort appeared, and the released steelhead darted into the clearing currents.

"One more," said Don, "and I'll be happy. Insurance."

"Perhaps the buck has a fair companion!" I said

I walked back up the pool, dealt myself in just a few casts above where the steelhead had struck my fly, and again began working the Winter Hope. As the fly was swinging through the holding lie, an enormous hen steelhead raced up at the fly with such momentum that the take occurred on the surface. I saw her dorsal fin roll through a slow-motion arc, saw her turn, and felt her weight on my rod as the fly gained a firm hold. The steelhead bolted for the heavy currents, gathered the river about her, and streaked for the Mixmaster. Seventy yards downriver she made a towering leap that carried her ten feet across the currents. "My God! She'll go eighteen pounds," I cried to Don. I was certain that that would be it, but the reel continued paying out line. "Better get the boat!" I called as I stumbled after the fish, astonished now that she was more than a hundred yards away, already the longest—and fastest—single nonstop run in all my years of steelheading.

She stopped abruptly and slowly came upstream on the same track on which she had departed. The steelhead was determined not to run downriver again, but remained a stone wall of resistance close in, fighting the rod as if it were a petty intrusion into her peace of mind. Twice I thought I had her when she staggered and wobbled in the shallows, but each time she spread her pectoral fins, steadied herself, and fought off the big rod by moving out and disappearing into deeper water. The last time I saw her clearly I had been able to move her into a couple of feet of water only a rod's length away.

I doubled the rod over parallel to the water and tried to drag her into sudden exhaustion. She would not roll over, and I could see her tense as I applied pressure. She moved upriver twenty feet, but before I could pressure her again, the hook came away.

When you've had your way with a steelhead this long, there is no loss. I was jubilant. No doubt Don was disappointed in equal measure. A portrait of this steelhead, a hen fish of rare beauty, could have fulfilled his expectations, too. We could not have scripted a more exciting meeting, and for both of us this steelhead would become the Skagit in our tales of fly fishing.

Joe Butorac helped me put that sense of the river into words.

One evening I was on the Mixer with Joe and Faith Holste. They were well below me, and I could watch them each time my fly began to swing. An hour before dark I saw Joe react to a steelhead's take, a strong pull that bested Joe's reaction. He changed from his Skagit Monster to a Half and Half, a smaller marabou fly that might entice the steelhead again. When this failed to bring the steelhead back, he pulled out. Joe and Faith were chatting on the beach as I continued fishing through. I think I found his steelhead, a pull, and then nothing. When I could not find the fish again, and I thought only twenty minutes remained of the day, I decided to reel in and change flies. I did this when the swing was nearly completed, bending over and reeling as fast as possible, the Winter Orange skidding across and up the river. Halfway back to me, and in water less than two feet deep, a steelhead slammed the fly so hard I wondered that it didn't break off. The fish jumped twice and drove for the middle of the river amid astonished laughter from Joe and Faith. As soon as I could collect myself, I began to laugh, too. Now I believed John Farrar's story: Jimmy Wright, a well-known Canadian angler, twice raised an April steelhead on a dry fly by standing exactly where I stood. How little we know about these winter steelhead of spring!

The steelhead became mine to release, a buck of ten pounds that glowed molten in the damp night air. Joe and Faith stood over me and studied the fish. "I've caught these steelhead on the last day of the season and you could still see through their fins," he said.

My hand ran along the flank of this steelhead, this ocean race only fleetingly of my river world, and lifted the broad tail. In the faint twilight I saw the clear outline of my fingers. I gave a gentle push. In a blink, the steelhead was gone.

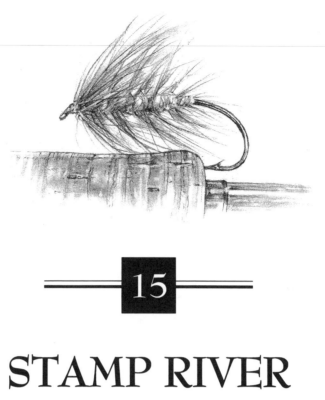

15

STAMP RIVER

T H I S pilgrimage began on an August day when the temperature had reached ninety degrees by midmorning. Vancouver Island's forests were tinder dry and all logging operations had been shut down, an enforced holiday for faller Mark Spence. He and I now trudged along an abandoned logging road, sweating hard in our waders and wishing for the sound of the river.

"We're almost there," he said, and pointed with his ten-foot drift rod to an opening in the woods. Mark sometimes guides to validate his passion for steelhead. I had come to enjoy the huge man's bonhomie and rascally sense of humor. "I   go get those wily steelheads," he would say each morning.

As we entered the clearing and first felt the coolness of the Stamp River, Mark mopped his face with a bandanna and waved it upstream and then downstream from our position at the bend of the dogleg.

"This is General Money's Pool," he said simply. I studied the run and thought it was at least seven hundred feet long. The water was impossibly clear, a lens of shimmering viscosities that brought into focus the splashes of orange and yellow on the freestone bottom. The greater depths, mostly on our side of the river, were filtered green, and ascending fish would easily disappear in the cover.

At the top end, from a shallows that ran from wooded bank to sweeping river bar, the Stamp broke cleanly to become several hundred feet of boulders and foam. A lone fisherman, nearly hidden in the

glare, cast roe, his large white float trailing a sparkling tail of monofilament as it arched through the sunlight. Directly before us the river slowed and deepened. Children were cannonballing its depths as their spaniel swam and barked from one geyser to another.

I asked Mark about the tiny feeder stream that trickled into the Stamp below our feet. "I've seen steelhead holding here at first light," he said. "One morning I counted eight." The long tailout was like the top end, but in slow motion and without the shallows of the gravel bar. Presenting a fly from the bank side would entail a deep and difficult wade with no room for a backcast. I would have a much easier time casting from the gravel bar across from us, and if I thought the pool held steelhead, it would take several hours to fish the entire run.

"Could the General have fished the pool from this side?" I asked. Mark saw the water as a drift fisherman, and the question was moot. We walked along the shore, located the best shallows, and started across. The river came to the very top of my waders. "I'm sure he never crossed the river to do his fishing," I added. We reached the far side and walked up the gravel bar to watch the bait fisherman continue through the pool.

General Money had a little cabin on the high bank across the river from where we stood. It was gone now. At least we could find no trace of it. The heavily wooded hillside still shaded the run beneath where the cabin must have been. From my new vantage, I saw how the General must have often fished Great Pool, as he called the water that now bears his name. Using his two-handed Wye rod, he would walk below his cabin and cover all the water with spey casts, the slowest part of the fly's swing taking place in the deep shadows along the bank, the crease of holding water I would reach briefly and only with difficulty. The General's approach was impossible to duplicate with my nine-and-a-half-foot rod and forward-taper line.

When the angler quit the water, Mark stepped in and began to search the lies, his float marking the course of the roe. He must have felt there was little promise in the exercise, for he made short work of it and joined me on the bar.

"Not a thing," he said. "Give it a go with your fly."

There was no doubt how I wanted to proceed. It didn't matter that there were no fish. I had tied on a low-water Atlantic salmon fly, an Orange Charm, and I would cast and mend and swim the sparsely dressed fly through the pool. That would provide great satisfaction, and in these relative ways Mark and I were fishing the river with different expectations. As I waded in and worked out my line, I wanted to tell him that my fly didn't possess any magical properties, that in fact I had more faith in his roe. It was just that my sense of historical propriety had determined how I wished this day to be joined with the past.

About halfway down the top end, a very large boulder lying just below the surface held up currents and caused unnatural drag. It took several casts to work out the mends, after which a very forceful upstream mend would eventually give me a proper presentation past this obstruction. The first time I was able to swing the fly into the downstream end of the boulder, I saw a flash and felt the steelhead take the fly. I was so astonished that I raised my rod and tightened too early. The steelhead was clearly visible as it sought to return to its station, but after several head shakes it panicked and began a downstream run. "Good for you!" cried Mark, and the fly came away. This had not been a large steelhead, probably no more than five pounds, but few trout had ever pleased me half so much.

The General, I thought, must be smiling.

BRIGADIER GENERAL NOEL MONEY

Brigadier General Noel Money first traveled to Vancouver Island in 1913, reportedly on the advice of his physician, who thought that any change from the English climate would provide a healthy antidote to a lingering illness. He was forty-six, a veteran of the South African War, and commander of the Shropshire Imperial Yeomanry when wounded in the Western Transvaal. At war's end in 1901, he

← Brigadier General Noel Money

resigned his army commission and returned to England and married. More than sixty years later I would come to know his son, Gordon.

If Money's health was his expressed reason for seeking out this remote corner of the world, a no-less-important motivation was the Campbell River's famous chinook salmon. The very English Canadians had brought to this extraordinary race meticulously crafted cane rods, finely machined reels, and a socially prominent salmon club to dispense buttons and badges commemorating the testing of wills and equipment. They distinguished salmon over thirty pounds as "tyee," and called lesser chinook "springs," names that survive to this day. No other salmon resort of the period so attracted an international clientele, and Campbell River justifiably called itself the "Salmon Capital of the World."

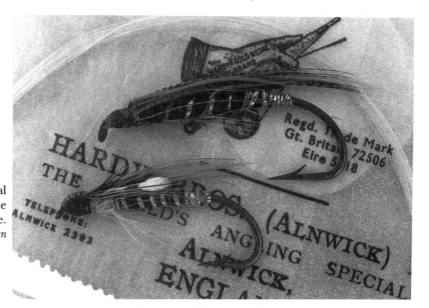

General Money # 2 tied by the general and saved by Ted Pengelley, the General's ghillie.
Photo credit: Arthur J. Lingren

Money saw business opportunities in these developments, and when he returned to England he sold the family estate, Culmington Manor in Shropshire, and left again for Vancouver Island. He settled with his family just south of Campbell River in the small coastal community of Qualicum Beach, and made plans to build a hotel for traveling salmon anglers. The enterprise, however, was delayed by the outbreak of World War I. Money took command of the 159th Brigade and was directly responsible for the liberation of Turkish-controlled Jerusalem. He was promoted to Brigadier General and retired once again to British Columbia, a revered old soldier, and an institution in the making, for his Qualicum Inn soon became an instrinsic part of the tyee experience.

Money's formal education in England had included a proper grounding in Atlantic salmon fly fishing. While a university student at Oxford, he had his first game book constructed. Leatherbound, with pages printed to record every category of fish and game, it could detail his fortunes on rivers and in the field. This was more than a logging-in of catches. He noted his companions, recorded his thoughts and the water conditions, and often headed the page with a photograph. Religiously keeping at this ever-expanding history—there would be nine game books in all—was a habit he maintained for more than half a century.

The General applied what he knew of Atlantic salmon to steelhead and found little reason to change long-practiced techniques. The steelhead were usually winter-runs, as are most in the waters of Vancouver Island's eastern slopes. The migrations came with a rush, and on the small rivers, half the annual escapement often occurred in six weeks, mostly in December and January, and their predictable abundance soon attracted a devoted angling following.

Summer steelhead were another matter. Common in West Coast streams and their remote canyon

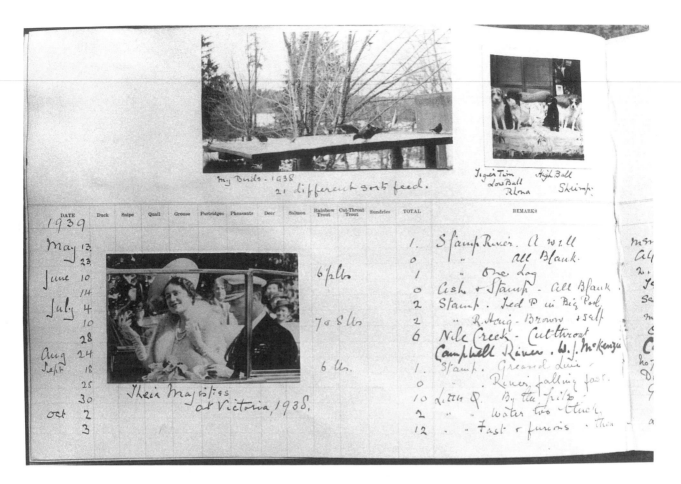

A page from the general's gamebook in 1939. The entry on July 10 marks a day Roderick Haig-Brown described in A RIVER NEVER SLEEPS. Note also: a) Entry for July 4: "Ted P," is Ted Pengelley. b) The General returned to the river on September 18 and took a 6 pound steelhead on the "greased line." c) Snapshot is of King George VI and Queen Elizabeth.

waters, the fish ascended inconspicuously and disappeared into deep pools, not to be seen again for weeks, even months. The spawning run continued in the company of freshly ascending salmon. Steelhead were obscured within these more massive migrations, and most were lost to angling. With the exception of the Stamp River, a summer steelhead was a single fish, encountered by accident.

Along the west coast of Vancouver Island, west and north of Washington's Cape Flattery, is Barkley Sound. Here is an immense kingdom of island groups, capes, and fjords. One of these arms of the sea, much longer than the rest, is Alberni Inlet, and it reaches so deeply into the island that it nearly makes two islands of the whole. Many rivers tumble into this sea, but none is so fine as those that begin with the Somass at Port Alberni.

The Somass is a short trunk of a river, a gatherer of other rivers and their lakes: only a mile upstream from tidewater, it splits to become the Sproat and the Stamp. Named for Captain Edward Stamp, a nineteenth-century English lumber merchant, the Stamp is joined, many miles upstream, by the Ash. All three rivers have flows sustained and tempered by very large lakes, and two of these, Sproat Lake and the Stamp's Great Central Lake, are sockeye-salmon lakes that have always been important to the commercial fishing industry of the area.

The first summer steelhead enter the Somass in June. They pass by Port Alberni on the flood tide before reaching the Stamp and the shelter of deep runs below steep hillsides and stately suburban homes. As the fish continue upstream, they enter a forest corridor honeycombed with logging roads and prairie farms, and anglers can find ways to follow them from salt water to their destination just below Great Central Lake.

Roderick Haig-Brown. *Photo by Mary Randlett*

General Money and his friends might sink a red or orange fly during periods of high water, but summer steelhead generally belonged to low-water dressings and the floating line. On the Stamp, as nowhere else, the rationale for fly selection and the methods employed for their presentation could be the same for Atlantic salmon and steelhead trout.

RODERICK HAIG-BROWN

By the late 1930s, Roderick Haig-Brown, a young Campbell River magistrate, was nearing completion of his monumental angling work, *The Western Angler*, published by The Derrydale Press in 1939, a definitive two-volume account of fresh- and saltwater angling in British Columbia. Whenever possible, he relied upon knowledge gained by local experts, and he combined this with his own considerable experience and the latest studies completed by provincial fishery biologists. Bill Nation, the father of Canadian Kamloops trout fishing, provided many original patterns and explained how best to make use of each on interior lakes. Tommy Brayshaw, twenty years Haig-Brown's senior, was a self-taught artist, and his brilliant paintings of Canadian gamefish illustrated the book. The author himself was wise in the ways of Campbell River salmon. During his youth in England he had learned how to work a Devon minnow in spate rivers for Atlantic salmon, so a transfer to winter steelhead was easy. His years of searching the Campbell River's Canyon Pool with a Steelhead Bee were still to come, and his knowledge of these more-elusive summer steelhead was now, at best, tentative. Not so the General's, and Haig-Brown gathered from their relationship an understanding of the Stamp River's steelhead and an idolatrous respect for his mentor. When *The Western Angler* was published shortly before the General's passing in 1941, it began with the following dedication: "To General Money of Qualicum Beach, finest of western anglers, and to his own Stamp River, loveliest and most generous of western streams."

I came to know these icons of western angling first through correspondence and ultimately in person. Tommy Brayshaw was a friend, and I discovered an original, two-volume copy of *The Western Angler* through him. I met Haig-Brown at a banquet in Portland, Oregon, and we had dinner together. The memory of that meeting and his letters to me are among my most cherished possessions. Gordon Money introduced me to his father through the General's game books. One afternoon we spent hours thumbing through the volumes, turning the pages and visiting Siberia and India, big game and upland game, Midlands trout and Scottish salmon. New World elk and salmon were there, too, as well as a consistent record of summer-run steelhead fly fishing. This was the archetypical Englishman taking his leisure, the sum total of a man's life measured neither by military deed nor by fortune gained, but by the intense pleasure his gentlemanly pursuits brought him. As we neared the end of the last game book, I came upon a single terse entry telling that on July 10, 1939, a day on the Stamp had been completed with "R. Haig-Brown." According to the ledger, they had killed two steelhead, a seven- and an eight-pounder.

Haig-Brown would later write about this experience with wonderful sensitivity in the "June" chapter of *A River Never Sleeps*. He had introduced the General to "a new method" of presenting a low water fly, the greased line, based on *Greased Line Fishing For Salmon*, the book Donald Rudd had written under the pseudonym Jock Scott.

The General took great pleasure in applying the method, and then hooking and successfully gaffing his catch.

"That's wonderful sport," he said. "We should have tried it long ago." He knelt beside his fish and freed the fly from the corner of the jaw. "I'm going to send away for the light rod as soon as we get home. You must help me pick one out from the catalogue." We took the fish back in the shade and sat down. "That's my day's fishing," the General said. "I'm getting old. But we've found something new for the river after all these years."

I do not know whether the General kept faith with his decision to purchase the new rod, but I think he did. He returned to the Stamp on September 18, more than two months later, and, as was his custom, he fished Great Pool. The game book records that he took a six-pound steelhead, and under the heading "Remarks" he wrote, "Greased line."

The two game-book entries signaled the passing of an angling heritage from one person who exemplified the best of our fly fishing traditions, to another who would communicate those ideals to future generations through angling literature of lasting importance. No small thing to be a direct descendant of such lineage!

STAMP RIVER STEELHEAD

Stamp Falls is a famous cataract four miles above where the Stamp joins the Sproat. Here the river gathers itself for a plunge into a pool that seems to possess no bottom. Because winter steelhead congregate in its depths, the Meat Hole, as it is inelegantly called by locals, is a popular place to dunk roe. Few of these fish continue their migration beyond this barrier, a habit established during eons when the falls was virtually impassable. Some years ago a fishway was constructed at the falls, and while this has assisted biologists in determining escapements and securing hatchery stock, it has also allowed a few winter fish to pass upstream. Historically, only the summer steelhead could best the tremendous currents of the falls, and today Stamp Falls still marks the nearly complete separation of the two seasonally distinct races.

Winter steelhead first enter the Somass in November, with peak escapement from late November to January. When rain is adequate, it becomes the rare November-run winter steelhead river. The majority of the escapement is over by March, though a few fresh fish are found well into April.

G. S. Horncastle, in his study, *Life History of Steelhead Trout from the Somass River on Vancouver Island,* 1981, determined that among winter steelhead, 9.2 percent were repeat spawners with females outnumbering males 7.5 to 1. Approximately sixty-five percent of the maiden steelhead were two-year ocean fish, while thirty-five percent were three-year ocean fish. (The one-year and four-year ocean categories were both represented by single fish from a sampling of 163 steelhead.) The two-year ocean steelhead averaged twenty-seven inches, or about seven pounds, and ranged from three to twelve pounds. Three-year ocean steelhead averaged nearly thirty inches in length and ten pounds, with a range of six to eighteen pounds. The "official" Stamp River record is a male winter steelhead of a little over nineteen pounds. A few local stories circulate of one or two steelhead of twenty pounds, but clearly these weights are the upper size limit for this race.

Horncastle's investigation of summer-run steelhead revealed a race significantly different from the winter-run. In the sampling of sixty-two wild steelhead, twenty-five percent were one-year ocean fish, and seventy-five percent were two-year ocean fish. Hatchery steelhead for the same age groups were sixteen percent and eighty-four percent respectively. *Steelhead with three or more years of ocean residency were totally absent from either group.* The one-year ocean fish averaged 23 1/4 inches; the two-year ocean fish averaged 27 inches, or about seven pounds, and exhibited considerable range—from about twenty-two to nearly thirty-eight inches. However, the great majority of Stamp summer-run steelhead were ten pounds or less; twelve pounds was exceptional. I asked Bob Hooton, senior biologist for the Fisheries Branch (1986), whether anything was unique about Stamp River steelhead. Without hesitation he replied, "Yes, their small size."

Among all wild steelhead, winter- or summer-run, the females outnumbered males by two to one, an expected imbalance due to the polygamous nature of the species. The ratio changes to one to one with hatchery stock; the reasons for this are not understood.

The summer fish spawn in late February and March, the winter-run about four weeks later. As the spawned-out steelhead, the kelts, pick their way downstream, they are met by thousands of May-run sockeye salmon migrating upstream for the lakes that receive their spawning tributaries. These steelhead, survivors of the season past, then enter Barkley Sound and join maiden summer steelhead of the new spawning year. Sadly, miles of sockeye gill nets document this passing of steelhead generations. About a thousand steelhead, mostly summer-run stocks, will perish in the nets, an incidental catch lost in a sockeye harvest numbering in the hundreds of thousands.

To mitigate these losses, the Robertson Creek Hatchery began releasing summer-run steelhead smolts in 1974. This program was increased in 1977, as a result of funding from the Salmonid Enhancement Program, a far-reaching joint effort by federal and provincial governments to increase salmonid stocks, including Atlantic salmon, to twice current levels, or to levels first exploited in the nineteenth century.

Robertson Creek Hatchery is located on the Stamp River at the outlet of Great Central Lake. Its primary function is raising several million chinook fry and a million coho fry. For ten years, the steelhead reared were summer-run stock. In 1986, about 60,000 summer-run and 125,000 winter-run steelhead smolts were released, the latter always the offspring of wild fish. The returns range from 3 to 7 percent for winter steelhead, to 1.5 percent for the summer run. In spite of this meager return, Bob Hooton estimated that at any given time in the summer there are 1,000 to 2,000 hatchery, and 200 to 250 wild summer-run steelhead in the Stamp.

Biologists discovered years ago that smolts released near the hatchery site returned to the hatchery as adults a year or two later with such determination and speed that they were in large measure lost to angling. At one point, steelhead were captured at the hatchery, trucked downriver, and released to repeat their upstream journey. Hooton found a better solution when smolts were released at points lower down in the system. These enterprising efforts have allegedly resulted in what some anglers call "The Miracle Mile," a mile or so of water just below the confluence of the Stamp and Sproat rivers where summer-run steelhead congregate for weeks before continuing upstream.

A few summer-run steelhead begin reaching the Robertson Creek Hatchery in June. Ten females and several males are secured each month for hatchery production. The other steelhead are collected at the hatchery and ultimately sold to a fish buyer who bids on the entire lot. When I visited the hatchery and discussed this with Mike Wolf, a federal fish culturist, we were staring into a pen containing several hundred steelhead from four to ten pounds. "We don't want these fish," said Wolf. "We want these hatchery fish caught."

At least part of the problem has been lack of angling pressure. The summer angler may dabble in brown trout from Great Central Lake, or he may spend a day or two hunting for steelhead in the Stamp, but basically, deep in his bones, he is a salmon fisherman. And no wonder: Port Alberni is famous for its tyee. One day I saw a sixty-three-pound chinook "in glass," the expression locals use to describe a salmon displayed on ice and under glass. This particular fish, the largest tyee that summer from Vancouver Island waters, was the source of considerable civic pride and served to justify the city's claim, "Salmon Capital of the World," a title they insist on sharing with Campbell River.

Mark would come to my campsite at Stamp Falls Provincial Park each dawn, and after coffee we would drive and then hike to his favorite water, a pool several hundred feet upstream from the top end of Money's. One morning here, where the Ash River met the Stamp, I raised a steelhead that had nosed up beneath the shallow turbulence of the confluence. Mark liked to fish farther down the pool, water that failed me completely, and a morning hardly passed without his finding a fin-clipped hatchery steelhead. After a few days, I began to feel that some combination of river depth and the manner in which steelhead held to the far side prevented my fly from slowing enough to encourage a rise.

After lunch, Mark and I would explore, sometimes driving to the upper Ash, or downstream to fish the Somass and Swanson Pool, a fly water every bit as classic as the General's. When I couldn't make a steelhead from two halfhearted rises, I became determined to return in November and cast a fly for the winter run. There would be many more fish then, tidewater steelhead fairly dripping with sea lice, and Mark thought that if the water were low the fishing would be grand.

"Not like chasing these ghosts of summer, eh?" I challenged.

"No! Those winter steelhead are *voracious*! You can't believe how strong they are—and they're *blue*! Wait until you see one against snow!" he answered.

The beautiful Ash River is a series of falls and extremely deep canyon pools. It has few access points, cannot be floated, and sustains little angling pressure. Biologists estimate that no more than one in fifty summer-run steelhead entering the Somass are Ash stock, but all of these are wild fish preserved as a natural gene pool.

Ash steelhead collect just below the river's confluence with the Stamp, exactly where Mark and I began each fishing day together. Rick Axford, provincial fishery technician, has frequently donned a wet suit and snorkled through the pool. He has counted as many as two hundred steelhead, the Ash fish spooky and temperamental by midsummer. Axford is also an enthusiastic angler who feels that these summer steelhead are easier to locate with a fly in late summer, just before the heaviest chinook and coho runs, or in November when most of the salmon have spawned.

The continuous recycling of the Stamp's hatchery-bred summer-run stock became a worry to biologists at the Robertson Creek Hatchery, and in 1986 they secured Ash steelhead to invigorate the Stamp gene pool. Biologists are certain that the use of wild winter steelhead for brood stock has been instrumental in maintaining that race's vigor and wild nature. It is hoped their efforts at enhancing runs of summer-run steelhead will be equally successful.

We returned to the Stamp every evening, I to fish the top end of Money's Pool, Mark to drift bait or bobbers below the mouth of the Ash. Just as the sun dropped below the mountains, a steelhead boiled beside my Green-Butt Skunk and did not take. I repeated the cast, and I felt only a tentative strike, more a pluck. I searched methodically down through the upper pool for a new fish and to rest the steelhead holding in the growing darkness. My concentration and the sound of the river so filled my head that I barely heard Mark's call, "Trey! I've got a big one!"

He was only a shadow against the firs, but the steelhead revealed his whereabouts with a jump that caught the last light of day on its flanks. I quickly returned to my steelhead, gave in to my scattered senses, and sent the fly directly across the heart of the run exactly as before. The take was solid, but there was no fish at the end of it. This had happened to me several weeks earlier on Oregon's Deschutes: On the fourth rise, in complete darkness, I had hooked a four-pound steelhead. This night would not be like that one, for the steelhead did not come back. I damned my lack of patience and wished I had waited ten more minutes until not even a crack of light remained.

I picked my way across the river and soon joined Mark on the bank. He was pumped from his experience, a man so fully restored by his catch and its release that the story came out rapid-fire as his pace kept me jogging in my waders. "Ah, that was a big bastard, at least twelve pounds," he said as we made our way down the path in the darkness.

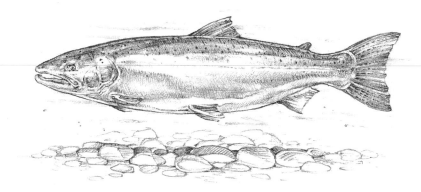

16

THOMPSON RIVER

AT first light, the bighorn sheep come down from the foothills of Arthur's Seat, the stone mountain throne that towers above the Thompson River's Lake Pool. White rumps flashing from the mists and chukar talk signal the band's passage through the scattered ponderosa pines. At least thirty animals pause along the bench immediately above the river to pasture on yellow grasses that grow around clumps of prickly pear. As the kids frolic, the ewes pick up a deeply rutted game trail and continue toward the river. Three rams linger to test the wind, to study the river below, and this morning, to watch Don Roberts and me cast our flies for steelhead.

The hollows and swards of tender new grass along the railroad tracks are the band's destination, passing boxcars of grain continuing to seed these bottomland pockets. When only the dominant ram remains, he drops to a ledge where a second ram has been waiting, and the two take the trail that leads to the river. In ten minutes, Don and I watch one of them drinking at the tailout while keeping an eye on our progress down Lake Pool.

When I introduced my friend to this band the previous evening, the sunset was silhouetting them on a commanding ridge. "The scene is too romantic to believe," he had marveled. We thought the sheep to be spiritually akin to the river's wild steelhead, a race famous for its great size and extraordinary strength.

David Thompson, after whom the river is named, was Canada's Lewis and Clark, an intrepid explorer and brilliant geographer who surveyed western Canada and became the first European to travel

219

the entire length of the Columbia River. He came this way in the 1800s, and today Thompson would probably feel that little has changed. Businesses here in eastern British Columbia never found enough timber on the hillsides or topsoil in the valleys to encourage more than skimpy enterprise. Some cattle are raised. The roadside fruit stands that open seasonally service backyard orchards. Tiny frontier settlements survive precariously by selling food and gas to motorists. Railroad tracks run on both sides of the river, and here and there a highway peeks into one's angling sanctuary. Mostly, however, there are the canyon waters, the mountains, and a sense of timelessness.

Fall rains ended the arid summer a month ago. Wildflowers and sagebrush sprinkled with pale yellow blossoms lend a springlike ambience to the northern desert. Early November is lush, invigorating, pungent. All the senses are embraced. The days are warm, the nights long, with hoarfrost mornings that set the tangle of riverside willows to shedding their leaves. I was here in mid-October when the river ran oily beneath thunderheads filled with arctic cold and the mountains got a dusting of snow. On that day, the surface river was a tepid fifty-eight degrees. Three weeks of benign weather had nudged the temperature down only six degrees. This was, however, less a matter of concern for steelhead metabolisms than for my wading comfort. These steelhead, like more northern races, remain active when the water temperature drops into the thirties. Bob York, an old Kispiox hand who chases after steelhead nine months a year, once told me of standing on rim ice in late December and raising Thompson fish to a dry fly.

One lazy fall afternoon I sat beside the river to soak up some sun while Harry Lemire tried to put the river's steelhead into perspective. "When I'm on the Dean, I think its steelhead are the strongest," he said, "but when I'm on the Thompson, I think its steelhead are strongest."

"Ah, yes," I said, "but Thompson steelhead are larger, the typical male running at least sixteen pounds, the female only a pound or two less. Aren't steelhead of less than ten pounds extremely rare? And Harry, wasn't your largest steelhead from this river a buck of thirty-seven pounds that took you a half-mile downriver?" I recalled that two friends of ours, Jimmy Hunnicutt and Sean Gallagher, had both taken huge Thompson steelhead on dry flies.

Comparing the Thompson to the Dean is as valid as comparing chocolate to vanilla. Harry was not comparing the races so much as distinguishing their steelhead from all others He applies many standards to his fly fishing, size of the fish being but one. Strength and response to surface flies are attributes he values more. In the end, I was happy that he dismissed my nitpicking with a wise smile.

The Thompson runs bigger than life, always a collection of superlatives when comparing steelhead stories. Certainly the vistas are grander, the river larger, and the currents more powerful than any other river in my experience except Idaho's Snake. The pools would seem too large to cover properly, too large to affect a personality and develop a following among fly fishers, but this is not so. Typically, the pools are shallow, the steelhead often choosing lies close to the beach, and if they are not disturbed, they may hold these exposed stations for hours. The best opportunity of finding such virgin water is at first light, and my willingness to rise in the dark when I'm fishing the Thompson is due only to that consideration.

Martel, Grease Hole, Rock Garden (the most treacherous water to wade in all of steelheading), John's Rock, Lake Pool, and Graveyard are but a few of the many, and each has its fly fishing faithful. There is, naturally, a strategy for fishing each, a "bucket," where the steelhead are most likely to hold, and secondary lies that must be searched confidently. The fly fisher will still be learning new approaches after a dozen trips through.

Long casts are helpful when searching for Thompson River steelhead; prodigious casts with double-handed rods are necessary when covering far distant lies. Throat-tightening caution is a fact of life for even the most audacious wader when he balances his life on huge, perfectly smooth rocks well-slimed with algae. A wading staff and stream cleats will reduce the number of times he falls in, and a few pools will call his number nearly every time. The largest steelhead lurk beyond his longest cast and dare him to wade deeper. Here the downstream-sprinting steelhead is a runaway until it has a

Graveyard Pool →

mind to stop—and some never do. Surely fly fishermen are spooled more frequently on the Thompson than on any other steelhead river.

I followed Don through Lake Pool, taking a somewhat different line by wading a little deeper, making a longer across-river cast, throwing deeper outside mends, and swinging a different fly. The 2/0 Ferry Canyon, a Randall Kaufmann tie, is a purple pattern with a flame butt that glows deeply in low light. I often go to it during periods of overcast, but particularly at dawn and dusk. We both fished floating lines, rarely mended to sink the fly, and generally were contented with a greased line approach. Occasionally I changed to a waking dry, a new variation of the reliable Waller Waker.

The Thompson summer-run are so free rising and surface oriented by nature that rarely is any other approach necessary. Only when heavy angling traffic has driven them into deeper lies do I occasionally wish for a sink tip line. Because the best lies are often flats with weak currents near the shore, the fast sinking shooting head becomes very troublesome, the fly fouling the bottom on nearly every cast.

When Don could go no farther, he quietly pulled out and watched the sheep browsing in the mountain's deep shade. I soon stood where he had fished and only grudgingly became convinced that the pool held no steelhead. While working down, I had occasionally felt the tap, tap of parr. The day before on the pool, a sharp little strike from a fourteen-inch rainbow had for a moment fooled me into thinking steelhead. These trout are not residualized premigrant steelhead, but a resident race, on the order of Deschutes "redsides." Biologists have told me that they grow to more than five pounds, but are uncommon to more than eighteen inches. My big flies rarely find them.

We took the short hike around the "lake" of the pool, picking up the river where it narrowed and plunged by so strongly that a shallow slot of holding water invited continued investigation with our flies. Don went through with a purple Muddler, a pattern he designed for Deschutes steelhead. I followed with the big Ferry Canyon, working down the short lie until the fly was swinging across the shallow flat. I was to my last cast when a buck came up behind the fly to grab it, nearly a direct downstream take, and as I tightened, it spasmodically completed a head-and-tail rise that brought it several feet upstream. The take, typical for large bucks, helped sex the steelhead for me; the single broad stripe confirmed it.

"I just fished my fly over that spot!" Don exclaimed.

"He's not well hooked. Never turned. He'll be hooked on the end of his mouth," I said, sure that the fly was about to come away. The steelhead swam upstream until it held only a dozen feet from me.

"He doesn't *know* he's hooked," said Don.

"Twenty pounds. Well, maybe. I got a good look at him."

As the steelhead began to fatigue, it lost its composure and moved out into the heavy current where it no longer tried to hold an upstream station and turned to run hard downriver. I stumbled after it, and when the steelhead slowed, I pressured it from the current. The entire sequence was repeated twice again until the steelhead was near the tailout. A good run would now take it over into a cauldron of white water. I saw the buck keel over, its pectoral fin waving in distress. With most races of steelhead, this would have been the end of it. I turned the rod horizontal to the water, locked down on the reel, and began easing the steelhead toward the beach. Too late. It righted itself and dashed back out into the current. Stop it or lose it, I thought, and locked down on the reel again. The steelhead was stopped, but again I failed to bring it to shore.

"Typical Thompson steelhead! You'll have to tail it. No decent place to beach him. One last time."

Don waded in, and when the buck again grew faint with exhaustion and turned on its side, I brought it directly in front of Don and pulled it half out of the river. Don had the steelhead by the tail and quickly drew the buck back into the river. It lay nearly motionless in six inches of water.

"Smaller than I thought," I said, "Eighteen pounds." The fly hung precariously from the very end of the buck's nose. When Don held the fly for a moment, it fell away. We measured the length at thirty-seven inches; eighteen pounds was a conservative estimate for the thickly muscled trout. When

Don turned the steelhead back, it darted from his grasp and disappeared into the tailout.

The railroad tracks were our trail back, a half-mile walk that sent the sheep scrambling up a hillside. They are hunted each September, full-curl rams only, an annual reduction of three or four animals from several herds in the area. A year earlier, I fished Montana's Madison River with a group of avid sheep hunters, two of whom had just returned from hunting Marco Polo sheep in Mongolia. They described for me the difficulties in securing a "grand slam," a trophy-class specimen from each of the four races of North American sheep, the Dall, Stone, Bighorn, and Desert. Though money was no object, the rare bighorn had eluded them. I thought of their frustration as a pair of hog-fat rams, their massive heads held low, bulldozed their way through the brush.

My truck was parked on the outskirts of Spences Bridge, the tiny railroad siding town, the half-boarded-up destination town for steelheaders that is located on the west side of the Thompson just below its confluence with the Nicola River. We drove to one of two restaurants still open. I stuck my head in the door. The place was empty of customers.

"Are the stream cleats okay?" I asked.

"Oh, sure!" said the waitress, as she waved us in. We took a table and ordered.

"Lots of places closed." I said. "Business is down?"

"I live on the river, and it used to be that when I looked through my window all I could see was fishermen. Now all I can see is river."

"The run of steelhead has been going down, too," I said.

"I don't know about that, but I know there are a lot less fishermen."

I wanted to explain to her that the no kill regulation in force this season had discouraged many anglers, that if some bait fishermen can't hit their steelhead on the head, they don't want to bother.

"So what are you trying to tell me? That fly fishermen are snobs?" she might have asked.

What these steelhead must go through just to get to Spences Bridge fills me with admiration for the race. Consider first that they enter continental shelf waters from two directions. Some pass down the Queen Charlotte Strait between Vancouver Island and the mainland through Johnstone Strait, Discovery Passage, and the Strait of Georgia before entering the mouth of the Fraser, the province's largest river and most important producer of sockeye salmon. Others may choose to enter the Strait of Juan de Fuca and pass between Washington State and Vancouver Island. The first route described puts migrating steelhead in the path of Canadian gill netters. Some of the steelhead will be caught incidentally and reported, though not as Thompson River stock. Others will be caught and will go unreported. Whether the steelhead will fare any better by taking the southern route is hard to say. They, too, will face Canadian gill nets set for sockeye and perish in this manner. But others will be lost to American gill nets. These Thompson River steelhead will *certainly* go unreported, for it is unlawful for an American commercial fisherman without aboriginal fishing rights to catch, possess, or sell any steelhead.

I live in a small town on the Olympic Peninsula. Many of our local commercial fishermen are gill-netters who fish in American waters for Canada's Fraser River sockeye. I am told about immense summer-run steelhead (the last one weighed nineteen pounds) that they sometimes find dead in their nets. Most fishermen I know will try to get away with keeping these steelhead, naturally preferring to save them for a barbecue rather than to deep-six them, an awful waste, regardless of how one views the matter. More to the point, no Puget Sound river possesses summer-run steelhead of this size, and no one seriously takes them to be anything other than Thompson River stock.

During the late 1980s, the run was estimated at "10,000 pieces," i.e., steelhead. Two thousand steelhead are subtracted from this figure to account for commercial interceptions. The great number of commercial fishing areas through which Thompson steelhead stocks pass makes this an arbitrary figure, and almost complete guesswork when American waters are factored in.

As the steelhead enter the lower Fraser, they encounter an aggressive sport fishery, and hundreds of fish become part of the Province's punch-card statistics.

More than fifty bands of Native British Columbians, mostly of the Sto:lo Nation, have aboriginal fishing rights between the Fraser's confluence with the Harrison River and Boston Bar. The gill nets set by the Indians for salmon and steelhead typically take five thousand steelhead, a staggering fifty percent of the escapement.

These interceptions—no longer "incidental"—have taken place only on the Fraser between the mouth and Lytton, the "Rafting Capital of Canada," situated at the confluence of the Thompson. At this point, if all the interceptions are added up, something like four of every five steelhead are already caught before the first Thompson River steelhead even reaches a Thompson River angler. When the anglers in the Spences Bridge area have pursued the steelhead through the sport-fishing season, approximately September through December with the four-week peak generally occurring from mid-October to mid-November, about a thousand to fifteen hundred steelhead have survived to spawn.

The typical angler at Spences Bridge is a gear fisherman. Not uncommonly, a father and son fishing together might span nearly a half-century of catch-and-kill on the Thompson. They resent that conservation efforts invariably begin by reducing their limit, when everyone, it seems, has already had a whack at their steelhead, a *sports fish* the last time they checked. In 1989, they had to give up their one-fish limit when the river went catch-and-release. The father can remember the halcyon days of his angling youth when he could kill six Thompson steelhead a day. Both will tell you that catch-and-release is a restriction, plain and simple. Only a simpleton would think otherwise. Why else do the fishery boys say that the river is *restricted to catch-and-release*? And, as always, it falls to those who pay for the support of the fishery, the license holders, to make the sacrifice. That's wrong. Furthermore, if an angler wishes to voluntarily practice catch and release, to embrace this ethic he has made a choice like choosing wildlife photography over hunting. Good for him. Give us back those eight thousand Thompson River steelhead and there won't be a problem.

The Native bands of the lower Fraser belong to several councils that have representation on the Indian Inland Fisheries Commission. In 1989, Ian McGregor, a senior Fisheries Branch biologist, was able to convince the Commission that a voluntary cutback of their subsistence fishery was the only hope the Province had for rebuilding Thompson steelhead stocks. This informal agreement, the first of its kind between sport and Native fishermen in British Columbia, noticeably increased the 1989 escapement.

McGregor reminded me that the Thompson steelhead was "the most fecund of any race of steelhead," the average female depositing more than twelve thousand eggs. He estimates that if only four thousand steelhead survive to spawn, the result will be a run of twenty-five thousand adults, a remarkable annual recovery. The catch, of course, is that four thousand steelhead must find a way to reach their spawning grounds.

LIFE HISTORY

Anglers and biologists alike are convinced that the "Thompson River steelhead" is actually two races: one with origins in the Nicola River, the other with origins in the tributaries of the Thompson above the Nicola, principally Deadman Creek and Bonaparte Creek.

Nicola steelhead are thought to be the slightly larger race, arriving mainly in late October, a week or two earlier than the Thompson stock. In either case, they can transit the Fraser in two weeks, and need, at most, a week more to travel the sixty miles from Lytton to Spences Bridge. However, these steelhead are notorious wanderers. Some will reach the inaccessible canyon waters of the lower Thompson and remain there the entire winter. Nicola steelhead are known to pass up the Thompson as much as seventy miles above the confluence of the two rivers and to stay for months. They may not reverse their movements and seek out the headwaters of their birth until late winter. Other steelhead may drop down into the deepest pools of the lower Thompson at the onset of winter. Also evident is that, although there are decided peaks in the runs, fresh fish will trickle into the system all fall.

Many interior rivers are known for their late run of summer steelhead, fish of October, even November. But the time needed to arrive at their spawning destination will be six weeks or more, and the steelhead's depature from salt water is actually in August or early September. Thompson steelhead may not leave salt water until October, a few even later, and they are unusual in this way. (In 1989, the Thompson run was somewhat later than usual; a test fishery on the Fraser in late November revealed that a run of Thompson steelhead had freshly entered. This is a time we associate with the first of the winter-run steelhead.)

Ian McGregor conducted the classic life-history study of Thompson River steelhead as the subject of his master's degree at the University of Victoria, in British Columbia. His thesis, "Freshwater Biology of Thompson River Steelhead (*Salmo gairdneri*) As Determined By Radio Telemetry," was completed in August 1986. The study was based on samplings from two different time periods. In 1976 and 1977, 391 and 286 adults were sampled from the sport fishery, and in 1984, 257 adults were sampled during the spring spawning migration in Deadman River, the fish processed through the counting fence. The sex of the steelhead was noted. Scales were removed and the ages determined, years in fresh water and years in salt water. Each fish's length and weight were recorded. (Not all the steelhead that could be sexed could be reliably aged.)

As I studied McGregor's findings, my immediate impression was of a giant race of steelhead with a growth rate equal to any yet investigated. Specifics that help describe this race include the following:

The ratio of males to females was 1:1.60, and 1:1.27 (1976 and 1977 sport fishery), and 1:2.67 (1984, Deadman River). The difference between fall and spring samplings was a six- to eight-month holdover period, a time presumably more stressful for the polygamous male. Average weights of the steelhead, fall and spring, reveal the more severe weight loss endured by surviving males.

MEAN (AVERAGE) WEIGHT

1976	female	13.86 pounds
	male	17.82 pounds
1977	female	13.86 pounds
	male	16.94 pounds
1984	female	11.66 pounds
	male	13.20 pounds

These figures illustrate an approximate body weight loss, of fifteen percent among females and twenty-five percent among males, that took place during the fall-to-spring holdover period.

The study revealed ten different age classes in 1976, fourteen in 1977, and fifteen in 1984. Repeat spawners made up 2.0 percent, 3.5 percent, and 7.1 percent of the sampling in those years with five different age classes identified. The repeat spawning life histories in Deadman Creek (1984) included 2.2S+ (4.3 percent), 2.2S1+ (1.2 percent), 2+.1S1+ (0.4 percent), 2+.2S+ (0.4 percent), and 3.2S+ (0.4 percent). Note that in the first and last life histories, the spawned-out steelhead returned to the ocean in the spring and then returned to the Thompson the next fall, and did not stay out an entire year. This was once thought to be atypical, but apparently it is not on the Thompson. The other age classes are more typical, with the steelhead remaining in the ocean for more than a year (1+) before returning to spawn a second time.

McGregor found no steelhead that had previously spawned twice.

The most common ocean age for steelhead spawning for the first time was two years plus several months (.2+). This time in salt water was found in approximately ninety percent of all steelhead. Steelhead with an ocean age of one year or three years were rare to uncommon.

The most frequent premigrant residency was two years (about eighty to ninety percent), followed by three years (ten to twenty percent), and one year (one percent or less). These are high-growth-rate residencies typical of more southern rivers, and a reflection of the longer growing season, warmer water, and abundant feed available in this desert river. Compare these growth periods to those for parr in the colder, less fertile rivers of the Skeena drainage and lower mainland, where they more typically spend three or four years as stream residents before smolting and migrating to sea.

When I discussed this aspect of the river's juvenile steelhead with Al Caverly, a Fisheries Branch biologist in Kamloops, it was the last week of November, and the Thompson remained a relatively warm forty-two to forty-four degrees. "There are mayflies hatching," he said, "and the parr are still actively feeding. There are other rivers on the lower mainland where the temperature is near zero [Celsius]. At that temperature the parr would be dormant and no longer feeding."

When the parr do smolt, usually in June and July, such an abundance of food is in the river that some smolts feed and grow before they actually acclimate to salt water. This growth shows dramatically in a scale reading (wider annulus rings after winter), and is described as 1+. or 2+., rather than 1. or 2., years of stream residency before smolting and migrating to sea.

Two facets of this steelhead's life history are most interesting: Males and females commonly have the same life history (2.2+ or 2+.2+); the three-year ocean males that make up the "trophy class" of the Babine, Sustut, and Kispiox rivers are very rare in the Thompson. The two sexes, for the same age, are remarkably similar in size. I believe that the Thompson River's female steelhead are possibly as large as any in the world, and that includes those of the Kispiox. Each year a female steelhead weighing twenty-five pounds and several weighing twenty-four pounds are caught. (I heard a story of a twenty-six-pound female but have not been able to substantiate it.)

McGregor found in his sampling that the females ranged from 26 to 41⅜ inches and weighed from 6.8 to 24.4 pounds. The males ranged from twenty-six to forty-four inches and weighed from 7.9 to 32.1 pounds. A typical Thompson River female is a 2.2+, 2+.2+, or 3.2+ fish thirty-three to thirty-four inches long and weighing thirteen to fifteen pounds. A male for the same ages will average 35½ inches in length and weigh approximately seventeen pounds. The two sexes will usually range in weight from ten to eighteen and ten to twenty-four pounds, respectively.

John Cartwright, Section Head, Kamloops Division, Fisheries Branch, described the brief history of the Thompson's steelhead enhancement programs. "Headwaters have been underseeded," he said, "the result of dramatically reduced escapements." Smolts, always the offspring of wild Thompson steelhead, were stocked in upper Deadman Creek beginning in 1980. "Results were so disappointing that the program was discontinued after four years." Currently some 400,000 fry from wild Thompson stock are planted annually in the Bonaparte River, upper Spius Creek, and the Coldwater River. "We've seen a difference," was Cartwright's guarded assessment.

A couple of kilometers above the mouth of the Bonaparte River is a falls that is impassable for steelhead. In 1988, a fish ladder gave migrating steelhead access to headwaters, and steelhead have been found as much as sixty kilometers (thirty-five miles) upriver. This additional spawning area holds great promise.

NOTES

Some of our finest steelhead fly fishers visit the Thompson each fall. Watching them take their pleasure on a pool with which they have grown comfortable is a special satisfaction for me. Where they enter their water, the manner in which they cover it, the fly line they employ to find their steelhead, and where they exit a pool are the sum of all their experiences, a live "how to" they freely communicate.

Among these anglers are friends and acquaintances of mine, and visiting with them is as important to me as wetting a line. A few of them are described elsewhere in this book. The chapters on Harry Lemire and Bob York provide some original thinking on the matter of Thompson River patterns. The

Trey Combs and Harry Lemire with a typical Thompson River buck.

Thompson River Rat by Ehor Boyanowksy, and the Green-Wing Bomber by Sean Gallagher are two dry flies that their inventors have found useful for their favorite river.

At one time or another I have seen every conceivable pattern work on the Thompson, from the General Practitioner and Squamish Poacher fished deep to Bombers plowing furrows across surface currents riffled only by canyon winds. The ubiquitous Muddler fished wet or waking, damp flies that include a number of caddis imitations, and a great variety of wet flies fished greased-line have all proven useful. If there is a "book" on pattern selection, it is to go on the drab and dark side, to appeal to this steelhead's "trouty" senses. Flies with black marabou wings, the General Practitioner in black, the Night Dancer, Coal Car, Ferry Canyon, and Signal Light are all fine low-light patterns.

The choice of rods is equally disparate, but they tend to be long. My favorite Thompson rod is a ten-foot 8-weight that controls a long belly forward-taper line with ease. This line is a lot of grains, but it carries 2/0 dubbed silhouette patterns heavy with water to lies ninety feet away.

When I wade into the Thompson, I tell myself, "If wishes were horses, beggers would ride." No part of the river is designated fly fishing only. There are no destination fly shops, and the fly-fishing heritage is best experienced by word of mouth on the gravel bars. My most optimistic expectation is for a rise a day. After all, I'm hunting for only ten to fifteen percent of the run, and on some days the river is as empty as the two motels in Spences Bridge. It is impossible not to wonder what this river would be like if the steelhead escapement were allowed to increase naturally by tenfold. The federal government's treatment of this race of steelhead, this national treasure, is pitifully shortsighted and economically wasteful. Obfuscating their way through the moral dilemma of Indians and commercial fishermen becoming the prime consumers of the province's steelhead is bureaucratic gridlock at its worst.

I think a lot about this sort of thing, and when my self-righteous whining begins getting the better of me, I think of Washington steelhead fly-fishing guide John Farrar.

John introduced me to a game. The rules are simple. If you had money and time in equal abundance, and could pick one different river each month, anywhere in the world, to provide the very best fishing for *Salmo* and *Oncorhynchus* in its most glamorous sea-run forms, Atlantic salmon, sea trout, steelhead, and sea-run cutthroat, what would be your twelve choices? The rivers of Norway, Scotland, Canada, and the United States get the imagination rolling. Including Argentina, with its opposite seasons, puts a nice spin on the game. Given these deceptively simple parameters, I hold that only one river stands singly and unassailably for a given month. The river is the Thompson, the month is November, and the fish, of course, is the steelhead. Raging debates attend nearly every other choice.

That remains my perception of the Thompson's steelhead, a race that ranks with any other salmonid regardless of the context, a world-class resource that it is my privilege to enjoy.

Author's note: Life history information described above also resulted from the following study: Moore, D. C. and W. R. Olmsted. 1985. An ecological study of steelhead trout (*Salmo gairdneri*) reproduction in Deadman River, B.C., 1984. Prepared for the Department of Fisheries and Oceans and the Ministry of Environment, Vancouver, by W. R. Olmsted & Associates, Inc. 43 pp. + appendix.

DEAN RIVER

ALDER Run is not a classic pool, at least not in the mold of Giant's or Rabbit or a host of other Dean River waters that possess great size and memorable character. It is distinguished by a stately row of black alders. Branches spread well above the river, but, save for dawn, the run is flooded with sunlight the entire morning. An angler presenting a fly from the gravel bar side does so with the sun to his back, and the steelhead must find that fly amid intense glare. At this time, the prospect for success is poor, and the appearance of the pool is so discouraging that the water is easily neglected.

In August, Alder begins slipping into shade by early afternoon. Hourly, the crease of dark currents sweeping against the bank grows wider, until the sun drops behind the mountain that rises from the river and leaves the pool in twilight for hours. Then the entire pool becomes holding water, and steelhead may be sought with confidence along its entire length.

John Farrar and I had spied Alder as we floated the Dean in his raft. I incorrectly thought the pool too small to support both of us and offered to fish a little run a hundred yards directly upstream. My water would still be in bright sunlight, but I wanted the pleasure of breaking it down with no regard to time and no respect to another's presence. I would take my pleasure with an eye on John as he fished Alder. I began at the upper end of my run, really too far up to expect a fish in heavy water that produced a very quick swing. If I failed to turn a steelhead, I would still be satisfied with my well-ordered approach.

Roland Holmberg on Giants. →

229

The river was still clearing from rains early in the week and had dropped six inches during the night. We had checked the water temperature that morning and found it, at fifty-six degrees, about midway in the optimum range. A waking dry fly could locate our fish, the water's touch of murkiness helping to obscure our presence. Neither of us would fuss much with pattern selection. Dark wet flies fished greased-line are *de rigueur* on the Dean, more so than on most steelhead rivers, and I began casting a 1/0 Black Gnat Bucktail. This size brings to mind a large fly, but the hook was dressed sparsely, three-quarters low-water. I moved no fish, and when I began working through the pool a second time, I changed flies to satisfy my sense of thoroughness and to provide a fresh approach.

Watching John was easy. I could look over my fly and see into his water. He cast a #6 Spade with the precise timing of a metronome, each new, tight loop identical to the last, the bright pink double-taper line passing from sunshine to shade. The little fly had been tied on a Wilson dry-fly hook and dressed to swim in the surface film, a silhouette that had attracted many steelhead for him.

When I reached the end of the pool a second time, the Green-Butt Skunk had found only parr. Nowhere are these trout more voracious than on the Dean, and I changed patterns as much to discourage their attentions as to attract a steelhead. I could now crowd John without guilt; he had been through his water twice, too. After tying on a large Purple Peril, I cast only to wet the fly and immediately turned a steelhead, its tail coming out of the water as it briefly held the fly. I had tightened hastily on a slow take, and I damned my reflexes. I cast a second time, and the steelhead took the fly and just as quickly blew it away. Getting skittish, I thought.

John's yell broke my concentration and brought my head up with a snap as his steelhead somersaulted into the air. When he looked over his shoulder to catch my attention, he missed the steelhead's second jump, a leap so prodigious that I could clearly see the fish above his head. My camera was with John in the raft, and I badly wanted to document his catch, but wouldn't a double be worth remembering? I again cast to the steelhead before me and made a strong back-mend to sink the fly. As the fly drifted easily through the swing, there was a telltale pluck and then nothing. The steelhead had not moved from its station. I put my rod down, leaving it on the gravel bar pointing exactly at the fish, and ran for the raft.

John was on his knees, and for a moment I was ready to console him—until I saw the steelhead. "Did you see him jump?" he said, his voice booming with excitement. "Five times! Look! Aren't these magnificent fish? He exhausted himself! They have such *character!*"

"There was a leap you missed. Higher than your head!" I said as I reached for the camera. The steelhead was coming around. I would have to hurry. Looking through the viewfinder, I could barely discern pink on the buck's gill plates. Along the lateral line were only ocean silver and ocean energy. "Sixteen pounds. I've never seen a more beautiful steelhead. Not a mark on it." I wanted to study the fish. John would not hold it a second longer than necessary. The steelhead suddenly bolted from his grasp and was gone.

"I'm working on a fish. Raised it three times already," I told him as I dropped the camera off and hurried back to the upriver pool, leaving my friend content in his reverie. The rod pointed to the little vein of holding water that now did not appear so familiar. I thought through the presentation and cast so that the fly would swing slowly over the uppermost end of the suspected station. I felt the steelhead take and held the running line tightly until tension brought the rod tip down to the water, the slow-motion take complete when the steelhead picked up the current and raced downstream. John was already crossing the side channel with my camera, his delight evident in his calls of encouragement. Once the steelhead had settled down, I could move her, and the ten-pound hen was soon resting in the shallows. She had the delicate sprinkling of tiny dots that distinguish female steelhead on the Dean, regardless of their size. I suspect this is a racial characteristic, though their dazzling appearance can addle one's powers of discrimination. We were perhaps sixteen river miles from the mouth of the Dean, the steelhead only a few days from life in the ocean.

John studied her for a moment. "She was a player."

"Yes, she came to the fly four times." When I eased her into water just deep enough to support her, the fly fell out, though the barbless hook had been well into the corner of her jaw. I was holding the steelhead firmly by the wrist of her tail when she twisted convulsively from my hand and disappeared into the river. "These steelhead release themselves," I said. John was still adjusting the camera.

Jimmy Hunnicutt and Bruce McNae were a pool or two upriver. The four of us had helicoptered in from the little village of Hagensborg to Clay Bank, a pool approximately twenty miles from the ocean. Each day, we would use our two rafts to leapfrog from pool to pool, until camp water and the dry fly brought us together. Most evenings the dinner dishes were washed by midnight, and sleep came instantly.

John and I could not find another steelhead in Alder, and we set off to find more river with deeply shaded pools. We soon came upon a run that offered good holding water only at the top end. It broadened quickly into a large, shallow tailout that braided around a dozen boulders for more than a hundred yards.

"Let's fish this," I said, and nodded for emphasis. I saw no evidence that other anglers had come this way today. The dark currents looked incredibly fishy, the presence of steelhead was palpable.

"We should set up camp first," he replied. John was the organizer, the person who, as he said, did the "strategizing." He was also a Washington steelhead fly-fishing guide on holiday, a man whose business card listed his specialty as "The World's Waterways." I found him flamboyant and mercurial, a world-class raconteur with more than a smidgen of off-the-wall looniness. He had once been a captain in U.S. Army Intelligence, and he still spoke Hungarian and German. All these qualities made for a grand companion who would gladly spend days discussing steelhead, the history of the samba, every piece of fly fishing literature ever written, and Sioux Indian culture, alternately or all at once.

"Can't camp wait? Let's fish. Aren't we setting up a spike camp? No tents. There'll be time," I assured him. John had long since resigned himself to my compulsive nature.

"Well, give me some room," he said. We divided the small pool in half, and I began casting the Purple Peril below him. I had barely started when the fly simply stopped, sometimes a sign of a large buck. The fish shook its head before rolling on the surface and starting down the long tailout in short spurts. After a run, it would reverse itself and give me a moment to skip after it from rock to rock. Each time I thought I could get below the steelhead, it would continue on downriver. I was applying a lot of pressure and was unable to feel the steelhead give in to it.

"If this is ten pounds, it is one very strong steelhead," I said to John. I began to work close to the fish until it held below me, only thirty feet away. John tiptoed downstream and stared into the black currents.

"My God, that steelhead is huge!" he called. The fish darted upstream, fighting both the river and my rod, and in two hundred feet I had him turned on his side, exhausted.

"You have your twenty-pounder," said John.

"Oh yes, at least that much," I answered.

Jimmy Hunnicutt suddenly materialized. "It's a doe!" he exclaimed.

"Look more closely," said John. The buck was so brilliant, still so sexually immature, that its head remained small. Enormous shoulder girth made the head look even smaller. I thought the buck was very much like an Atlantic salmon in contour. I tailed the steelhead for pictures and then eased it into deeper water for the release.

DEAN CHANNEL

During the next few days, we caught a half-dozen steelhead, from ten to thirteen pounds, with fresh wounds from encounters with gill nets. Curiously, no large steelhead bore net marks. I think this was a matter of luck, for the nets do not discriminate.

We expected to see these mutilated steelhead. This was the second week of August, and the chum salmon fishery at the entrance of Dean Channel was well advanced. (No commercial netting is allowed in the channel itself.) Here, miles of gill nets are set directly in the path of steelhead bound for the Dean River. Thousands perish and are legally sold.

When a Canadian commercial fisherman sells his catch to a fish buyer, he notes the statistical area from which the fish came. Failure to do so can supposedly result in the loss of his license. This data includes steelhead; most Dean River steelhead are caught in Area 8.

While steelhead may be canned as "sea trout," "deep-sea trout," or simply as steelhead, most are sold fresh, and they occupy the same price range as coho salmon. However, George Dodman, an executive with B.C. Packers told me in 1988 of steelhead selling in Vancouver, B.C., deli markets for as much as fifteen dollars per pound.

All saltwater fish in Canada—and this includes salmon—are under the authority and management of the Department of Fisheries and Oceans, a federal department. Conversely, all freshwater fish—and this includes steelhead in their rivers—are managed by the Ministry of Environment, a provincial agency. Information gained about steelhead is not always shared between these two agencies, sometimes because of their separate natures, and sometimes by design. Beyond any internecine mixing of fishery management and fishery politics is the fact that ocean steelhead fall into a grey area and are not the direct responsibility of anyone. This is astonishing, considering the fact that more steelhead are killed incidentally in the ocean than are killed by anglers fishing in rivers.

Steelhead generally make up only a very small percentage of the total commercial take of salmonids. In Area 8, during the period when gill nets took 200,000 chum salmon, seine nets accounted for millions of sockeye and 250,000 more chums. These are staggering numbers, compared to the suspected take of 10,000 steelhead and the recorded commercial take of 2,478 in 1988. Several factors contribute to the disparity.

If only a few steelhead are found in the nets, they often end up on the galley stove, in the home canner, or in the smokehouse, and they are never recorded. This practice may be more common when the steelhead have a lower market value than the targeted salmon—sockeye (red) and chinook, for example. Off Dean Channel, some of the steelhead caught in commercial nets in June and July will be kelts, either Dean summer-runs or Bella Coola winter-runs, an April and May escapement. These fish have little or no market value as fresh fish. Also, some steelhead are likely tossed in with salmon during canning runs. Finally, an unknown number of Dean River steelhead are netted in waters other than Area 8.

Commercial fishermen are becoming increasingly sensitive about the loss of these steelhead from the sport-fishing sector. Many are themselves steelheaders, and the entire matter of net-caught steelhead has become a politically contentious issue. New netting restrictions crop up each year in an effort to save steelhead in various mixed-stock fisheries, and they are never at the convenience of the commercial fishermen. Many fishermen in the gill net and seine net fleets now make an effort to release steelhead from their nets, even when the steelhead have only a marginal chance of surviving. Seine nets, in particular, can bring in undamaged steelhead. Some fishermen will make an effort to scoop out as many steelhead as possible before stowing their catch. It is impossible to know how many of these steelhead are thus saved, or how many die after being removed from the gill nets. "The commercial boys don't tell us a thing," one provincial fishery technician told me.

Escapement figures for Dean River steelhead are general, and subject to considerable fluctuation from year to year, but *may* range from seven thousand to twenty-five thousand. Natural fluctuation is due to a number of factors. Spawning and hatching success and the growth of parr are enhanced by mild winters and spring runoff of sufficient moderation that spawning redds are not scoured out. The ocean environment is not static, either, and in some years, climate and available food supply contribute to highly successful returns. Beyond natural mortality, the impact of the commercial fishing industry on steelhead populations is governed by the numbers of salmon present and the resulting "open" days available to commercial fishermen. Heavy runs of salmon can (and do) coincide with low steelhead returns, with devastating results to steelhead numbers.

The Ministry of Environment must now find a solution to this vexing problem. Solutions are certainly not going to come from either the Ministry of Fisheries and Oceans or the commercial fishermen, whose unions are strong and militant. Each organization is somewhat a prisoner of the other, and neither, of course, is responsible for steelhead except for keeping track of how many come off the boats. Before any meaningful solutions are found, however, it must be understood how steelhead enter Area 8, and how they behave once they are in this area of intense commercial activity.

To that end, in 1987, the Fisheries Branch of the Ministry of Environment began a sonic tag study. I discussed the study with Jack Leggett, Section Head, Cariboo Fisheries, and Dennis Wilders, Fisheries Technician, in their office in Williams Lake, British Columbia. Both were active in the study, which was ongoing at the time of the interview in August 1988.

The study consisted of capturing steelhead in the Dean Channel and placing three-inch by half-inch stainless tubes, the sonic tags, down their throats. The steelhead were fin-clipped and released. (Anglers catching these fish were asked to kill the fish so that the tags could be returned.) The steelhead were tracked for at least twenty-four hours. The range of the nine hundred dollar tag was only two hundred meters or so, and following the fish required constant vigilance. This was exhausting work, but worth the effort, for an accurate picture of the steelhead's saltwater movements in Dean Channel emerged. The steelhead generally traveled between one hundred and three hundred feet from shore, within the upper two meters and, usually, within the upper four feet of water. The steelhead traveled at a rate of only one to two nautical miles per hour, and *only in the daytime*. At night, they milled around without any particular direction. The fish invariably stopped before each freshwater inlet to nose around, presumably to smell out trace elements, though different water temperatures could have been a factor. Movements in the lower river were generally steady, but not always. One signal continued from a single pool for a couple of weeks, until biologists became convinced that the fish had disgorged the sonic tag. Then the fish suddenly continued its migration; no one knows what prompted this behavior.

Using this information, cooperation between federal and provincial fishery agencies could modify current salmon harvest practices to reduce the incidental take of steelhead. Nets could be set at least four feet below the surface and three hundred feet from shore. Chum and sockeye are not so surface-oriented, and the change would not reduce the commercial harvest of these salmon.

The huge incidental catch of steelhead should be a grotesque violation of *someone's* stewardship. After all, this is the loss of a sport fishing resource that has vastly more recreational value to British Columbia than commercial value to Canada. But the net wounds serve as reminders that steelhead trespass many jurisdictions in their travels. The ocean is the dark side of their life, the mysterious source of their beauty, size, and wildness, and the reason I pursue them with such passion.

EARLY ANGLING

The Dean River is still accessible only by air and by sea. Hundreds of islands guard the outer coast of British Columbia, while the great fjords that cut deep into the mainland enforce the sense of isolation. One can observe wolves and bear walking island beaches. Virgin stands of hemlock, fir, and cedar cover much of the surrounding land. Waters still teem with fish, and the intertidal zones are impossibly rich in shellfish. In many respects, the area is little changed from when Captain George Vancouver first charted it for Great Britain two hundred years ago.

Well east of the protected "Inside Passage" is the entrance to Dean Channel, a sixty-mile-long reach that ends at Kimsquit and the entrance to the Dean River. Kimsquit is what Canadian cartographers call a "locality." It certainly isn't a village. If anything, it is a landing strip, a crossroads on the north side of the river where people and supplies are ferried in and out. During August, the place is humming.

Only thirty years ago, almost nothing was known of the Dean as a steelhead river. Before World War II, some Indian families from the Bella Coola area had ancestral fishing grounds on the Dean and would set up camps there each summer. Ultimately, the Indians became part of a Bella Coola reserve, and they currently net the Bella Coola River for both salmon and steelhead. They maintain a camp on the lower Dean below the falls, but only as a summer cultural center. Netting no longer takes place.

Logging commenced in the Dean Valley in 1961. Initially, this was on a very modest scale, but it grew dramatically when Mayo Logging began operations in 1964. The following year, a massive wooden bridge was constructed across the river just above the canyon so that heavy equipment could be taken to the south side of the Dean. A landing strip was built below the canyon, as well. Though all this was to facilitate the logging operation, the area opened up for visiting anglers, who now had easy access to both sides of the Dean. Mayo Logging shut down in 1968, but Crown Zellerbach logged the area through 1969. Mayo Logging returned to harvest logs in the area until mid-1976, when the bridge had become so battered by flood waters that it was no longer safe to use. Mayo moved upriver to log the Sakumtha and Kalone areas in early 1976, but withdrew all its heavy equipment and dismantled its buildings. Today, all that is left of those enterprises is a logging road that parallels the Dean for twenty-five miles or so, a footbridge that is a shambles, and a lot of stumps. (When I returned to the Dean in 1989, the bridge had either washed out—or been blown up.)

Dick Blewett and Bob Stewart first explored the valleys of the Bella Coola and Dean rivers with Dick Poet in his Cessna 180 floatplane during the late 1950s. They landed for the first time on the Dean River several miles upstream of the canyon in September 1957. After inflating their rubber rafts, Blewett and Stewart camped and fished their way to the takeout above the canyon. They were seeking coho salmon, and they caught many, along with the odd steelhead, little realizing that the main run of steelhead was already past them. They returned again in the fall of 1958 and 1959, always for the coho. When they returned in 1961, it was in August, the choice of time somewhat happenstance, and for the first time, they encountered the main run of Dean River steelhead.

The next year, the two men opened the first guide camp on the river, nine miles from the mouth, the site chosen because a floatplane could be landed safely there. "Camp" was some tents that housed a few anglers.

Two additional fishing camps were established on the Dean in 1965, taking advantage of the newly built landing strip. Rimarko Ranch was located a mile above tidewater, while Double Haul Enterprises built their camp on Kimsquit Bay by the mouth of the Dean. That year, an estimated 140 anglers fished the Dean.

In 1968, Daryl Hodson moved from Ocean Falls to build a fishing lodge at Mile 7.5, the old "Net Hole" of the Bella Coola Indians. That same year, forty miles up the Dean, Dick Blewett and Bob Stewart established a second camp, which could be reached only by helicopter. A competing helicopter camp opened the following year, but both closed in 1970, when the entire Dean River above Kalone Creek, Mile 21, was closed to fishing and preserved as a spawning area.

Dick Blewett sold his interest in the camp to Bob Stewart's son, Rob, in 1973. While Duncan Stewart, Rob's brother, eventually bought out his father's interests, Rob Stewart has managed the Lower Dean River Lodge since 1973. (During these years, Bob Stewart has successfully operated Stewart's Lodge on Nimpo Lake, a Canadian institution near the headwaters of the Dean River.) Today, Stewart's and Hodson's are the only two licensed lodges operating on the Dean.

In 1971, the Ministry of Environment initiated a creel census to determine the annual number of "angler days." (An angler day, or rod day, is any part of a day fished by one angler. For example, if a visiting angler fished for five days, regardless of the number of hours he fished each day, he would contribute five rod days to the annual total.) There were 937 angler days in 1971, and 2,636 by 1975. The 1989 estimate was that the Dean supports approximately five thousand angler days annually, more than three thousand of the days in August. The Ministry of Environment feels that these numbers for August are much too high and threaten the quality of the wilderness experience. I discussed this with Fisheries Branch biologists Jack Leggett and Dennis Wilders. Both expressed concern that the rapidly building number of anglers visiting the Dean each summer shows no sign of abating. "This is currently our biggest problem in managing the Dean," said Wilders. Final plans were being developed for a limited-entry system to go into effect in 1990, the first of its kind in British Columbia.

DRY FLIES

Each morning, John would wake up and begin singing, a Spanish folk tune mostly, but when a cold drizzle greeted us one dawn, he switched to Christmas carols. Coffee fueled his hearty delivery, and we had all brought bags of gourmet coffee. After breakfast, John would set up the camp table, attach a vise, dig out some fly-tying materials, and fall silent. We knew he was once again working on a new steelhead dry fly.

On Anchor Pool, John and Bruce went through twice with wet flies without turning a fish before deciding to work the tail of the pool with some of the large dry flies that festooned Bruce's felt hat. He had a lot of Bombers and some Waller Wakers, the pattern that Lani Waller had recently developed for use on the Babine River. Each of them raised a good fish three times to a Waker by throwing a downstream mend, the hard-dragging fly setting up a very visible commotion. But when Bruce solidly hooked a steelhead at last light, it was to a spidery low-water wet.

John had thought hard on the matter. Some of the water he covered that evening was seventy feet out, easily within range of his ten-foot 7-weight rod. But even when holding the rod straight up and raising his arm, it was hard, in broken water, to keep the dragging fly from going under. A more buoyant, higher-riding fly was possible, but its hooking qualities could be suspect. John's fly tying was an effort to solve the problem of keeping a dry fly waking through distant lies.

Jimmy Hunnicutt and I hiked downriver to fish Rabbit, a quarter-mile-long pool between ancient stands of red cedar. Earlier in the year, he had been climbing peaks in the Andes, and he remained whippet hard and nearly as fast, even in waders with aluminum cleats. As I wheezed along after him, he talked of trout fishing near his boyhood home in North Carolina's Great Smoky Mountains and of his most memorable West Coast steelhead. Since moving to Washington ten years earlier, he had fished just about every important steelhead river worth the name, a recreation schedule he maintained throughout the year.

Two hours before dark I hooked a hen of fourteen pounds that swept up my Green-Butt Skunk on the run. She raced down from the head of the pool to jump fifty yards below the hookup, the kind of blistering run that Bill McMillan calls, "a reel meltdown." She bore no net scars, and we rejoiced in her safe release.

Jimmy is given to drab greased-line flies with roughly dubbed bodies that produce a very buggy appearance. His Blue Mole was a deadly low-water creation that had already accounted for a number of Dean steelhead. But late on this day, with the water before us a little turgid from headwater rains, I suggested a brighter fly and offered him my box. Jim chose a Midnight Sun, an orange and yellow pattern, and almost immediately hooked a large steelhead. Because of an eight-pound tippet, he played the fish carefully. When the buck was beached, we estimated its weight at twenty pounds. "That fish paid for my trip," he said.

There was no doubt where we wanted to camp the next night.

Jimmy and I returned to Anchor at last light to listen with interest as John and Bruce described their experiences with the dry fly, but we were not moved to change from the elegant wet flies we had been fishing. The conversation turned to why these steelhead struck so readily, why they were so "trouty" in their behavior while still so "ocean" in their appearance. Like most steelhead fly fishermen, we were seeking to know what relationships existed between the fauna of the steelhead's world and the artful and fanciful flies conceived in our imaginations. As theories were tossed about, caddisflies whirred in the hissing lantern light and gave a good approximation of the indigenous species. While picking them from the light for identification, a huge caddis fluttered up the side of the glass. I first thought it was a moth.

"Look! An October caddis!" said John. He held it to the light; the dirty orange body was diagnostic. Bill Bakke's October Caddis steelhead pattern was better known to me than the insect itself.

"I had no idea they were found this far north. I think of them as an Oregon caddis," I said. Then

I was struck by another similarity. "You know, the Blue Mole has some of that very burnt orange in the butt section. I wonder if that is why it's so effective."

Who is to say why a steelhead strikes a fly, I thought. We try to flirt with their reasoning, and then hope that they attack our flies for noble reasons, that they take our General Practitioner for a prawn and not, God forbid, for roe. Beyond such gratuitous prejudices is the more certain relationship between the steelhead's eagerness to strike flies suggesting insects and their premigrant environment in an insect-rich river.

When we reached the Dean, I had immediately noticed thousands of nymphal skins left on rocks by emerging *Pteronarcys*. This was the very end of the hatch, but the next day I watched a parr chase an enormous winged adult down the river. My amusement changed to astonishment when it finally took the stonefly down. (My admiration for the parr would turn to despair when I couldn't keep them off the flies I wanted to fish, and I was reminded of this incident again and again. Fishing a Blue Charm proved especially hopeless.) That same day, John discovered a golden stone in one of the coolers. Smaller stoneflies were about, and mayflies often sprinkled down on midday runs. I became so impressed with this abundance that I regretted our lack of a field guide on stream entomology. The hatches reminded me of more southern rivers, especially those with cottonwoods and sagebrush, and I wondered if Dean steelhead reflected these differences. I suspected that they did, and on this night in the wilderness I took satisfaction in that.

The next morning we moved to Rabbit and set up camp beneath the huge cedars. The abundance of good lies eliminated any anxiety over their allocation, and each of us sought a piece of water to suit his approach. Jimmy, ever restless, rowed John across the river, and the two hiked to a long slick they

Jimmy Hunnicutt with one of his back to back 20 pound steelhead.

had glimpsed on the quick float down. Bruce McNae eyed the immense tailout and thought it had been heaven-sent; he would seek no other part of the pool during the next two days. The elbow at the head of the pool fixed my attention, and I would be happy in its turbulence, the river thundering in my ears as I drove the fly for the far side.

By midafternoon, Jimmy had beached his second steelhead of over twenty pounds and had lost another of nearly equal size, a fish that had left him with only six feet of backing on his reel. "Yeah, another twenty-pounder," he said, "larger than the first." His drawl was Tarheel deadpan, but he had the aura of a man beatified. "No, that never happened before, never back to back," he said in answer to my question. Jimmy recalled a larger Thompson steelhead that had come to his Sweet Loretta, but trying to put this day in perspective was not easy.

John had lost a steelhead right in front of camp. "High in the teens, maybe twenty pounds," we all agreed.

Bruce remained anchored at the end of the pool, a tiny figure beneath Rabbit's several mountains, and we speculated whether he was going to homestead the area. That seemed fitting, because he raised thoroughbred racehorses in Washington, described himself with convincing humility as "a farmer," and possessed the disarming equanimity of landed gentry.

John had spent much of the day tying his new dry-fly creation. When he handed me the first example, I called it a Top Knot, for the crest of bright orange polar bear over the body of spun deer hair. But after John had tested the fly at a variety of distances and observed with satisfaction the commotion it made, he called it the Sputterkicker.

SPUTTERKICKER

Body Two clumps of deer body hair loosely spun on to form the body. The first clump is at a point above the hook point, the second just back of the loop of the eye. Clip to shape.
Wing Orange polar bear fur
Head Caribou, spun loose and clipped to shape. Square off the head so it creates a maximum of surface disturbance.

As the three of us discussed the fly, we heard occasional yells and groans from the tailout. There was no "Yahoo!" mixed in, the signal that Bruce was fast to a steelhead. "He's not being eaten by a grizzly," I said. We could discern a feverish casting stroke, but not one of self-defense "He's not drowning either," I added. We knew Bruce would happily double-haul his way over a falls. The man was that keen. His flailing, we decided, was no distress signal. The long "Yahoo!" that soon echoed up the valley turned into a kind of screaming death rattle. Bruce appeared, looking uncharacteristically frazzled.

"Those splashes aren't salmon. They're steelhead! I've been raising steelhead all afternoon on dries, on the Sputterkicker! Rose one five times!"

"How many rises did you have in all?" I asked. This set Bruce to counting back, and he was sure he could remember eighteen.

"Did you manage to hook any?"

"Twice steelhead came up and took the fly down. No splashes. No false rises. I was sure they were hooked. When I finally raised my rod—nothing. But I did hook a fish!"

"On the Sputterkicker?"

"No, on a low-water wet. A steelhead hit the fly and ran out of the pool and down the river. Never stopped. When most of my backing was gone, the fly came out."

Bruce's experiences were not unusual, the dry fly a great indicator of where a steelhead may be

John Farrar tails an 18 pound buck that rose to his Sputterkicker.

holding, offering a chance to follow up with a different dry, or a greased-line wet, with or without a hitch. But hooking one straightway on a dry can sometimes be a frustrating experience, and I admired Bruce's determination.

The next day, John and I were well below Rabbit. He was fishing his Sputterkicker, happy to go fishless if that was the result of his choice. He wanted time to sort out the pattern as a primary approach, not as an alternate to a failed wet fly.

Rain continued off and on throughout the day, the river now rising and showing a bit of color, but not enough to discourage John's dry-fly efforts. He raised a good fish five times without a solid take. I watched each rise, and several times the surface boiled six inches from the Sputterkicker. When the fish would not come back, I covered the lie with an Orange Charm fished with a hitch, but the steelhead was gone. I thought that would be the end of it, but John soon located another steelhead. After the fish had come to the fly twice, he called me over to watch. John made no effort to rush the fish, and he presented the dry fly by casting well across the river and executing a strong back-mend to produce a long, downriver, drag-free float. I watched him with satisfaction, for I often cast a dry fly downstream in just such a manner. John grew tense when the fly began to drag. He led the fly through the swing and was again over the fish. There was a huge boil beside the fly.

"There, did you see him?"

"Yes! I don't know what to say. The steelhead came right to the fly, but he didn't take it down. Try again."

John repeated the cast, exactly as before, and when the fly began its swing, it followed the track of the previous drift. In a blink, the steelhead lunged at the fly, its head completely out of the water. It missed, and, catlike, pounced again—and again failed to catch the deer-hair fly bouncing about in the current. Such audaciousness often leaves a steelhead cautious, as if its predatory nature has been triggered so involuntarily that it doesn't know what to make of it. I was not encouraged.

"Are you going to rest the fish?"

John's line trailed downstream. He was collecting himself, too. He shook his head and went right back at the fish. I would not have done this, and I would have been wrong. The steelhead came head-and-shoulders out of the water and crushed the fly.

"Fish on," said John. His voice, grim and intense, was barely audible. The steelhead jumped once before clearing the pool and tearing down the long run of broken water. We staggered in pursuit along the slickly cobbled shore as the fish disappeared around a bend. When I reached the bank above the river to better keep track of the steelhead, it occurred to me that John's big Hardy Perfect must be nearly emptied. "I thought about it, and dared not look at it," he would tell me that evening. John called out, asking if he could get around a tree jutting into the water. I was sure the deep currents would sweep him away. I reached for his free hand, pulled him up the bank, and we continued our mad scramble. John was below the steelhead when it finally paused to turn upstream and maintain a holding station. This was the break he needed. A few minutes later, some three hundred yards from the hookup, the eighteen-pound buck was on his side, motionless in his exhaustion. The Sputterkicker, now a fly with a past—and an auspicious beginning—was still securely fastened in the corner of his jaw.

DEAN RIVER STEELHEAD

The "Dean River Steelhead" is at least two very distinct races, long separated by headwater destinations. First is a spring run of steelhead bound for the Takia River, a main branch of the Dean some forty-five river miles from the ocean. These fish come through so quickly they often overrun themselves, and they may drop back downstream during the warmer periods of late summer. They are sexually immature, average eight to nine pounds, and appear greyer than mainstem Dean River steelhead. I think this race would compare very much to the springers in Washington's Kalama, Washougal, and Wind rivers. The peak of the run is usually found by gear fishermen seeking chinook salmon in June and early July along the lower two miles of the Dean. Each year, a few eighteen-pound Takia steelhead are caught. I am not aware of any scale analysis studies conducted on the race. By means of a creel census, anglers often provide fishery biologists with hard escapement data, but the Takia River is closed to angling, and save for run timing, there is no certain way to separate the two races on the lower river.

Bobby Cunningham is a carpenter and master boat builder from Kamloops who camps along the Dean just below the falls for several months each summer. I met him near Kimsquit, and we motored along the lower river in his plywood jet boat, studying the steelhead lies now filled with chum and pink salmon. For Bobby, whose steelhead fly fishing is confined mostly to the Dean and Thompson rivers, the Takia race is a breed apart, the strongest of all steelhead. "They will pop a seventeen-pound tippet like nothing," he told me. The large, early July Takia steelhead had Bobby searching for superlatives. "They still have sea lice hanging on them, and they haven't wasted any energy getting over the falls. There is nothing like them."

Few anglers have the experience to make such an emphatic racial distinction. Dean steelhead caught from below the falls at any time of the year are steelhead of legendary strength. Many fly fishermen will claim that the same fish caught from above the falls have, at worst, lost only a step, and they vie with Thompson River steelhead as the "hottest" in North America.

I believe several factors contribute to these claims. Dean steelhead possess remarkable girth, their robust shape rarely conforming to the usual weight-to-length ratio associated with summer-run steelhead found elsewhere. (At twenty-four inches, a steelhead will weigh four pounds. For each additional inch in length, add a pound. Thus, a thirty-inch steelhead is typically ten pounds.)

In their study, *A Resumé of the Dean River Sport Fishery: 1971–75*, J. W. Leggett and D. W. Narver gave the following correlation of ocean age to mean (average) length and weight: a) 2 + ocean males were 72.6 cm and 4.9 kg (28.6 inches and 10.8 pounds); 2 + females were 71.4 cm and 3.9 kg (28 inches and 8.6 pounds); b) 3 + males were 88.8 cm and 8.9 kg (35 inches and 19.6 pounds); 3 + females were 81.5 cm and 6.8 kg (32.1 inches and 15 pounds).

My general impression of the most robust male steelhead was that their girth-to-length ratio was often as great as those typically found on the Kispiox, the generally accepted standard against which other steelhead are measured.

Several explanations could account for their robust size and strength. Great physical effort is required to overcome the falls on the lower Dean. It is impossible to imagine this not being part of a natural selection process at work. (Interestingly, the less-athletic pink and chum salmon spawn below the falls, while chinook and sockeye salmon spawn well above the falls. Biologists do not believe that Dolly Varden char are capable of passing up the falls. Below the falls they are saltwater in much of their orientation, feeding freely on chum spawn and salmonid smolts in tidewater. Upstream, these fish are strictly residential.)

The majority of Dean steelhead, as well as those steelhead that enter the Kispiox, Sustut, Babine, and Bulkley rivers, enter fresh water at approximately the same time. The Dean has a reputation as a July and August sport fishery, while the famous tributaries of the Skeena are notable for their fall fishing. The major difference, of course, is the distance the steelhead must travel before reaching water that can be fished with a fly. Dean fish are immediately available to anglers, and their condition is superb. Time spent in fresh water is a period of advancing sexual maturity. Bucks in the upstream tributaries of the Skeena are typically highly colored, and are often sluggish, despite their great size and strength. No steelhead's condition is improved by a month or more spent ascending its river.

Leggett and Narver collected scale samples from Dean River steelhead killed by anglers between June and September 1973, 1974, and 1975. The steelhead's freshwater and ocean age in years were thus determined. (Repeat spawners will be discussed later in this section and are omitted from these figures.)

TABLE 1	Freshwater Age				Ocean Age		
	2	3	4		1+	2+	3+
Percent (1973)	14.9	82.6	2.4		8.0	74.0	18.0
(1974)	28.1	70.8	1.1		5.6	82.0	12.4
(1975)	9.3	88.4	2.3		3.4	85.2	11.4

TABLE 2	Total Age							
	2.1+	2.2+	2.3+	3.1+	3.2+	3.3+	4.1+	4.2+
Percent (1973)	.8	7.3	6.8	6.5	65.8	10.3	1.9	.5
(1974)	1.1	22.5	5.0	5.0	58.4	7.9	——	1.1
(1975)	——	7.0	2.3	1.2	77.9	9.3	1.2	1.2

Note: The "+" beside each numbered year of saltwater residency tells that the fish is in the next year of its saltwater life. For example, a 2+ steelhead had passed through two complete years in salt water, and was in its third year in salt water when it entered the Dean.

Freshwater residency is typically three years, midway between what is found among Washington and Oregon steelhead (two years) and the more northern races found in the Skeena drainage (four years). These differences do not necessarily produce different-sized smolts. I believe the longer freshwater residence of steelhead parr as one goes north is a necessary result of the slower growth rates experienced in more frigid, less fertile waters, and the shorter, temperate period of rapid growth.

If the sampling is representational, it is evident that some years show stronger runs of steelhead with longer ocean residencies. I have discussed this with numerous fly fishermen, and many are certain they have experienced this in their fishing. There are "trophy years" when, for reasons beyond our understanding, a river will have more than the usual number of large fish. I am just as certain that, within the months of total escapement, a few weeks each year offer the greatest opportunity at a trophy-size steelhead. This period is not necessarily the time of peak escapement, though I believe it is so on the Dean.

The ratio of male to female steelhead was approximately 1:1.60, even among the one-year ocean fish. There was no true run of "jack steelhead," the sexually precocious males evident on some other rivers.

In addition to the above sampling, 100 repeat spawners were examined. They represented 11 percent of the run in 1974, and 17.9 percent in 1973. Most were of age 3.2S1S+, primarily female steelhead that had spawned after two years in salt water, spent a year in the Dean followed by a year in salt water, and were captured while in the Dean a second time, steelhead in their eighth year of life. One female steelhead was returning to spawn a fourth time, a fish at least in its ninth year.

An evaluation of twenty-two repeat spawning Dean River steelhead by the Ministry of Environment in 1979 revealed the following life histories:

TABLE 3	Total			
	3.2S1+	3.2S1S1+	3.3SS	4.2S1S1+
Number	17	3	1	1
Percentage	77	13	5	5

Note: The 3.3SS steelhead returned to spawn a second time without an intervening year in salt water, a remarkable—and anomalous—post-smolt history.

The 4.2S1S1+ was a steelhead in its eleventh year of life returning to spawn a third time, a record for longevity on the Dean.

REFLECTIONS

We came off the Dean late in the afternoon, having exhausted the seven-day permits issued by the Ministry of Environment. The take-out is just above the canyon where the sound and energy of many river miles is compressed into a quarter-mile of boulder-studded violence. A dirt road meets the river here, and it led me to the condemned bridge that spanned the canyon, or to the Kimsquit landing strip several miles away.

I hiked out onto the bridge, looked down into the upwelling of lethal hydraulics, and experienced a rush of giddiness. No passage remotely existed for even the most nimble of boatmen. How had Blewett done it? Twenty-five years before no road existed, and transporting gear and supplies to the lower river was overland and back-breaking. One day, disgusted with this prospect, Dick Blewett stuffed air mattresses into his rubber raft to provide back-up flotation, and dropped down into the chasm. This was no glory ride at any cost, but an effort to master this section of river in late summer's low water and connect his lodge enterprise to the lower river.

"I had barely started when the rocks broke both my oars in half," he told me. "From then on I kept pushing myself off with a pole." Dick chuckled at the memory, and was mildly incensed when I told him I'd heard that the run nearly killed him. No one ever tried this again, and Blewett's experience is the most enduring of all local tales.

The four of us stacked all of our gear at the take-out and camped by the river. An employee from Tony Hill's Nakia Lodge would haul our gear to the airstrip in the morning. I was tired and satisfied, my mood reflective; the wait would not be taxing.

A young man I had passed earlier in the day happened by, and we talked about Dean steelhead. I remembered him both for the Bogdan reel he was fishing and for the casts he made while standing to his armpits in the currents. He was using a very-fast-sinking shooting head spliced to a lead-core sink tip, and he had successfully dredged the bottom for several fine steelhead. Two more would come to his fly that evening, but I had no desire to follow him up the river. I had enjoyed wonderful fishing all week using only floating lines, and I broke down my rod as we spoke.

Nakia Lodge is near the landing strip, a convenience perhaps offset by its distance from the river. By means of Honda three-wheelers, guests can shuttle themselves back and forth. After days of quiet solitude, this little fleet of motorcycles should have produced culture shock, but the quicker, more competitive pace of the last few miles of river had prepared me for them.

As John Farrar and I stood on the strip, I felt detachment far out of proportion to my sense of impending departure. Upriver pools were still blotting out most of the here and now. I was more comfortable two days before, and most comfortable the day before that. I like solitude; I lose myself in it. My recreation is solitude and fishing, together, but in that order.

Gerhardt Trolitsch was looking for a conversation when he motored up on one of the three-wheelers. Weeks alone in the game cabin by the take-out made him anxious for company. A hearty, good-natured man and a brilliant wildlife artist, Gerhardt had been contracted as a fisheries technician for the summer. He had known the river for many years and had a long memory for local minutiae. "I don't think the Dean steelhead are as large today," he said. "Twenty pounds is exceptional today, but not twenty years ago. That was just a good fish then." I wondered if large fish were like cold winters and deep snow, a product of youthful memories that make the past unassailable. He could recall extraordinary steelhead, including one just over thirty pounds, but that did not at all seem like an impossible expectation of the present river.

I heard the sound of an airplane and thought at first that it was ours, but the direction was wrong, and soon a Cessna came out of the bank of rain clouds and put down on the river. Buzz Fiorini, late in his seventies, was flying in Bob Stroebel and Harry Lemire, a trio of steelheading legends. I had first heard about the Dean from Harry Lemire many years ago. He had returned from the river with the largest steelhead ever caught on a dry fly, one well over twenty pounds. I knew the story by heart. Now, I wondered if anyone had ever done better on the Dean. I hoped not.

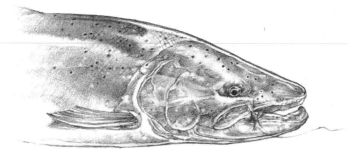

18

BULKLEY RIVER

"I cast right to the fishing lane, about thirty-five degrees from downstream," said Collin. There was no back-mending and no part of the drift that was drag-free in his nuts and bolts approach. The Mouse was driven out sixty feet, its big head designed to send out streams of bubbles on the swing, and with the rod tip held almost to the water, the fly began waking.

Collin Schadrech is a grizzled bear of a man, fiercely emphatic when explaining the dry-fly methods that have come to define his steelheading. As the outfitter continued to lecture, he made quick little mends while intently studying the Mouse's progress across the slot of holding water. "You want to slow the fly down. Usually the larger the steelhead and the colder the water, the slower you want that fly to swing." Collin dropped down a step, picked up his line, and made another cast. "You don't want to wade too deep. The steelhead may be holding in only two feet of water, even less when the river is at its lowest in early fall." He thought for a moment and then added. "And they will be holding the same stations when the river is in spate. We've caught them on drys in six feet of water."

I found pleasure in watching Collin as he delivered his comments with textbook clarity. He claims to have caught over four thousand steelhead, half this number on a dry fly, a figure too staggering to contemplate, even if the total were halved. The majority have come from the Bulkley River, the tributary of the Skeena that supplies forty percent of the watershed's annual run of steelhead. Neighboring Skeena-bound rivers such as the Babine and the Kispiox are celebrated for annual numbers of trophy steelhead, but their runs are paltry by comparison. A banner year on the Bulkley may see twenty thousand steelhead ascending to spawn in rivers tributary to the main stem, and in the Bulkley itself.

"There! Did you see the boil?" I searched the currents and couldn't detect the fish on additional casts. "The steelhead may be a little sluggish," Collin said. Water temperature was forty-three degrees, still warm enough on this late October day to expect a steelhead on a dry.

Chris Reeser, a lead guide for Collin, told me of raising steelhead on drys well into November, when surface currents had dipped into the high thirties. These experiences had convinced him that water temperature was an overvalued factor with these free-rising steelhead. Even when plummeting air temperatures froze fly lines in the guides, steelhead would still respond to the active dry.

Years of guiding on the river have made Collin acutely aware of water levels and the fly-fishing implications of each. He was certain that on this day the river was running 5,700 cfs. "Anything over six thousand cfs brings a rapid decline in the dry-fly fishing," he explained. Maximum flow occurs in June throughout the Skeena drainage, and the Bulkley, just above its confluence with the Skeena, can run over 18,000 cfs. Then the river cuts away at banks and drops huge cottonwoods into its rushing currents to be deposited on downstream bars. Rapids rated II or III become IV—or worse—and every year the early summer Bulkley claims unwary rafters.

Collin and Shari Schadrech own Far West Lodges in Telkwa, British Columbia. The main lodge is their home, a riverside creamery they have completely refurbished and filled with fly-fishing memorabilia. Farther downriver is Seaton's, a simpler but no less comfortable lodge, housing guides and additional clients.

Collin and his guides, in the course of servicing seventy-six miles of the Bulkley River, have identified more than seven hundred pieces of holding water. These waters are divided between the Creamery Waters and Seaton Waters, the latter containing Twin Creek, the river camp I would reach this day near last light. Enormous maps hung on the Creamery's walls break down the water into tenth-of-a-mile increments. They pinpoint every piece of holding water that lends itself to the fly, and the guides understand how the fly is to be presented on each pool. Great economy and little wasted motion result from this approach. General prospecting is reserved for newly discovered runs; keen hunting is practiced on those many waters with fly fishing histories. Collin and his guides are so certain where the steelhead will hold that they won't hesitate to move a fly fishing client a single step one way or the other.

Collin calls the section of the Bulkley River where we were fishing the "upper canyon water," a nineteen-mile float completed in two very full days. Where we launched the McKenzie boats the river was freestone, open, and accessible, the highway and passing traffic a frequent reminder of civilization. The highway soon falls away as ledge rock and canyon walls replace freestone channels. Here the river gradient increases, and boats must be lined down in places.

Collin first rafted this water in 1983, and calls the experience "my greatest days of steelheading." He later returned by helicopter with two friends from Los Angeles. "We were," Collin said, "fishing water no one had ever fished before—even though the highway was only three and a half miles away." The two trips inspired him to open up a river camp, and many of his clients now consider Twin Creek the best of the Bulkley experience.

I shared the McKenzie boat this afternoon with Royce Hall, a physician from Florida who was long on saltwater experience. His trout fishing had consisted mostly of hunting down steelhead with Collin over six seasons. They were fast friends and took special delight in maligning each other, verbal darts that Royce's southern drawl would dignify with subtle hilarity. Contrary to Collin's dictum, Royce was using a wet fly, and that morning he had beached a brace of steelhead, the largest exactly a yard long.

Collin raised a steelhead in each of the first three pools we fished, but none came to the fly with determination, and I don't think any of them returned a second time. I was not faring even that well, and Royce told me that he had not received so much as a touch. We knew many steelhead were in the river, both the fresh, mint-bright arrivals, and the "sun-tans," steelhead that had darkened after some weeks in the river. As always, the males exhibited this change most dramatically.

The first steelhead of the season show in these pools as early as mid-August, and by early September probably twenty percent of the run is in the main stem of the Bulkley. This figure increases each week, and by late October, at least ninety percent of the entire run is distributed throughout the Bulkley system. Many of these fish will reach a certain destination and then drop downstream, sometimes for miles. The reasons for this are not fully understood. I know that on some rivers severe drops in water temperature can trigger such movements, but this does not seem to be the case with Bulkley fish. Regardless of what governs their movements, by Collin's reckoning, some steelhead were now going upstream, a lesser number were going downstream, and a lot of steelhead were holding a station and, at least temporarily, satisfied with their whereabouts.

The wind that began blowing through the canyon that afternoon signaled a massive storm system. I would have taken pleasure in the scudding black clouds and rattling forests of barebone alder had those winds not made fly casting a labor. As much to penetrate the wind as to reverse my declining expectations, I changed from the Mouse to a Night Dancer, but by the time we approached Twin Creek we were still fishless, and Collin and I were speculating on the effects of barometric pressure on steelhead. As we pulled the boat into camp water, the wind suddenly passed through, replaced by mists of soft rain that muffled every sound and enhanced our sense of remoteness.

River lodges and their less-grand relation, river camps, are situated with great care. If the lodge is to be serviced by floatplane, then suitable landing water naturally becomes the first priority when selecting camp water. There is an extra bonus if this same water can provide memorable angling. Gary Miltenberger managed this on the Sustut; and Surprise Pool, which graces Steelhead Valhalla Lodge, is one of the great pieces of water in all of steelheading. River camps, however, are placed almost solely for the fishing they can provide. Camp water must give first-light anglers a leg up on their steelhead-per-day definition of good fishing. It must be a hole card for anglers returning from a long day who are fatigued and perhaps discouraged. By consent, common and unspoken, the hard-luck angler, the less-skilled angler, can be turned loose on this water and have fortunes changed and enthusiasms rekindled. Finally, because fellowship and good whiskey are never far away when it is time to reflect on the day, camp water carries the burden of the river's angling tales.

Myron Kozak was guiding Don Payiva and Warner "Bud" Brackett below us all day, and I had glimpsed their boat from time to time. We had joined them for lunch, and then lost them in the afternoon. Now in the final few minutes of twilight, Myron watched his clients with satisfaction as they worked their flies down through the turgid currents at Twin Creek with sink-tip lines. I wondered whether to take up the end of this pool, then thought better of it. I had been concentrating for hours on the fishing, a period of draining intensity, and more fishing would have been mere work. I walked up the bank and deposited my rod beside the two quonset-style, twelve-by-fifteen-foot tents made nearly permanent with gas lighting and wooden floors. When I turned, I saw Don's rod take a sudden set and a steelhead break clean from the tailout. I hurried downstream to photograph the thirty-two-inch buck, and as I was trudging back, Bud hooked a thirty-seven-inch hen. Don found a third steelhead and rose still another in almost total darkness before he quit the pool and joined the rest of us for steaks and wine. All in all, it was a remarkable turn of activity from a sweet spot no larger than the floor area of our dining tent. Collin had picked his camp water well!

In the morning, Collin called to me, "We're off to Paradise!" I followed him up the steep trail behind camp that led to an empty pasture. Royce was left the camp water, while Myron and his clients continued on downstream.

"Paradise?"

"Yes, we have a Paradise Found, a Paradise Lost, and a Paradise Regained."

Wasn't Milton an indigestible, dry-as-dust subject that bullied budding intellects? Fishing Paradise Found would have an element of skipping school about it. The thought made me smile.

We pushed on through an alder break and followed the rude trail back down to the river. Morning sunshine found slots in the overcast to illuminate this beautiful pool. Collin was in no hurry to fish, and I asked him about the steelhead races within "Bulkley/Morice" steelhead. I had always found the subject confusing, mostly because of how the river and its principal tributary are designated.

Collin explained that far upstream of where we were fishing, the Bulkley splits into two tributaries.

The largest of these, carrying at least eighty percent of the flow at the confluence, is called the Morice River. The other tributary is the Bulkley. Bob Hooten, Section Head, Skeena Branch, Fisheries Division, told me that the Bulkley headwater is insignificant as a spawning area. Conversely, the Morice holds many spawning fish, but has a reputation for small steelhead, those in the four- to five-pound range. Bob's opinion was that "Bulkley" steelhead generally spawn throughout the system, meaning the Morice, too. Even though the Morice River is simply the upper reaches of the Bulkley, do the two rivers, in fact, possess different races of fish? Collin thought so.

"The earliest fish in the system are of Morice stock. They may be found in the Bulkley from July on, though in the area where we fish we don't pick many up at that time. We used to find them by the end of July or the first of August in the forty-odd miles upriver from Telkwa." Collin was certain these steelhead were smaller, on average, than main-stem Bulkley stock below the confluence with the Morice. Well downstream in the Bulkley system is a fragile run of Suskwa steelhead, a "super race," and "among the largest strain of steelhead to be found in the entire Skeena system," according to Collin. They are characterized by a very robust shape and great size. The fourth major strain, the Telkwa River stock, is probably indistinguishable from main-stem Bulkley fish. Collin's experience has been that these genetic strains can be in very specific places at certain times of the year. Generally, the early-arriving Bulkley fish "only go so far up and wait until water levels are conducive for them to go up a major tributary, the Telkwa for instance."

At midmorning, I finally cast my Night Dancer on Paradise. A Dolly Varden surprised me, its sharp strike an adrenaline rush, and, as always, I was disdainful of the fish when I discovered the truth. Collin called to me from his rock perch, "We get them as sea-runs to five pounds." I could not, however, find anything glamorous in this fish, and my disappointment was keen.

We returned to Twin Creek to find Royce still casting his fly on camp water. He told us that after several trips through the pool he had hooked a steelhead, his only rise all morning. The buck was very large and had given him some bad moments during a struggle that lasted over half an hour. Beaching the fish proved particularly difficult, but Royce had kept his head and was able to measure the trophy carefully, thirty-eight inches, his largest steelhead.

Collin said that, as a general rule, the late-season Bulkley steelhead average ten to twelve pounds. Furthermore, each year his clients take a dozen or more steelhead over twenty pounds, sometimes much more. During a couple of days in October 1987, there were steelhead of twenty-two, twenty-four, and twenty-nine pounds, all on waking dries. Carl J. Sieracki of Burlington, Connecticut, used a #6 tan Mouse to catch a buck 41 1/2 inches long that must have weighed at least twenty-five pounds. (No girth measurements were taken.) Collin finds nothing unusual in even the largest steelhead coming to a dry when conditions promote its use.

The rain now began in earnest. A fluorescent golf ball left on the shore the previous evening to mark the rising water indicated the river was up six inches. Water clarity was deteriorating too; I could barely see my boot tops in waist deep water. I didn't want to fish a dry and told Collin so.

"Do you have something in orange?" he asked.

I held up a sheepskin fly book filled with Squamish Poacher-type winter shrimp patterns in hot orange and Krystal Flash.

"Too much," he said to the dazzling array.

I went through my boxes of summer flies and finally selected a sparsely dressed 1/0 Macks Canyon, a floss-bodied Halloween pattern that would show up well and, if back-mended, sink like a stone.

We continued our float until we arrived at a riffle so long that all three of us could be accommodated by wading down the shallow center of the river and casting toward shore.

"This is an awesome run," Collin called down to us.

As I followed Royce through, a hen steelhead struck my fly and streaked away in a single motion, the backing knot following her down the river an instant later. She was a splendid fish, strong and in magnificent shape. I was anxious about her capture, because I wanted to photograph her. Collin came downstream, and when the hen was close in and tired, he took the rod while I returned to the boat for my camera. He took pains not to stress her, and we worked fast to shoot the close-up pictures I desired. After freeing the barbless hook, Collin held the hen for another picture and then sent her on her way. I guessed her weight at a shade over ten pounds.

Though loathe to give up the dry fly, Collin now fished behind me with a General Practitioner, and very shortly rose a buck of perhaps twelve pounds that jumped as much as my hen ran, an active male fish, very typical of Bulkley River steelhead.

As we continued downstream, Collin commented that coming up shortly was an obscure piece of water that to his knowledge had never before been fished. He had noted the lies in low water, but remained uncertain of its promise. Now was the right time to go though it with a fly. This aggressive sense of discovery expands Collin's knowledge of holding water, and I was happy to oblige, though I became somewhat skeptical when we came upon the water. From my upstream position, the river along the shore seemed almost without current, and trees crowded the shore in a variety of attitudes. There was no beach, and I was to my knees in the river with my back nearly against the bank. I discovered that there was a ledge a dozen feet from the river's edge. Collin saw me start to stumble and smiled with amusement.

"You found the drop off!" He motioned me back. "You're too far out." It was an appraisal of my wading that I had heard repeatedly. "You West Coast steelheaders aren't happy unless you're wading up to your chest!"

As I fished the run, I lost sight of the entire river and studied only what my fly could reach with a modest spey cast. The run fished surprisingly well, the currents mending my line and bringing my fly through the swing on a tight line. Halfway down, a steelhead took with such force and resisted the rod with such determination that I badly overestimated its size, even when the fish rolled and its tail came up like little flukes. "This steelhead is in the teens for sure," I stated.

"Eight pounds," said Collin.

"Not possible," I called back. As the fish flashed by, I was still thinking large steelhead, and I continued to think so until it was easy to move. That is rarely possible with a heavy fish. As I eased the steelhead over my open hand, I knew he was right. Collin materialized with a tape to settle the matter. The hen was just over twenty-six inches long, massive in girth, like a silver football.

"Well, it's the fight in the dog that counts," I offered.

Telkwa is a little village at the confluence of the Bulkley and Telkwa rivers, a meeting its residents observe from the Bulkley side. From my room at the Creamery, I could see both rivers through a row of huge cottonwoods that landscaped a narrow riverside park. Even with my view somewhat obscured, I could see that the single river ran as two, the badly muddied Telkwa flowing down the west side of the Bulkley, while the Bulkley itself remained green, still very much the dry-fly river. Where the two rivers did not mix was as clearly defined as a median line, sharply evident even as the river left town and ran north and west before Hudson Bay Mountain, the regal backdrop for Telkwa and her rivers.

I had taken a day off from fishing and now found myself wondering how long this separation was maintained. To find out, I hiked to less than a mile below town and watched a powerful eddy send the Bulkley back upstream to swing away from shore and into the Telkwa's currents. All that remained from the mixing was a thin green line along my shore, a graphic demonstration of how the Telkwa divides the Bulkley. As I began my walk back to the Creamery, I saw that the guides had abandoned their cherished canyon water and were arranging to fish their clients above the Telkwa. With continued rain in the forecast, this would be the last major piece of steelhead fly water in the Skeena country to go out.

The town of Telkwa is more than a division of angling perceptions. Upstream, the river valley broadens until it reaches its widest point at the junction of the Morice River. Downstream from Telkwa, the river valley narrows until the benchlands disappear altogether and the mountain slopes become canyon walls. Miles below my last cast with Collin, a series of cataracts contain present day Moricetown, and just below these lies Hagwilget, the ancient summer salmon camp of the Wet'suwet'en. A few river miles later, the Bulkley joins the Skeena, the meeting known as Forks almost from earliest exploration.

Prospectors began wintering here on the banks of the Skeena in the 1860s, and in 1868 the tiny settlement adopted the name of Hazelton for the abundant hazel bushes growing on the flats above the river.

The Skeena is navigable from the sea to its confluence with the Bulkley, a distance of 150 miles, though Hazelton can hardly be called a deep water port. When the Hudson's Bay Company established a store in Hazelton in 1880, supplies shipped from the coast were relayed to remote fur trading forts throughout the region. Hazelton grew steadily, and it came to tie mining interests to the coast just as Telkwa supplied farmers in the river valley it headed. The two towns, unconnected commercially but similarly sited, should have entertained equally sanguine futures. That they did not was a direct result of the Grand Trunk Pacific Railroad and a completed line from Prince Rupert to Prince George in the spring of 1914. The line generally followed the Bulkley River, and when it was determined that several "divisional points"—yards, shops, and residences for railroad employees—were needed, Telkwa ended up on the wrong side of the river. A new townsite, a dozen miles east of Telkwa, was chosen. It was called Smithers, after A. W. Smithers, chairman of the Grand Trunk Pacific.

Smithers is now the hub of the Skeena wheel, the steelhead angler's destination on jet flights from Vancouver. Telkwa, literally on the wrong side of the tracks, is slowly going nowhere and doing so with dignity and neatness, something Smithers can't match. As I wandered back through town on this cool October day, I found the quiet pace of its frontier atmosphere a tonic.

The Wet'suwet'en Indians once owned the entire basin of the Bulkley River and called their river Wet'sinkwha. This confederation of matrilineal families with ancestral food gathering locations was eradicated as a condition of British Columbia's entry into the Dominion. The subject can be left at that, save for this footnote—bizarre, and a little pertinent.

A work party of 150 men invaded their lands in 1866, with the intention of laying a telegraph cable to Siberia via Russian Alaska and the Bering Sea. The work would continue across the vast steppes of Asia until the cities of Europe and North America were connected. This bold scheme was the brainchild of Perry Collins, an American, who sold the idea to the newly formed Western Union Telegraph. Their receptivity to Collins's proposal was due entirely to Cyrus Field's repeated failure to lay a telegraph cable across the floor of the Atlantic.

The British Columbia link in this vast chain was a route up the Fraser River, east down the Bulkley to the Skeena, and up the Kispiox until reaching the Nass drainage. The cable crossed the Bulkley at Moricetown, the principal Wet'suwet'en village. The Indians observed this enterprise with great curiosity. For most, it was their first intimate association with whites.

Colonel Charles S. Bulkley was put in charge of the construction through British Columbia. By all accounts he managed the project well enough, for when word reached Bulkley that Field had successfully laid the Atlantic cable, work parties were forty miles up the Kispiox River. Naturally, Bulkley ordered the work stopped. Most of the men returned home, but a few stayed in the area, took up prospecting, and settled in Hazelton.

The telegraph line worked as far as it went, but it arrived from nowhere and went nowhere, and it soon fell into disrepair. The Wet'suwet'en, a clever people, set upon the miles of abandoned cable with saws, and used it to fence their fields and strengthen their bridges, one of the few windfalls they were ever to experience in their relationship with whites. What Colonel Bulkley thought of the river that bears his name is not recorded. He played no further role in the history of the region.

DRY-FLY DAYS

I had never seen a summer in the valley of the Bulkley hang on as it did in 1989. The wisps of fog that typically strung the lowlands together burned off by midmorning. Ospreys that might otherwise have been riding Mexican thermals were etched against a hard blue sky, hawking over the dry fly flats for parr. Alder were still green, the dogwood only rarely blushed with pink. Even the cottonwoods,

ic blendings of new yellow and old green. Only the aspen flut-
announced the season.

a half-century had glutted the river and spent itself in a million
e fish still littered the cobblestone shore and floated downriver,
inst the back of my waders, often in midcast.

mon had tilled the river, an aeration of gravel and detritus that
rms of stoneflies and mayflies precipitating from the flows and
wly arrived steelhead. The fish greedily gobbled up loose spawn,
n, some with sink tip lines and simple yarn flies, others with
mph patterns.

obably no better than the fishery technicians had predicted. A
een at the Trout Creek boat take-out each day since the first of
d only widespread disappointment. The most optimistic assess-
g to be late this year.

d at so prosaic an explanation. They blamed the offshore drift
an gill nets off Prince Rupert with equal disgust. One devil was
ial antipathy was born out of a sense of helplessness. Gossip on
ead had gone into the pink salmon harvest and were purposely
s another can of steelhead coming off the line. The most de-
f the Bulkley steelhead was being permanently restructured for
systematically eliminated from the race by commercial fishing

e fishing was not, a common enough refrain in steelheading. I
and Denise Maxwell, dry-fly purists who have long practiced a
rn, their own Telkwa Stone, a simulation of a stonefly, genus
n the Bulkley. The run, such as it was, would by now contain
ture of the river was hovering around fifty degrees. Under these
lhead like no other method.

Bulkley near Telkwa, and on this day Mike's son, Mike Jr., was
sco dentist, and his friend, Evelyn Peck. They were an elegant
ompletely natural strolling through the Smithers hotel lobby in
cing a year to master the two-handed rod, a steelhead on a dry
no idle companion. She managed her own water with a single-
meticulous determination.

coffee merchant of Dr. Craig's vintage, had never before caught
cast well enough and had the stamina of a man half his age.
sure thing, though now I was far from confident of anyone's

tion is a long drag-free float. As the fly sails downriver, slack line
t brisk enough to cause the fly to jerk erratically, but not to drive
lhead from its station as it drops downriver with the fly. The
es under tension, often the very moment it begins to drag. Then
of line released to assure additional slack as the rise takes place.
en it attempts to return to its station, the drag of the line pulling
s mouth and setting the hook firmly into the hinge of its jaw.
this from atop the ridge of Coal Seam pool. A few times they
leaders, tossed it into the river to float over a waiting steelhead,
seen a remarkable transformation when the fly has been entic-
d records of exactly where in the swing the rise occurs continue
sentation.

Mike Maxwell presents a Telkwa Stone with a double spey cast. →

Denise Maxwell is a cheerful woman who picks up more line than most fly fishers can cast. Some men find this disconcerting, until they discover that she is a former world champion distance caster, the story of her l70-foot tournament cast smoothing out a lot of ego. But it is not the distance cast that impresses so much as the line control she exhibits. She is an expert fly fisher.

I really try to please the Maxwells by duplicating their somewhat involved presentation. I watch the fly intently, and I don't mend into the drift quickly enough. The fly drags too early. I pull the fly under on the mends.

"Denise," I say, "why don't you go through first? I'll watch you as I follow."

She is all business. No wasted motion. Short cast, medium cast, long cast, mend and feed line, move on and begin again. All the water is covered.

Mike is standing by the jet boat, pulling line off his big English reel. He flips his double-handed rod and throws twenty feet of line on the river. As he continues to strip line, a steelhead a yard long and at least sixteen pounds takes the bouncing fly from the surface. I share his astonishment. Twenty minutes later, as the fish is landed, the leader parts.

With the mood jollied up, my presentation begins to fall into place, but I am still dragging the fly under on the mends. When I reel in and place a hitch just behind the head, the fly is nearly unsinkable. A cast or two later, a boil beside the Telkwa Stone is followed by a perfect head-and-tail rise. The steelhead takes the fly all the way down before I tighten on the twenty-nine-inch hen. Denise hears the commotion and comes up to help me take some pictures. She is beaming. "That steelhead rose to my fly, a big splash just to let me know she was there. Wouldn't come back."

Denise shares a secret: When she and Mike are guiding clients, they fish the Telkwa Stone with the hook bent all the way around, the point pushed up into the body. When she raises a steelhead she marks the station. "I think I had a boil over there," she tells her sport. "Why don't you give it a try?"

Denise laughs shyly at the ruse. "I used to cut the hook off at the bend. Steelhead would feel the sharp edge and not come back. Once a fish took one of these flies, raced across the river, thrashed around and shook its head. I said, 'How can this be happening? There is no hook!'"

"So much for the theory that steelhead keep their mouths open after they take the fly," I said. Mike nodded. He told me that he had a steelhead clamp down so hard it forced the bent hook through the fly's body. The little point stuck the steelhead and kept it on for a few minutes.

"Denise was really ready to give it to me!" he recalled.

During lunch we drift past Dr. Craig and Evelyn. They round a bend, stop to fish, and Dr. Craig spey-casts his dry fly for male steelhead of thirty-three and thirty-four inches.

I have seen no river that is the equal of the Bulkley for an abundance of dry-fly water. The low gradient and shallow channels have produced immense flats of light current that comfort steelhead and bring just the right amount of action to waking dries. One of the very finest pieces of water is Home Pool below the Maxwells' house. It is a short, remarkably well-defined piece of holding water, the kind I call a "gut," where I'll often find a buck steelhead. Eustis was taking the lead, for he had not yet caught a steelhead, and his first fish was more important than anyone else's second. He called to me when his fly disappeared, and he could feel only dead weight.

"Trey, I've hooked bottom!"

"With a dry fly?"

"No. Wait! I've hooked a salmon!"

"How do you know its a salmon?"

"It won't *jump.*"

"Eustis, you've hooked a buck steelhead, for sure."

"I thought steelhead were supposed to jump!"

The fish rolled up a wide rose-colored stripe and confirmed Eustis's prospects. If he was shaken, he did not show it. He grimly hung on and tried to compute all the advice I was offering. The steelhead was safely beached and carefully measured, thirty-four inches, easy. I photographed him making the release.

Denise Maxwell, the only woman who holds a guide's licence for steelhead in Canada.

"Eustis," I said, "when you're back home knocking back a bourbon with a few good old boys and the name of the game becomes one-upmanship, tell them about the thirty-four-inch rainbow you took on a dry fly!"

"Oh man!" he·said.

LIFE HISTORY

The Bulkley River above its confluence with the Morice is a minor tributary of the Bulkley. A small population of coho salmon and a remnant chinook run are known to ascend to its headwaters east of

Houston. A few steelhead are presumed to be in this mix, but little else can be said for its anadromous runs.

The Morice *is* the main-stem Bulkley above the confluence. With a forty-five-mile length and a drainage of a thousand square miles, it is by far the larger of the two headwater systems. The majority of all salmonids that enter the Bulkley at Hazelton are bound for the headwaters of the Morice River. They include sockeye, pink, coho, and chinook salmon, and steelhead trout. Typical of most sockeye rivers, the Morice is lake-headed. Morice Lake, large, cold, and deep, lies in a depression on the eastern slope of the Coastal Mountains. It tempers the river's flow and sediment load and helps to prevent extremes in water temperature. This moderating influence maintains the Morice—and much of the Bulkley—in a temperature range of forty to sixty degrees, and keeps it flowing clear except during prolonged periods of rain.

Morice steelhead enter the Skeena in July and August, during the peak of the commercial gill-net fishery. Half of the run is taken incidentally to the targeted stocks of sockeye and pink salmon. Indian gill nets set along the Skeena and lower Bulkley are part of a subsistence fishery, and although they are intended to intercept salmon, they are as indiscriminate as saltwater gill nets. Steelhead ascending this canyon water pass through their last obstacle at Moricetown Falls only to face an Indian gaff fishery. For a hundred miles above this point, they are available to sports fishermen on the main stem of the Bulkley and Morice rivers.

Steelhead appear in the Morice as early as mid-August, and by September they are well distributed in the drainage. They overwinter just below the outflow of Morice Lake and will spawn there in late May and June. Kelts negotiate their return to salt water quickly, but June spawners are late-June- or early-July-mending kelts, which once again puts them at the mercy of an intense commercial gill-net fishery.

Two important life history studies pertaining to Morice/Bulkley steelhead are current. They are: *Bulkley River Steelhead Trout: A Report on Angler Use, Tagging, and Life History Studies Conducted in 1982 and 1983,* by M. J. O'Neill and M. R. Whatley, Skeena Fisheries Report, 1984; and *Morice River Steelhead Trout: The 1976 and 1977 Sport Fishery and Life History Characteristics from Anglers' Catches,* by M. R. Whatley, W. E. Chudyk, and M. C. Morris, Fisheries Technical Circular No. 36, July 1978.

The Bulkley River study was conducted between Smithers and the confluence, but included three miles of the Morice River above the confluence. (It did not include the Bulkley above the confluence.) The Morice River study included the Morice to the confluence and the Bulkley River below the confluence to Barrett. The overlap of at least ten miles is part of both studies. If the studies had revealed clear racial distinctions between Bulkley and Morice steelhead, the overlap would have proven troublesome. Such differences were not expected, and, in these studies, were not encountered. Nevertheless, most anglers believe the Bulkley steelhead is definitely a larger race. Compelling reasons may support that contention.

I think of the Skeena as merely a conduit to famous tributaries and their unique races of steelhead, somewhat like the nondescript trunk of a tree leading to the profusion of branches. Four famous branches are the Babine, Kispiox, Sustut, and Copper. These steelhead have developed over the millenia and exhibit certain racial characteristics for contour, weight, and run timing. The headwaters of the Skeena itself are extremely remote and not well known, but no angler of my acquaintance who has fished them suggests that their steelhead are larger than those in the Sustut, Babine, or Kispiox. My own fly-fishing experiences on both the upper Skeena and the Skeena below its confluence with the Kispiox support this view. What we have are some tributary races that are greater in size than headwater main-stem fish.

Something similar may be at work on the Bulkley system of rivers. There are several tributary races. One of these is the headwaters of the Bulkley, water that we call the Morice River. Two others are the Telkwa and Suskwa races. There are also steelhead that spawn in the main stem of the Bulkley below the confluence and are known to arrive later than those that spawn just below Morice Lake. I think it is quite possible that these steelhead are races distinct from the Morice. The October angling record certainly seems to support the plausibility of this theory.

The Morice River study covered a period of two fishing seasons and was based on an angler creel survey of 5l8 steelhead, divided between 225 males and 293 females. Their life histories break down as follows:

Age Group	Percent of Total
2.1+	.4
3.1+	11.4
3.2+	10.8
3.3+	.2
3.1Sl+	.4
3.2Sl+	.8
4.1+	38.2
4.2+	25.5
4.3+	.9
4.1Sl+	2.9
4.2Sl+	2.1
4.2SlSl+	.2
5.1+	5.4
5.2+	.8
5.1Sl+	.2
15	100.0

Notes: The two-year freshwater age was represented by a single male fish. The other freshwater ages, as years of residency before smolting, were these percentages of the total sampling: 3 years = 23.5 percent, 4 years = 69.9 percent, 5 years = 6.4 percent.

Size at the time of smolting for these ages was typical of races in these nothern latitudes: 5.4, 6.7, and 8.7 inches, respectively. The slower growth rates exhibited by these premigrant steelhead is due to a colder environment, less-abundant insect life, shorter growing season (i.e., periods of lowered metabolic activity during long winters).

Male and female steelhead with an ocean age of 1+ made up over fifty percent of the total sampling. The average weight was 4 pounds for males and 3.5 pounds for females.

Male and female steelhead with an ocean age of 2+ made up over forty percent of the total sampling. Their average weight was 9.9 pounds for males and 8.1 pounds for females.

Three-year ocean steelhead were all males and totaled only six fish. They weighed from 15.8 to 21 pounds.

Repeat-spawning steelhead represented 6.2 percent (1976) and 6.8 percent (1977). The ratio of females to males was approximately 2:1.

The Bulkley River study of 877 steelhead was based on a creel census for 1982 and 1983. Of the scale samples gathered from this number, 503 were "readable." A summation of these results is interesting for its similarities and differences from the Morice study.

Most (90.3 percent) Bulkley River premigrants smolt at age three. Compare this to 23.5 percent for Morice steelhead where the premigrants more typically smolt at age four. The difference suggests that the Bulkley is a less hostile environment that promotes faster growth.

Only nine different adult age groups were identified, dominated by four. (Compared to fifteen on the Morice.) One+ ocean steelhead (3.1+, 4.1+) ranged from 37.2 percent (1982) to 68.5 percent (1983); 2+ steelhead (3.2+ and 4.2+) ranged from 59 percent (1982) to 27.2 percent (1983). Variation of this magnitude from one year to the next is not rare, and supports the belief commonly held by anglers that there are years when steelhead are unusually large or small.

When ocean years are lumped together, 1+ steelhead made up 53.7 percent of the run, 2+ steelhead contributed 45.7 percent of the run. Only three steelhead were 3+, two males and a single female.

These life-history figures were, for all practical purposes, identical to those describing Morice steelhead. In short, the Bulkley study described a race in which half of the steelhead were small one-year ocean fish, and the remaining half were two-year ocean fish weighing eight to l2 pounds. In either case, the three-year ocean male, the trophy class of steelhead on other Skeena tributaries, was rare.

Wally and Carol Booth's son stares at his father's 35 pound Kispiox steelhead.

19

KISPIOX RIVER

MIKE Craig and I stood on the grassy bank and waited for Richie Montella to bring the raft. We could look directly downstream into Lower Potato Patch, but the pool's legendary properties were not immediately evident. The currents seemed stilled by the October cold, and the river flowed without character or sound until it broke unevenly along the tailout far below.

"More trophy steelhead have been caught from this pool than from any other," Mike said, his Virginia accent hardened only slightly by his years as an outfitter on Montana's Bighorn River. He did not say from any other pool on the Kispiox, but from *any* other, a remarkable claim, considering the small number of fish that make up the run.

Kispiox steelhead for the year usually number no more than two thousand sexually mature adults. They first collect off the coast of British Columbia in August, between Porcher and Smith islands, a dozen miles south of Prince Rupert, and no more than ten miles from the mouth of the Skeena River. This generally describes Area 4, a statistical designation by Canada's Department of Fisheries and Oceans. Here the steelhead join millions of Skeena-bound sockeye and pink salmon, and here they are an incidental catch by gill- and seine-netters who are targeting the salmon. Though the steelhead can pass through Area 4 in four days or less, their numbers are devastated, more than forty percent of the run is lost. A subsistence gill-net fishery by landed Indians takes an additional ten percent of the run as the steelhead ascend the Skeena for the Kispiox. Current sport-fishing laws allow only one

Kispiox steelhead per season to be killed, and this must occur in October. Thus, during a typical year, less than a thousand Kispiox steelhead may survive to spawn.

These few, however, are the steelhead against which all others are measured. Mike believes, as I do, that they are, at the least, the largest steelhead in the world. Other attributes, such as heart and responsiveness to the dry fly, are less measurable and more subjective but invariably complement the race's genetic advantage for size.

As we studied the pool we were about to fish, we did so as one might study a painting, trying to gain a sense of what makes it special, to divine its essence, and to see if those impressions would translate into a fly perfectly fished.

How a pool fishes often isn't appreciated until the water immediately above and below it are understood. Each becomes a contributing factor in determining where the fish will hold, and even how they might behave in the pool between. When I searched the shallow riffles below the tailout, I felt they provided few places for an ascending fish to rest. The rigors of ascending this section would likely promote the security enjoyed in the deeper run. Here, anglers could find steelhead "stacking up" to collect themselves before pressing on. The very head of the pool ran narrow and deep, posed no problem to their continued migration, and might even contribute to spreading the fish out through much of the pool. At least the steelhead would not collect just below the head, because there was nothing intimidating in its nature. I made a final observation. Though steelhead reached the pool with some difficulty, they could leave it in a flash. Across the river from our vantage point, the sweeping gravel bar ended at the tailout; below, the forest ran hard by the river. There would be a special kind of hell to pay for the runaway.

The edge of the field where we stood had not been tilled in a generation. Its former purpose had given this and neighboring pools their names, for there was a total of four "potato patch" pools. They were more spread out than is suggested by the name they had in common, but a trail connected them by four-wheel-drive, and a day could be passed fishing all four.

Richie appeared with the little raft on top of his truck. We launched it below the bank and paddled across to the gravel bar. Richie sometimes used the raft to make short river floats, but its central function was to chase large steelhead that could be followed in no other way. For this purpose alone, the one-man raft is uniquely popular on the Kispiox. Of course, it happens that after being chased downstream, the fish reverses itself and passes upstream and around a bend or two, leaving the angler a little crazy. Nevertheless, the raft is an article of faith here, like a fighting butt or a saltwater reel, trappings of angling that reflect the reality of hookable fish that may be unlandable.

Mike invited me to enter the pool first, and I did so midway, he and Richie would enter above and fish behind me on the first pass through. The current was deceptively fast, the river deeper than I expected. We cast very-fast-sinking shooting heads, and not one of us touched bottom. The steelhead were summer-runs, and I was certain they would move to the fly. This confidence was reinforced when I stopped fishing to check the water temperature, forty-one degrees, warm enough to bring them up to a waking dry.

Richie is a Bighorn guide who works for Mike. New Jersey is his first language; there is no second. He is never awake without a cigar, which he simultaneously smokes and eats. He is also a superb fly fisherman, refreshingly unfettered by the mystique of the "gentle art." When I pulled out at the bottom end of the pool, I met Richie on the bar and asked him what pattern he was using. "I call dis deh Black Fly," he replied, holding up a 2/0 fly heavily dressed in black bear. I had tied on a similar, though slightly smaller, fly called Night Dancer; now the name sounded a little pompous.

The three of us fished through the pool for the next hour, each lost in the task of dividing the water into a certain number of casts, sweeps that would eventually locate and hook the unseen fish. The discipline necessary to complete this was not fueled by any certainty that a steelhead was present. It was rather a desire to cover the water properly, to fish the river with a concise rhythm and grace, businesslike yet artistic, and to find simple satisfaction in that approach. In this context, we grew less contented and began to suspect that the flies would have to be deeper to attract. "We'll have to hit them on the head," Mike said finally, and he left the river to change lines.

When a gauzy mist had settled into the riverscape of butter yellow cottonwoods, I changed from the dark pattern to a Skykomish Sunrise, a fly I favor on late afternoons like this. It was thinly dressed on a stout salmon hook, and would sink well. The floss body of fluorescent cerise glowed especially bright in the poor light. This choice also reflected my conviction that the timeworn adage, "bright day, bright fly; dark day, dark fly," was not nearly so true in steelheading as "bright day, dark fly."

I made a long cast across the even-flowing current, took four long steps downstream with the fly, and fed additional line into the drift as the fly began swinging across the river. This gave the fly additional time to sink, and on the first cast I felt a satisfying tick as it hit the bottom. In this manner, I began working quickly through the pool until my fly was passing through in the flat of water above the tailout. A steelhead stopped the fly, and my strike did little more than remove some slack from the deep running line. I took a couple of turns on the reel and struck the steelhead again, coming up against it hard only at the end of the strike. I didn't feel good about this, but the fish was on and holding in the current. When additional pressure didn't move the fish in the least, I was certain the steelhead was exceptionally large.

I became vaguely aware that line was very slowly leaving the reel, that the steelhead was exiting the pool, and doing so at a rate actually slower than the current. Even as it slipped into the more broken water, the pace did not change. I realized that the fish was still holding its upstream position, that no sense of panic had yet entered its consciousness, that it had simply picked up and floated downstream. I wanted now only to see such a fish, to see what size would permit this behavior, but it was not to be. I was running after the steelhead to close the distance between us when the hook came away.

I returned to my fishing, but I did so with little enthusiasm, for my thoughts were still with the unseen steelhead. This was not so much a case of dwelling on a lost fish as on a steelhead that was assuming a size of fantastic proportions. The legacy of the Kispiox has always been tales of steelheading that run bigger than life. Some of the world's finest fly fishermen swear that they have had encounters with steelhead of forty pounds. I did not entertain such a conviction, but I was left wondering.

I had heard of a fly fisherman who fought a Kispiox steelhead for over six hours. Observers claimed that the fish was over forty pounds, and for the most part it swam upstream and downstream with almost casual disregard for the angler. I was also told of a desperate angler who late in such a struggle attempted to shoot his steelhead. Fay Davis, for many years a Kispiox regular who had beached several steelhead in the thirty-pound range, once hooked a steelhead so huge that the long struggle left him totally exhausted. As the fish was being beached, it rolled on the line, but at that moment Davis fainted. When he regained consciousness, the great fish lay on its side in the shallows. He crawled to the steelhead, cut it free, and ultimately staggered back to camp. Davis thought the fish would have weighed forty pounds. And so it goes, one more story in a pantheon of legends that gives the fishing here an elevated sense of destiny.

Not that all the large steelhead escape, or can't be documented, for some can. The current world record fly-caught steelhead of thirty-three pounds came from the Kispiox in 1963. Karl Mausser killed the buck and carefully weighed it, documenting his record in the time-honored fashion. The longevity of the record would seem to cast doubt as to the authenticity of much larger fish hooked and lost, except that some of these steelhead were not lost, but *released*.

We have gone from a "Kill your limit" standard, through a more enlightened "Limit your kill" phase, to a current uncompromising and dogmatic "Release your catch if the steelhead is wild, or face censure by your peers." This puritanical approach may or may not save threatened Kispiox stocks, but the angler must now rely on less direct methods of determining the size of his catch. Length and girth in inches can be measured carefully, and using the formula $\frac{1.33 \times L \times G^2}{1000}$ the weight determined. The method is only as accurate as the measurements taken, but anglers are usually quite general, taking either a whole inch or, at best, a half-inch. Some anglers eschew any calculations, and ascribe general weights

Clay Carter and his great steelhead.

based on length. A forty-inch Kispiox steelhead is thus, "about twenty-five pounds." Any buck much over forty inches can make thirty pounds, with the angler pretty much guilt-free. No one minds this feigned casualness. Certainly, the lack of emphasis on "getting a record," once a staple motivator here, is healthy for the sport and for the river. Yet documenting these fish by size and by life history (scale analysis) would greatly benefit conservation efforts. I think knowing exactly what is being lost *to* commercial interests, and what is being saved *from* commercial interests, must be hammered home in a manner the public can immediately understand. It is fine to appreciate that this particular race is a rare and wondrous thing that we cannot recreate. It is absolutely necessary to know that in this river swim the largest rainbow trout in the world.

Several years ago, Clay Carter of Ketchum, Idaho, beached an enormous steelhead at Lower Patch. Careful measurements were made and many pictures taken, and it was determined the buck weighed thirty-seven pounds. Carter released the fish and gave up any hope for a world record, but he gained no little fame for his classy gesture. Had he killed the steelhead for the world record it was, the record would not have been a popular one. These are the fish that genetically energize their race, and their preservation is seen as a sacred trust among fly fishermen. We have come a fair piece since Mausser's record. (Karl Mausser has for many years practiced catch-and-release.)

After thirty years of intense angling scrutiny, we still do not know with certainty the maximum size Kispiox steelhead can reach. Rich stories of steelhead lost leave the potential for size up to unbridled imaginations. Releasing a giant fly-caught steelhead underscores this latitude while charming the memory as nothing else can. As Mike, Richie, and I quit the river and returned to camp, the river remained a delicious mystery.

I awoke in the night to the sound of a light drizzle on Mike's Airstream trailer. Through the gloom, I could make out the vague outline of Olga Walker's famous lodge. Steelhead had burst through tailouts to find their freedom in a dozen dreams. The scene had repeated itself again and again, the outcome always impossible to change. I thought of the rain and a comment Richie made. "The Kispiox should be called the River Out," he had said in reference to how easily the river can muddy, or even flood, the result of unwise timber-cutting practices years ago. Maybe that's it for a week. I closed my eyes, and the steelhead reappeared; sleep did not return easily.

Morning was glorious, a fall day of such brilliance and warmth the fishing could only be good. The drizzle proved to be almost entirely sound on the aluminum trailer, for the river remained extremely clear and low. We did not rush the day, and it was midmorning before Mike's raft and Richie's truck were in place. As we floated downriver, Mike chose our first water to fish, a rather meager run with a boulder-filled tailout. It was an easy read, and we drove the big flies across the river to a favorable slot we imagined held fish.

I covered the water without difficulty with a 7-weight outfit. A compact saltwater reel that held two hundred yards of backing provided additional confidence, though some regulars on the river would have found the outfit light. After a second complete pass through the run, I honed the hook to needle sharpness and again began reaching for the far side, now purely for the enjoyment it gave. I was certain this water held no fish.

The first time the fly reached into the tailout on this pass through, it was struck so solidly that I needed only to tighten on the line to solidly hook the fish. The steelhead ran to the end of the pool, paused for a second or two, and raced on downriver, a hot fish with a big current behind it. I saw the fish roll a hundred yards below, just above a cottonwood that had fallen into the river, and the flash of color sexed the fish for me. I was running now, away from Richie and through Mike, as I called to the fish to stop before it disappeared into the tangle of branches. I soon reached a tiny point on a gravel bar with the river on both sides. Unable to continue, I stood waiting for the inevitable. Mike and Richie had better sense, and I was scooped up as they floated by in the raft. They quickly brought me to the far side of the river, where I could draw the fish away from the tree and the heavy currents. Rod pressure brought the fish to me, and I never lost control of the buck after that. Five minutes later, it was laboring to stay upright in the shallows.

The steelhead was quintessential Kispiox: Massive hardness in every dimension and a double row of rose along its flanks. Richie weighed the fish in a net, and though it was scarcely more than a yard long, the steelhead went nineteen pounds, just above average for the river. It was then returned to the Kispiox without suffering further indignity.

I did not catch another fish that day. Late in the afternoon, Mike hooked a bright steelhead that weighed twelve pounds, and he could not recall another buck so small. The next morning I returned home and left Mike and Richie to spend ten more days on the Kispiox.

Richie eventually made his way back to Fort Smith, Montana, while Mike wintered in New Zealand. I was on a long fishing trip that winter, and did not read Mike's Christmas card until late January. The fishing had remained spotty, he said, but one day on one pool Richie got a buck of twenty-four pounds, and he followed with one of twenty-eight pounds. Just like that—one, two—only a few minutes apart. Afterwards they had sat on the bank to let their good fortune percolate, for they knew a lifetime could pass without a repeat.

LIFE HISTORY

The Kispiox originates in the glaciers of the Skeena Mountains to its north, and in the many tiny low-gradient creeks that feed the lakes and bogs of its northwestern headwaters. These branches join and run south to pick up outflows from the sockeye lakes, a tempered increase in the river's narrow-gauge passage through ancient stands of fir and hemlock. The confluence of the Nangeese River marks the upper end of the Kispiox Valley and the start of a public road that generally parallels the river for fifty miles until the Kispiox joins the Skeena just north of Hazelton.

Kispiox Valley Road is the arterial to this angling world, connecting launches, take-outs, dirt access roads, trailheads, and dozens of named waters. Fly fishermen rarely bother to know them all. Their favorite dry-fly riffles of late summer and wet-fly pools of fall may be concentrated in only a few miles of river. Certainly those pools from Raisin Bread and Dundes to Lower Airport, fly-grabbing Cotton-wood below these, and the Potato Patch waters near the mouth, are names frequently heard in any conversation where steelhead is spoken.

In the valley are working farms and a number of vacation cabins that are deserted by fall. A few residences are situated so that one could cast successfully for steelhead from their lawns. I recall Mike Craig intently working a run one day while a backyard full of dogs howled out their displeasure. Mike forgot the distractions when a steelhead took him on a sprint to the gravel bar below the house.

The Kispiox Valley is a transition zone between conifer-rich coastal drainages and the arid interior slopes of sagebrush and ponderosa pine. This is not evident until fall, when the somber river corridor is set ablaze with the electric yellows of aspen and cottonwood. Talk turns to hunting—a lot of moose and bear stories—and a stranger quickly learns that the Kispiox reaches into grizzly country. There are wolves somewhere to satisfy the frontier soul, and, of course, the great fall steelhead.

The steelhead actually enter the estuary of the Skeena in July and August; they are true summer-run fish, though they ascend slightly later than most other Skeena stocks. Steelhead can be in the main stem of the Kispiox by mid-August, usually young females, but they are rare. Not until early September is the run present in numbers. Anglers commonly believe that the fish come in two waves, early to mid-September, and an October run that is less a wave than a constant trickle. I am certain that fresh steelhead arrive all fall, and I suspect that a few steelhead enter during winter freeze-up, when there may be only patches of ice-free water, or none at all. Olga Walker has told me of observing fresh, bright steelhead after ice-out in late winter. Neither of us knew what to make of this, but we didn't believe the steelhead to be winter-runs.

Mike Whatley wrote *Kispiox River Steelhead Trout: The 1975 Sport Fishery and Life History Characteristics from Angler's Catches*, published in May 1977. It is the classic study on this race of steelhead.

Anglers were asked to report their success on creel-census forms made available at the three resort lodges in the Kispiox Valley. Whatley collected additional life-history information by collecting scale samples from steelhead both killed and released. A total of 219 anglers responded in the creel survey and reported 114 steelhead killed and 389 released.

Two hundred nine steelhead were sampled that supplied 195 sets of readable scales. A total of eighteen age groups were identified during 1975. (These figures would certainly change from one year to the next. Some rare age groups would not appear each year.) These figures are particularly interesting, for each age group is broken down by sex.

Age Group	Number Steelhead	Males	Females	Percent
2.1+	1	0	1	0.5
2.2+	2	1	1	1.0
3.1+	4	3	1	2.1
3.2+	29	8	21	14.9
3.3+	29	24	5	14.9
3.1S1+	1	1	0	0.5
3.2S1+	14	0	14	7.2
3.3S1+	1	0	1	0.5
4.1+	4	3	1	2.1
4.2+	59	26	33	30.3
4.3+	20	15	5	10.3
4.1S1+	1	1	0	0.5
4.4+	5	4	1	2.5
4.2S1+	18	3	15	9.2
4.5+	1	1	0	0.5
4.2S1S1+	1	0	1	0.5
5.2+	3	1	2	1.5
5.3+	2	1	1	1.0
	195	92	103	100

Notes: One-year ocean steelhead are rare, typical of all the Skeena tributaries except the Morice River.

Two-year ocean steelhead were dominated by females, fifty-seven to thirty-six. A similar balance was found among Sustut steelhead with the same age.

Three-year ocean steelhead were dominated by males, forty to eleven. This trend was also evident among the Sustut steelhead.

Here are three first-spawning categories I have not seen elsewhere: 4.4+, 4.5+, and 5.3+. These steelhead (six males and two females) are remarkably old for first-time spawning. The 4.5+ age class was a single male steelhead. This is the first documentation of a steelhead with a five-year ocean life. (Apparently its weight was not recorded, because it does not appear below.)

Repeat-spawning steelhead, all ages, made up 17.9 percent of the total. I find this figure remarkable, for the Kispiox steelhead are "old" when they spawn for the first time. Compare this figure to the Sustut (five percent), and to the Bulkley (6.2 percent and 6.8 percent). Note also the 3.3Sl+ female steelhead. This is the first three-year ocean steelhead I have found that returned to spawn a second time; the fish was in her ninth year. The oldest Kispiox steelhead in the study was in her eleventh year (4.2SlSl+).

The freshwater ages (winters in the Kispiox before migrating to sea) of the adult Kispiox steelhead were as follows: two year = 1.5 percent, three year = 40 percent, four year = 55.9 percent, and five year = 2.6 percent.

The average weight and range for weight and length was determined for each ocean age of first-spawning steelhead.

WEIGHT—POUNDS

Sex	Ocean Age	Average	Range	Number
Male	1+	5.7	3.5–11	5
	2+	14.3	7–27	32
	3+	21.6	15–27.5	37
	4+	22.4	17–27.5	4
Female	1+	5.1	4–6	3
	2+	11.2	7–22	56
	3+	15.2	8–20	12
	4+	22		1

LENGTH—INCHES

Sex	Ocean Age	Average	Range	Number
Male	1+	24	20.5–28	6
	2+	33	23–41	31
	3+	38	33–42	35
	4+	40	39–43.5	5
Female	1+	21	19–22	3
	2+	31	21–39	45
	3+	34	31–39	13
	4+	39	—	1

Notes: Even a cursory examination of these figures reveals the potential for great size in a short time. Male steelhead weighed as much as twenty-seven pounds after only 2+ ocean years and had an average weight of 14.3 pounds. This is about twice what an average two-year ocean steelhead would weigh in Washington and Oregon.

Three-year ocean males averaged 21.6 pounds and thirty-eight inches in length. This is a typical Kispiox male steelhead—massive contour regardless of its length. Almost any other race of steelhead would weigh several pounds less for this length.

Unfortunately, this sampling was very small and covered but a single year. I would like to have seen a few life histories of steelhead over thirty pounds. However, knowing that these remarkable steelhead can reach weights of nearly thirty pounds after only two years in the ocean, one can reasonably assume that male steelhead with three, four, or even five ocean years will grow to over forty pounds.

No doubt, fly fishermen have hooked steelhead of over forty pounds. Indians on the Skeena have also taken Kispiox steelhead of over forty pounds from their nets. How much more is a question that is never asked of any other race of steelhead.

Mike Craig with a buck steelhead he estimated at 28 pounds.

Nearly forty years since its "discovery" by fly fishermen, anglers concede that it is unlikely any race of steelhead larger than those of the Kispiox will be found. No hint of such steelhead has been encountered in the Nass, Stikine, or Taku river systems to the north. Indeed, if a size trend exists as we go north of the Skeena, it is that the steelhead are smaller. The uniqueness of this race is underscored by the races of Skeena steelhead that are relatively average by comparison.

The Kispiox is the environment for spawning adults and the nursery for their young, and steelhead rivers everywhere are handmaidens in no less a manner. When these steelhead are raised in hatcheries, or hatched in rivers different from those of their racial origins, they are not the same. Kispiox steelhead have good genes, but they cannot be replicated elsewhere. In some manner beyond our understanding, the waters of the Kispiox possess magical properties. Our knowledge of this race is best displayed when we admit that Kispiox steelhead are giants only as native steelhead born and reared naturally in the Kispiox.

20

BABINE RIVER

I first thought of myself as a serious student of fly fishing while I was living in Tacoma, Washington. I had custom-built a wonderful little pram with the single thwart seat placed so that I could only row forward while facing rising trout. After work, I would join friends who had identical boats and cast Royal Bucks and Pink Lady Nymphs for cruising rainbows on our lowland lakes. Occasionally we would find a holdover trout of fifteen inches, a bragging-rights size sure to be mentioned at the wet fly session of our local fly-fishing club.

One evening Morrie Kenton and I fished a lake containing a tiny outlet creek that led down to a bay. When a series of rises sent him off in pursuit, I stopped fishing to watch. Morrie would cast the Royal Buck, find he was short, row furiously, curse the fast moving fish, and cast again. The rowing became faster, the casts longer, and the curses louder until I was shaking with laughter. His final cast was a tremendous effort that snaked out eighty feet and dropped the fly lightly in front of the trout. The take was almost imperceptible. Moments later, a steelhead shot four feet into the air before taking off across the lake and winding up Morrie's automatic reel one last time. When the steelhead broke off, my friend was already in a catatonic haze.

Those few seconds fixed my angling future. I now made any excuse to avoid lowland lakes and their hatchery trout. My pram became my first drift boat. When I nearly drowned my four-year-old son while trying to run the Satsop River rowing forward, I knew I was kamikaze crazy for steelhead. God, I was happy!

The steelhead of my summers were those of Puget Sound. They were one-year ocean fish of five pounds or so, rarely more than seven, that ascended the North Fork of the Stillaguamish River for Deer Creek. I knew about winter rivers, too, especially those of the West End, the Hoh, Queets, and Quinault, darkly mysterious Indian rivers that tumbled down the weather side of the Olympic Mountains.

267

Joe Brooks
Photograph courtesy of
Outdoor Life.

The winter fish were larger, seven to eight pounds. The potential for great size seemed to increase right through winter, until huge male fish were sure to slip in during the first days of spring. At first I hunted for them with bait-casting gear and lures, even though I fished the fly for summer steelhead. That did not last long, for the challenge of taking one of our very largest steelhead on a fly, a fish of possibly twenty pounds, was too great.

Twenty pounds. That was the barrier. I knew of only two men, Wes Drain and Ralph Wahl, who had done it, and both were legendary figures. Few other anglers had even come close.

My perception that the largest steelhead were found in the winter did not change when my frame of reference expanded to include several rivers in southwest Washington and Oregon's Deschutes. It did change, with jarring suddenness, when I learned that extraordinary fall steelhead over twenty pounds were being caught regularly from British Columbia's Kispiox River. I first assumed them to be early-returning winter-runs, and I just as wrongly thought their size devalued my steelhead fly fishing. Washington had steelhead well over twenty pounds, too, I told friends. Indian nets killed a few. Some angling encounters hinted at steelhead of thirty pounds, a size almost beyond my comprehension. My protests ceased altogether when Karl Mausser took, from the Kispiox, his thirty-three-pound world record on a fly.

At this confused juncture in determining my steelheading values, I read an article by Joe Brooks, the fishing editor of *Outdoor Life*, and a hero of mine. He told of visiting a river named the Babine and hooking a behemoth of a steelhead that would have weighed over *forty pounds*. The fish ran God only knows how many miles this way and that way while beating up on Joe before making its escape. I was now certain that the steelhead of these fabled rivers could reach cosmic sizes and, of course, I, too, wanted to be soundly thrashed by one. To wish for anything less was tantamount to launching my pram once again for hatchery trout.

SILVER HILTON

Lani Waller reached into a plastic bag containing dozens of 2/0 Signal Lights and grabbed a handful. "You'll need these," he said. I accepted his offer without question. Randall Kaufmann's large silhouette pattern with the black marabou wing well larded with Krystal Flash was an appropriate choice.

"This is a hell of a way to start a week of dry-fly fishing!" I said.

We had just flown in from Smithers to Bob Wickwire's famous Silver Hilton Lodge on the lower Babine, the pilot landing the lumbering DeHavilland Otter on the second bounce. From the air, I saw the river flowing the color of fresh cement, a sure sign of glacial runoff. This was Saturday, turn-around day, and the anglers leaving were decidedly grim. No one had fished since Wednesday. "Good luck. You'll need it," one man said as he boarded the plane.

Lani began sorting through a bag of sinking lines. "We'll find some fish," he said. "Maybe even on top with a dry." His carefree manner reassured me.

"We could use some cold weather?" I asked. The Babine was basking in a strong Pacific high, T-shirt weather, with black flies in evidence by midday on this first week of fall.

"The temperature needs to drop below freezing at night," said Lani. "The river would then be clearing by the next afternoon; it takes a while for the clearing water to work its way down. We'll fish above the Shalagiyote tomorrow."

"That's putting the Babine out?"

"Yes, that and the Nilkitwa that joins the Babine just below Babine Lake. The Shalagiyote runs in just upstream. Both rivers have glacial sources. They are the enemy!"

"Could the Babine be out all week?"

"That would be very unusual. Even in off weeks you always get a few days of good fishing."

We finished stowing our gear in the cabin we would share with John Pytka from Slippery Rock, Pennsylvania, and Jeff Williamson from Cambridge, Maryland. They were friends in Eastern Shore waterfowl hunting who, literally, had a world of fly-fishing experience between them—everything from Florida tarpon to Alta River salmon.

The cabins were luxurious. Hot showers morning and night. A fire set in the stove before our return. Ice for our drinks. Coffee served to us in bed each morning at seven. Jerry Lou Wickwire's meals: "You'll gain weight this week," Lani predicted. The condition of the Babine became less critical to my happiness.

Lani has been coming to the Babine from his home in San Rafael, California, for more than ten years. "The Babine is my home river. I know almost every rock in the lower river," he told me when we first talked of fishing the river together. This wasn't said boastfully, more a matter-of-fact synopsis of his angling life. Lani has had a hand in naming many of the Babine's pools, and has been influential in refining tackle and techniques for its steelhead. In some measure, this influence has come as the result of a 3M fly-fishing video that detailed both Lani's Babine angling methods and his popular steelhead dry fly, the Waller Waker.

When he first fished the Babine, the preferred tackle was 9- and 10-weight rods, shooting heads, and egg patterns. (The Babine Special, either in red or orange, remains popular in Alaska for resident rainbows and is sometimes used on steelhead rivers during the winter.) The presentation was straight-forward: you stood up to your waist in the river, cast as far as you could, and made ready to set the hook.

How different our tackle was today! My choice was a ten-foot 7-weight, Lani's a nine-and-a-half-foot 8-weight. We were both using thirteen-foot sink-tip lines, mine a IV sink rate, his a V. Our leaders were about four feet long with tippets of twelve- or fifteen-pound test Maxima. "There is always the possibility that on the next cast you'll hook a thirty-pounder," Lani said.

Dale Schneider was our guide. His wife, Cynthia, works with her dad, Bob Wickwire, who guides at the satellite camp upriver on the great Triple Header Pool. Judd Wickwire manages the main camp, while his mom, Jerry Lou, keeps the dining tables overflowing with down home cooking. This is a family operation.

Either lodge would look at home in an upscale neighborhood. It was easy to forget that most of the building materials came in by helicopter. Fishing parties traveled by twenty-foot jet boat, the guides linked together by radio telephones. A dozen anglers filled both camps and were swallowed up in twenty miles of river. Pools were always properly rested. Slow mornings weren't so slow when word crackled over the phones that thus and such just got a big buck. "Sorry, no details. You'll hear about it tonight," the guide would say. Miraculously, there came new life to the old arm.

The first morning, the river had no more than eight inches of visibility. Lani fished whatever little pockets he could find, while putting me on the larger runs with flats and guts easily readable even in the muddy water. It was soon evident that I wouldn't do justice to his generosity. With the river so discolored, creeping the fly across the bottom was necessary. Even then, a holding steelhead would see the fly only for a second. At the end of a short dead drift, I was making outside mends to slow down the fly's swing and finding IV sink rate insufficient to hold the fly down once all slack was out of the line. Feeding additional line into the drift and throwing additional line into outside mends helped, but after hours of fishing I had lost only a couple of flies. Lani's flies littered the bottom, and he had soon landed as fine a brace of hen steelhead as one is ever likely to see. One was thirty-four, the other thirty-five inches; both were thick, still deeply silvered, and free of net scars. A peculiar aspect to their capture was that neither would make long runs. I asked Lani about this.

"The water is so muddy that the steelhead can't see where they're going," he said. "They will tend to hold where they were hooked. You'll see the difference when the water clears!"

Lani doesn't work through a run so much as dissect it. His casts are short and completely controlled. He routinely stands in the river and alternately casts to the shore and to the middle. If he is convinced that a slot in front of or behind a midchannel rock may hold a steelhead, he will cast again and again to the area. Nothing was methodical about his approach, no step between casts, no slogging along. I watched him and tried to remind myself not to overfish by working too fast, casting too far, or wading too deep. Occasionally I did all three—at once. "This is more like fishing for trout," he said, "except that the trout are a yard long." I began to understand, and when he hooked a third steelhead, I took his approach to heart: Be selective in the water fished, beat on it hard, and concentrate. The tempo of greased line fishing in clear water doesn't apply. Even when you know this, it is easy to put your fishing on auto pilot and daydream your way down a run. Once I had determined where an unseen steelhead was holding, I cast to that unseen fish with complete faith that it was there. The broken-up nature of the water made this approach absolutely necessary.

Jud Wickwire regularly videotapes his clients during their fishing day and then entertains them during the cocktail hour by playing back their exploits on the dining room's VCR. One evening we watched some remarkable footage of a steelhead rising to a Riffle Express, a new dry fly of his own design. After dinner, I asked Jud about the fly and how he fished it. He got out his fly box and presented me with an example. The fly had a white calf-tail tail, a thin body of deer hair, and a flared-deer-hair head/wing that had been coated with Goop, a shoe repair cement, and trimmed in a circle about the size of a nickel. The hard circle was tilted forward at a bass popper angle. "It's, uh, an *unusual* fly," I said. The Riffle Express was hardly traditional. If fished drag-free, and I was doubtful that it even floated very well. It was, in fact, the best of a new type of steelhead fly designed to wake on top of any water that can be expected to hold steelhead. The design of the fly and the velocity of the current, rather than the inherent flotation of its materials, keep the fly on top. I had seen other examples of this design coming out of the Skeena area: The Bulkley Moose, in which the Goop-stiffened head is split and trimmed like, well, *moose antlers*; the Bubble Head, in which the Goop-coated head is the short half of flared moose wing; the new Waller Wakers, in which the calf-tail wing is short, fanned out (not divided), and stiffened with cement.

Jud Wickwire's dry fly underscores how intensely studied the Silver Hilton's Babine has become in terms of the dry fly. Given several feet of visibility and a temperature range of fifty-eight degrees (first week of September and unseasonably warm), to thirty-six degrees (the coldest the guides have experienced), Jud and Bob Wickwire and Dale Schneider will confidently urge clients to fish a dry fly.

The other outcome of guests leading with the dry fly has been the expansion of the lodge's understanding of holding water. Soft water that is almost free of current, small slots, eddies, and runs along banks that would otherwise be ignored, reveal their steelhead secrets when a dry fly wakes their surfaces. Flinging a shooting head into these microholds is, by comparison, a coarse and unrewarding approach.

The dry fly is now so appreciated that many of the Babine's Silver Hilton pools are first thought of in this context. Beaver Pond, Triple Header, Dead Tree, American Hole, Dave's Drift, Eagle, and Wolverine are classic dry-fly waters. None of these pools so captured my fancy as the Dry Fly Diner, upon first inspection an uninspiring piece of water. Located in front of a pool called Camera Rock, it is a slow-moving, circular flat into which large steelhead, especially males, ease to rest. Howard West of Scientific Anglers once took two large steelhead on drys from the little pool, an event that inspired the name. Lani's contribution built on the gear fishermen's habit of describing outsized steelhead as "hogs." At the Silver Hilton, a steelhead of twenty pounds or more is called a "piggy." "Piggies just love the Dry Fly Diner," says Lani. "It's an automatic." And he adds, "I never met a piggy I didn't like."

The man knows how to have a good time.

The next day the river was clearing, and by midafternoon I could see my fly through eighteen inches of water. Lani and I were finding steelhead, rolling up some large bucks in the morning and losing them all. Late in the afternoon, I began working down from the very top of a run that was locked in deep shade, tossing my fly in the shallow riffles, and letting it wobble off to quarter into a slot of deeper water. This was too much turbulence for a buck to find comfortable, I thought, a better place for a hen to hold before exiting the pool.

The steelhead took going away, a shocking strike that caused my reel to overrun. I was watching the slack line hit the reel and was frantically able to strip away line and save the fish. The reel overran again, well into the backing, as the steelhead surged into the tailout. That should have been the end

Lani Waller prepares to release his 35-inch hen steelhead.

of it, but the fish stopped, pausing just long enough for me to get things under control and begin to wear her down. Lani was there when I beached the hen. Ten pounds? "Oh, a pound or two more than that," he offered.

"I can't recall a more incredible strike. Caused my double pawl reel to overrun. That's never happened before!"

"We'll be fishing Marvin's Pool," said Lani. "It was named for this guy who clamped down on his reel every time he got a strike. Broke three reel handles off during the week!"

"I would rather raise a steelhead like this one than a twenty-pound buck that just sits and shakes its head."

"Yeah, we call those 'pet fish,'" said Lani.

"It was nice to get one on the beach. You must lead the way on the next pool."

"Now that you're *healed*?"

"Now that I'm healed!"

On the next pool, Lani fished behind me again, though starting higher in the run. He was swinging his fly well out from where I had entered the river when a steelhead of twenty pounds stopped his fly. I heard his whoop as the buck ran downriver along the beach and sent me backpedaling to avoid being run over. We discovered that the steelhead—its colors not yet dingy, its rainbow still light pink—had a small head with a distinctively snooklike profile. One finds that steelhead are very individual in their appearance, behavior, and character. I think the most memorable steelhead are those that strongly appeal to our sense of beauty. Such was this fish. Long after Lani had made the release, I was still studying its wildness, wondering about its life before this meeting, and feeling not at all sanguine over its prospects for a safe return to the ocean. I would like to have seen it three weeks before, and three weeks before that, when it was hunting just below the surface of Chatham Sound.

We would find more steelhead, though never with a dry fly; never, in fact, with a floating line. Lani pressed the Dry Fly Diner with a big Waller Waker, the still dingy water canceling out his skillful efforts. Watching the fly come alive on the currents was a pleasure he keenly enjoyed, and I enjoyed watching him. I have never characterized dry-fly fishing as a liberating alternative to the drudgery of wet-fly fishing, even when using a sinking line. If I wanted to fish the Babine with a dry fly, I would have to travel again to this extraordinary river.

Exactly how and why a certain river wears so well says a lot about us. Lani told me the Babine was his home river, and I didn't have to ask why. A home river is, after all, where your heart and head reside. Rarely is this relationship built solely upon the convenience of where the river is located. I would soon join him again at the Silver Hilton, and thus begin edging closer to his notion of a home river.

Jud Wickwire guided Lani and me one afternoon. As we sat in the jet boat munching sandwiches, Lani told how they had met.

"When I first came up to the Babine, I didn't get a steelhead the first couple of days. All the guides were busy, and I was put with this twelve-year-old kid. That was Jud. I thought, what can he know? Well, we came to this pool, and Jud pointed out a little slick of holding water, told me where to cast, said there might be a good fish there. I followed his directions and hooked a twenty-pound steelhead. I said, 'God, you're a genius! Do you know any other spots that hold twenty-pound steelhead?' Jud said 'No.'"

Jud remembered and smiled. Twelve years old wasn't too young to guide when you had grown up in the wilderness.

Bob Wickwire came north to the Skeena Country in 1961 with Larry Stanley, a buddy from their high school days. Magazine articles had set the odyssey in motion. Babine Lake and the Babine River, they read, were a fisherman's paradise, the concentration of rainbow trout, steelhead, lake trout, chinook salmon, coho salmon, and immense runs of sockeye and pink salmon unequaled in North America.

Bob had been dividing his time beween clerking in Larry's Sports Center in Oregon City, Oregon, and guiding for steelhead on the Clackamas River. His dream was to live the wilderness life, to hunt and fish, to guide, and to operate a lodge. This desire was then, as now, a common-enough litany by tethered souls in love with the outdoors, but Bob would succeed where others failed. Realizing his dream would take twenty often desperately hard years.

Their search led them to a partially completed lodge on Morrison Arm (then called Hatchery Arm) on the far northwest corner of 120-mile-long Babine Lake. Financing secured the buildings, and they made ready for business. That first year they took in approximately five hundred dollars, could not make their payments, and nearly had the lodge repossessed. The upside of Bob's year occurred when he returned to his home in Cottage Grove, Oregon, and married Jerry Lou.

The Wickwires bought out Larry Stanley before selling the operation and purchasing a lodge at the mouth of the Babine River at Nilkitwa Lake. This they named Babine River Rainbow Lodge. A second lodge, the Babine River Steelhead Lodge, was built in 1974 on the Babine River, seven miles down the lake entrance. For several years they owned and managed both lodges simultaneously before selling all their holdings in 1977 and 1978. They managed the steelhead lodge for the new owners before moving farther downriver and building the Silver Hilton. Construction was completed in 1983. Triple Header Cabin, their satellite camp, was completed in 1988.

The Babine River Steelhead Lodge is now owned and managed by Chick and Marilyn Stewart.

This brief chronology would be incomplete without mentioning Ejnar Madsen. He and Cecil Brown ("Brownie" to his many friends) built a luxurious lodge near Fort Babine on the narrow western arm of Babine Lake in the early 1950s. In those days, guests were driven the fifty miles from Smithers to Smithers Landing, where they were met by a boat for the twenty-mile ride to the lodge. The lodge opened June 1, and did not close until November. Lodging, meals, and a guide came to twenty-five dollars per day. It was not a long run from the lodge to Nilkitwa Lake (actually more of a widening of the Babine River) and the Babine River. Guests could fish for steelhead from mid-September through October and, weather permitting, a week into November. Eventually a second camp for steelhead was built below Nilkitwa Lake on the Babine. For a decade, the most direct link to the wonders of the Babine River and her steelhead was through Ejnar Madsen and his Norlakes Lodge.

Pierce and Debbie Clegg currently own and manage Norlakes Lodges. They are a young couple who have taken an active role in the fight to preserve the wilderness nature of the Babine watershed.

SOCKEYE

The lake-headed nature of the Skeena watershed has created one of the world's most prolific sockeye spawning areas. These salmon pass rapidly upriver until reaching the lake. (In the case of the Babine, the transit time from the mouth of the Skeena to Babine Lake is but eighteen to thirty days.) The salmon hold in the lake for a month or more until they reach full sexual maturity. Then they ascend the many small streams tributary to the lakes, where they spawn and die, a matter of several weeks.

Approximately twenty-one lakes and sixty tributary streams support sockeye salmon, but none is remotely as important as Babine Lake. Historically, this huge lake—the second largest in British Columbia—produced sixty-five percent of all the sockeye in the entire Skeena system, a run of over a million fish.

The sockeye early on attracted commercial fishing interests. Inverness Cannery was built in 1877; by 1926, fifteen canneries were in operation along the lower Skeena. Sockeye stocks declined through the late 1920s and 1930s. A hatchery was constructed on the Morrison River, and a counting fence—the

"Babine fence"—was placed on the very upper end of the Babine River so that the sockeye escapement could more accurately be determined. Commercial fishing pressure continued to increase through World War II, and the sockeye runs continued to decline.

In 1951, a rock slide that blocked sockeye from reaching Babine Lake occurred on the Babine River, a potential catastrophe for the region's commercial fishing industry if it were not quickly removed. Temporary fish ladders assisted fish over the obstruction, and a road was punched in to the site from Hazelton. Heavy earth-moving equipment was brought in and the slide cleared. Nevertheless, for a year or two afterwards, the run of sockeye was dramatically depressed; full recovery of affected stocks would take years.

This event became the impetus for an intensive federal program to restore Skeena sockeye stocks to historic levels. Rehabilitation efforts centered on the installation of two artificial spawning channels in the Fulton River and one in Pinkut Creek. These streams had always been important spawning tributaries of Babine Lake, accounting for approximately thirty-two percent of all Skeena sockeye. Following completion of the channels in l968, these two remote streams supplied sixty-five percent of the Skeena's sockeye escapement, an increase that boosted the Babine's overall contribution to the Skeena's sockeye run to ninety percent. The Fulton River and Pinkut Creek literally became the economic lifeline for Prince Rupert's commercial fishing industry.

This success had disastrous side effects.

Sockeye were divided into two main categories, Babine and non-Babine, or intensely managed and not managed. Because there was no way to separate the two stocks in the ocean, the non-Babine sockeye were soon threatened, their numbers even more depressed than before. Even within the Babine system itself, the numbers of sockeye in the upper Babine River and Morrison River declined as they were incidentally harvested at levels too high to allow for rebuilding.

Large numbers of chinook salmon were caught incidentally, especially those mid- to late-running chinooks with Kalum, Ecstall, Babine, and Morice river origins. Runs of pink salmon and sockeye overlap, creating problems when one run is imminently harvestable and one run is not. Coho stocks, already severely depressed because of poor logging practices, continued to decline as a result of being incidentally caught in the sockeye and pink fishery. Some races of coho faced extinction.

This was just the beginning.

The discovery by the outside world in the late l950s that the largest steelhead in the world lived in the Skeena watershed led to a burgeoning sport fishery. Lodges were built on every major steelhead tributary of the Skeena. By the mid-1970s, adventurous anglers were coming from all over the world for the opportunity to catch thirty-pound steelhead, and by the mid-1980s the Babine, Kispiox, Bulkley, Sustut, and Copper rivers were confidently ranked, in the minds of the world's fly-fishing fraternity, with the great Atlantic salmon rivers of Scandinavia, Canada, and Iceland.

The growth of this sport-fishing industry paralleled the rehabilitation of the sockeye runs in the Fulton River and Pinkut Creek.

The "fall run" of steelhead actually began entering the Skeena in June, peaked in July and August, and declined in September. Early returning stocks, particularly those of the Morice and Sustut rivers, were hammered so thoroughly that the early part of their runs were eliminated altogether. Restructuring of gene pools continued on all the rivers, the late-run segment of each river's race of steelhead the least affected, the early returning segment of the runs exploited to below recovery levels. Depressed stocks became threatened stocks, and then they were either eliminated altogether or were so reduced as to no longer be a viable segment of the area's sport fishery.

Ironically, of these races of summer steelhead, Babine stocks ascend unusually late and have been the least affected by the commercial fishing industry.

During the l950s, Ejnar Madsen advised those guests who wanted to come to Norlakes Lodge for Babine steelhead to wait until October l. Then, as now, the very first steelhead of the year moved into the lower Babine the third week of August. This means that these same steelhead passed through the

Trey Combs and Lani Waller with a typical
Babine Buck.

sockeye and pink commercial fishery of Chatham Sound in July, at or near peak concentrations of these salmon. Babine steelhead have not been spared.

This conflict, between the sport and commercial fishing sectors of British Columbia, between the Province's Ministry of Environment and Canada's Fisheries and Oceans is the most contentious such conflict in North America. The pros and cons of the many solutions offered would fill a small library. There is, however, a single bottom line. A more sophisticated method of harvesting salmon must be found. Casting nets blindly into the sea no longer makes any sense. It is wasteful, destructive, and totally out of touch with current management practices.

LIFE HISTORY

As the Skeena River follows its convoluted course southward, it picks up three major tributaries from the east, the Sustut, Babine, and Bulkley/Morice rivers, and one from the west, the Kispiox. All are, to one degree or another, lake-headed, and all possess medium gradients with long, classic steelhead pools. While steelhead races in the five rivers are, in my estimation, quite distinct, those of the Kispiox and Babine are almost certainly the largest in North America.

(The Sustut probably belongs with this pairing. The current sampling of sport-caught fish is very small when compared to either the Kispiox or the Babine, but it has revealed a number of fly-caught steelhead over twenty-five pounds, and one over thirty pounds.)

Male Babine steelhead are likely to be less massive for their length, possibly due to genetic factors, possibly a product of the greater distance Babine steelhead travel from salt water. Nevertheless, they have been caught and released weighing more than Karl Mausser's fly record, the aforementioned Kispiox buck of thirty-three pounds. Judd Wickwire told me of anglers who chased after steelhead that were never controlled, but were seen, and these, he said, would be pretty close to forty pounds. He reminded me, "It takes a lot of luck to land a thirty-pounder." A forty-pounder? Look to the gods and pray for divine intervention.

I have found the hen steelhead of either race to be extremely massive, altogether magnificent, and, from a casual examination, indistinguishable. In a very general sense, they average about eighty percent of the weight of the average male fish for the same age.

The classic 1969 study of Babine steelhead, *Age and Size of Steelhead Trout in the Babine River, British Columbia*, by David W. Narver, was based on scale samples collected from 121 sport-caught adult steelhead in September and October 1967 and 1968. The ratio of males to females was 1 to 1.33. One hundred seventeen steelhead were spawning for the first time. Four steelhead, all females, were spawning for the second time. No steelhead were found returning to spawn a third time. The most common age for both sexes was 3.2 + (Three years in fresh water, two winters in salt water and returning to spawn during the third summer in salt water). The second most common age was 3.3 +. Male steelhead showed a stronger tendency to spend one or three years at sea, and females a stronger tendency to spend two years at sea. Steelhead were observed spawning in March, April, and May in the uppermost part of the Babine between the counting fence and Nilkitwa Lake.

Among the 117 first-spawning steelhead, 100 had readable scales for freshwater residencies. They broke down as follows: 2.= two percent, 3.= eighty-two percent, 4.= fifteen percent, 5.= one percent.

All 117 first-spawning steelhead had readable scales for saltwater residencies. These broke down as follows: .1 + = 10.2 percent (seven males, five females); .2 + = 69.5 percent (twenty-eight males, fifty-four females); .3 + = 20.3 percent (seventeen males, six females).

The steelhead that had spawned previously were as follows: 2.2 + S1 + (14.3 pounds), 3.2 + S1 + (14.96 pounds), 4.2 + S1 + (18.04 pounds), 3.2 + S + (9.02 pounds). Note that in the last example, this atypical steelhead did not return to the ocean for an entire year after spawning, but migrated to sea in the spring and returned to the Babine the following fall, an ocean residency of approximately four months.

The weight in pounds of first-spawning steelhead by ocean age group and sex revealed the following:

	FEMALE STEELHEAD		MALE STEELHEAD	
Ocean age	**Average**	**Range**	**Average**	**Range**
.1 +	5.28	(3.08–7.48)	4.84	(3.3–7.04)
.2 +	10.56	(5.94–13.86)	13.42	(7.92–18.04)
.3 +	18.26	(14.52–22.0)	22.44	(18.04–27.72)

It can be seen from the above that there really is no such thing as an "average" Babine steelhead.

The sampling covered September and October, but no week by week breakdown was given, and there was no way to determine from the study whether the male steelhead's tendency to migrate upriver two or three weeks later than the female was also typical of Babine steelhead.

The percentage of male steelhead with a .2+ ocean residency is higher for the Babine than either the Kispiox or Sustut, rivers where the majority of male steelhead is a .3+ fish. Nevertheless, the second most common life history for male steelhead on the Babine is 3.3+. That age group, when combined with the 4.3+ steelhead (single fish), has an average weight of 22.44 pounds. This translates into hundreds of steelhead that will weigh twenty pounds or more in the river's annual escapement.

Escapement estimates for the Babine and other Skeena tributaries are subject to considerable variation from one year to the next. Fisheries Section personnel estimate the Babine steelhead run to be 6,616 mature fish (1986), approximately that of the Sustut and Kispiox rivers combined. A commercial harvest of 2,710, a native harvest of 781, and a sport harvest of 207 are subtracted from the total, leaving 2,918 steelhead to spawn, or forty-four percent of the total. Changes in the Babine's escapement from one year to the next doesn't change the fact that among major Skeena tributaries, only the Bulkley/Morice system has a greater steelhead escapement than the Babine.

So although the Babine has a lower *percentage* of trophy-class steelhead than the Kispiox, its much greater escapement probably contains a higher *number* of steelhead over twenty pounds than any other steelhead river in the world.

21

SUSTUT RIVER

M A R K'S excited voice came through my headphones. "There she is Trey, the crown jewel of the Skeena!"

The helicopter swept down from timberline toward the distant ribbon of blue, the Sustut River, least known and most remote of the Skeena's legendary tributaries.

The ravines and creeks below were a tracery of gold, fall cottonwoods and aspen in a somber sea of evergreens. We followed the lines in a dizzying descent to the river corridor. Just after passing Steelhead Valhalla Lodge, a complex of five log cabins, I spotted a man standing on a gravel bar. His hands were jammed into the pockets of a heavy wool coat, and he wore a large stetson. Fixed to his hatband was a variety of colorful flies. When the helicopter touched down, I grabbed my bags and ran in a crouch to the waiting figure.

"Gary Miltenberger?" I said.

"Good to see you, Trey!" he affirmed. The lodge owner exchanged greetings with my companions on the hundred-mile flight from Smithers, British Columbia: Bob Allen, a retired Bechtel executive; Walt Balek, a Spokane physician; and Mark Pinch, Gary's brother-in-law and an old Sustut hand whose commentary had inspired my awe.

"Lunch is waiting," said Gary. He assigned us to our cabins, and after dropping off our gear, we headed for the lodge, where Dennis Farnworth joined us. Dennis, the lodge co-owner, had arrived only minutes before, piloting his Aeronca Chief floatplane to a safe landing on Surprise Pool, the lovely stretch of camp water before us.

Beside each of the two dining tables was a fly-tying bench piled high with hot fluorescent hackles and furs. The honey-colored log walls were covered with huge photographs of happy anglers releasing trophy steelhead. The ambience placed me in every picture. Gary added to my growing excitement.

"We're having the best escapement in years," he said over soup and sandwiches. "The sockeye run is depressed, and commercial fishermen in Prince Rupert are down to one day a week."

I appreciated the significance of this. Gill-net and seine-net sockeye fishermen in the Department of Fisheries and Oceans' "Area 4," essentially Chatham Sound to the mouth of the Skeena, annually take about half the steelhead escapement for the entire Skeena watershed. Besides the Sustut, this includes the Kispiox, Babine, and Bulkley, rivers considered sacred by the world's fly-fishing community.

Gary told us how clear skies had continued through their chinook-salmon fishing in August and the early September run of steelhead. Shallow tailouts sometimes held a dozen steelhead, and clients had successfully worked low-water wets and waking dries for their fish. Dredging conventional wet flies through the pools proved almost worthless. Now, late September rains had ended the drought and ushered in the short-lived fall, a time that has traditionally brought the peak fishing of the year.

"The river rose two feet and was out for a day; then the fish were hard to find." said Gary.

"But it dropped eight inches in one night. She comes down in a hurry," Dennis added.

"We flew over Bob Wickwire's Babine camp on the way in, and the river looked out," I said.

"Until it gets colder, the Babine gets a lot of glacial runoff," Gary answered. "It goes out more quickly than the Sustut; takes longer to clear, too."

One way or the other, we all wanted to know how the fishing had been.

"The females so far have outnumbered the males five to one," said Gary. "We expect the big bucks in any time. Last year, they were here a week ago."

We discussed Sustut steelhead patterns, which from Gary and Dennis's lead are large—1/0 and 2/0—and gaudy. Among the most popular dressings are the Purple Ugly, Purple Porcupine, and Sustut Boss.

After lunch, Bob and I loaded our fishing gear into one of the three twenty-four-foot jet sleds. We would fish downstream with Gary; Walt and Mark would go upstream with Dennis. Each day the sequence would change.

Our initial run to the lower river introduced me to a series of classic pools with heads that ran deep through freestone channels before shallowing by long rocky beaches. Often a tailout could be waded from bank to bank, and steelhead might hold in any part of it.

Bob was the first to hook a steelhead, a hen of ten pounds, and when she was beached, we had time to study her. I noted the unusually robust shape and splendid coloration, a blend of gray and silver with a light pink lateral line that ended with a splash of rose on the gills.

"This is about as small a steelhead as you'll find on the Sustut," said Gary. "Only Kispiox steelhead can run heavier for their length."

We fished another pool, where I had a deliberate, almost ponderous take and felt the full weight of the fish before it was gone. I checked the hook and found it broken. A slow backcast into the rocky slope behind me, I rationalized. After a summer of casting a floating line, the fast sinking shooting head was proving a quicker exercise. But I despaired. A steelhead per day anywhere is an immutable standard of excellence. I replaced the fly with another Night Dancer, a very dark pattern I particularly favor, and after a few casts I was solid to a strong fish. When the steelhead tired, Gary was there to net the hen.

"Notice the net marks?" he asked.

"I've read that gill-netters will sometimes cut a live steelhead free."

"Perhaps. She just may have been able to back out," he said as he freed the fish from the net and the fly.

In recent years, gill-net mesh size has been reduced to five and a half inches in an effort to reduce the incidental take of the much larger chinook salmon, a conservation measure that may also help large steelhead.

Gary measured the fish's length and girth—thirty-two and seventeen inches—and estimated its weight at thirteen pounds. He tagged it by injecting a thin stainless steel wire beside the dorsal fin. The exposed part of the wire was plastic coated, color coded, and carried an identification number. As gently as possible, so as not to injure the fish, Gary removed several scales and placed them in an envelope. Fishery Branch technicians would later "read" these scales, and provide him with the fish's life history: premigrant years in the Sustut and years in the North Pacific.

Late in the day, we returned to Surprise Pool, water of such length and variety that I could happily fish it all day. Bob soon had a very handsome buck on the beach. Typically, it was more highly colored than the females, proved to be more reluctant to jump, and, at fifteen pounds, was barely average for the river.

Steelhead Valhalla Lodge is situated five miles above the confluence of the Sustut and Skeena rivers and sixteen miles downstream from where Bear Creek enters. Above this point, for sixty to seventy river miles, the Sustut is closed to fishing. Steelhead may ascend to spawn just below Johanson and Sustut lakes, nearly at timberline, five thousand feet. This waterborne climb from sea to the very origins of the Sustut is 270 miles, a journey that begins from mid-July to early September for about thirty-six hundred steelhead. As many as two thousand become victims of the commercial fishery. An additional three hundred are lost to the Indian food fishery, taken either by gill net or gaff. Under these circumstances, no fish killed by anglers can be considered negligible, and, unless mortally hooked, all steelhead caught by lodge guests are released.

Early the next morning we began casting from the sled on a long, even-flowing pool near where the Sustut joins the Skeena. Little distinguished those pockets and slots where steelhead might be holding, and the usual sense of expectation was missing. Experience had taught Gary that most of the steelhead would be within twenty feet of the shore, and he repeatedly urged us to continue to fish the fly dead downstream after the swing was completed. Bob and I did this, and the slowness of the fishing was made pleasant by the warm sun and Gary's stories.

He had been on the pool the previous year with two clients. Each man was wading and fishing from an opposite shore when both suddenly hooked extremely large steelhead, bucks in the twenty-five-pound range. Soon one of the fish raced downstream and left the pool. Gary loaded the man in the sled, and they followed the fish to the pool below, where the struggle was resumed. Gary returned upstream to encourage the other client. This running back and forth continued until both fish were lost.

About halfway down the pool I had a slashing take as I was stripping back the fly for another cast. This startled me, and I felt fortunate that the line piled loosely at my feet followed the streaking fish without fouling. The hen measured out at twelve and a half pounds and remained our only steelhead from the pool.

Gary took the best fish of the day, a buck of nineteen pounds. The fish came to a flame-and-yellow calf-tail pattern that had been fished through the drift and left to hold in the surface. When the buck was worked into shallow water, we could see that it was tagged. A few minutes later, with the fish secure in the net, Gary noted the number. That evening he searched the catch book, and the buck's tag number was located. A client of Dennis's had caught the steelhead a couple of weeks before in a pool a mile or so upstream.

Mark Pinch had been fishing his own Riffle Dancer, a clever and very effective dry fly. The water temperature was forty-three degrees, warm enough to bring steelhead up. Nevertheless, on some pools he had come back behind the dry to fish a wet with a sink-tip line. Walt Balek was sticking with wet flies, generally a Flashabou Skunk dressed with a wing of pearl Flashabou. They were finding few fish.

Gary strongly advocated a long-casting shooting head system for the Sustut. We both commonly used a fast-sinking head (Type III), though this proved to be too much sink on the broad tailouts. I could avoid changing lines for a while by quartering my casts well downstream, but eventually the change became necessary. The jet sled carrying my tackle bag was never far away, and I could afford the convenience of a spare reel with a floating forward-taper line. (I had a floating head in my jacket and would have fished it, given no other choice.) Other anglers in our group carried two complete outfits to the sled. However it was accomplished, a change from a sinking to a floating line was sometimes necessary on the single run.

Gary also recommended rods of at least 8- to 9-weight. "A straight eight is too light," he insisted. We happened to fish identical nine-and-a-half-foot rods that had the power to move big fish without wringing the last drop of life out of our arms.

Gary had emigrated to Canada from Washington State to work as a guide on the Babine and Bella Coola rivers. His goal was to open a lodge of his own, and ultimately he was granted a lease on the Sustut by the Ministry of Lands and Forests. He discussed his plans with Dennis Farnworth, another transplanted American, when the two were working at Bob Wickwire's Silver Hilton Lodge. A partnership resulted, and under Dennis's guidance they spent the next two summers in the bush, falling trees and constructing the lodge and sleeping cabins. "Dennis," Gary told me, "can build anything."

They enlisted the services of Okanogan Helicopters and began the expensive task of flying in the building supplies. Dennis prefabricated a 24-foot jet sled out of plywood in Smithers and assembled the boat at the building site. Supplies flown by bush plane to an upriver landing strip could also be transported to the site. Corrugated steel for the roofs, window frames, pumps, generators, stoves, a freezer, furniture, and even carpets were brought to Surprise Pool. Dennis constructed two more sleds in Smithers. A small spruce tree was attached to the transom of each sled for stability, and the boats were towed in by helicopter. Steelhead Valhalla Lodge was opened for business in the fall of 1984.

Their lodge was not the first. In 1969, Doug Robertson built Suskeena, a tent camp twelve miles above the Sustut's confluence with the Skeena. Beautiful pools filled no one's memory. Miles of river awaited investigation with the fly. The right of naming new water would be granted to the guest who first took a steelhead from the water. The choice of names came to recall the angler's good fortune, to honor a woman in his thoughts, to distinguish some part of the pool, or to introduce to those who followed his sense of whimsy. However chosen, the names of these pools now lend substance to the river and fortify the spirit during long hours between strikes: Betty's Bend, Fennelly's Fox Hole (named for John Fennelly, author of *Steelhead Paradise*), Martin's Garden, Anderson's Alley, Blueberry, Forget-Me-Not, and Surprise, the future site of Steelhead Valhalla Lodge. Gary and Dennis built on this tradition strictly as fly fishermen and further distinguished the river: Junction, Lookout, Boulder, Fishtrap, and 319, among others.

On the third morning, the barometer was dropping, a bad sign according to Gary. He mistrusted change one way or the other, but the soft rain of this grey dawn pleased him. "Perfect steelhead weather," he said.

Upstream, Mark was getting rises to his Riffle Dancer, but none of us yet shared his unshakable faith in that fly, and we all stayed with patterns and methods we trusted. By late in the morning, both Bob and I had put nearly identical ten-pound hens on the beach.

As I fished through the top end of Forget-Me-Not Pool, Bob and Gary cast from the boat downstream where the pool fanned out beside jackstraw logs. Suddenly, an enormous buck took to the air.

"Trey! I've got a hog!" Gary called.

"How large is it?" I answered on a dead run as the steelhead jumped again.

"Over twenty pounds, for sure!" The fish leaped clear of the river a third and fourth time.

"Over twenty. Easy," I said to no one and then whispered, "Thirty pounds?" It seemed possible. I wasn't a good judge; at these sizes, a few inches in length can translate into a lot of pounds.

Gary passed the rod to Bob and motored for the beach. The steelhead jumped again and worked toward the end of the tailout. Gary took the rod again and palmed hard on the reel.

"He's close to going over," I said nervously.

"You'd be amazed at how fast I could follow this fish through that white water." Gary said this with the steelhead a good seventy yards downstream and holding just above the dangerous raceway.

Thirty pounds had become a barrier for Gary and Dennis. Kispiox and Babine fishermen have fly-caught a few steelhead over this weight. During each of the past two seasons, guests of Steelhead Valhalla Lodge have hooked these fish also, to perhaps thirty pounds, but all have been lost. The lodge record stands at twenty-eight pounds. (On September 15, 1987, John Holmes of Juneau, Alaska, took a 41½-inch by 22½-inch buck that weighed thirty-one pounds. Dennis was guiding him at the time, and he weighed the huge steelhead before its release.)

"Anyone who catches a thirty-pound steelhead gets a free week at the lodge next year," they both told me.

Gary was counting the leaps and asked for confirmation. "Eight!" he exclaimed after twenty minutes, and we agreed.

The fish was close now, the fly-line splice working up and down the guides, and we got our first glimpse. Through the glare of the pewter currents, the buck's tail looked a foot wide.

Gary declined Bob's offer to net the fish; he would lose or land the steelhead himself. Five minutes later, the exhausted buck was tailed in shallow water. After being measured, it was slipped into a net and weighed. "Over twenty-four pounds, the largest steelhead I've caught from the Sustut. Only a pound less than my best, a winter-run fish from the Bella Coola."

Gary asked if I could shoot some extra pictures for him. "Perhaps I could get a mount for the lodge," he explained. His request underscored the lodge's "no kill" policy. Any guest who wishes to have his trophy steelhead mounted can do so if supplied with length and girth measurements and enough pictures to get the nuances of color and shape just right. The resulting synthetic mount can be exact in every detail, becomes easier to maintain, and most important, may be secured without killing the steelhead. This would seem to be a reasonable, even superior, way of keeping a trophy fairly won, but not all prospective clients have agreed, and cancellations have resulted. Beyond the conservation issue is the matter of keeping a steelhead for up to a week in the bush. "Not practical," said Gary. "We simply don't have the facilities. You need a refrigerator or freezer just for that purpose. Then the helicopter must take the fish out, and weight restrictions make this difficult."

After the tagging was completed and the scale samples obtained, the steelhead was freed to continue its journey. We moved downstream, and the weather continued to clear, the swirling mists around the mountains opening to reveal slopes freshly dusted with snow. At Surprise Pool I got out to wade the head, while Bob again cast from the boat off a slot of water that had yet to fail him. I had completed but a single pass through my water when a yell told me that Bob's good fortune held. Gary called to say they were slipping downstream after the fish. Did I want to go? I had seen the fish leap, and from the flash of silver I knew it to be a female and not a remarkable one at that. However, I never had enough pictures, so I joined them in the sled. We beached the boat, and in spite of the steady pressure from Bob's rod, the steelhead stubbornly continued to run on the backing. After some minutes, the fish was moved to the shallows on our side of the river. Gary waded downstream to net the hen and to tow her to shore.

"You guys had better take a look," he called. "This fish is larger than you think." I waded over, the fish growing with each step. Suddenly, it just doubled in size.

"That's one of the most magnificent steelhead I've ever seen," I exclaimed. After a few measurements—the hen was a good yard long and had an eighteen-inch girth—Gary called the weight at eighteen pounds. It was almost a pity to take even one scale from such a sea-bright specimen.

For Bob, a man as familiar with *Madam Butterfly* at La Scala as he is with pounding out a big bucktail on an Illiamna stream, the steelhead was a milestone, his largest rainbow ever.

We motored to the last pool we would fish this day, 319 Pool, water named when three nineteen-pound steelhead came from it in one day.

I was only a cast or two into the pool when I hooked a steelhead and began to reel in the slack line while maintaining proper tension to the fish. But when the steelhead turned to run, the fly came free. I was chewing on the usual blend of bile and inner rage over this lost opportunity when Gary called out from his anchored boat.

"You need to strike first, *then* clear your line."

"Thought I had," I called back. These flies are large and the takes deliberate. Hitting the fish hard was necessary when fishing a deep running line, and I had not done so.

The shoreline water below me was too deep to wade, and a jumble of trees uprooted during a long-past winter flood made the rocky bar impassable. I walked into the bush and around a back eddy now only glistening mud. Wolf and bear tracks pocked the area, a reminder that this was a wilderness experience. Dennis had recently counted ten wolves on a Sustut bar while flying his plane. Last year a lone male had stood across the river from the lodge and stared forlornly at Dennis's Malamute bitch. Black bears are routine sightings. The uncommon grizzly is encountered each year, especially when the August run of chinook salmon has filled the lower Sustut.

Clouds had moved down from the mountains, the misty rain enclosing the river in twilight. I changed to a fluorescent Skykomish Sunrise and was immediately into a fish. Each time I thought the steelhead had tired and that heavy pressure would bring her to net, the hen would turn and run well out into the pool. When Gary finally slid the net under her, we could see that she was slightly smaller than Bob's steelhead. Gary called the weight at sixteen pounds.

This was our last steelhead of the day. Tired and jubilant, we began the upstream run to the lodge. Though it was nearly dark when Dennis passed us, his raised fingers counted several steelhead and told us there was joy in his boat, too.

Bob and I were soon glowing from both our fishing and dollops of Crown Royal. As we sat before steaming platters of roast moose and fresh vegetables, I looked down the dining table. "Well, Walt, how did you do?" I began. This had been his best day yet; a hen of thirteen pounds and a buck of fourteen pounds had come to his Flashabou Skunk, both fish from the bottom end where Gary had caught the nineteen-pound buck. "And Mark?" I continued.

"Ah, Mark! He has tales to tell!" Walt's eyes were fairly dancing with pleasure. Mark, having caught a shower before dinner, now joined us and clearly savored the moment. His determination with a waking dry had paid off.

"I wasn't sure I'd had a rise; there was just this tiny dimple in the current. I cast to the spot again, and this time got a boil beside the fly. On the third cast, the buck's entire head came out, and he had the fly."

"How large did the fish go?" someone asked.

"Nineteen pounds," he said. Mark shook his head in wonderment. "A buck, and it was tagged."

The wheels were turning in our heads.

"Not the same fish!" we cried.

"Yes," said Mark. "'Marvin' again! He was released to keep *that kind of steelhead* in the gene pool!"

This remarkable nineteen-pound steelhead highlighted what collectively would be our best day on the Sustut, eight steelhead landed with an average weight of fifteen and a half pounds. As I write this (in the winter of 1986), "Marvin" is resting safely above the Bear Creek confluence, where he will remain even as the river freezes completely over. Males are polygamous, and this buck will spawn repeatedly after ice out. After passing downstream with smolts of the new year, he will reach salt water and immediately face miles of gill nets. If he is fortunate, he will pass through unharmed and head out to sea, too old to ever return. Mark was right. This steelhead must continue to be part of the Sustut gene pool. Maybe we'll see his likes again. It was a nice thought.

During the next few days, Bob and I would fish with both Dennis and Gary, and our fortunes would decline. I managed a twelve-pound buck, while Bob lost several fish. Conversely, Mark and Walt were finding steelhead, and one day while fishing with Dennis, all three beached fish using the Riffle Dancer.

Upstream is canyon water, ledge rock, and basaltic walls, and the good pools are few, with none possessing the classic charm that so characterizes the pools in the lodge area. Access to this water is not without price. The boulder-strewn rapids are extremely narrow and twisting. Despite the great care taken when negotiating this water, the sleds almost invariably suffer some damage. Still, there are a few pools, such as Glory Hole, that when filled with steelhead can provide angling of storied quality.

The remarkable 19-pound Sustut buck that was hooked and released three times.

The steelhead can leave the small pool for the white water below, and following the fish is impossible. Fly fishermen seek this challenge with relish, but their memories are likely to contain more than the usual share of heartbreak. Lodge records, thirty-pounders, it is said, have been all-too-brief encounters.

Late on the sixth day, we were returning from a long upstream run to Glory Hole when Bob pointed back upstream and said to Gary, "Moose!"

Standing beside the river, about 150 yards distant, was a moose that didn't seem the least perturbed by either the sound of the jet sled or our presence. Gary soon determined that this was a bull, and drew his .375 Winchester from the console.

"Would you guys mind putting your heads down?" he asked. I did this with the muzzle over my head and my fingers in my ears. The rifle roared three times. I saw the moose's legs buckle slightly before it sauntered, unhurried, into the bush, coming out beside a small creek which cut through a boggy meadow. Gary parked the boat and headed into the stand of scrub willow. Four more shots rang out. Gary emerged, his broad smile confirming that the moose had been blasted to smithereens.

"We'll drag the moose down the creek to the river," said Gary. "Then we'll put it into the sled."

I immediately had doubts. A bull moose is a colossal animal. Canadians, I thought, must be made of sterner stuff. After thirty minutes of dragging and cursing, we had skidded the beast to the river, and after another herniating period we had the moose's chin and four inches of lolling tongue over the sled's gunwale. The rest of the moose remained firmly nailed to the stream bottom. We decided to tow the moose several miles downstream to camp. This bizarre tow pretty much eliminated the steering. The rapids, in cavelike darkness, were especially memorable. My appreciation of moose meat was forever heightened.

On my last morning on the Sustut, with the air temperature well below that of the water, I was working the tailout of 319 Pool and feeling as cold, as completely frozen through, as I could remember. Dennis motored by to report that Walt had just put two steelhead on the beach by waking a Riffle Dancer. His words still hung in the clouds of his breath as the sled disappeared downriver. A dry fly? I shivered deeper into my pile jacket, alone again in a riverscape now touched by winter.

As I continued to cast and mend my way downstream, I tried to put this and other events of the week into perspective. I had come to feel that the Sustut was among the very finest of our steelhead rivers. I certainly thought it would be the last river of this caliber discovered within the steelhead's natural range. It still astonished me that a few six-week seasons and a handful of anglers were this river's entire fly-fishing heritage. But that made me a pioneer, too, and my fly fishing had been accompanied by a constant sense of discovery.

I thought of the angler who had averaged a steelhead over twenty pounds per day during a week in 1985. Dennis said something about an angler who took two steelhead on two consecutive casts one day at Boulder Pool, and that each fish went well over twenty pounds. Wasn't there a story about a steelhead that guide and angler estimated at forty-four inches before it was lost? The stories piled one atop the other. Would these steelhead become the object of pilgrimages, one of those very necessary experiences if a lifetime of trout fishing was to be called complete?

A pang of anxiety cut short these rhetorical musings. The Sustut, I knew, had once been a July steelhead river, too. Gary and Dennis now search in vain for a steelhead before the third week of August. As with the Bulkley River, the early-returning races have been systematically and permanently removed, victims of a commercial fishing industry that continues to ravage all these summer-run races regardless of run timing. Natives are determined to establish an interior commercial salmon fishery on rivers in the Skeena drainage. If this becomes a reality, steelhead stocks will be threatened still further.

The Sustut steelhead's future has always been in the hands of those individuals who have had the power to guarantee its survival. While I took scant comfort from that fact, I hoped that an outgrowth of British Columbia's commercial fishing conflicts included the preservation of this remarkable race of steelhead.

LIFE HISTORY

What we presently know of the Sustut steelhead's life history is due, in great measure, to the efforts of Gary Miltenberger and Dennis Farnworth. As described earlier in this chapter, each steelhead caught by their clients is carefully measured, has a few of its scales removed, and is darted with a tag before being released. The temperature of the water is noted and recorded. At the end of each fishing season, the scales are sent to Smithers, where they are read by Ron Tetreau, a fisheries technician for the Fishery Branch of the Ministry of Environment. The length and girth measurements provide a very close approximation of the steelhead's weight. The date and the sex of the fish indicate run timing, and how the run proceeds for each sex. The scales reveal the steelhead's life history, its years in fresh water and in salt water. From this raw data, physical attributes and freshwater migratory habits emerge sufficiently to define the race in terms of angling. The picture is not a whole, but the image grows sharper each year, reinforcing my conviction that Sustut steelhead are one of the few true giant races of summer steelhead.

Gary has sent me the results of this research from 1985 to 1989. In the following discussion, I have used data gathered from 1985, 1986, and 1987. My comments are based on my interpretation of this raw data.

The life-history categories are those found in three seasons covering an evaluation of over 650 steelhead caught from late August to late October. Some common categories change in strength from year to year. Not all are represented each year. A few rare categories may be found one year, only to be totally absent for some years to come.

The 3.2+ steelhead consisted of seven females and two males averaging 11.53 and 14.52 pounds, respectively. The 4.2+ steelhead consisted of twenty-nine females and thirteen males (10.73 and 13.62 pounds average). Extremes in size for 2+ ocean steelhead were three females weighing fourteen pounds, and a single male of twenty pounds. *Females (thirty-six) outnumbered males (fifteen) by better than two to one.*

The 3.3+ steelhead were made up of three females and twelve males (15.4- and 20-pound averages).

SCALE SAMPLE ANALYSIS 1985

Age	Number of steelhead	Percentage
3.1	2	2.3
4.1	——	——
R.2	——	——
3.2+	9	10.3
4.2+	42	48.3
5.2+	——	——
R.3+	2	2.3
3.3+	15	17.2
4.3+	12	13.8
5.3+	——	——
3.4+	——	——
3.1S1+	——	——
3.2Sl+	2	2.3
4.2Sl+	3	3.4
5.2S1+	——	——
4.2S1S1+	——	——
5.2S1S1+	——	——
3.2S1S1S1+	——	——

TOTAL 87

OCEAN AGES

Age	Number of steelhead	Percentage
1+	2	2.3
2+	51	58.6
3+	29	33.3
4+	——	——
3.2S1	2	2.3
4.2S1+	3	3.4

TOTAL 87

Note: One-year ocean steelhead are generally very rare in the Sustut. The two fish were a male of 7 pounds and a female of 4.4 pounds. The size of the male is remarkable for a year and a month or so of ocean life, and helps one appreciate how these steelhead get to weights of over thirty pounds.

The 4.3+ steelhead were essentially identical; the two females and ten males averaging 15.5 and 19 pounds. When the R.3+ steelhead (freshwater years undetermined) are added, the 3+ ocean category is made up of twenty-five males and five females. This is a reversal of the trend observed among the 2+ ocean steelhead, and no explanation can be offered. Evident in this sampling is that the male fish tended to maintain their ocean residency for an additional year.

I also examined the scale-sample analysis to see whether these male 3+ ocean steelhead were predisposed to arrive later in the main stem of the Sustut than the 2+ ocean females. Gary has experienced an early run of steelhead dominated by females by as much as five to one. He also spoke of the "big bucks" that appeared later, though in truth outsized male fish could be found at any time during the run. Given the seasonal variability of steelhead runs, I wondered if such a trend would show up clearly, or whether those "big bucks" were also the steelhead best remembered.

Ninety-five steelhead were actually in the study; eight were left out because no scales were removed. However, these fish were sexed. The first steelhead was caught August 23, the last on October 20. In a season covering approximately sixty days, the first half saw twenty-two steelhead caught, the second half totaled seventy-three steelhead. If we break the sixty days down roughly into twenty-day periods and sex the escapement, we get a clear trend: 8/23–9/16: seventeen (eleven females, six males); 9/17–9/30: thirty-seven (twenty-two females, fifteen males); 10/1–10/20: thirty-nine (seventeen females, twenty-two males).

This supports Gary's theory that the greatest percentage of the male trophy-class steelhead is likely found late in the steelhead's fall escapement. How and when this run peaks fuels fascinating speculation. Getting in and out of the Sustut after the third week in October on a fixed schedule is difficult, and as a consequence, the lodge business is pretty much shut down. A few balmy days with reliable flying weather in late fall will someday allow a few hearty souls the opportunity to answer these questions.

Five repeat-spawning steelhead were represented, four females and a single male. The females ranged from 9.9 to 18.9 pounds; the male weighed 13 pounds. As always, steelhead spawning a second, third, or even a fourth time are rarely the largest members of their generation, regardless of their age. Rapid growth occurs in the ocean, not in rivers where little, if any, growth takes place and where metabolisms are geared to reproduction.

A second, larger sampling of 385 steelhead covers two seasons and describes a few remarkable life histories.

SCALE SAMPLE ANALYSIS 1986/87

Age	Number of steelhead	Percentage
3.1+	———	———
4.1+	3	.78
3.2+	86	22.34
4.2+	169	43.90
5.2+	14	3.67
R.2	7	1.82
3.3+	29	7.53
4.3+	51	13.25
5.3+	2	.52
R.3+	3	.78
3.4+	1	.26
3.1Sl+	1	.26
3.2Sl+	4	1.04
4.2Sl+	10	2.60
5.2Sl+	1	.26
R.2Sl+	1	.26
4.2SlSl+	1	.26
5.2SlSl+	1	.26
3.2SlSlSl+	1	.26

Total 385

OCEAN AGES

Age	Number of steelhead	Percentage
1+	3	.78
2+	276	71.79
3+	85	22.08
4+	1	.26
.1S1+	1	.26
.2S1+	16	4.16
.2S1S1+	2	.52
.2S1S1S1+	1	.26

Total 385

Note: The last two life histories may be records for longevity, both females in their twelfth years of life. I have never before found documentation for steelhead so old. The last steelhead was returning to spawn a fourth time. After surviving to become a sexually mature adult, it successfully survived the gill-net fishery four times as an ascending fish, and three times as a mending kelt!

Not a single steelhead that spawned after three ocean years was found to have returned to spawn a second time. As has been true on other rivers, the great fish of steelhead legend are seen but once.

The differences between 1985 and 1986–87 are not dramatic and are probably typical for the Sustut. The reader will note a decline of the 3+ ocean steelhead and a slight increase in the 2+ ocean steelhead from 1985 and 1986–87. Such fluctuations are within the normal range and are typical for the Sustut.

During the sampling, 374 smolts were examined. They were the following ages: three years–32.62 percent, four years–62.57 percent, five years–4.81 percent. The Sustut, like the Morice, is relatively cold and infertile. Growth of juvenile steelhead to smolting age and a length of eight to nine inches typically takes four years.

Salty Saltzman and Billy Pate discuss the merits of a dressing for the North Umpqua.

PART THREE

THE
ANGLERS
AND
THEIR
FLY
PATTERNS

Anadromous steelhead grow from two worlds. Streams are their nursery; their food is the mayflies, caddisflies, stoneflies, and terrestrials of trout-fishing lore. We hope they can remember these premigrant years when we cast greased-line wets and waking dries for them. We understand the foods that fuel their ocean years less well. What we know and what we suppose inspire patterns in remarkable variety, but often modeled after Atlantic salmon ties. Bright prawn and streamer flies may or may not imitate life, but they are surely art, each a talisman capable of magical turns of fortune.

The anglers in the chapters that follow are experts at tying and presenting flies that attract steelhead. Specialists, generalists, and figures of folklore, they invite you to look into their fly boxes and to fish their home rivers. Whether their steelhead rise from the mists of deep winter or race down pools in the darkness of a summer evening, their methods are worth dwelling upon.

Frank Amato

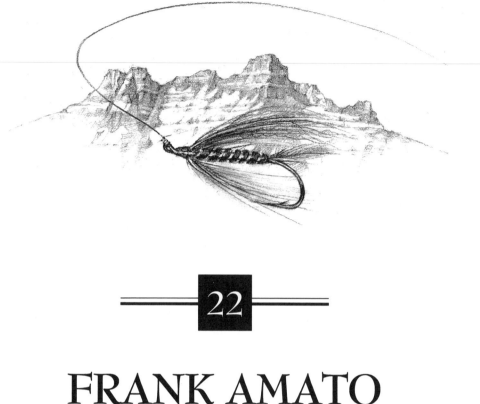

22

FRANK AMATO

THE flickering lantern light played host to innumerable caddisflies as Frank Amato and I stood on either side of the makeshift table. We viewed each other's surreal likeness through a cloud of erratic flights, picked fallen celebrants from our cups of wine, and reflected upon our day on the Deschutes River.

Dick Lawson was still at Lower Music. He had left a couple of hours earlier in the canyon's gathering darkness. Now the ridge tops were black holes, the night sky without stars. The Deschutes fishes well as late as any steelhead river I know. Still, I was relieved to hear his footfalls behind the tiny grove of white alder that Frank had claimed for a campsite.

Dick, usually cool to a fault, but now hardly able to contain his delight, told us that well past where he had expected to find a steelhead, a wonderful fish had hit his dark fly, a Queenie. The steelhead was ultimately brought to shore, where he guessed its weight at twelve pounds.

I knew the fly was from a pair of new steelhead fly dressings, one dark, one bright, that Frank had recently developed. He was fishing them alternately, water conditions and time of day factors in his choice of which fly to fish.

The bright pattern was called the Patriot. I had used nothing else for three days. My first steelhead of the trip, a hen of nine pounds, had struck the fly as hard as any steelhead in my memory. The impact knocked the reel's pawls out of alignment, and only by frantically palming the free-running spool was I able to prevent a massive override. This success would not have prevented me from trying

293

out the Queenie, a silhouette pattern in its element in the shadow-water of dawn and last light. But the next evening I raised a fish that toyed with the Patriot from time to time for an hour and a half, until I was left in the total darkness of canyon night. Then, the steelhead took the fly without hesitation. That a thin, yellow-bodied fly should prove so effective in zero light had generated in me a strong prejudice for the dressing.

Nevertheless, I listened to Dick's story with a twinge of regret. I should have given the dark fly more time on the water. Maybe my reluctance to use the fly stemmed from my dislike of its name. There was nothing "queenie" about the fly's dressing or developing reputation.

"Frank," I said, "you've always had lovely names for your steelhead flies. There was the Sicilian Gold. Now there is the Patriot. But, Queenie?"

"Perhaps I should call it Thatcher's Red," he answered with a laugh.

"But the fly isn't *red*," I countered.

Months later, as I was preparing for my first trip to British Columbia's Sustut River, Frank sent me a small package that contained several examples of the Patriot, and a fly he called Night Dancer, a pattern I recognized as the Queenie from our days together on the Deschutes. I liked the new name. The enclosed message read: "Use these flies with confidence."

I tied copies, using larger hooks, 1/0s mostly, and I hooked two Sustut steelhead with the Night Dancer only a few hours after my arrival. I fished no other wet-fly pattern, and after five days my supply was nearly gone. I reluctantly tied on one of the two originals and hooked a twelve-pound buck, which tried to swallow the fly. This is a steelhead habit that I have come to associate with dark patterns in general and with the Night Dancer in particular.

The Night Dancer has become a favorite of mine, and I would include it in any list of five best patterns. I don't fish the Patriot as much, though there is no other yellow steelhead pattern I care for half so much.

The originals as tied by Frank Amato:

PATRIOT

Tail Red hackle fibers
Body Yellow floss ribbed with flat silver tinsel

Hackle Deep purple
Wing White calf tail or bucktail

Note: The yellow floss turns translucent when wet, and the black hook shows through if the body is thinly dressed. This can be avoided by underwrapping the hook with silver tinsel. The result is dazzling. I find it convenient to make the underbody, tag, and ribbing one length of flat silver tinsel.

NIGHT DANCER

Tail Red hackle fibers
Body Black floss ribbed with silver tinsel

Hackle Deep purple
Wing Black calf tail or bucktail

I have invested so much time in its use that I currently tie the Night Dancer in several styles. I like the original dressed somewhat low-water with a reduced wing of black squirrel tail or black marabou, and a body of either floss—a handsome, trim tie—or dubbing, which can give the fly a very nymphlike appearance. This variation has been productive for me on the Deschutes and Klamath rivers in sizes 4 to 8. For the Skeena's rivers, the Dean, and the Thompson, I dress the fly more fully in 1/0 and 2/0, dub the body, and add an underwing of purple Krystal Flash. Recently, I've been tying the Night Dancer as a spider on light-wire hooks by thinning out the entire dressing and overwrapping the wing with a collar of Chinese pheasant rump dyed extremely dark purple. Most of the pheasant rump is gathered above the hook to sweep back and blend in with the black wing. This is a wonderful fly to fish greased-line, with or without a riffling hitch.

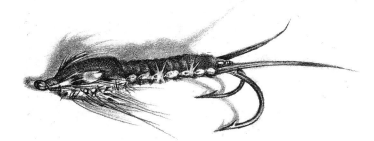

JIM GARRETT

I F fly fishing, the "gentle art" of presenting a fly to a trout, is the sport, then fly tying, the art of dressing a hook with feathers and fur, is surely the hobby. And one recreation can be exclusive of the other. I know fine anglers who possess neither the time nor the aesthetic inclination to enter the arcane world of fly tying. Conversely, some fly tyers rarely fish, but they possess such dressing skills that their complex flies are displayed in museums, and a single fly may sell for several hundred dollars.

Considerable resolve is necessary to master both the sport and the hobby. The effort is supported by fluency in the very large body of literature that is devoted to fly fishing, and it is fueled by a lifelong passion for our rivers and still waters. Athletic skills must be learned, but fly casting is grace, too, and the finest casters seem to be born to it. Numerous fly dressing techniques must be mastered, and our most celebrated tyers mix in a kind of creative wizardry that can defy duplication.

Among the handful of western anglers possessing these attributes is Jim Garrett, guru of Olympic Peninsula fly fishers, who lives where he works, at the Beaver Springs salmon hatchery on the Sol Duc River. An entire room of his home is given over to fly tying. Prime fishing water is within earshot. He keeps a saddle horse and a pack horse for high-country travels. A cassette library fills his evenings with country music, but the sweetest sound in all his world is the answering call of a properly bugled bull elk. His wide-brimmed Stetson and his soup-strainer mustache seem anachronistic. Whitewater

Jim Garrett

canoeing and bow hunting are also passions. He has survived a massive heart attack and open-heart surgery; a profound sense of his mortality guides his life.

I got together with Jim early in 1989 in order to better understand the rationale behind his fly designs. His fly-tying bench was littered with bits and pieces from a variety of wildlife: golden pheasant, jungle cock, peacock, teal, gadwall, partridge, deer, and bear. No eye of newt here, but I found the results to be no less artistically alchemic. Jim's supple hands worked over the vise with wonderful dexterity as esoteric parts were secured to the hook with floss and thread. The procedure was quick and sure, the Olympic Stonefly dressing finished in ten minutes.

"Give it a try?" Jim said. I've been tying for twenty-five years and can do a decent job of it. His marvelous performance made me unsure. "I'll talk you through it," he offered. My fumble-fingered result was clearly not up to his standard. He seemed not to notice and praised the result. I liked him for that.

Garrett is a native Washingtonian, born forty-odd years ago in White Salmon. In answer to the inevitable question of how he came to hold fly fishing so dear, he says simply, "I've been fishing since I could walk." He recalls being a spin fisherman until the age of seven, when he received his first fly rod. Two years later, he caught his first steelhead on a dry fly. Naturally, he had tied the fly himself. After a stint in the Navy, he attended Peninsula College in Port Angeles and became a fisheries technician. He has since worked for the Washington Department of Fisheries in their salmon culture programs at hatcheries on the Dungeness, Klickitat, and Elwha rivers.

Jim returned to Peninsula College to teach fly tying, a practice he has continued for more than ten years. "I especially like to work with gifted tyers who put a little bit of their soul into it," he told me. The classes he taught paralleled his growing interest in steelhead fly fishing. When the Peninsula Fly Fishers was organized, he was one of its founders, and he served as president for many years.

"When I first came up to the Peninsula twenty years ago, nobody was fly-fishing for steelhead," he said. Jim cast all the conventional attractor patterns then in vogue and examined the steelhead runs accordingly. The Elwha River became a favorite proving ground for his own experiments in fly design. These years at streamside gave him an understanding of run timing and revealed the racial characteristics of steelhead from river to river, and season to season. The result is a collection of steelhead flies designed uniquely for fishing Olympic Peninsula waters. They are broken down into a number of series for the steelhead races of summer and those of winter under a variety of conditions: late summer's low-water fishing ("Septober," says Jim); frigid winter currents; summer's gin-clear dry-fly water, spate rivers discolored from rain and snowmelt.

Jim and fellow members of the Peninsula Fly Fishers have fought for less liberal fishing regulations, preached a catch-and-release angling philosophy, and campaigned for fly-only water. The Hoko River is their proudest achievement.

The little Hoko meets the sea west of Clallam Bay after a short and busy run down from the Olympics. It is a nowhere river that supports a nominal Indian fishery. Bait fishermen enjoy its lower reaches and curse its tackle-grabbing ways. Little else would call attention to it save for a remarkable fact: The upper Hoko is one of only three fly-fishing-only steelhead rivers in Washington, and the only such river for winter steelhead. It now supports a statewide following, and its canyon waters are becoming a hallowed retreat for fly fishers.

When I last visited Jim, we fished the Hoko together. On this warm day in late February, every piece of holding water spoke to him, and he told their stories well.

"This is a river with large steelhead, over twenty pounds. A seventeen-pound buck took a Trinity just this side of that rock by the feeder creek, and then took me around the bend!" Jim laughed merrily over the recollection. So it went, the anecdotes building one upon the other until a coherent picture of the river and its steelhead emerged.

We drove far upstream and then walked along the river that remained but a headwater creek, too small to properly swing a fly and perhaps abandoned for that reason. The river hardly made a sound, and in the stillness, our voices dropped to nearly a whisper. This was where Jim's steelhead were born.

Redds were evident. Fresh tracks of otter and bear were etched in the wet sand of the river bar. Bald eagles, gone with the last of winter's salmon, again searched the river corridor.

"What do you see?" Jim suddenly asked. I wasn't sure what he was driving at, and I looked into the Hoko's clear water until he answered his own question. "I love it here. This is where I go to get away from it all."

Not to fish or hunt, I thought. Here you can listen for an answer to a prayer. I nodded, and we left to catch his favorite pool on the lower river while there was still light.

OLYMPIC STONEFLY SERIES

Nothing else in fly fishing is quite like Jim Garrett's Olympic Stonefly series of steelhead flies. "I originated this fly on the Elwha River in the early l970s. I had many a memorable day with the Orange and Black, and then developed the other variations."

The original dressing, large and elegantly crafted, imitates *Pteronarcys californica*, the salmon fly or "dark stonefly" in the nymphal stage. This large stonefly, with its bright tangerine orange body, is found hatching each spring on Pacific Coast streams from British Columbia to California, and is abundant on some rivers, such as the Rogue and the Deschutes. It is locally common in the Olympic Peninsula, especially on the Elwha and Sol Duc rivers, where the adults hatch late in April. This time corresponds to the end of the winter run of steelhead, and no one suspects that these fish feed on hatching adults. We do not know how actively the winter- or summer-run feed on the nymphal form, but it is likely intermittent. No doubt premigrant steelhead feed aggressively on stoneflies in all life stages, including the huge adults. I suspect this early conditioning is why adults so readily take nymph-like steelhead flies.

ORANGE AND BLACK OLYMPIC STONEFLY

Tail Peacock primary feather dyed black (Garrett uses peacock because it is wider and sturdier than goose)

Tag Fluorescent flame floss. This is tied in first to help split the tail of peacock.

Underbody Black polypropylene. This is tied from the middle of the hook back. Black chenille is tied in at the same point to give the body additional bulk. The black polypropylene is then wound forward over itself and over the black chenille up to the thorax region and tied off.

Overbody Narrow-diameter black chenille and hot orange yarn. The two contrasting materials are used to construct the woven body. Using the "opposite hand," the bright material is grasped, the dark color overhand-knotted, and the dark color passed over the hook shank. This is repeated until the woven body is completed into the thorax area. The two contrasting materials are drawn tight to make each knot while the hands are held parallel to the fly-tying bench. This assures that the bright lateral line of the fly will be even.

Caseback Tie in six strands of polypropylene at the head and bind down to midsection. Then tie in natural black webby neck hackle and flame yarn at the midsection. Wind yarn forward and tie off. Wind hackle forward and tie off. Bring caseback forward and tie off.

Cheeks Jungle cock

Head The inner construction of the fly is done with single-strand black floss. Change to fine-diameter Danville mahogany thread only when nearing completion. When the metallic stoneflies are constructed, use three or four strands of single-strand silver or gold lamé. This is a tarnish-resistant thread for sewing machines or hand embroidery. The thread is manufactured by Easy International, 130 Grand St., Carlstadt, New Jersey, 07079.

The metallic color variations were inspired by the favorite colors incorporated in plugs, the "hot-shots" used on Peninsula rivers. The complete series includes four additional patterns. "Wherever I have taken them in Washington, they have caught steelhead," Jim says.

Jim fishes the flies on a dead drift until they come under tension and begin to swing. He believes that the polypropylene assists in hooking the steelhead. It is soft and catches on their teeth, even during a light, tentative take. The dressings are effective for both summer- and winter-run steelhead.

BLACK AND SILVER OLYMPIC STONEFLY

See above.

BLACK AND GOLD OLYMPIC STONEFLY

See above.

BLUE AND SILVER OLYMPIC STONEFLY

(Woven body consists of four strands of silver lamé and royal blue Flashabou. Caseback is entirely of blue Flashabou.

GREEN AND SILVER OLYMPIC STONEFLY

(Woven body consists of insect green Krystal Flash and silver lamé. Caseback is emerald green Flashabou.

This series invites other color combinations if one uses the many colors of Krystal Flash and Flashabou. "Feelers" may be added using peacock primary-feather sections dyed black. Jim ties some of the patterns on 2/0 long-shank double hooks by Partridge. They keep the fly riding evenly in heavy currents. He particularly favors their use when fishing Olympic Stoneflies from a boat.

TRINITY SERIES

The Orange Trinity was first tied in 1968 for pink salmon on the Dungeness River. Its effectiveness led Jim to use the fly for chum and chinook salmon and steelhead. This pattern and two variations have become reliable standbys for winter steelhead. He ties them from size 4 to 2/0 and gives the following rationale for the size range: "My experience has been that when winter steelhead first come into the rivers they will not take a large fly. The longer the steelhead are in the river, and the more sexually mature they become, the larger the fly they will take."

ORANGE TRINITY

Tail	Golden pheasant crest dyed hot orange	**Hackle**	Orange
Body	Three "balls" of fine fluorescent orange chenille divided equally by embossed gold tinsel. Take two turns of tinsel at the tail for a short tag.	**Wing**	White polar bear, or bucktail
		Head	Purple

HOT ORANGE TRINITY

Substitute flame chenille.

CHRISTMAS TRINITY

Substitute chenille in the sequence of orange, flame, and lime green, tail forward. Hackle is lime green mixed with flame.

FEATHER-WING FLIES

Jim Garrett's feather-wing steelhead dressings are among the most beautiful in steelheading. He begins his argument for their use by bemoaning the general loss of such elegant and simple low-water feather-winged flies as the Silver and Mallard. Today's anglers, he says, are "enamored of hairwings."

The aesthetic qualities brought to steelheading by this type of feather-wing fly are obvious. But Jim finds practical value in their use during late summer and early fall and during the occasional low-water periods of March and April, when very aggressive, sexually mature winter steelhead have adopted broad, shallow tailouts for spawning. "The flies," he says, "have a translucency that only certain feathers possess, producing an effective blending of colors that could not exist in a hairwing fly. Study the Kate underwater in bright sunlight, and observe the radiance that occurs when the colors blend. The effect is unobtainable with any other materials."

TERESA'S TEASE

Tail Golden pheasant crest dyed hot orange
Body Rear half red yarn ribbed with embossed gold tinsel. Front half peacock palmered with soft, black hackle.

Throat Guinea
Wing Drake green-wing teal flank

D'ANA MARIE

Tail Golden pheasant crest dyed hot orange
Body Rear half hot orange floss, front half red wool. Rib entire body with embossed gold tinsel. Body is then palmered with orange hackle.

Throat Guinea
Wing Ring-neck pheasant tail sections from secondary flight feathers
Cheeks Jungle cock

SARA TEEN

Tail Golden pheasant crest dyed hot orange
Body Rear half embossed silver tinsel, front half black chenille, rib entire body with embossed gold tinsel

Hackle Guinea
Wing Four white hackle tips
Topping Amherst pheasant crest
Head Wine tying thread

BOBBIE JEAN

Tail None
Body Hot orange floss ribbed with embossed silver tinsel, and palmered black neck hackle
Wing Brown mallard flank

Topping Amherst pheasant crest dyed wine
Cheeks Jungle cock
Head Wine

QE–3

Tail Golden pheasant crest dyed flame
Tag Embossed gold tinsel
Body Rear half fluorescent cerise floss over silver mylar. Front half, four peacock herls wound as a chenille and palmered with ring-neck pheasant rump. Rib entire body as a continuation of the tag.

Hackle Golden pheasant flank (reddish brown)
Wing Teal flank
Cheeks Jungle cock
Head Claret

KATE

Tag Embossed silver tinsel
Body Red floss over silver mylar; rib with a continuation of the tag
Hackle Red, palmered on the front half of the body

Underwing Two golden pheasant flank feathers, face to face
Wing Greenwing teal flank
Cheeks Jungle cock
Head Claret

T.C.–3

Tail Golden pheasant crest dyed flame
Body Rear half fluorescent white floss, front half fluorescent flame floss. Wrap body over silver mylar. Rib with embossed gold tinsel.

Hackle White, palmering the front half of the body
Cheeks Jungle cock
Head Flame

HELLEN'S FANCY

Tail Golden pheasant crest dyed orange
Butt Black ostrich
Body Rear half fluorescent lime green floss over silver mylar tinsel; front half, fluorescent flame floss over silver mylar tinsel.

Rear Hackle Fluorescent lime green palmered over front half of body
Hackle Golden pheasant flank (reddish brown)
Wing Teal
Cheeks Jungle cock

NIGHT TRAIN

Tail Amherst pheasant over golden pheasant tippet flanked with single strip of red goose, long
Butt Black ostrich
Body Rear half fluorescent orange floss over silver mylar tinsel; front half black ostrich. Rib entire body with embossed silver tinsel.

Rear Hackle Red, palmered over forward half of body
Hackle Natural black
Wing Teal

MAC GARRETT

Tail Golden pheasant crest dyed flamed
Butt Black ostrich
Body Rear half fluorescent lime green floss over silver mylar tinsel; front half black ostrich
Hackle Natural black
UnderWing Strips of purple goose secondary flight feathers, back to back

Wing Teal
Topping Golden pheasant crest dyed flame
Shoulder Small, whole golden pheasant tippet dyed flame
Cheeks Jungle cock

FATHER BILL

Tail Wood-duck flank
Butt Black ostrich
Body Medium embossed silver tinsel
Hackle Orange palmered over front half of body
UnderWing Strips of red-goose secondary back to back

Wing Teal
Topping Golden pheasant crest dyed flame
Cheeks Jungle cock

SOUL DUCK

Tail Wood-duck flank
Butt Yellow ostrich
Body Yellow floss ribbed with embossed gold tinsel
Rear Hackle Fluorescent yellow palmered over the front half of the body

Hackle Teal flank
UnderWing Strips of red-goose secondary back to back
Wing Teal

SOFT-HACKLE FLIES

Jim developed a series of soft-hackle flies for summer-run steelhead when rivers are low and clear. He is convinced that when the steelhead are really fresh in the river the brighter fly is more effective, while darker patterns work better as the season progresses. When steelhead are late into their spawning migration, he goes to black flies. The series reflects these color options.

The examples pictured were tied on Alec Jackson gold-plated Partridge hooks. The hook color glows through when the floss becomes wet and somewhat translucent. A similar effect can be obtained by underwrapping the body with gold tinsel, if the hook is black.

CANDY MONTANA

Body Rear half fluorescent lime green floss, front half flame floss. Rib entire body with embossed gold tinsel, the tinsel dividing the two colors evenly.

Hackle Hungarian partridge
Head Flame tying thread

DENISE MONTANA

Body Red floss ribbed with embossed gold tinsel
Hackle Belly feather of a ring-neck pheasant dyed black

Head Purple tying thread

DANA MONTANA

Body Rear half orange floss, front half red floss. Rib entire body with embossed gold tinsel.

Hackle Hungarian partridge
Head Purple tying thread

LIBBY'S BLACK

Body Rear half black floss ribbed with embossed silver tinsel. Front half black ostrich, no rib.

Hackle Soft webby hackle from the belly of a ring-neck pheasant, dyed black
Head Purple tying thread

LOW-WATER FLIES

During periods when steelhead are holding in water extremely clear and low and nearly stagnant in flow, Jim turns to this series of flies, casting them on leaders as long as fourteen feet. With care, the fly can be worked repeatedly over a dull fish without spooking it. The range of colors runs from attractor style, to several that when fished greased-line, resemble emerging insects.

I think these flies would be excellent used as searching patterns on broad, shallow tailouts. I would try them with a Portland hitch and use them as follow-up patterns, after steelhead have shown themselves behind an erratic surface pattern such as a Bomber.

PETERSON M.D.

Body Red floss over silver mylar, rib with flat silver tinsel. Palmer with black hackle.

Wing Midnight blue metallic mallard secondary
Cheeks Jungle cock

JOHNSON M.D.

Tail Golden pheasant crest dyed flame
Butt Black ostrich
Body Claret thread ribbed with flat silver tinsel

Hackle Red, palmered
Wing White-tipped mallard secondary
Cheeks Jungle cock

SEPTOBER CANDY

Tail Golden pheasant crest dyed flame
Body Flame floss over silver mylar. Rib with embossed gold tinsel. Palmer forward half of the body with lime green hackle.

Hackle Red
Wing Mallard terciary, white-tipped
Cheeks Jungle cock

SEPTOBER PHEASANT

Tail Golden pheasant crest dyed flamed
Body Rear half claret floss or thread; front half black ostrich. Rib entire body with embossed gold tinsel.

Hackle Fluorescent orange palmered over front half of the body
Wing Matching sections from back feather of a ring-neck pheasant

SEPTOBER ORANGE

Tail Golden pheasant crest dyed flame
Body Embossed gold tinsel
Hackle Brown, palmered over the front half of the body

Wing Orange primary sections
Cheeks Jungle cock

HOKO HUMMERS (SERIES)

This all-season series is somewhat on the order of Woolly Buggers. They are easily tied and carry a lot of action to the steelhead. Variations are endless. Four patterns are offered.

#1 TAIL/CASEBACK: BLACK MARABOU

Body Fluorescent orange chenille
Hackle Hungarian partridge

Head Black ostrich

#2 TAIL/CASEBACK: BLACK MARABOU

Body Hot orange chenille
Hackle Hungarian partridge

Head Black ostrich

#3 TAIL/CASEBACK: BLACK MARABOU

Body Silver tinsel chenille
Hackle Belly feather of ring-neck pheasant, dyed black.

Head Black ostrich

#4 TAIL/CASEBACK: BLACK MARABOU

Body Red wool
Hackle Hungarian partridge

Head Black ostrich

Septober Caddis Series

Though originally tied to be fished on a dead drift in Washington's Columbia River tributaries, the male and female are excellent greased-line dressings. The unusual wing construction provides a a lot of surface action in soft water, especially if the fly is dressed on a light-wire hook and given a riffling hitch.

LARVAE

Abdomen	White surgeon's glove over white acrylic yarn. Rib with single-strand gold lamé.	**Eyes**	Striped pheasant stem. Clip after tying with figure-eight turns.
Thorax	Peacock herl	**Head**	Claret
Legs (hackle)	Natural black		

FEMALE

Butt	Lime yarn, clipped short	**Hackle**	Hungarian partridge
Abdomen	Orange polar bear dubbed over a loop of gold lamé and twisted	**Wings**	Ring-neck pheasant philo plumes (dampen and pinch to length before tying)
Thorax	Otter dubbing		

MALE

Abdomen	Fluoresent orange chenille, fine	**Wing**	Ringneck pheasant philo plumes (dampen and pinch to length)
Thorax	Otter		
Hackle	Hungarian partridge		

GARRETT'S SHRIMP

Tail	Large golden pheasant crest dyed hot orange. Small additional hot orange feather at the base for added color.	**Wing**	Red bucktail taken from the back side of the tail (the color is a wine shade)
Body	Hot orange polar bear dubbing. Palmer body with orange hackle and rib with embossed gold tinsel.	**Cheeks**	Jungle cock
		Head	Wine

This blending of colors makes a superb winter pattern. Independently of Jim, I came up with a nearly identical dressing. Instead of dyed bucktail, I used golden pheasant flank.

ALEC JACKSON

T H E best-known hook in steelhead fly fishing bears his name. The Alec Jackson Spey, a sweeping low-water design with a subtle Dublin point, is marketed under Alec's label, Yorkshire Fly Fisher. He first noted the hook in a 1929 Hardy Brothers catalog, and when he brought it out in 1985, it bore only slight changes from the original. That this hook has come to embody our devotion to English-born Atlantic salmon traditions, and the direction steelhead fly tying has taken, is due in no small measure to Alec himself. As one of steelheading's most literate spokesmen, he has helped us cultivate a taste for the finer aspects of fly fishing. This has taken the form of elegant dressings, finely crafted cane rods, handmade reels, and the most noteworthy literature of our sport. If we sometimes find ourselves infected with a touch of grace and gentility, the condition is likely the result of Alec's gentle persuasion.

Alec Jackson grew up in the small Yorkshire village of Selby, in northern England, where coarse-fishing was the commoner's angling and match-fishing the expert's sport. Thus, when he left home at age twenty, he knew more of dace, roach, and chub than he did of trout, and he knew almost nothing of fly fishing. The single exception was quite memorable for the wonder it elicited—and for the promise it extracted. He recalled it for me one evening over dinner:

When I was a prepformer in boarding school—I was not yet ten—we had a geography master named Mousey Mitchell. We actually drove him crazy. When we left the classroom, he went straight to the lunatic asylum. We got a new geography master, and we called him Jack Harrison. He had been in Canada before he came to teach in England and had this propaganda from one of those Canadian tourist boards. I saw this photograph of two steelhead in the publication. It was kept in a big old oak cabinet. I can remember picking the lock to steal that photograph because they were the most beautiful fish I'd ever seen.

Alec went to New Zealand, where he worked for the forest service, learned about fly fishing, and bought his first cane rod, a nine-and-a-half-foot Hardy Knockabout. When he arrived in Washington State in 1956 to attend graduate school, he says, "I knew I was in the home of the steelhead."

He was also a long way from home. The colonies, he soon learned, had their own way of doing things.

I can remember going out—I didn't even know there was such a thing as fly fishing for steelhead—and seeing the people on the river fishing with pencil lead and egg clusters, and thinking, 'What a terribly primitive way to fish for a fish like a steelhead!' I thought it was pagan because in any civilized country fishing with salmon roe was outlawed a hundred years ago.

Alec told me, "I learned you could catch steelhead on a fly through an individual named Ron Hicks. That's when I met the likes of Bob Stroebel, Harry Lemire, Al Knudson, Walt Johnson, and Wes Drain."

Bob Stroebel—"old blue heron" in Alec's *Fly Tyer Magazine* column—became his friend and mentor. Alec followed him around for nearly a year, hardly ever fishing, but watching and learning. One day, while they were together on the Sauk River, Alec landed a spawned-out hatchery steelhead at Slide Hole. This occurred in the late 1960s. It is no overstatement to say that, in one form or another, Alec has since devoted his life to steelhead and fly fishing.

As a collector of rare flies, books, and fishing tackle, Alec often plays the role of broker, locating and purchasing a particularly fine item for a discriminating customer. Rose Jackson told me that she once watched her husband display his Bogdan reels, more than twenty in all, on the dining room table. Like King Midas, he had sat and gloried in the display of wealth. She insists that that was when he decided to begin selling. He demurs, but admits to profiting on many of those Bogdans, a few reels by Walker, Leonard, and Vom Hofe, and selling more cane rods than he cares to remember.

Alec has represented the Federation of Fly Fishers, and currently represents Washington Trout on The Deer Creek Policy Group, a committee that has for years dedicated itself to rehabilitating Deer Creek, the sole spawning tributary of the famous Deer Creek steelhead. These unique one-salt fish of the Stillaguamish River's North Fork are close to extinction due to a half-century of logging that contributed to the silting of their spawning habitat. If the Deer Creek steelhead survives, Alec Jackson and his friend Bob Arnold deserve a splash of single malt whenever the river and its lovely native steelhead are toasted.

Alec is the consummate storyteller of our sport. Drawing from a wealth of personal experience and a vast knowledge of angling literature, he can be, in turn, gossip, historian, or polemicist. John Shaw, George M. Kelson or Dr. T. E. Pryce-Tannatt are visited with nary a misstep, and Alec's understanding of Arthur Wood exceeds Donald Rudd's. Certainly, to discuss greased-line fishing with him is as close as anyone is likely to come to joining Wood at his Cairnton beat on the Dee. Alec's tales of contemporary angling are no less redolent with history. He enjoys writing in uncapitalized Yorkshire slang, and tells of the pools *toughtit* and *backaleathersis*, of the characters *millhand*, *redneck*, and *weasel*. There are feuds, whiskey, and great silver steelhead racing for tailouts. One expects to meet Mr. Toad fishing a double-handed rod. But despite their allegorical charm, his stories are factually told, the players very real, and the waters still the sacred fly drifts of the Stillaguamish River's North Fork.

Alec fishes a few rivers and knows them extraordinarily well. The Wenatchee in early October and the Sauk in late April may be less than twenty pools, but a considerable task to know in high water and low, sunshine and overcast, and where and for how long steelhead will hold in each. These are summer-run waters that lead Alec quickly into winter, and winter-run waters that are often the best summer days of his angling year. These contrasting flavors heighten his senses and have come to

Alec Jackson

balance his love for the sport. Other rivers take the edge off cabin fever—the upper Skykomish and North Fork are examples—he admits that the Sauk often gives up its steelhead begrudgingly, and that the Skagit is usually more generous. But this man is a romantic with strong convictions who wears his choices more comfortably with each passing year.

Alec cares to fish only a few summer, greased-line, patterns, but tied in a variety of sizes, styles, and hook weights. He wrote in the fall 1986 issue of *Fly Tyer*: "First, I don't want to see my fly skating as it swings across the current. If it does, I put the same fly on a heavier wire hook. Second, if I tighten slightly (by lifting the rod), I want to see my fly pop to the surface. If it does not, I put the same fly on a lighter wire hook."

This versatility is accomplished by dressing the Skunk—long his favorite steelhead pattern—on three different-weight hooks, from heavy salmon to a light-wire, in sizes from 3/0 to 6. The smaller light-wire examples are usually reduced dressings. Only rarely does he tie a thin floss-bodied Skunk, and each season he carries a few Skunks tied as full-winged streamers for high-water sink-tip conditions.

He likes his greased-line flies overhackled and portly, a tapered "pumpkin seed" body that produces a stronger silhouette than Arthur Wood's slimly elegant Blue Charm or Silver and Mallard.

His Coastal Skunks are for fresh fish and are slimmer. His Inland Skunks are quite fat, "for steelhead removed from the salt by time and distance." A typical example:

SKUNK

Tail Red hackle fibers (cock)	**Hackle** Black "cockey" hen for large flies; hen for
Body Black chenille with a built-in silver tinsel rib	small flies (Cockey hen: stiff, fine-stemmed hen hackles)
	Wing Polar bear mask

In recent years Alec has made his own chenille for his Skunks, using eight strands of either peacock herl or ostrich, or a combination of the two. These strands, and a length of oval silver tinsel, are tied in to the underside of the body, secured with hackle pliers, and twisted into a rope until the individual fibers stand out at right angles. The whole lot is then wound on the body. Alec may coat the hook with very thick head cement first, in which case the body is not gripped until the cement has dried. This precaution prevents the body from matting on the wet cement.

A final variation to Alec's remarkable arsenal of Skunks is one he dresses heavily with a body of black seal fur. It is an intensely buggy affair not unlike Jimmy Hunnicutt's Sweet Loretta (see Chapter 38).

Of the homely little Spade, Alec says, "It is the only dark pattern that is the equal of the Skunk. I tie them in more styles and colors than you can count, but bodies of black ostrich and/or peacock dominate."

First, the original as tied by Bob Arnold:

SPADE

Tail Natural brown deer hair	**Hackle** Grizzly
Body Black chenille	

Alec has added guinea, mallard, or teal after the grizzly, or added a tag, or substituted dik-dik, mouse deer, mink, or fitch tail for deer hair to make the Spade more attractive. This led him to two variations that have become well known in the Northwest, the Claret Guinea Spade for failing light, and the Yellow Guinea Spade for bright days. Alec usually uses a long leader, twelve to sixteen feet, a floating line, and leads the fly across soft currents for savage strikes. In faster water he goes to sink tips (Type II), and shorter leaders of seven to nine feet to better keep the fly below the surface.

CLARET GUINEA SPADE

Tag Red Gantron Firefuzz
Tail Dark brown mink or fitchtail
Body Black chenille with a built-in silver tinsel rib. In the example pictured in the fly plate, the body is of a chenille made with black ostrich and oval silver tinsel. *Note:* Mylar tinsel will stretch and break. Flat metal tinsel will cut the body material. Alec's choice is old-fashioned metal oval silver tinsel.

Hackle Grizzly tending toward dry-fly quality followed by a doubled claret grizzly

YELLOW GUINEA SPADE

Substitute a tag of yellow Gantrol Firefuzz. Guinea hackle is yellow, tied as above.

Alec also ties a Fancy Spade in which the body is divided, the aft half thin with peacock herl, the front half plump with black ostrich "rope." If red ostrich is substituted, the fly becomes the Fancy Red Spade. Presumably, other colors could also be substituted.

Jacob's Coat is really another Spade, a "hedge your bets" pattern, says Alec. To obtain the variegated effect, he uses a single strand of peacock herl and six strands of ostrich, all of different colors, usually whatever is on the bench. The hackle is hen grizzly in any color that blends nicely with the body color.

Alec's "Whaka Blonde," a delightful tale of life after death and sentimental madness on the Wenatchee's Orchard Drift, was published in the winter 1986 issue of *Fly Tyer*. The central incongruity in the story was the Whaka Blonde, an all-purple hackle fly he dressed in the inland-river fashion of his Spades and Skunks.

WHAKA BLONDE

Tail Purple cock hackle
Body Purple ostrich with a built-in silver tinsel rib

Hackle Purple hen neck

Shrimp and grub flies for British salmon are on the far end of the aesthetic spectrum, but more functional than the best of Victorian England's full-dressed patterns that primarily simulated one's social station. In Alec's skilled hands, these ties in steelhead colors become a handsome cross-pollination of angling cultures.

The Sauk River Grub and Sauk River Shrimp, winter patterns named for his favorite winter-run river, have, Alec says, "a tremendous track record."

The Shrimp's long tail is missing in the Grub. Save for this difference, the two flies are identical.

SAUK RIVER SHRIMP

Tail Orange bucktail at least as long as the hook
Body Ostrich dyed red and twisted into a rope chenille. Take full turns of orange hackle to evenly segment the body. (The body is not palmered.) Segment the body in four places with each hackle progressively larger.

Hackle Orange, the fifth hackle station in the dressing

Les Johnson

25

LES JOHNSON

N O steelhead held on Graveyard's flats. The fishery technician had said as much while completing his creel census. The pool had been hammered all day, and any steelhead about—likely not many—had certainly been driven off the broad shallows for the security of deeper lies. In the early morning a fish might ghost out of nowhere to hold along the shore of this enormous pool of the Thompson River, but not now.

The spot where Les Johnson and I believed the steelhead would hold was beyond our longest casts and our deepest wade. A few of my casts had sent the end of the fly line through the guides, and even then the fly would barely reach the sweep of deeper current. Control of the forward-taper line was impossible at this distance, and I could not keep the fly swinging properly through the water.

On these fall afternoons, the Thompson at Spences Bridge possesses a grandeur almost unmatched among steelhead rivers. Intense satisfaction with our whereabouts, and no doubt a perverse stubbornness, kept us booming out casts long after the sun had dropped behind a ridge. Les followed me through as the river turned dark, the one time of day when I expect a fish on every cast, when any rise to my fly does not surprise me. Anglers with better sense had long since given up on the water, a show of pessimism that I did not share.

"I'm going to try upstream," Les said. He pulled out and started toward a knot of bait fishermen above the head of the run, where deep water and drop-offs were not for the fly. I thought he could do no worse, and I bade him good luck as he disappeared behind the scrub willow of the shoreline.

311

I grew weary during the last few minutes of twilight and decided to look for Les to see if I could pull him away from the river for a toddy of Drambuie in the comfort of the rustic cabin we shared. Les had also quit the river and was coming my way, his breath condensing in the frosty evening air.

"Hooked the largest steelhead of my life," he exclaimed, and pointed to the water below us. "Right there!"

"My God, Les, how big was that?" Some exceptional steelhead have come his way on the Kispiox; "largest," always relative, has special significance here.

"Big buck took the fly only forty feet or so from shore, jumped, and nearly crossed the river before the fly came out. He had a red stripe down his side this wide." Les held his hands six inches apart. "Twenty-five pounds, anyway."

"That's possible," I said. "Remember the steelhead we saw beached today?" We had observed several anglers staring down at a freshly caught steelhead, a white mound that from a hundred yards away looked like a little beluga whale. One of them had killed the fish, and we heard that it bottomed out their scale, which registered to twenty-eight pounds.

Les's huge trout was still in the river, and their meeting would turn in his head for seasons to come. He doesn't dwell on what causes premature releases. Such thoughts only erode his peace of mind. For this reason I find him a serene angling presence, and an altogether delightful companion.

I first became aware of Les Johnson many years ago, when I was hopelessly addicted to outdoor magazines. I read them all, and Les was hard to miss. He was prolific, interesting, and apparently a maniac for every kind of fishing. Years later, we met when both of us were writing books for the same publisher. His book, *Sea-Run Cutthroat Trout*, Frank Amato Publications, 1979, remains the classic reference on the subject.

Les took early retirement from his job as Director of Advertising and Public Affairs for Weyerhaeuser Company in Federal Way, Washington, to become retail manager of the Eddie Bauer store in San Francisco. He became a regular on the California coastal streams from the Russian to the Navarro, winter steelhead waters, many with estuaries at their mouths.

The estuaries typically are big, sandy pools, and in summer when their rivers are low, sandbars build up and block their low-gradient flows from reaching the ocean. Heavy storms, high tides, and rain-swollen rivers pound away at these barriers all winter, opening the rivers for steelhead to ascend. Fly fishermen have long been aware of these dynamics, and estuary fishing has an enthusiastic following in California.

Often, when kelts reach the estuaries in late winter and spring, their return to the ocean is blocked. As the brackish water of the estuary brightens up their pewter flanks, the steelhead begin to feed actively on shrimp. Estuary anglers have used steelhead patterns suggesting shrimp for generations, though until recently they were, at best, crude imitations.

ESTUARY SHRIMP

Les initially designed his Estuary Shrimp series of steelhead patterns for California rivers, where spawned-out steelhead were actively feeding from January through May. He later used them successfully when fresh fish were entering the estuary. "What you were looking for then was a high tide at two or three in the morning. The fish came in on the tide and held in the estuary as the tide started to drop." He has also fished the flies as winter patterns on the Gualala and Navarro rivers, "down to size 10, when the rivers were very clear." Les found it was hard to hold steelhead on sizes smaller than 10.

Les explains his rationale for the fly's design: "I wanted a lot of movement, a wispy look with plenty of light through it. The estuaries have lots of sunlight, and I wanted to take advantage of that."

Partridge Seastreamer hooks are used when they are available, and Eagle Claw 1197 gold hooks are used for the Tan Estuary Shrimp.

BLACK ESTUARY SHRIMP

Tail Black calf tail and pearl Flashabou, thin
Body Black dubbing, rib with pearl tinsel
Hackle Black, sparse

Wing Black calf tail and pearl Flashabou
Topping A few strands of hot orange calf tail
Head Flame tying thread

ORANGE ESTUARY SHRIMP

Tail Orange calf tail mixed with pearl Flashabou
Body Orange dubbing ribbed with pearl tinsel
Hackle Orange

Wing Pearl calf tail and pearl Flashabou
Topping White polar bear hair
Head Hot orange tying thread

PINK ESTUARY SHRIMP

Tail Pink calf tail and pearl Flashabou
Body Pink dubbing ribbed with pearl tinsel
Hackle Pink

Wing Pink calf tail and pearl Flashabou
Topping White polar bear hair
Head Flame tying thread

GREEN ESTUARY SHRIMP

Tail Lime green calf tail and pearl Flashabou. (You may have to dye white calf tail to get this color. Use Rit or Veniard dye, if available.)
Body Lime green dubbing ribbed with pearl tinsel

Hackle Lime green
Wing Lime green calf tail and pearl Flashabou
Topping White polar bear hair
Head Lime green tying thread

TAN ESTUARY SHRIMP

Tail Brown squirrel tail and pearl Flashabou
Body Gold tinsel
Hackle Grey pheasant rump

Wing Brown squirrel tail and pearl Flashabou
Topping Greenish grey pheasant rump
Head White tying thread

A general order of preference for steelhead is: Black, Orange, Pink, Green, and Tan. The Pink Estuary Shrimp has been very effective for rainbow trout in Alaska's Iliamna region. The Orange Estuary Shrimp incorporates the proven colors of the old Polar Shrimp but with a far more enticing blend of colors, highlighted by the fine Flashabou. The Green Estuary Shrimp is, according to Les, "a much better salmon pattern than a steelhead pattern." Lime green patterns are being used more frequently for steelhead, particularly on interior desert rivers such as Idaho's Clearwater. The Tan Estuary Shrimp is fished when the water is extremely clear, the fly allowed to sink to the bottom and retrieved very slowly. Sometimes the hook digs in a bit on the bottom. Les believes that the fly acts like a ghost shrimp.

In contrast to the Tan Estuary Shrimp, all the other dressings are fished near the surface with slow-sinking shooting heads or cut-up monocore "slime" lines. Spot-casting to cruising steelhead is often possible. Seven- and 8-weight outfits are preferred, fished with nine-foot leaders tapered to six- or eight-pound tippets. Les secures the fly with a Duncan loop.

These graceful flies have been used for both steelhead and salmon in Oregon, Washington, and British Columbia. Les has taken many chinook salmon with the flies, particularly at the mouth of Oregon's Elk River.

Walt Johnson

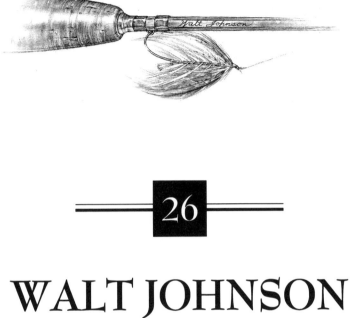

26

WALT JOHNSON

THE story of how steelhead made it into Walt Johnson's consciousness always makes me smile. After fifty years, his recollections are tinged with awe, and I know these events still embody what sea-run rainbows mean to this revered Northwest angler.

"Reuben Helm worked for my father, and he really wasn't a fly fisherman. One day, he wandered into Enos Bradner's Seattle bookstore and heard about Stillaguamish steelhead and the Washington Fly Fishing Club. I think this was early in 1940. The Club was just starting out, and Bradner invited him to join. Well, Reuben told me about this, and he said he wasn't much for joining things, and I said I'd join with him. Neither of us knew anything about steelhead then. It wasn't long after this that some friends invited Reuben to fish the South Fork of the Stilly. The next morning he was on the river kind of dabbing at the water with a fly. He saw this big rock, and when he got his fly behind it, an eight-pound steelhead grabbed the fly and went tearing off downriver. Reuben had one of those automatic reels, and the steelhead wound it up tighter and tighter until the reel exploded. Parts were all over the place. He was in a state of shock."

Reuben's experience so impressed Walt that he visited Bradner to get more information about these steelhead. Bradner would one day become the Outdoor Editor of the Seattle *Times*, and something of an angling institution, but at the time his passion was for steelhead, the fly, and the North Fork of the

Stillaguamish. He toiled for the preservation of this association and, as the newly elected president of the Washington Fly Fishing Club, he was spearheading a drive to have the North Fork restricted to fly-fishing-only during the summer-run steelhead season. It was a revolutionary concept.

Walt was a lowland lake angler and not a fly tyer, but he knew that Dawn Holbrook tied flies professionally in a little space rented in a Seattle barbershop. A quick demonstration from Holbrook was enough. Walt had a few crudely tied Orange Shrimp and his trout gear when he left Seattle for the North Fork.

Drizzly night air was still hanging over Deer Creek Riffle when he reached the tiny valley community of Oso. Walt walked down to the river at the first hint of light and almost immediately hooked a steelhead. When he attempted to strip the line in, the fish broke him off. He tied on a new fly, cast, and a second steelhead broke him off. During the next two hours a third, fourth, fifth, and sixth steelhead had identical sport with him as his hands shook more and more violently. By late morning, Walt was out of flies and nearly out of his mind. Time to go home and regroup! He thought hard on this calamitous morning, and the next week, when a steelhead again rose to his Orange Shrimp, he was ready. "It was not a large fish, only six pounds. I kept telling myself, 'play the fish on the reel,' and 'stay calm!' until I finally got the steelhead on the beach."

Walt and fly fishing would never be the same Three years later, he and his wife, June, had a log cabin built above Elbow Hole on the North Fork. To the front door he nailed a metal casting of a steelhead that read, HAVE ROD WILL FISH. A sign hung from the eaves of the porch carried, on one side, the angler's refrain, YOU SHOULD HAVE BEEN HERE YESTERDAY, and the optimistic promise, JUST WAIT UNTIL TOMORROW, on the other. Here they lived each summer for forty years while Walt became one of fly fishing's most venerated figures (see Chapter 12).

Near the end of World War II, The Charles F. Orvis Company in Manchester, Vermont, announced in magazine advertisements their intention to manufacture fly rods using the same impregnated epoxy process they had employed in the manufacture of bamboo ski poles. Walt wrote the company and was able to purchase an 8-foot 4 1/4-ounce bakelite bamboo rod, the equivalent of today's 6-weight, and "light" by the standards of the day. He took many steelhead with the rod, including some on dry flies presented upstream and drag-free. (Skating and waking dry flies under drag were techniques then unknown in steelheading circles.)

Walt believes it was about 1950 when he first became aware that Lee Wulff was taking Atlantic salmon on a midge rod, an Orvis Deluxe Superfine, six feet long and weighing only 1¾ ounces. (Lee Wulff is pictured playing a salmon with this rod in his classic book, *The Atlantic Salmon*.) Walt wrote Orvis again, explaining that he intended to use the rod for steelhead dry-fly fishing. Duckie Corkran, then the owner of The Orvis Company, wrote back asking if he would consider writing an article for the Orvis catalog. Walt obliged, and the article appeared opposite one by Lee Wulff, each man singing the praises of the midge rod for his steelhead or salmon. Later, Corkran sent Walt Orvis's six-foot one-piece Superfine with his compliments. Using these rods, Walt took many steelhead to nearly twelve pounds on dry flies.

"My goal," Walt told me, "was to catch steelhead on the lightest gear possible." Other bamboo rods followed: the Paul Young Midge, from Detroit, six feet, three inches and 1 3/4 ounces; and his current choice, Heritage Rods' six feet, nine inches and 2 1/2 ounce 3-weight model built by Art Weiler.

Walt Johnson is best known in steelhead fly-fishing circles for developing some of the most beautiful—and most effective—wet flies in all of angling. Readers of *Steelhead Fly Fishing and Flies* may recall Walt's flies pictured on Plate VIII: Lady Coachman, Migrant Orange, Red Shrimp, Thompson River, Indian Summer, and Evening Coachman (Dry). Walt still uses these dressings, with the Migrant Orange his choice for early-season fish, and a relatively new pattern, the Deep Purple Spey, his favorite all-season pattern for a variety of conditions.

DEEP PURPLE SPEY

Hook	Partridge single Wilson (low water, 4X long)	**Body Hackle**	Dark brown Chinese pheasant rump feather tied spey-style
Tail	None	**Hackle**	Deep-purple-dyed hen hackle
Body	Deep purple mohair ribbed with flat silver tinsel	**Wings**	Strips of red golden pheasant body feathers tied close to the body

"The Deep Purple Spey was a derivative of Ken McLeod's Purple Peril. I fished this for years, and it worked real well. Eventually I wanted a fly with a little more action. My first example was a fly I called the Violet Nymph. It had a purple wool body and purple pheasant rump wound on and looked a lot like a Carey Special. The fly was excellent under all water conditions—bright sun, off-colored water—whatever. It seemed to be the ideal steelhead fly. Then, in the early 1960s, I met Syd Glasso on the Stilly, and I saw some of his spey flies. I went over and fished with him on the Olympic Peninsula and decided to try something in the spey version. The red golden pheasant breast feather seemed like an ideal color to use for the wing."

I've been with Walt when he fished this pattern. Describing it is hardly the same as seeing it in action. It possesses tremendous action and high visibility, the bright brick red wing showing beneath the surface for a considerable distance. Walt says the very best brown pheasant rump is found on wild birds. He ties the pattern in sizes 6 to 1, the larger sizes solely for winter steelhead.

GOLDEN SPEY

Hook	Partridge single Wilson (4X long)	**Body Hackle**	White-black heron breast dyed golden olive
Tail	None	**Hackle**	Hen hackle dyed orange toucan
Body	Fluorescent yellow floss overlaid with deep yellow seal's fur dubbing. (*Note*: Angora goat is a satisfactory substitute.) Rib with flat embossed gold tinsel.	**Wing**	Two light brown hackles tied low on the body
		Topping	Golden pheasant crest

ROYAL SPEY

Hook	Partridge single Wilson (4X long)	**Body Hackle**	White-black heron breast feather dyed fluorescent pink and tied spey-fashion around the pink body section
Tail	None		Hackle Fluorescent pink hen hackle
Tag	Silver tinsel overlaid with cerise floss	**Wing**	Two light blue hackles set low on the body
Body	Peacock herl divided by a narrow band of fluorescent pink fire fiber or wool	**Cheeks**	Lady Amherst tippets dyed blue

RED SHRIMP

Hook	Partridge single Wilson (4X long)	**Hackle**	Hen hackle dyed red
Tail	None	**Wing**	Red-dyed hackles set low over the body
Body	Fluorescent orange floss overlaid with red dyed seal fur. Rib with flat silver tinsel.	**Topping**	Golden pheasant crest
Body Hackle	Dark brown Chinese pheasant rump tied spey-style		

The Red Shrimp was the first of his spey series and has been a favorite winter pattern for Walt since the 1960s. The Golden Spey and the Royal Spey are more recent. All four reflect Walt's conviction that steelhead are prone to taking flies that resemble something they have recently been feeding on in the ocean—shrimp, prawns, and the like. He believes that the spey-type flies in particular simulate these forage foods.

He remains equally convinced that water clarity and the color of the stream bottom must be taken into account when selecting a particular fly. This consideration explains the color variations he incorporates into these spey patterns: the darker flies with dense color performing well when the river bottom is dark, the water clear or dingy; the light-colored dressings his choice for low and clear rivers where the gravel bottom is light-colored.

SPRINGER GREEN

Hook	Partridge single Wilson (4X long)	**Hackle**	Orange-toucan-dyed hen neck hackle
Tail	Orange-toucan-dyed hackle fibers	**Throat**	Barred wood-duck breast feather
Tag	Flat silver tinsel overlaid with light fluorescent green floss	**Wing**	Light tan rabbit, fox, or similar fur
Body	Rear half light fluorescent green wool; front half deep fluorescent green. Rib entire body with flat silver tinsel.	**Cheeks**	Highlander-green-dyed hackle points

The Springer Green was intended for early-returning summer-run steelhead, the "springers" of southwest Washington. "I tried to get something that would work on those rivers where you are fishing in that spring light," says Walt. "Green, yellow, and gold all seem to be good colors for a fly in that type of water."

DUSTY COACHMAN

Tag	Fluorescent yellow floss	**Throat**	Widgeon
Tail	Golden pheasant crest	**Wing**	Yellow or beige Antron
Body	Fluorescent yellow wool dividing ostrich dyed gold	**Topping**	Golden pheasant crest

"Years ago we used an awful lot of yellow on the Stilly, the Yellow Hammer, for example. Of course Al (Knudson) fished his Spider. I liked yellow, especially in the late spring and early summer. The color is more obscure and not so gaudy as the other steelhead colors."

SPECTRAL SPIDER

Hook	Partridge single Wilson (4X long)	**Hackle**	Several wraps of stiff grizzly before over-wrapping spider-fashion with barred mallard flank that extends to the end of the body
Tail	Fluorescent yellow Antron nylon fibers or any acrylic fake fur		
Body	Pearlescent mylar ribbed with flat silver tinsel	**Cheeks**	Blue chatterer or kingfisher-blue back feathers
Wings	Layered, from the bottom: cerise, orange, green, and blue Antron nylon in very small bunches. One cream badger hackle is set lengthwise down the hook shank on each side.		

Dry fly alternate: Substitute a long golden pheasant crest for the tail and provide extra wraps of grizzly hackle.

Preston J. Jennings, author of the Derrydale classic, *A Book of Trout Flies*, expressed great interest in the role light refraction plays in the vision of trout. The prismatic effect water can have on sunlight was duplicated in the rainbow-hued series of streamers he developed during the 1930s. The Iris Series, the Lady, Lord, Murky, and Dark, supposedly matched the seasons from spring through winter. The Lord Iris, in particular, has been popular among steelhead fly fishers willing to master the details of its complicated construction.

Walt found his inspiration for the Spectral Spider in Jennings's Lord Iris, but the subtle flash and movement of Antron nylon incorporated into the carefully stacked wing, and the veiling of the barred mallard, produce a far more lifelike baitfish imitation. It was originally intended for sea-run cutthroat, he told me, designed to be stripped back on the swing. (Walt holds the unofficial state record, a sea-run cutthroat of five pounds, twelve ounces caught on October 13, 1972.) "The first time I ever fished the pattern, those big cutthroat wouldn't leave it alone. They would come out of the brush piles and just nail it. The beauty of it was that I could fish it dry, just under the surface, or sunk."

During a fall cutthroat outing, Walt discovered that the Spectral Spider also attracted steelhead. "I was casting on this hole above town, where I normally expect to find a cutthroat, and as I started stripping it in, this steelhead—I bet this thing would have gone eighteen or twenty pounds—came out of there, and grabbed that fly, and started down the river." After a long and merry chase, the fish was lost when the light leader parted. "It took me a couple of months to get over that," said Walt. He's been using the Spectral Spider on summer-run steelhead ever since.

DAMP DRAKE (Dry)

Hook 4 to 10 fine-wire
Tail Grizzly hackle fibers

Body Yellow polypropylene or wool
Hackle Grizzly. Overwrap with drake mallard

This is basically the Yellow Spider, a wet fly developed by the late Al Knudson, but with a heavy underwrap of grizzly hackle and a body of polypropylene. As its name suggests, the fly rides very low—damp—in the water.

YELLOW ANT (Dry)

Hook Size 8 fine-wire
Tail Strands of mottled brown deer body hair
Body Fluorescent yellow fire fiber or wool

Hackle Light brown
Wings Two light hackle tips tied back to back

For many years the Yellow Ant has been Walt's first choice when dead-drifting a dry fly. He feels it is an especially good choice for the middle of the day in bright light. He fishes both dry flies on a seven-and-a-half-foot leader tapering to a four-pound test tippet.

Randall Kaufmann

27

RANDALL KAUFMANN

RANDALL and I stood in the Queets River opposite where it joins the Clearwater. The southerly rain that swept in from the ocean during the early morning hours had left behind a blustery March day and a badly muddied Clearwater. The Queets, its headwaters protected in Olympic National Park, ran clear until this meeting. Now, along its southern shore, roiled currents fanned out to discolor the Queets and disguised the many gill nets set at tidewater.

Clay Butler, our friend from the Quinault Indian Reservation, explained how we might fish the long pool. "The steelhead will hold right to the edge of the Clearwater's flow. They are all through the run, though. Best to find them from there, down." He pointed to the ledge line where the rivers joined.

"Which part do you like?" asked Randall.

"I don't care," I said with a shrug. This was all virgin water, reservation water where only the nets were fishing. We were well below where the river was open to the public. When Randall insisted I choose my water, I waded downstream to fish below the confluence. I was soon reaching hard for the midriver crease of holding water and barely able to keep my balance in the heavy currents.

From time to time I looked upriver to watch as Randall picked his way to the very top of the run, above the confluence, in water barely knee-deep. This was a good place to start fishing if nothing had moved over the water to startle a fish in the shallow lies. I would have thought better of his prospects if it had been first light, when a steelhead could still feel secure with only its nose beneath a saucer-sized piece of frothy turbulence.

I grew discontented with the water before me. The currents were too swift for even the Teeny line, and I couldn't imagine a steelhead so determined that it would run my fly down through any part of the drift and swing. Randall's faint cry broke through my feckless mood. His rod arm was raised high as the steelhead beat a quicksilver path from the top-end shallows. I pulled out and jogged up the bar to share in his good fortune, a twelve-pound hen only hours from the ocean. Randall's touch was deft and sure, the steelhead's labors strong and not extended once it was in the shallows. Such a trout is all too rare, and we admired her beauty.

I've known Randall and his brother, Lance, for more than twenty years. When I first met the pair, they operated a tiny fly shop in Tigard, Oregon, their own version of a third-world sweatshop. Lance tended the merchandise and Randall tied the flies they sold. Even today, Randall describes fly tying as "a part-time hobby and full-time disease." Soon their mother, Oda Kaufmann, was doing shipping and office work, and the business began taking off. Today they manage three Kaufmann Streamborn fly-fishing stores, a retail mail-order business (their catalog is a great read), and Kaufmann's Fly Fishing Expeditions, Inc., which books anglers for fly-fishing adventures in every corner of the world. As Randall cradled the steelhead for a photograph, his deep tan reminded me that only the week before he had been fishing for bonefish at Los Roques, Venezuela, with Fred Arbona. His routine includes all manner of exotic destinations. Our conversations have taken me from Iceland to Alaska, from South America to New Zealand. Randall is equally at home on spring creeks and wind-swept bocas. As much as anyone I know, he personifies the new breed of international angler.

I remember seeing the very rough draft of Randall's *American Nymph Fly Tying Manual*, and wondering about his new choice of careers. Of course, the book was a huge success, and others soon followed, including *Lake Fishing with A Fly*, written with Ron Cordes, *Fly Tyers Nymph Manual* and *Tying Dry Flies*.

I think the Deschutes is Randall's first love among rivers because it so appeals to his eclectic tastes. The redside rainbow offers all the challenges of trout in an arena of great hatches; the steelhead is a higher-voltage proposition and more a mystery of location. Randall, an angler-entomologist without peer, is an expert steelhead fly fisherman because he reads water so well. The river balances his angling interests as no other.

In 1979, he and Lance purchased a house on the Deschutes River for their fly-fishing school, and to accommodate their guides and clients returning from day-long floats. Randall frequently stays at the Maupin residence, joins in the floats, and shares his experiments in steelhead fly design. Dressings found to be especially effective are marketed commercially. These experiments have resulted in a series of extremely effective dark steelhead patterns that are now popular far beyond their Deschutes origins.

Randall Kaufmann's comments follow each fly pattern.

FREIGHT TRAIN

Tail Purple hackle fibers
Body Divided into three equal parts from the tail forward: fluorescent flame wool, fluorescent red wool, and black chenille. Rib entire body with silver tinsel. (The fly is very effective if purple chenille is substituted for the black chenille.)

Hackle Purple
Wing White calf tail

"During the 1970s and early 1980s, I was fortunate to spend most summers fishing the Deschutes. When we commenced our fishing schools at Maupin, the Deschutes became, more or less, my summer residence.

"Early-arriving steelhead are as bright and as hard as Carson City silver dollars, and it was never difficult to convince visiting anglers to chase steelhead in lieu of trout. With a steady flow of eager anglers, it was easy to 'test' many new patterns and cover a great deal of unknown water. I was fishing flies that incorporated colors of the most productive patterns and finally ended up with a favorite combination, but it didn't have a name. One hot, windless summer evening, I was fishing a long riffle when a freight train rounded the bend. My attentions were caught up in the loud rumbling of the diesel engine, and as I watched the train roll up the canyon, the powerful pull of a heavy steelhead jolted me back to the river. The fish ran upstream much like the freight train, and I had a name for the fly. The Freight Train has since become our most popular steelhead pattern; it is a real favorite with Deschutes anglers."

KRYSTAL FLASH FREIGHT TRAIN

Same as the original in all respects, except for a wing, equally divided, of pearl over blue Krystal Flash.

"During the mid-1980s, highly reflective materials came into vogue in steelhead flies, the new patterns resembling the glitzy neon marquees in Vegas. These materials caught on, and soon even the old standards were being dressed in the new flashy fashion.

"The Krystal Flash Freight Train is exactly like the Freight Train, except for a wing equally divided of pearl over blue Krystal Flash. The iridescent effect attracts fish from a greater distance and is especially useful in off-color conditions.

"The White River originates from the White River glacier on Mt. Hood, and empties into the Deschutes a few miles below Maupin. During exceptionally hot weather, the White River will carry a heavy load of glacial silt, which can color the Deschutes murky white. The Krystal Flash Freight Train is especially productive during such times. I also like to fish it over hard-fished steelhead that have 'seen it all.'"

SIGNAL LIGHT

Tail Purple hackle fibers
Butt Fluorescent red fuzzy wool
Body Divided into thirds: flame fuzzy wool, fluorescent green fuzzy wool, and black chenille. Rib entire body with oval silver tinsel.

Hackle Purple
Wing Underwing, three to five strands each of pearl, wine, lime green and blue Krystal Flash; overwing, black marabou

"At present, this is my favorite steelhead pattern. I find myself knotting it onto my leader on legendary steelhead rivers from Oregon to British Columbia. I vary the size according to conditions, generally preferring a larger fly for big water, big fish; smaller sizes for smaller water and smaller fish. It can be weighted and fished deep, weighted and fished slightly subsurface in fast water, or dressed sparse for a greased-line or "damp" presentation. The marabou wing is a deviation from the classic style fly, but creates excellent animation, even in slower currents. I believe this to be an important factor in triggering steelhead to grab the fly. Good color visibility further enhances the Signal Light. I think it is an excellent pattern under all situations. The color combination reminded me of the signal lights, which are spaced out on the Deschutes railroad tracks, hence the fly's name."

PURPLE FLASH

Tail Purple hackle fibers
Body Purple chenille ribbed with oval silver tinsel
Hackle Purple

Wing Underwing, two to five strands each of wine, pearl, lime green and purple Krystal Flash; overwing, purple marabou

"This pattern is a take-off on the Purple Marabou and Street Walker patterns. The marabou and Krystal Flash of the wing meld together nicely, creating animation and attractability. If fishing a dropper-fly setup, I like to weight this fly slightly and fish it on the point, thus keeping the fly just subsurface on the swing. The dropper fly will often be selected to skate on the surface, allowing the angler to cover two mediums, surface and subsurface, on the same cast. Also, I will select two different colored patterns, thus offering more color choices."

FERRY CANYON

Tail Purple hackle fibers
Butt Fluorescent flame (fire orange) fuzzy wool
Body Purple chenille ribbed with oval silver tinsel

Hackle Purple
Wing Underwing, two to five strands of wine, pearl, red, and blue Krystal Flash; overwing, purple marabou

"The Ferry Canyon area of the Deschutes River has long boulder-filled runs that I fish early in the season with this pattern. The Purple Peril has been somewhat popular on the Deschutes for years. The Ferry Canyon has these basic colors, with the added kick of a fluorescent butt. It has lots of animation and visibility and is especially useful in off-colored water. Purple, like black, offers consistent visibility under low light."

COAL CAR

Tail Black hackle fibers
Body Rear half evenly divided, fluorescent orange and flame (fire orange) fuzzy wool, balance black chenille. Rib entire body with narrow oval silver tinsel

Hackle Black
Wing Black squirrel tail; add a few strands of black Krystal Klash as an underwing

"Often the most productive and pleasant time on the water is after evening shadows have faded from purple to near black. The warm evenings of the east slope desert country always seem to lend themselves to one last cast. During such times I switch to a black fly, because it is more easily seen by the steelhead. Hold a light-wing or light-colored fly up to the evening sky, and you will notice that the dark fly offers a more solid silhouette. It was for this reason that I converted the Freight Train into a Coal Car. Don't be afraid to fish a larger-than-usual fly after dark, as it too will be more easily located."

FLAT CAR

Tail Black hackle fibers
Butt Fluorescent green wool
Body Black chenille. Rib entire body with narrow oval silver tinsel

Hackle Black
Wing Black marabou mixed with a few strands of black and pearl Krystal Flash

"A fly for the last light of day when the strongest possible silhouette is desirable," says Randall. Inspired by the Green-Butt Skunk, this most recent dressing (1989) is especially effective as a reduced low-water dressing. "Then I tie it with a tag of fluorescent green floss over an underbody of flat silver tinsel, and dub in a body of black seal."

Author's Note: My usual habit is to underdress summer patterns for greased work, converting chenille-bodied flies to dressings with thinner bodies of dubbing. This is not simply a matter of taste. I believe the result is more nymphlike, certainly "buggier" when viewed from any angle, especially from below, and is easier to control for depth placement. If the pattern is dark—purple, black, grizzly—so much the better. I tend to take flies with split, two-part bodies, and tie in the bright aft section as a small tag, but always with an underwrap of silver tinsel so that the tag glows brightly when wet. If the fly has a three-part body, the aft-most section becomes the tag, the second section is no more than one-third of the body, while the balance (black or purple) is usually dubbed. I will sometimes palmer this forward section with dyed pheasant rump. I often reduce the Krystal Flash to a few strands or eliminate it altogether, and I often substitute black squirrel tail for black marabou, because it is more durable. I have found that Randall's dark patterns invite this sort of tinkering for low-water conditions like no other series in steelheading.

Harry Lemire

28

HARRY LEMIRE

I had just stepped into the very top end of Rabbit when Bobby Cunningham's graceful freighter jet broke through the hot glare of the afternoon tailout. He motored up the long Dean River pool and held the boat in the currents well below the swing of my fly, an invitation for me to catch up on river gossip and discover how friends of mine had fared below. I reeled in to join him.

"Griz on the beach down there," he said "I made some noise and sent it off into the bush."

"I'll keep an eye out." Grizzly bears are in the Dean watershed, there to mind their own business and fuel campfire horror stories. I had never heard of a serious confrontation. Bobby also told me of a steelhead caught earlier in the month that was twenty-seven pounds and forty inches, and I asked him about the ups and downs of the run.

"The fishing a couple of weeks ago was plenty hot," he said.

"So I heard. The commercial fishing strike helped. This week has been pretty fair."

"Did you know Lemire was here then? There were so many steelhead he cut the point off his flies. Just got a jump and run out of them!"

"That sounds like Harry!" I said.

Harry Lemire's recreation is fly fishing in all of its many facets. How a new hybrid line fishes, a new fly swims, or a prototype rod casts are questions he studies intensely. The far narrower demands of quantity have never held his interest, and I have never heard him describe a trip in terms of numbers of steelhead. When Bobby opened the throttle and kicked the boat around for the bottom end of the pool, I was thinking about Harry, a bracing pick-me-up that provided a new sense of discipline.

There is no more complete steelhead fly fisherman, but Harry so understates his own genius that he seems to succeed with mirrors and magic. He does not write, make videos, operate a fly-fishing store, guide, or otherwise commercially indulge his love for the sport. He is a famous angler because of his creative skills at tying a fly and then presenting it. I've known him for many years, and I never cease to marvel over the travels of his imagination.

How would Harry have fished my water? Certainly, it would be a dignified exhibition of grace and equanimity. I imagined the scene. I saw him picking a good-size wet fly, his Green-Butt Spey, to swing in the heavy currents before finding a Fall Caddis more ideal where the currents eased, and then thinking the Grease Liner a delicious offering on the glassy sweep of tailout. I would gladly have quit the pool to watch such a show!

Harry Lemire has been coming to the Dean each year since 1971. Maybe he has missed a year or two, but he has long since become a revered fixture on the river. When I first met him, he was already making the grueling annual drive through the Chilcotin, the "Freedom Road," from Williams Lake to Bella Coola, for the short charter flight into the Dean. Harry returned with stories of twenty-pound steelhead on dry flies, tales from steelheading's outback that left the rest of us dazzled. Now, Buzz Fiorini flies Harry, and often Bob Stroebel, in his Cessna 185 floatplane to either Shillings or Victoria Drift. The three fish together for a week, and this is the high point of Harry's angling year.

He told me that his brother had introduced him to fly fishing, "the only way I've ever fished," he says, when they were kids living in Woonsocket, Rhode Island. Harry joined the Air Force and was stationed in nearby Cape Cod when he met Marlene Barnhart, his wife-to-be, a Wenatchee, Washington, girl also serving in the Air Force. After leaving the service, the couple made a visit to Wenatchee to meet her parents. When their short visit lasted three months, Harry got a job with Boeing, and they moved to West Seattle. It was 1957, and steelhead fly fishing was still an eccentric pastime. He recalls:

I had heard about steelhead back home. When I came out here, I was really going to find out about the steelhead, and I wanted to talk with some steelhead fly fishermen, but you know, you would hear names. There's a guy by the name of Wes Drain, or Walt Johnson, or Syd Glasso. But these guys were like ghosts. You'd hear the name but you'd never meet the person. Finally, I went into Roy Patrick's fly shop in North Seattle, and there I started meeting and talking to people who were steelhead fly fishermen. That was great. There were not very many of them.

Harry was soon a regular on the Skagit, Stillaguamish, and Skykomish rivers. The Green became his home river when he moved out of the city to the little town of Black Diamond. The Kalama and other Columbia River tributaries helped fill out the seasons. The sport's legends were traveling to the Skeena country, and Harry joined them in 1965. He divided his time between chasing big steelhead in the Kispiox and dry-fly fishing the Morice, but by 1970 the crowds and boats were too much, and his annual vacation was devoted to the Dean. This has always been an August trip, one part of a complicated annual steelhead circuit.

Harry has been tying his own flies for as long as he's been fishing for steelhead. Among the different patterns he has used, many are now nearly forgotten, some have survived after thirty years of refinement, as his tastes changed and his skills sharpened, and a couple have become standards in steelheading. All are quite traditional, even Old World. He takes little pleasure in flies that resemble nothing in life. He will not add Krystal Flash or Flashabou to a dressing. He says: "I try to tie my flies with natural materials that have life in them. I want the flies to move, act alive. I use squirrel, long, webby hackle, and when you have a fly like that and *you swim it*, it is moving all the time."

GREEN BUTT SPEY

Hook Partridge low water, 2/0–6

Butt Fluorescent chartreuse floss over flat silver tinsel. Rib with three turns of oval silver tinsel. Apply three coats of colorless nail polish.

Tail Golden pheasant crest feather tied with curve pointing down

Body Black tying thread ribbed with flat silver tinsel and palmered with spun black rabbit between rib wraps

Hackle Gadwall or teal, one turn only

Wing Gadwall over grey squirrel tail

Eyes Matching pair of quail flank feathers

Harry's assessment: "The combination of rabbit and gadwall for lifelike movement, and a shiny green butt for attraction, has made this fly very productive for me for both summer and winter fish, with either wet or dry lines."

The key to the fly's effectiveness is the thin body overwrapped with spun rabbit, a method of using this material not found in any other steelhead pattern. The tying technique provides plenty of denseness without the bulk of rabbit-strip leeches or matukas. Even the lightest currents set the fur in motion and make the fly come alive. This particular pattern, at once nymphlike and graceful, certainly invites color variations.

First used in 1985, the Green-Butt Spey is now one of Lemire's most dependable dressings, especially favored for use on the Thompson, Clearwater, and Snake rivers.

LEMIRE'S WINTER FLY

Hook Partridge single salmon 2/0–4

Tip Flat silver tinsel

Tail Salmon and red hackle fibers

Body Salmon-colored dubbing ribbed with medium flat silver tinsel under thin red embossed tinsel. (*Note*: It may be necessary to shop in the notions department for the red tinsel.)

Hackle Salmon colored, long and soft

Wing White polar bear or goat, sparse

Head Red tying thread

"I dislike using lure or bait-type flies," says Harry, "but with a lot of winter conditions, it is necessary." This is his single "bright" pattern for off-colored winter water, to my eye one of the most elegant in the sport. He adds: "When conditions dictate, I fish this fly with a deep, slow, dead drift."

FALL CADDIS

Hook Partridge Wilson size 4–8

Body Burnt orange dubbing ribbed with bronze mylar or bronze wire

Underwing Gray squirrel tail

OverWing Game-hen hackles tented over the squirrel wing

Hackle and Head Moose body hair. Hackle and head are formed by spinning moose body hair and trimming away to form a bullet-shaped head that is then trimmed flat on top and bottom and cemented to keep its shape.

The Fall Caddis, a low-riding waking pattern, was first tied for the upper Green River in 1984. As the name implies, it suggests the orange-bodied caddis found on many steelhead rivers in the fall. It is a clever tie, the head trimmed to leave a few hairs streaming over the entire fly, the resulting silhouette remarkably lifelike. Harry normally does not fish it with a hitch, and from time to time the fly will drop below the surface film. Burnt orange is his favorite clear-water color to incorporate into waking dries, but he will tie the Fall Caddis in a variety of colors.

Several years ago, Harry was fishing the Thompson River below the old bridge with a series of submerged pilings below him, when he rose a steelhead twice. The buck came back for the fly a third time. "It was," said Harry, "like a submarine pulling out." He almost reached the pilings on the first run, but Harry was able to ease him back and walk him downstream past the pilings. "I mesmerized him," he says. The struggle continued to take both fish and angler downriver until Harry thought the next bridge would claim his prize. But the fishing gods were smiling that day. "I could not believe the size of him. His head was huge." This was the largest steelhead Harry had seen in thirty years of fly fishing. Before its release, careful measurements were taken. The steelhead was forty-one inches long and had a *twenty-six-inch girth!* This works out to a little more than thirty-six pounds!

THOMPSON RIVER CADDIS

Hook Partridge low water, size 2–6
Body Insect green dubbing ribbed with black tying thread

Wing Green-phase pheasant back feather over a small bunch of pheasant rump feathers
Hackle and Head See Fall Caddis, above

Harry describes this damp pattern as "a simple-to-tie caddis imitation and a favorite of mine." He fishes it greased-line, but not with a Portland hitch, allowing the fly to mix in the surface film. Of course, a hitch could be used to keep the fly up.

GREASE LINER

Hook Partridge Wilson, size 4–8 for a dry fly, size 2–8 low water for a waking fly
Thread Black Nymo, size A
Tail Fine chestnut colored deer body hair
Body Black dubbing, or any color to match egg-laying caddis in the area fished

Hackle Grizzly, sparse and tied wet
Wing and Head Body length same as tail. Head is formed by allowing 3/16 inch of wing material to extend past two tight overlapping wraps of tying thread. Whip-finish to complete.

In 1962, Harry was fishing the mouth of the Wenatchee River when a steelhead boiled behind his dry fly. Additional casts wouldn't bring the fish back. While resting the steelhead, Harry picked through his box and tied on a no-name dark dry fly with hackle crushed across the bottom from improper storage. He was still unable to move the steelhead, until he inadvertantly raised his rod tip and dragged the fly across the surface. The steelhead lunged, and for a moment was hooked.

That fish was gone, but it did get me thinking about a new way of dry-fly presentation for steelhead. Since then, I've found that a dry fly that is allowed to swing on a tight line from the center of the drift into shore is just as likely to raise a fish as a drag-free drift, and possibly more so.

It was at that time I started designing a fly that would swim along the top of the water without biting into it and being pulled under. In reality, it's like fishing the greased-line method with a dry fly.

After some trial and error, I came up with a fly designed to sit up on the water, causing a slight depression and providing a noticeable silhouette for a drag-free drift. When the fly line begins to belly from the current and the fly begins to be pulled, the butt ends of the wing will cause a resistance against the water, and the fly will wobble and swim with more life than usual.

Thus was born the Grease Liner, first waking dry specifically designed for steelhead. It remains as popular as ever, and would fill most lists of "Ten Best Steelhead Flies." Harry fishes it with a black body on rivers that usually run with some color, such as the Dean, and with a burnt-orange body on clear running waters, for example the Thompson, Green, and Morice.

LEMIRE'S IRRESISTIBLE

Hook Partridge Wilson, size 4–8
Tail Fine black deer body hair
Body Dyed-black deer body hair, spun and trimmed to shape

Wing Fine black deer body hair tied upright
Hackle Black saddle

Lemire's note: Trim the hackle and body hair flat. This allows hackle, body, and tail to sit flatly on the surface film, giving the fish a good silhouette of the fly.

This high-floating skater pattern, trimmed to maintain tension with the surface film and provide a better silhouette, has been a special favorite of Harry's since he took a twenty-three-pound Dean River buck with it in 1973. (The details of this catch are described in *Steelhead Fly Fishing and Flies*.)

HARRY KARI BUCKTAIL

Hook Size 1–8
Tail Red hackle fluff from butt end of hackle
Body Yellow and black chenille, yellow in back of black, wrapping simultaneously

Hackle Pheasant back, sparse
Wing Black bear

The Harry Kari Nymph was originated in 1957 for trout, and was tied on a 3X long #6 hook. The fly was extremely effective when twitched while drifting in a boat. Later a black bear wing was added and then shortened to regular length for use on summer and fall steelhead. At that time it was re-named the Harry Kari Bucktail.

SQUIRREL AND TEAL

Hook Low water, size 2–6
Tip Oval gold tinsel
Tail Golden pheasant crest feather
Body Dark grey dubbing ribbed with oval gold tinsel

Hackle Blue dun tied as a beard
Wing Grey squirrel with teal tented over and combed out
Cheeks Jungle cock (optional)

Harry calls the Squirrel and Teal "a neat little fly that doesn't frighten or startle fish in low, clear water." And he adds: "Expect a natural take, not a smashing strike." If fishing the fly on the upper Green, he will likely be casting an eight-and-a-half-foot cane rod and an all-wood Nottingham fly reel. The aesthetics of wood glowing beneath coats of varnish is in keeping with this most elegant of steelhead patterns.

BLACK DIAMOND

Hook Size 1–8
Tip Flat silver tinsel
Body Black dubbing ribbed with flat silver tinsel
Hackle Guinea hen tied as a beard

Underwing Four peacock-sword fibers
Overwing Guinea hen and grey squirrel, mixed
Cheek Jungle cock (optional)

When jungle cock is not used, hackle with one complete turn of guinea hen.

This pattern, named for the little coal town in Washington where the Lemires make their home, has been a favorite of his since its development in 1963. He says, "where grease-lining, a little black bug is required, especially during the summer and fall."

I have long favored black and guinea for shallow tailouts when the light is low. The compact and classically beautiful Black Diamond fills that need perfectly.

GOLDEN EDGE YELLOW

Hook	Size 1-6	**Hackle**	Guinea hen tied as a beard
Thread	Yellow	**Wing**	Bronze mallard and gray squirrel, mixed
Tip	Flat silver tinsel	**Topping**	Golden pheasant crest
Tail	Golden pheasant crest	**Cheek**	Jungle cock (optional)
Body	Yellow dubbing ribbed with flat silver tinsel	**Head**	Yellow tying thread

GOLDEN EDGE ORANGE

Identical to the Golden Edge Yellow except for orange thread, head, and body.

The Golden Edge patterns, first appearing in 1970 (yellow), and 1971 (orange), remain the backbone of Harry's wet-fly fishing. The smaller sizes are used when greased-line fishing, the largest for winter fish, when fishing with sink-tip lines or fast-sinking heads.

LISA BELL

Hook	Size 1–6	**Hackle**	Hungarian partridge tied as a beard
Thread	Red	**Wing**	Gray squirrel and teal tented over
Tip	Flat silver tinsel	**Cheeks**	Jungle cock (optional)
Body	Red dubbing ribbed with flat silver tinsel		

The Lisa Bell, most frequently a clear-water winter fly, reminds me of the English lake and sea trout patterns such as the Peter Ross or Teal and Red.

STEELHEAD SCULPIN

Hook	Size 1–4	**Beard**	Pine squirrel, sparse
Body	Grey wool. Rib with pearl mylar tinsel and over-rib with copper wire. The copper ribbing can be wound *counter* to the mylar ribbing to keep the ribbing from being torn loose.	**Cheeks**	Red wool
		Head	Deer body hair. Trim to a flat shovel shape.
Matuka Wing	Three "ratty" badger or grizzly neck hackles all flowing the same direction. The current will hit this bend and cause the fly to wobble.	**Top of Head**	Small bunch of fine black bucktail

One April, several years ago, I was camped at the Skagit River's Steelhead Park. I had heard that Harry and Jimmy Green were on the river too, working their double-handed rods, and taking a few late-winter steelhead. I had just ordered one of these long rods and was hoping to get some advice on its use. As luck would have it, I awoke one morning to find Harry already fishing the camp water. With balletic moves, he was launching a series of hundred-foot double-speys from the wooded shore. Only the high-wind sound of the sixteen-foot rod sweeping through the air told of the explosion of energy taking place. I watched, fascinated. When he quit the pool, I joined him, Green, and John Farrar for a day on the water below the confluence of the Sauk.

Harry was fishing the most nondescript winter fly I'd ever seen. He had been on the river for several days and all his steelhead had come to it. Did it have a name? I asked. Could he give me the recipe? Is it fished in a special way? Harry laughed. "Oh, it's still in research and development!" he said.

Two years later, he had only unabashed enthusiasm for the pattern, which now had a name. Harry fishes the Steelhead Sculpin throughout the year on both floating and sinking lines. "I fish it right in the surface film, and when the fish comes, you see the boil. I make one mend and then swim it by, allowing drag to set up in the line and pull the fly. In the winter I'm using heads, but I'm swimming it the same way. That's normally how I present a fly."

When fishing those winter heads, Harry makes his initial mend to straighten the head around, and then slips line to give the head time to sink. When the desired depth has been reached, he tightens and swims the fly around.

Mike Maxwell

29

MIKE MAXWELL

NEAR the end of the first winter I fished a two-handed rod, I was still unable to handle it skillfully enough to justify its use. Some days, the rhythm of my overhead casting was satisfactory enough, but my spey casts, both single and double, were pretty sorry. My ignorance was producing only bad habits. To remedy the situation, I visited Mike and Denise Maxwell at their shop, Gold-N-West Flyfishers, in Vancouver, British Columbia.

Despite all the recent ballyhoo in steelheading over two-handed rods, very little instruction regarding their proper use has been available. But Mike produced a one-hour video and wrote an exhaustive instruction manual on the subject. These two items, combined with Mike's "hands on" instruction, remained the most complete course of its kind in the Northwest—and probably in North America. He does not leave the subject at that. Mike builds what many anglers consider the finest spey-casting two-handed rods available anywhere. He has also engineered his own hybrid sink-tip lines, which are superior to any spey-casting lines currently marketed.

Our time together at the casting pond led me to join him and Denise on the Bulkley River. Here they have a second home and operate The Maxwell's Bulkley River Steelhead Guide Service, a summer steelhead camp specializing in dry-fly fishing. Mike provides casting and dry-fly fishing lessons in this natural setting, but only Denise may guide. She is a Canadian citizen; Mike continues to maintain his British citizenship. To my knowledge, she is the only woman licensed to guide for steelhead in British Columbia.

Though born in India, the son of a professional soldier, Mike grew up in southwest England, an area of chalk streams and rich angling traditions. His early fishing consisted of poaching on the River Test with the proverbial bent pin and worm. Gamekeepers kept dragging him home, until one day his irate father turned his angling education over to a local blacksmith who was both a skilled fly fisherman and a local tackle maker. "What followed," says Denise, "was a complete grounding in angling, from still-water fishing with float and bait, to spey-casting with a double-hand rod."

That was fifty years ago. When this former tank commander and structural engineer emigrated to Canada, his keen interest in fly fishing was rekindled. There were blue ribbon trout streams, Kamloops lakes, and salmon and steelhead streams of the coast. Steelhead soon became central to his angling interests.

After glumly watching the Kispiox go out one day some years ago, Mike retreated to the Bulkley River. As was the custom, he fished big wet flies with a sinking line. During a midday lunch break, he and his companions noticed a steelhead resting in four feet of water. As they studied the fish, it rose to sip in a small caddisfly. It repeated the performance again and again. They had absolutely no doubt; the steelhead was actively feeding.

This incident might have become only a curiosity in Mike's memory save for an experience the following spring. He returned to the Bulkley in search of resident trout and found only parr and smolts. Just as significantly, the river teemed with stoneflies, the clumsy insects often crashing into the river. When this happened, immature steelhead and salmon would dash for the stonefly, which was often scarcely smaller than the little fish. The steelhead usually arrived first and took it down.

Mike was familiar with stoneflies, having spent many springs in Montana, where a very rough delivery with a Sofa Pillow would create enough surface disturbance to excite big browns.

Late that summer, Mike noticed a man on the Bulkley River who was fly fishing with what looked like a ball of fur. On each cast, the fly was slapped down on the water and allowed to drag. To Mike's surprise, the man rose a steelhead. A second steelhead followed. Mike thought the man was trying to imitate a stonefly, but he incorrectly reasoned that a dead drift would accomplish infinitely more. He fished along with the angler with very discouraging results. Mike thought that perhaps the action of the fly was at the heart of the matter. It did not seem possible for these steelhead to be so residential in character, but Mike could reason no other explanation. To better understand what was required, he carefully noted the habits of the female stonefly.

The stonefly was *Acroneuria abnormus*, brownish and, at one and a half inches long, only slightly smaller than the huge *Pteronarcys californica* of salmon-fly fame. The female, fluttering constantly over the water on two sets of wings, releases her eggs by dipping the tip of her abdomen just below the surface. The current frequently catches and rolls her under the water. When she reappears, wind may blow her across stream, even upstream. This activity triggers a feeding response among the premigrant steelhead in the spring, an identical response to that produced by the dry-fly imitation when it is properly fished over adult steelhead in the fall.

Since making these observations, Mike has worked at refining both the dressing imitating *Acroneuria abnormus*, and the manner in which it is fished. He has codified both. His instructions for the dressing and how it is fished are very specific and detailed.

PRESENTATION

Mike divides the presentation sequence into three parts: mend and feed, swing, and retrieve.

He begins his fishing by wading into the river to barely above his ankles, in order to avoid casting his fly beyond holding steelhead. Fly line is stripped off the reel until fifty feet are beyond the rod tip—thirty feet to be cast and twenty feet to be held in reserve. The cast is made, followed immediately by a back-mend and a release of part of the line. The fly makes a short dead drift and then comes

TELKWA STONEFLY (Dry)

Hook Wilson by Partridge (#4) or Tiemco 8089 (#2 or #4), a "stinger" style hook used for surface bass flies. The Tiemco hook is considerably heavier, but much stronger and, unlike the Wilson, will not straighten out on large fish.

Body and Tail Use golden-colored A rod-wrapping thread throughout the tying sequence. Tie in one-quarter inch from head a one- quarter-inch bunch of moose body hair and bind down by wrapping to the bend of the hook and spacing the wraps to give the body a segmented appearance. Throw a loop of thread around the body about one-eighth of an inch past the hook bend and pull in the direction of the tail as tension is applied. Take fly out of the vise, turn upside down, and take several additional turns. Trim body evenly. Apply a very small portion of dark brown dubbing to the waxed thread. Any good seal imitation will do. Mike uses Imiseal, a Canadian product. Wrap dubbing around the very end of the body. This bump of dubbing represents the egg sac. Perhaps more important, it provides additional flotation, which is necessary when using the heavier Tiemco hook. Tie in the split tail of dark brown goose quill. The bump of dubbing keeps the goose quill spread nicely. Wind the thread forward over the previous wraps and take a number of wraps forward of the body to build up a base for the head.

Wing Mike likes to use light elk on bright days and dark elk for overcast days and evening fishing. Cut a one-quarter-inch bunch of elk body fur. *Don't stack or you'll get a shaving-brush effect.* What you want to achieve is a more blurred appearance that wings in motion would produce. Line up wing and trim even with hook eye before tying down. Complete a soft loop, bind down wing, and take several turns. Pull back the head and take additional turns to force the head up. Apply dubbing to your tying thread and wrap just as the tail was completed. Tie in the split goose quill for head antennae. Apply head cement to underside of the wing.

under tension. At that point, a second mend takes place, with additional line released into the mend and following drift. With each mend, the fly is certain to act erratically, popping with a discernible bubble. When all the slack line has been used, the fly will begin to complete the swing. This swing can be repeated with a large mend that throws the fly back into the downstream channel. When the swing has finally been completed, the retrieve should be made slowly, for a steelhead may follow the fly. When the twenty feet of "feeding line" has been stripped in, the cast can be repeated.

Mike makes three casts at each of three distances: thirty feet, forty to forty-five feet, and fifty-five to sixty feet. In this manner, about nine casts are made at one station if the angler is confident that there may be a steelhead holding somewhere in this range.

The steelhead can see the fly coming for a long distance. As the fly comes over his station, the steelhead will likely pick up and drop back with the fly, turn, and continue following it downstream. If it does not take when the fly comes under tension, the steelhead loses interest, leaves the fly, and returns to its station. The cast may be repeated several times before the fish takes.

Unless a mend is being made, the rod is held upright. As the steelhead takes the fly down, it will return to its original station. A quick strike at this point will either pull the fly out of its mouth, or hook the fish at the edge of its mouth. But if the rod tip is dropped, line drag will bring the fly across the steelhead's mouth until the hook point penetrates the back hinge of the jaw. For this to work properly, the hook point must be extremely sharp.

The angler's reactions must be very disciplined. Fly fishermen have learned to strike on the rise. This is so ingrained as to be virtually automatic. The sudden appearance of a trout as large as a steelhead is certain to cause an involuntary strike, with discouraging results.

Mike told me of fishing with Craig Mathews from the Blue Ribbon Fly Shop in Montana. "His reactions were so fantastic that he would strike immediately. One day he pulled the fly out of a fish's mouth seven times. Finally, when I saw the fish coming I said, 'Craig, look at the bald eagle!' He looked up, and boom! He had the fish on!"

Bill McMillan

30

BILL McMILLAN

BILL pointed to the soft break in the Washougal River, a string of stream-worn rocks, each about as large as a man could carry, and told me how he had deposited them just so to change the character of the well-scoured riverbed. This was a tremendous labor, but worth the effort if steelhead paused behind them on their upstream migration. That did not happen. The capricious hydraulics of flood and drought altered the river and sent the next season's steelhead up a different channel to hold farther across the river. Bill was philosophical and mildly self-mocking about his efforts, and he drew my attention to the new travel lanes with a wry smile.

Our remarkable vantage was Bill's study, a small hideaway on the second story of the house that he and his wife, Wanda, started building many years ago. His fly-tying bench is his writing table, and it sits before a large window, so that a glance up from either activity looks down into what is literally his home pool. If he sights a steelhead, Bill needs but a few minutes to slip into waders, grab his rod, and cover the lie. This convenience is but one facet of a remarkable intimacy with the Washougal River that Bill has maintained throughout his adult life.

Not since Roderick Haig-Brown has a western angler written so intelligently on the passage of life in an anadromous river. No other western writer, past or present, has drawn so many important conclusions from his steelhead fly fishing and from his years of careful observation. A good many of his articles document this. His book, *Dry Line Steelhead*, a collection of articles and letters, is a cerebral tour of his world, and a graduate course in steelhead fly fishing.

Bill has long despaired over the practice of stocking summer-run steelhead in the Washougal. Native steelhead began disappearing years ago, to be gradually replaced by Skamania hatchery clones, large, selectively bred fish that stack up in the deepest pools and remain unresponsive to the fly. "Great sport for snaggers," Bill says sarcastically. In contrast, he describes the spirited, native, one-year ocean steelhead of five pounds as his "bread and butter fish." These steelhead of greased-line lies and sparkling riffles have been genetically eliminated from the river. "I could once come home from work and, in a hour or two, raise a half-dozen of these steelhead," he says wistfully. When we visited in the spring of 1988, the native Washougal summer-run steelhead was very nearly extinct, only a couple of hundred two-year ocean steelhead in a hatchery run of thousands.

Bill rails against this wrongheaded assault on his river's steelhead. He dares to suggest that the quality of the fishing is linked to the quality of the steelhead, that for all of the taxpayers' money spent on hatcheries and "enhancement" programs, the actual quality of the sport is *declining*. He says bluntly and emphatically that numbers of steelhead, per se, are meaningless, and that hatchery steelhead are a sorry excuse for the native race. This thinking is, of course, blasphemy to any state's entrenched hatchery-oriented bureaucracy, and it has taken years for his crusade to dent their heads.

Bill has a lot of company today. The serious questions he raised years ago are now being discussed thoughtfully among the agencies entrusted with managing our steelhead. He tells me that there may soon be a recovery program for the native Washougal steelhead, but their numbers are so small, their gene pool so fragile and threadbare, that the effort may now be too late. Native steelhead are currently given complete protection on some rivers, and they are afforded partial protection on others. Catch and release is sometimes required as an alternate means of increasing steelhead stocks. Hatcheries are now seen neither as a quick fix nor as a long-term solution. Working to protect our watersheds against the unnatural loss of steelhead stocks is a commonsense bottom line supported by every environmental group worth its name. We may finally be getting the horse back in front of the cart. If so, Bill can take a bow; he has been both carrot and baseball bat.

For all of Bill's good works on behalf of our native steelhead, his reputation rests most durably on the steelhead fly-fishing techniques he has perfected. These were first described in a series of landmark articles for Frank Amato's *Salmon Trout Steelheader* magazine in 1973. Bill cast an "old fashioned" double-taper floating line, practiced greased-line techniques, dead-drifted the wet fly on long leaders in winter, and skated dry flies for steelhead in summer. He disdained as uncouth and unnecessary fast-sinking shooting heads, then very much in vogue. In his virtuoso approach, steelhead fly fishing could still be grace and tradition. The articles were a genteel sell of enormous appeal by a quiet, almost diffident man, country squire and Thoreau in equal measure.

Bill uses only a few steelhead fly patterns, but each was designed to be fished in a specific manner under specific conditions. The four dressings described here, and his comments that follow each, sum up his steelhead fly fishing methods.

STEELHEAD CADDIS

Hook	Size 12–6 Wilson dry fly (Partridge)
Tail	None
Body	Originally hare's mask (orangish fur at the base of the ear), but any tan, orange, brown, olive, black, or yellow dubbing provides alternates to the original
Wing	Mottled turkey wing tied tent style
Collar	Spun deer hair, light tan
Thread	Brown 6/0 prewax

"The Steelhead Caddis is essentially a sparse, low-water variation on the Muddler Minnow that is meant to ride up on the surface with a trailing wake when fished against the current, or to float in the surface film when greased and fished on a dry-fly natural drift.

"I developed the pattern in September 1975, as a representation of two large caddisfly species, of the family Limnephilidae, that are common to Northwest rivers during the fall months. These caddis are very large, and due to the commotion of their egg-laying activities on the surface of the rivers, they tend to be very attractive to steelhead. I've observed steelhead actively feeding on these insects, and in the days when I kept some fall steelhead, the adult caddis and their pupal forms were common stomach contents.

"I now fish the Steelhead Caddis anytime conditions warrant—primarily with water temperatures at forty-three to forty-four degrees or more—and have hooked steelhead on this pattern every month of the year. The pattern is effective with or without caddisflies in evidence, and it is a fair-to-good representation of numerous stoneflies, alder flies, termites, carpenter ants, larger mayflies, or even an injured minnow (depending on its body color).

"While the pattern was originally designed to wake in the surface through careful manipulation of the line—I fished it in this manner for more than three years—I have since come to use a riffling hitch with it to ensure a good wake on every cast.

"On smaller rivers, where steelhead are less inclined to follow a fly very far out from their lies, I cast the caddis very tightly downstream to bring it into immediate tension against the current. I immediately use greased-line 'control mends' to hold the fly in a skimming hang just above a visible or suspected steelhead's lie. The rod tip must be at a forty-five-degree angle so that when the steelhead comes with a mouth-gaping rush, I can immediately drop the rod point to parallel the surface and provide two or three feet of slack. This allows the steelhead to suck the fly down, grasp it, and make his downstream turn. Then, and only then, do I lift up with a delayed strike response.

"On larger rivers, or on water that promotes a steelhead to leave his lie, I will cast the caddis less downstream and sometimes very nearly cross-stream. Then, rather than mend the line, I will simply lead the fly across the stream with an advancing rod tip. This puts the skimming fly into a very broad arc that, from the angler's point of view, seems almost too fast to attract a fish. However, from the fish's observation angle, I think the effect is quite different, that the fly is actually working both downstream and cross-stream, and that the cross-stream speed, very fast to the angler, is actually not more, and generally somewhat less, than the downstream speed of the current being fished. Whatever, 'tacking' current speed on the fly seems to be an important stimulus for drawing a steelhead out of its lie for what can be a long, long follow with multiple rises at the fly—or then again, an immediate 'grab' only a few feet out of the lie."

WASHOUGAL OLIVE

Hook Size 2–1 (cold water), Mustad 7970, or size 5–3 (warm water) Alec Jackson Spey	**Throat** Golden-olive-dyed calf tail
Tail Golden-olive-dyed calf tail	**Wing** White calf tail
Body Gold tinsel or mylar	**Head** Black

"I developed the Washougal Olive in February of 1968 as a late-winter through late-spring pattern that would fish effectively under full-volume, winterlike water flows without skidding to the surface when fished on a floating line. The typical chenille-bodied, bucktail-winged steelhead patterns of the era, tied on medium-weight wet-fly hooks, fished satisfactorily in the lower volumes of summer on a floating line, but in the higher, winter-type volumes, these patterns would merely skid to the surface when quartered down and across.

"The solution to this problem seemed to be a combination of better hook choice and improved fly design. The first angling book that was truly my own was *How To Fish From Top To Bottom*, 1955, by Sid

Gordon. I purchased it as a twelve-year-old, through *Outdoor Life*'s Book of the Month Club in 1957. Gordon approached his angling very scientifically, not unlike Edward Hewitt, although less abrasively, more humbly, and with more reliance on observation than on computed theory. I don't know how many times I read the book, but it was often, and Gordon has undoubtedly had a strong formative impact on my own angling approach. One important lesson was how to make varying hook styles and wire weights work to the angler's advantage. To this day, I am surprised at how few anglers make the best possible use of the hooks available, particularly for wet fly fishing. When one insists on using only a floating line, an understanding of hooks is critical for effective wet-fly fishing.

"My hook choice was the Mustad 7970, a short, stout hook of 5X-diameter bronze wire. Some anglers consider this hook unappealing due to the large hook eye and the big barb (necessitated by the heavy wire), but long ago I learned to judge beauty in differing ways, not the least of which is the beauty of efficient function. I've found this hook is irreplaceable in floating-line steelhead fly fishing where a relatively small-size fly must be presented at considerable depth. Flies tied on this hook are also easier to cast than are leaded flies on light-wire hooks.

"At the time, no steelhead patterns made substantial use of the color green. I found this bothersome, because a common stonefly on the Washougal River in late May and early June is olive in color, and the dominant coloration on the river in the spring is varied tones of green, both above and beneath the surface. The Northwest in spring is an emerald fairy tale land, yet there were no steelhead flies to blend with the surroundings. I was also very attracted by two Atlantic salmon patterns of green coloration, the Green Highlander and the Cosseboom, both with solid fish-catching reputations. I set about filling the green steelhead fly void and hoped that the new fly would be attractive to the best of all steelhead, the very early running summer steelhead, the "springers" that return to several southwest Washington streams in March, April, and May.

"When the water becomes low and very clear, I'll dress the Washougal Olive on Alec Jackson's spey hooks and fish it greased-line just under the surface film. At other times, I'll fish it on the stout hook on a deep, natural drift, nymph-style. But for the most part, I fish it on the stout hook quartered initially upstream if the water is at full winter height, or quartered downstream if the water is lower, with takes expected on the broad swing or as the fly holds directly downstream at the completion of the swing.

"While I don't use the Olive as often as I used to, it remains one of my favorite patterns. It has moved some of the most memorable and difficult steelhead I've ever encountered in the late winter and through the spring.

"I haven't the vaguest notion as to what food form the Olive represents to a steelhead. Its design was based strictly around coloration, with no attempt to suggest a specific imitation."

PAINT BRUSH

Hook	Mustad 7970	**Hackle**	Purple, veiled by turquoise blue
Tail	None	**Wing**	None
Body	Wide gold mylar or tinsel palmered with red-orange hackle	**Head**	Red 6/0 prewax thread

"The Paint Brush was developed in February 1973 as a winter pattern that fished effectively on a dead drift with a floating line.

"As in all wet-fly fishing with a floating line, the choice of a proper hook was my first consideration in developing a new pattern. I already had a preferred pattern for fishing winter steelhead on a deep wet fly swing, the big Winter's Hope. However, a dead-drift pattern posed a different set of problems. A swinging fly is a searching pattern that is designed to bring a fish to the fly, and a dead-drift pattern is fished in a manner that brings the fly to the fish. A swinging fly is fished against the current, which ensures that all of a pattern's varied materials will be swept back along the hook shank with well-animated movement. The drifting fly must possess an inner movement of its own as it glides in suspension with the current.

"I decided to stick with the proven primary colors of the Winter's Hope—blue, purple, and deep orange—but it seemed that a smaller-size fly might be better accepted when it was coming right at the fish with the current. The best hook for putting a lot of weight into a small pattern was the Mustad 7970, and it was my immediate choice.

"I always prefer simple patterns that use a minimum of materials because: 1) they sink better; 2) I am a very slow fly tyer; 3) I don't like to pretend that a fish is more complicated than the rather primitive animal it is; and 4) intricate fly patterns are for the human mind, not the fish's. As a result of this inclination, the pattern turned out to have only two materials, tinsel and hackle. The body was palmered with red-orange hackle over gold tinsel, and the front hackles were purple veiled by turquoise blue. The hackles were tied with a tiered effect, gradually tapering larger toward the eye of the hook. All hackles were chosen for maximum web so that they would absorb water and be soft enough to provide a pulsing movement while drifting with the current.

"The pattern provided remarkable winter fishing that first February. Thirty-three steelhead were hooked under very low-flow conditions, and twenty of these fish came to the new pattern I had named Paint Brush, due to its resemblance to the mountain flower, Indian Paintbrush.

"I strictly fish this pattern on a natural dead-drift by quartering the cast upstream. I quickly throw one to three back-mends to provide slack, and then concentrate on the tip of the floating line as an indicator of the steelhead's subtle take. Unlike the wet-fly swing, the angler wants to position himself directly across the stream from a visible fish or suspected steelhead lie. At this point, the drifting fly should have reached its maximum depth. If the take comes, the line point will typically bow into an upstream arc that requires an immediate and forceful strike to take up the slack line."

WINTER'S HOPE

Hook	2/0 to 6/0 Partridge salmon	**Topping**	A few strands (six to ten) of golden olive calf tail
Tail	None		
Body	Wide silver tinsel or mylar	**Head**	Burgundy 6/0 prewax
Hackle	Purple over turquoise blue, long and weepy		
Wing	Two yellow hackle tips enclosed by two deep orange hackle tips		

"I began to develop the Winter's Hope in 1971, during my search for a fly specifically designed to fish for steelhead with a floating line on cold-water flows typical of Northwest rivers from November through March. The steelhead patterns typical to that era were dressed on size 2 to 8 medium-weight wet-fly hooks with thick chenille bodies (creating considerable resistance to the current), buoyant bucktail wings, and relatively short, stiff saddle hackles that absorbed very little water and had very little movement without some outside manipulation, such as a rod twitch. Essentially, they were flies that depended on a sinking line to pull them down from their natural inclination to skid to the surface when fished against the current on a wet-fly swing.

"The quest to develop the Winter's Hope came to symbolize my personal reaction against the use of a sinking line. In the late 1960s, I turned occasionally to Atlantic salmon patterns, and by 1970 I began to employ simplified versions of them on a few 2/0 and 4/0 down-eye bronzed hooks that I'd found in a dusty corner of a Portland tackle shop. It slowly dawned on me that here was the solution to making the preferred floating line a useful winter steelhead tool even in December's and January's formidable flows. After all, the rivers of Scotland had been yielding Atlantic salmon in January and February for a century or more to anglers wielding huge flies without the benefit of Dacron or lead-core lines. I was particularly attracted by the classic Silver Doctor and Silver Wilkinson, and by Preston Jennings's Lord Iris, but I was not attracted to either their complicated ties or to their thick-built lack of movement in the water.

"Then, as now, there were all sorts of color-perception theories and their applications in angling. Nearly all of them expounded some sort of mathematical justification as "proof," and I chose to incorporate a few of these notions that were attractive to my less-technical sense of logic, and more important, those colors that were aesthetically pleasing to my eye, if not necessarily to the fish's. I liked the notion that blues and purples, being at the shortest end of the light spectrum, are the least impacted by reductions in available sunlight. One is commonly confronted by very dim light conditions in a Northwest winter, and it seemed important to include these colors. At the other end of the spectrum were the reds and oranges that had long been proven effective for taking steelhead.

"Beyond colors, I wanted the fly to give the impression of considerable bulk in order to veil the large hook. Yet if the fly was to sink quickly and resist the currents while on the swing, it would require a minimum of materials. Time and again, I had demonstrated to myself that a heavily dressed, bulky fly tended to trap air, the sheer quantity of materials tending to parachute a fly's sink rate with delayed suspension. By contrast, a bare hook will plummet through the water. I knew that a fly pattern that only suggested bulk, but in reality approached the sink rate of a bare hook, would be necessary if the fly was expected to fish deep strictly because of its design, and not through the use of a sinking line.

"In order to provide the illusion of bulk, I chose long and webby neck hackles with fibers consisting almost entirely of web. Such hackles flow back naturally along the hook shank, and they are so soft as to allow the current to play on them freely in perpetual movement. The tinsel body kept with the notion of a bare hook while providing an element of flash. There was no need for a tail, because I chose the soft, extended movement provided by hackle-tip wings. In order to complete the rainbow-like spectrum of colors, I chose a few strands of golden olive calf tail as a final topping over the wing.

"As this final version was clamped in my vise on a January evening in 1972, there was, I thought, new hope for my winter fly fishing—thus the fly's name.

"Those anglers who have spent much of their lives casting into the swollen expanse of a winter river know that they must tenaciously cling to some strength deep within themselves in order to accept, perhaps even enjoy, the seemingly empty hours of casting required to move a winter steelhead to a fly. During every one of those thousand or more casts, the angler must cling to a silent prayer that is forever a winter's hope, no matter what the actual fly pattern.

"In the mid-1970s, I developed a hairwinged version of the Winter's Hope that was layered with calf tail, olive, yellow, and orange, from top to bottom. I abandoned it after several years of ineffective use. Some anglers did well with it, though.

"I fish the Winter's Hope in only one manner. The fly is initially quartered upstream with from one to three back-mends that throw coils of slack line upstream of the leader junction. This slack allows the fly to sink freely away from the floating line if a long, ten- to twelve-foot, leader is used. This initial drift of the Winter's Hope is used to gain depth to the steelhead's suspected lie well downstream of the angler. As the fly reaches the end of its natural drift, the current will pull the line into a crossing arc that lifts the fly into a cross-stream swing. The angler must then control the speed of this swing through more typical greased-line control mends that maintain a slight arc in the line through the fly's swing. One can expect the steelhead's take to come at any point from the time the fly begins to lift into its swing until it hangs below the angler at the completion of the swing.

"I typically fish the Winter's Hope in size 5/0 for normal and high winter flows. In very low winter flows, I drop down to a 3/0 or 2/0."

31

DAVE McNEESE

ONE July afternoon I was following Dave McNeese's speeding truck along the winding North Umpqua road that led from our campsite at Horseshoe Bend to the "holy waters" of Steamboat. When he veered across the oncoming lane for a pull-out set precariously along the edge of the canyon, I obediently followed, and shortly was peering down into the boiling currents to see what had caught his fancy.

"This is Redman Pool. I hooked my first steelhead here," he said by way of explanation. Almost immediately, he located a steelhead secure beneath a canopy of turbulence. After several minutes of coaching, I *thought* I saw it, too. Soon, Dave detected two more steelhead. He told me where they often held, a slot of water across the river beside a tabletop-size beach. The mountainside cliff offered no access, while our side of the river was a steep, rubble-filled slope. Locating the steelhead was the easy part.

"Where did you catch your steelhead?"

"Right there in that slot." Dave looked puzzled, as if I hadn't been listening.

"How on earth did you get over there? Did you have a raft?"

"Oh no. I crossed over a way upriver, hiked along the ridge, climbed over the mountain, and came down the face of the cliff. This pool was almost always open. No one else bothered to fish it."

"I see," I said.

Dave McNeese

"Well, are we going to try for those steelhead?"

"I don't think I'm up to going through all that," I said, pleased with my tactful bit of understatement. But Dave's enthusiasm was remorseless.

"Oh, no! We'll fish from this side."

I looked down into the canyon and judged the steelhead to be ninety feet away from the base of the nearly perpendicular rock slide. Not even Dave could roll cast that distance. "There's no room to cast down there!" I said.

"No, no," he said, "we'll fish from the highway."

Ah, I thought, this must be a joke. Those steelhead are at least 120 feet away and 30 feet down.

"Dave, you can't do that," I said. I gave a conspiratorial snicker to let him know I had caught on, but he seemed not to notice and pointed behind me to where the highway had cut away the hillside.

"There's room for a backcast!" His earnest manner resolved the matter. Between passing logging trucks and speeding campers, Dave would double-haul his way from one mountainside to another. Not Bunyanesque, I thought, just vintage McNeese. I insisted that we continue on toward Steamboat, where mere mortals fished. He shrugged, and we were off.

Dave was born and raised in Camp Creek, a little Oregon town on the Willamette River just east of Eugene. His first fishing experiences were with his father, and he was soon fly fishing for trout every day, a serious angler while his peers were still shooting marbles. He recalls removing screens from his house to sift through the Willamette's insect-rich muck and discover what his trout had been eating. A full-service fishing and hunting store became his teenage dream, but the realities of his finances necessitated a less expensive investment. In 1971 he began operating a fly-tying supply company out of his garage, advertising his wares in national magazines. The young entrepreneur's name soon became synonymous with fly-tying materials of the highest quality.

Dave told me a story about himself that I found most revealing. He realized early on that what he wanted to know about fly tying could not be taught in Eugene. He was only twenty-two, and all facets of the hobby, from full-dressed Atlantic salmon flies to ethereal likenesses of mayflies, were his obsession. He bought every book he could find on the subject, including Art Flick's *Master Fly Tying Guide*, an anthology of notable angling personalities and their fly-tying methods. The book so profoundly influenced him that nothing less than a pilgrimage back East to meet the masters and learn the secrets of their craft would do. Eric Leiser, Walt and Winnie Dette, Ray Smith, Harry and Elsie Darbee, Buck Metz, Ted Niemeyer, and Art Flick grounded him well. Dave still takes great pride in properly tying a Catskill dry.

A second turning point in his fly-tying education occurred in 1976, when he saw his first Syd Glasso steelhead fly. Glasso worked in Forks, Washington, as a schoolteacher and tied the most finely crafted steelhead flies in the world, bringing to our sport the tying excellence, the traditions, and the aesthetics of Old World tyers. (He would go on to greater fame as a tyer of Atlantic salmon flies. Some of his very best work adorns the luscious fly plates in Joseph Bates's *The Art of the Atlantic Salmon Fly* (1987, David R. Godine Publisher, Inc.).

When Dave opened up McNeese's Fly Shop in Salem, Oregon, obtaining exotic fly tying materials and dyeing them in shades found nowhere else became an important service to his customers. He invented new steelhead patterns, testing them on dozens of friends, and he tied old standards in new ways by incorporating hot orange and electric purple while emulating the style and craftsmanship perfected by Glasso.

His favorite waters for testing new patterns are, alternately, the Deschutes, the North Umpqua, and the North Santiam, the latter a nearby tributary of the Willamette that he describes, without hestitation, as his home river. Historically, the Willamette supported only runs of winter steelhead. Efforts to establish Siletz summer steelhead in the Santiam failed, and Skamania hatchery steelhead from the Washougal River were introduced. These plants took, and they became the basis for a splendid annual run that has built up to over twenty thousand summer steelhead.

Dave's early-season water is between Stayton and Green's Bridge. The steelhead move upriver with the passing of summer, above Mill City in July and August, and above Pack Saddle Park in the fall. He hunts for them anytime during breaks in his frantic schedule, with first and last light his obvious preferences, late afternoons avoided whenever possible. He casts a big fly, usually full-dressed 1/0 or 2/0 patterns that will move steelhead five or six feet. He is a powerful caster, quite comfortable with his ten-and-a-half-foot 10-weight rod. Dave's approach is total command of the water, long casts quartering well down and immediately swinging through the lie.

McNeese's Fly Shop is an institution of higher learning for steelhead fly fishermen. Dave invites fly-tying luminaries such as Bob Veverka to instruct classes on Atlantic salmon flies. He organizes Deschutes fly-fishing classes, and operates an annual seminar on Santiam steelhead. He has perhaps the finest private collection of historically important steelhead flies. His remarkable library of rare books on Atlantic-salmon flies qualifies as a research center. He custom-builds rods. He trades and stocks rare fly-tying materials for his most discriminating customers, and he raises his own jungle cocks.

Although his steelhead flies exhibit his fine sense of craftsmanship, they are not show flies. They have been thoroughly tested on steelhead and are designed to fish as well as they look. Between Dave and his friends, each dressing has accounted for at least 150 steelhead. Furthermore, he has donned a wet suit to observe and photograph all of these flies under actual fishing conditions. Dave's brief comments highlight each dressing.

Note: Dave obtains feathers from exotic birds only by legal means. Substitutions are freely invited in his steelhead dressings.

DESCHUTES MADNESS

Tag	Fine flat silver tinsel	**Hackle**	Purple
Tail	Golden pheasant crest, dyed red	**Wing**	White polar bear or pearl Krystal Flash
Ribbing	Fine oval silver tinsel		
Body	Rear third fluorescent orange floss over flat silver tinsel; front two-thirds purple seal fur, thin		

"The fast currents of the Deschutes River are perfect for flies with flashing wings and fluorescent butts. They will entice a quick response."

Note: The Deschutes Madness, a "McNeese standard" since 1978, is close to an all-around steelhead dressing. I would not hesitate to substitute a wing of white marabou over a small bunch of pearl Krystal Flash.

GOLDEN DEMON II

Tag	Fine flat silver tinsel	**Wing**	Wide furnace hackle tips
Tail	Golden pheasant crest	**Roof**	Bronze mallard
Body	Flat gold or copper tinsel	**Topping**	Six to eight golden pheasant crests
Ribbing	Fine oval silver tinsel	**Cheeks**	Jungle cock
Hackle	Long, hot orange from center		

"This is a pattern I often use in bright sunlight. The multiple crests—a dressing habit found in some Atlantic salmon flies—make the fly just glow in the water. The same effect can be achieved on other steelhead patterns as well, the Redwing for example."

GOLDEN HERON

Tag	Fine flat silver tinsel
Rib	Fine oval silver tinsel
Body	Medium flat gold tinsel
Hackle	Long black heron or dyed pheasant rump
Wing	An underwing of four golden macaw breast feathers or dyed substitute
Roof	Thin section of bronze mallard
Cheeks	Jungle cock
Red Heron:	Identical except for a wing of red macaw or hen hackle tips dyed red.

"I use this elegant pattern in riffles on the North Umpqua and North Santiam rivers. The Red Heron is especially good in the fall.

I use the Gold Heron, Purple Prince, and Red Wing when the sun is on the water and I've worked a fly through like a Green-Butt Skunk or Silver Hilton. If I know there's a steelhead there and I haven't raised it, I'll put one of these brilliant flies on—something that has extraordinary color— and I'll often take the fish."

HILTON SPIDER

Tag	Fine flat silver tinsel
Tail	Strip of pintail flank
Ribbing	Medium oval silver tinsel
Body	Black seal
Hackle	Long pintail flank
Wings	Four wide grizzly hackle tips

"This has proven to be a very effective version of the popular Silver Hilton. Perfect in both fast and slow runs. The fly may also be hackled with heron or pheasant rump."

An alternate to this dressing is the Green-Butt Silver Hilton, the "green butt" one-third the body length tied with fluorescent green plastic chenille.

KNOUSE

Tag	Fine flat silver tinsel
Tail	Golden pheasant crest dyed purple and Indian crow substitute
Ribbing	Medium oval silver tinsel
Body	Fluorescent red floss butt; rear half hot pink seal, front half hot purple seal
Hackle	Long, hot pink flank starting at purple seal
Throat	Long purple pintail flank
Wing	Purple pintail flank topped with golden pheasant crest dyed purple
Cheeks	Jungle cock

Notes: This pattern honors Stan Knouse, one of the original Steamboaters and a North Umpqua regular for many years. Below Takahashi's Pool is Knouse's, the lowermost of Steamboat's famous waters. A bronze plaque, "In Memory of Stan Knouse," has been set in the ledge rock to commemorate Knouse's work for the preservation of this great steelhead river. One evening in 1986, Dave hiked down from the Mott water to take a lovely brace of steelhead at the tailout of this pool, using a nameless but consistently reliable hot pink pattern. As a young man, he had seen Knouse fish this water. The bronze plaque triggered that memory and gave him a name for this beautiful dressing.

Dave says of the Knouse, "I use this pattern for both summer and winter steelhead. It's a good British Columbia pattern in large sizes, and a particular favorite of mine for deep runs such as Knouse's."

MCNEESE MADNESS

Tag Fine flat silver tinsel
Tail Fluorescent orange floss
Body Fluorescent orange floss, built up, ribbed with four turns of plastic purple chenille counter wrapped with fine silver wire

Hackle Hot pink Krystal Flash and purple hackle
Wing Hot purple polar bear mixed with purple Krystal Flash
Cheeks Jungle cock

"This is a great Deschutes pattern that has become more popular every year."

Note: When Krystal Flash came out, Dave tied up a number of different patterns incorporating this material and then tested them on the Deschutes. He found that this dressing was much more effective than any other. He also gave samples to friends to fish. In this manner, the McNeese Madness has been successfully used in British Columbia for steelhead and on Atlantic salmon rivers in Norway, Iceland, and Canada.

Dave has a strong preference for hot floss tails. The material is durable and shows up well under water. He prefers to make the bodies of his flies full-length (note color plate), a factor in their construction that prevents a floss tail from wrapping around the bend of the hook.

PALE PERIL

Tag Flat silver tinsel
Tail Golden pheasant crest dyed purple
Body Flat silver tinsel ribbed with oval silver tinsel

Hackle Purple, full
Wing Purple over white polar bear mask
Cheeks Jungle cock

"This fly was inspired by the old Purple Peril. The 'Pale' version is a good summer pattern; my clients and I have taken a lot of fish on it."

PALE PERL

Tag Fine flat silver tinsel
Tail Golden pheasant crest dyed red
Ribbing Medium oval silver tinsel
Body Purple Poly Flash tinsel
Hackle Long, hot purple or pintail flank dyed purple

Wing White polar bear over six strands of pearlescent Krystal Flash
Topping A small bunch of bluish purple polar bear

"A proven pattern from British Columbia to California, a fly that has produced more steelhead for me on the North Santiam than any other. It is my favorite morning fly (in the evening I often fish the Green-Butt Skunk). I first tied it in 1976. The Pale Perls I have fished are stuck in the wall and are just shredded."

PURPLE BRAT

Tag Fine flat silver tinsel
Tail Golden pheasant crest dyed red
Ribbing Medium oval silver tinsel
Body Rear third, half fluorescent orange floss and half fluorescent red floss; front two-thirds, hot purple seal fur

Hackle Long, hot purple from third turn of tinsel
Wing Hot orange polar bear containing a few strands of orange Krystal Flash, topped with purple polar bear
Cheeks Jungle cock

"I use the Purple Brat everywhere, for both winter and summer steelhead, with great success."

Note: This pattern is a variation on the Brad's Brat, a steelhead pattern Enos Bradner developed almost a half-century ago for use on the North Fork of the Stillaguamish River. Dave has a second variation of this reliable old favorite, a classic dressing he calls Bronze Brad's Brat.

PURPLE HILTON

Tag	Fine flat silver tinsel	**Hackle**	Hot purple mallard flank
Tail	Golden pheasant crest dyed red	**Wing**	Four purple grizzly hackle tips
Ribbing	Medium oval silver tinsel		
Body	Rear third, half fluorescent orange floss, half hot orange seal fur; front two-thirds, hot purple seal fur		

"Purple is a tremendously efficient color, and this pattern is possibly more effective than the popular Silver Hilton. I first tied this variation of the original in 1985. Since then, I've had a lot of anglers write back to me about using the fly. It has been good on British Columbia rivers, too."

PURPLE POLAR BEAR MATUKA

Tag	Fine flat silver tinsel	**Hackle**	Long purple mallard flank
Tail	Long purple polar bear and four strands of purple Krystal Flash	**Cheeks**	Jungle cock
Ribbing	Medium oval silver tinsel		
Body	Purple seal fur		
Wing	Set in four sections as the body is being made. Each wing section is slightly longer than the section before it so that the tips are even. Add a few strands of purple Krystal Flash.		

"I first tied this fly for fast water in 1978. Typically, I fish fairly far downstream, but there is fast water where you can cast across and strip back. The Matuka then gives a very broad outline to get the steelhead's attention. Of course, you may also fish it downstream.

"Though the Purple Polar Bear Matuka has become a popular fly on the Santiam system, I have found it to be effective on all of our rivers. I can never have enough tied to satisfy customer demands even when charging three dollars a copy."

Note: Dave uses the Matuka construction as described above on other patterns, notably the Thor, Polar Shrimp, and Brad's Brat. The full white wing, set in four sections, is highly visible, and has tremendous movement.

I particularly like the Matuka style for its ability to carry an abundance of color while penetrating heavy water without laying over. My own series of winter flies with modest hackle at the throat and large wings essentially have Matuka proportions. Substitute hot orange for purple in the above for an effective winter pattern. Many so-called General Practitioners in marabou—the all-black variation, for example—are really Matukas. No matter. They ride better than the traditional G.P.

PURPLE PRINCE

Tag	Fine flat silver tinsel	**Hackle**	Hot purple pintail flank
Tail	Golden pheasant crest and Indian crow substitute	**Throat**	Long pintail flank
Ribbing	Fine oval silver tinsel	**Underwing**	Hot orange hackle tips
Body	Rear half fluorescent red floss; front half fluorescent hot orange seal	**Overwing**	Purple golden pheasant flank
		Topping	Two golden pheasant crests
		Cheeks	Jungle cock

"I developed this pattern just for the North Santiam steelhead. It is a beautiful pattern with movement and enough color added to be effective for both winter and summer fish."

PURPLE SPEY

Ribbing	Medium oval silver tinsel	**Throat**	Very long pintail flank
Body	Rear third, fluorescent orange floss over flat silver tinsel; front two-thirds purple seal fur	**Wing**	Golden pheasant flank dyed purple
		Topping	Two or three golden pheasant crests dyed purple
Hackle	Long black heron or pheasant rump dyed black	**Cheeks**	Jungle cock

"The Purple Spey was a new pattern when Keith Mootry and I fished it on the South Santiam on October 1, 1978. He took six steelhead and I took four that evening. Typically, I have continued to use this fly in the evening."

SPAWNING PURPLE

Tag	Fine flat silver tinsel	**Hackle**	Two turns each of long hot orange, long hot purple, and long guinea or pintail flank
Tail	Long hot orange polar bear holding a few strands of orange Krystal Flash		
Body	Hot orange seal spun on a loop to form a fuzzy, ball-shaped body	**Wing**	Four hot purple hackle tips or purple Flashabou

"This is an old favorite of mine. I first tied it in 1977, for winter steelhead in clear water. (The Spawning Spey is a more recent 'feathery' version.)

"I give the loop of seal fur only a few turns and use varnish to cement it to the hook. The body will stay together for a long time."

SPAWNING SPEY

Tag	Fine flat silver tinsel	**Throat**	Long, hot purple pintail flank
Ribbing	Fine oval tinsel	**Wing**	Four hot purple hackle tips
Body	Rear third, half fluorescent orange floss, half fluorescent red floss; front two-thirds, fluorescent orange seal	**Topping**	Two to four hot purple golden pheasant crests
Rear Hackle	Hot orange heron or long hackle beginning at second turn of tinsel	**Cheeks**	Jungle cock

"A favorite winter steelhead pattern, slender but with lots of motion to entice sluggish winter steelhead."

STRATMAN FANCY

Tag	Fine flat silver tinsel	**Throat**	Purple pintail flank
Tail	Golden pheasant crest dyed purple	**Wing**	Pearlescent orange and purple Krystal Flash, four strands each. Top with purple polar bear.
Ribbing	Medium oval silver tinsel		
Body	Purple tinsel		
Hackle	Hot orange pintail flank wound from middle of body		

"I named this pattern for Roger Stratman, a fine steelhead angler and a fishing friend. It has mobile hackles, plenty of flash, and all the right colors. A great producer."

REDWING

Tag	Fine flat silver tinsel	**Wing**	Matching pair of golden pheasant tippet feathers
Tail	Golden pheasant crest		
Body	Rear third fine flat silver tinsel, front two-thirds red macaw breast feathers or redwing blackbird shoulder feathers, or the tips of white hen hackle dyed red, tied in as clumps around hook shank, four to six clumps to make a complete red body	**Topping**	Golden pheasant crest
		Cheeks	Jungle cock

"I never use the Redwing as a standard pattern. I like to use this fly in quiet pools and tailouts. On the North Santiam, there are many pools like this, three to four feet deep. When I go through a pool and can't find a steelhead and just *know* one is there, I'll put this fly on. Many, many times it has then been a producer.

"I usually fish it fairly small, sixes and eights, often tying it on double hooks I make myself. The tippet feathers tend to make the fly cock a little and the double hook keeps it riding straight in the water.

"The breast feathers stick out nearly at right angles to the body as the fly floats down. The feathers still stick out when the fly is under drag. This gives the fly a lot of movement. Adding more topping with additional crest feathers (four to six) produces an even more intense glow in the water."

Note: Dave also fishes the Redwing for salmon. While fishing Oregon's Trask at tidewater in November 1989, he landed a sixty-two-pound chinook salmon on a Redwing, size eight. After the hour-and-forty-minute struggle, the salmon was weighed and released. The fly joined others that are retired and displayed in Dave's shop.

CADDIS FLASH (Dry)

Tail	Orange polar bear over orange Krystal Flash	**Hackle**	Orange Krystal Flash
		Wing	Deer or elk body hair
Body	Hot orange plastic chenille		

The Caddis Flash, a waking pattern, is constructed on the order of Harry Lemire's Grease Liner, but with the addition of "hot" new materials. This recent introduction has been so effective that the dressing will surely invite other color combinations using Krystal Flash and plastic chenille.

Gary Miltenberger

32

GARY MILTENBERGER

A F T E R flying to Bear Lake, Gary Miltenberger and
Rai Thomas packed their raft and gear down Bear Creek to the Sustut River, twenty miles above its
confluence with the Skeena. Gary thought they might need ten days to pick their way along the lower
Sustut, to fish the pools and determine lies, to count the pools in terms of rods, and to study the pools
as landing sites for a float plane. With luck, the fall 1982 trip would end his five-year search for a site
to build a steelhead lodge.

Miles below the Sustut confluence, the Skeena gathers in the Babine and Kispiox rivers before joining with the Bulkley River at Hazelton, their planned takeout. Almost nothing was known of the
Skeena River between the Sustut and Babine rivers, and as a precaution the two men left an itinerary
with the Royal Canadian Mounted Police in Hazelton.

Though this was Gary's first trip to the Sustut, the river was well known to him. Years before, he
had thrilled to John Fennelly's book *Steelhead Paradise,* the story of fly fishing for steelhead in the
Skeena Country. Fennelly had fished the Sustut all the way to the spawning headwaters below Sustut
Lake. Now, only the lower twenty miles of the river was open to fishing. Otherwise, little had changed.
The river was still wilderness, a hundred-mile fly-in from Smithers, and it remained the least fished
of all the Skeena's famous tributaries.

About halfway through their float on the Sustut, they stopped at Suskeena Lodge, a tent camp built
by Doug Robertson in 1969. The business was for sale, and Gary had unsuccessfully dickered over the

355

price with Robertson. He hoped that somewhere below Suskeena he would find his site.

About six miles from the mouth, they came upon a pool that was long and open enough for a fully loaded float plane to land and take off. They camped there for days. Gary fly fished for a twenty-three-pound buck, at the time his largest summer steelhead, and one afternoon he shot an enormous bull moose. After dressing out the animal, he hiked to Suskeena to have the quarters transported to the airfield aboard the little scooter used by the Takla Lake Band of Carrier Indians to transport goods along a deserted railway line. The heart and liver were put in a cooler in the raft.

On October 20, snow began falling, and with the lateness of the steelhead season pressing upon them, they drifted out of the Sustut and into the Skeena. The next day, with snow still falling and about a third of the trip behind them, they entered the Skeena's almost inaccessible canyon waters. Gary explains:

> We hit a drop in the river with a reversal at the bottom. It looked kind of innocuous—we had gone through some hellacious water the day before—but damned if this reversal didn't suck us back upstream. Water coming over the raft pushed me out into the river, and I swam for shore. My partner got control of the raft and rowed over to extract me from the rock face, but I was so weak I couldn't just bounce into it. "Rai," I told him, "I'll have to catch you downstream. Go over the next rapid, and I'll get you down below." He was out of position on the next rapid, and the raft flipped. When I watched the raft go over, I thought, Oh God, we're in big trouble. That was the last I saw of him.

Gary climbed along the canyon wall, a tangle of snow-covered slide alder and devil's club, and made his way downriver in search of the raft. Near last light he found shelter beneath a rock outcropping and started a fire with a flare. He spent the night drying out.

Rai Thomas awoke on a beach to find himself still half in the river. Shaking violently with hypothermia, his legs useless, he dragged himself out and sought to build a fire. He ultimately accomplished this by lighting off a patch of latex cut from his waders. Thomas drifted in and out of consciousness for the next day, and he suffered from extensive frostbite, but as with Gary, the fire saved his life.

The cooler had washed up on the beach, and Thomas was able to roast some of the moose liver. Gary was less fortunate. Five days later, a helicopter rescue team located the men and evacuated them. Until then, each assumed the other had perished.

Gary remembered the great pool called Surprise, and he shared his discovery with Dennis Farnworth, a cabinet-maker from Smithers. The two transplanted Americans had met two years before at Bob Wickwire's Silver Hilton Lodge on the Babine. Gary was guiding, while Dennis completed work on some new construction. A partnership in a lodge business had grown out of the meeting. After Gary moved from Bella Coola to Smithers the following spring, they obtained a lease for a lodge site from the Ministry of Crown Lands. They then set to work constructing the series of log cabins on Surprise Pool that would become known as Steelhead Valhalla Lodge.

Gary calls the following steelhead patterns the "Sustut Seven," the result of input from hundreds of clients and his own inspiration at the vise.

PURPLE UGLY

Tail Wine red calf tail
Body Purple yarn ribbed with flat silver tinsel
Hackle Fluorescent red saddle hackle

Wing Wine red calf tail
Head Bead-chain eyes with red thread

Gary first tied the Purple Ugly for the Bella Coola River's late winter run, and the Dean River's famous summer run of steelhead. He also found the fly to be effective on the Kispiox and Babine rivers. When he first began fishing the pattern, he discovered that his friend Les Karoluk of the Bela Coola Atnarko Guide Service was tying a pattern that was virtually identical. Whatever its origins, it is a Sustut standard and typical of the large, gaudy flies used on the river.

SUSTUT BOSS

Tail Large, thick tag of fluorescent cerise or pink yarn

Body Black chenille ribbed with wide flat gold tinsel

Wing Black bear fur under, pearl Flashabou over

Head Bead-chain eyes tied with red thread

This pattern, a kind of Egg Sucking Leech in reverse, doesn't win any prizes for beauty, but it is very effective. Gary first tied it during the 1984 season, and late that October, Danish angler Keld Olsson was fishing it when he landed a twenty-eight-pound buck, a lodge record that stood for several years.

PURPLE PORCUPINE

Tail Purple Flashabou under, purple marabou over

Body Black chenille palmered with wide black saddle hackle

Head Fluorescent red or hot pink chenille

Gary told me that Warren Wiley, a professional fly tyer from Missoula, Montana, sent some variations of the Egg Sucking Leech to Steelhead Valhalla Lodge in September, 1986. These samples were varied only slightly to obtain the Purple Porcupine. Gary used the fly when he caught a twenty-three-pound hen, still a Sustut record, and still one of the largest hen steelhead ever taken on a fly.

When I was visiting Frank Moore on the North Umpqua in 1989, Claude Batault handed me a fly and said, "Try this on the Dean." The fly, another variation on the Egg Sucking Leech theme, had no name. It could be called a "Black Porcupine." The fly was entirely black except for a head of fluorescent flame chenille. Under low light, the pattern proved to be amazingly effective.

SUSTUT SUNRISE

Tail Orange bucktail or calf tail under, purple Flashabou over

Body Fluorescent flame chenille ribbed with large flat gold tinsel

Hackle Deep purple saddle

Wing Orange bucktail or calf tail

Head Red tying thread

When lodge guests began requesting a bright pattern that would contrast to the standard purple and black dressings, Gary tied the Sustut Sunrise, "with apologies to the McLeods," a reference to Ken and George McLeod, who gave steelhead fly fishing the famous Skykomish Sunrise fly. In 1987, Dr. Fred Miller christened the new pattern with a twenty-seven-pound buck from the Glory Hole.

PURPLE JESUS

Tail Purple bucktail under, fuchsia Flashabou over

Body Fluorescent pink yarn palmered with purple saddle hackle

Hackle Deep purple saddle

Wing Purple bucktail

Head Red tying thread

The fly-tying bench in the dining room of Steelhead Valhalla Lodge gets big play during the cocktail hour. A drink in the hand and the events of the day have inspired more than a few patterns that became personal favorites.

One evening while Gary was taking his turn at the vise, a guest wandered up and remarked, "Jesus, look at that purple thing." Gary found in the comment a name for the fly, and a new pattern was born. It can be a pretty fly if dressed down a bit.

I substitute purple Krystal Flash and place it under the wing, spin a pink angora wool body, and rib with silver tinsel, all really minor changes from the original.

Row 1 Purple Ugly, Sustut Boss, Purple Porcupine
Row 2 Ultimate Leech, Ghost Leech
Row 3 Sustut Sunrise, Purple Jesus

ULTIMATE LEECH

Tail Pearl Flashabou
Body Gold tinsel
Wing Black rabbit tied Matuka-style

Throat Black rabbit fur
Head Bead-chain eyes tied with red thread

Terry Roelofs, a professor at Humboldt State University, popularized a black leech pattern for use on the North Umpqua River. Jim Van Loan, owner of the North Umpqua's Steamboat Inn, brought the "Roellofs' Leech" to the Sustut in 1987. The fly was unique for its articulated body, barbell lead head, and almost weedless disposition. "We 'slaughtered' them," Gary recalls. He regards his simplified version, "The best of all the Sustut patterns." Because lodge guests sometimes experienced short takes, Gary began cutting the wing short so that it extended no more than an inch past the bend of the hook. This hasn't reduced the fly's effectiveness.

GHOST LEECH

Tail Pearl Flashabou
Body Gold tinsel
Wing White rabbit tied Matuka-style. Add a very small bunch of black rabbit fur behind the head

Throat Black rabbit fur
Head Bead-chain eyes tied with red thread

Gary has successfully fished the Ghost Leech under all water conditions and at all times of the day, including bright midday sunlight, but he feels the dressing is especially effective at dusk. He recalls one evening when, after wading into a thoroughly fished pool, he "banged two fish, right behind clients."

Mel Krieger and Les Johnson fish variations of the Ghost Leech (see Chapter 38).

Author's note: Mike Montaigna, Olema, CA, builder of extraordinary "quad" rods, tied the first articulating black leech pattern and introduced it to the North Umpqua in 1985. Terry Roelofs adopted the fly, and so popularized it that the fly is commonly identified with his name.

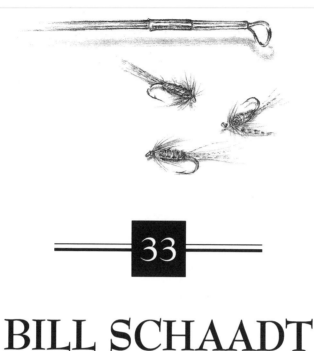

33

BILL SCHAADT

O N E February day several years ago, I flew out of a Seattle snowstorm and into a San Francisco downpour to visit Bob and Helena Nauheim in nearby Santa Rosa. Bob and I were to join Bill Schaadt on the Gualala River for a few days of fly fishing. Bill was staying in his trailer somewhere up on the river, and Bob was sure he could find him. The two were old friends, often companions on the Smith River when great ocean-bright chinook first filled the pools above tidewater in October, and on the Russian when it was still California's finest winter steelhead river. "Maybe you can talk with Bill in the evening," Bob had said. "Otherwise he'll be fishing. He won't stop for anyone."

I knew at least that much about Bill Schaadt. Mostly I knew that sometime in the long ago of steelhead fly fishing he became so much bigger than life that his reputation bordered on the mythical. Romantics said he embodied angling in its purest form, that he was a natural with boundless determination who fly-fished only for the fun of it. Nothing else really mattered to him—neither money, nor possessions, nor station in life.

Many tales gave rise to the legend. I'd heard at least two before we met. In one, Bill is driving along the Eel toward the pool he is to fish at first light, when his car goes out of control, slides off the road down an enbankment, and flips upside down. He gets out, finds his gear undamaged, and goes fishing. At the end of the day, he calls a tow truck and has the car pulled out. Another story was a magazine article by Russell Chatham that I read maybe fifteen years ago. Bill is fishing the Smith River one

Bill Schaadt

afternoon when he hooks an immensely strong chinook salmon. The fly is dressed on a #8 hook, the tippet but eight-pound test. Bill presses every imaginable advantage, but the salmon seems invincible, and the hours pass into night. Incredibly, the struggle lasts more than eleven hours before the forty-two-pound salmon is beached.

I stuffed my canvas duffles into the rental car, glumly aware that the fishing trip was a bust. Newspaper headlines read, "Wind, Rain Rips Area." Less than two hours later, I was at the Nauheims' mountaintop home.

I've known Bob Nauheim for years as the owner of Fishing International. He is a cheerful broth of a man, given to stories of his African safaris, trips to Norway's salmon rivers, and the latest fly pattern sure to be deadly on permit. He does not tell you he is the inventor of the famous Crazy Charlie, a fly pattern long synonymous with bonefish on tropical flats. His house is decorated so eclectically that I called the style Contemporary Museum. He has genuine Cro-Magnon spear points, ancient Pomo Indian flutes, a zebra skin rug, and displays of antique fly-fishing reels. A greater kudu looms over his baronial living room. It's a great show.

Bob had helped me plan several saltwater fly-fishing trips, and along the way had educated me on some finer points of California steelheading. "You know the rivers are out," he said by way of a greeting. "They won't be in for days. Two inches of rain in one night! Bill brought his trailer down. He knows you're coming. We'll drive over to his house and see if he's there. He's around. I called his neighbor. He doesn't have a phone."

We drove north through the Irish-green hill country of pastures and live oak until we reached the caramel-colored Russian. The river took us west, into a moist coastal valley filled with second-growth redwood. Bill lives here in Monte Rio, a tiny village just off the river. For a generation, he has been an inveterate collector of junk, and all manner of scroungings fill his yard to the height and density of Iowa corn. Until the police got after him, a wave of scrap metal was washing out onto the street. A lot of this is bicycle parts, and in time Bill combines them into serviceable bikes that he gives away to neighborhood kids. Because finding a trail to his front door is difficult, he often sleeps in the travel trailer parked out front. Bob left the dinner invitation on the trailer window, and we continued on to Jenner, searching for Bill along the lower Russian until we reached the mouth and the colony of seals that were, as usual, eating hatchery steelhead. When we couldn't find him on those nearby creeks that Bob knew would clear first, we returned to Santa Rosa. An hour later, Bill called and was on his way for dinner.

I met a tall, gracefully athletic man of sixty-seven, whose hair was still full and dark, a gift from his Portuguese mother. Schaadt is German, pronounced "Shad, like the fish," he explained. Only the day before, Bill had offered to usher an angler into the hereafter for serious and repeated breaches in stream etiquette. He called to Bob, "I took out my teeth and said, 'Okay, let's go!'" The sidelong grin was gone, and the eyes became predatory, gunfighter slits. His enormous, thickly calloused hands, described as "great bats" by Russell Chatham in *The Angler's Coast*, flapped about in pantomime. Bill turned to me. "I got your letter," he said, tidying up a bothersome scrap of his past. "That was some time ago. Something came up. Can't remember. Never answered it."

"You have a good memory!" I replied, "That was, ah, twenty-some years ago? I never knew you got it. No matter. It's good to see you."

I had written to William E. Schaadt, General Delivery, Monte Rio, California, asking for a fly, some advice, some tangible evidence that he was a real person. When I didn't hear from him, he remained the subject of apocryphal tales and campfire scuttlebutt. I eagerly participated in this, and tried hard to add to the folklore. That's the way I turned him over in my mind, a star-struck fan playing to his iconoclastic ghost of the foggy north coast. I imagined we met each year, when his name appeared in the *Field & Stream* fishing contest under "rainbow trout," chinook salmon, and striped bass. I nodded knowingly when I read about him in articles, but it was ten years before I learned to pronounce his last name.

Temporarily unable to fish, Bill would do the next best thing and talk about it. The three of us ate

Bob Nauheim displays a trophy steelhead from the North Umpqua. *Photo credit: Rune Alm*

Helena's cooking and drank Bob's bourbon for two days and found no memory nor theory nor opinion too insignificant to worry and pick over. I had known Myron Gregory, understood the early history of Paper Mill Creek, had fished a few of Bill's coastal rivers, and could give you Jim Pray and Lloyd Silvius, chapter and verse. His recollections were the other part of a puzzle I had waited years to complete.

Bill Schaadt graduated from San Francisco Junior College with a degree in art and then moved to Monte Rio and the Russian River in 1946. When it was convenient to do so, he worked as a sign painter, usually in late spring when the rivers were between runs of salmon or steelhead. Bill judged that with artists starving from Sausalito to Fort Bragg, a good sign painter would never lack for work, and he hasn't.

The quick-rising summer steelhead of the Klamath were his introduction to fly fishing. Bill bought flies from Jim Pray, cast a nylon HCH line on a dreadful old bamboo rod, and sometimes hooked a winter fish in the Russian's and the Gualala's low-gradient delta pools. He learned where the fish were likely to collect, or stack up, and positioned himself to be "in the bucket."

Lloyd Silvius, a neighbor and friend of Pray's in Eureka, California, brought out the Fall Favorite Optic in 1946, and in only a few seasons it became a winter standard, with or without the optic head. On Christmas Eve, 1953, Bill was on the Gualala, casting the optic variation with a Herter's rod and Hardy reel when he hooked and landed a seventeen-pound steelhead that placed third in the annual

Field & Stream fishing contest. Other California rivers that year accounted for second place, a twenty-pound six-ounce buck from the Mad River and a state record for the fly, and a fourth, sixth, and seventh, the latter a fourteen-pound eight-ounce Garcia River steelhead by Jon Tarantino. It is interesting to note that Tarantino was using a new fiberglass rod sold under the name of a young designer and fellow tournament caster named Jim Green.

During the early 1950s, the Golden Gate Angling and Casting Club could claim among its membership the finest fly casters in the country. Winter steelhead fly fishing came to be centered on those rivers immediately north of San Francisco: Paper Mill Creek, the Russian, Gualala, and Garcia rivers. Myron Gregory introduced the shooting head to fellow club members, and Tarantino was the world champion distance caster. (Bill Schaadt could and did hold his own against Tarantino.) Experimentation with new fly designs began in earnest. The Comet fly was born, one-half of the winter steelhead equation that shortly included sinking fly lines of polyvinyl-chloride (Wet Cel) and those of lead core. Myron Gregory's shooting head now had great winter application. For ten years, Bill Schaadt took *hundreds* of winter steelhead on a fly each season, mainly from the Russian, then, arguably, the most productive winter steelhead river in the country. He recalls those days with nostalgia, and the story of the Comet fly is especially dear to him. No other dressing so symbolizes the period, and even today, no California wet fly is so popular for winter steelhead and fall chinook salmon. "I was on the ground floor," he likes to say at the start of a story. He often interrupts himself to ask, "You follow me?"

Years ago, Jack Horner's fishing circuit started with Montana, and he would fish up there for a couple of months. From what I understand, he was quite a trout fisherman. He had to be pretty good. When you're associated with the Golden Gate Angling and Casting Club, it was kind of automatic. He had several flies credited to him. I think his most famous one was the Horner Shrimp. Anyway, Jack made a few dollars selling tackle on the side. When we fished the Eel (that was years ago), Jack spent most of his time on the shore shooting the breeze with the people. From what I understood, this Comet fly came into being when he sold some fly tying gear to a young fellow, and this kid came up with this kind of fly. You know, it looks like some amateur would tie it, really, out of proportion and all. He never actually used the fly himself, but at the time there was a friend of his in the city named Joe Paul, who also was associated with the Golden Gate Angling and Casting Club and was into tournament casting. He gave some of these flies to Joe Paul to try out. Joe used them, but I looked at the damn things and thought, "A fish would never catch that!" Well, it happened that Joe Paul, a fellow named Alan Curtis, and I were fishing up on the Gualala after the season ended. At the time, the river was closed February 28, but there was a little clause in the law that left the Gualala open at tidewater. Tidewater was at least a mile up the river, and that mile encompassed most of the best pools. The three of us went up there one day in March and proceeded to hook a lot of downstream fish as we went from pool to pool. The first pool we hit was the Switchhill Pool. There was no competition, and we caught several fish out of it. I dropped down to the next pool, maybe two hundred yards, called Snag Hole, and I caught a few fish out of there. Pretty soon, Joe and Al followed me down and they were doing really well, too. I got down to the Donkey Hole and I hooked four or five fish. It was loaded with steelhead. I yelled for Al and Joe to come down. At the time I was using a Fall Favorite, maybe a size four, and it had been my favorite fly up to that time. I had been very successful with it and had landed some pretty big steelhead on this particular fly. Alan Curtis had introduced me to the fly. I think it was one of Jim Pray's flies. My largest on it was nineteen pounds, ten ounces. Anyway, they came down to the Donkey Hole, and Joe was using this Comet fly. He threw out and hooked this fish. He threw out and hooked another. And another. Meanwhile, I couldn't touch another fish. When Joe had hooked, let's see, number five, Al says, "Give me one of those damn flies." Al throws out and he's got one. Back and forth they went, and I never got another one. They hooked at least ten. I could not believe the success they were having with this ridiculous long-tailed fly. It wasn't like I was a weekend fisherman.

At the time I was palling around with with an old retired gentleman from Los Angeles. He was very interested in fly fishing, and I told him about this incident. I tied him some to show him what I meant. This was March, and the Russian River was clear. He took a few of the flies and went down to Austin Riffle—this was long before there were dams on the river—where fish collected, and he literally knocked the socks off of them on this fly. He was all enthused over this thing, and went down to one of the two local shops in Guerneville. Johnny Ferenz had one of them. This fellow had talked old Johnny into stocking some fly-tying equipment. In the meantime, Grant King had a store in conjunction with driving a truck for one of the oil companies. The store was just a hole-in-the-wall affair his wife ran. But Grant tied flies commercially on the side to supplement his income. Anyway, Johnny tied up some of these Comets and began selling them. And then Grant heard about them. The Comet soon got to be a popular fly and it all started right there in the Donkey Hole.

Note: Bill called his variation of the Fall Favorite a "Shad Roe." The nineteen-pound ten-ounce steelhead was caught on January 6, 1955, and placed fourth in the *Field & Stream* fishing contest. George McLeod won the contest with a twenty-nine-pound two-ounce Kispiox steelhead, and this started the fly-fishing run on that river. Other anglers who placed in the contest that year included Ralph Wahl, Enos Bradner, and Al Knudson.

The original Comet was all orange with a bucktail tail twice the length of the hook. Bead-chain eyes and an underbody of lead wire were added to help take the fly down. So many variations quickly followed the original that "Comet" gained a generic connotation, and a fly was sometimes said to be tied in the Comet style. (There was soon a gold, silver, and fluorescent variation of the original called the Howard Norton Special.) Among these new Comets was the Boss, an orange and black pattern developed by Virgil Sullivan of Forestville, California. Forty years after its development, it remains one of steelheading's most popular flies.

Virgil Sullivan was known from the Russian to the Navarro as a fine fly fisherman. Bill found him secretive, for when he discovered Sullivan on a pool, the man would quit fishing and quietly slip away. Eventually, the two men met, and they exchanged fly books to find what the other was using. Back then, Bill stuck pretty much to two patterns, the orange and red Fall Favorite, and a nondescript black fly. This may or may not have been the inspiration for the Boss. Shortly after the Comet became popular, Sullivan brought the idea for the Boss to Grant King, who was soon tying the fly commercially. Bill said, "Grant thought the world of this guy."

"We might get lucky in the fall," Bill explained, "and it wouldn't rain until the first of the year. The water was low and clear. You can't imagine the steelhead that came into the lower part of the Russian! And just stayed there! I mean hundreds and hundreds of steelhead. It was nothing to land two hundred steelhead in a season."

These water conditions could also find the steelhead spooky and stale and nearly immune to the seductions of every conventional approach. Bill's solution would change the flavor of winter steelhead fly fishing for the next generation of anglers.

Years ago, fishing the Russian—this was back in the 1950s—I was over this pile of fish using a big fly, a size four, and I was hooking fish. They would grab it and let go. I'd get them on for a short time, and they'd come off. I got to thinking that if I used a smaller hook it would penetrate easier than the big hooks I was using. Well, I tried it, and it worked. I broke off the first few fish. I'd been using leader proportional to the flies, 15- and 10-pound test, but now I was using three-pound tippet. Once I got the technique down, all the fish had to do was touch the fly and they were hooked.

I cut off the bottom of the hackle because it interferes with the point of the hook. These steelhead always lay in a school. If I can go through and bump a fish, sometimes prick the fish in the dorsal or in the tail, I know where the fish are holding. I call the flies "Feeler Flies," because if you feel them [fish] there is no sense in moving.

I had lost many fish, and people finally hooked fish that had one of my small flies in it. That was the only way they found out. I want to tell you, I hooked hundreds. For a time I had these people going absolutely crazy!

When you're using the small flies, it's the difference between night and day. And the smaller the better. I use size twelve and fourteen and tippets to two-pound test. What a challenge when you hook those big winter-run fish on that light leader. You've got the ultimate, especially in this particular river when you are only a mile from the ocean.

Bill and I spent hours pawing through his fly boxes. He rarely bothers to name the tiny patterns, though their recipes have been consistent for years. I found him to be a harsh critic of any fly that did not meet expectations. He treasures the truly effective patterns, though he never romances aesthetics. He ties the flies roughly, can complete one in a couple of minutes, and loses them by the gross.

FEELER FLIES

BROWN NYMPH

Tail Teal
Body Dark brown wool

Hackle Brown

GOLD NYMPH

Tail Lemon wood duck
Body Gold mylar tinsel

Hackle Grizzly dyed orange

GREY NYMPH

Tail Lemon wood duck
Body Grey wool

Hackle Brown

NASTI NYMPH

Body Light grey wool palmered with brown
hackle

SCHAADT'S NYMPH

Tail Teal
Body Brown wool

Wing Grizzly hackle tips dyed orange
Hackle Brown, tied as a collar

Tying Note: Bill ties in the tail and body, winds the body forward, and temporarily holds the end with hackle pliers. The tying thread is then wound forward to rib the body and further secure it. If tying a tinsel body, the same approach is used, except the thread is simply brought forward under the body. Bill calls this "speed tying," because there is no bobbin at the head of the fly to get in the way of winding on body material, regardless of the material used.

"The Russian was in its prime in the early 1960s," Bill said, as he began to recount the loss of his favorite river. Its escapement of winter steelhead was phenomenal, certainly in the tens of thousands, the fish filling a vast watershed that began in the mountains in Mendocino County and gathered tributaries through Sonoma County before reaching the ocean. The river could always take considerable rain. When it rose and grew discolored, Bill's shooting heads and big bright comet flies soon had the steelhead located. The steelhead rarely exceeded fifteen pounds, but they routinely weighed ten pounds, splendid thick-bodied fish often caught within hearing distance of the ocean surf.

"They decided to put a dam on the river," Bill continued, "and they put this up by Ukiah, without any provision for a fish ladder. Then we had a crooked politician, a county supervisor, who had a lot of friends who owned property along the river, and they started digging gravel from the river. We had an early fall, the river is supposed to be clear, and the river is muddy. It stayed muddy all year, and I couldn't figure it out, because we had no rain. This went on for two or three years, and there were enough fish being caught on bait that no one gave a damn. This really hurt my soul! I knew the steelhead were there, but I couldn't fish for them!"

Bill called Myron Gregory, who sought help from fellow members of the Golden Gate Angling and Casting Club to stop the graveling. "Eventually this happened," he said, "but it took twenty years to do it. In the meantime, we had another dam built on the river, new highways went in, and finally it just went to hell. Now the seals have taken over."

Bill was probably the first local angler to discover that the river's shad would take a small, sparsely dressed silver-bodied fly with a red head, a pattern he knew had been used successfully on the Connecticut River. (He would ultimately catch shad on dry flies and poppers.) When Ted Trueblood visited the Russian to write an article on its shad fishing, he and Bill fished together. They became friends and sometimes camped on the Klamath for fall steelhead in the area of Perch Creek Camp.

Striped bass were no less a passion, and Bill chased them from the Russian River to San Francisco Bay. He mentioned several times that he had fished the coastal rivers, especially the Russian and Gualala, every year since 1946, except for one year. "And that year?" I finally asked.

He told me that he frequently went to the lower Russian to cast for stripers, usually got "winded out," and though unable to launch his little pram, nevertheless found the odd fish. But on one evening in September, "It was flat as a pancake, and for a mile the place was churning with stripers. I mean it was *boiling*! If you hooked one and lost it, you got another. You couldn't get your fly back!" Bill fished through the night and was promptly arrested the next morning for fishing after dark. He was fined fifty dollars, his tackle was confiscated, and his fishing license was revoked for one year. In only a couple of weeks he would have been up on the Smith with his lead-core shooting heads, hunting for chinook salmon. (Bill had landed one of 56½ pounds, a world record for the fly, and several others over 50 pounds.)

As combative as ever, Bill got together with Syd Green, a longtime friend, and drove up to Oregon to find another Smith. "Damned if they were going to put me down!" he remembers.

The first stream they came to was the Chetko. They hiked downriver until they came to a pool that later would become known as Morrison Hole. "There wasn't a soul there, and the place was moving with salmon! I said, 'I can't believe this thing!'"

Bill went back to town, got a license, and was told that no one fished with flies for the salmon. "If you get one to take a fly, let me know," said the store owner.

"I don't know if there were simply a lot of salmon, or if the salmon were just stupid. It was nothing to catch twenty-five in a day," Bill comments.

Of course, that kind of showmanship gets around, and the store owner was soon stocking flies and talking patterns. Within a couple of years, the Chetko joined the Smith as one of the finest rivers in North America for chinook salmon on the fly.

Since then, Bill has traveled to Alaska with Ed Rice and Jim Teeny to fish for chinook salmon. Once he and Russ Chatham drove across the country to spot-cast for cruising tarpon with Tom McGuane, a novelist friend then living in Key West, Florida. In 1974, Bill and Grant King, Bob Nauheim, Frank Bertainia, Bill Collins, and Bob Wickwire flew to Costa Rica to chase tarpon on the Rio Colorado and pelagic gamefish in the Pacific. He made trips to Montana, too. But Bill does not usually stray far from home, and he dismisses much of this other fishing with vague recollections. Describing the Russian and Gualala for winter-run steelhead, or the Smith for chinook salmon, is another matter. He reaches hard for the right adjective and booming passion is in every recounting. These are his rivers and his gamefish. He was here first with a fly, and I suspect that in fact or fable he'll remain here for generations to come.

A final story that Bill told about himself illustrates the many facets of his personality, from compassion for his gamefish to intolerance of his fellow anglers.

If a Smith River angler hooks a salmon anywhere but in the mouth, continuing to play the fish is illegal, and it must be broken off. Often this is not done, and the foul-hooked salmon can extend the struggle for hours. If Bill is around, he will inform the angler of the situation in none-too-charitable terms. Whether the angler doesn't know what's going on—or doesn't want to know—this news is never well received. At one time, Bill would continue to raise no end of hell to make his point, but no more.

He has devised a remarkable fly that has razor blades brazed top and bottom at the bend of the hook to form a V. The excess is trimmed away. The hook is then dressed conventionally. This "fly" is tied to the end of a lead-core shooting head. As Bill rows about "seaching for new water," the fly is trolled behind. Soon, the offending angler and his salmon go their separate ways. When Bill finished telling me of this strategy, I had the temerity to ask whether it really worked or whether this was a fantasy still in research and development.

"Work?" he roared. "Hell, I've probably saved an entire run!"

Collin Schadrech

34

COLLIN SCHADRECH

C O L L I N and Sharie Schadrech operate Farwest
Lodges from the Creamery, their home on the south bank of the Bulkley River in Telkwa, British
Columbia. Since 1980, Collin and his guides have placed an ever-increasing emphasis on the use of dry
flies for steelhead. No doubt, Collin and neighbor Mike Maxwell (Gold-N-West Flyfishers) have had a
strong effect on how anglers visiting the Bulkley approach their fly fishing. I don't think there is
another steelhead river in North America where dry-fly fishing has become such a basic strategy, where
the many variations on the dry fly approach are so single-mindedly pursued. In steelhead fly-fishing
circles, the dry-fly purist lives for the Bulkley.

Collin claims to have caught something like four thousand steelhead in nearly thirty years of angling,
half that number on dry flies, nearly all of them from the Bulkley. However vast the actual number,
his first steelhead were winter fish from the rivers of the lower mainland and Vancouver Island. Small
floats cut from commercial net floats marked the downriver passage of his bait. The occasional winter
steelhead, often a March fish, inexplicably rose to take the float down while ignoring the bait—the first
surface takes he ever witnessed. Several years later, Collin made his first trip north to fish the Skeena
area. "Like everyone else," he says, "I had a Hi-D line." On the Copper and the Bulkley, Collin found
that the wet-fly was sometimes still on the surface when the take took place. "I wondered why I was
doing this wet fly business, this arm-wrenching Hi-D business, when my fishing could be done on the
surface."

Collin's break with steelheading's wet-fly tradition, up to then incremental and tentative, changed almost overnight. "We had a pilgrim appear in our midst in the fall of 1977. He was fishing big clipped deer hair flies on a floating line and taking his two fish a day." By the following fall, Collin was fishing the first of the Mouse patterns, "a straight tan fly with no color whatsoever," he says.

The early Mouse was sparse, as much a wet as a dry fly, beginning as a spun deer-hair variation on the Burlap. During two years of experimentation, Collin often found himself fishing the pattern between anglers casting wet flies with sink-tip lines. He estimates that about eighty to ninety percent of the time, the wet and dry flies did equally well, and when they did not, the wet fly proved more effective. Collin had the fly tied progressively larger and denser to float better and be more visible for the clients he was guiding. When this "improved" Mouse was fished, he began to experience false strikes, the steelhead aggressively coming up behind the fly and not touching it. At such times he began to come back at the steelhead with the thinly dressed original and get the fish to take. Thus began Collin's "finder and catcher" approach, whereby the first fly was fished to locate the steelhead, and a second fly fished to actually hook the steelhead. With refinements, this is essentially the approach that he uses today.

His finder (or locator) fly of choice is a high-riding Bomber, basically the yellow-black-yellow spun deer-hair pattern that Don Hathaway first introduced to Northwest steelheaders a dozen years ago. "As soon as we have a steelhead up on the Bomber, we change to the Mouse," Collin says.

On dull days, or days when rain has turned the water murky, Collin fishes a very large tan Mouse, depending on the disturbance it makes to bring a steelhead up. If he experiences false rises, he downsizes, going to a #6 or #8. The smaller fly rides deeper, digging into the surface film, and the steelhead will likely return to take the fly with confidence.

On bright days, as a locator Collin fishes the Bomber or the black Mouse anglers have nicknamed "Disco Mouse." "On really bright days I prefer to have the fly in the surface film as much as possible, and I'll downsize considerably."

MOUSE

Tail A small bunch of 1/32-inch Flashabou or Krystal Flash, often gold or silver for the tan Mouse, and pearl for the black Mouse. This is optional and is often left out on the smaller sizes.

Body Fly-tying thread worked forward

Head and Wing A bunch of deer body hair tied down and clipped to shape. Head is large. (Note chapter illustration and Mouse selection in the color plates.) Do not spin hair on, because the bottom of the fly is bare of all materials except the tail. The broad, flat underside of the head and wing provide a great deal of concentrated surface area flotation.

(The original Mouse was developed by Jimmy Wright and refined by André Leport for West Lodges.)

Collin told me of having a steelhead come up as many as seventeen times on thirty casts, a "player" not able to resist rising to the fly, but not a "grabber," either. This may happen regardless of whether the dry floats high or low, is large or small, bright or dull. Our mutual experience has been that this situation can be resolved if the angler changes to a sparsely dressed low-water wet fly, a drab, soft-hackle, or spider dressing being an especially good choice.

When I fished with Collin, I commented on how his method of presenting a dry fly differed from that of some other anglers I had observed. "One of the things you see waking dry fly fishermen do is hold their rod up high. They are kind of skating their fly along. I don't do that. I fish the fly the same way I would a wet fly, that is, I seldom cast more than thirty-five degrees to the current. I do small mends, popping the fly a bit, somewhat like Atlantic salmon twitches. Generally, the takes on the Mouse are very, very positive."

His departure from this total swing approach occurs late in the season when water temperatures drop, or when he is working over a particularly large steelhead. Then, Collin slows the swing down with additional mends and holds the dry fly over the steelhead—or the steelhead's lie—for a longer time.

35

JIM TEENY

I first met Jim Teeny nearly twenty years ago at an outdoor show. He was a young entrepreneur with a box full of simple, almost crude flies tied entirely with fibers from a pheasant's tail. Each fly had a black tag explaining that, to safeguard against its duplication, a patent application had been filed. "Look for the fly with the tag!" exclaimed the message. I was incredulous. There was not the slightest doubt in *my* mind that the man had lost *his* mind. It seemed to me that violating the patent would be like tearing off mattress tags. Who could say what I could or could not tie at my fly-tying bench?

Of course, I missed the point entirely. Jim was crazy like the proverbial fox. The patent protected him against other manufacturers and brought fame to the fly called the Teeny Nymph. It soon became evident that the fly was more than a clever marketing strategy. At one time or another, Jim would hold nine International Game Fish Association freshwater world records using the nymph. Ten more world records would fall to other anglers using the nymph, especially for sockeye and chum salmon. Many *Field & Stream* fishing-contest winners used the Teeny Nymph for trophy chinook salmon. The fly proved deadly on steelhead, Alaskan rainbows, grayling, lake-dwelling trout, even bass and panfish. Today, few other flies can match it for versatility and effectiveness in fresh water.

The original Teeny Nymph was—and still is—ringneck pheasant tail fibers wound on a hook with a few additional fibers tied in for a beard. That's it. A dozen of the flies can be tied in a few minutes.

As a kid growing up in Portland, Oregon, Jim would invent new trout patterns and present them

Jim Teeny

to his father for approval. On one occasion, his father said, "Not ugly enough," and sent Jim back to tying up some rougher variations. The result was a dressing Jim called the "Abduli," a simple wet fly of pheasant tail fibers. When he and Danny Shocker first fished it in May 1962 on Oregon's East Lake, they had a phenomenal day. "We were really slamming big trout," Jim remembers. He was sixteen years old, and he did not know it at the time, but the Teeny Nymph was born.

Shortly after Jim had established the Teeny Nymph Company in 1971—the "patent pending" fly, marketed for trout, was the company's sole product—he was winter-steelheading on Washington's Kalama River. A very slow day prompted him to fish his Teeny Nymph. A chrome-bright steelhead took the drab fly, and Jim was soon bleaching and dyeing pheasant tail in a variety of hot "steelhead" colors. Not surprisingly, the new flies found wide acceptance among salmon fly fishermen. Additional colors resulted from requests by other anglers. The black might represent a leech, the green a damselfly larva, the antique gold a stonefly nymph, the ginger perhaps a caddis nymph.

Howard West of Scientific Anglers came out from Minnesota to fish with Jim on the Kalama in the mid-1970s. Jim was asked at the end of a day how he liked their fastest sinking line, the High Speed Hi-D. "Howard, they're the best sinking lines on the coast," Jim replied. "But if you want to fish the British Columbia, Washington, and Oregon rivers, you need a line that will sink two to three times faster. With such a line, we wouldn't have to put split shot on our leaders or cast a mile upstream to get the fly down."

West returned to Scientific Anglers, and with these comments in mind, asked research and development to come up with Deep Water Express. Prototypes of the line were sent to Jim. "I went out and tripled my steelhead hookups," he told me. Jim then used the new line to design a sink tip line that would run deeper than anything currently on the market. The results were the now-famous Teeny lines, twenty-four feet of sink tip spliced to extra-heavy-diameter running line, marketed in 200, 300, 400, and 500 grains.

Use of the Teeny lines rapidly spread far beyond the steelhead and salmon rivers of the Pacific Coast. Most saltwater fly fishermen now carry a few. One of my largest fly-caught dorado, a bull of thirty pounds, came to a 4/0 Deceiver while I was casting a Teeny 400 off Loreto, Mexico. I've packed the Teeny 300 from Alaska to Argentina and wouldn't be without one. I usually fish with the full twenty-four-foot length, but the sinking portion can be trimmed back to suit local needs and specific rod requirements.

The super-fast-sinking lines and compact, effective, easily tied flies came to suit Jim's very direct approach to his steelhead fly fishing. "If you spot him, you've got him," he likes to say. Jim *hunts* for his steelhead by using polarized glasses (switching to amber on overcast days) and carefully studying the river until he locates a holding steelhead. He then works into position slightly below the fish and casts upstream, so that the dead-drifting fly will reach the steelhead's level by the time it reaches the lie. Jim may give a twitch to his Teeny Leech, or give it a slow strip retrieve to provide additional action. If necessary, additional weight is added to the leader at the junction of the tippet. The take will be soft, though the strike can be very hard if the dead drift is finished and the fly is quartering on the swing. If the steelhead refuses the fly, Jim will persist, changing flies and changing his position. He feels that the steelhead will take the fly about eighty percent of the time. If he finds the steelhead in an unfishable lie, he may "rock him" with a fist-sized rock tossed so judiciously that the steelhead is moved a short distance. The fishing is then resumed, to better advantage.

For much of this unorthodox approach Jim relies upon either a T-300 or T-400 line and a three-foot leader consisting of twelve inches of twenty-pound butt perfection looped to twenty-four inches of twelve-pound test tippet. He never uses less than eight-pound test and presses his fish hard for a quick release.

Donna Teeny

If the water is shallow, Jim uses the Teeny Mini-Tip, a floating line with a five-foot Deep Water Express sink tip. The leader is typically ten feet long, the depth of the fly controlled by mending.

Donna Teeny is often at Jim's side for clinics, outdoor shows, and slide presentations. She is an expert fly fisher and has caught many steelhead and salmon with the flies and lines she and Jim promote.

TEENY NYMPH, TEENY LEECH, AND FLASH FLY

Pheasant tail and tying instructions can be purchased from the Teeny Nymph Company, P.O. Box 989, Gresham, Oregon.

Fibers stripped from the center tail feathers of a ring-necked pheasant provide the basic material in all these flies. The body is wound on tightly from the bend of the hook and tied off at the head. Additional fibers form a throat, and a wing in the larger sizes. The Leech has a long tail, and a body and throat tied in as with the Nymph. On #4 and #2, the throat—or feelers—may be tied in twice, first bisecting the body and then at the head. The Nymph and Leech are tied entirely of one color. Jim prefers drab colors for hard-fished waters; they are not so likely to spook wary steelhead. The Flash Flies often have a wing and body of contrasting colors. They are tied just like a Nymph, but have a wing topped with Krystal Flash. Besides the natural colors, the flies are tied in fluorescent cerise, hot orange, and purple. Jim told me that many of the popular combinations he now markets originated with anglers experimenting with various color combinations.

36

LANI WALLER

FLY fishers know Lani Waller as the star of three 3M videos in which he shares his steelheading techniques with the viewer. Together they experience the Deschutes, Dean, and Babine rivers, fly-fishing adventures that eventually lead to enormous steelhead rising to the Waller Waker, the big dry fly of Lani's own design. The series, an instructional windfall for neophyte and expert alike, has achieved great popularity, and the success of the videos is due primarily to Lani. His friendly demeanor, craggy good looks, and soft Missouri drawl give his screen presence great charm.

The first time I fished with Lani, I quickly learned that the man is the genuine article, a fishing maniac with laser eyes and the concentration of a tai chi master. "Lani," I've told friends, "could find a steelhead in a rain barrel—and then raise it to a fly."

Fishing, especially fly fishing, was just about the only thing Lani ever wanted to do. For years, he was a self-confessed "fishing bum" in Chico, California, before "turning professional" in 1974, and writing a column called "Angler's Corner" for a local newspaper. Two years later, he formed a partnership with Dave Inks and Andy Puyans and opened Creative Sports III in San Rafael. Lani developed a small travel program on the side and led fishing parties to Alaska. After six years, he shut down the shop. "The essence of fly fishing was not sitting behind the counter," he told me. Shortly thereafter he was managing the fly-fishing department of the Eddie Bauer store in San Francisco. The fly-fishing travel program he developed in conjunction with this job got the attention of Bob Nauheim and Frank

Lani Waller

Bertainia of Fishing International, and they hired him to handle all their steelhead fly-fishing accounts. In 1987, Lani established his own fly-fishing travel business, called Lani Waller's International Angler.

Irwin Brown, an executive of 3M, and Howard West, who managed Scientific Anglers for 3M, were in the audience when Lani narrated a slide show at the l986 San Mateo outdoor show. They were so impressed with his presentation that Lani was offered the opportunity to make a series of steelheading videos.

The production of these videos ultimately took Lani to the Dean River, where some of the dry-fly sequences were shot. On a pool that came to be called Moviemaker, John Fabian, the director and head camerman for the production crew, urged Lani to tie up a dry fly that would be highly visible. The result was the Waller Waker, a remarkable achievement in steelhead dry-fly design.

WALLER WAKER

Hook Tiemco 7089 light salmon or Partridge Bartleet. Sizes 2 and 4 are most frequently used, but also tied on 8 to 1/0.

Tail Very stiff moose

Wing White calf tail. Tie in wing and tail dry-fly fashion. Set wing well forward. Isolate the wings and tail section by folding pieces of Scotch Magic Tape around each wing. This helps to prevent the wings and tail from being cut accidentally when the body is trimmed.

Body Alternate bands of black-dyed deer body hair and natural moose. For best results, *fold* the clumps of deer body hair with the bottom of the V pushed up against the hook shank. Tie it down in this position. This keeps almost the entire body riding above the hook shank.

Throat Stiff moose extending to the base of the tail

Variations Lani ties two variations of the original. In the first, fluorescent yellow calf tail is substituted in the wing to provide even greater visibility. The body is then alternate bands of dyed brown deer body hair and natural moose. In the second variation, sometimes called the Bumblebee, the tail and throat are natural moose, and the body is banded black, orange, and black with deer body hair. The wing of the Bumblebee Waker is natural elk. The Bumblebee is tied in smaller sizes, usually 4 to 8.

Tying the body above the hook as described, rather than spinning the deer hair on, achieves several important goals. The hook gap is maintained, the hook rides below the surface while the fly rides on and above the surface, and the fly is an excellent floater even in broken water. The design rarely makes a riffling hitch necessary. If a hitch is made, it can be looped behind the wing and throat. Once the body and wings have soaked up some water, however, the fly will tend to ride on its side. Keeping the wings on the short side helps to reduce this tendency. My preference is to loop the hitch behind the head. This reduces the advantages of a hitch on the Waker, but it keeps the fly riding properly. The very clean construction around the head makes securing both a double turle knot and a hitch easy—no small thing when fishing over a promising lie in last light.

The Waller Waker is remarkably versatile, both as a searching and an "eating" pattern. "It works well dead-drifted, skated across, or downstream on a wake," claims Lani.

I have many times watched Lani fish the Waker. One particularly effective approach he uses—not unlike the technique employed by the Maxwells—involves casting slightly upstream for a drag-free downstream float, throwing outside mends when the fly comes by to continue the float, and letting the fly sweep downstream before it turns and begins to wake. Another method is greased line, a straight-across cast and the fly twitched back as it is mended on its swing across the current.

At all times, the rod is held upright at a forty-five-degree angle to the water. When the steelhead takes the dry, Lani lets the fish take the fly down and holds the running line firmly before raising the rod on an already tight line. The raised rod allows a little slack, which enables the steelhead to turn so that the fly, it is hoped, penetrates the tough hinge area of its jaw.

If a steelhead boils but does not take as the fly is swinging, Lani repeats the cast exactly as before, but makes it two to three feet shorter. He does this in case the steelhead has moved upstream several feet from its original station. The third cast is identical to the first. His fourth cast is about four feet longer than the first. If the steelhead still refuses to come back, Lani changes to a fly that is different in both color and floating/waking characteristics. His alternate pattern of choice in recent years has been Bob Wagoner's Steelhead Skater, a high-riding Wulff-like dressing with inverted wings (see Chapter 38). The Skater is presented as in casts two, three, and four using the Waller Waker, that is, short, the original distance cast, and then long. Lani feels that nine times out of ten, the Skater will trigger a rise. But for that one-in-ten steelhead, he goes to a small, drab, natural looking wet fly, a Burlap or Spade-type, for example. It is most unusual when he can't bring a steelhead back during some part of this sequence.

Lani Waller, like most steelhead dry-fly fishermen, feels that, given the right conditions, any steelhead, regardless of size, can be brought up to a dry. His own best with the Waker was twenty-one pounds. Howard West reportedly landed two steelhead, each weighing about twenty-two pounds, using the pattern. I've heard of other anglers taking steelhead to twenty-five pounds using the fly. While these reports have all come out of the Babine and the Silver Hilton Lodge, the Waller Waker is a highly regarded standard on all the major steelhead rivers where a large, unsinkable dry is called for.

Lani manages the big, wind-resistant Waker with a nine-and-a-half-foot 8-weight rod and a weight-8 or 9 long-belly forward-taper line. (This is his choice for wet-fly fishing as well.) He chooses a leader diameter of .010 to .013, ten- to fifteen-pound test in abrasion resistant Maxima.

Lani's choice of wet flies centers mostly around the Boss, Silver Hilton, Green-Butt Skunk, Burlap, and his own variation of the Polar Shrimp, called the Polar Flash. It is the basic Polar Shimp dressing but with a wing of white marabou over pearl Krystal Flash. If a large silhouette pattern is called for in discolored water, Lani fishes Randall Kaufmann's Signal Light in sizes 1/0 and 2/0. The Boss dressings that Lani intends to fish right on the bottom are tied on a hook used by bass fishermen to secure a plastic worm. The hook has a keel bend and will turn upside down when fished, making the fly nearly weedless.

The Boss by Lani Waller.

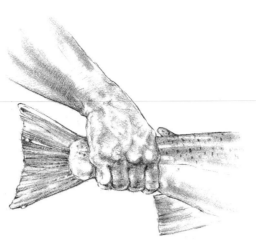

37

BOB YORK

W H E N I answer the phone, the voice is familiar, but distant and nicked by static.

"Hi! Trey! It's Steelhead Bob!"

"Bob! Where are you?" Good question. This time he is dropping quarters down an ancient pay phone in Ketchikan, Alaska.

"Just flew out from a stream in Boca de Quadra Inlet! Good for the fly! Big steelhead! My largest went twenty-three pounds!"

He continues to relate his latest adventure. A new chapter in my steelhead education has begun.

Bob York's pursuit of steelhead is one part holy crusade, one part devout pilgrimage. He engages the sport passionately, resolutely, and without quarter. His life is built around this singular obsession like no other person I know. He sometimes calls himself a "Steelhead Bum," a title he claims with pride. The bottom line is this: The man fishes for steelhead eight months a year, day in and day out, and has done so for as long as almost anyone can remember.

Each year from May through July, since the 1950s, Bob has fished commercially in Bristol Bay for sockeye salmon on his wooden gill-netter. These months of round-the-clock work fund his other months of fly fishing, including the occasional jaunt to South America.

I first met Bob on the Kispiox one October, at Olga Walker's lodge. We had coffee together and discovered that we would both be in Bariloche, Argentina, the same week in January. Couldn't we fish

Bob York

for trout and hoist a glass of wine together? Bob agreed. But when I arrived in that city in the Andean foothills, I found no Bob and no message. His hotel's receptionist could only say that he had left four days earlier. I assumed that this was a case of passion over reason, that somewhere in Patagonia, probably on a windy *boca*, Bob was firing a Zonker out ninety feet and having the time of his life.

I was wrong. As I struggled to make myself understood to the desk clerk, my friend was driving north from his Seattle home, headed for the Queen Charlotte Islands and the Yakoun's fabled run of winter steelhead. I never did find out what soured him on Argentina that year. Bob had left a message for me, but apparently no one at his hotel could understand his brand of Spanish. Nor mine, for that matter.

I found him later that year, once when he was coming off the Dean with Salty Saltzman, and again while I was floating the Bulkley River Canyon. He was blasting upstream in his famous (or infamous) jet boat, the *Rainbow Chaser*. Bob claims he can reach reach freeway speeds when he isn't carrying his inflatable jet boat. When water gets too thin for the big boat, he pumps up the inflatable and is on his way.

Dozens of rivers mark his year. Bob may get as far south as the North Umpqua, and he spends months in southeast Alaska. The Skeena system draws him like a magnet. He calls the Kispiox his home river.

Bob confesses he was a "stone age fisherman"—his title for gear fisherman—back in 1973, when after a four-hour struggle, he beached a thirty-four-pound buck from the Kispiox's Dundas Drift. He still cannot recall a stronger steelhead among the four thousand he has caught, but he remembers the fish more for marking his conversion to fly fishing.

Late each summer, Bob tows his trailer north to the Kispiox River Resort and stays the fall, fishing the Kispiox when water conditions permit, and using the area as a springboard to new, yet-to-be-discovered steelhead waters. He charters helicopters and float planes, and his jet boats transport him up uncharted rivers or across the straits and channels of southeast Alaska. There is no major river that he has not fished.

Several years ago on the Kispiox, he beached a thirty-one-pound steelhead using a General Practitioner. Four minutes later, he hooked a second steelhead on a Green-Butt Skunk. It too went thirty-one pounds. No, it wasn't the same fish—Bob took measurements each time. Although this is his best story of catching lightning in a bottle, he can hardly remember a year when his largest steelhead did not make twenty-five pounds.

Bob normally fishes several sink-tip lines, depending on conditions and river, but he changes to a forward-taper floater under low-water conditions. With either line A or B (see below), his running line of choice is weight 4 Scientific Anglers.

Line A: Twelve-foot weight 8 Hi-Speed Hi-D spliced to sixteen-foot floating-weight 10
Line B: Seventeen-foot weight 11 Hi-Speed Hi-D spliced to ten-foot floating-weight 12 to 13
Line C: Teeny 300, containing twenty-four-foot sink tip of Deep Water Express

The rods used to fish these lines are a nine-and-a-half-foot for a 9-weight and a ten-foot for an 8-weight.

KISPIOX BRIGHT

Tail Red calf tail mixed with a few strands of yellow Krystal Flash
Body Purple chenille ribbed with silver tinsel
Hackle Hot orange

Wing White bucktail topped with yellow bucktail that is mixed with yellow Krystal Flash (FisHair may be substituted for bucktail)

Bob likes this dressing when water conditions are high, but not too discolored. "When the water is brown on the Kispiox, you are lost if using a bright fly." His choice then is any extremely dark fly, black and purple his first choices.

Early in their migration, Bob calls the Kispiox steelhead "coastal in character." After they have acclimated to the Kispiox, he says they display "interior characteristics," becoming "trouty," and "much like Thompson steelhead."

KISPIOX DARK

Tail Black bucktail
Body Green floss ribbed with gold tinsel
Hackle Grizzly, tied as a beard

Wing Black bucktail mixed with black Krystal Flash
Head Small lead "eyes" on each side for additional weight, optional

The Kispiox Dark is a standard when water is off-colored, even brown. Bob feels that green is an especially good Kispiox color if there is some visibility to the river.

SKEENA WOOLLY BUGGER

Tail Golden pheasant tippet
Body Black wool palmered with grizzly hackle
Wing Black Krystal Flash, thin

Hackle Hot orange as a collar over the wing
Head Orange tying thread

This is actually a pattern for the Bulkley, the "finest steelhead river in the world for the dry fly," according to Bob. He believes that black and orange are especially effective colors. The dressing is large, 1/0 and 2/0 normally, and never smaller than 2. The fly can be effectively fished sunk or greased-line.

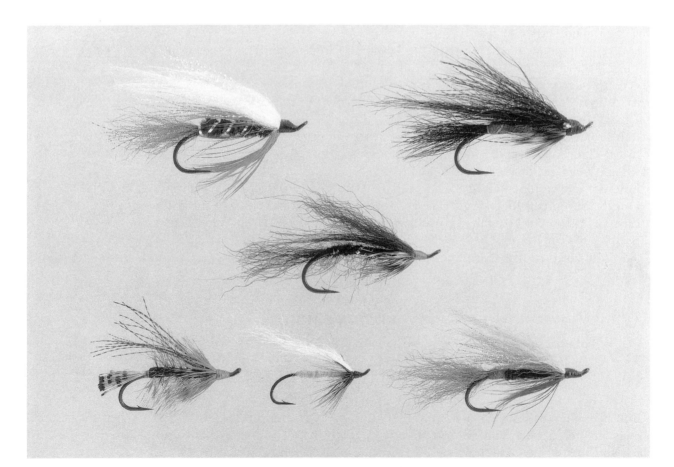

Row 1 Kispiox Bright, Kispiox Dark
Row 2 Thompson Special
Row 3 Skeena Woolly Bugger, Low Water Green, Spring Favorite

SPRING FAVORITE

Tail Red calf tail
Butt Green wool
Body Red chenille

Hackle Red
Wing Orange calf tail over a few strands of orange Krystal Flash

Bob has used this pattern for many years for late-run winter steelhead on Washington's Skagit and Sauk rivers, and on British Columbia's Bella Coola. It is tied in sizes 2 to 2/0.

THOMPSON SPECIAL

Tail Brown calf tail
Body Black wool, thin, ribbed with silver tinsel
Hackle Grizzly

Wing Brown calf tail over a few strands of black calf tail
Head Orange

Bob told me that with this dressing he gets a "buggy pattern for interior-type fish," a description that best describes the Thompson's late-arriving summer run. He feels a long slender fly is especially good on the Thompson.

This river fishes well for Bob right through December, even when the water temperature falls into the thirties.

LOW WATER GREEN

Tail None
Body Insect green wool, thin

Hackle Furnace
Wing White calf tail

Bob uses this fly only on the Kispiox during very low water conditions, always fishing it in #4 or smaller. The dressing reflects his prejudice for green on this river.

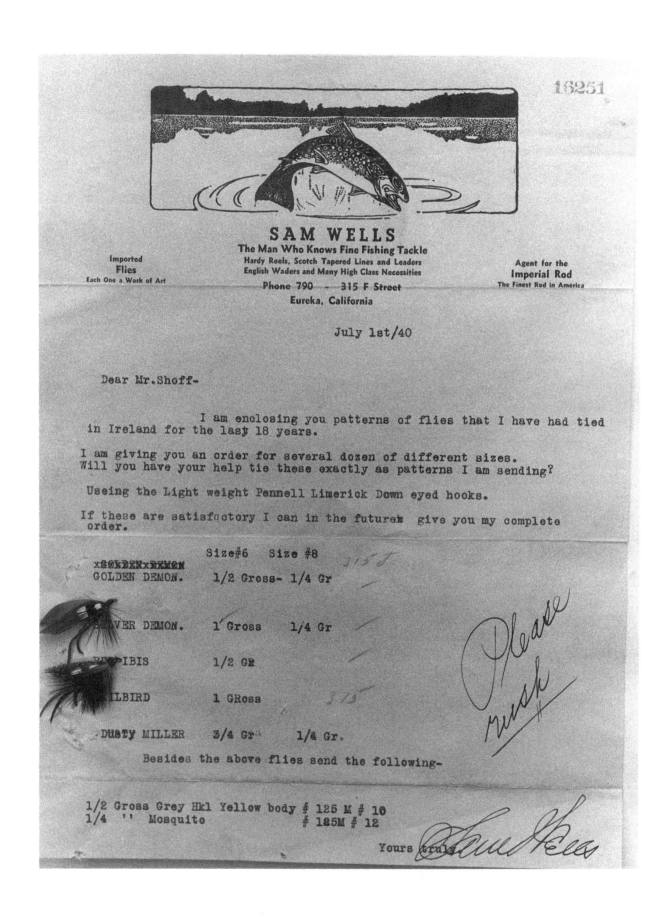

16251

SAM WELLS

The Man Who Knows Fine Fishing Tackle

Hardy Reels, Scotch Tapered Lines and Leaders
English Waders and Many High Class Necessities

Imported
Flies
Each One a Work of Art

Agent for the
Imperial Rod
The Finest Rod in America

Phone 790 - 315 F Street
Eureka, California

July 1st/40

Dear Mr.Shoff-

      I am enclosing you patterns of flies that I have had tied
in Ireland for the last 18 years.

I am giving you an order for several dozen of different sizes.
Will you have your help tie these exactly as patterns I am sending?

Useing the Light weight Pennell Limerick Down eyed hooks.

If these are satisfactory I can in the future give you my complete
order.

	Size#6	Size #8
xGOLDENxDEMON GOLDEN DEMON.	1/2 Gross-	1/4 Gr
SILVER DEMON.	1 Gross	1/4 Gr
RED IBIS	1/2 Gr	
RAILBIRD	1 GRoss	
DUSTY MILLER	3/4 Gr	1/4 Gr.

      Besides the above flies send the following-

1/2 Gross Grey Hkl Yellow body # 125 M # 10
1/4 '' Mosquito   # 125M # 12

Please
rush

Yours truly

38

NEW STEELHEAD FLY PATTERNS

ATLANTIC SALMON

Nineteenth-century Atlantic salmon dressings came to steelheading embodying the most aristocratic of all angling heritages. Slips of feathers from a dozen different exotic birds were crafted into a single fly that was an attractor of fish and a metaphor for peerage, propriety, and the salmon mystique. A Jock Scott or a Thunder and Lightning spoke to us, grounded us, gave our sport a necessary infusion of soul. We traded on this association, and our steelhead flies, always the product of plebeian enterprise, needn't ever be graceless confections. Married strips of dyed goose, silk tags, ostrich butts, heads of peacock herl, and golden pheasant crests embellished ties, bastard creations that nevertheless required a thorough knowledge of fly tying. A British ghillie would have considered them coarse as he noted parts missing from the classic originals, but the flies gladdened our untutored frontier anglers and filled them with confidence. A steelhead fly is nothing if it can't do that.

The earliest "fly shops" were hardware stores that sold fishing and hunting licenses. At a back counter beneath elk heads and stuffed salmon, one could purchase anything from deer rifles to snelled trout flies imported from Ireland and Scotland. In the larger sizes, these wet flies were among the first steelhead patterns, the Royal Coachman, Black Gnat, Professor, and Red Ibis, for example. Steelhead flies would come to have red tails and white wings and, as often as not, cheeks of jungle cock. When they came to be constructed of bucktail and chenille, these simple trout flies were easily converted.

The elaborate Atlantic salmon patterns were not. For more than thirty years, the proliferation of bright, showy steelhead bucktails became a distinctly American art form and symbolized the sport of steelhead fly fishing. In these many dressings, Atlantic salmon flies survived mostly as trace elements.

Two men in particular, Sam Wells and Joe Wharton, strongly influenced the early development of steelhead flies. Wells's shop at 315 F Street in Eureka, California, serviced fly fishermen bound for the Eel River, certainly the first American river where summer-run steelhead were routinely pursued with a fly. His own Wells Special, John Benn's Railbird, and Sumner Carson's Royal Coachman were locally popular steelhead dressings. Beginning in 1922, Wells had these and other steelhead patterns tied for him in Ireland. "Imported flies" meant British, and that mattered greatly to West Coast anglers taking their first tentative steps toward sorting out steelhead with a fly. According to Wells's letterhead, he could advance the angler's needs with "Hardy Reels, Scotch Tapered Lines and Leaders, English Waders, and Many High Class Necessities."

Joe Wharton's store changed from hardware to sporting goods, and by the 1930s, his location at 104 South Sixth Street in Grants Pass, Oregon, was a landmark. He helped outfit Zane Grey for an expedition down the Rogue in 1926, and Grey had urged him to begin stocking English and Scottish fly tackle. The writer told about his Rogue adventures in *Tales of Freshwater Fishing,* and Wharton became a celebrity. He took to calling himself the "Sage of the Rogue," and wrote extravagantly about its steelhead. Wharton's "#1 Special" became the Rogue River Special, and his "Turkey and Red" became an early favorite of Grey's.

Not all the steelhead flies being sold were imported. Commercial fly tying was always something of a cottage industry, often a sideline occupation that attracted women who could work from their homes. Overhead was minimal, the flies readily marketed through local sporting goods stores.

"The Bunnell Sisters," Ardath and Irene, grew up in Goldendale, Washington, and learned their craft from Wharton and Wells. They did a mail-order business, Oregon Waters Fly Company, from Portland, Oregon, and called their product "Water Call 'Scotch tied' Flies." These flies reflected the fashion of the 1930s, when steelhead flies became hairwings, a bucktail wing vastly out of proportion to the body, three or four times the length of the hook. Anglers found the dressings extremely unstable, a characteristic that led to the use of double hooks, especially on the Rogue. Among the fifteen "steelhead" patterns the Bunnell Sisters listed in their catalog were the Durham Ranger and Jock Scott as simplified feather wings, and a hairwing Silver Doctor.

Glen Evans, Inc., a tackle and lure manufacturer in Caldwell, Idaho, was the largest commercial tyer in the West through the 1940s and 1950s. John Joy worked for Evans and had invented the sewing-machine "vise," a treadle operation in which the hook spun around and could be dressed in seconds. Eventually, over a hundred women tied flies for Evans on these machines, including Joy's daughter, Audrey.

Audrey Joy left Idaho in 1945 to find work in Portland, Oregon. At the time, Polly Rosborough was quitting his job as a fly tyer in the sporting goods section of Meier and Frank, a Portland department store, and the job became available to Joy. For more than twenty years she tied at her sewing machine—an estimated 300,000 flies, and her little booth became a shrine. She is best remembered for refining the Rogue River Special and Juicy Bug to more compact double hook dressings.

Perhaps the most influential of the sporting goods dealers was Shoff's Tackle in Kent, Washington. Though little known outside of Puget Sound, Clarence Shoff wholesaled flies and fly-tying materials to many other businesses, including Sam Wells, Joe Wharton, and C. Jim Pray. By the 1930s, Zane Grey was ordering flies directly from Shoff. In a handwritten letter dated April 7, 1935, he wrote: "I rec'd the 6 dozen flies and they sure are swell. I confess that collecting flies is a passion with me. But some of them I use. Tie me a dozen Gold Demon Bucktails for the size hook enclosed. Also, one dozen each of Hair Coachman in 10-8-6-4 and the size I enclose. Put in a little more bucktail."

This last request is interesting. At the time, Washington steelhead fly fishers were tying their flies on larger hooks and along sparser lines. Grey, still operating from a California-Southern Oregon frame of reference, wanted flies with longer streamer-style wings and tied on regular-length hooks.

Zane Grey's next letter to Shoff, dated May 22, 1935, illustrates the West Coast angler's ambivalence about Atlantic salmon dressings that persisted in steelheading. "One dozen each of numbers 6, 4, 2,

01, size hooks, Jock Scott pattern only with gold body (not gilt) with red streamer running out from the body."

By the 1940s, steelheading had its own cherished fly patterns, home-grown and winged with bucktail or polar bear. Jim Pray's Optics and Thor, the Umpqua Special and Skunk from the North Umpqua, Ken McLeod's Skykomish Sunrise and Purple Peril, Enos Bradner's Brad's Brat, and Clarence Shoff's Polar Shrimp were standards that would soon beget hundreds of similar patterns.

The steelhead bucktail was something of a one-dimensional approach. It was usually fished on a sinking line, commonly a shooting head system by the 1960s, weighted for summer fishing, and heavily weighted for winter rivers. Hook size ran to 6s, 4s, and 2s in regular length, with turned-down eye. Its typical symmetry was a fairly long hackle tail, a wing that came to the end of the tail, and hackle that reached just to the point of the hook. Overdressed by today's standards, it did not penetrate strong currents well on a floating or slow-sinking silk line, and was likely to plane across the surface on its side. Weighting the fly helped to sink it, but this made it even less stable, and not uncommonly, the fly passed through a hard swing upside down.

Anglers sought to fish these flies well sunk because of their general conviction that the fly needed to be carried to the steelhead, that it was less effective—or not effective at all—when working in the surface film. Gradually, our perceptions changed.

Twenty years ago, steelhead fly fishing began a tremendous growth that corresponded to a truly remarkable renaissance in steelhead fly tying. For inspiration, tyers returned to their spiritual roots, to the Atlantic salmon flies of both the past and the present. They dusted off *Greased Line Fishing*, studied it carefully, and tied low-water flies that functioned as beautifully as they were formed.

Since the 1930s, hairwing Atlantic salmon flies, particularly those from New Brunswick's Miramichi, had been slowly replacing the classic full-dressed Atlantic salmon patterns. Harry Smith's Black Bear series, John Cosseboom's lovely full-collared patterns, and Roy Angus Thompson's now famous Rat series (RAT for his initials), were examples of highly original Atlantic salmon ties using bear, squirrel tail, and fox—not bucktail. At the same time, complicated married-wing dressings were dressed down—"reduced"—and, when possible, simply tied with wings of hair. These and other dressings were given a "Portland hitch" so that the leader came from the throat of the fly, forcing the fly into the surface film where it caused a visible and erratic wake. By the 1960s, a spun-deer-hair dry fly, the Bomber, was fished under intentional drag on a downstream swing and "skated" in a manner impossible to achieve with Wulffs and Steelhead Bees. It, too, could be given a "hitch" and made nearly unsinkable.

These developments in Canada ignored Scottish spey flies, an omission resolved by Syd Glasso of Forks, Washington, with spey flies that are still among the most beautiful in steelheading. Syd inspired an army of disciplined, studious followers, and I think the Northwest—including British Columbia—has a larger number of truly outstanding fly dressers than any other area of the world.

We had gleaned so much from Atlantic salmon anglers, that by the 1970s, our heads were filled with many new approaches to tying and fishing steelhead flies. New materials, and traditional materials dyed in exciting hot colors, were appearing, challenging the imagination still further. Using Atlantic salmon dressings for their graceful proportions and better swimming characteristics, anglers began the cross-pollination that has created a generation of steelhead flies at once new and classic.

This renewed fascination with Atlantic salmon flies sent many of us searching through any books we could find on the subject. Lee Wulff's classic, *The Atlantic Salmon*, was my starting point. Joe Bates's *Atlantic Salmon Flies and Fishing* was next. However, it was Art Flick's *Master Fly-Tying Guide* that had the greatest effect on me. One of the chapters, "Salmon Flies," was written by Ernest Schwiebert. Here the inimitable author describes and discusses a group of hairwing Atlantic salmon patterns and the roles each has played in his angling fortunes. I tied up five of the dozen described, the Orange Charm, Blue Charm, Green Butt (a.k.a. Black Bear), Black Fitchtail, and Minktail, and rose steelhead to all of them. I fished them on doubles, low water singles, dressed them modestly, and dressed them very sparse, wound the hackle under the wing, tied it on as a throat, and sometimes with the Green Butt and Black Fitchtail, gave the fly a tiny head by finishing it with a black collar tied back and blending into the wing and hackle. The only notable change I made, however, was to combine the tag and tip by winding the floss over most of the silver tinsel tag. This produced a dot of bright color visible for a remarkable distance.

Green Butt by Bob Veverka. This famous Vermont tyer's Atlantic Salmon dressings are equally useful on Northwest steelhead rivers.

ORANGE CHARM

Tag Flat silver tinsel
Tip Yellow-orange fluorescent floss. (I use fluorescent orange—*not* "hot," or "flame" orange.)

Tail Golden pheasant crest
Body Black floss ribbed with flat silver tinsel
Throat Bright orange hackle fibers
Wing Red squirrel tail

BLUE CHARM

Tag Flat silver tinsel
Tip Fluorescent yellow floss
Tail Golden pheasant crest

Body Black floss ribbed with flat silver tinsel
Throat Bright blue hackle fibers
Wing Red squirrel tail

BLACK FITCHTAIL

Tag Flat silver tinsel
Tip Orange-yellow fluorescent floss (see Orange Charm for my comments)
Tail Golden pheasant crest

Body Black floss ribbed with flat silver tinsel
Throat Black hackle fibers
Wing Black fitchtail (I substitute black squirrel tail)

GREEN BUTT

Tag Flat silver tinsel
Tip Bright green fluorescent floss
Tail Golden pheasant crest
Body Black floss ribbed with flat silver tinsel

Throat Black hackle fibers
Wing Black fitchtail (I substitute black squirrel tail)

MINKTAIL

Tag Flat silver tinsel
Tip Fluorescent yellow floss
Tail Golden pheasant crest
Body Black floss ribbed with flat silver tinsel

Throat Iron blue dun hackle fibers
Wing Light brown mink or fitchtail (I usually use very fine buck tail from the backside of a tail)

Jim Vincent handed me this bizarre, spiderlike version of the classic original. "I call this the Black Bear—with its head up its ass," he said. "The fly's a killer on the Kispiox." The tail, wing, and hackle were all black bear fur. The butt of fluorescent green wool wrapped around small bead chain "eyes." No ribbing adorned the body of black chenille or dubbing.

BOMBERS

Joseph Bates, in *Atlantic Salmon Flies and Fishing*, credits Francois de B. Gourdeau with the Bottlewasher, a dressing built entirely of hackles wound tightly around a light-wire hook. Bates describes "its counterpart in hair-body" as the Bomber, an Atlantic salmon fly "developed in approximately 1967, for use on New Brunswick's Miramichi River, where it has been very effective." Rev. Elmer J. Smith, a Miramichi regular in the late 1960s, tied the Bomber that illustrates Bates's book, but he is not honored as its inventor, though that was apparently the case.

The Miramichi was the scene of intense experimentation in fly design during the 1950s and 1960s. The Butterfly, a splayed-winged pattern developed by Maurice Ingalls in 1957, was fished dry, wet, and with a hitch. Hairwing flies were used routinely, and the Butt series, essentially a Black Bear with an orange-, red-, or green-silk butt, were extremely popular. Long-hackled dry flies were cast upstream and "skated," drag-free. Hairwing dries were "skittered" under drag on a downstream swing, the basic waking approach. Bombers, spun with natural brown, grey, or white deer hair, were fished upstream drag-free, downstream under drag, or even sunk and fished wet. This multidimensional approach to a sport long ruled by sacred and hidebound traditions was soon felt in steelhead fly-fishing circles as well. Certainly any study into the genealogy of steelhead flies and how they are presented could do no better than to look to the Miramichi. The Bomber is a case in point.

The Bomber has become so popular as a steelhead dry fly that many anglers will fish nothing else. It is tied in an endless variety of colors and styles. It has been referred to as a "locator fly" and a "guides' fly" for its ability to cause a steelhead to show itself, and a "skater" for its erratic, high-floating characteristics. At no time, however, does the fly ride on its hackle points. In fact, many Bombers are tied without any hackle, palmered or otherwise.

No one has yet taken credit for bringing the Bomber West for steelhead. Anglers were likely experimenting with the fly for steelhead only a few years following its introduction on the Miramichi. By 1975, Steve Pettit and Keith Stonebreaker were using it regularly on Idaho's Clearwater. The original:

BOMBER

Tail Deer body hair or white calf tail
Body Deer body hair spun on and clipped to shape, tapering at both ends. Most of the body is clipped away under the hook to avoid reducing the hook gap. Palmer with brown saddle hackle.
Wing Single bunch of deer body hair or white calf tail. An additional turn or two of hackle is sometimes taken around the wing.

Comments: The wing does not assist in floating the fly. A wing of white calf tail is preferred because, as with Bi-visible flies, the touch of white makes the fly more visible in poor light. Leroy Hyatt (see Hyatt's Caddis) ties a variation called the Grizzly Bomber. The tail and wing are white calf tail. (Use the end of the tail for the wing so that the wing curls back naturally.) Body is palmered with grizzly saddle.

Modifications to the original were not long in coming. In the late 1970s, Don Hathaway, a commercial fly tyer from Nampa, Idaho, worked in Bill Hunter's fly-fishing shop in New Boston, New Hampshire. He took classes in tying full-dressed Atlantic salmon flies and became familiar with the Bomber, which he knew was sometimes fished on the Clearwater and Grande Ronde rivers. When Don returned home several months later, he began tinkering with the Bomber's design and color. For inspiration,

Don Hathaway

he used caterpillars he had observed in British Columbia. One was yellow and black, the other orange-red and black, the so-called Woolly Bear or Woolly Worm. Samples of the Yellow and Black and the Orange and Black were given to friends to try in British Columbia, on the Copper, Bulkley-Morice, and Kispiox rivers. Results were immediate and spectacular. Within a couple of years, these gaudy "bumble bee" bombers were more popular than the original. Other color combinations followed, including a Bomber in contrasting shades of violet and purple. Canadian Bombers still tend to be larger—6s and 4s, even 2s—than those commonly used on U.S. waters. Along the way, Don dropped the soft calf-tail wing and tail for a short, *horizontal* wing of stiff moose or javelina.

See the Bomber color plate for Don's Yellow and Black, Orange and Black, and Purple Bomber.

The single wing of the Bomber has a lot to do with how the fly fishes. When tied with calf tail or squirrel tail and left fairly long, the wing fills with water and tips the fly over. The wing's tension with the surface pins the fly down in that position. This is not fatal. I have raised many steelhead with a Bomber in this position. Tying a riffling hitch—usually a good idea when fishing a Bomber—will not change this. In fact, a hitched Bomber lying over on its side creates a sizable wake on the swing.

Black and Yellow Bomber—Don Hathaway

Several things can be done to reduce this tendency. Shortening the wing is one, and following Don Hathaway's approach is another. Tying the wing upright and divided will set the Bomber rocking on the swing, each wing helping to prevent the fly from lying over. Keeping the wing short and fanned out and saturating part or all of it with glue is yet another solution. The wing then tends to force the fly up on the surface as long as the fly remains waking under tension. Some anglers add a few strands of moose at the throat, which helps to skid the fly on top to behave even more erratically.

The Bomber is made more stable when the cylindrical body is clipped flat on the bottom. Anglers sometimes shave the underside of the fly with a razor blade as close to the hook shank as they dare, both to stabilize the fly and to maximize the hook gap. Some Bombers are clipped nearly flat on the bottom *and* the top, creating an oblong saucer shape that skates and wakes its way across currents without rolling over.

BLACK BOMBER

Tail White calf tail
Body Black deer body hair spun and clipped to shape. Palmer body with grizzly saddle hackle.

Wing White calf tail

This combination of colors is a favorite of mine. If the wing is kept short and full, I can take the hitch behind the wing. The resulting Bomber, if dressed well, keeps waking for hours.

Keith Stonebreaker, of Lewiston, Idaho, has been using Bombers on the Clearwater River since 1975. He fishes his own variation called the Cigar Butt in #8 and #10, and believes that it is more difficult to move steelhead to the larger sizes.

CIGAR BUTT

Tail White calf tail
Body Natural deer body hair. No hackle.

Wing White calf tail
Optional: Add a small bunch of moose as a throat

Bill McMillan fishes a Bomber called a Moose Turd, his standard steelhead dry. (A variation on this fly is the Tundra Turd. I'm told it's a good Alaskan fly for rainbows.)

MOOSE TURD

Tail White calf tail
Body Black deer body hair spun and clipped to shape. No hackle.
Wing White calf tail, upright

Bill McMillan also ties the Air B.C., a bizarre and wonderful pattern bearing the name of a Canadian airline. It looks like a cross between Bill Bakke's Dragonfly and a Red Bomber, its stubby wings churning a waking path through an arching swing.

AIR B.C.

Tail White calf tail
Body Red or brick red deer body hair spun and clipped to shape. Leave tufts of deer hair on both sides for the wings. (I think the fly would fish better if elk were used to form the wings. The wings could be tied in first and covered with tape so that they wouldn't get cut when trimming the body.)
Wing White calf tail. Select calf tail at the end of the tail with a natural curl. Tie in so that the wing curves forward like a cresting wave.

Sean Gallagher, of Enumclaw, Washington, usually ties his Green-Wing Bomber with a wing upright and divided for the stable float this provides. He has taken many steelhead with it on the Dean and Thompson in Canada, and the Green and Skykomish in Washington. He may go as large as a #2 on some Canadian rivers and prefers to use his sixteen-foot two-handed rod to turn the big flies over.

GREEN-WING BOMBER

Tail Grey squirrel tail dyed green
Body Natural deer body hair spun and clipped to shape and palmered with short grizzly saddle hackle

Wing Green squirrel tail set forward but upright and divided

Bombers can be fished successfully in nearly any color combination. Danny Diaz, of Lewiston, Idaho, ties one using the colors in pistachio ice cream. Jerry Cebula, of Golden, Colorado, incorporates his school colors—orange and black—into one of his Bombers, a pattern he calls the Princeton Tiger. His Steelhead Bomber accounted for a forty-one-inch Bulkley River steelhead in 1988, possibly the largest taken that year on a dry.

STEELHEAD BOMBER

Tail Orange calf tail
Body Deer body hair dyed black and palmered with orange saddle hackle

Wing Javelina, set forward and divided (the bristly hair of the javelina is very stiff)

Bob Clay, a Kispiox River guide and writer of steelhead lore, showed me his Purple Bomber when we fished together in 1990. He had been given a dried moose hide, which he cut into one-foot squares with a circular saw. These he dyed hot purple and converted into *a lot* of Purple Bombers. Bob explained that Don Hathaway first tied a Purple Bomber using deer hair and peccary. Bob's slightly different version—the fanlike wing of moose would help almost any Bomber—is invariably fished with a hitch.

PURPLE BOMBER (Bob Clay)

Tail Moose dyed with a combination of purple and fluorescent pink dye, which creates a hot purple with a pinkish tinge. The tips of the hair take almost none of the dye.

Wing A single bunch of moose, flared, and set forward

Body Moose, but cut tips off before spinning the hair. The base of the body hair is naturally cream-colored, and takes the dye far more intensely than the tips.

Ehor Boyanowsky of Vancouver, British Columbia, 1991 president of The Steelhead Society of British Columbia, and steelhead fly fisher extraordinaire, named this strange relative of the Bomber for his favorite river.

THOMPSON RIVER RAT

Tail Deer body hair dyed pale green

Body Natural caribou, spun and clipped to shape

Wing Long, pale green, any pliable synthetic fur

Head Red tying thread

Two additional Bombers, the Orange and Rusty, fill out this list. Both are excellent. The Orange Bombers I've purchased from Kaufmann's Streamborn had bodies clipped very flat. They have produced quite well for me on Canadian rivers. The Rusty Bomber is a marvelous pattern if the wing is not tied too long. My preference is for the wing to be short, somewhat flared, and the base saturated with fly dope or Goop.

ORANGE BOMBER

Tail White calf tail

Body Deer body hair dyed deep orange and palmered with orange saddle hackle

Wing White calf tail

RUSTY BOMBER

Tail Rusty brown squirrel tail

Body Deer body hair dyed brown

Hackle Brown saddle hackle

Wing Rusty brown squirrel tail

BOB BORDEN

Bob Borden, the creative genius behind Hareline Dubbin, his fly-tying-material business in Monroe, Oregon, developed two of steelheading's most important dressings of the past decade. The Krystal Bullet, in myriad color combinations, almost overnight became a standard winter fly. Borden's Prawn, a larger and more ambitious tie, produces action unmatched by any General Practitioner, and is now certain to become a popular alternative to that classic dressing.

Bob began tying flies commercially in the mid-1970s, and began marketing rabbit dubbing in twenty-four colors (thus Hareline Dubbin), always pouring his profits back into the fledgling company as he searched for new fly-tying products to market. Ten years later, a close friend of Bob's returned from New Zealand with samples of a neon, hairlike plastic used in fishing lures. Bob located the manufacturer and worked out an exclusive for its American distribution. He called the material Krystal Flash, and steelhead fly tying hasn't been the same since. The material is now an essential ingredient in many "traditional" patterns, particularly in flies intended for winter steelhead.

Bob knew about the Thunder Creek series of minnow-imitating flies, and decided to use Krystal

← Bob Clay and an "alligator head" on a Purple Bomber.

Bob Borden

Flash to create the same type of bullet head in an attractor-type steelhead fly. This, of course, became the Krystal Bullet series.

The Borden Special, Bob's long-hackled sea-run cutthroat pattern, is now considered a standard pattern in the sport. Bob hunts for his favorite gamefish along the upper stretches of the intertidal Siletz River. He ties the fly as follows: Tail and hackle are an even mix of fluorescent pink and yellow hackle. The body is fluorescent pink Hareline No. 4—you can substitute fluorescent pink chenille—ribbed with flat silver tinsel. The sparsely tied wing is white—arctic fox, calf tail, or a similar fur. Many anglers have successfully used the Borden Special for steelhead, including summer-runs. Bob said, "Marty Sherman told me that the largest summer steelhead he ever caught on the Deschutes was caught on this fly. I think he said it was fourteen or fifteen pounds."

KRYSTAL BULLET

Thread Pink
Body Fluorescent pink chenille
Hackle Hot pink Krystal Flash
Bullet Head The "hackle" is tied down in two steps. First, spin the Krystal Flash around the hook at the head and tie down just behind the eye with the tips extending forward. Wind the thread down the hook and tie in the tail, five to seven strands of Krystal Flash. Tie in the chenille, wind the thread forward, bring the chenille forward, and tie off. Draw the Krystal Flash toward the rear of the fly and bind down the "hackle." (Bob finds it helpful to use a ball-point pen without the liner, or a similar tube, to force over the eye of the hook and evenly spread out the Krystal Flash.) These steps create the Bullet's "head."

Comments: Endless color combinations are possible with this quick and very effective fly. Bob says, "The black and purple are good for summer-run, the bright colors best for winter-run. And the lime green is really great for chinook salmon!"

BORDEN'S PRAWN

Hook	Single or double salmon, 6 to 3/0	**Body**	Strip of rabbit cut side to side so that when wound the rabbit will fold back naturally
Eyes	Pair of Hareline pearl bead-chain eyes		
Rostrum-Head	Hareline Dubbin	**Back**	Dyed golden pheasant rump (not flank) feathers. Use two feathers on a #6, three on larger sizes.
Antennae	Dyed golden pheasant tippet and ten to twelve strands of Krystal Flash		

Tying Instructions: Wrap thread to bend of hook and secure a pair of pearl bead-chain eyes. These can be colored black with a permanent marker. Continue to wind thread to halfway down bend, dub thread, and wind back up the bend, around the eyes, continuing up the shank until above the point of the hook. Cut out the tip from a tippet feather and secure at the butt end. Dub around the tie-in area. Tie in the cross-strip of rabbit that has been tapered at the tie-in end. Wind forward. The fur will lie down naturally, pointing toward the eyes. Five to eight wraps will be needed to complete the fly. After the first three wraps, tie in ten to twelve strands of Krystal Flash that extend nearly to the end of the tippet fibers. Tie in a single golden pheasant rump feather over the Krystal Flash. At the midpoint of the fly, tie in a second rump feather. (Omit if using #6 hook.) Wrap the fur to the head of the fly, add a third rump feather, and tie off.

Bob offers seven color variations of the Borden Prawn:

Pattern	Thread	Eyes	Rostrum/Head	Antennae	Body	Krystal Flash	Back Feathers (Golden pheasant rump)
Red	Red	Black	Fluorescent red	Red	Red	Pearl	Fluorescent red
Hot orange	Hot orange	Black	Hot orange	Fluorescent orange	Hot orange	Fluorescent fire orange	Fluorescent orange
Crayfish	Hot orange	Black	Rusty orange	Fluorescent orange	Crayfish	Fluorescent fire orange	Fluorescent orange
Yellow	Yellow	Black	Yellow	Natural	Yellow	Hot yellow	Natural
Hot pink	Hot pink	Black	Fluorescent Hot pink	Hot pink	Hot pink	Fluorescent shrimp pink	Hot pink
Purple	Purple	Pearl	Purple	Purple	Purple	Dark purple	Purple
Black	Black	Pearl	Black	Red	Black	Pearl	Fluorescent red

STEVE BROCCO

Steve Brocco is a familiar figure to those who regularly attend the Federation of Fly Fishers conclaves. He can be found in the fly tying section, sharing his special techniques, explaining the finer points, "what a single wrap of thread will do," as he likes to say. His "class" is eager to learn—and determined to get the sample fly being tied! Steve's flies are valued treasures.

When I last visited Steve, he had just returned from an international fly tying exposition in Holland. In the main, he found the tying skills of his European peers quite mediocre. "The best tyers in the world are in the Northwest," he told me matter-of-factly. "We're on the verge of a whole new level in fly tying, very different from the old style."

Steve has a Ph.D. in marine zoology from the University of Washington. "I currently use my degree to imitate freshwater aquatic insects." He is only half joking. Several years ago, with employment op-

Steve Brocco

portunites slim to nonexistent, he and Neil Herrett started Eastside Anglers in Redmond, Washington. When he's not at work selling tackle and tying flies, he mounts and frames flies for other anglers, work that is of museum quality. The Snoqualmie River is a stone's throw away from the shop, and it holds steelhead, winter and summer.

The following flies are proven patterns. Steve originated all of them, except Hardy's Favorite and Rusty Rat. He discovered Hardy's Favorite in my book, *Steelhead Fly Fishing and Flies*, and improved upon it both as a tyer's specimen, and an effective steelhead fly.

BLACK WITCH

Tip Narrow oval gold tinsel
Tag Fluorescent green floss
Body Black seal fur ribbed with narrow oval gold tinsel
Hackle Pheasant rump dyed black
Wing White polar bear
Facing Hackle Teal flank

ORANGE WITCH

Tip Narrow oval gold tinsel, five turns
Body Orange seal fur ribbed with five turns of narrow oval gold tinsel
Wing White polar bear
First Hackle Golden pheasant flank
Facing Hackle Bronze mallard
Head Orange thread

PURPLE WITCH

Tip Five turns of narrow oval gold tinsel
Tag Deep purple floss
Body Purple seal fur ribbed with narrow oval gold tinsel
Wing White polar bear
First Hackle Golden pheasant flank
Facing Hackle Bronze mallard
Head Red thread

HARDY'S FAVORITE

Tip Narrow oval red tinsel, five turns
Tail Speckled guinea fibers topped with a small clump of red golden pheasant. Entire tail is short and sparse.
Body Red floss. Secure peacock herl at the head and wind to the tail and back. Rib with red floss (strengthen peacock herl by winding in a couple of strands of tying thread).
Hackle Red golden pheasant flank

Wing Brown pheasant rump fibers. Split wing material in half and tie in the first half. Cover the butt ends of this with a facing hackle of bronze mallard, and then tie in the remaining wing. This approach will reduce the wing bulk so that a small, neat head is possible.
Head Red tying thread

HARLEQUIN SPEY

Tip Narrow oval gold tinsel, five turns
Tag (optional) Red floss
Body Deep orange, red, and purple seal fur, divided equally. (Place the materials in sequence in a dubbing loop.)

Hackle Red golden pheasant flank
Wing White polar bear
Facing Hackle Bronze mallard
Head Red tying thread

Note: In the example tied for the color plate, Steve omitted the rear section of deep orange but retained the tag of red floss.

RUSTY RAT

Tying thread while constructing the body: Primrose yellow

Tag Narrow oval gold tinsel, five turns
Tail Peacock sword fibers
Body Rear half rusty orange floss, front half peacock herl. Rib entire body with narrow oval gold tinsel. Where body divides, tie in several strands of rusty orange floss, the tie-in point covered with the peacock herl.
Wing Grey squirrel, silver monkey, or grey fox
Hackle Grizzly. Tie in by the tip over the wing butts. This will result in a tiny red head, little more than a couple turns of tying thread.

MIKE BROOKS

Mike Brooks's home waters are the steelhead rivers near his home in Veneta, Oregon, most notably the lower McKenzie downstream from Leaberg Dam, and also the Middle Fork of the Willamette, the North Fork of the Umpqua from Glide to Whistler's Bend, the South Fork of the Santiam, and the Siuslaw above Mapleton. I found him to be a pragmatist with strong opinions based on twenty years of steelhead fly fishing. "I am a nut about fly patterns," he says. "I really believe that the fly is more important than presentation or tackle or technique."

For Mike, steelhead means both modern and classic Atlantic salmon dressings presented with a ten-foot High Speed Hi-D sink-tip line. This is just about the only kind of line he has ever used. The salmon flies, however, are much more recent, and he is convinced that they are primary to his success.

The colors of most of the effective Atlantic salmon flies are natural; bright colors, especially fluorescent colors, are used only as tints and highlights. The bodies are dubbed furs, not wrapped wool or chenille. The wings are made of soft guard hair like black bear, stoat tail, woodchuck, squirrel, and fox, or are of soft flowing feathers. As opposed to steelhead flies, I am struck by the subtlety of salmon flies. Take two similar flies as an example, the Green-Butt Skunk and the Black Bear Green Butt. The Green-Butt Skunk is a very popular steelhead pattern that I have fished and found singularly ineffective. I believe this to be due to the fact that almost everything about this pattern is wrong. Everything in the fly is dyed except the wing. Then, the body is made of chenille. In the water, chenille just goes dead. Chenille has no inner color, no sparkle, no life, no soul! Secondly, the wing is made of bucktail, or even worse, of polar

Row 1 Fiery-Brown, Gibbs Shrimp, Mckenzie Sapphire #1, McKenzie Sapphire #2.
Row 2 Orange Blossom, Beully Snow Fly, Polar Shrimp
Row 3 Red Dog, RVI (purple body), RVI (light orange body)
Row 4 Steelhead Rat Series

bear! Both of these materials are very stiff. The only place I use these materials on my flies is when I want a stiff underwing to support my soft fibered main wing. [*Note*: Mike uses Mongolian ringtail.] The Black Bear Green Butt is a relatively modern Atlantic salmon fly with a slim silhouette. The tail is usually made of a natural golden pheasant crest feather. The natural champagne yellow fibers glisten. The body is made up of a small fluorescent green tip of floss and then translucent seal dyed black, or better yet, natural black-bear underfur. The soft errant fibers sticking up from the body provide movement and create the illusion of life. The translucence of the natural fur dubbing passes and reflects light, furthering the illusion. The wing is made of black-bear guard hairs, usually from a yearling bear, or of natural black squirrel tail. These furs move with the slightest amount of water pressure and whisper to the fish, "I'm alive!"

Mike calls the RVI, General Practitioner, Rat, and Sapphires his "essential patterns." He says, "They account for ninety percent of the fish I take." In the summer, the Rats are usually fished on droppers and kept small, sixes and eights, to contrast to the larger point fly.

His method of presenting the flies is worth noting: "I usually fish classic wet fly style, but a lot more slowly than anyone else I see. I usually take five minutes or more to fish each cast, paying special attention to keep my fly over fish or likely water as long as possible. I start out with a dead drift, but on subsequent casts to the same water I will impart *very slight* action to the fly. At the end of a cast, I never just bring the fly in. Instead, I strip in a little line, eight inches or so, and let most of it out again, and then let the fly dangle in the current. I may repeat this action thirty or more times per cast."

Mike has additional comments regarding individual patterns. This assortment of flies is worth studying. I like his use of golden pheasant, and I find his Rat, RVI, and Sapphire series, and the Gibbs Shrimp, especially noteworthy.

BEAULY SNOW FLY

Hook Size 4 to 5/0 Partridge ("If you can find them, use Partridge low-water hooks 6X long.")

Thread Orange

Body Kingfisher blue seal. Rib with medium flat silver tinsel followed by medium oval gold tinsel. Palmer with black heron, doubled (substitute black Chinese pheasant) from second turn of tinsel. Counterwrap hackle with fine oval silver tinsel.

Wing Strands of bronze peacock herl (make a good-size bunch; they slim down somewhat, like marabou)

Collar Two or three turns of body hackle reaching at least to the bend of the hook

Head Hot orange rabbit guard hair spun in a dubbing loop to encircle the wing and collar

Note: "I always have one or two of these flies with me. The peacock and low flowing hackle seems to attract steelhead when everything else fails."

FIERY BROWN

Hook Size 10 to 6 Partridge low-water

Tag Narrow flat gold tinsel

Tail None

Body Blended fur from the ears and cheeks of hare's mask dyed hot orange ("Because of the natural dark barring of the hare's mask, the dye takes unevenly over the

mask. When the lighter cheeks and almost black ears are mixed together the result is the most beautiful fiery brown you have ever seen.")

Wing Fiery brown guard hairs from a woodchuck, sparse and tied short

Note: "I use this pattern during extreme low water conditions when fish are crowded into pools and wary."

GIBBS SHRIMP

Hook Size 8 to 1/0 Partridge low-water double

Thread Hot orange

Tag Medium oval silver tinsel, four wraps

Rear Hackle A long red golden pheasant body feather, three wraps, veiled on each side by bright blue kingfisher body feathers

Body Two sections of wide flat silver tinsel ribbed with medium oval silver tinsel. In the middle of the body is a butt of flame seal followed by three turns of long claret

saddle hackle veiled by two bright blue kingfisher body feathers. At the front is another butt of flame seal, three turns of claret saddle veiled by two kingfisher blue body feathers.

Wing A pair of very long jungle cock eye feathers reaching to the bend of the hook

Collar Three turns of long red golden pheasant body feathers

Note: "This is a beautiful fly that is admittedly difficult to tie. Nonetheless, it is well worth the effort. I use it as a change of pace from the General Practitioner."

McKENZIE SAPPHIRE #1

Hook	Partridge low-water, size 6 to 2, or Tiemco 7999, 2 to 2/0, when deep-sinking the fly	**Hackle**	Two turns of bright blue neck hackle
Tip	Fine oval silver tinsel	**UnderWing**	Four strands each, mixed, of light blue, red, yellow, and green bucktail
Tag	Yellow floss over flat silver tinsel	**Wing**	Any soft white hair, sparse (Mike generally uses Mongolian ringtail)
Body	Black seal ribbed with flat silver tinsel palmered with bright blue neck hackle starting at the second wrap of tinsel (*Note*: I would substitute saddle if running the fly deep.)		

McKENZIE SAPPHIRE #2

Same as above except that the overwing is black squirrel tail.

ORANGE BLOSSOM

Tag	Fine oval silver tinsel and yellow floss	**Wing**	Woodchuck guard hairs
Tail	Golden pheasant crest	**Cheeks**	Jungle cock (optional)
Butt	Black ostrich	**Collar**	Hot orange hackle slightly longer than yellow hackle
Body	Rear third flat silver tinsel, front two-thirds bright yellow seal palmered with bright yellow saddle hackle. Rib entire body with medium oval silver tinsel, five turns.		

Note: "This is my favorite 'bright' fly. I fish it deep on a short leader during winter and early spring." Woodchuck guard hairs were not used in the original Orange Blossom.

POLAR SHRIMP

Thread	Hot orange or flame	**Wing**	Soft white hair to end of tag
Tag	Medium flat gold tinsel	**Collar**	Red golden pheasant body feather reaching to the bend of the hook.
Tail	Tip of red golden pheasant body feather		
Body	Bright orange seal fur ribbed with five turns of medium flat gold tinsel. Palmer with hot orange saddle hackle following the tinsel from the second turn.		

Note: "This is a good example of how the Polar Shrimp should look when tied with proper materials. Compare this to the dead-looking 'traditional' pattern tied with chenille and polar bear. I've never had a steelhead take the traditional version even though I fished it for several years. Yet this pattern is one of my favorite winter flies and accounts for several fish every season."

RED DOG

Hook Size 4 to 2/0 Partridge Bartleet (*Author's note*: To tie this lovely spey fly, I would use the Alec Jackson Spey, formerly by Partridge, now by Daiichi.)

Tag Flat silver tinsel

Body Bright red Berlin wool ribbed with wide flat silver tinsel followed by medium oval silver tinsel, five to six turns. Palmer with heron dyed brown or natural Chinese pheasant or brown spey cock.

Hackle Teal, folded

Wings Bronze mallard

RVI

Hook Size 6 to 2 Partridge Wilson for greased line; Size 4 to 2/0 Tiemco 7999 if running deep

Tying Thread Flame

Tag Flat silver tinsel beginning at hook point

Tail Golden pheasant body fibers, gap-width in length

Body Rear one-third silver tinsel or pearl Flashabou over tying thread. Front two-thirds orange seal. Rib entire body with flat silver tinsel.

Hackle Palmer seal body with teal flank. Counterwrap with narrow oval gold tinsel (optional)

Wing Four golden pheasant body feathers, red, tied Dee style, i.e., set low and tented over hook. The wing should extend to the tip of the tail.

Note: "For the past several years from mid to late summer I have had evenings where steelhead took this fly on every cast. I rose ten fish and landed seven on my best evening with the light orange version. My favorite colors for the RVI are light orange, green, and purple. This fly is named for Ron Van Iderstine, a guide from Springfield, Oregon, and the best steelhead and salmon guide I have ever known."

STEELHEAD RAT

Hook Size 10 to 4 Partridge low-water

Tag Flat or oval gold tinsel starting at the hook point

Tail Fiery brown guard hairs from the base of a fox squirrel. Do not extend beyond the bend of the hook.

Body Rear third fluorescent green wool or floss, balance peacock herl. Rib entire body with fine oval or flat gold tinsel.

Hackle Grizzly, palmered, follow ribbing through the peacock herl

Wing Woodchuck guard hairs showing white and black bars

Collar Natural black hen hackle, two turns

Alternate dressings Substitute fluorescent flame, orange, blue, or grey for rear one-third. Mike's Steelhead Rat series is based on the Pack Rat, an Atlantic salmon fly.

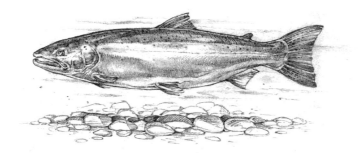

BULKLEY MOOSE

Tail Dark moose, full. Wrap hair forward, trim at the head. This forms the body.

Wing Large clump of moose body hair, tips extend to bend of the hook. Bind down hard enough to cause the butts to flare. Set slightly forward, divide and coat with Goop. When dry, cut on angle as shown.

The stiff "antlers" will keep on the surface while the fly is under tension. The fly may also be tied with the forward two-thirds of the body dubbed with seal, angora goat, or similar material. When seen from below, this dubbing gives the fly an especially buggy appearance.

If you visit John Mintz's fly shop, The Fish'N Factory in Smithers, British Columbia, you find a long fly-tying bench with holes cut out beneath each vise so that the cut-away dressing materials drop neatly into a waiting trash can. Customers are invited to sit down and tie a few flies, sip some coffee, and talk steelhead with John. When I visited with him in the fall of 1989, he had recently come up with the Bulkley Moose dry fly, a strange-looking dressing that floated drag-free, churned and wobbled over the water on the swing while remaining all but unsinkable and, to hear John tell it, drove steelhead crazy. It fished on somewhat the same principal as Judd Wickwire's more radically designed Riffle Express.

Another tie somewhat on the same order as the Bulkley Moose is the Bubblehead, an extremely simple yet effective tie, also from the Bulkley River. The tail of stiff moose is tied in as with the Moose, and the wing secured about halfway down the hook. The butt ends are bound down toward the head and then tied down hard enough to cause the hair to flare into nearly half a circle. This is coated with Goop and trimmed in a semicircle.

BULKLEY RIVER SAMURAI

Tail Two matching blood-plume marabou tips containing a few strands of pearl Flashabou

Body Black chenille palmered with black saddle hackle

Wing Strip of black rabbit approximately two to three inches long, depending on hook size

Hackle Black, long

I first saw this leech pattern in use on the Kispiox in 1987. A few anglers and a couple of guides were fishing it and remaining very closemouthed about it, one of those "secrets" that couldn't last, and didn't. Two years later, the unnamed dressing was a mania on the Kispiox and, at least on the Bulkley, had a name. Basically, this big silhouette pattern is a Matuka in which the end is not secured, the strip of rabbit waving in the current and giving the fly tremendous action.

The Samurai can be dredged on a sinking line or fished more conventionally on a sink tip and floating-line swing.

This approach to tying silhouette dressings should certainly include purple, perhaps white, and even hot fluorescent colors for off-colored winter rivers.

DEAN RIVER LANTERNS

I first heard about the "Dean River Lantern" pattern years ago, but I was never able to run down its source. The "lantern," I was told, referred to the glow the pattern emitted. A friend said this was accomplished by winding monofilament over a hot floss body that covered a tinsel body. This, in fact, may have been a variation. Bob Wagoner, a commercial fly tyer from Lewiston, Idaho, sorted me out on the matter. "The Dean River Lanterns," he explained, "were developed by a gentleman named Dr.

Art Cohen of San Francisco, California. He discovered Edge Bright as a fly tying material." Bob now uses Edge Bright in steelhead flies, bonefish flies, and nymph casings. By itself, the material is not spectacular, but wrapped over silver tinsel, it possesses an amazing "lantern" glow. Bob offers four examples.

GREEN DEAN RIVER LANTERN

Tail Squirrel tail dyed black to length of hook shank, cocked slightly

Body Silver tinsel overwrapped with green Edge Bright

Hackle Dark green to match body color

YELLOW DEAN RIVER LANTERN

Tail Squirrel tail dyed black to length of hook shank, cocked slightly

Body Silver tinsel wrapped with fluorescent yellow Edge Bright

Hackle Yellow or chartreuse to match body color

RED DEAN RIVER LANTERN

Tail Squirrel tail dyed black to length of hook shank, cocked slightly

Body Silver tinsel wrapped with fluorescent red Edge Bright

Hackle Red or fluorescent red to match body color

ORANGE DEAN RIVER LANTERN

Tail Squirrel tail dyed black to length of hook shank, cocked slightly

Body Silver tinsel wrapped with fluorescent orange Edge Bright

Hackle Orange or fluorescent orange to match body color

FAY DAVIS

Fay Davis has been traveling to the Kispiox each fall since 1973, a fragile wisp of a man who was still attacking Cottonwood Pool with his big Winston rod when December ice rimed the shore and his fly dropped between pieces of flow ice. He remembers when water temperatures were well down in the thirties. "You could see the steelhead come right after the fly. They're as active then as any other time of the year except September. One day, the air temperature was twenty degrees, and the line froze in the guides after each cast. I beached four steelhead that day, including a buck too large to follow."

Fay went north to "break Mausser's world record," an often-expressed ambition among early Kispiox anglers. "But I gave that up within a year. I knew that when my time came I would release that fish."

And he did, probably many times, certainly a couple of times, for he has put his tape on seven 43- to 45½-inch Kispiox steelhead that he thinks would have broken the record. He came close to killing one of these giants. From the very first visit, Fay always stayed at Olga Walker's Kispiox Steelhead Camp, and in time they became fast friends. One day, just below the lodge, Fay hooked a huge steelhead that took him nearly two hours to beach. Olga sometimes dropped down to visit with Fay, but this day she was working in her garden. "If Olga had been there, I would have kept it," he told me. "Olga would have floated the bill to have it mounted. She didn't show, so I released it."

Fay's greatest steelhead came to a FAD 78 on September 11, 1984, at the Cottonwood water just below Walker's lodge. The buck was measured—45½ inches by 26 inches—and scale samples removed. The length and girth worked out to an estimated forty-one pounds. Mike Whatley, a fisheries biologist, determined the fish's age to be 5/3+, a steelhead that was in its ninth year after having spent more than three years in the ocean and five years as a premigrant resident.

Fay developed the habit of inventing a fly pattern and naming it for each new season, a system that has helped him to sort out the years. Most of the flies were not used after that season, even if memorable steelhead came to them. A few patterns, however, became his standards, flies he believed were especially suitable for the Kispiox. The FAD 75 and FAD 78 are such examples.

FAD 74

Tail Black calf tail
Body Gold or silver mylar piping ribbed with red floss

Hackle Black, dry-fly quality
Wing Center tail fibers from the ring-necked pheasant

FAD 78 (Also known as Fay's Black Fly)

Tail Black hackle tips
Body Black hackle, dry-fly quality
Hackle Red, forward of black
Head Bead-chain eyes

Fay says, "Dry-fly hackle was used on the original (FAD 78) and proved very effective. Later, wet-fly hackle was used, and though it worked, it was not as good. It seems to me that vibrancy rather than undulation is needed on this particular tie."

Both patterns fish well on either a floating or sinking line. Fay's sinking-line system is worth noting. He cuts nearly the entire front taper from a forward-taper saltwater line, and splices to the lead seven to ten feet of Hi-Speed Hi-D line.

When I visited Fay in October 1988, he had been staying in one of Olga's cabins for more than a month. The Kispiox flowed only a few feet away, but he hadn't once made it to the river. As always, he was living mostly on coffee and cigarettes. Emphysema had reduced his weight to a hundred pounds. I doubted he would last the winter, and he almost didn't. He lived on the upper Skagit River, in the little town of Marblemount. When I checked on him the following spring, his doctor had taken his cigarettes away, and he was sounding spry, even a little ornery. I thought the odds were at least even that he would make it north again.

KEN DRIEDGER

Ken Driedger, of Smithers, British Columbia, sent me a box of strange-looking flies he called "The .08." A note explained that the fly was conceived when he was "on intimate terms with fermented spirits," his blood alcohol above the legal limit for driving in Canada, .08. I told him that many of our steelhead patterns were invented under similar working conditions, and that there was no law against tying while intoxicated. What mattered was whether steelhead liked the result. Anticipating this, Ken had produced a long list of anglers in the Smithers area who would testify to the fly's effectiveness on Bulkley River steelhead. And he admonished, "Don't discount this pattern. Tie one on and observe the transformation when the fly is wet. You'll want to step on this critter!"

THE .08

Tail Tuft of purple marabou one-half- to three-quarters-inch long

Body Pink and black wool woven with the pink under. Palmer entire body with grizzly, three to four turns, with the first turn at the base of the tail.

Wing Purple marabou, thick, half the body length

GENERAL PRACTITIONER

I don't know of another fly pattern that has impacted steelhead fly fishing as much during the last ten years as the General Practitioner. It has a nickname, G.P., and endless variations—some crude, others quite complicated and extremely lifelike. It is to winter steelheading what hopper patterns are to Rocky Mountain angling; everyone seems to have his own version.

Anglers tell me they've been fishing G.P.s for all eternity, but some rigorous soul-searching usually leads them back to Joe Bates's *Atlantic Salmon Flies and Fishing*, published in 1970. Bates tells how Colonel Esmond Drury tied the original prawn imitation in 1953 to circumvent a British ban on the use of the natural prawn as bait for Atlantic salmon. By all accounts, the dressing was an immediate sensation.

The British tied the fly on either double or treble hooks, 2X long or thereabouts, a custom either illegal or disdained by Americans. Otherwise, the dressing, just as the originator tied it, quickly attracted a small army of Northwest supporters during the 1970s.

GENERAL PRACTITIONER (Original)

Tail Ten hot orange bucktail hairs extending two inches beyond the hook bend. In same tying point, secure a golden pheasant neck feather, concave side upward. Tie in slightly forward a second golden pheasant neck feather, concave side upward, that lies over and matches the first.

Body Tie in hot orange "cock's hackle" and fine oval gold tinsel. Dub tying thread with pink-orange mohair or seal fur. Wind dubbing forward to halfway point and secure. Rib and secure. Wind hackle to this point and secure. Tie in golden pheasant neck feather. Tie in the "eyes" of the shrimp by cutting a V from a golden pheasant tippet and secure this feather so that it lies flat on the neck feather. Dub additional tying thread and wind to half remaining distance. Secure. Rib and secure. Wind hackle and secure. Tie in neck feather of golden pheasant large enough to extend to end of golden pheasant tippet. Repeat as before with dubbing, hackle and neck feather, with the neck feather larger and veiling the one before it. The final neck feather will be the fourth in the sequence.

Note: Rather than wind the hackle forward, I prefer to tie in a hackle and take a turn or two at each segment. I often omit the tinsel. This makes the dressing a lot simpler. If one *must* have it, narrow oval gold tinsel can be used to spin a dubbing loop. Orange Krystal Flash is often mixed with the tail material. If it's available, I prefer polar bear. Entire golden pheasant skins can now be purchased dyed red, hot orange, and purple. This can make for some interesting G.P.s.

This original General Practitioner, tied on a double hook, sank quickly and was very stable on a swing even in heavy currents. The same dressing on a single hook is not so advantaged. If the body is weighted with lead wire, the fly is likely to ride upside down. This is not altogether bad, and is probably more disconcerting to the angler than to the fish. Nevertheless, I do not weight these flies, and usually fish them on 1/0 and 2/0 heavy-wire hooks.

Left unweighted, and fished on a sinking line, the General Practitioner will float over obstructions that would catch many other deep-sunk flies. It is at its best in water suitable for spey flies—the soft flats, guts, and easier tailouts where steelhead are holding in relatively shallow water. Though the dressing in smaller sizes is successfully fished greased-line in these types of water, I have a strong prejudice for the pattern as a winter and spring fly for winter-run steelhead.

Stew Wallace of Portland, Oregon, ties an absolutely stunning variation using scarlet seal fur and hackle, with the tippet and polar bear tail dyed red. The golden pheasant neck feathers of the carapace are natural. "One word of caution here," says Stew. "This is a fly that fish will either race across the stream to take, or run from in total fear."

On some rivers such as Washington's Skagit, Sean Prawn's more popular than the original General Practitioner.

Sean Gallagher calls the first of his variations Sean's Prawn. The tail is of Krafty Fur (available in dime stores) between a few strands of polar bear. The body is kept thin and on the sparse side. Three tying stations of natural golden pheasant neck feathers form the top, with the first feather halfway up the hook. A turn or two of very deep cerise hackle at the head completes the fly. When tied in sizes 2/0 to 5/0, the fly sinks like a stone and swims without rolling over. Sean sometimes bends the shank of the hook to give the fly a more "shrimpy" look. His other fly is the Black Marabou Practitioner, one of the finest all-season dressings in steelheading.

BLACK MARABOU PRACTITIONER

Tail A small bunch of Krafty Fur between a few hairs of black polar bear, long. At this tying point, secure golden pheasant tippets, short, extending just past second black bar, one clump on each side of the tail.

Body Black seal ribbed with pearl mylar and palmered with black saddle hackle

Wing Matuka style, with first wing dividing the body, the second wing at the head

Head Black

When we fished on the Skagit, Sean told me, "I gave a Black Marabou Practitioner to Jerry Wintle, and he reported hooking four winter fish on it before breaking it off on a rock. Those Canadians love black flies!" I met Sean that fall on the Thompson, just after he had released a fifteen-pound fall-run hen, "a screamer," he said, that took his Black Practitioner on the run. When I last spoke with him, he had had a good day on the Skykomish River with chrome-bright January steelhead. Again, the fly of choice was this wonderful dressing.

This is a pattern with tremendous action, one highly visible under all water conditions that can be considered remotely fishable.

HORNY SHRIMP

Tail Salmon marabou, 1½ inches long

Eyes Modeling pins with black heads

Body Fluorescent salmon chenille palmered with light orange hackle

Wing/ Carapace Red marabou slicked back with head cement

Head Flame single-strand floss

Sean Gallagher

Joe Butorac reasons that shrimp may be the last item in the steelhead's saltwater diet before they ascend their rivers.

STEVE GOBIN

Steve Gobin is a Tulalip Indian who fly-fishes for steelhead with cane rods, English reels, and Scottish spey flies that would be the centerpiece in any angling museum. The first time I examined his flies, I said, "You don't really fish with these!" Steve assured me that he did, including flies with braided gut loops for eyes. "I think the loops give the fly better action," he said. When we hunted for summer-runs on the Stillaguamish, he fished a black-bodied spey fly with wings of white goose tented low over the body, tied on an Alec Jackson Spey hook. The fly wobbled with an erratic action quite unlike anything in my experience.

The Tartan, complete with a braided gut loop, is one of the many Scottish spey flies Gobin uses in his steelhead fly fishing.

Steve Gobin

Later that summer, when Steve traveled to eastern Canada to fish for Atlantic salmon with Bob Veverka, the two master tyers cast only full-dressed Atlantic salmon patterns. Both men assured me that a Jock Scott, if true in every respect to the original, fished with tremendous action.

I told Steve, "You guys are lucky someone didn't kill you for your flies!" Either man can command hundreds of dollars for a single one of his full-dressed flies.

"Fly fishing gives me a reason to tie," he says. "I've been at it since I was a kid." A childhood illness kept him in bed for weeks, and an uncle brought him a fly-tying kit to help pass the time. In a few years, he had read every book he could find on the subject.

Steve fishes commercially for salmon. He also does stream surveys and redd counts, and tags wild steelhead on the Snohomish River and its major tributaries, the Snoqualmie and Skykomish, for the Tulalip Fishery Department.

When I asked him about his surname, he said, "My dad should tell you that story!"

Bernard Gobin told me that some five generations ago, even before Issac Stevens, Washington's first Territorial Governor, negotiated a reservation treaty with the Tulalips in 1855, a marauding band of Tlingits swept down from Alaska in great ocean canoes and raided Tulalip lands. They captured the chief's daughter, a girl of only seven or eight, and returned north with her. The girl was an adult before she was able to escape and return to her people. For reasons no longer understood, the Tulalips ostracized her, and she eventually married a Frenchman named Antoinne Gobin, Steve's great-great grandfather.

As the following flies suggest, and the color plates illustrate, Steve ties along traditional lines, whether the dressing is a steelhead fly of his own invention or a classic Atlantic salmon pattern borrowed from George M. Kelson or T. E. Pryce-Tannatt.

POLAR SHRIMP (Dark)

Tip One or two turns of narrow oval silver tinsel

Body Rear half rose red silk, front half rose red seal, rib with flat silver tinsel and narrow oval silver tinsel. Palmer with rose red hackle. (The color rose red is achieved by combining a mix of two-thirds hot orange and one-third magenta.)

Throat Guinea, one turn

Wing Bronze mallard

POLAR SHRIMP (Light)

Tip One or two turns of narrow oval silver tinsel

Body Rear one-fourth deep orange silk, balance hot orange seal. Rib with narrow oval silver tinsel. Palmer with hot orange hackle.

Throat Pintail, one turn

Wing White goose

SKYKOMISH DARK

Tip Two turns of narrow oval silver tinsel

Body Rear one-fourth orange silk, balance red seal. Rib with flat silver tinsel and narrow oval silver tinsel. Palmer with yellow hackle.

Throat Pheasant rump dyed black

Wing Bronze mallard

Head Red tying thread

SKYKOMISH LIGHT

Identical to the Skykomish Dark except for a throat of golden pheasant rump.

CARRON

Two versions, a full spey and a reduced spey, are pictured in the color plates. In the full spey, the schlappen hackle is tied in butt-first. In the reduced, low-water variation, this hackle is reversed and tied in tip-first.

Body Orange floss ribbed with red floss. Partially covering the red floss is a rib of oval silver tinsel. The body is then palmered with black schlappen in the direction of the rib. A second rib of very narrow gold tinsel is then wound in the opposite direction, crossing each turn of hackle at right angles.

Throat Teal

Wing Bronze mallard

CLARET SPEY

Butt Small, very short tuft of yellow wool
Body Claret seal ribbed with oval silver tinsel

and palmered in the same direction with black schlappen

PURPLE SPEY

Body Rear one-fourth hot pink floss, balance deep purple floss. Rib with oval silver tinsel and palmer with schlappen dyed deep purple.

Throat Guinea
Wing Bronze mallard

GREY HERON

Body Rear one-third yellow floss, balance black floss. Rib with flat silver tinsel and follow with oval silver tinsel of the same width.

Body Hackle Heron
Throat Guinea
Wing Bronze mallard

ORANGE HERON

Body Rear one-fourth orange floss, balance hot orange seal. Rib with flat gold tinsel and oval silver tinsel. Palmer with black schlappen in the same direction as the ribbing. A third rib of very narrow oval silver tinsel is at right angles (or so) to the hackle.

Throat Teal
Wing Bronze mallard

PURPLE KING

Body Deep purple floss ribbed with a single strand of deep purple floss with oval tinsel set on the floss rib. Palmer with black schlappen, and rib at right angles to the hackle with gold thread.

Throat Guinea
Wing Bronze mallard

HYATT'S CADDIS (DRY)

Hook Size 4 to 8
Body and Wings Alternate small sections of Hareline Dubbin and natural elk body hair. The first section of elk should extend only slightly beyond the bend of the hook. Four clumps of Dubbin and four wings completes the body.
Head/Collar Natural elk body hair spun on (pack tightly) and clipped to shape

Hyatt's Caddis

LeRoy Hyatt, of Lewiston, Idaho, is a magician at spinning deer hair, and this is reflected in most of his patterns, including his Hyatt's Caddis, a complicated, nearly unsinkable dry that is tied in a number of body colors: fluorescent orange wool, yellow, tan, grey, and peacock herl, for example. He told me that this trout and steelhead dry was first tied with stiff saddle hackle, an even mix of grizzly and brown, and called the All-Purpose Caddis. Eric Leiser renamed the fly Hyatt's Caddis in an article he wrote for the *Lewiston Morning Tribune* in 1984. Bob Wagoner, a close friend of LeRoy's, suggested the spun-deer-hair head. LeRoy now ties the fly in either style, generally preferring the spun-deer-hair head for steelhead. He recently sent me the peacock-body version with a topping of pink calf tail. Steelhead don't appreciate this, but the fly is far more visible to the angler. He also has an all-black variation, a fine silhouette dry for low-light conditions.

DAVE HALL

Annually since 1980, Dave Hall has averaged more than 120 days guiding and fishing on the North Umpqua. When not operating his Jade River Guide Service, he works as Umpqua Feather Merchants' Quality Control Supervisor, responsible for overseeing the tying of flies all over the world.

Though this single river is much of his life, he says, "I don't call myself an expert; in fact, in over two decades of fishing here, I don't know *any* experts on this river's summer steelhead. There are no hard, fast rules that lend themselves to these fickle fish. I have seen many of the so-called legends, and for the most part, the majority of them are far better storytellers than summer steelhead fishermen. Most of them are not familiar with hundred-foot casts, roll casts of sixty to eighty feet, and tough wading. They don't take to being skunked, and on no other river have I seen egos as crushed as they get here on the North Umpqua."

Dave got into fishing these incredibly "buggy" patterns when the standard, more traditional patterns weren't working. "I'm not trying to match the hatch in any traditional sense," he says. "But these flies do represent insects prevalent in the North Umpqua, bugs that were part of the juvenile's diet at one time.

"The Hammerdown Caddis and Golden Stonefly are patterns I've been using for trout for years with great success. I just enlarged them to accommodate steelhead and varied some techniques in their

Dave Hall

presentation. The Flashback Nymph was a fairly standard all-purpose nymph pattern. As with the Hammerdowns, I enlarged it, and used some pearl Flashabou to give it sparkle. The Crawlers were an extension of the soft-hackle flies that I included in my buggy patterns. You'll notice all the flies use a soft hackle that when wet makes for lot of movement and a great silhouette. The silhouette is the key. It is far more important in clear water than color. I want a fly that moves and exaggerates its presence in the water, a fly that moves naturally and can be 'pumped' in the drift to add further action. This is a far better material than rubber legs, which I detest!"

Note: Heavily weighting nymphs is standard on the North Umpqua, because it is necessary to be able to run a fly along the bottom of the narrow holding channels. This is best accomplished with a floating line and a leader of fourteen feet or more. A strong back-mend gives the fly a few seconds to get down, the rod then leads the fly through the dead drift and swing.

HAMMERDOWN OCTOBER CADDIS

Body Sparkle blends fifty percent #39 crawdad orange, fifty percent #9 march brown. (Any rusty-colored dubbing will do.)

Tail Dark grey or black deer hair

Wing Dark grey or black deer hair tied down one-third back

Legs Soft brown or furnace saddle hackle. Legs should be at least as long as the body.

The pattern is tied weighted or unweighted, depending upon what type of water you're fishing. Hook size is 1/0 to 6.

Golden Stone Hammerdown, Flashback Nymph, and Black Crawler

GOLDEN STONE HAMMERDOWN

Body Sparkle blend #14 goldenstone or similar-colored dubbing. Rib with stripped stem of brown saddle hackle.

Tail Natural-colored deer hair

Wing Natural-colored deer hair tied one-third back

Legs Soft brown saddle hackle at least as long as the body

The pattern is tied weighted or unweighted, depending on what type of water you're fishing. Hook size is 2 to 6.

FLASHBACK NYMPH

Body Dubbed black rabbit. Rib with pearl Flashabou.

Tail Black saddle hackle and five to eight strands of pearl Flashabou

Wing Case Dark turkey tail feather

Legs Soft black saddle hackle at least as long as body, one strand of pearl Flashabou on each side the same length

Tied in weighted sizes 2 to 8.

NATURAL CRAWLER

Body Dubbed hare's mask up to thorax. Rib with "smoke" larva lace wrapped up to thorax.

Tail Long black saddle hackle

Legs Black saddle, long and soft

Head Danville #505. Use thread to tie in a small tag under the tail.

BLACK CRAWLER

Body Dubbed black rabbit. Rib with larva lace wrapped up to the thorax.

Tail Long black saddle hackle, five to eight strands

Thorax Black rabbit

Legs Black saddle, long and soft

Head Danville #505. Use thread to tie in a small tag under the tail.

Tied in weighted sizes 2 to 8.

ICEBERG

Tail Red hackle fibers

Body Pearl crystal chenille ribbed with flat silver tinsel

Hackle Blue

Wing Squirrel tail dyed blue

Keith Stonebreaker, of Lewiston, Idaho, first tied the Iceberg for the Deschutes River. "I simply wanted a blue fly," he said when I asked about the source of his inspiration. The pattern is coming into more frequent use for Idaho waters. Bob Wagoner, Keith's neighbor in Lewiston, commercially markets the fly in his business, The Fly Den.

MIKE KINNEY (SPEY FLIES)

Mike Kinney's dressings are a lovely blending of somber colors and classic proportions. Names like Boulder Creek and Car Body are for favorite pools on the Skagit River.

I first met Mike Kinney one spring morning when Dale Edmonds and I were running big marabou flies through the Skagit's famous Mixer. This was Dale's first experience with winter-run steelhead. I put him at the pool's upper end, and on his fifth cast he was into a steelhead. He eventually lost the fish and continued to work down as two anglers entered the pool above him. I hooked a steelhead, too, and the fly did not come away until it was being beached. When I pulled out and started up the beach, one of the anglers called to me.

"Where are you going?"

"To start at the top end again," I said. "I hooked my fish." The man was casting a sixteen-foot two-handed rod and clearly seemed to know what he was about.

"Oh, you don't have to do that. Go ahead and fish through."

I thought about this. To violate common courtesy and custom at another angler's request is danger-ous. I reasoned that perhaps he didn't want anyone fishing down on him. I resumed fishing, and in

Mike Kinney

a single cast hooked another fish. The steelhead was gone in a moment. Now I was determined to quit the pool, and the angler did not wave me back, but instead joined me, my second surprise. One does not casually lose one's place on the Mixer.

This was Mike Kinney. I'd read about him in an article by Bob Arnold, a caring and insightful treatment, and I'd heard about his spey flies, true working flies at once beautiful and practical. I knew that he lived his life on the Stillaguamish and Skagit rivers so completely that his understanding of people and steelhead bordered on the mystical. Bob said that though Mike is only forty, Stilly locals refer to him as the "Old Man of the River." Mike thinks of himself as a "River Keeper."

"He's Irish, has the soul of a poet and the look of a Leprechaun," I later told Dale.

We became friends, hung out together from time to time, and promised ourselves we would fish the Stillaguamish the next summer. This led me to his one-room cabin behind Oso's general store and within earshot of the Stilly. His clothes are stored with his fly-tying materials, and he ties during the day because the cabin is without electricity—or running water, for that matter. So Mike bathes in the river and shares a communal outhouse. His son, Benjy, lives in the cabin too, and Mike counts this as his greatest blessing.

For much of his life he has guided bait and gear fishermen on the Olympic Peninsula, and now fly fishermen on his home waters, winter and summer. Like Walt Johnson, his neighbor across the Stilly, Mike can sometimes be found in the summer casting dries for steelhead with a six-foot midge rod, and in early fall he takes time off from guiding to hunt for sea-run cutthroat on the lower river. But when I think of Mike, he has his big two-handed rod and a box full of spey flies, and his fly is swinging through a lie a hundred feet away.

BOULDER CREEK

Body Black floss ribbed with flat chartreuse mylar tinsel and palmered with black hackle

Throat Kingfisher blue and guinea

Wing Matching golden pheasant flank

Topping Two golden pheasant crest feathers

CAR BODY

Body Black dubbing ribbed with chartreuse mylar tinsel. Palmer with deep purple saddle hackle.

Throat Kingfisher blue

Wing Matching pheasant rump dyed purple (color is nearly black)

DARK DAZE

Body Black dubbing ribbed with chartreuse mylar tinsel. Palmer with black saddle hackle.

Throat Saddle hackle dyed Veniard's Highlander Green

Wing Matching pheasant flank dyed black

DRAGON'S TOOTH

Tip Several turns of narrow oval silver tinsel

Body Purple dubbing or wool palmered with long deep purple saddle hackle. Rib with flat silver tinsel and narrow oval silver tinsel.

Throat Pintail

Wing Matching golden pheasant flank (red). Partially veil with golden pheasant body feather on each side (yellow).

TURKEY TRACKER

Body Black wool or dubbing ribbed with embossed gold tinsel and palmered with brown turkey beginning about two-fifths forward

Wing Hackle tips dyed Veniard's Highlander Green. Veil with short golden pheasant flank (red).

Throat One turn each of pintail and purple saddle

IMPROVISED PRACTITIONER

Mike's simplified version of the General Practitioner is a quick tie, appears quite shrimpy, and has proven to be an effective winter pattern.

Tail A dozen strands of orange bucktail. Two small matching golden pheasant feathers (red).

Body Hot orange wool and ribbbed with flat silver tinsel. At midpoint in body, tie in golden pheasant tippet feather. Hackle with pheasant rump dyed orange.

Wing Two small matching pheasant rump feathers dyed orange and a single golden pheasant rump, natural red

Hackle Teal, long, dyed orange

KALAMA RIVER DYNAMITE

Body Wind red thread three-eighths-inch down the hook and halfway back. Tie a piece of heavy yarn that extends to the bend of the hook.

Wing A clump of deer body hair tied down at same point as the yarn. The deer hair will flare. Clip front for a small head.

When it is my turn, I say, "Three candy bars and a cup of coffee." As I place them on the counter, the woman rings up the sale. I am uneasy, but I ask, "Can you tie me up some Dynamites?" Dawn Grytness smiles. "Sure honey, but let me get this other customer first." In a few minutes, Mahaffey's General Store is empty, and she has attached a fly tying vise to the counter. Her hands fly about the hook, a dozen turns of red thread, a piece of black yarn, a bunch of bucktail, and the fly is done. A second fly is started. To break the silence, she tells about the fly. "A woman came into Prichard's one day—this was after Al sold it to Blacky and Thelma Tidd—and asked him to tie a fly with the colors of a single egg yarn fly she had been fishing. She'd caught a lot of steelhead on it. You know, red and black. Took Blacky awhile to get it right, but that was the first Kalama River Dynamite. Best fly on the river."

"Does Blacky still tie the fly?"

"Blacky's gone. Wayne and Barb Orzell own the store now. It's called Prichard's Western Angler."

Dawn completes a third fly. She has been doing this for seven years. No wasted motion. She hands me the flies. Maybe two minutes have passed.

"Honey, if you want to hitch the fly, tie the wing farther back. Here," she says, and points out the spot.

"Just the red thread around the hook shank will give the hitch a secure seat?"

"Yes, but set the hitch in front of the bubblehead," she says.

The "bubblehead" is the fan of deer hair she has left in front to form the head. Black yarn gives the fly a great silhouette, like a Black Bomber, but the tie is more the low-riding damp, not at all a skater.

I thanked Dawn and left the store. I felt ancient, "older than God" as Salty Saltzman likes to say. How many years ago was it when Bill Bakke first told me about the Portland Hitch, when he read from Jock Scott's *Greased Line Fishing* and tied Toys and carried a few Redshanks and Blueshanks in his sheepskin fly book? Twenty-five years? I had been getting my fly patterns from *Professional Fly Tying, Spinning and Tackle Making Manual and Manufacturer's Guide* by George Herter. Looking back, I think going from George Herter to Arthur Wood nearly gave me the bends. Now, I'm getting the latest advice on waking dries at the checkout counter of the local market!

Bill tied the first waking dry I ever saw. We were fishing the Wind River, and he showed me a new pattern he called a Dragon Fly. It had the spun head of a Muddler, deer-hair wings that stuck out from each side nearly horizontal to the water, and a deer-hair tail. It floated well, but extremely low, and then came alive under tension. The wings became little paddles as the fly rocked back and forth and churned a bubbly wake through the swing. Steelhead devoured his entire supply that day. It seems like one of us was into a fish constantly. I remember taking them on a drag-free float and on a waking swing. The flies were a wonder. It was years before I heard about Bombers.

Bill Bakke was ahead of his time in other ways, too. Twenty-five years ago, the Kalama River already had a ten-year history of stocking hatchery steelhead. The first plants were a mixture of Cowlitz and Elochoman winter steelhead. And in 1957, the Kalama received Washougal and Klickitat summer stocks, those selectively bred Skamania Hatchery stocks of the Washougal River that came to be transplanted everywhere, even in the Great Lakes.

The Kalama naturally had fresh steelhead every month of the year. It was famous for its springers, sexually immature summer-runs that came in as early as March, with the winter fish. The main summer-run month was July, the perfect fishing month in the Northwest. Upriver, in the area of Pigeon Springs, was a short fly-fishing-only section. Add to these resources the prospect of an ambitious hatchery program, and you have angling Nirvana. Send a tiny fish to sea, argued hatchery proponents, and get back a steelhead weighing seven or eight pounds. This arrangement with Mother Nature would be a bargain at twice the cost! Hatcheries were nothing less than integral to the American way of guaranteeing that more anglers would catch more steelhead. Punching your card out meant your annual limit of thirty steelhead had been realized. This is what your license money paid for, and a skilled angler expected to get his money's worth. The Good Old Boy Network could tell you who was and who wasn't.

Bill Bakke spoke to me in a strange reactionary tongue. He talked of catch and release, gene pools, racial diversity, and why he hated hatcheries. In his mind, they were a covenant with the Devil, the state getting off cheap for sucking the life's blood from the watershed. Whether that was dewatering, deforestation, dams, or the kind of massive erosion that turns spawning gravel into concrete didn't matter. Native steelhead were races unique to each river, ten thousand generations had seen to that. The most perfect Kalama River steelhead was a wild fish, naturally born and bred. They existed and flourished because of the pristine watershed. Dumping a weird genetic mix of hatchery steelhead into the Kalama—and a hundred other rivers as well—was a rape of the native strain's genetic integrity. Bill believed that. In time, I believed it too.

Bill Bakke became the driving force behind Oregon Trout, and presently works as its politically wise Executive Director. He and game departments now speak a far more common language. I think they have met Bill halfway, and only have halfway to go.

KISPIOX RIVER SHRIMP

Hook 1/0 to 3/0, heavy-wire, down-eye. Weight with twenty wraps of 3/0 wire.

Body Flame orange fluorescent yarn. Palmer with orange saddle hackle. (Mike likes to start winding with the fluff-end of the hackle.)

Back Orange Krystal Flash covered with heavy clear plastic. Leave the Krystal Flash one inch long. Tie this down to represent downward-pointing feelers. Rib entire body with heavy copper or gold wire. (The wire, digging into the clear plastic, segments the body.)

Head Silver bead-chain eyes

Mike Craig's Kispiox Shrimp looks like a huge scud, a natural inspiration for him. He operates the Bighorn Angler in Fort Smith, Montana, and books more floats on the Bighorn River than any other outfitter in the country. Scuds, in a variety of colors, are popular patterns on the river, and Mike sells them by the gross.

With no wing, plenty of hackle, and weighted, the Kispiox Shrimp tends to roll around and may even be upside down on the swing. This doesn't matter to the steelhead. They'll take the fly in any attitude.

Mike dredges the fly through runs either with heads with a sink rate of IV (High Speed Hi-D), or sink tips of Deep Water Express.

MARABOU

Steelhead fly design in the 1980s was characterized first by the routine use of marabou in dressings, and later by the many new synthetic fly-tying materials that helped to create altogether new patterns, or to add visual spice to traditional dressings. Today, marabou is often mixed with Flashabou, Krystal Flash, Edge Bright, and Diamond Braid. In the hands of expert tyers, these materials are mixed to produce flies of classic beauty. But marabou is not popular for its aesthetic advantages. The material possesses movement in the water that is matched by nothing else. Its only shortcoming is its lack of durability compared to any of the furs.

In 1980, John Farrar was experimenting with a technique developed by Poul Jorgensen for fashioning "hackle" from rabbit's fur. Guard hairs were placed in a dubbing loop and twisted. The fur was then dampened a bit and wound around the hook just like a wet-fly hackle. John used this technique with the fine blood plumes of marabou. The butt ends of the individual barbules could be trimmed to whatever length hackle he desired. Palmered, it was a fine substitute for heron in spey flies. Colors could be stacked in the single loop so that one color veiled the other. Different colors could be mixed to blend perfectly into shades obtainable no other way. Saddle hackle was often wound on first to keep the marabou wing full, and a second saddle was wound on to veil the marabou wing. With the addition of Flashabou and Krystal Flash, the creative variations were endless.

"Other tyers working with marabou use different techniques," John told me. "Bob Aid, frustrated by the dubbing loop, discarded the technique and simply wound the plume around the hook by means of the stem. George Cook turned wizardry into art, mingling tarpon, steelhead, and Alaskan salmon patterns to produce a concoction called the Alaskabou."

John believes it's a mistake to overdress his Marabou Spey. "Keep it light," he insists. "This is a sunk fly. You want it to sink well and fill and move easily in the water."

MARABOU SPEY

Hook Size 2 to 2/0

Body Gold mylar tinsel. One-third down the body, secure dubbing loop and fill with any two contrasting colors, the darker color to go in last. (John's first preference is red over orange, but cerise over pink, even black over white is used.) Wind loop to the head and tie off. Double a golden pheasant flank feather and wind two or three turns. (John also uses teal, particularly if the marabou is black.)

Wing Matching sections of bronze mallard set low and not extending past the bend of the hook. The body may also be covered with floss, or dubbed, and then ribbed before the loop of blood plumes is used to palmer in the "spey" hackles.

Four specific patterns are offered. As their names suggest, all evolved from John's years of guiding fly fishermen on the Skagit during March and April.

George Cook

SKAGIT SPEY SERIES (JOHN FARRAR)

BLACK SKAGIT SPEY

Tag Flat gold tinsel

Body Rear one-fourth orange floss over underbody of flat gold tinsel. No rib. Tie in six to eight strands of orange polar bear hair. Forward three-fourths black seal ribbed with fine oval silver tinsel and palmer with black marabou

Throat Teal

Wing Bronze mallard

Cheeks Jungle cock

ORANGE SKAGIT SPEY

Tag Flat gold tinsel

Body Rear one-fourth orange floss over underbody of flat gold tinsel. No rib. Tie in six to eight strands of orange polar bear hair. Forward three-fourths, hot orange seal. Rib with fine oval gold tinsel. Palmer with black orange marabou followed by a single turn of red. (Proportion the dubbing loop accordingly.)

Hackle One turn of magenta

Throat Golden pheasant and pintail, one turn each

Wing Bronze mallard

Cheeks Jungle cock

WHITE SKAGIT SPEY

Tag Flat gold tinsel

Body Rear one-fourth red floss. No rib. Tie in six to eight strands of white polar bear hair. Forward three-fourths, light grey dubbing over flat gold tinsel. Rib with narrow oval gold tinsel. Palmer with light grey marabou.

Throat Mallard

Wing Bronze mallard

Cheeks Jungle cock

YELLOW SKAGIT SPEY

Tag Flat gold tinsel

Body Rear one-fourth hot orange floss. No rib. Tie in six to eight strands of white polar bear hair. Front three-fourths yellow dubbing over flat gold tinsel. Rib with narrow oval gold tinsel. Palmer with white marabou followed by yellow, last turn.

Throat Mallard flank over a small bunch of magenta hackle fibers

Wing Bronze mallard

Cheeks Jungle cock

Bob Aid, manager of the Kaufmann's Streamborn store in Seattle, has been an avid steelhead fly fisherman for more than twenty years. In the early 1980s, he and John Farrar operated a guide business called "The Gilly Service." During this time, Bob developed his own marabou fly-tying technique, which has become the standard approach for winter flies. There are two keys to Bob's approach. First, he ties in a shoulder of dubbing before winding on the hackle. Second, the hackle is wound on by tying in the tip first. The short barbules of the blood plume and the dubbing shoulder help to keep the marabou from matting down against the hook. He says, "The 'Steelhead Marabou Spiders' evolved from John's Marabou Spey about 1980 because they were easier for me to tie. They are very effective both in winter and in the higher flows of summer."

BLACK AND ORANGE

Body Gold mylar

Shoulder Orange angora goat

Hackle Black marabou followed by an orange hen hackle

Collar Guinea dyed orange

ORANGE AND RED

Body Silver mylar

Shoulder Orange angora goat

Hackle Orange marabou followed by red marabou

Collar Black pheasant rump

PINK AND RED

Body Silver mylar

Shoulder Pink angora goat

Hackle Pink marabou followed by red saddle or red hen hackle

Collar Guinea dyed red (optional)

PURPLE AND BLUE

Body Silver mylar
Shoulder Purple angora goat

Hackle Purple marabou followed by a smaller amount of teal blue marabou

SKAGIT SPECIAL

Body Silver mylar
Shoulder Orange angora goat
Hackle Yellow marabou followed by orange marabou

Collar Guinea dyed orange

STEELHEAD PINKIE

Body Silver tinsel
Shoulder Pink angora goat

Hackle Pink marabou followed by a smaller amount of blue marabou

George Cook guided at Alaska's Alagnak Lodge in 1983. Using pink and purple saddle hackle, he tied up tarpon-style flies for the fresh runs of chum salmon. When the camp ran out of saddle hackle, George substituted marabou. "Looks like a Las Vegas showgirl," said a client. For a couple of years he continued to tie it tarpon-style and called the powder-puff dressing "Showgirl." Each season he returned to the lodge and, in 1985, guided Gordon Nash and Randy Stetzer, his fellow employees at Kaufmann's Streamborn in Tigard, Oregon.

The Showgirl had become an Alaskabou and grown more sophisticated. Marabou was mixed with Flashabou and tied in two layers, the first halfway down the hook, the second at the head. When asked for the name of the tricolored marabou pattern he was tying, George remarked, "I don't know, maybe a popsicle," a reference to the red, white, and blue "cherry pops" he ate as a kid. Thus was born the Popsicle, an orange, red, and purple fly that became tremendously popular in Alaska for salmon, and in British Columbia and Washington for steelhead.

While George Cook's Popsicle refers to a single pattern, the Alaskabou is a series, the Tequila Sunrise, Candy Cane, Pixie's Revenge, and Showgirl. The patterns are tied in approximately the same manner. A clump of marabou is tied in two-thirds of the way up the hook shank. The second clump of marabou, sightly shorter in length, is tied in just forward and obscures the head at the first clump. A smaller third clump—omitted in some Alaskabous—veils the other two. This sequence helps to keep the fly from fouling, and prevents the head from bulking up. A full collar of saddle hackle finishes the fly. Krystal Flash and Flashabou is incorporated throughout the tie.

TEQUILA SUNRISE

First Wing Salmon marabou topped with twelve strands of pearl Krystal Flash
Second Wing Orange marabou, repeat pearl Krystal Flash

Third Wing Sparse, but like second wing
Collar Red saddle hackle

CANDY CANE

First Wing Cerise marabou mixed with fifteen to twenty strands of silver Flashabou and ten to twelve strands of wine Krystal Flash

Second Wing Repeat as in first wing
Collar Red saddle hackle

PIXIE'S REVENGE

| **First Wing** | White marabou mixed with fifteen strands of gold Flashabou. Top with eight to ten strands of orange Krystal Flash | **Third Wing** | As in second wing |
| **Second Wing** | Orange marabou. Repeat gold Flashabou and orange Krystal Flash. | **Collar:** | Magenta saddle hackle |

SHOWGIRL

| **First Wing** | Cerise marabou and fifteen strands of purple Flashabou | **Second Wing** | Repeat as in first |
| | | **Collar** | Purple saddle hackle |

Note: George has used the Showgirl primarily on chum and silver salmon.

POPSICLE

No tail or body. Head is red. First clump is orange, second is red. Add a collar of short purple marabou at the head.

Mike Kinney fishes marabou spiders in a number of color combinations for winter fishing on the Skagit, Sauk, and Stillaguamish rivers. Each fly is hackled with one or two blood plumes, and finished with a contrasting color of saddle hackle. His favorite combinations of marabou and hackle include purple/Highlander green, purple/orange, purple/kingfisher blue, Highlander green/black, and yellow/orange. For "dirty" water Mike likes these flies, marabou and saddle hackle, in purple, black, and gentian violet.

Kevin Cooney calls his purple marabou dressing the Acid Flashback. The pattern has a tail of red hackle fibers mixed with pearl Krystal Flash, a body of purple chenille ribbed with flat silver tinsel, purple hackle, and a wing of purple marabou over a few strands of pearl Krystal Flash.

Jimmy Hunnicutt's Blood on the Waters, the "Blood," is one of our most beautiful steelhead flies, a blending of fluorescent cerise and red marabou that glows in low light. First fished for late-winter steelhead on Washington's Sauk, it has been used during all seasons when cold or turgid water calls for a highly visible well-sunk fly. I recall one August day several years ago on the Dean when the Blood ended two dead-slow days for Jimmy. I watched a sixteen-pound hen take the fly—and Jimmy—downriver and around the bend, all in one motion. I've been a fan of the pattern ever since.

The fly is loosely constructed to move in the lightest currents, but it does not sink well without a sinking line. Jimmy looks for the broad, shallow tailouts that harbor late winter-run steelhead to fish the Blood, often covering the water with his sixteen-foot double-handed rod.

BLOOD ON THE WATERS

Tail	Golden pheasant tippet dyed red	**Collar**	Grizzly saddle dyed red. Tie back to blend with the wing.
Butt	Red seal fur		
Body	Flat silver tinsel. Forward one-fourth, red seal fur.	**Cheeks**	Jungle cock
		Head	Red
Underwing	Red polar bear fur		
Overwing	Cerise marabou is wound first, followed by red marabou		

Sean Gallagher, one of the Northwest's most knowledgeable steelhead fly fishers, ties his Electric Blue in a similar fashion. Its long royal-blue wing of blood plumes is wound on to envelop the hook. A long red collar is followed by a shorter purple collar, both of saddle hackle. The three contrasting colors are dazzling. This is a winter fly, more fully dressed than the Blood, and always fished on a sinking line.

ELECTRIC BLUE

Body	Flat silver tinsel ribbed with oval gold tinsel		ever color surrounds it, and he uses it sparingly.
Wing	Royal blue marabou mixed with several strands of pearl Krystal Flash. Sean feels that the Pearl Krystal flash takes on what-	**Collar**	Red, long, followed by purple, short
		Head	Black

Bob Arnold, another longtime regular on Washington's winter rivers, ties his marabou flies in a conventional manner, a long clump for the wing, a slightly shorter one—but the same color—for the throat hackle, and a collar (à la Bob Aid) that contrasts with the wing and hides the tying wraps that secure the wing and throat. The final product has a tiny red head. Bob says, "I want the body visible and consider it an important part of the fly, so I utilize a reduced tie whenever the river isn't raging."

Bob fishes his two favorite marabou patterns, the Deer Creek and Royal Flush, on a sinking-line cast quartering downstream. He mends slack line into the drift until he feels the fly touch bottom downstream as it completes its swing. If feeding additional mends doesn't accomplish this, Bob casts across or even slightly upstream when trying to reach down into an especially deep hole.

DEER CREEK

Tail	Red hackle fibers		for metallic French tinsel. Unfortunately, it is now often hard to find.)
Body	Flat silver tinsel ribbed with oval silver tinsel. (Mylar tinsel breaks easily, and an oval tinsel rib will help to protect it. This problem is the reason I have a strong preference	**Upper and Lower Wing**	Purple marabou
		Collar	Silver doctor blue or Laxa blue

ROYAL FLUSH

Body	Dark blue chenille ribbed with flat silver tinsel	**Upper and Lower Wing**	Red marabou

If Bob adds a few strands of red Krystal Flash, he calls the pattern a Royal Flush.

Don Hathaway developed the Purple Bad Habit while working as a guide at Bristol Bay Lodge in Alaska. It was one of many different marabou patterns for silver salmon with which he experimented. Only the Habit, however, was also outstanding on steelhead. He now calls it "My pride and joy!"

PURPLE BAD HABIT

Tail	Purple marabou to body length, full	**Hackle**	One turn or more of red, purple, and magenta
Body	Silver mylar braid		
Underwing	Purple marabou, full, to just past end of tail	**Head**	Hot orange
Overwing	Purple Flashabou followed by magenta Flashabou		

Steve Gobin, a tyer known for his Scottish spey flies and full-dressed Atlantic salmon flies, ties a single marabou pattern for winter steelhead. It is a beautiful fly of remarkable contrasts and has been very productive for him. In Steve's hands, the fly is a work of art.

PURPLE MARABOU

Body Deep purple floss ribbed with oval silver tinsel and palmered with red schlappen

Wing Purple marabou wound full and long
Hackle Guinea, one or two turns

Joe Butorac told me the Skagit Monster resulted from his collaboration with Dick Sylbert, a fly for "big water, late-season winter fish."

The Monster is just that, the largest fly I have seen used for March and April steelhead, whether the river flows muddy or clear. Joe often begins with the Monster and follows up a pull with the more petite Half and Half. Both dressings are quick to tie and have proven records.

SKAGIT MONSTER

Hook 2/0 to 5/0
Wing Marabou blood plumes are wound on by the tip first. Each turn is carefully wound forward of the previous turn. Pick out any snarls with a bodkin. Each color represents a full hackle tip: Fluorescent yellow, fluorescent orange, and red.
Head Flame single-strand floss

HALF AND HALF

This simple fly of red over orange is constructed from the blood-plume tips of marabou. The stem supplies stiffness and prevents the fly from wrapping on the hook. Head is flame single-strand floss. No body.

Dan Reiff, a regular on Washington's Skagit and Skykomish rivers, swears by his two winter patterns. He ties the Scarlet Lightning on the order of Bob Aid's Marabou Spiders, the ball of orange chenille under the marabou giving the body a fuller shape. The Semi-Respectable sinks well and remains stable in strong currents. Using this dressing, Dan has caught some of the largest winter steelhead ever taken on a fly.

SCARLET LIGHTNING

Hook Size 2 Mustad 9049
Body Flat silver mylar. At forward end wind in a three-eighths-inch ball of orange chenille.

Hackle Red marabou blood plume wound full and long
Wing Cockatoo breast feather or white equivalent two-thirds length of marabou

SEMI-RESPECTABLE

Tag Flat silver tinsel
Tail Pink hackle fibers, long
Body Fluorescent orange chenille ribbed with flat silver tinsel, the rib a continuation of the tag

Hackle Pink
Wing Matched scarlet marabou feathers tied twice the length of the hook shank

Note: Dan sometimes ties in cheeks of flicker breast feathers to eye the fly and calls the result The Respectable.

Several years ago Tony Sarp, owner of Alaska's Katmai Lodge, came up with a gaudy bottom-dredging pattern, the Sarp's Seducer. He fishes it on hybrid lines, sink-tip combinations of floating level looped to an eighteen-foot section of floating-level 10-weight line looped to lengths of Deep Water Express from two to eight feet. Depending on the size of the hook used—1 to 5/0—the fly may be heavily weighted and will likely ride upside down.

I like this pattern dressed down a bit on 2/0 hooks without additional weight, fuse wire, or bead-chain eyes. A collar of black saddle hackle and a head of red tying thread also dresses it up a bit.

Tony practices what he preaches. When I last met him on the Skagit he was giving the river hell with his Seducer.

SARP'S SEDUCER

Tail	Pearl Flashabou one-third length of hook shank, full	**Overwing**	Medium blue Flashabou, full, veil over entire wing
Weight	Eight-amp fuse wire. (Omit in large size.)	**Eyes**	Silver bead chain
Underwing	Black over red marabou, full, two blood plumes for each color.	**Head**	Black

These artists with marabou are found elsewhere in this chapter, or in various river chapters. Randall Kaufmann's popular marabou flies are detailed in Chapter 27.

There is no hard-and-fast rule for selecting one color over another. Generally, black, purple, and fluorescent flame are my choices for discolored water. If the water has reasonable clarity, I like orange. For clearer water and overcast days, fluorescent cerise and hot pink are good colors. Touches of red or purple with these colors are additions steelhead appreciate. I do like fluorescent colors for low-light mornings and evenings.

I have my own approach to tying marabou flies that, like Randall Kaufmann's, generally duplicates a conventional tie. I rarely dress them on anything less than a 1/0 hook, and prefer the 2/0 size for the hook's greater weight, which helps, even on a fast-sinking line, to take the fly down and keep it there. They are not generously dressed, but swim nicely through a swing even in hard-running riffles. (See Winter Series.)

I love to fuss with these flies. Blending the many shades of fluorescent marabou, larding their brilliance with Krystal Flash, and incorporating dyed golden pheasant, guinea, and various duck flank into the aesthetic equation can be immensely satisfying. They are the largest flies I fish for steelhead.

MUDDLED SKUNK

Hook	Size 12 to 2/0
Tail	Black bucktail
Body	Pearlescent mylar
Wing	Black bucktail, white polar bear (or synthetic equivalent), and black bucktail in three equal clumps
Head	Black deer body hair spun Muddler-style, but with the entire collar trimmed away

Gene Parmeter first fished his Muddled Skunk in 1978, on Alaska's Anchor River, where it proved effective on both steelhead and coho salmon. He next took the fly to Montana and discovered that Madison River browns and rainbows were equally fond of it. When Gene settled in Bellingham, Washington, his "Skunk" became a steelhead pattern, raising fish for him on many Northwest rivers, including the Methow, Stillaguamish, Skagit, and Thompson.

MUDDLER MINNOW

Tail	Matching sections of brown mottled turkey wing quills
Body	Gold tinsel, flat or embossed
Wing	Matching sections of mottled brown turkey wing quills over grey squirrel tail
Head and Collar	Deer body hair spun on and clipped to shape

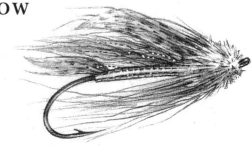

Don Gapen conceived the Muddler Minnow in 1937, a long, loosely spun deer-hair streamer intended to imitate the freshwater sculpin, the "muddler minnow." He first called his creation Gapen's Special Fly, and fished it in Ontario's Nipigon River for the huge brook trout that were his lifelong passion.

Dan Bailey of Livingston, Montana, popularized the fly Gapen would ultimately rename the Muddler Minnow. He made the fly less gainly, tied it densely, and trimmed it more carefully, giving it the well-rounded head anglers now associate with the pattern. The Muddler soon became synonymous with catches of trophy brown trout from the Madison, Yellowstone, and Bighorn rivers. Bailey added a pale version, the Missoulian Spook—a dead end as far as steelhead fly fishing is concerned— and developed the Marabou Muddler series, probably angling's best big trout flies. Years later, he crossed the Muddler and the Spruce Fly to produce the Spuddler.

Dave Whitlock, a genius at spinning deer hair, developed the Whitlock Sculpin, a "Matuka Muddler" that is tremendously lifelike. A variation on this theme is Harry Lemire's Steelhead Sculpin, a new all-season pattern that shows wonderful promise (see Chapter 28).

The Muddler Minnow has been used on steelhead rivers as a waking dry, a greased-line fly, and a deeply sunk winter fly. When tied commercially it is often overdressed, the thick, short collar killing the fly's action and making it nearly worthless. I prefer to tie the fly sparsely, spinning a long collar and then trimming most of it away. This collar then blends nicely with any fine hair that is barred black and brown. Squirrel tail and very fine bucktail are excellent. I may also include a few strands of orange Krystal Flash in the wing. If the Muddler is to be fished greased-line or as a waking dry, the head should still be loosely spun, trimmed small, and blended somewhat into the collar "shoulders" of the pattern. As a dry, tie the pattern on a low-water light-wire hook and follow the double turle knot with a riffling hitch. In either case, the sparser dressing helps to keep the Muddler riding upright in riffles and swimming in a more supple and lifelike manner.

The Muddler has inspired so many steelhead variations that today one could fish only these and the original during any season and never be without the right fly. Below are a few of the Muddlers that have proven especially effective on steelhead.

BLACK KRYSTAL FLASH MUDDLER

Tail	None	**Throat**	One complete turn of a dubbing loop of red angora wool
Body	Embossed gold tinsel		
Wing	Small bunch of black squirrel tail mixed with Black Krystal Flash below matching sections of dark mottled turkey wing quills	**Head and Collar**	Black deer body hair spun on and clipped to shape

PURPLE KRYSTAL FLASH MUDDLER

Tail	None	**Throat**	One complete turn of a dubbing loop of red angora wool
Body	Purple Diamond Braid		
Wing	Grey squirrel tail dyed purple mixed with purple Krystal Flash under matching sections of dark mottled turkey wing quill	**Head and Collar**	Purple deer body hair spun on and clipped to shape

OLIVE KRYSTAL FLASH MUDDLER

Tail	None	**Throat**	One complete turn of a dubbing loop of red angora wool
Body	Peacock Glitter Body		
Wing	Olive green Krystal Flash under matching sections of dark mottled turkey wing quill	**Head and Collar**	Natural deer body hair spun on and clipped to shape

John Hazel, a steelhead guide and store manager for Kaufmann's Streamborn, developed this slim trio of Muddlers when Krystal Flash first became available a few years ago. They are very well proportioned, provide a lot of flash and action, and offer a good silhouette even to #6. He fishes the flies as waking dries—though he may cast them upstream first for a drag-free float—as greased-line flies, and as wet flies. He told me, "Be sure you trim the head flat on the top and bottom. You want the fly to slide right in the surface film when greased-line fishing." He explained that as the collar works in the currents, the band of red, the "throat" or "gills," will be exposed.

In early 1990, Randall Kaufmann told me, "Our sales of regular Muddlers have plummeted since John introduced these Krystal Flash Muddlers."

COON MUDDLER

Tail	None
Body	Embossed gold tinsel
Wing	Matching slips of wood-duck flank under a small clump of raccoon guard hairs

Head and Collar	Natural deer body hair spun on and clipped to shape

Joe Howell ties steelhead flies for the Blue Heron Fly Shop, which he and his wife, Bonnie, operate on the North Umpqua River in Idleyld Park. The Muddler Minnow is a frequent request, but expensive to tie commercially with genuine oak turkey. The "eyed" feather of wood duck flank and raccoon hair were cheaper substitutes. The resulting Coon Muddler is, in Joe's opinion, at least as effective as the original.

Joe regularly fishes two other Muddler variations of his own design, both tied to be fished dry.

ORANGE SCOOTER

Tail	Orange Krystal Flash
Body	Fluorescent orange wool, thin

Wing	Orange Krystal Flash, black bucktail over
Head	Spun deer body hair dyed black

The Orange Scooter meets Joe's need for a high-visibility silhouette pattern that can be waked on a floating line, or fished subsurface on the swing with a sink-tip line.

GOLDEN STONE

Tail	Moose
Body	Gold wool palmered with furnace saddle
Wing	Natural elk (tan in color). Tie in a brown saddle hackle at the head.

Head	Deer body hair dyed gold, spun and clipped to shape. Palmer head with brown saddle.

The golden stone (*Acroneuria californica*) is abundant on the North Umpqua in June, with sporadic hatches taking place through July and August. Joe's Golden Stone matches this hatch. Though dressed full, the fly rides low, its large head setting up a sizable wake on the swing. This is an excellent floater, and I wouldn't be without a few for midsummer fishing on the pools below Steamboat.

PURPLE SMUDDLER

Hook	Mustad 9674 or Tiemco 300, #2 or #4
Tail	None
Body	Purple Poly Flash or Sparkle Braid
Underwing	Black calf tail

Wing	Black marabou holding a few strands of purple Krystal Flash
Head and Collar	Black deer hair spun on and clipped to shape

Don Roberts, a longtime friend of mine from Bend, Oregon, swears by this Purple Smuddler. He says, "Credit for this pattern—yet another variation of the celebrated Muddler Minnow—belongs to Greg Smith, a graphic designer from Portland, Oregon. The secret of Greg's Smuddler lies in its sleek silhouette and, because of the sparse layering of soft, pliant materials, its unbelievably lifelike swimming motion when fished slower than the current. I think that this is probably the single most consistent and productive pattern for probing clearly defined water and pockets in small to mid-size steelhead streams. I am so sold on the Purple Smuddler's enticing action that I use it everywhere, in every kind of water and stream condition."

STEELHEAD MUDDLER

Tail	Orange calf tail
Body	Gold tinsel chenille or flat gold tinsel
Underwing	Orange calf tail to bend of the hook
Wing	Matching grizzly hackle tips, face to face, not flared, slightly longer than orange wing
Head	Deer body hair spun and clipped to shape. Leave the head large so that a substantial wake is produced.
Collar	Tips should extend three-fourths to wing tips

BLOODY MUDDLER

Substitute white calf tail for the tail and red calf tail for the underwing. Otherwise, identical to the above Steelhead Muddler.

LeRoy Hyatt (see Hyatt's Caddis) developed these two steelhead dries to be fished in sizes 6, 8, and 10. "The Bloody Muddler," he says, "is my all-time favorite fly for both trout and steelhead. But both patterns have worked very well for me on the Clearwater and Grande Ronde rivers during the fall season."

MARK NOBLE

Mark Noble is the resident expert and owner of the Greased Line Shop in Vancouver, Washington. His home rivers range from the Kalama on the west to the Klickitat on the east, with the East Fork Lewis his "fall favorite." The fly patterns to follow are a reflection of these relatively small rivers and the demands they make upon the fly fisher.

His greased-line drys are large wakers that ride low and make a lot of commotion, an advantage where flies must be visible in violent and very localized currents. One pattern suggests the October caddis, the other a general approximation of a grasshopper. Both have accounted for many steelhead.

Mark's steelhead versions of the Muddler Minnow are also high-visibility patterns that create distinctive silhouettes. In tight little creases of holding water, a graceful conventional swing is out of the question. These are flies that slide and dart in braiding currents to stop and wiggle above suspected lies. One can go right at the fish. By comparison, fine low-water dressings often lack the bold silhouette necessary to trigger a response on such waters.

Mark Noble

GREASED LINE FALL CADDIS

Tail Deer body hair
Body Orange seal, or substitute (Seal Clone, opossum, angora goat) palmered with stiff brown saddle hackle
Wing Deer body hair. Bind down to cause butts to flare. Trim butts, leaving a quarter-inch bubblehead above the head. Wind tying thread on both sides of the wing butts. Coat head and base of wing butts with cement. The bubblehead will help to keep the fly waking when under tension.

GREASED LINE HOPPER

Tail Red hackle fibers
Body Yellow, in any material described above. Palmer with brown saddle hackle. Take several extra turns at the head.

Wing Brown deer body hair as above

AFTER DINNER MINT MUDDLER

Tail Medium green Krystal Flash
Body Green Diamond Braid
Underwing Grey squirrel dyed green. Top with medium green Krystal Flash.

Wing Natural brown turkey
Head Deer body hair spun and clipped so that the head is flattened like a sculpin's head

BLUE McGOON

Tail Light purple Krystal Flash
Body Violet Diamond Braid
Underwing Light purple Krystal Flash under grey squirrel tail dyed purple

Wing Natural brown turkey
Head Black deer body hair spun and clipped to shape so that the head is flattened like a sculpin's head

Mark Noble's Caddis Pupae nymph dressings are heavily weighted and designed for the small stream. Using a floating line and ten-to-fourteen-foot leader, Mark casts across and slightly upstream, the nymph sinking like a stone. After an initial mend, the rod tip follows the fly's passage through the dead drift, and leads it through the swing. A steelhead may take the fly at any time.

In this manner, Mark dissects his rivers, dropping his Caddis Pupae down narrow channels and dredging the bottom, or going up top with strong silhouette dressings. Except for a couple of low-water dressings for the broad tailouts that lend themselves to the greased-line presentation, I would quite willingly fish Mark's rivers with just these few patterns.

BEIGE CADDIS PUPAE

Body Beige cactus chenille
Collar Hungarian partridge

Head Black ostrich

BURLAP CADDIS PUPAE

Body Burlap, or grey wool
Collar Pheasant rump

Head Black ostrich

ORANGE CADDIS PUPAE

Body Orange Seal or substitute (Mark uses Seal Clone)

Collar Hungarian partridge
Head Black ostrich

PEACOCK CADDIS PUPAE

Body Peacock herl
Collar Pheasant rump

Head Black ostrich

SCOTT NOBLE

Scott Noble's world of steelhead fly fishing comprises a wealth of experiences tied to four remarkable dressings, two dry, two wet, each thoughtfully conceived and skillfully tied. Winter and summer, he is a familiar figure on the Skykomish, Snoqualmie, and Green rivers, waters easily reached from his home in Renton, Washington. Besides being one of the Northwest's most gifted tyers, Scott makes his own cane rods, "flamed and based on the Garrison taper," he says, and fishes them with reels Stan Bogdan custom built for him. The man is *serious* about his steelhead fly fishing.

STEELHEAD DRY

Hook Partridge Wilson, size 10 to 16
Tail Elk
Body Alternate bands of dubbing, the light center band of opossum separating dark bands of muskrat
Wings Elk, upright and divided
Hackle Two or three brown neck hackles, #1 dry-fly quality, full

Scott Noble

Scott's Steelhead Dry, a high-floating pattern inspired by Roderick Haig-Brown's Steelhead Bee and Lee Wulff's Grey Wulff, is usually tied in sizes 12, 14, and 16. The fly is cast slightly upstream, the line mended, and the fly floated drag-free for a short distance. As the fly comes under tension, it is led skating through a swing. He feels that about ninety percent of the takes occur just when the fly begins to skate, and ten percent while the fly is still drag-free. The careful record Scott has kept of the rises, and time spent with each size, reveal that the smaller the fly, the more rises it induces. For example, in 1987 he had forty-seven rises to dry flies. These broke down as follows: twenty-two on size 16, fifteen on size 14, eight on size 12, and two on size 8. I asked Scott if he experienced any problems holding steehead on hooks as small as 16? He assured me that he didn't. "I've caught steelhead to sixteen pounds on the size 16. For example, in 1985, I had sixteen rises on the size 16. Of these, I hooked eight and landed six."

The Steelhead Dry is a general simulator, but Scott thinks it is most effective when sedges, the large late-summer caddis, are on the water. Scott has twice seen a steelhead take one of these caddis out of the air.

AUTUMN SEDGE

Hook Partridge Wilson, size 10 to 14 (Scott ties the Sedge in 16 and 14 for sea-run cut-throat)

Body Wrap with thread. Secure clump of elk dyed rust red. Clip off tips, and leave bobbin at bend. Pull elk forward and wind tying thread forward for the rib. Wings are also elk dyed rust red. Tie in upright and divided. The antennae are the stem of a blue dun neck hackle. Scott runs his thumbnail down the stem so that it curls at the end. These must be tied in before the wings.

Hackle Three reddish brown neck hackles, #1 dry-fly grade, full

"I think this fly does a better job of imitating the October Caddis than any other fly I've seen," says Scott. "It skates beautifully, swinging back and forth like an egg-laying October caddis." He fishes the Autumn Sedge as early as July on the Snoqualmie, and never fishes it in sizes larger than 10.

When I fished with Scott, he cast the same Autumn Sedge for hours. The fly is a wonderful floater, skating like thistledown through each swing. At the time, I was fishing my hairwing version of the Lady Caroline, a fly I hackle with red golden pheasant before winging the fly with brown bucktail and winding on a collar of brown barred duck flank. My wet fly was the same color as his dry, and I think that fishing the two in sequence has merit.

PRISMATIC SPEY

Tag	Three turns of flat gold tinsel, wound over itself, and hung with hackle pliers. A continuation of the tag will become the rib.	**Wing**	From bottom to top, three fibers magenta, two purple, two green, two blue, two yellow, and two orange. A single strip of red is then laid down on top and running down the center. As completed by Scott, the wing has the appearance of prismatically running together. The thread must be reversed to keep the wing balanced.
Body	Rear half hot orange floss, front half hot tangerine seal (a mixture of red and orange). Rib with four wraps of tinsel. Palmer with yellow schlappen stripped on one side.		
Fore Hackle	Hot orange, doubled, two to three turns	**Head**	Flame
Underwing	Hot orange goose primary, short, no more than one-fourth inch long. This is tied in solely to help support the wing.		

MIDNIGHT SPEY

Tag	Flat silver tinsel, three turns	**Wing**	From bottom to top, five fibers of green, five of blue, and seven to eight of purple. The purple section tents barely over the green and blue fibers, but has the appearance of being married.
Body	Rear half purple floss, front half purple seal. Rib as a continuation of tag, four turns of flat silver tinsel. Palmer from second turn with purple pheasant flank.		
Fore Hackle	Blue schlappen, doubled, two turns	**Head**	Flame
Underwing	Purple goose primary, short, no more than one-fourth inch long. This is tied in solely to support the wing.		

The late Syd Glasso, a master tyer who introduced spey flies to steelheading, was a friend of Scott's and became the inspiration for his Prismatic Spey. "There is a lot of Walt Johnson's Spectral Spider in the fly, too," says Scott. Its companion dressing, the Midnight Spey, also has its origins in the Deep Purple Spey, another of Walt's ties. I found the prismatic effect of both reminiscent of Preston Jennings's Lord Iris. Regardless, these patterns are uniquely Scott's, and no other flies in steelheading are remotely like them.

When Scott first shared his spey flies with me, I could see they were brilliantly crafted, but delicately so, and I dismissed them as fanciful show flies. I was wrong. They are his day in, day out wet flies, dressings that produce dazzling high-visibility images in clear and turgid currents. Scott says, "I feel that blue is an underused color in steelhead flies." He mixes blue with purple in the Midnight Spey, the result an "electric" shade of both—effective for steelhead in any season. Of the Prismatic Spey, Scott says simply, "Strictly a winter fly. Beautiful in the water."

NYMPHS

Kaufmann's Stone

Nymphs for steelhead are commonly large versions of standard trout patterns. Dave Hall took this route when developing his Hammerdown and Crawler nymphs for the North Umpqua. For years, Billy Pate has fished a Montana Stone on this river. Strike-indicator advocates often fish the Hare's Ear and Puyan's Nymph. Mark Noble's Caddis Pupae series would doubtless be effective on resident browns. I have nymphed both the Girdle Bug and Kaufmann's Stone for steelhead. Brad Jackson's Ugly Bug is a highly regarded steelhead version of many rubber-leg trout patterns. The Brindle Bug and the Mossback are steelhead nymphs that have been popular wet flies for years.

In these largely impressionistic examples, the weighted fly is fished on a dead drift and then led strongly through the swing.

Small weighted nymphs are more easily fished with a strike indicator. This approach has particular application when working over stale fish, or when trying to slide a very small nymph down a narrow holding channel.

Rarely are steelhead nymphs tied to represent specific insects. Mike Maxwell's Telkwa Nymph is a notable exception. He says, "When a steelhead keeps rushing up to my Telkwa Stone, and refuses to take, I tie on the Nymph and get it every time!" Mike's presentation is accomplished with a two-handed rod and sink tips of five to fifteen feet. "I cast quartering upstream and mend. The nymph will come straight downstream on a dead drift. Then I lead the fly around. This is like the "biological drift," the nymph tumbling downstream, trying to grab on to a rock to work toward shore where it will pupate."

TELKWA NYMPH

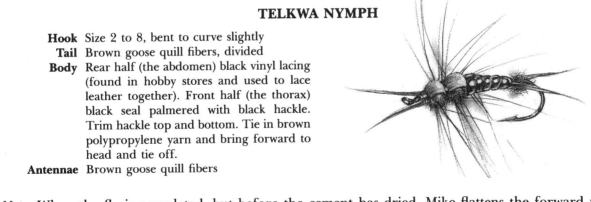

Hook Size 2 to 8, bent to curve slightly
Tail Brown goose quill fibers, divided
Body Rear half (the abdomen) black vinyl lacing (found in hobby stores and used to lace leather together). Front half (the thorax) black seal palmered with black hackle. Trim hackle top and bottom. Tie in brown polypropylene yarn and bring forward to head and tie off.
Antennae Brown goose quill fibers

Note: When the fly is completed, but before the cement has dried, Mike flattens the forward part of the body with pliers.

OSO SPECIAL

Tail Fluorescent hot orange floss
Body Rear three-fourths hot orange chenille, front one-fourth black chenille

Hackle Black
Wing Black moose mane

"Down on the river I found me a lady," sings Charlie Gearheart in "Oso Special," a Bluegrass song from the album, *Goose Creek Symphony*. He explains, "She has straight black hair and a nice curvy body." And promises, "Put her in the river and the fish come running."

This fly that is "Oh, so special" to Gearheart is an old-time Stillaguamish pattern, named for the tiny one-store town of Oso, which borders the river. Gearheart himself is a North Fork regular who fishes there whenever he isn't traveling with his band.

PINK SHRIMP

Body Pink chenille palmered with pink hackle   **Head** Fluorescent red tying thread
Carapace/Tail Fluorescent red Kraft Hair

When I gave a talk to the Evergreen Fly Fishers in Bellingham, Washington, I was told about a simple but very effective fly local anglers swore by for winter steelhead. Jerry Wells, a member of their club, had developed it. "You must get the pattern for your book," I was told.

DAN REIFF

Pity the poor angler who must follow Dan Reiff through a pool! I know. This Bellevue, Washington, nutritionist so skillfully locates winter steelhead that he rarely fails to put a fish on the beach, and he often manages several. Like most experts, he knows his water intimately, and he fishes hard.

In the mid-1970s, Dan began using a General Practitioner on winter steelhead rivers, and he remembers it was years before he saw other anglers fishing the fly. He used a thin hook to dress the fly but could never get it to swim correctly, particularly on the swing under tension. (We agree that the dressing fishes much better when tied like the original, on a double hook.) The Reiff's Shrimp is a less complicated tie that sinks well, remains upright when under tension, and takes steelhead at all levels. Dan fishes it down to size 8 for summer steelhead and 2 for winter-runs. His largest steelhead, a Skagit buck $42\frac{1}{8}$ inches long, and weighing something over twenty-five pounds, came to this fly. This is one of the largest winter-run steelhead ever caught on a fly.

REIFF'S SHRIMP

Tying Thread Red
Underbody Burnt orange seal fur from bend of hook to head of fly
Throat Red polar bear or like fur to hook point, sparse
Carapace Red polar bear, extending beyond the hook the length of the body. Tie in at the head, hold down over the body, and segment in five places by winding the thread aft.
Eyes Insect mounting pins. Color heads black with an indelible marking pen. Insert pins

down the sides of the dubbing until only the head protrudes. Wind the tying thread just behind the head with several figure eights of thread. Tie off the fly at this point.

BLACK BEE (Dry)

Hook Wilson size 8   **Hackle** Black hen
Wings and Tail Black squirrel   **Body** Black and yellow seal (or equivalent)

Dan designed this variation of Roderick Haig-Brown's Steelhead Bee—sometimes called the Mohammad-All-Bee—for late evening fishing when the fly's well-defined silhouette and good surface wake will trigger a rise.

The long wing is divided, set well forward, and angled only twenty degrees above the horizontal. It combines with the long tail to keep the body on or above the water.

RIFFLE DANCER

Mark Pinch, of Spokane, Washington, tied up one of his Riffle Dancers for me in 1986, while we were fishing out of Steelhead Valhalla Lodge on the Sustut River. The first time I fished the fly, I told my companion that it acted as if it ran on batteries! Given a downstream mend to cause drag, the big flat paddles set to work, and the fly seemed literally to crawl up and down waves. I'd never seen anything quite like it, and I knew that Mark had a brilliant design.

Like the Riffle Express that follows, it is a most unconventional tie.

Hook	Size 4 to 2, Mustad 36890. Take the forward third of the hook and bend upward thirty degrees.
Tail/Body	Deer body hair is tied in and crisscrossed forward with a double wrap of thread. The tail/body ends at the bend.
Upper Body	Large clumps of deer hair are spun on and clipped to fill the upper two-thirds of the remaining hook shank. Trim nearly even with the back, but allow to extend about a quarter of an inch below the hook. This becomes a kind of skid that the fly will surf on when it comes under tension.
Wings/Head	The wings are formed by gathering the collar, half to each side, soaking the base with head cement, and squeezing the wings flat. The butt ends of the hair form

the head. Most of this hair should remain on top. Let the hair extend past the eye and trim. To stiffen the head, and to help keep the fly's head up, a small bunch of moose is tied in on top of the head and trimmed even with the end. The butt end of this extends an eighth of an inch or so over the upper body.

Mark has worked wonders with this dressing on the Morice/Bulkley, Sustut, and various Idaho and Washington rivers. During a week on the Sustut, he took a nineteen-pound buck on it. The fly was revised again and again for three years before Mark was satisfied, and the result is truly extraordinary. Though a labor-intensive tie, the Riffle Dancer deserves a great following.

RIFFLE EXPRESS

Tail	White calf tail. Take several turns under to set the tail pointing up at a forty-five-degree angle. (The tail will be visible to the angler.)
Body	Tie in a thin bunch of deer body hair at head, bring to the tail, secure, and tie down to the head so that the body is crisscrossed. When the head is reached, bind down deer hair hard so that it flares evenly in all directions. Coat with black Goop or a like adhesive. When dry, trim

deer hair in a perfect circle. Make sure the circle tilts forward at approximately a thirty-degree angle.

Jud Wickwire

Jud Wickwire manages the main camp at Silver Hilton Lodge on the Babine River. Following Lani Waller's lead, the dry fly has become very popular with Jud, his guides, and their clients when conditions favor its use. In the fall of 1988, Jud introduced the Riffle Express, a fly that incorporates a new approach in steelhead dry-fly design. Unlike other dry flies, which are tied with materials that keep the fly floating, the Riffle Express is constructed so that it can't sink as long as it is under tension in the current. In fact, I doubt the fly would float more than a few feet on a dead drift before sinking. The key to this is the dime-sized circle of deer hair centered at the head of the fly and tilted forward at a thirty-degree angle. (When Jud first showed me the fly it reminded me of the spinner blade of the Panther Martin.) This "hackle" keeps the fly wobbling and chugging across and over currents even after an errant wave "drowns" it. Steelhead rise to it with complete confidence.

The Riffle Express is one of several new patterns that employ this principle (see Bulkley Moose).

RIPPA'S REVENGE

Tying Thread Red
     Tail Red hackle fibers
     Body Rear third pink seal, balance black seal. Rib with flat silver tinsel.

Hackle Black
     Wing White polar bear over blue bucktail (Pearl Flashabou or Krystal Flash can be substituted for polar bear)

Stew Wallace, of Portland, Oregon, first tied this popular dressing in 1979 and named it for the late Bob Rippa, a regular on the Deschutes River for many years. "Blue is the least used and understood color in steelhead fly fishing," says Stew. "It combines well with most colors, and in many cases, combines in such a way as to give an impression of movement, of life."

I've fished on Oregon's Clackamas River with Stew and his wife, Kitty, who are both excellent anglers. Stew is also a fine artist, his work often illustrating articles published in *Flyfishing* magazine.

Skeena Nymph

Hook 1/0 to 3/0
Tail Black bucktail the length of the hook
Body Black sparkle chenille. This has a built-in rib of mylar. Palmer with soft neck hackle, long.
Throat Black bucktail. Tie in bucktail so that it extends at least to the hook point. The butt ends are not trimmed at the eye, but are left extending to three-eighths to one-half inch past the eye.

(A similar fly is also known as a "Road Warrior"; it was originated by Jim Holcomb of Hailey, Idaho, for the Kispiox.)

Bob Hull, of Telkwa, British Columbia, designed this ragged looking dressing, a kind of a nymph-Woolly Bugger combination, to be fished on a dead drift when water temperatures in the Skeena Country run thirty-three or thirty-four degrees. He uses a five-foot sink-tip line and a stack cast, that is, a cast made quartering upstream, and as the fly dead-drifts down to a point opposite the angler, slack line is cast on top of the fly. This gives the fly time to get right on the bottom. He depends on the floating part of the line to act as a strike indicator, because the take will be very soft. A steelhead has to do little more than open its mouth. "A large, easy meal without any energy," says Bob of the fly. When necessary, he also fishes it on the swing in deeper water with longer sink tips.

Spade

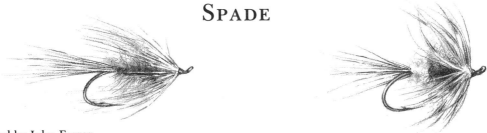

The Spade as tied by John Farrar

The original Spade as tied by Bob Arnold.

John Farrar once said to me of the Spade, "Everyone has his favorite black fly. This is mine." I knew his faith was well-placed. I had watched him and Jimmy Hunnicutt fish it to great advantage on the Dean. I, too, had experienced the fly's magic on summer waters. Though a remarkably simple pattern, and largely unheralded outside the Northwest, it is standard on the great summer rivers. Many experts who are certain they cannot live without the McLeod Ugly are equally sanguine about the Spade.

Bob Arnold originated the Spade in 1964. This occurred when the North Fork of the Stillaguamish was so low and clear that even the red tail of his Woolly Worm seemed gaudy. He recalls, "I was losing a lot of flies on the bottom, and I wanted to tie up a fly that was fast, one with just three parts." The simple and somber Burlap was his inspiration. He tied the original Spade with a tail of grey-brown deer body hair, a body of black chenille, and then hackled the fly with soft grizzly—in effect, a black Burlap. That was it—no ribbing, no tail. He could knock out a dozen in a few minutes.

Bob often fished the new fly below Deer Creek at the Elbow Hole. He introduced the fly to Bill Stinson and Ed Weinstein, who would, in time, devise their own variations to the dressing. Jerry Wintle

Bob Arnold

sometimes joined him, and one evening twitched and stripped the Spade so effectively that Bob came to "work the fly." Jerry was soon fishing the Spade on the Morice. Other Canadian anglers began taking a wrap or two of orange hackle ahead of the grizzly when the fly was fished in turgid water.

John Farrar brought a little culture to the rough pattern by dressing it on a size 6 or 8 Wilson dry-fly hook, using fine brown bucktail for the tail (the body hair flared too much), and dubbing the body with glossy black seal that he picked out before hackling in soft grizzly. In John's version, the hackle extends to two-thirds of the way to the point of the hook. This is the pattern I know as the Spade.

The best-known variation has one-third of the dubbing loop of orange seal and two-thirds of black. This gives the fly an orange butt and simulates an emerging October caddis pupa. Many anglers feel this Orange-Butt Spade is more effective than the original.

Bob Arnold now ties the Spade in a number of variations. Sometimes he ties in a butt of fluorescent green chenille, or divides the body equally with orange dubbing and then black dubbing, or gives the dressing a body of red dubbing, or changes the somber grizzly hackle for one mixed with red and yellow.

When we were fishing together on the Dean, Jimmy Hunnicutt came up with two variations. Both are tied on Wilson dry-fly hooks, #6 or #4. The body is dubbed like the Orange-Butt Spade except the forward dubbing is iron blue dun. The hackle is kept short, and the body is picked out until it appears very course and ragged. I called this fly the Blue Spade, and his second variation the Polar Spade for its ice blue appearance. It has a tail of white polar bear, a butt of greenish blue seal followed by black seal. The short grizzly hackle is overwrapped with teal. It, too, is thoroughly picked out.

Jimmy Hunnicutt's Blue Spade

These Spades, like Farrar's variation and Bob Arnold's original, are well-dubbed hackle flies. The seal gives them a translucent silhouette and an extremely buggy appearance that steelhead find irresistible.

Stan Young ties an Umpqua Spade with a tail of dark brown deer body hair, a body that begins with a single band of fluorescent green chenille (lime colored) and continues with black leech yarn. The grizzly hackle is stiff and short. It is the least Spadelike of the variations.

No less an authority than Alec Jackson ties two well known variations of the Spade that are elegantly beautiful, and dressed on Alec Jackson Spey hooks, sizes 5 and 7. The Claret Guinea Spade and Yellow Guinea Spade follow the same tying approach. The tail is extra-fine deer body hair (or dik dik, mouse hair, impala). Black ostrich is substituted for seal. Alec takes a couple of turns of dry-fly-quality grizzly at the head before winding on the dyed guinea. The result is a pulsating, very three-dimensional dressing that he usually fishes on a sink-tip line.

Joe Butorac, of Arlington, Washington, claims these crosses between a Spade and a Skunk "combine the best of both flies." He feels the natural deer-hair tail is more effective than a tail of red hackle. The "Hairy" version, a larger silhouette for low light and slightly off-colored water, was suggested to Joe by Dick Sylbert.

SKPADE

Tail Natural brown bucktail, fine
Body Black sparkle chenille
Wing White bucktail extending to the bend of the hook

Hackle Black, tied in front to blend into the wing

HAIRY SKPADE

Tail Natural brown bucktail, fine
Body Black sparkle chenille palmered with stiff black saddle hackle

Wing White bucktail

Butorac's Steelhead Stick incorporates those colors found in Randall Kaufmann's better-known Flatcar. This fast-water greased-line fly fishes best from late evening to dark and is said to simulate an emerging October Caddis, the long hackle suggesting its folded wings.

STEELHEAD STICK

Tail Fluorescent green yarn, short
Body Black chenille or black sparkle chenille

Hackle Long, black, extending nearly to the end of the body

Spey Flies

I recall tearing into the box, pulling away the covering that described the contents in Palmer-perfect handwriting, and staring at my first batch of Syd Glasso spey flies. They were a new series of steelhead flies that he was developing for the Olympic Peninsula streams near his home in Forks, Washington. Each was tied on a size 2 or 1 low-water hook and flowed with either genuine heron hackle or the

Syd Glasso's Orange Heron

largest saddle hackle available. The wings were usually hackle tips or mallard, and their butts disappeared into a tiny dot of varnish and a wrap or two of thread. I had never seen steelhead flies remotely their equal. Later, a second box of Syd's flies arrived, with this note below the recipes: "Identical flies sent also to Harry Lemire."

I don't know how many other Northwest anglers received Glasso's flies. Not many, I'm sure, for he tied them painstakingly slowly. Each was a treasure, and each created a sensation when he shared it with friends. They illustrated both *The Steelhead Trout* and *Steelhead Fly Fishing and Flies*. For many steelhead anglers, these photographs marked a turning point in their fly tying habits. Glasso's flies were maddeningly difficult to duplicate, and their design stretched everyone's tying skills. That the growth of steelhead fly tying became a commitment to excellence, to the craft of fly tying, was due in large measure to Syd Glasso. And I think that his impact is felt more profoundly today than ever before.

Glasso's inspiration was the Atlantic salmon flies of Scotland's River Spey. These tended to be somber patterns, with bronze mallard wings tented over a wool body palmered either with the hackle from a great blue heron, or the largest saddle hackles from a "Spey cock," a capon common on Spey Valley farms a century ago. A strand or two of ribbing wound in the opposite direction helped to secure the stem of the feather. The dressing was likely on fine-wire, long-shanked (approximately 2X), Dee-type hooks, a development from the nearby River Dee. These Spey flies were essentially utilitarian, very unlike the more purely aesthetic, fancy, full-dressed flies that gradually replaced them late in the nineteenth century.

Syd Glasso tapped into the strong historical mystique that surrounds the use of spey flies. These romantic notions were further served aesthetically when he incorporated the brighter "steelhead" colors into dressings already among the loveliest in all of angling.

Joe Bates wrote, in *Atlantic Salmon Flies and Fishing*, that spey flies "are designed for fast-water fishing." "Fast" is so relative as to be nearly meaningless, especially when comparing Atlantic salmon lies with steelhead lies. Bates also quotes "famous English angler" Geoffrey Bucknall from an article he wrote in *Trout and Salmon* magazine: "They are for me, the best flies to use in low, clear, though fast, water." And, "I've no experience with their effectiveness as a deeply-sunk fly, though my reading leads me to conclude that they were used as such in days of yore."

My experience is generally contrary to these opinions. A spey fly does not sink well, and in fast currents does not stay upright well when under tension. If dressed full and fished greased-line, the long hackles quickly lay the fly over on the swing. These tendencies are more severe when the spey hackle is not stripped on one side, or when the hackles are unusually long. My opinion on this extends to flies palmered with marabou blood plumes as well. If I'm going to fish the kind of water Bucknall describes, the spey will have to be much reduced—something of a contradiction, for when I palmer only the forward half of the fly with the hackle stripped on one side, I'm no longer fishing a spey fly.

I believe the spey fly is most effective in steelhead fly fishing when fished deeply sunk in "soft water," the quiet flats and guts running beside heavy mainline currents. Here the fly's resistance to currents is an advantage, as it is not so likely to foul the bottom, while even the faintest current will breathe life into the long hackles.

Syd Glasso, The father of the Steelhead Spey Fly. *Photo Credit: Bob Arnold*

Syd Glasso, who usually fished his spey flies "deeply sunk" for winter steelhead, often spoke of the difficulty in obtaining just the right hackle to palmer the fly. He would purchase loose saddle hackles by the pound, yellow and natural brown, and hunt through the lot for the single perfect feather for a Courtesan or Sol Duc Spey dressing. As with the original spey flies, the widest "spey hackle" was found among the last several feathers of a complete saddle. Unless the fly was solely for show, few anglers would be that uncompromising. Today, however, a number of retailers are capable of meeting such sophisticated needs—for a price, of course.

Syd told me how he could convert almost any steelhead fly to a spey fly. For a white wing, he would use a half-dozen or more perfectly matched saddle hackle tips, tenting them just enough so that they set low and short over the body. The result was quite beautiful.

I often try to copy Syd's spey-fly style using the Admiral (red and white) and Polar Shrimp (orange and white) color schemes. I double the saddle hackle and add a touch of magenta at the throat of the Shrimp so the resulting dress is quite full. I tie them on extra-heavy-wire hooks, 2X long, the dubbed body in red or orange over an underbody of flat silver tinsel. I also like to use pheasant rump in my spey flies, especially as a lighter dress for summer steelhead. A particularly fine dressing for this sort of fishing is the Lady Caroline. (Pheasant rump feathers are short in the stem, and it may be necessary, with large flies, to start the palmering at the second turn of tinsel.)

Joe Howell's spey flies clearly reflect the Syd Glasso legacy. He fishes them on the North Umpqua during all seasons, but saves the Orange Heron for the native run of late fall and winter steelhead. The fly has been effective on a dead drift, hard swing, but often when making short strips as the fly is on a swing. He calls the Silver Streak, the most traditional of the series, "my favorite fly." Joe has taken both winter and summer fish with it in sizes 2 to 4/0. "Of course," he says, "the larger the fly, the harder it is to get hackle for it, and heron is always difficult to obtain."

ORANGE HERON 1

Tag	Flat silver tinsel
Body	Rear half fluorescent orange floss, front half hot orange seal fur. Rib entire body with fine oval gold tinsel.
Spey hackle	Dyed black heron, or extra-wide saddle hackle. Joe always strips one side first.
Wing	Four matching hackle tips dyed fluorescent orange
Throat	Two turns of teal (strip feather on one side)
Cheeks	Jungle cock

Note: Bob Veverka gave Joe a tip he has found useful. Before tying in the wing, match the four tips together and mash the butt end with a flat-jawed plier.

ORANGE HERON 2

Tag	Flat silver tinsel. Rear half orange floss, front half hot orange seal fur. Rib entire body with fine gold oval tinsel.
Body Hackle	Heron
Throat	Teal, two turns
Wing	Matching strips of peacock secondary-wing quills

SILVER STREAK

Tag	Flat silver tinsel
Body	Flat silver tinsel ribbed with oval gold tinsel. According to Joe, the body is then palmered "with heron hackles as long as I can get."
Throat	Guinea dyed blue
Wing	Bronze mallard

GOLD STREAK

Tag	Flat gold tinsel
Body	Rear half orange floss, front half hot orange seal fur. Rib entire body with narrow oval gold tinsel.
Body hackle	Heron, natural grey
Throat	Guinea dyed orange
Wing	Bronze mallard

Jimmy LeMert, manager of Patrick's Fly Shop in Seattle, ties the Amethyst Spey, one of steelheading's most beautiful dressings.

Twenty-five years ago, Roy Patrick wrote *Pacific Northwest Fly Patterns*, the "bible" for a generation of Northwest fly tyers. His fly shop on Eastlake Avenue was an institution, while Patrick himself gave wise council to every current expert on the subject.

AMETHYST SPEY

Hook Alec Jackson Spey
 Eye Twisted and soaked silk gut
 Tag Fine silver French tinsel
Butt Red floss
Body Four strands of peacock sword fibers ribbed with narrow oval French silver tinsel. Palmer from first turn with either blue heron or blue-eared pheasant.

Throat Red over purple neck hackle
 Wing Mallard dyed purple, tented and set low

Hairwing alternate: Alec Jackson Spey size 5 to 7 for summer; 1½ to 3 for winter use. Omit spey hackle. Substitute purple squirrel tail. Dressing is otherwise identical to the Amethyst Spey.

SPIDERS (WET)

Al Knudson's Wet Spider, circa 1940

A hackle fly, a bit of wool wound on a hook and a feather wound at the head, is as old as fly fishing. A spider, wet or dry, suggests very much longer hackle, though no strict rules govern the separation. Dry spiders must, by the nature of their construction, be very small, because the entire fly glides on its hackle points like so much thistledown. A wet fly does not suffer from such constraints, and may be almost any size. Pheasant rump and duck flank, for example, enable tyers to dress spiders to streamer length. What, exactly, such a spider represents is known with certainty only to a trout. But to my eye, the fine barring of duck flank suggests the scale highlights of a minnow. Walt Johnson's exquisite Spectral Spider, a steelhead and sea-run cutthroat fly of considerable renown, simulates a small fish by means of his clever use of mallard flank and spectral stacking of Antron fibers (see Chapter 26).

This basic split in spider design, from a hackle fly suggesting an insect to a streamer fly suggesting a minnow, describes the two approaches to wet-spider patterns in steelheading. Inspiration for the former is lost in antiquity. The latter, however, is the singular achievement of Al Knudson.

I used to visit with Al at his apartment in Everett, Washington. We sat at his kitchen table around a huge pickle jar filled with flies he had tied, dating back to the 1920s. He would grab a handful, toss them out on the table, and pick through them. Each led to a discussion, stories that took him back to his early commercial-fly-tying days on the Rogue River. There were prehairwing Silver Doctors, and Royal Coachmen with peacock herl heads, other patterns we could only guess at, the earliest marabou flies used in steelheading, and the first Al's Spider—or simply Wet Spider—I had ever seen. They were originally trout-size flies of yellow chenille and mallard flank that grew to size 4 as they came into use for steelhead.

Al Knudson's original steelhead spider inspired friends to tie more sophisticated variations. Besides Walt Johnson's Spectral Spider, examples include Mark Canfield's Low & Clear Spider ("'difficult fish,' fly," he says), and Bob Bettzig's San Juan Spider.

LOW & CLEAR SPIDER

Hook	Alec Jackson Spey, bronze, sizes 3 and 7	**Body**	Rear half, flat gold tinsel; front half sienna-colored seal
Tag	Fine oval gold		
Tip	Golden yellow floss	**Wing**	Pine squirrel (low and divided), with a pair of jungle cock eyed feathers down the middle
Tail	Lemon wood-duck fibers and golden pheasant crest dyed red		
Butt	Bronze peacock	**Hackle**	Lemon wood duck

SAN JUAN SPIDER

Hook	Mustad 38941, #6	**Shoulder**	One or two turns of fluorescent yellow hackle
Tag	Flat silver tinsel		
Tail	Fluorescent yellow hackle fibers	**Hackle**	Mallard flank dyed yellow
Body	Fluorescent orange sparkle chenille	**Topping**	Sparse red synthetic fur or bucktail

Most steelhead fly fishers carry a few long-hackled spiders—usually unnamed, but beautiful, practical flies when dressed on Alec Jackson Spey or Partridge Wilson light-wire hooks. I don't think a better fly exists for greased line fishing in soft-water flats and tailouts when rivers are low and clear. They are also superb follow-up "eating flies" when a steelhead can't be brought back to a dry. Their only shortcoming is that their long throat hackles will lay the fly over during its swing through fast riffles. Sparser conventional ties are more appropriate for these conditions.

I've included a few examples that may inspire the reader to try other combinations. The first pair of spiders are the work of the late Karl Hauffler, a pioneering steelheader whose fondest memories were of his days on the Kispiox. The flies do not have names. With apologies to Karl, I've called them the Purple Spider and Gold Spider. Both are tied on Alec Jackson Spey hooks.

GOLD SPIDER

Butt	Peacock herl	**Hackle**	One wrap of golden pheasant flank, followed by two wraps of brown pheasant. Finish with one wrap of lemon wood duck.
Body	Rear half flat silver tinsel, front half gold seal fur		

PURPLE SPIDER

Tail	Purple hackle, a few fuzzy barbules from base of hackle	**Hackle**	Two turns of deep purple hackle followed by several turns of pheasant rump dyed black.
Body	Rear half, flat silver tinsel; front half purple seal or angora goat	**Head**	Wine

Sean Gallagher developed the Steelhead Carey, a thin-water spider that has raised many steelhead for him. He says of the dressing, "The fly has been extremely effective on the Green and Skykomish rivers during late summer and early fall low-water periods. I like to fish the Steelhead Carey with the traditional greased-line method."

A variation on his Carey theme is the Black Green-Butt Spider, a superb greased-line pattern for summer steelhead.

STEELHEAD CAREY

Tag Cerise floss

Body Black seal fur palmered with short black hackle and ribbed with fine oval silver tinsel (Alternate: Substitute purple seal fur for black)

Hackle Grey-green pheasant rump

GREEN BUTT SPIDER

Tail Red hackle fibers

Butt Fluorescent green floss over flat silver tinsel

Body Black seal fur ribbed with fine oval silver tinsel

Hackle Pheasant rump dyed black

Bob Pierce of Talent, Oregon, an angling regular on the upper Rogue, swears by his Orange Spider, a portly tie with a body of hot orange chenille and hackle of mallard flank. His L.P. Special has a body equally divided, the rear half of hot orange chenille, the front half fluorescent green chenille. The hackle is black, "hackle" length rather than "spider" length. These quickly tied patterns represent a popular approach to spider patterns followed by hundreds of Northwest anglers for steelhead and sea-run cutthroat.

SQUAMISH POACHER

Tail Orange bucktail, sparse

Body Orange chenille. Palmer with orange hackle, the longest fibers to the rear of the hook. Two glasss eyes are tied in at the bend of the hook.

Carapace Fluorescent orange surveyer tape. Silver tinsel, copper wire, or tying thread can be used to segment the body. Start about two-fifths the hook length from the tail. This will create a head around the eyes. Wind toward the head of the fly. The tape can be cut at the head of the fly to create a 'tail.'

Joe Kambietz of Vancouver, British Columbia, developed this prawn lookalike, and in many winter steelhead fly-fishing circles, it has all but replaced the General Practitioner, a considerably more complicated tie.

STEELHEAD BEE (BRIAN DOUGLAS)

Brian Douglas' Steelhead Bee

Twenty years ago, Roderick Haig-Brown sent me two Steelhead Bees. I knew something about the dry fly from his book *Fisherman's Fall*. But Haig-Brown's published description did not fully prepare me for their appearance. They had been fished and were nearly flat, the wings set well forward, the hackle swept back along the belly of the fly. This was a low-riding fly, one designed to be fished drag-free, though later I found it would wake under moderate tension. Typical of hairwing dries incorporating soft furs, the fly tended to nose in and then spin when under moderate tension. But in my mind, the Bees were a departure from the higher-riding Wulffs and Humpies, and a vast improvement over the Bivisibles I sometimes fished. I realized that the hackle on the dressing had nothing to do with its flotation, and that set my mind to working in many directions.

Today, most steelhead dries are fished primarily as waking and skating patterns, though small Wulffs and Humpies have been rediscovered as a follow-up "eating fly." Because anglers now look downstream instead of upstream when casting a dry, the split-wing dry often has wings stiffened with Goop to help the fly plane up and through the currents. Brian Douglas gets around this problem by using the tips of moose hair. It is exceedingly stiff, and when set forward provides a good planing surface. The tail is fairly long; the fly has no tendency to tip over on its head. Hackle is fairly full and gives the fly a buggy appearance when waking.

I met Brian at Driftwood Lodge, the old-fashioned fishing hotel his brother Keith has built just outside Smithers, British Columbia. Bob Hull, a guide at Stewart's Dean River lodge, introduced me to the dressing. He and other guides swear by it. Brian gave me the following tying instructions.

STEELHEAD BEE

Hook Mustad 94840, size 10 to 6
Tail Moose with a couple strands of pearl "Starline," a material very much like Krystal Flash

Wing Moose set forward and well cemented
Body Ginger sparkle yarn divided by a band of orange seal
Hackle Two, black

STEELHEAD BUNNY

Mel Krieger's Steelhead Bunny

Les Johnson introduced me to the Steelhead Bunny when we were fishing the Skykomish River for winter steelhead. He manages a few steelhead each year with the pattern, usually in white, but he also fishes the Bunny in black and purple. I was reminded of the huge White Leech patterns I had fished during my stay at Ted Gerkin's Iliaska Lodge. Monster rainbows running out of Lake Iliamna had annihilated a few of these flies; I wasn't surprised that steelhead liked them, too. Les was quick to point that out the fly didn't originate with him. "Talk to Mel Krieger," he told me. Later that year, I met with Mel to discuss the origins of his Bunny Leeches, and to find how he applied them to his steelhead fishing.

Late in the 1960s, Mel went to New Zealand, where he discovered the Kiwis fishing a rabbit-strip pattern tied Matuka-style over a number of different body colors. Mel brought the idea home and tied a version of the fly to replace the plastic worms he normally used in his bass fishing. He was soon casting the fly for trout and Alaskan rainbows. "It really took off twelve to fourteen years ago, in Alaska," he said. The ginger version suggested the decaying flesh of sockeye, the white a parasitic flatworm, the black something too edible to resist.

When fishing for steelhead, Mel uses a sink tip line or shooting head to take the fly down. He normally doesn't fish it weighted and likes it in black and purple, but also in olive and tan. He hasn't yet fished it white, the color Les Johnson uses to advantage in winter steelhead fishing.

Mel's flies are as thinly dressed as Les's are massive, no doubt the difference between summer and winter perceptions. To tie Mel's Steelhead Bunny, secure a strip of rabbit about a quarter inch from the head of the fly. Tie down again halfway down the body and above the point of the hook. Take a short piece of rabbit and "hackle" with a full turn of rabbit at the head of the fly. Mel uses red tying thread, and he wraps the body before securing the rabbit for the first time. Thus, the head and body are red, but other tying thread colors are used. For all of its effectiveness, this is a pretty casual tie.

Mel Krieger holds a 25 pound, 40-inch Sustut buck taken on a Steelhead Bunny.

STEELHEAD BUNNY (Les Johnson)

Tail Strip of rabbit fur, one or two inches long (strips can be purchased pre-cut for Zonker and Leech patterns)

Underbody Lead wire

Body Strip of rabbit fur wound forward and tied off at the head. A couple strands of Flashabou may be added to each side

Head Fluorescent tying thread

STEELHEAD CHARLIES

This had to happen, and it makes perfect sense. The Crazy Charlie, Bob Nauheim's wonderful bonefish fly conceived on Andros Island, was converted to a steelhead fly. Why not? It is nearly weedless. With its sparse dress and bead-chain eyes, it sinks like a stone. Add Edge Bright to give it a hot glow, and you have an irresistible steelhead combination. Bob Wagoner developed these conversions. He was thinking of cold-water steelhead and has explored their possibilities along these lines. Early results are very encouraging.

GREEN STEELHEAD CHARLIE

Wing Dyed green squirrel tail tied under to encase the hook point

Eyes Silver-bead chain eyes tied on top of the hook

Body Silver tinsel wrapped with green Edge Bright

All other Steelhead Charlies are tied in this manner.

ORANGE STEELHEAD CHARLIE

Edge Bright is fluorescent orange, and wing is squirrel tail dyed orange.

RED STEELHEAD CHARLIE

Edge Bright is fluorescent red, and wing is squirrel tail dyed red.

CHARTREUSE STEELHEAD CHARLIE

Edge Bright is fluorescent chartreuse, and wing is squirrel tail dyed black.

BLUE STEELHEAD CHARLIE

Edge Bright is fluorescent blue, and wing is squirrel tail dyed blue.

STEELHEAD SKATERS

I remember holding up Bob Wagoner's Steelhead Skater and admiring its compact, bushy silhouette, before I realized that I was holding the fly upside down. This is easy to do, for the fly is built upside down. And it has created a sensation in steelhead fly-fishing circles. Lani Waller swears by it, using the Skater as a follow-up fly for his own Waller Waker. He and Howard West, of 3M/Scientific Anglers, have raised Babine steelhead to the Skater with surface currents holding in the high thirties. Collin Schadrech fishes the fly with equal enthusiasm, alternating it with the Mouse, a waking pattern he has popularized for Far West Lodges, his Bulkley River lodge operation in Telkwa, British Columbia.

Bob ties commercially (The Fly Den) from his home in Lewiston, Idaho. He is a former over-the-road truck driver who returned full-time to his lifelong fascination with fly tying when diagnosed as a diabetic. He remains a man of energy and great good cheer who fishes the Clearwater and Grande Ronde when he isn't at his tying bench. At any given time, a dozen anglers are trying out new patterns he is developing.

The Skater is just that, a fly that skates on the surface rather than waking on—and in—the surface film. When fished as a finder fly across and down, it rides on its downward-pointing wing bristles and tail through the swing, dancing erratically over the currents yet creating a wake as its wing tips take a little bite. It is also a fine follow-up "eating" pattern when fished as described, or cast upstream and twitched on a drag-free float over the steelhead that has showed but refused the skated or waked fly.

Bob describes the development of the Skater: "I first thought of this fly in 1973 while in California attending a fly-tying class by a famous tyer. As he lectured about the floating attributes of elk, deer, and moose hair, I thought to myself, 'if it floats so damn well, who don't you put the wings under the hook where it will float instead of on top of the hook, where they just look pretty?' Carrying this thought around with me for years, I finally sat down one day and started tying wings under the hook. What I ended up with was a lot of blood from the holes I punched in my fingers. With a little effort and lot of swearing, I finally mastered tying the wings on first under the hook. This was on a size twelve hook. Keith Stonebreaker happened to stop by a couple of days later, and I showed him—with a little bragging—the results. Keith immediately said that it would be an excellent steelhead fly. He and a couple of friends took the Skater to British Columbia that fall and had excellent results with the pattern. I've had very good sales of the fly [Bob Marriott's Fly Fishing Store, Fullerton, California], and had a recent article written about them ["Sensational Skater for Steelhead and . . . ," Dave Enger-bretson, *Scientific Anglers' Fly Fishing Quarterly*, Fall 1989]. I have continued to receive excellent feedback from steelhead fly fishers who have been fishing the Skater.

"I started out tying the Skater in as many colors as there are in the rainbow, but after testing all of these, I've narrowed the successful colors down to just four patterns and have kept them as simple as possible."

BROWN HACKLE PEACOCK

Wings Black moose, set forward

Tail Black moose, one and a half times the body length

Body Three to four strands of peacock herl reverse wrapped with fine gold wire and palmered with brown saddle hackle

Hackle Three to four brown saddle hackles tied from the butt end and wrapped in front and behind the wings

GRIZZLY HACKLE PEACOCK

Wings, tail, body, as above. Palmer and hackle with grizzly saddle hackle.

SALMON FLY

Wings and Tail As above. Palmer and hackle with brown saddle hackle.

Body Orange Krystal Flash

Tying Instructions (Bob Wagoner)

"Use a rotating vise. After placing the hook in the vise, turn it over and attach thread. Cut a section of black moose and secure to the hook shank, end of the hair pointing to the front of the hook. Pull the hair upright, tie under, and divide with figure eight wraps. Cover the base of the wings with

Bob Wagoner

cement. (I prefer a mixture of Duco cement thinned with acetone.) Tie in the black moose tail one and a half times hook shank. Tie in hackle at the tip, shiny side to you, and gold rib. Tie in body material and wrap to base of wings. Tie off body materials and reverse-wrap with gold wire on peacock-herl bodies. Palmer the hackle with the shiny side down. This will force hackle to lie toward the hook point, giving you a nice tapered body. Tie in three or four saddle hackles and wrap them in back and in front of the wings. I have found you can push the wings out of the way when wrapping and not hurt them at all."

LeRoy Hyatt, a friend of Bob's, recently tied the Steelhead Skater with a spun deer hair body. "There are a few guys around here using them with some success, but Steve Pettit has been knocking the socks off the steelhead with this skater." He ties them with a tail and wing of elk body hair dyed black. The bodies are natural grey, rusty brown, and black. The black Skater is palmered with black saddle; the other two variations are palmered with brown saddle hackle.

The average tyer is no LeRoy Hyatt, and the spun deer hair Skater, the "Ultimate Skater," will take some practice. The results, however, should be well worth the effort.

STEELHEAD WOOLLY BUGGERS

If limited to a single fly pattern to fish all the world's trout water, I would choose a Woolly Bugger, probably in olive, and then feel terrible that I couldn't have the dressing in black, too. I've used it in white for Iliamna rainbows, black for Tierra del Fuego sea trout and West Coast steelhead, and in olive for rainbows in Chile, where my guide said it represented a *pancora*, a kind of crawfish. It is a nymph, and it is a leech. Like the ubiquitous Muddler, it doesn't exactly look like anything, but it looks something like everything. A few years ago I went tarpon fishing in Costa Rica with Richie Montella, a Bighorn River fly fishing guide. He showed up with some Woolly Buggers—in 7/0! Russell Blessing, a Pennsylvanian often credited as the inventor of the Woolly Bugger, would have been impressed.

Bob Wagoner told me, "When I first received Crystal Chenille in February 1988, I thought, 'Woolly Buggers will never be the same.'" In his skillful hands, the Crystal Chenille Steelhead Woolly Bugger is *almost* handsome! He ties it in four colors: red, orange, purple, and black.

CRYSTAL CHENILLE STEELHEAD WOOLLY BUGGER

Tail Two matching marabou blood hackle tips. A few strands of Krystal Flash in the same color is tied between the bloods. (*Note:* By using hackle tips containing the stem, some stiffness is maintained. This will help to keep the tail from wrapping around the hook, a common problem with Woolly Buggers.)

Body Crystal Chenille palmered with saddle hackle of the same color

Hackle Long, webby saddle hackle, three to four turns

Joe Butorac introduced these comet-like bucktail versions of the Woolly Bugger:

BLACK STEEL WOOLLY

Hook 1/0 to 2/0 (winter), 1 to 2 (summer), 2X long

Tail Black bucktail, one and a half times the shank length

Body Braided silver tinsel palmered with black saddle

Hackle Black, stiff

Head Black

RED STEEL WOOLLY

Body As above. All other colors are red.

Head Flame single strand floss

Randy Stetzer

RANDY STETZER

Randy Stetzer and I first fly-fished together on Baja California's Sea of Cortez for dorado, sailfish, and striped marlin. At the time, he was a group leader for Kaufmann's Streamborn, and responsible for the egos of fifteen fly fishermen. He brought to this impossible task such patience and good humor that I've been his admirer ever since.

Randy describes Bill McMillan as "my mentor and close friend," a man who "has had a strong influence on my angling ethics." Bill taught him the finer points of steelhead fly fishing in the mid-1970s on the Washougal. Randy has since fished most of the major steelhead rivers from southern Oregon to Alaska. For much of the year he works as a full-time trout and steelhead guide on the Deschutes.

Randy is now (in 1991) completing work on a book of fresh- and saltwater flies. He is widely recognized as one of the Northwest's premier fly dressers, and he tied the hundreds of flies that will be featured in his book, from tiny emergers to spey flies to Streakers. Randy also tied the flies that illustrate David Hughes's *American Fly Tying Manual* (Frank Amato Publications, 1986).

The four dressings to follow, a dry, a low-water wet, and two beautiful spey flies are an all-season assortment. Randy's comments follow each.

FLUTTERING TERMITE (Dry)

Hook	Partridge Wilson size 10 to 12	**Wings**	Moose body hair or black bear mask, very stiff, divided and set slightly forward
Tail	Natural fox squirrel tail	**Hackle**	Brown
Body	Orange poly pro lightly spun with hot orange seal or goat		

"The Fluttering Termite was conceived on the Washougal River. I tied it to match the wood termite that hatches in the fall. These insects are on the water then and steelhead start taking them. The termites fight and flutter trying to get off the water, and this triggers the steelhead's response. The fly is also effective late in the season when the big October Caddis are out. The fly has produced very well, fished on either a dead drift or a controlled drag."

PATRICIA

Hook	Size 1/0 to 8, Tiemco 7999	**Body**	Claret seal or goat, rib with oval gold tinsel
Thread	Wine 6/0 prewaxed	**Hackle**	Claret
Tag	Fine oval gold tinsel	**Wing**	White polar bear
Tail	Claret hackle fibers		

"I first tied the Patricia for the Deschutes River, but it has proven its worth on many other rivers as well. I've always leaned toward darker colors for my standard wet flies, feeling that in all light and water conditions they give a better silhouette. In clear water the somber tones are less likely to spook fish, and in dirty water the flies are more easily seen. Also, I have long felt that steelhead fly fishers greatly underrate claret."

OCTOBER SPEY

Hook	Size 3/0 to 2
Thread	Black
Body	Hot orange seal or goat, thin, ribbed with oval gold tinsel and fine gold wire
Body hackle	Black heron
Throat	Mallard or teal flank, dyed hot orange
Wing	Bronze mallard

Randy Stetzer's October Spey

SPRING SPEY

Hook	Size 3/0 to 2	**Body Hackle**	Gray heron
Thread	Light olive	**Throat**	Mallard or teal flank, dyed grass green
Tail	Golden pheasant crest	**Wing**	Bronze mallard
Body	Grass green seal or goat, thin. Rib with oval gold tinsel and fine gold wire		

"I've always admired the style and look of the spey flies that the late Syd Glasso brought to prominence in steelhead fly fishing. I feel they are far and away the most effective wet fly one can fish for steelhead. The movement of the long-flowing hackle and sleek swimming action are perfect!"

STREET WALKER

Hook	Eagle Claw 1197, size 2 to 8	**Hackle**	Purple saddle
Tail	Purple hackle fibers	**Wing**	Clear Flashabou.
Body	Purple chenille ribbed with oval silver tinsel		

Gordon Nash, a Deschutes guide for Kaufmann's Streamborn since 1980, introduced the Street Walker in the early 1980s. He feels the nickle-plated hook combines with the Flashabou to make a better attractor. The Street Walker has proven to be a very reliable summer dressing for Gordon and his clients.

STRING LEECH

String Leech by Bob Hull
(Mike Montaigne brought the first String Leech to the Dean and passed it on to Terry Roelofs; Bob Hull's String Leech was the product of that development.)

"Whatever happened to jungle cock?" Lani Waller looked amused as the two of us studied Bob Hull's six-inch-long snakelike fly.

"This still has the animal attached!" I said. The "body" was a length of extra stout shoemaker's thread, the "string," with one end clinch-knotted to a 1/0 hook. A loop six inches away was the "eye." Just behind the loop, a strip of rabbit was secured with tying thread. To accomplish this, Bob had driven a nail into the wall opposite his vise, and had run a rubber band to the hook. This put the string body under tension. A bunch of blue Flashabou secured under the strip of rabbit finished the fly. A couple of split shot pinched on the string just behind the head, or lead barbells tied down at the head, would help to drown the beast.

Bob Hull and I were sharing a cabin located behind Bob Clay's house in the Kispiox Valley. Both Bobs were fly-fishing guides on vacation, Hull a guide at Stewart's on the Dean, Clay an independent guide on the Kispiox and Skeena rivers. When Lani flew in from the Babine, our party was complete.

Bob Hull holds a 20 pound hen steelhead that couldn't resist the String Leech he worked along the Skeena's rocky shore.

"You can make it do tricks." Bob Hull stroked it a few times. Lani and I watched as the fly curled up a bit and rolled over.

"When the river is low and clear, do you go to smaller flies?" I tried not to sound too eager.

"Larger flies!" he said. "This big!" He held his hands ten inches apart.

Bob sat on his bed and searched his fishing log. "Let's see, I was fishing with Keith Douglas. Okay. 'Hooked two at King's Crown, five at Rainbow Ranch, each caught one at Island; hooked seven at Gang Bang, beached five.'"

Bob Clay told us he had once watched a snake try to cross the Kispiox. A steelhead rose to it, and the snake disappeared in a huge swirl.

My Wheatleys only went to 2/0, row after row of pitiful little things. "Murphy's Law," I said, "the fly they're taking is the only one you don't have."

Bob Hull was the first to tie this String Leech. He got the idea for the fly from clients on the Dean. Their rabbit leeches were like those on the North Umpqua, where a hook clipped at the bend is connected to a trailing hook with heavy Dacron line. This was a no-frills giant version of the Black Leech, a.k.a. "Bimbo" and "Road Kill." The hook he used had a turned down eye; I would have secured it with a double turle knot instead of a clinch. Either way, the fly has a raw Outback flavor to it.

For the next several days we fly-fished the Kispiox and Skeena and found fresh steelhead. As usual, Lani liked his Boss, and we both raised fish on dries. Bob stayed with his String Leech; he couldn't keep the steelhead away. When he beached a twenty-pound hen steelhead, Lani and I switched to sink-tip lines. "The lines from hell," said Clay, happy with his full-floater and Purple Bomber. We began dickering with Bob Hull.

"I'll give you four of my new improved Wakers," began Lani.

"I really need one of these flies for my book," I said.

SUNDOWNER

Bob Wagoner's Sundowner series is only as recent as the advent of Krystal Flash, 1986, though he had sorted out the basic color schemes in more mundane materials some years before. The flies are simple to tie, carry a lot of flash, and raise steelhead. His firsthand experience with these fly patterns is mostly on the Clearwater and Grande Ronde rivers. "The original," says Bob, "was inspired by the colors in the Sundowner rose."

BLACK SUNDOWNER

Wing	Orange Krystal Flash	**Body**	Fluorescent green wool
Tail	Orange hackle fibers	**Collar**	Black hackle
Butt	Silver tinsel	**Head**	Black
Hackle	Black, palmered		

ORANGE SUNDOWNER

Wing	Black Krystal Flash	**Body**	Fluorescent green wool
Tail	Black hackle fibers	**Collar**	Orange hackle
Butt	Silver tinsel	**Head**	Orange
Hackle	Orange, palmered		

PINK SUNDOWNER

Wing	Pearl Krystal Flash	**Body**	Red wool
Tail	Fluorescent pink	**Collar**	Fluorescent pink
Butt	Silver tinsel	**Head**	Pink
Hackle	Fluorescent pink, palmered		

PURPLE SUNDOWNER

Wing	Pearl Krystal Flash		**Body**	Fluorescent orange wool
Tail	Purple hackle fibers		**Collar**	Purple
Butt	Silver tinsel		**Head**	Black
Hackle	Purple, palmered			

RED SUNDOWNER

Wing	Pearl Krystal Flash		**Body**	Fluorescent red wool
Tail	Red hackle fibers		**Collar**	Red
Butt	Silver tinsel		**Head**	Red
Hackle	Red, palmered			

JIM GREEN SPECIAL

(*Note*: This latest Wagoner dressing honors Jim Green, the great tournament caster and rod designer who lives in retired splendor above the lower Grande Ronde. While not really a Sundowner, it has that resemblance, and was photographed with them in the color plates.)

Tag	Flat silver tinsel		**Body**	Flat silver tinsel palmered with black sad-
Tail	Black hackle fibers			dle hackle
Butt	Fluorescent green wool		**Collar**	Fluorescent green hackle

Tying instructions: First tie in the wing pointing over the front of the hook, but leaving room for four to five turns of hackle. Trim Krystal Flash to half the length of the tail. Tie in the tail and take one turn of tying thread under to cock it up. (Tail and wing should be cocked at the same angle.) Tie in silver tinsel and take five to seven turns for the butt. Tie in hackle at the tip and palmer over the silver tinsel body. Fold wing back and secure. Tie in hackle and take four to five turns for the collar. Tie back. Lacquer head with two coats of cement.

SWEET LORETTA (JIMMY HUNNICUTT)

Hook	Alec Jackson Spey
Tag	Very short strand of flame yarn
Body	Black seal. Do not over twist the dubbing loop. The body must be extremely ragged if it is to create the necessary silhouette
Hackle	Black, long
Wing	None

I asked Jimmy Hunnicutt, a true romantic and one of the Northwest's premier steelhead fly fishers, how the Sweet Loretta got its name.

"Ah, she had bright red lips and raven black hair," he began.

"But a little ragged looking?" I said.

Jimmy looked disappointed. He told me about a forty-one-inch Thompson River doe hooked in a canyon. The Sweet Loretta had brought her up, a violent take right on the surface. He could not follow the runs that took her far downriver. It was forty minutes with his sixteen-foot two-handed rod before the great fish was brought to his casting station and the fly recovered.

I told Jimmy the fly reminded me of Roderick Haig-Brown's Carpenter Ant. But Jimmy's liberal use of seal in his variation of the Spade birthed the dressing.

The fly works right in the surface film, sometimes "damp" as much as wet, and the takes are quite visible.

THE STEWART

Tail Golden pheasant tippet
Body Black floss ribbed with oval gold tinsel
Hackle Black

Wing Black squirrel
Topping Hot-orange calftail

The Stewart is the brainchild of Marty Sherman, editor of *Flyfishing* magazine and longtime steelhead addict. I'm not sure whether I carry the pattern because it fishes so well, or because of its traditional beauty. Either way, this is a fine silhouette pattern, useful in clear and off-colored water in both shade and sunshine. I have raised fish to it in sizes up to 2/0. My own preference is to tie The Stewart with embossed gold tinsel and to add a tag of fine gold wire.

TIGER'S PAW

Tag Oval copper tinsel
Tail Black hackle fibers
Body Black chenille or dubbing ribbed with oval copper tinsel

Hackle Black
Wing Orange Krystal Flash

Joe Howell's Blue Heron Fly Shop in Idleyld Park, Oregon, marks the beginning of the North Umpqua's legendary section of fly-fishing-only water. Joe first tied the Tiger's Paw when Krystal Flash became available from Hareline Dubbin in the mid-1980s. It became a favorite local pattern in sizes 2 and 4, its popularity soon spreading to the Rogue, where anglers fished the fly in sizes 6 and 8. Canadian anglers are equally enthusiastic about the dressing in sizes 1 and 1/0. "Steelhead really climb on this fly," says Joe, "winter or summer."

TUBE FLIES

I first met Roland Holmberg one January in Buenos Aires. I was returning from a memorable week of sea-trout fishing in Tierra del Fuego on Jorge and Jacqueline Carrera's estancia, which contained many of the finest meanderings of the Rio Grande. The mysteries of sea-run brown trout were new to me, but one day Juan Lincoman and I had found eleven of them with our big Marabou Muddlers. These trout, as lavender silver as any winter blackmouth salmon, were only hours from the ocean and averaged nine pounds.

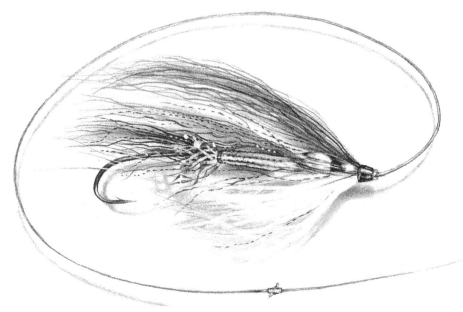

Roland Holmberg's Herring Sea Habit

Roland Holmberg

Roland was the Carreras' lead guide at Kau Tapen Lodge, but he had learned his sea-trout lore on the River Em in his native Sweden. Each summer, he guided some of the world's best-known anglers on Norway's Gaula and Aa rivers for Atlantic salmon. I knew him well by reputation. When I called the Carreras to thank them for their hospitality, Roland was having tea with Jacqueline, planning their new January-through-March season. Twenty minutes later, he joined me at the Hotel Bisonte to begin two days of delightful debriefing. Roland thought hard on my stories. Every detail counted for something. The previous season, he had successfully introduced the dry fly to Kau Tapen's sea trout. His head was full of innovative ideas. We spent hours discussing lines, flies, and presentation techniques. Over Chilean wine and Argentine beef, we became fast friends. "You must come steelhead fly fishing with me," I said to him. "The Dean would be a perfect introduction!"

"Yes, I would like that very much. I have heard of the Dean. I have had clients who talked of this often," he replied.

Eighteen month later, we met in Vancouver, British Columbia. After a few days at my home to chase jet lag, we drove to Hagensborg, where a chartered helicopter took us to the upper river. Rain soon raised the river and turned the water snowmelt dirty.

"Help yourself to any of my flies," I said as we got ready to fish. "I made up an extra box for you."

"I will do that. Yes. But I want to experiment. I want to try some of my own patterns." Roland showed me his ancient aluminum fly box, rows of metal prongs holding an assortment of tube flies. Most were chewed ratty and snarled. He had killed forty-nine salmon to twenty-eight pounds on the Gaula that summer, and before that, released more than fifty sea trout in Tierra del Fuego.

"Give it a go," I said, "but treble hooks are illegal."

"Oh, yes. I've been using a single salmon hook jammed up the plastic tube." Roland showed me that with the fly unable to rotate, the pattern could have a dorsal and a ventral surface, a wing and a hackle, for example. His tube flies were not just a mixed clump of FisHair and Flashabou spun around a tube. Roland's Herring Sea Habit made perfect sense.

One evening in my study, Roland had tied several of these very lifelike baitfish imitations on 1/0 single hooks, since I had no suitable tubing. They were pale blue and white mixed with pearl mylar and Flashabou. Jungle cock eyed each fly. "Pretty things," I'd said. "These aren't steelhead colors, but who knows?"

Roland ran the fly across his mouth several times to wet the Herring Sea Habit and judged its contour. He held the fly up and asked, "How far are we from the ocean?"

"Twenty miles," I said. "The steelhead can come through quickly. They are often very fresh." Satisfied, he tied the fly on and began fishing, a series of long casts that reached to the rock wall on the far side. A slick of holding water ran along its base, but a fly drifted there for only a moment before being swept away by the main flow. For that reason, I did not like the water and worked my side of the river off the main flow. About halfway down, Roland dropped a cast to the far side, and as the fly began dragging away, a steelhead tore after it. The buck caught the fly a dozen feet down the pool, charging it with such abandon that the fly impaled the fish outside its mouth. The steelhead, held briefly for photographs, would have weighed sixteen or seventeen pounds.

If Roland was astonished over his good fortune, he gave no sign of it. He told me that of the thirty-two salmon he had caught the past summer from the Aa's Sea Pool, fifteen came on the Sea Habit. And the Gaula's great Gaulfoss Pool, where the Sea Habit was a wonder, was fifteen miles from the ocean.

Roland had satisfied one curiosity and now sought to satisfy another. He next fished a Garry Dog, a tube fly of red and yellow FisHair mixed with Flashabou. The fly looked four inches long, but no matter, steelhead liked the Garry Dog. And they liked a green tube fly, too. Roland cast the fly and bobbed the rod tip up and down through the swing, a maneuver that kept the long, serpentine fly jerking erratically. Not until the river dropped and cleared did Roland switch to my box of greased line flies.

In retrospect, I think my spey flies worked as well as Roland's tube flies. But the advantages of his tube flies became very evident to me. The fly was not lost when the hook point became badly blunted or the hook broke. Likewise, the hook—but not the fly—could be left in a steelhead if removing the hook would injure the fish. A relatively small hook—a #2, for example—could be used on a very large fly. Large tube flies do not possess the weight—or sink rate—of the big irons, the 3/0 to 5/0 flies some anglers associate with winter steelhead. This means that more delicate rods, 7-weights, for example, can cast and work very large flies on fast-sinking lines so long as the lies are not too deep.

The bodies for tube flies can be purchased in plastic, aluminum, and brass. Regardless, the hole down their center is sleeved in plastic and will permit only the tippet to pass through. (Sleeving in plastic prevents the tippet from chafing on bare metal.) This is fine so long as the tube fly pattern has no top and bottom characteristics. Roland prefers to purchase tubing with an opening just large enough to permit the eye of the hook to pass with some difficulty. In effect, the tubing becomes an extension of the hook. The tubing is cut to the desired length, two inches or so. To tie the materials to the tube, he takes an extremely long-shanked hook in the largest size obtainable and cuts off the eye. This hook is set in his vise and the plastic tube slipped over it before the tying begins. He begins to tie about one-eighth inch from the end because, when the fly is completed, he presses this end against a very hot piece of metal. The tube melts just a bit and forms a ridge, which prevents the head from slipping. (Presumably, this step could be completed before the tying begins.)

HERRING SEA HABIT

Tail	White and blue FisHair mixed with light blue Krystal Flash
Body	Silver mylar tubing
Wing/Hackle	White marabou blood hackle wound at the head. Light blue Krystal Flash or Flasha-

bou tied in on top and a few strands on the bottom. Tie in a small bunch of blue FisHair (dorsal part of herring).

Cheeks Jungle cock, the fish's "eyes"

UGLY BUG (BRAD JACKSON)

Brad Jackson's Ugly Bug

Dennis Black once invited me to fish a favorite water. A dirt road leads to a long slab of ledge rock, literally the jumping-off point. Across the river is a riffle, two hundred feet of boulder-filled lies that never fail to hold a few steelhead in August. This morning was no exception. Through the North Umpqua's clear currents, we counted three.

"I've raised some forty fish here," said Dennis. "Most on dries. Why don't you start through with a dry. Do you have one?"

The pool is only a few minutes from Glide, where Dennis owns and manages his business, Umpqua Feather Merchants, and from his home in Idleyld Park. He catches the water on the way to work, during a lunch break, or perhaps after dinner.

I waded in above the pool, and made a preliminary cast to judge the distance and strip off some line. The Rusty Bomber had just started swinging when the water erupted beneath it. The fish would

Dennis Black prepares to sink an Ugly Bug with a shooting head.

not come back, and I changed to a #6 Royal Humpy. This produced a halfhearted rise, a boil, and part of a back.

As I fished down the pool, Dennis worked clean-up, first with a greased line wet, then with a shooting head and weighted black leech that plummeted down the ledge-rock wall and swam weedless between the rocks. Neither of us found a steelhead that wanted our flies badly enough to take solidly, and I arrived at the tailout with no excuses. Dennis, however, tied on a nondescript black nymph with rubber legs and went after the fish one more time. He fished the simple fly as before, and in a few minutes enticed one of the steelhead, a bright six-pound hen. After releasing her, Dennis cut off the fly and gave it to me. "An Ugly Bug," he said.

Brad Jackson, inventor of the Ugly Bug.

Brad Jackson, an outdoor writer and lecturer from Redding, California, originated the Ugly Bug. He first fished nymphs for steelhead back in the 1970s, while working at Time Flies, Larry Simpson's fly-fishing store in Arcata, California. The pattern was Simpson's Rag Doll Nymph. "A Hare's Ear nymph hybrid," says Brad. "An alternative to conventional patterns sometimes found to be damagingly gaudy. Simpson insisted that active summer- and fall-run strains fed at times. Consequently, he believed that the fish responded much better to trout tactics and impressionistic nymph patterns than to traditional steelhead patterns."

Brad tried dead-drifting a few of his own nymph designs, with exciting but inconsistent results. Two summers of guiding out of Jim Danskin's Tackle Shop in West Yellowstone led Brad to a *Pteronarcys* nymph of his own design, Brad's Stonefly Nymph. It was heavily weighted and had rubber feelers. When Brad opened his own business, The Fly Shop, in Redding, California, he regularly fished the upper Trinity for its steelhead. One afternoon, he dead-drifted his nymph exactly as he would have done on the Madison for Montana browns and hooked four steelhead in succession, including a seven-pound hen, a gigantic fish for the Trinity.

Brad remembers. "I was too inexperienced to recognize the implications of the dead-drift hook-up." Six years passed before he could settle in with the concept. He recalls one morning at Steamboat on the North Umpqua with Phil Haight, "the day it all happened."

When we reached the river after breakfast, I walked into the first pool, saw a fish flash deep in the green currents, and dropped my nymph about ten feet upstream of that spot. I threw slack, fed a little line and allowed the fly to penetrate the water column, and led the nymph past the steelhead. I'll never forget that moment, because what happened next validated years of theorizing and speculating. The fish flashed again, the tip of the floating line moved, and I set the hook crisply. One hundred twenty-five yards downstream and ten minutes later I landed that bright buck—with my nymph seated in the corner of its mouth.

I whooped it up. No swinging fly. No gaudy tinsel or Day Glo theatrics. No sinking line. Just a dead drifted nymph like I'd used for fat rainbows on the riffles of Hat Creek. Phil and I landed so many fish in the next two hours we were oblivious to the intensifying downpour.

They shared their discovery, giving flies to Kenny Gleason and Dennis Black. "We couldn't have done a better job of spreading the word if we'd hired a publicist. We had given our ugly bugs to two of the most experienced and talented steelheaders in the Northwest!"

ORIGINAL

Hook Size 2 to 8; 2 is the most popular size, with sizes 4 to 8 used when imitating instars.

Thread Black

Body Small to medium black chenille. Taper to duplicate the natural *Pteronarcys* nymph.

Weight Large-diameter lead. Double-wrap the thorax to enhance the taper. Use a double wrap if fishing deep-holding water, a single wrap for shallow riffles. (Brad says, "Matching the amount of lead to the water type is vital to the fly's effectiveness.")

Tail Two black rubber hackles, 8 to 10 mm long

Legs Three pairs, 6 to 20 mm, each pair a single piece of black rubber hackle secured in the middle at right angles to the hook. Evenly space and figure-eight in place. Wind chenille forward over lead foundation. (Don't try to figure-eight chenille around rubber legs.) Tie off and secure two black rubber hackle at the head for antenna, 20 to 30 mm long. Rubber tail, legs, or antenna can be made longer if more action is desired.

VARIEGATED UGLY BUG

Same as the original except the chenille is variegated black/yellow chenille and tied in sizes 4 to 8. This variation is used to imitate the golden stonefly.

FLASHABOU UGLY BUG

Same as the original except several strands of pearl Flashabou is added to each pair of legs. "The sparkle of this fish-attracting material will, at times, add to the pattern's effectiveness. Some anglers report success when substituting Krystal Flash," says Brad.

FLUORESCENT UGLY BUG

Same as the original except for substituting a tail of white rubber hackle, and a body of fluorescent fire orange chenille. (Danville Fire Orange is recommended.) Brad says, "Great for winter steelhead in off-colored water, as well as ocean-fresh summer-runs and the huge three-salt summer fish of northern British Columbia. It can be fished dead-drift or with a conventional down-and-across swing. At times a teasing twitch elicits a strike at the end of the drift."

North Fork Stillaguamish hen (Deer Creek native)—six pounds, July. *Photo credit: Dan Reiff*

Skagit River hen, fourteen pounds, April

Dean River hen, sixteen pounds, August

Deschutes River buck, six pounds, August

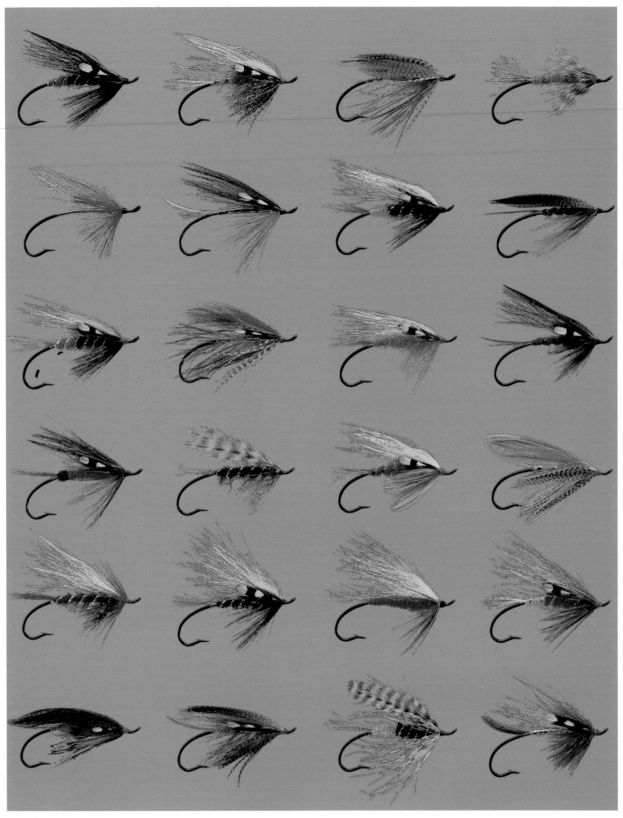

Plate 1

Row 1 Black Gordon, Brad's Brat, Brown Heron, Burlap
Row 2 Fall Favorite, Golden Demon, Green Butt Skunk, Lady Caroline
Row 3 Macks Canyon, Orange Heron, Orange Shrimp, Purple Peril
Row 4 Red Ant, Silver Hilton, Skykomish Sunrise, Sol Duc
Row 5 Del Cooper, Skunk, Thor, Umpqua Special
Row 6 Blue Boy, Bronze Brad's Brat, Green Butt Silver Hilton, Pale Peril

All flies in Plate 1 were tied by Dave McNeese

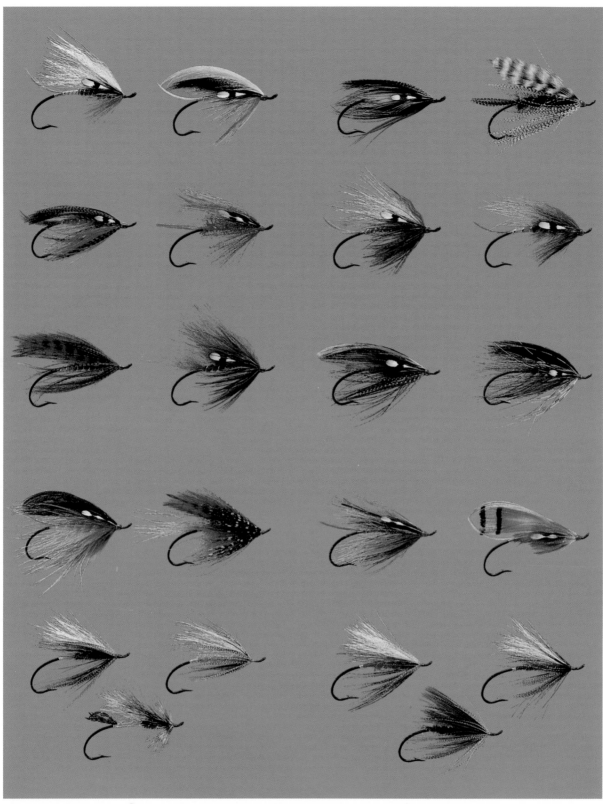

Plate 2

Row 1 Deschutes Madness, Golden Demon II, Golden Heron, Hilton Spider
Row 2 Knouse, McNeese Madness, Pale Perl, Purple Brat
Row 3 Purple Hilton, Purple Polar Bear Matuka, Purple Price, Purple Spey
Row 4 Spawning Spey, Spawning Purple, Stratman Fancy, Red Wing
Row 5 Black Witch, Orange Witch, Harlequin Spey, Purple Witch
Row 6 Rusty Rat, Hardy's Favorite

Rows 1, 2, 3, and 4 tied by Dave McNeese
Rows 5 and 6 tied by Steve Brocco

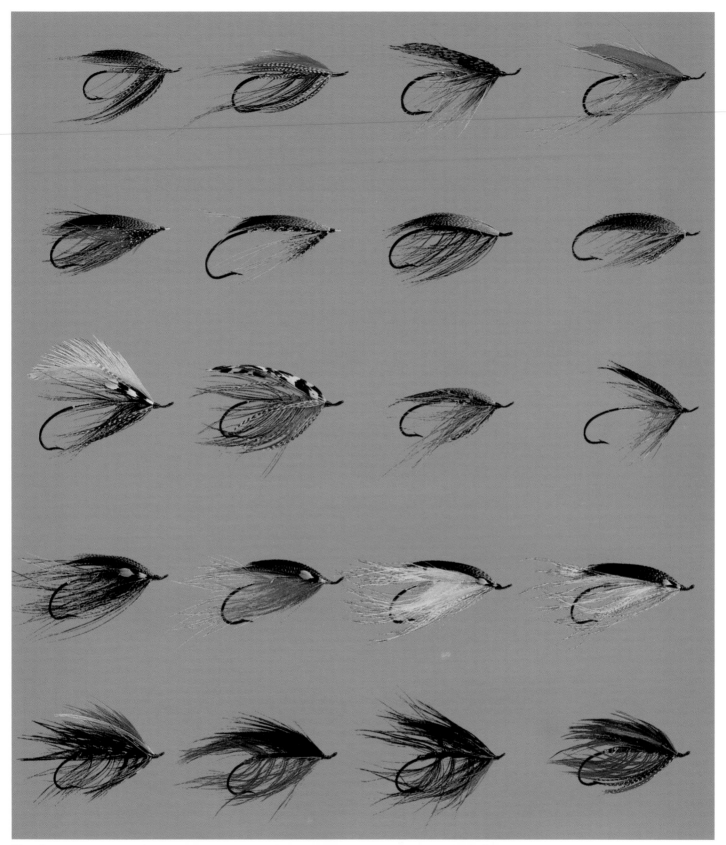

Plate 3

Row 1 Gray Heron, Orange Heron *(Syd Glasso)*, Brown Heron, Orange Heron *(Pat Crane)*.
Row 2 Purple Spey, Gray Heron, Claret Spey, Gray Heron (reduced) *(Steve Gobin)*.
Row 3 Orange Heron #1, Orange Heron #2, Silver Streak, Gold Streak *(Joe Howell)*
Row 4 Black Skagit Spey, Orange Skagit Spey, Yellow Skagit Spey, White Skagit Spey *(John Farrar)*
Row 5 Boulder Creek, Car Body, Dark Daze, Dragon's Tooth *(Mike Kinney)*

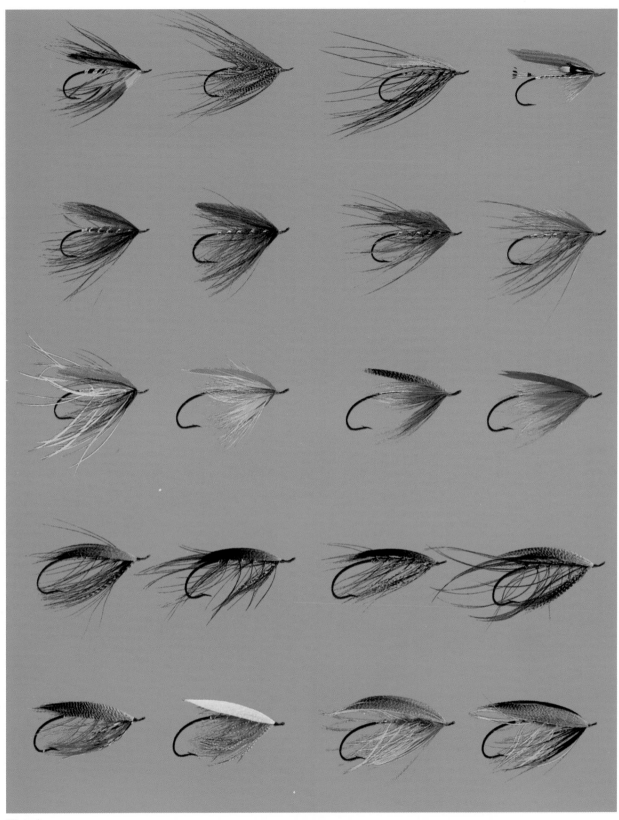

Plate 4

Row 1 Black and Orange Heron, Blue Heron, Green Heron, Lord Iris
Row 2 Purple Heart, Purple Heart Spey, Purple Sol Duc Spey, Rusty Heron
Row 3 Sol Duc Spey, Orange Sunset, Blue and Bronze Sunset, Steelhead Sunset
Row 4 Orange Heron, Purple Kind, Carron (reduced), Carron (full)
Row 5 Polar Shrimp, Polar Shrimp (white wing), Skykomish Light, Skykomish Dark.

Rows 1, 2, and 3, Bob Veverka
Rows 4 and 5, Steve Gobin

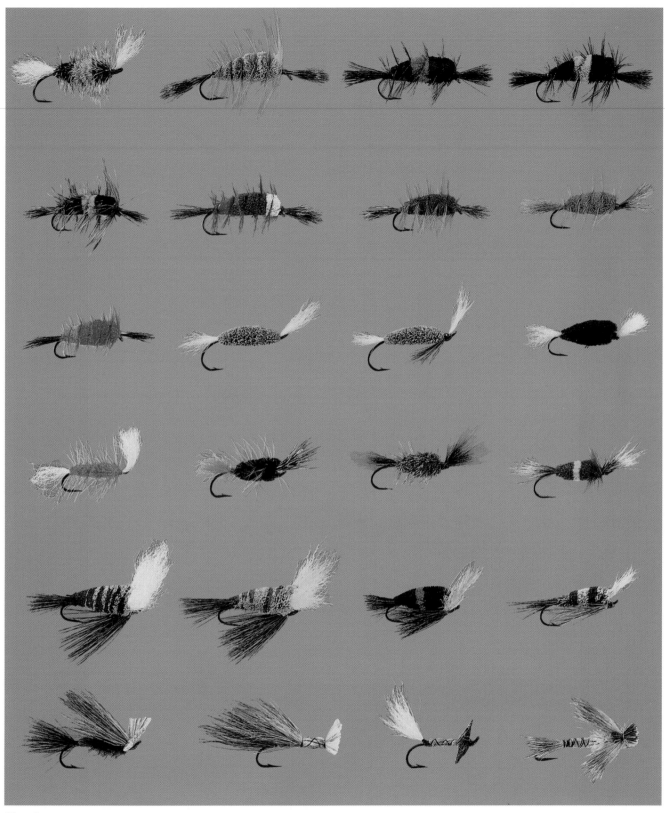

Plate 5

Row 1 Bumble Bee Bomber *(Warren Duncan)*, Orange and Black Bomber, Yellow and Black Bomber *(Don Hathaway)*
Row 2 Yellow and Black Bomber (grizzly hackle), Purple Bomber, Brown Bomber, Rusty Bomber *(Don Hathaway)*
Row 3 Orange Bomber *(Don Hathaway)*, Cigar Butt, Cigar Butt (moose throat), Moose Turd *(LeRoy Hyatt)*
Row 4 Orange Bomber *(Kaufmann's Streamborn)*, Steelhead Bomber *(Jerry Cebula)*, Green Bomber, Steelhead Bee Bomber
(Sean Gallagher)
Row 5 Waller Waker (original), Waller Waker (low light), Bumble Bee Waker, Waller Waker
(original with short wing stiffened with Goop) *(Lani Waller)*
Row 6 Bulkley Moose, Bubblehead *(John Mintz)*, Riffle Express *(Judd Wickwire)*, Riffle Dancer *(Mark Pinch)*

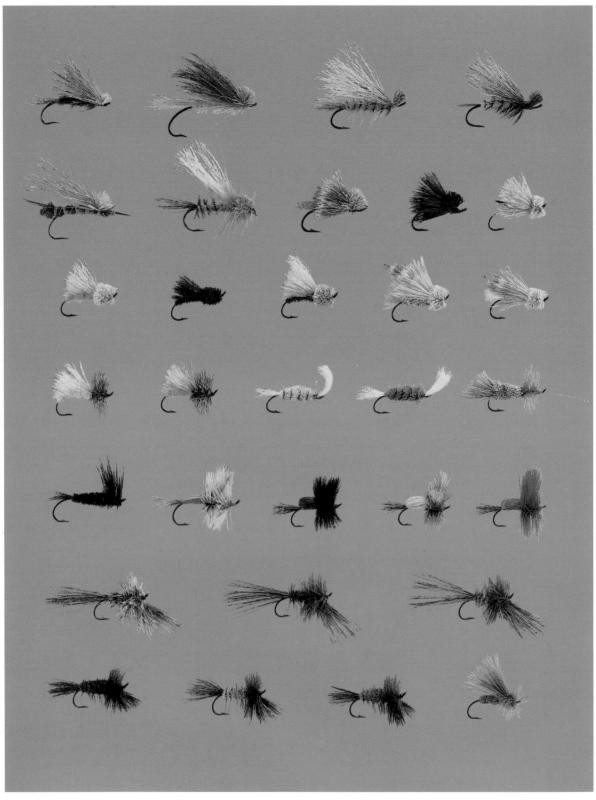

Plate 6

Row 1 Grease Liner *(Harry Lemire)*, Caddis Flash *(Dave McNeese)*, Greased Line Fall Caddis, Greased Line Hopper *(Mark Noble)*
Row 2 Telkwa Stone *(Mike Maxwell)*, Golden Stone *(Joe Howell)*, Bulkley Mouse (original), Bulkley Mouse ("Disco Mouse")
(Andrée Laporte) October Caddis *(LeRoy Hyatt)*
Row 3 Hyatt's Caddis (orange), Hyatt's Caddis (black), Hyatt's Caddis (peacock), Steelhead Muddler, Bloody Muddler *(LeRoy Hyatt)*
Row 4 Hyatt's Caddis (gray hackle), Hyatt's Caddis (orange hackle) *(LeRoy Hyatt)*, Bomber, Rusty Bomber, Goddard Caddis
(Umpqua Feather Merchants)
Row 5 Lemire's Irresistible *(Harry Lemire)*, Royal Humpy *(Umpqua Feather Merchants)*, Steelhead Humpy: black, tan, red *(Don Hathaway)*
Row 6 Steelhead Skater: Grizzly, Brown Hackle Peacock, Salmon Fly *(Bob Wagoner)*
Row 7 Steelhead Skaters (spun deer hair bodies): Black, Natural, Rusty Brown *(LeRoy Hyatt)*, Autumn Sedge *(Scott Noble)*

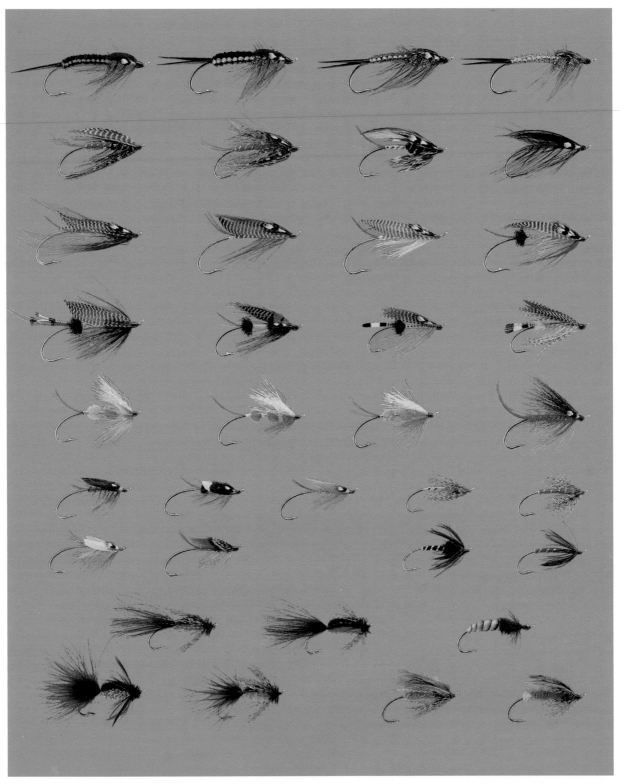

Plate 7

Row 1 Olympic Stonefly: Orange and Black, Black and Silver, Blue and Silver, Green and Silver
Row 2 Teresa's Tease, D.Ana Marie, Sara Teen, Bobbie Jean
Row 3 QE 3, Kate, T.C. 3, Hellen's Fancy
Row 4 Night Train, Mac Garrett, Father Bill, Soul Duck
Row 5 Christmas Trinity, Hot Orange Trinity, Orange Trinity Garrett's Shrimp
Row 6 Peterson M.D., Johnson M.D., Septober Orange, Candy Montana, Denise Montana
Row 7 Septober Candy, Septober Pheasant, Libby's Black, Dana Montana
Row 8 Hoko Hummer #1, Hoko Hummer #2, Septober Caddis Larvae
Row 9 Hoko Hummer #3, Hoko Hummer #4, Septober Caddis Male, Septober Caddis Female

Rows 1–9, Jim Garrett

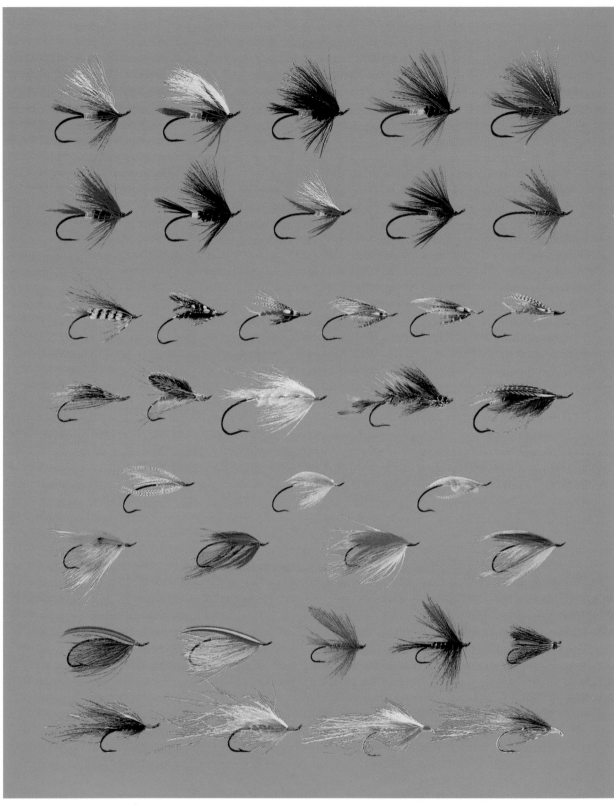

Plate 8

Row 1 Freight Train (original), Freight Train Marabou, Coal Car, Signal Light, Purple Flash *(Randall Kaufmann)*
Row 2 Ferry Canyon, Flat Car, Signal Light (low water), Coal Car (low water), Purple Flash (low water) *(Randall Kaufmann)*
Row 3 Harry Kari Bucktail, Black Diamond, Lisa Bell, Golden Edge Orange, Golden Edge Yellow, Squirrel and Teal *(Harry Lemire)*
Row 4 Thompson River Caddis, Fall Caddis, Lemire's Winter Fly, Steelhead Selpin, Green Butt Spey *(Harry Lemire)*
Row 5 Spectral Spider, Springer Green, Dusty Coachman *(Walt Johnson)*
Row 6 Royal Spey, Deep Purple Spey, Red Shrimp, Golden Spey *(Walt Johnson)*
Row 7 Midnight Spey, Prismatic Spey *(Scott Noble)*, Blue Sky, Black Sky, Thompson River Caddis *(Stan Young)*
Row 8 Estuary Shrimp: Black, Orange, Pink, Brown *(Les Johnson)*

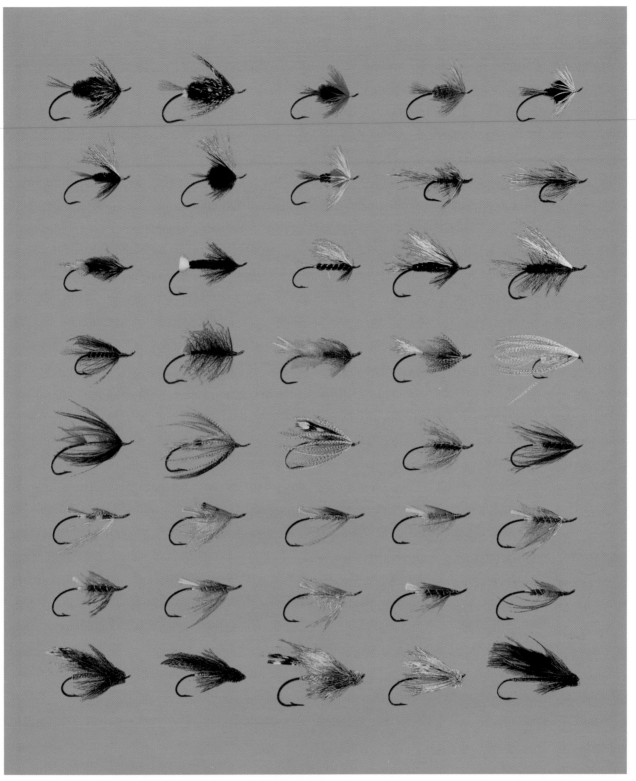

Plate 9

Row 1 Claret Guinea Spade, Yellow Guinea Spade, Whaka Blonde, Jacob's Coat, Fancy Spade *(Alec Jackson)*
Row 2 Coastal Skunk, Inland Skunk, Fancy Red Spade *(Alec Jackson)*, Spade (original, Spade (brown) *(Bob Arnold)*
Row 3 Gordon Spade, Steelhead Stick *(Joe Butorac)*, Skunk *(Wes Drain)*, Skapade, Hairy Skapade *(Joe Butorac)*
Row 4 Night Dancer *(Frank Amato)*, Sweet Loreta, Spade, Polar Spade *(Jimmy Hunnicutt)*, Wet Spider *(Al Knudson)*
Row 5 Purple Spider, Gold Spider *(Karl Hauffler)*, Low and Clear Spider *(Mark Canfield)*, Steelhead Carey, Green Butt Spider *(Sean Gallagher)*
Row 6 Low Water Bee, Blood and Brandy, Brazen Lady, Bright Sienna, Creme-de-Menthe *(Dick Van Demark)*
Row 7 Dark Ale, Mai Tai, Optical Black, Royal Blue *(Dick Van Demark)*
Row 8 Purple Krystal Flash Muddler, Black Krystal Flash Muddler *(Kaufmann's Streamborn)*, Coon Muddler *(Joe Howell)*, Steelhead Caddis *(Trey Combs)*, Purple Smuddler *(Don Roberts)*

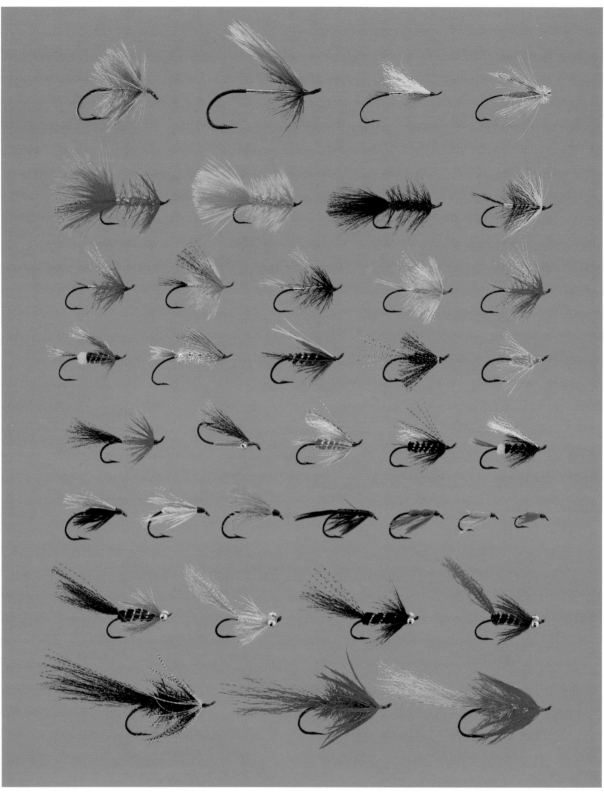

Plate 10

Row 1 Paint Brush, Winter's Hope, Washougal Olive, Steelhead Caddis *(Bill McMillan)*
Row 2 Steelhead Wooly Buggers (3): Red, Orange, Black. Jim Green Special *(Bob Wagoner)*
Row 3 Purple Sundowner, Orange Sundowner, Black Sundowner, Pink Sundowner *(Bob Wagoner)*
Row 4 Purple Skunk, Iceberg *(Bob Wagoner)*, Street Walker *(Kaufmann's Streamborn)*, Black Krystal Bullet, Orange Krystal Bullet
(Bob Bordon)
Row 5 Dean River Lantern, Steelhead Charlie *(Bob Wagoner)*, Skykomish Sunrise, Skunk, Green Butt Skunk *(Kaufmann's Streamborn)*
Row 6 Teeny Flash Fly (1, 2, 3), Teeny Leech (4), Teeny Nymph (5, 6, 7) *(Jim Teeny)*
Row 7 Boss, Orange Comet, Black Comet, Purple Comet *(Kaufmann's Streamborn)*
Row 8 Black Estaz Comet, Purple Estaz Comet, Red Estaz Comet *(Kaufmann's Streamborn)*

Plate 11

Row 1 Skykomish Sunrise, Winter Red, Pink Pearl, Winter Orange *(Trey Combs)*
Row 2 Winter Purple (three-part wing), Coal Car, Deer Creek, Winter Purple (two-part wing) *(Trey Combs)*
Row 3 Sauk River Grub, Sauk River Shrimp *(Alec Jackson)*, Blood on the Waters *(Jimmy Hunnicutt)*, Polar Bear Matuka
(Generic. Note partially dyed wing.) *(Dave McNeese)*
Row 4 General Practitioner *(Trey Combs)*, Black Marabou Practitioner *(Sean Gallagher)*, General Practitioner *(Stewart Wallace)*
Row 5 Horny Shrimp *(Joe Butorac)*, Reiff's Shrimp *(Dan Reiff)*, Sean's Prawn *(Sean Gallagher)*
Row 6 Kispiox Shrimp *(Mike Craig)*, Borden's Prawn *(Bob Borden)*
Lower left: Herring Sea Habit, Garry Dog *(Roland Holmberg)*
Center: Steelhead Bunny *(Les Johnson)*
Right: Steel Woolies *(Joe Butorac)*

Plate 12

Row 1 Deer Creek, Royal Flush *(Bob Arnold)*, Electric Blue *(Sean Gallagher)*
Row 2 Alaskabou series. Pixie's Revenge, Tequilla Sunrise, Popsicle *(George Cook)*
Row 3 Purple Marabou *(Steve Gobin)*, Skagit Monster, Half and Half *(Joe Butorac)*
Row 4 Skagit Special, Purple and Blue, Pink and Red *(Bob Aid)*
Row 5 Black and Orange, Steelhead Pinkie, Orange and Red *(Bob Aid)*

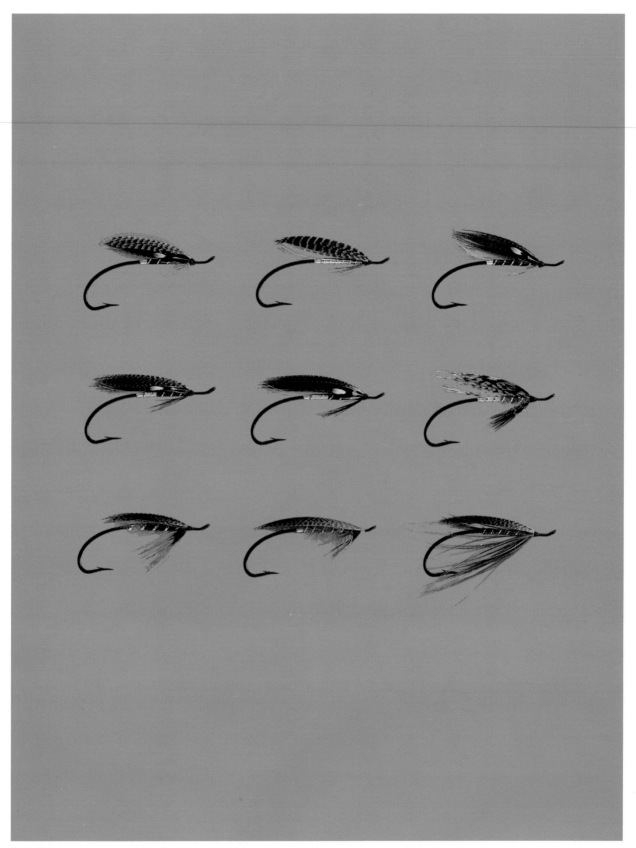

Plate 13

Row 1 Blue Charm, Silver Blue, Logie
Row 2 Jockie, Jeannie, March Brown
Row 3 Bumbee, Claret Alder, Lady Caroline

All flies tied by Steve Gobin

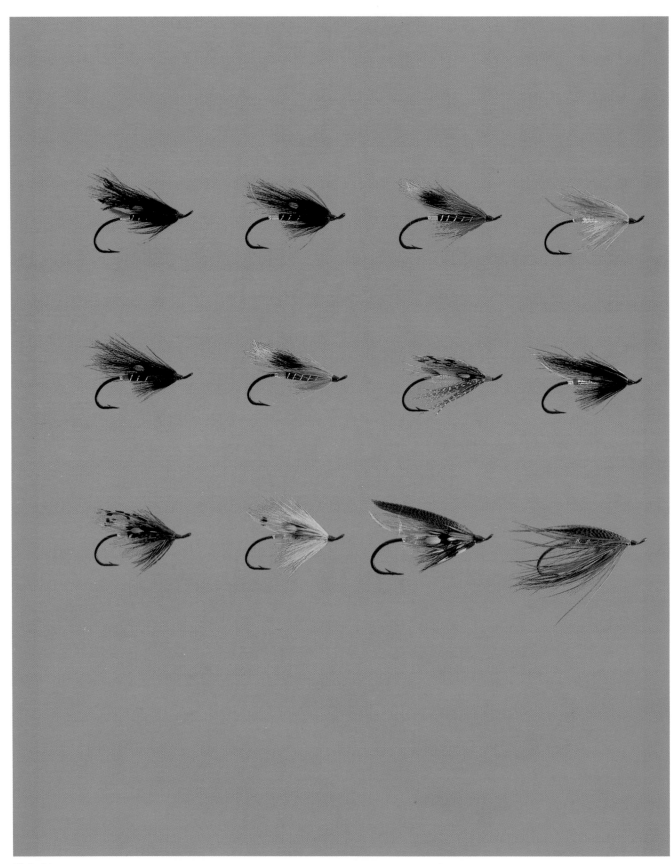

Plate 14

Row 1 Black Dose, Black Bear Green Butt, Blue Charm, Orange Blossom
Row 2 Black Bear Red Butt, Orange Charm, Blue Baron, Nite Hawk
Row 3 Thunder and Lightning, Green Highlander, Jock Scott, Lady Caroline

All flies tied by Bob Veverka

DICK VAN DEMARK

Moulin Rouge

Dick Van Demark of Bellingham, Washington, calls these flies his "flat-winged Flymph low-water steelhead series." The name with the pedigree may not catch on, but the flies should. Not because they're unique or even beautiful, but because they're pragmatically designed from the ground up, with only modest consideration given to traditional form. Dick carefully thought out every aspect of their design, and the result is as significant as it is provocative. The "salients," as he likes to call them, are many. The hackle varies, but whether long-fibered pheasant, grouse, or duck flank, it provides luxurious movement in the water. The top of the hackle is clipped off and a few hairs tied in for an underwing. This helps to support the wing and gives a sprinkle of color to the wing. The wing, "a concession to the fish's perspective from below the fly," is feathers set flat over the hook, somewhat on the order of "damp" caddis patterns. This feature gives the fly considerable silhouette for all the lightness of its dress, and serves as a planing surface when the fly is riffle hitched. Dick calls his use of matching fluorescent flosses for the tail and the tag an "attraction at a distance." He accomplishes this by tying in the tag as it should be, with an underbody of mylar so that it glows rather than dulls when wet. It is the dubbed body, however, that Dick, the artist, most labors over. He chooses a material that is highly translucent, and dubs it loosely so that the fibers don't matt and loose their refractive qualities. The color combinations are made on the basis of "optical blending," mixing two or more colors that are opposite each other on the color wheel. The colors are intensified because of their mutual contrast. In this manner, a red and yellow from a distance appears to be orange, but when close at hand the component colors appear vivid and contrasting. Dick's theory is that this excites steelhead into more readily taking the fly.

He uses substitutes for seal, including angora goat, imitation seal, and synthetic yarns chopped up with scissors and run through a blender. Examples of these yarns are: 100 percent unspun Kodel polyester knitting yarn, Dawn Odyssey yarn by American Thread Co., and Aunt Lydia's heavy rug yarn. Dick prefers to dub on a spinning block, the thread-spun fur bodies stored on a notched card for later use. The bodies may also be spun from a dubbing loop made while tying the fly.

Dick reminded me that the flies that appear in the color plates were tied with small heads for aesthetic purposes. "I usually leave space during the tying operation for a somewhat longer-than-normal head. This provides space for the use of a Portland hitch which I occasionally employ."

Pete Hidy first described for Dick the dubbing techniques that he and Jim Leisenring had developed for their "flymph" emerger patterns. Later, angling author Rick Hafele demonstrated, at the vise, their methods and how to use a spinning block. Dick has been applying these methods to his low-water series ever since.

BLOOD 'N BRANDY

Thread	Flame or red
Tip	Gold mylar
Tag	Flame floss
Tail	Four or five strands of flame floss
Body	Dubbing mix in three equal parts of fluorescent orange, fluorescent yellow, and scarlet
Dubbing Silk	Orange or red. Rib with gold rope.
Hackle	Mallard flank dyed fluorescent orange
Underwing	A few strands of red hair
Overwing	Two golden pheasant crest feathers dyed scarlet

BRAZEN LADY

Thread Flame or dark brown
Tip Silver mylar
Tag Flame floss
Tail Four or five strands of flame floss
Body Copper tinsel yarn

Hackle Red-orange golden pheasant body feather
Underwing A few strands of red hair
Overwing Two ruddy brown feathers from shoulder of golden pheasant

BRIGHT SIENNA

Thread Brown
Tip Gold mylar
Tag Fluorescent yellow-orange floss
Tail Four or five strands of fluorescent yellow-orange floss
Body Mix of two parts burnt sienna—a vivid reddish brown—and one part fluorescent orange

Dubbing Silk Orange or yellow. Rib with gold rope.
Hackle Reddish orange golden pheasant body feather
Underwing A few strands of yellow hair
Overwing Two ruddy brown feathers from shoulder of golden pheasant

CREME-DE-MENTHE

Thread Olive
Tip Gold mylar
Tag Fluorescent yellow-orange floss
Tail Fluorescent yellow-orange floss
Dubbing Silk Yellow or olive
Body Dubbing mix of three parts olive and two parts chartreuse (lime green). Rib with gold rope.

Hackle Greenish-grey Chinese pheasant rump
Underwing A few strands of white hair
Overwing Two greenish-grey feathers from Chinese pheasant rump

DARK ALE

Thread Brown
Tip Gold mylar
Tag Fluorescent salmon-orange floss
Tail Four or five strands of fluorescent salmon-orange floss
Dubbing Silk Orange

Body Dubbing mix of three parts dark brown and one part maroon. Rib with gold rope.
Hackle Well-marked English grouse body feather
Underwing A few strands of orange hair
Overwing Two reddish orange golden pheasant body feathers

LOW WATER BEE

Thread Brown
Tip Gold mylar
Tag Fluorescent yellow-orange floss
Tail Red saddle hackle
Body Alternate bands of medium brown, yellow, and medium brown dubbing. The center band of yellow is one part fluorescent yellow and one part regular yellow

Hackle Brown Chinese pheasant rump
Underwing A few strands of red hair
Wing Two Hungarian partridge body feathers with a pale center stripe

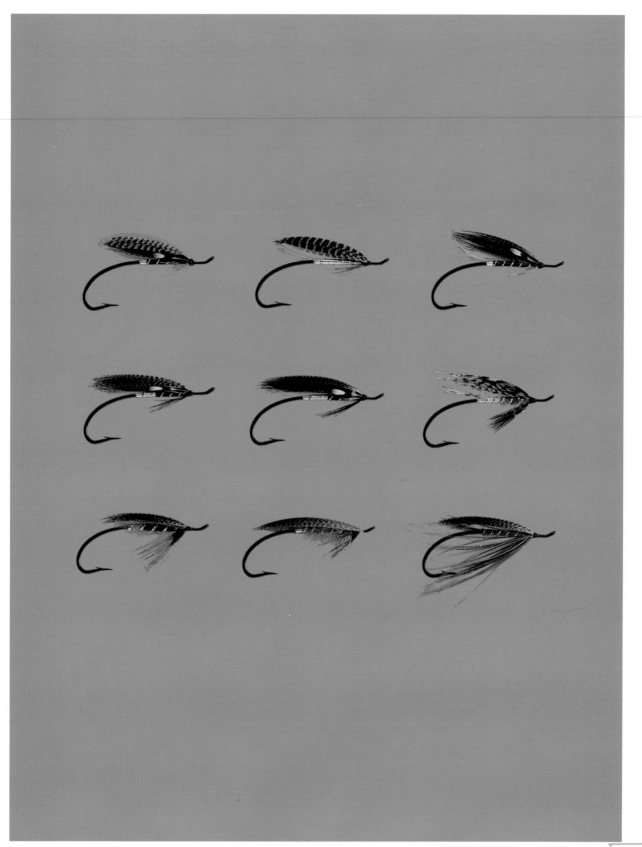

Plate 13

Row 1 Blue Charm, Silver Blue, Logie
Row 2 Jockie, Jeannie, March Brown
Row 3 Bumbee, Claret Alder, Lady Caroline

All flies tied by Steve Gobin

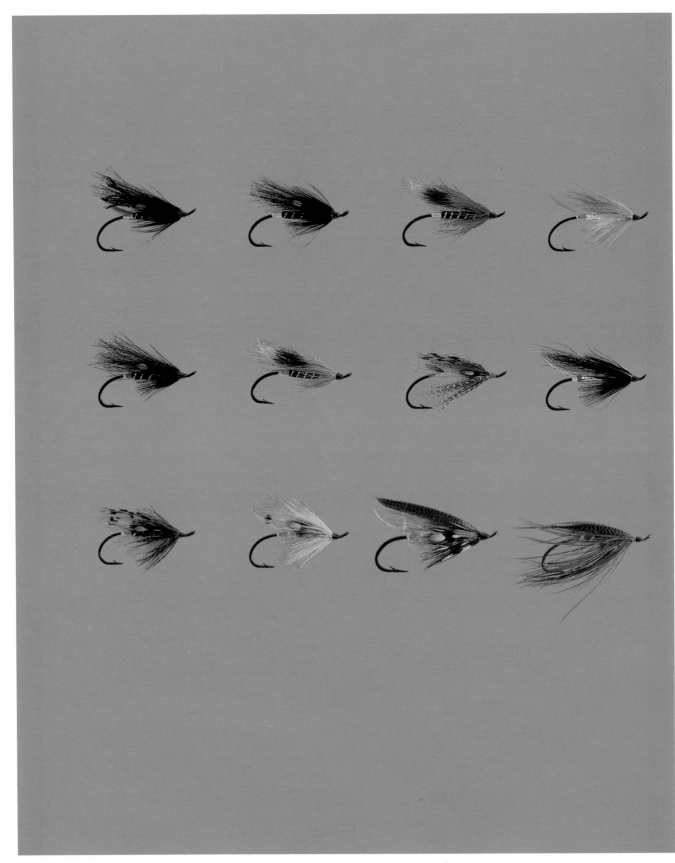

Plate 14

MAI TAI

Thread	Red
Tip	Silver mylar
Tag	Fluorescent yellow-orange floss
Tail	Four or five strands of fluorescent yellow-orange floss
Dubbing Silk	Orange or red
Body	Dubbing mix of two parts fluorescent orange, three parts scarlet, and two parts maroon. Rib with silver rope.
Hackle	Chinese pheasant rump dyed red, which gives a shade of maroon
Underwing	A few strands of orange hair
Wing	Two Hungarian partridge body feathers with a pale center stripe

MOULIN ROUGE

Thread	Flame or red
Tip	Gold mylar
Tag	Flame floss
Tail	Four or five strands of flame floss
Dubbing Silk	Red or orange
Body	Dubbing mix of equal parts of scarlet and fluorescent orange. Rib with gold rope.
Hackle	Greenish grey Chinese pheasant rump
Underwing	A few strands of red hair
Wing	Two reddish-orange golden pheasant body feathers

OPTICAL BLACK

Thread	Black
Tip	Silver mylar
Tag	Fluorescent salmon-orange floss
Tail	Reddish orange golden pheasant body feathers
Dubbing Silk	Purple or red
Body	Dubbing mix in four equal parts of dark blue, crimson, dark green, and black
Hackle	Reddish orange golden pheasant
Underwing	A few strands of red hair
Wing	Two ruddy brown shoulder feathers of golden pheasant

ROYAL BLUE

Thread	Black
Tip	Silver mylar
Tail	Royal blue hackle fibers
Dubbing Silk	Orange
Body	Rear half royal blue dubbing, front half mix of one part yellow and two parts scarlet. Rib with silver rope.
Hackle	Mallard flank dyed royal blue
Underwing	No more than 6 strands of silver Flashabou (may be omitted)
Wing	Two mallard breast feathers dyed scarlet

TAWNY PORT

Thread	Red
Tip	Gold mylar
Tag	Fluorescent salmon-orange floss
Tail	Four or five strands of fluorescent salmon orange floss
Dubbing Silk	Red or orange
Body	Dubbing mix of two parts of fluorescent orange and three parts maroon. Rib with gold rope.
Hackle	Reddish orange golden pheasant body feather
Underwing	A few strands of yellow hair
Wing	Two small orange golden pheasant crests

Bob Veverka

BOB VEVERKA

Bob Veverka, of Underhill, Vermont, is a prodigious fly-tying talent, arguably the finest tyer of full-dressed Atlantic salmon flies in the world. No more than a half-dozen tyers belong in his select company. If the reader doubts this lofty claim, examine Joseph Bates's *The Art of the Atlantic Salmon Fly.* Bob's flies are on display beside those of the late Syd Glasso, a man many consider the most gifted tyer of full-dressed Atlantic salmon flies our country ever produced.

Bob Veverka began tying trout flies as a fifteen-year-old high school student on Long Island. The classic New England streamer flies by Helen Shaw inspired him and became a specialty even after he had learned the intricacies of full-dressed salmon flies. When Joseph Bates first saw Bob's streamer flies, he was working on his new book about Atlantic salmon flies. "I want to see your salmon flies!" he said.

Bob may spend hundreds of dollars securing the rare—and largely secondhand—materials that go into a single full dressed fly. Dave McNeese has one such fly. "I wouldn't sell it for a thousand dollars," he told me.

Commercially tying hairwing, spey, or dee-strip salmon flies for a very discriminating clientele fills Bob's time. In the early 1980s, he traveled to Washington to study Syd Glasso's flies and the Olympic Peninsula rivers, and to steep himself in the Glasso mystique. More trips followed, to fish the Skagit with Alec Jackson, the Santiam with Dave McNeese, the North Umpqua with Joe Howell. Now he ties steelhead flies in the tradition of Syd Glasso, the following set his working dozen.

BLACK AND ORANGE HERON

Body Rear half black floss, front half orange seal fur. Rib with two narrow strands of oval tinsel with a single strand of fluorescent orange silk between.

Hackle Black and orange
Wing Two orange hackle tips flanked by two black hackle tips

BLUE HERON

Body Rear half deep blue silk, front half blue seal. Rib with flat and fine oval silver tinsel.

Hackle Grey
Throat Teal
Wing Two matching blue hackle tips

GREEN HERON

Body Rear half fluorescent green silk, front half green seal. Rib with flat and narrow oval gold tinsel.
Hackle Black

Throat Hooded merganser flank
Wing Four matching fluorescent green hackle tips

LORD IRIS

Tag Oval silver tinsel
Tail Golden pheasant tippet
Body Flat silver tinsel ribbed with narrow oval silver tinsel
Underwing Two orange hackles flanked by two badger hackles

Wing Married strips of red, orange, green, and blue goose
Sides Jungle cock

PURPLE HEART

Tag Oval silver tinsel
Tail Amherst crest
Body Rear half purple silk, front half red seal. Rib with flat silver and narrow oval silver tinsel.
Hackle Red

Throat Black
Wing Four red hackle tips followed by a single purple hackle tip on each side, three-fourths length of wing
Topping Amherst pheasant crest

PURPLE HEART SPEY

Body Rear half fluorescent red silk, front half purple seal fur. Rib with flat silver and narrow oval silver tinsel.
Hackle Purple

Throat Black
Wing Two red hackle tips flanked by two purple hackle tips

PURPLE SOL DUC SPEY

Body Rear half fluorescent red silk, front half purple seal fur. Rib with flat silver and narrow oval silver tinsel.
Hackle Purple

Throat Black
Wing Two red hackles flanked by two purple hackles

RUSTY HERON

Body Rear half fluorescent orange silk, front half orange seal. Rib with flat silver tinsel and narrow oval silver tinsel.
Hackle Grey

Throat Golden pheasant body feather (red)
Wing Two yellow hackle tips flanked by two orange or red hackle tips

SOL DUC SPEY

Body Rear half fluorescent orange silk, front half orange seal. Rib with flat silver tinsel and narrow oval silver tinsel.

Body Hackle Yellow
Throat Black
Wing Four orange hackle tips

BLUE AND BRONZE SUNSET

Body Flat silver tinsel veiled above and below with golden pheasant crest
Hackle Blue, followed by claret

Throat Golden pheasant body feather
Wing Bronze mallard

ORANGE SUNSET

Body Flat gold tinsel veiled above and below with golden pheasant crest
Hackle Yellow, followed by orange

Throat Golden pheasant body feather
Wing Strips of orange goose

STEELHEAD SUNSET

Body Flat silver tinsel veiled above and below with golden pheasant crest
Hackle Magenta, followed by claret

Throat Golden pheasant body feather (red)
Wing Strips of claret goose

WINTER SERIES (TREY COMBS)

My Winter Series of steelhead dressings developed from my need for a fast sinking winter fly that would swim well under tension. This series includes both traditional patterns, tied in a very specific manner, and new patterns.

Our finest swimming winter flies, the marabou spiders, General Practitioners, and spey flies with the body hackle doubled, carry an abundance of color to the steelhead. But the luxurious hackle below the hook—and very little material above the hook—make these slow-sinking styles unstable. Under substantial tension they roll over or even turn upside down. Winter lies are often so soft that flies dressed in these traditional styles are ideal, for great swimming movement is maintained in even faint current and the slow sink rate becomes an advantage. Conversely, conventional flies with a hairwing, short tail, and hackle are poor swimmers in light currents, the fly looking quite dead and riding butt-down when led through the swing. My Winter Series flies sink well in deep pools and attract in soft currents, yet swim upright through heavy tailouts—where the take often occurs.

The tail is tied in solely to supply lift. The slim, hard body is made from the single strand floss I'm using as a tying thread. Each body, unless black, is underwrapped with silver tinsel and thus glows when wet. The ribbing is a continuation of the tinsel tag. I find the clean lines of the body and the sparse throat hackle allow the hook to act as a keel for the wing of marabou blood plumes.

I remove the marabou in bunches and tie it down exactly as I would bucktail. Each wing is three parts, the first tied down at the center of the looped eye, the second, shorter, wing slightly forward and hiding the butts of the first. The final wing is shorter still. The butts of this wing are covered by the collar of hackle. The general contour of the entire wing is that of a Matuka, a comb of blood plumes across the top of the fly.

I do overdress some of these Winter Series patterns, the Coal Car and Winter Purple, and Winter's Hope, for example, for badly discolored water. I like the Pink Pearl, Midnight Sun, Skykomish Sunrise, and Winter's Hope for water with some color. I find that the Winter Orange attracts steelhead in both clear and discolored water. When dressed down with a shorter, three-part, wing, it is a fine clear-water pattern in sizes 1 and 1/0. I think of the Winter Red as a clear-water pattern, and generally fish it then, though the combination of red and fluorescent cerise is "hot" and very visible.

These patterns work equally well on high, discolored summer water and for fresh spring-run steelhead. Jimmy Hunnicutt took two Dean steelhead in the twenty-pound range with the full-dressed Midnight Sun. I have caught some fine summer fish with the Midnight Sun, Skykomish Sunrise, Pink Pearl, and Coal Car dressed down and fished greased-line. All swim much better than originals tied with fur wings, or with long marabou wings that tend to wrap around the hook.

I prefer to use French tinsel with these flies. The material is strong, permitting me to bind down very hard on the floss body. This is necessary to keep the tinsel from sliding around on so slick a surface. A more durable fly is produced if a bead of head cement is laid down along the dorsal surface of the floss body after it is ribbed, with additional cement in the wing butts and under the tag of tinsel.

WINTER ORANGE

Tail	Orange hackle fibers	**Throat**	Orange marabou fibers
Body	Fluorescent orange floss over flat silver tinsel.	**Second Wing**	Orange marabou
		Third Wing	Red marabou, sparse
Tag and Rib	Flat silver tinsel.	**Hackle**	Rose red or red. Sometimes I like to give this fly a final turn or two of magenta hackle.
First Wing	Orange marabou over several strands of orange Krystal Flash, full		

Note: I have had excellent results when tying this fly with a wing of orange polar bear mask. The result is very shrimpy, and I've had winter steelhead come from a considerable distance to hit the fly.

WINTER RED

Tail	Fluorescent cerise hackle fibers	**Second Wing and Throat**	Fluorescent cerise marabou
Body	Fluorescent cerise floss over flat silver tinsel	**Third Wing**	Red marabou
Tag and Rib	Flat silver tinsel	**Collar**	Red hackle
First Wing	Extending to the end of the tail, fluorescent cerise marabou over several strands of pearl Krystal Flash.		

WINTER ROSE

Tail	Pink hackle fibers	**Second Wing and Throat**	Pink marabou
Body	Fluorescent pink floss over flat silver tinsel.	**Third Wing**	Deep rose-pink marabou
Tag and Rib	Flat silver tinsel	**Collar**	Magenta hackle fibers
First Wing	Pink marabou over several strands of pink Krystal Flash		

MIDNIGHT SUN

Tail	Orange and yellow hackle fibers	**Second Wing**	White marabou
Body	Fluorescent orange floss over flat silver tinsel	**Throat**	Orange and yellow marabou
Tag and Rib	Flat silver tinsel	**Third Wing**	Orange over yellow marabou
First Wing	White marabou over several strands of pearl Krystal Flash	**Collar**	Rose-red hackle

PINK PEARL

Tail	Fluorescent cerise hackle fibers	**Second Wing**	White marabou
Body	Fluorescent cerise floss over flat silver tinsel	**Throat**	Hot pink marabou
Tag and Rib	Flat silver tinsel	**Third Wing**	Hot pink marabou
First Wing	White marabou over several strands of pearl Krystal Flash	**Collar**	Fluorescent cerise hackle

COAL CAR

Tag	Flame floss over flat silver tinsel	**First, Second, and Third Wing**	Black marabou blood plumes
Tail	Black marabou blood-plume fibers		
Body	Black floss ribbed with flat silver tinsel		
Underwing	Four to five strands pearl Flashabou	**Collar**	Black saddle
Hackle	Black saddle		

SKYKOMISH SUNRISE

Tail	Cerise and yellow hackle fibers	**Second Wing**	White marabou
Body	Fluorescent cerise floss over flat silver tinsel	**Throat**	Fluorescent cerise marabou
Tag and Rib	Flat silver tinsel	**Third Wing**	Fluorescent cerise marabou and yellow marabou, half and half
First Wing	White marabou over several strands of pearl Krystal Flash	**Collar**	Fluorescent cerise hackle

WINTER'S HOPE

Tail	Orange hackle fibers	**Second and Third Wing**	Orange marabou
Body	Fluorescent orange floss over flat silver tinsel		
Tag and Rib	Flat silver tinsel	**Throat**	Orange marabou
First Wing	Yellow marabou, full	**Hackle**	Deep purple followed by kingfisher blue

Note: I sometimes do this in a speed tie. I eliminate the tail and floss body and substitute the traditional body of flat silver tinsel. I then increase the length of the yellow marabou so that it extends well beyond the bend of the hook. The wing butts are covered by winding a full blood plume of orange marabou over the yellow. The collar is tied in as above.

STAN YOUNG

Stan Young, of Bellevue, Washington, says of himself, "I am a relative newcomer to the sport of steelhead fly fishing, having not discovered its appeal until about 1978." Since his retirement from the National Park Service in 1982, he has devoted all his free time to steelhead fly fishing on rivers from the North Umpqua to the Kispiox. Between trips, Stan writes articles about steelhead and champions the cause of wild fish.

"I favor smallish flies, even in winter, and either a dry line or short sink tip," he says. His water, "essentially the edges, riffles, tailouts, and pockets," favor these lines. "My impression is that steelhead are more attracted to the smaller flies (they have truly remarkable eyesight) and that the small flies are better at hooking and holding the fish."

BLUE SKY

Hook Mustad 36890, size 1/0 to 4 in winter and Tiemco 7989 or Mustad 90420, size 6 to 10 in summer.
Tail Blue hackle fibers
Tag Silver tinsel
Body Blue yarn or floss ribbed with oval silver tinsel

Hackle Blue hen, long and soft, wrapped full on both sides of the wings
Wing Blue hackle tips tied back to back
Head Black

"The long, soft hackles and the wings tend to lie back over the fly once it is being fished, giving it a spey appearance. This is the fly I have come to depend upon most and one I use on all rivers and during all seasons and under all water conditions. The only thing I vary is its size. If I were permitted only one pattern, this would be it."

BLACK SKY

Hook Mustad 90420, size 1/0 to 4
Tail Black hackle fibers
Tag Silver tinsel
Body Black yarn or floss ribbed with gold tinsel

Hackle Black hen, wrapped full, on both sides of the wings
Wings Black hackle tips
Head Black

"Many steelhead fly fishers swear by a black fly under almost all water conditions. I use the Black Sky mainly during winter and spring when waters range from low and clear to high and discolored."

RUSTY SKY

Hook Mustad 36890, size 1/0 to 4
Tail Rust or orange hackle fibers
Tag Flat silver tinsel
Body Rust or orange yarn or floss ribbed with gold tinsel

Hackle Rusty hen, long and soft, wrapped full on both sides of the wing
Head Black or red

"An excellent fly any time waters are somewhat high and colored."

STEELHEAD IRRESISTIBLE

Hook Tiemco 7989, size 6 and 8
Tail Dark brown deer body hair
Body Dark brown deer body hair spun and trimmed to taper at both ends

Wings Dark moose, set forward and divided

"This fly planes and rises out of the water if there is any current at all, producing a wobbly wake, much like a Bomber. The faster the current the higher it rides. Fish often go after it violently and repeatedly."

THOMPSON RIVER CADDIS

Hook Tiemco 7989, size 6 to 10
Body Rust colored floss ribbed with gold oval tinsel
Wing Two brown golden pheasant neck feathers set flat over the top of the body

Hackle A clump of deer, elk, or moose evenly spun around the body. The front will flare. Clip so that a small head remains.

"This fly is fished with a floating line. When the current speeds up the fly often lifts out of the water and wakes."

39

TRADITIONAL STEELHEAD FLY PATTERNS

T H E list of traditional steelhead fly patterns is short, several dozen or so, some of them no longer in common use. For the sake of historical continuity, I've made reference to these classics throughout the book, and from that standpoint alone they should be listed. These are also the dressings that inspire the many variations that become the "new" patterns with each generation, and they are still a frequent starting point for me when I'm experimenting at my fly-tying bench.

I've credited the originator whenever possible. A more detailed accounting of these dressings can be found in my book, *Steelhead Fly Fishing and Flies*, Frank Amato Publications, 1976.

ADMIRAL (Rear Admiral Eustace Baron Rogers, U.S.N. 1855—1929)

Tail Red hackle fibers
Body Red wool ribbed with gold tinsel

Hackle Red
Wing White bucktail

AL'S SPECIAL (Al Knudson)

Tail Red hackle fibers
Body Yellow chenilleribbed with oval silver tinsel

Hackle Red
Wing White bucktail

Wes Drain *Photo credit: Ralph Wahl.*

BLACK ANT

Tail Red hackle fibers.
Butt Peacock herl
Body Red floss

Hackle Brown
Wing Black calftail, upright and divided

BLACK GNAT BUCKTAIL

Tail Red hackle fibers.
Body Black chenille

Hackle Black
Wing Natural brown bucktail

BLACK GORDON (Clarence Gordon)

Body Rear 1/3 red yarn, front 2/3 black yarn, rib with narrow oval gold tinsel.

Hackle Black
Wing Black or very dark brown bucktail

BLACK PRINCE

Tail Red hackle fibers
Body Rear 1/3 yellow yarn, front 2/3 black yarn. Rib with oval silver tinsel.

Hackle Black
Wing Black bucktail

BLUE CHARM

Tip Silver wire
Tail Golden pheasant crest
Body Black floss ribbed with oval silver tinsel
Hackle Light blue

Wing Mallard.
Topping Slip of teal flank and golden pheasant crest

BOSQUITO (Roy Donnelly)

Tail Red hackle fibers
Body Yellow chenille.

Hackle Black
Wing White bucktail

BOSS (Virgil Sullivan)

Tail Black bucktail at least as long as the hook shank
Body Black chenille ribbed with flat silver tinsel.

Hackle Red
Head Silver bead chain eyes

BRAD'S BRAT (Enos Bradner)

Tail Orange and white bucktail
Body Rear half orange wool, front half red wool, rib entire body with flat gold tinsel.

Hackle Brown
Wing White bucktail.
Topping Orange bucktail

BRINDLE BUG (Lloyd Silvius)

Tail Natural brown hackle tips
Body Black and yellow variegated chenille wound with the first turn under the tail to turn it up.

Hackle Brown

BROWN HERON (Syd Glasso)

Body Rear 2/3 orange floss, front 1/3 hot orange seal. Rib with medium flat silver tinsel, overlay with narrow oval silver tinsel.
Hackle Grey heron, one side stripped, palmered along rib

Throat Teal
Wing Bronze mallard
Head Red

BUCKTAIL COACHMAN

Tail Red hackle fibers.
Body Peacock herl.

Hackle Brown
Wing White bucktail

BURLAP (Arnold Arana)

Tail Grey or light brown bucktail
Body Strands of burlap. Score to give a ragged appearance.

Hackle Grizzly

CARSON (Sumner Carson)

Tail Golden pheasant tippet fibers
Body Peacock herl with a scarlet-floss center
Hackle Brown.

Wing White bucktail
Topping Red bucktail

Note: This dressing is also known as the Carson Royal Coachman. Early versions of the fly were tied with white and red goose primary.

CHAPPIE (C. L. "Outdoor" Franklin)

Tail Tips of two grizzly hackles, face to face
Body Orange wool ribbed with orange silk thread

Hackle Grizzly
Wing Two grizzly neck hackles tied back to back and set high off the hook

CHAVENEY

Tail Golden pheasant tippet fibers
Body Grey wool ribbed with silver tinsel

Hackle Grizzly
Wing Natural brown bucktail

Note: The wing is often tied upright and divided on this Rogue pattern. The Blue Rogue is a variation of the Chaveney. It has a slate blue wool body, but is otherwise identical.

COMET

Any fly with an extremely long tail and hackle at the head qualifies as a Comet. Usually the fly is tied with bead-chain eyes. The original Comet is now called the Orange Comet. It had a tail of orange bucktail, a body of orange chenille ribbed with gold tinsel, and orange hackle at the head. (See Chapter 33 for a complete description of this development.)

CUMMINGS (Ward Cummings/Clarence Gordon)

Body Rear third yellow floss, front two-thirds claret wool, rib entire body with silver tinsel

Hackle Claret
Wing Natural brown bucktail

CURT'S SPECIAL

Tail Yellow hackle fibers
Butt Hot orange chenille
Body Silver tinsel

Hackle Orange.
Wing Natural brown bucktail, upright and divided

DEL COOPER (Mike Kennedy)

Tail Red hackle fibers
Body Purple wool ribbed with silver tinsel

Hackle Red
Wing White bucktail

DRAGON FLY (Bill Bakke)

Tail Deer body hair
Body Dubbing, any color
(*Note*: I like either black or burnt orange.)

Wing Deer body hair, divided and set nearly flat to the water
Head Deer body hair spun and clipped to shape

Note: The wing and head involve separate operations.

EVENING COACHMAN (Dry) (Walt Johnson)

Tag Flat silver tinsel, fluorescent orange floss over
Tail Golden pheasant crest feather

Body Peacock herl divided by a narrow band of fluorescent red floss
Hackle Stiff saddle, grizzly

FALL FAVORITE (Lloyd Silvius)

Body Flat silver tinsel
Hackle Red

Wing Orange bucktail

GENERAL MONEY NO. 1 (General Noel Money)

Tail Golden pheasant breast fibers
Body Rear two-fifths oval silver tinsel, front three-fifths black dubbing. Rib entire body with oval silver tinsel.

Hackle Burgundy
Wing Orange goose primary sections
Cheeks Jungle cock

GENERAL MONEY NO. 2 (General Noel Money)

Tail Golden pheasant crest
Body Black, wool or floss, ribbed with gold tinsel

Hackle Yellow
Wings Red goose primary sections

GOLDEN DEMON (Zane Grey)

Tail Golden pheasant crest
Body Embossed gold tinsel

Hackle Orange
Wing Natural brown bucktail

GOLDEN GIRL (Roderick Haig-Brown)

Tail Yellow or orange hackle fibers
Body Flat gold tinsel
Hackle Yellow

Wing Two golden pheasant tippet feathers matched back to back and enclosing orange polar bear hair
Topping Golden pheasant crest

GREEN BUTT SKUNK (Dan Callaghen)

Tail Red hackle fibers
Butt Fluorescent green chenille
Body Black chenille ribbed with flat silver tinsel

Hackle Black
Wing White bucktail

HORNER SILVER SHRIMP (Jack Horner)

Tail Gray bucktail. Tie in a second bunch of bucktail for the carapace.
Body Oval silver tinsel over a floss core. Space tinsel and palmer grizzly hackle in the spaces. Bring bucktail forward and tie off at the head.
Head Large, black, painted with a white iris and black pupil

JUICY BUG (Ben Chandler/Ike Tower)

Tail Red hackle fibers
Butt Black chenille
Body Red chenille ribbed with silver tinsel
Wing White bucktail tied upright and divided
Cheeks Jungle cock

KALAMA SPECIAL (Mooch Abrams)

Tail Red hackle fibers
Body Yellow chenille or yarn palmered with badger or grizzly
Wing White bucktail

This pattern is also known as the Kennedy Special after Mike Kennedy.

KISPIOX SPECIAL (Karl Mausser)

Tail Red polar bear
Body Hot orange chenille
Hackle Red
Wing White bucktail

LADY HAMILTON (Ralph Wahl)

Tail Red goose primary
Body Red floss ribbed with embossed silver tinsel
Wing Red over white bucktail, evenly divided
Head Black with a white iris and black pupil

LORD HAMILTON (Ralph Wahl)

Tail Red goose primary strip
Body Yellow floss ribbed with embossed silver tinsel
Wing Red over white bucktail, evenly divided
Head Black with a white iris and black pupil

LORD IRIS (Preston Jennings)

Tail Golden pheasant tippet fibers
Body Flat silver tinsel
Hackle Orange
Underwing Two orange saddle hackles, peacock sword fibers, two badger hackles
Overwing Red, orange, green, and blue goose primary strips married
Topping Golden pheasant crest

MACKS CANYON

Tail Orange and white hackle fibers, mixed
Body Rear third hot orange chenille or wool, front two-thirds black chenille. Rib entire body with flat silver tinsel.
Hackle Black
Wing White bucktail
Topping A few strands of orange bucktail

McLEOD UGLY (Ken and George McLeod)

Tail Red hackle "fuzz" from the base of the hackle

Body Black chenille palmered with grizzly hackle

Wing Black bucktail

MIGRANT ORANGE (Walt Johnson)

Tag Fluorescent orange floss over flat copper tinsel

Tail Fluorescent orange bucktail or hackle fibers, long

Body Fluorescent orange wool ribbed with flat copper tinsel

Wing Fluorescent orange bucktail

NITE OWL (Lloyd Silvius)

Tail Yellow hackle fibers

Butt Two turns of red chenille

Body Oval silver tinsel

Hackle Orange

Wing White Bucktail

OLD MARE

Tail Orange hackle fibers

Butt Green chenille

Body Red floss ribbed with narrow silver tinsel

Hackle Brown

Wing White bucktail, upright and divided

Note: This dressing is one of the many variations of the Rogue River Special.

OPTIC (Jim Pray)

Simple bucktail fly with a large head made from a split-brass bead or built up with tying thread. The head is painted with a large eye. Colors commonly used: Red, black, and red-and-yellow.

ORANGE HERON (Syd Glasso)

Body Rear two-thirds orange floss; front third orange seal. Rib entire body with medium flat silver tinsel.

Body Hackle Heron, one side stripped, wound beside rib

Throat Teal flank

Wing Four matching hot orange hackle tips, short, set low on the body

Head Red tying thread

ORANGE SHRIMP

Tip Gold tinsel.

Tail Red hackle fibers

Body Orange wool or chenille

Hackle Orange

Wing White bucktail

PARMACHENE BELLE (Henry P. Wells)

Tail Red and white hackle fibers

Body Yellow wool ribbed with silver tinsel

Hackle Red and white, mixed

Wing White bucktail

Topping Red bucktail

POLAR SHRIMP (Clarence Shoff)

Variation of the Orange Shrimp that substitutes white polar bear for the wing. Pattern is otherwise identical.

PURPLE PERIL (Ken McLeod)

Tail Purple hackle fibers

Body Purple; floss, chenille or wool dubbing.

Hackle Purple

Wing Natural brown bucktail

RAILBIRD (John Benn 1838–1907)

Tail Claret hackle fibers

Body Claret wool palmered with claret hackle

Hackle Yellow

Wing Teal or mallard

Cheeks Jungle cock

RED ANT

Tail Golden pheasant tippet fibers

Butt Peacock herl

Body Red floss

Hackle Brown

Wing Brown bucktail

Note: Wing is tied upright and divided on a double hook when fishing the lower Rogue.

ROGUE RIVER SPECIAL

Tail Orange hackle fibers

Body Rear third yellow wool, front two-thirds red wool. Rib entire body with silver tinsel.

Hackle Brown

Wing White bucktail or calf tail, upright and divided

ROYAL COACHMAN

Tail Golden pheasant tippet fibers

Body Peacock herl divided by a band of scarlet floss

Hackle Brown

Wing White bucktail

SILVER BLUE

Tip Silver wire

Tail Golden pheasant crest

Body Flat silver tinsel ribbed with narrow oval silver tinsel

Hackle Light blue

Wing Pintail flank

SILVER BROWN (Roderick Haig-Brown)

Tail Indian crow breast feather

Body Flat silver tinsel

Hackle Natural dark red

Wing Golden pheasant center tail strips

SKUNK (Mildred Krogel and Wes Drain, independently)

Tail Red hackle fibers

Body Black chenille ribbed with silver tinsel

Hackle Black

Wing White bucktail

SKYKOMISH SUNRISE (Ken and George McLeod)

Tail Red and yellow hackle fibers, mixed
Body Red wool or chenille ribbed with flat silver tinsel

Hackle Red and yellow, mixed
Wing White bucktail
Head Red tying thread

SOL DUC (Syd Glasso)

Tip Flat silver tinsel
Tail Golden pheasant crest
Body Rear half fluorescent orange floss, front half hot orange seal. Rib entire body with four or five turns of flat silver tinsel.

Hackle Yellow, starting at the second turn of tinsel
Throat Teal, one turn
Wing Four matching hot orange hackle tips
Topping Golden pheasant crest

STEELHEAD BEE (Roderick Haig-Brown)

Tail Fox squirrel, long
Body Divided into three sections of brown-yellow-brown dubbing or floss

Hackle Natural red
Wing Fox squirrel, divided and set well forward

THOR (Jim Pray)

Tail Orange hackle fibers
Body Red chenille

Hackle Brown
Wing White bucktail

UMPQUA SPECIAL

Tail White bucktail
Body Rear third yellow wool, front two-thirds red wool. Rib entire body with silver tinsel.
Hackle Brown

Wing White bucktail with a few strands of red bucktail on each side
Cheeks Jungle cock

VAN LUVEN (Harry Van Luven)

Tail Red hackle fibers
Body Red wool ribbed with silver tinsel

Hackle Brown
Wing White bucktail

WET SPIDER (Al Knudson)

Body Yellow chenille
Hackle Several turns of mallard flank. Grizzly is sometimes wound in first so that the mallard flank flares out.

WOOLLY WORM (Don Martinez)

Tail Red hackle fibers

Body Black chenille palmered with grizzly

BIBLIOGRAPHY

Anderson, David M., David P. Liscia and David W. Loomis. *North Umpqua River Fish Management Plan.* Oregon Department of Fish and Wildlife, 1986.

Arnold, Robert C. "Homage to Ken McLeod." *Flyfishing,* January–February 1986.

———"Walter Johnson, A Life on a River." *Flyfishing,* November–December 1987.

Bates, Joseph D., Jr. *The Art of the Atlantic Salmon Fly.* Boston: David R. Godine Publishers, Inc., 1987.

———*Atlantic Salmon Flies and Fishing.* Harrisburg: Stackpole Books, 1970.

Behnke, Robert J. "Still a Rainbow—By Any Other Name." *Trout,* Winter 1990.

———"The Family Tree: Origins of Trout and Salmon." *Trout,* Spring 1990.

———"How Many Species?" *Trout,* Summer 1990.

Brownlee, M. J. *An Update on the Fisheries Resources and Habitat Issues of the Skeena River Watershed.* A paper presented to the British Columbia Wildlife Federation's Skeena River Conference in Terrace, 1985.

Carrey, Johnny, Cort Conley, and Ace Barton. *Snake River of Hells Canyon.* Cambridge, Idaho: Backeddy Books, 1979.

Cassidy, Maureen and Frank Cassidy. *Proud Past, A History of the Wet'suwet'en of Moricetown, B.C.* Moricetown: Moricetown Band, 1980.

Chatham, Russell. *The Angler's Coast.* Livingston, MT: Clark City Press, 1991.

Cox-Rogers, S. *Scale Pattern Analysis of Skeena River Steelhead Trout (Salmo Gairdneri) Harvested Incidentally in the Area 4 Commercial Salmon Fishery: 1984–1985,* Smithers: SCR Bio-Resources Ltd., 1986.

Crawford, Doc. *North Umpqua Angler's Guide.* Portland: Frank Amato Publications, 1989.

Davy, Alfred G., Editor. *"The Gilly" A Flyfisher's Guide*. Portland: Frank Amato Publications, 1985.

DeVoto, Bernard, Editor. *The Journals of Lewis and Clark*. Boston: Houghton Mifflin Company, 1953.

Ecology and Management of Summer Steelhead in the Rogue River. Fishery Research Report Number 7, Oregon State Game Commission.

Engerbretson, Dave. "Sensational Skater for Steelhead and . . ." *Scientific Anglers' Fly Fishing Quarterly*, Fall 1989.

Fennelly, John. *Steelhead Paradise*. Mitchell Press Limited, 1963.

Fessler, James L. *An Ecological and Fish Cultural Study of Summer Steelhead in the Deschutes River, Oregon*. Portland: Oregon Wildlife Commission, 1973.

Flick, Art, Editor. *Art Flick's Master Fly-Tying Guide*. New York: Crown Publishers, Inc., 1972.

Grey, Zane. "The Best Fishing River in the U.S.A." *Argosy*, March 1973.

_____"North Umpqua Steelheads." *Sports Afield*, September 1935.

_____*Tales of Fresh-Water Fishing*. New York: A. S. Barnes and Company, 1928.

Haig-Brown, Roderick. *A River Never Sleeps*. Toronto: Collins, 1944; new edition, Lyons & Burford, 1991.

_____*The Western Angler*. New York: William Morrow and Company, 1947.

Holbrook, Stewart H. *The Columbia*. New York: Rinehart and Company, Inc., 1956.

Hopelain, James S. *Age, Growth, and Life History of Klamath River Basin Steelhead (Salmo Gairdnerii) As Determined From Scale Analysis*. State of California Department of Fish and Game, 1987.

Horncastle, G. S. *Life History of Steelhead Trout from the Somass River on Vancouver Island*, 1981.

Hydroelectric Development and Fisheries Resources on the Clackamas, Sandy, and Deschutes Rivers. Portland General Electric, 1988.

Jordan, David Starr and Barton Warren Evermann. *American Food and Game Fishes*. Doubleday, Page and Company, 1923.

Kiefer, Sharon Wallace. *An Annotated Bibliography on Recent Information Concerning Chinook Salmon in Idaho*. Idaho Chapter of the American Fisheries Society, 1987.

Koski, Charles H., Stephen W. Pettit, and John L. McKern. *Fish Transportation Oversight Team Annual Report—FY 1989, Transport Operations on the Snake and Columbia Rivers*. U.S. Department of Commerce: March 1990.

Kreider, Claude M. *Steelhead*. New York: G. P. Putnam's Sons, 1948.

Leggett, J. W. and D. W. Narver. *A Resumé of the Dean River Sport Fishery: 1971–75*.

Large, R. Geddes. *The Skeena: River of Destiny*. Sidney: Gray's Publishing Ltd., 1981.

Light, J.T., S. Fowler, and M.L. Dahlberg. *High Seas Distribution of North American Steelhead as Evidenced by Recoveries of Marked or Tagged Fish*. (Document submitted to the International North Pacific Fisheries Commission.) Seattle: Fisheries Research Institute, University of Washington, 1988.

_____C.K. Harris, and R.L. Burgner. *Ocean Distribution and Migration of Steelhead (Oncorhynchus mykiss, formerly Salmo gairdneri)*. Seattle: Fisheries Research Institute, University of Washington, 1989.

McGregor, Ian. "Freshwater Biology of Thompson River Steelhead *Salmo Gairdneri* As Determined By Radio Telemetry." University of Victoria, 1986.

McMillan, Bill. *Dry Line Steelhead.* Portland: Frank Amato Publications, 1987.

_____"What Remains When Hatchery Steelhead Fail?" *Salmon Trout Steelheader,* April–May, 1986.

Mott, Major Lawrence. "Umpqua Steelheads." *Forest and Stream,* July 1930.

Murphy, Leon W. and Howard E. Metsker. *Inventory of Idaho Streams Containing Anadromous Fish Including Recommendations for Improving Production of Salmon and Steelhead, Part II Clearwater River Drainage* U.S. Department of the Interior, 1962.

Narver, David W. *Age and Size of Steelhead Trout in the Babine River, British Columbia,* 1969.

Nehlsen, Willa, Jack E. Williams, and James Lichatowich. *Pacific Salmon at the Crossroads: Depleted Anadromous Fish Runs of the West Coast.* (Text of presentation given at American Fisheries Society, Oregon Chapter meeting.) February 1990.

O'Neill, M.J. and M. R. Whatley. *Bulkley River Steelhead Trout: A Report On Angler Use, Tagging, and Life History Studies Conducted in 1982 and 1983.* Smithers: British Columbia Ministry of Environment, 1984.

Proposed Mainstem Flows for Columbia Basin Anadromous Fish. Portland: Columbia Basin Fish and Wildlife Authority, 1990.

Raymond, Steve. *The Year of the Angler.* New York: Winchester Press, 1973.

Rogue Basin Fisheries Evaluation Program Adult Progress Report. Portland, U.S. Army Corps of Engineers, 1982.

Ryan, Jim, Jeff Cedarholm, Louis Halloin, and Jerry Thorson. *Preliminary Report Deforest Creek Landslide of March 1984.* Washington State Department of Natural Resources, 1984.

Scott, Jock. *Greased Line Fishing for Salmon: Compiled from the Fishing Papers of the late A. H. E. Wood, of Glassel.* London: Seely, Service, and Co. Ltd., 1935.

Spence, C. R., M. C. Beere and M. J. Lough. *Skeena River Steelhead Investigations 1986.* Smithers: British Columbia Ministry of Environment, 1990.

Sundborg, George. *Hail Columbia, The Thirty-Year Struggle for Grand Coulee Dam.* New York: The Macmillan Company, 1954.

Van Fleet, Clark C. *Steelhead to a Fly.* Boston: Little, Brown and Company, 1954.

Van Loan, Sharon and Patricia Lee. *Thyme and the River.* Portland: Graphic Arts Publishing Company, 1988.

Wahl, Ralph. *Come Wade the River.* Seattle: Superior Publishing Company, 1971.

Wharton, Joe. "Game Fish of Rogue River." *Forest and Stream,* June 1928.

Whatley, M. R. *Kispiox River Steelhead Trout: The 1975 Sport Fishery and Life History Characteristics from Anglers' Catches.* Fisheries Technical Circular No. 30, Smithers: Ministry of Recreation and Conservation, 1977.

_____W.E. Chudyk and M.C. Morris. *Morice River Steelhead Trout: The 1976 and 1977 Sport Fishery and Life History Characteristics from Anglers' Catches.* Smithers: Fish and Wildlife Branch, 1978.

Wulff, Lee. *The Atlantic Salmon.* New York: A. S. Barnes and Company, 1958; new edition, Lyons & Burford, 1982.

INDEX

A

Abrams, Mooch, 478
Acid Flashback, 422
Acroneuria abnormus, 336
Admiral, 473
Admiral Spey, 442
After Dinner Mint Muddler, 429
Aid, Bob, 420–21, Plate 12
Air B.C., 391
Al's Special, 473
Alaskabou, 421–22
Alec Jackson Spey (hook), 305
Allen, Zeke, 112, 113
Alspach, Bill, 158
Amato, Frank, 9, 130–35, 138–43, 292–94, Plate 9
American Fisheries Society's Committee on Names of Fishes, 6
Amethyst Spey, 443
Anchor River, 425
Arana, Arnold, 476
Arnold, Bob, 177–79, 195, 414, 423, 437–38, Plates 9, 12
Asam, Fred, 113
Ash River, 218

Association of Northwest Steelheaders, 162
Autumn Sedge, 68, 431–32
Axford, Rick, 218

B

Babine Lake, 274–76
Babine River, 267–78
Babine River Steelhead Lodge, 274
Bailey, Dan, 426
Bakke, Bill, 66, 130, 416–17, 477
Balek, Walt, 279, 284
Bardon, Claude, 96, 102–03
Bates, Joseph, 405, 442, 466
Beamer, Eric, 202, 206
Beardsley Trout, 5
Beauly Snow Fly, 399
Beige Caddis Pupae, 430
Beitelspacher, Ron, 149
Bella Coola River, 235
Benn, John, 480
Bergman, Ray, 118
Bertainia, Frank, 366
Bettzig, Bob, 443

Black and Orange Heron, 467
Black Ant, 474
Black Bear, 64
Black Bee, 434–35
Black Bomber, 391
Black Crawler, 411, 413
Black Diamond, 331
Black Estuary Shrimp, 313
Black Fitchtail, 388
Black Gnat Bucktail, 475
Black Gordon, 475
Black Krystal Flash Muddler, 426
Black Leech, 124
Black Marabou Practitioner, 406
Black Prince, 475
Black Skagit Spey, 419
Black Sky, 471
Black Steel Woolly, 450
Black Sundowner, 454
Black Witch, 396
Black, Dennis, 459–60
Blessing, Russell, 450
Blewett, Dick, 236, 244
Blood 'n Brandy, 463
Blood on the Waters, 422
Bloody Muddler, 158, 428
Blue and Bronze Sunset, 468

Blue Charm, 64–65, 388
Blue Heron, 467
Blue Heron Fly Shop, 456
Blue McGoon, 430
Blue Sky, 471
Blue Spade, 438
Boat Pool, 113
Bobbie Jean, 300
Boldt Decision, 203
Bomber, 370, 389
Bonneville Dam, 4, 146–47
Borden Special, 394
Borden's Prawn, 395
Borden, Bob, 393–95, Plates 10, 11
Bosquito, 475
Boss, 364, 475
Boss (Waller), 378
Boulder Creek, 415
Bowlin, Bert, 154
Boyanowsky, Ehor, 203, 227, 393
Brad's Brat, 64, 475
Bradner, Enos, 169, 175, 176–77, 315, 475
Brayshaw, Tommy, 215
Brazen Lady, 464
Bright Sienna, 464
Brindle Bug, 84, 475
Brocco, Steve, 395–97, Plate 2
Brooks, Joe, 268–69
Brooks, Mike, 397–401
Brown Drake, 84
Brown Hackle Peacock (Skater), 449
Brown Heron, 475
Brown Nymph, 365
Brown, Cecil, 274
Bucknall, Geoffrey, 440
Bucktail Coachman, 476
Bulkley Moose, 69, 492
Bulkley River, 245–57, 404
Bulkley River Samurai, 402
Bulkley, Colonel Charles S., 150
Bunnell Sisters, 386
Bunny Leech, 446
Burlap, 84, 476
Burlap Caddis Pupae, 430
Burnham, Fred, 97, 113
Butler, Clay, 321

C

Caddis Flash, 353
Caddis Pupae (Series), 430
Cade Canyon, 85
Callaghan, Dan, 120, 477
Candy Cane, 421
Candy Montana, 302
Canfield, Mark, 443, Plate 9
Capilene, 38
Car Body, 415
Carron, 409
Carson, 476
Carson, Sumner, 476
Carter, Clay, 262
Cartwright, John, 226
Caverly, Al, 226
Cebula, Jerry, 70, Plate 5
Celilo Falls, 135
Chandler, Ben, 478
Chappie, 84, 476
Chatham, Russell, 359, 366
Chaveney, 476
Chetco River, 366
Church, Frank, 153
Cigar Butt, 155, 391
Clackamas River, 274
Claret Guinea Spade, 309, 439
Claret Spey, 410
Clay, Bob, 71, 392, 453–54
Clearwater River, 144–67
Clegg, Pierce and Debbie, 274
Coal Car, 64, 324
Coal Car (Combs), 470
Cohen, Dr. Art, 402–03
Columbia River, 145–49
Comet, 476
Cook, George, 419, 421, 422, Plate 12
Coon Muddler, 123, 427
Cooney, Kevin, 422
Corkran, Duckie, 316
Cosseboom, John, 387
Craig, Mike, 259–63, 418, Plate 11
Crane, Pat, Plate 3
Creme-de-Menthe, 464
Cruickshank, Glenn, 157
Crystal Chenille Steelhead Woolly Bugger, 450

Cummings, 476
Cummings, Ward, 476
Cunningham, Bobby, 327
Curt's Special, 476

D

D'Ana Marie, 300
Damp Drake, 319
Damp flies, 68
Dana Montana, 302
Dark Ale, 464
Dark Daze, 415
Davis, Fay, 403–04
Dean Channel, 233–35
Dean River, 229–44
Dean River Lanterns, 402–03
DeBernardi, Joe, 114, 116
December Gold, 162
Deep Purple Spey, 317
Deer Creek, 172–73, 177–79
Deer Creek (Marabou Spider), 423
Deer Creek Policy Group, 178, 306
Deer Creek Restoration Fund, 178
Del Cooper, 477
Denise Montana, 302
Deschutes Madness, 348
Deschutes River, 130–43
Diablo Dam, 191
Diaz, Danny, 162
Disco Mouse, 370
Dodman, George, 234
Donnelly, Roy, 84, 475
Douglas, Brian, 69
Dragon Fly, 69, 417, 477
Dragon's Tooth, 415
Drain, Wes, 169, 198, 269, 480, Plate 9
Driedger, Ken, 404–05
Driftwood Lodge, 446
Drury, Colonel Esmond, 405
Duncan, Warren, Plate 5
Dusty Coachman, 318
Dworshak National Fish Hatchery, 4, 154
Dworshak, Henry, 153

E

Edge Bright, 403
Edmonds, Dale, 413–14
Electric Blue, 422–23
Elk River, 313
Elwha River, 297
Estuary Shrimp, 312–13
Evans, Glen, 386
Evening Coachman, 477
Ewell, John, 112, 113
Exum, Ed, 71

F

Fabian, John, 377
FAD 74, 404
FAD 78, 404
Fagerness, Doug, 150–51
Fall Caddis (Harry Lemire), 68, 131, 329
Fall Caddis (Mark Noble), 69
Fall Favorite, 477
Fall Hopper, 69
Farnworth, Dennis, 279, 285
Farrar, John, 35, 204, 227–33, 237–40, 418–20, 437, Plate 3
Farwest Lodges, 246, 369
Father Bill, 301
Fauna Boreali Americana, 5
Feeler Flies (Bill Schaadt), 364–66
Fennelly, John, 355
Ferry Canyon, 64, 324
Fiery Brown, 399
Fiorini, Buzz, 244, 328
Fishing International, 377
Flash Fly, 373
Flashabou Ugly Bug, 462
Flashback Nymph, 411–12
Flat Car, 324
Flick, Art, 388
Fluorescent Ugly Bug, 462
Fluttering Termite, 69, 452
Fly boxes, 41
Fly lines, 17–22, 24–28
Fly lines (Bob York), 381
Fly presentation, 56–76
Fly presentation (Mike

Maxwell), 336–37
Flymph (low-water series), 463–65
Franklin, Outdoor, 84, 476
Fraser River, 223–24
Freeman, Jim, 85
Freight Train, 322–23
Fulton River, 275

G

Gairdner, Dr., 5
Gallagher, Sean, 227, 406–07, 422–23, 444–45, Plates 5, 9, 11, 12
Gapen, Don, 426
Garrett's Shrimp, 304
Garrett, Jim, 295–304, Plate 7
Garry Dog, 458
Gearheart, Charlie, 434
General Money No. 1, 477
General Money No. 2, 477
General Money's Pool, 209
General Practitioner (Original), 405–06
Ghost Leech, 358
Gibbons, Dr. William P., 5
Gibbs Shrimp, 399
Gibson, Rainbow, 104
Glasso, Syd, 439–42, 466, 475, 479, 481, Plate 3
Gobin, Steve, 407–10, 423–24, Plates 3, 4, 12, 13
Godfrey, Will, 162
Gold Demon, 477
Gold Nymph, 365
Gold Spider, 444
Gold Streak, 442
Gold-N-West Flyfishers, 335
Golden Demon II, 348
Golden Edge Orange, 332
Golden Edge Yellow, 332
Golden Gate Angling and Casting Club, 363
Golden Girl, 477
Golden Heron, 349
Golden Spey, 317
Golden Stone, 123, 427
Golden Stone Hammerdown,

411–12
Gordon, Clarence, 110, 118, 119, 475, 476
Gore, Rusty, 166–67
Gorge Dam, 191
Grand Coulee Dam, 147
Grave Creek, 91
Graziosi, Jorge, 128
Greased Line Fall Caddis, 429
Greased Line Hopper, 429
Greased Line Shop, 428
Greased line, steelhead, 56–57
Greased line, traditional, 57–62
Greased Liner, 68, 330
Green Ant, 157
Green Butt, 388
Green Butt Skunk, 64, 477
Green Butt Skunk (Jimmy Green), 157
Green Butt Spey, 329
Green Butt Spider, 445
Green Dean River Lantern, 403
Green Drake, 84
Green Estuary Shrimp, 313
Green Heron, 467
Green, Jimmy, 157, 162, 196–97, 363
Green, Larry, 85
Green-Wing Bomber, 227, 392
Gregory, Myron, 362
Grenvik, Tim, 85–87
Grey Gordon, 119
Grey Heron, 410
Grey Nymph, 365
Grey, Loren, 116
Grey, Romer, 97, 114, 116
Grey, Zane, 94–104, 118, 128, 174, 386–87, 477
Griswold, Morley, 137–38
Grizzly Bomber, 389
Grizzly Hackle Peacock (Skater), 449
Grytness, Dawn, 416
Gualala River, 359

H

Hafele, Rick, 463
Haig-Brown, Roderick, 174–75,

184, 214–16, 445, 477, 480, 481
Haight, Phil, 461
Hairy Skpade, 439
Half and Half, 424
Half-pounders, 81–82
Hall, Dave, 411–13, 433
Hammerdown October Caddis, 412
Happy Camp, California, 85
Hardy's Favorite, 397
Hareline Dubbin, 393–394
Hargis, Merle, 111–12, 114
Harlequin Spey, 397
Harry Kari Bucktail, 331
Hathaway, Don, 390–91, 423, Plates 5, 6
Hauffler, Karl, 444, Plate 9
Hazel, John, 427
Headrick, Frank, 169, 176
Hellen's Fancy, 301
Helm, Reuben, 315
Hemingway, Jack, 162, 163
Herring Sea Habit, 456, 458–59
Hidy, Pete, 463
Hill, Tony, 244
Hilton Spider, 349
Hodson, Daryl, 236
Hoko Hummers (series), 303
Hoko River, 297–98
Holbrook, Dawn, 175
Holding water, 51–55
Holmberg, Roland, 54–55, 157, 230–31, 456–59, Plate 11
Hooks, 43–47
Hoopa Valley Indian Reservation, 88
Hooton, Bob, 217
Hopkins, Bill, 113
Horner Silver Shrimp, 478
Horner, Jack, 363, 478
Horny Shrimp, 406–07
Howard K. Miller Steelhead Park, 192
Howard Norton Special, 364
Howell, Joe, 121–25, 126–27, 427, 442, 456, Plates 6, 9
Hull, Bob, 437, 453–54
Hull, Royce, 246
Hume, Robert, 96

Hume, William, 146
Hunnicutt, Jimmy, 188, 189, 233, 237–38, 422–23, 438, 455, Plates 9, 11
Hunter, Cliff, 85–87
Hyatt's Caddis, 410
Hyatt, LeRoy, 158, 160–63, 410, 428, Plates 5, 6

I

Iliamna, Lake, 6
Iliaska Lodge, 446
Improvised Practitioner, 416
Inks, Dave, 375
Iris (Series), 318
Iron Gate Dam, 88

J

Jackson, Alec, 9, 178, 305–09, 439, Plates 9, 11
Jackson, Brad, 459–62
Jacob's Coat, 309
Jade River Guide Service, 411
Jennings, Preston J., 318, 478
Jim Green Special, 455
Johnson M.D., 303
Johnson, Alan, 155
Johnson, Les, 189, 310–13, 446, Plates 8, 11
Johnson, Walt, 128, 169–80, 198, 314–19, 415, 477, 479, Plate 8
Joy, Audrey, 386
Juicy Bug, 478

K

Kalama River, 417
Kalama River Dynamite, 416
Kalama Special, 478
Kambietz, Joe, 445
Kamchatka Peninsula, 4, 7
Kamloops Trout, 5
Kate, 301
Kaufmann's Streamborn, 322,

451, 453, Plates 9, 10
Kaufmann's Stone, 433
Kaufmann, Lance, 131, 322
Kaufmann, Oda, 322
Kaufmann, Randall, 131, 320–25, 427, Plate 8
Kelson, George M., 409
Kennedy, Mike, 477
Kimsquit, B.C., 235
King, Grant, 363, 366
Kinney, Mike, 413–15, 422, Plate 3
Kispiox Bright, 381
Kispiox Dark, 382
Kispiox River, 258–66, 381, 403–04
Kispiox River Resort, 381
Kispiox River Shrimp, 417
Kispiox Special, 478
Klamath River, 81–89
Knots, 30, 33–34
Knouse, 349
Knouse, Stan and Yvonne, 120
Knudson, Al, 168, 198, 443, 473, 481, Plate 9
Koler, Steve, 141
Kozak, Myron, 247
Kraemer, Curt, 172, 204–06
Krieder, Claude, 83–84, 118, 184
Krieger, Mel, 446–47
Krogel, Mildred, 121, 480
Krystal Bullet, 393–94

L

L.P. Special, 445
Lady Caroline, 65
Lady Hamilton, 478
Lambuth, Letcher, 175
Lannigan, Craig, 162
Laporte, Andre, Plate 6
Lawson, Dick, 293–94
Leaders, 32
Leggett, Jack, 235
Leisenring, Jim, 463
Leiser, Eric, 410
LeMert, Jimmy, 442–43
Lemire's Irresistible, 331

Lemire's Winter Fly, 329
Lemire, Harry, 68, 131, 188, 193–95, 220, 244, 326–33, Plates 6, 8
Leven, Mel, 152, 163
Lewis and Clark Expedition, 135
Lewiston Dam, 88
Libby's Black, 302
Lisa Bell, 332
Lochsa River, 155
Lord Hamilton, 478
Lord Iris, 467, 478
Low and Clear Spider, 444
Low Water Bee, 464
Low water flies, 62–64
Low Water Green, 383
Lower Granite Dam, 162

M

MacGarrett, 301
MacIntosh, 123
Macks Canyon, 64, 478
Mad River, 363
Madsen, Ejnar, 274
Mai Tai, 465
Managing hooked steelhead, 77–78
Marabou Spey, 418–20
Marabou Spiders (Bob Aid), 420–21
Martuch, Leon, 184
Mathews, Craig, 337
Matuka Muddler, 426
Mausser, Karl, 261–62, 478
Maxwell, Denise, 251–55, 335–36
Maxwell, Mike, 67, 73, 250–55, 334–37, 433, Plate 6
McGregor, Ian, 224
McGuane, Tom, 366
McKenzie River, 397
McKenzie Sapphire, 400
McLeod Ugly, 175, 479
McLeod, Ken and George, 169, 176, 198, 479, 480, 481
McMillan, Bill, 9, 57, 73, 130, 338–43, 451, Plate 10
McNae, Bruce, 233, 239

McNeese Madness, 350
McNeese's Fly Shop, 347–348
McNeese, Dave, 66, 345–53, Plate 1, 2, 6
Meiggs, BJ, 139–40, 200
Methow River, 51
Meyers, Kate, 8
Midnight Spey, 432
Midnight Sun, 470
Migrant Orange, 479
Miller, Lynn (Radar), 163–67
Miller, Russ, 186–87
Miltenberger, Gary, 9, 279–89, 354–57
Minktail, 388
Mintz, John, 402, Plate 5
Miramichi River, 155
Missoulian Spook, 426
Money, Brigadier General Noel, 210–13, 215–16, 477
Mono loops, 30
Montella, Richie, 259–63
Moore, Frank and Jeanne, 119–21
Moose Turd, 391
Morice River, 248
Mott Trail, 113
Mott, Major Jordan Lawrence, 112
Moulin Rouge, 465
Mouse, 69, 369–70
Muddled Skunk, 425
Muddler Minnow, 64, 425

N

Nakia Lodge, 244
Nash, Gordon, 453
Nasti Nymph, 365
National Marine Fisheries Service, 149
Natural Crawler, 413
Nauheim, Bob, 359–62, 366, 447
Navarro River, 9
Nicola River, 51
Night Dancer, 64, 294
Night Train, 301
Nite Owl, 479

Noble, Mark, 69, 428–30, Plate 6
Noble, Scott, 430–32, Plates 6, 8
Norlakes Lodges, 274
North Fork Stillaguamish River, 168–80, 316
North Pacific Fisheries Commission, 4
North Santiam River, 347
North Umpqua Lodge, 118–19
North Umpqua River, 109–29
Nymphs, 433

O

O'Byrne, "Umpqua Vic", 128
Ocean Migration of Steelhead, 3, 4
October Caddis, 66
October Spey, 452
Old Mare, 479
Olive Krystal Flash Muddler, 426
Olympic Stonefly Series, 298–99
Oncorhynchus, 6–7
Optic, 479
Optical Black, 465
Orange and Black Bomber, 390
Orange Blossom (Mike Brooks), 400
Orange Bomber, 393
Orange Caddis Pupae, 430
Orange Charm, 64–65, 388
Orange Dean River Lantern, 403
Orange Estuary Shrimp, 313
Orange Gordon, 119
Orange Heron, 410, 479
Orange Heron I, 442
Orange Heron II, 442
Orange Scooter, 123, 427
Orange Shrimp, 479
Orange Skagit Spey, 420
Orange Spider, 445
Orange Sundowner, 454
Orange Sunset, 468
Orange Witch, 396
Orange-Butt Spade, 438
Oregon Trout, 417

Orleans Barber, 84
Oso Special, 433–34

P

Paint Brush, 342–43
Pale Peril, 350
Pale Perl, 350
Parkening, Duke, 152
Parmacheene Belle, 479
Parmeter, Gene, 425
Pate, Billy, 129, 290, 433
Patricia, 452
Patrick's Fly Shop, 442
Patrick, Roy, 443
Patriot, 293–94
Peacock Caddis Pupae, 430
Pelton Dam, 136
Pero, Tom, 125
Peterson M.D., 302
Pettit, Steve, 148–49
Pierce, Bob, 445
Pinch, Mark, 279, 284, 435,
    Plate 5
Pink Estuary Shrimp, 313
Pink Pearl, 470
Pink Shrimp, 434
Pink Sundowner, 454
Pinkut Creek, 275
Pixie's Revenge, 422
Poet, Dick, 236
Polar Flash, 378
Polar Shrimp, 387, 480
Polar Shrimp (dark), 409
Polar Shrimp (light), 409
Polar Shrimp (Mike Brooks),
    400
Polar Shrimp Spey, 442
Polar Spade, 438
Polypropylene, 38
Popsicle, 422
Port Alberni, B.C., 213
Portland Creek, 65
Potlatch Corporation, 154
Powell, Walton, 85
Pray, Jim, 184, 362, 386–87,
    479, 481
Prichard, Al, 416
Princeton Tiger, 153

Prismatic Spey, 432
Pryce-Tannatt, T.E., 409
Purple Bad Habit, 423
Purple Bomber, 390, 393
Purple Brat, 350
Purple Flash, 324
Purple Heart, 467
Purple Heart Spey, 467
Purple Hilton, 351
Purple Jesus, 357
Purple King, 410
Purple Krystal Flash Muddler,
    426
Purple Marabou, 424
Purple Peril, 64, 480
Purple Polar Bear Matuka, 351
Purple Porcupine, 357
Purple Prince, 351
Purple Skunk, 155
Purple Smuddler, 427–28, Plate
    9
Purple Sol Duc Spey, 467
Purple Spey, 352, 410
Purple Spider, 444
Purple Sundowner, 455
Purple Ugly, 356
Purple Witch, 396
Puyans, Andy, 375

Q

QE-3, 300
Queets River, 321–22

R

Railbird, 480
Rain gear, 40–41
Rainie Falls, 97
Raymond, Steve, 175
Red Ant, 480
Red Dean River Lantern, 403
Red Dog, 401
Red Shrimp, 317
Red Steel Woolly, 450
Red Sundowner, 455
Redwing, 353
Reels, 28–29

Reeser, Chris, 246
Reiff's Shrimp, 434
Reiff, Dan, 206, 424, 434–35,
    Plate 11
Reily, Eustis, 251–55
Rice, Ed, 366
Riffle Dancer, 69, 282, 435
Riffle Express, 69, 435–36
Riffling hitch, 65, 416
Rippa's Revenge, 436–37
Rippa, Bob, 436
Roberts, Don, 125, 206–08,
    219–23, 428
Robertson Creek Hatchery, 217
Robertson, Doug, 355–56
Rock Creek Hatchery, 111
Rockport, Washington, 192
Roelofs, Terry, 358
Rogue River, 90–108
Rogue River fly patterns, 105
Rogue River Special, 480
Ross Dam, 191
Round Butte Dam, 136
Royal Blue, 465
Royal Coachman, 480
Royal Flush, 423
Royal Humpy, 67
Royal Spey, 317
Royal Wulff, 67
Rudd, Donald G., 57
Russian River, 361, 365–66
Rusty Bomber, 393
Rusty Heron, 468
Rusty Rat, 397
Rusty Sky, 471
RVI, 401

S

Salmon Fly (Skater), 449
Salmon River, 163–67
Salmon, sockeye, 274–76
Saltzman, Salty, 290, 381
San Juan Spider, 444
San Leandro Creek, 5
Santiam River, South Fork, 397
Sara Teen, 300
Sarp's Seducer, 425

Sarp, Tony, 424–25
Sauk River, 192
Sauk River Grub, 309
Sauk River Shrimp, 309
Scarlet Lightning, 424
Schaadt's Nymph, 365
Schaadt, Bill, 84, 359–67
Schadrech, Collin, 245–49, 268–70
Schneider, Dale, 270
Schwab, Peter, 84
Schwiebert, Ernest, 388
Scott, Jock, 57–63
Sean's Prawn, 406
Selway River, 155
Semi-Respectable, 424
Septober Caddis Series, 304
Septober Candy, 303
Septober Orange, 303
Septober Pheasant, 303
Seth, LeRoy, 162
Sherars Falls, 137
Sherman, Marty, 157, 394, 456
Shoff, Clarence, 386–87, 480
Shoshone-Bannock Tribes, 149
Showgirl, 422
Sieracki, Carl J., 248
Signal Light, 64, 323, 378
Silver Blue, 480
Silver Brown, 480
Silver Hilton, 84
Silver Hilton Lodge, 269–74, 436
Silver Streak, 442
Silvius, Lloyd, 84, 362, 475, 477, 479
Simpson, Larry, 89
Siuslaw River, 397
Skagit Monster, 424
Skagit River, 190–208, 413–14
Skamania steelhead, 179, 417
Skating flies, 68
Skeena Nymph, 437
Skeena Woolly Bugger, 382
Skpade, 439
Skunk, 64, 480
Skunk (Alec Jackson), 308
Skykomish Dark, 409
Skykomish Light, 409
Skykomish River, 4, 181–89

Skykomish Sunrise, 175, 182, 481
Skykomish Sunrise (Combs), 470
Smith River, 366
Smith, Harry, 387
Smith, Jedediah, 100
Smithers, A.W., 250
Smithers, British Columbia, 250
Snake River, 156
Snohomish River, 181–82
Snoqualmie River, 181
Sol Duc, 481
Sol Duc River, 295
Sol Duc Spey, 468
Somass River, 213
Soul Duck, 301
Spade, 437–39
Spade (Alec Jackson), 308
Spawning Purple, 352
Spawning Spey, 352
Spectral Spider, 318
Spence, Mark, 209, 218
Spences Bridge, British Columbia, 223
Spey Flies, 439–43
Spiders, 443–45
Splices, 30–31
Spring Favorite, 382
Spring Spey, 452
Springer Green, 318
Sputterkicker, 239
Squamish Poacher, 445
Squirrel and Teal, 331
Stamp River, 209–18
Stamp, Captain Edward, 213
Steamboat Creek, 111
Steamboat Inn, 119–20
Steelhead Bee, 67, 481
Steelhead Bee (Brian Douglas), 69, 445–46
Steelhead Bomber, 70, 392
Steelhead Bunny, 446–47
Steelhead Caddis, 66, 68, 340–41, Plate 9
Steelhead Carey, 444–45
Steelhead Charlies, 447–48
Steelhead Dry, 68, 430
Steelhead Irresistible, 472
Steelhead Muddler, 428
Steelhead Rat, 401

Steelhead Sculpin, 332
Steelhead Skater, 70, 378
Steelhead Skater (LeRoy Hyatt), 450
Steelhead Skaters, 448–50
Steelhead Stick, 439
Steelhead Sunset, 468
Steelhead Valhalla Lodge, 279, 356
Steelhead Woolly Buggers, 450
Steelhead, Babine River life history, 276–78
Steelhead, Dean River life history, 241–43
Steelhead, distribution, 7; life history, 7; taxonomy, 6–7
Steelhead, Kispiox River life history, 263–66
Steelhead, Klamath River life history, 88–89
Steelhead, Morice River life history, 256–57
Steelhead, Rogue River life history, 106–08
Steelhead, Stamp River life history, 216–18
Steelhead, Stanley Basin, 166
Steelhead, Sustut River life history, 286–89
Stetzer, Randy, 138, 451–52
Stewart, Bob, 236
Stewart, Chick and Marilyn, 274
Sto:lo Nation, 223
Stonebreaker, Keith, 153, 155, 156, 448
Stratman Fancy, 352
Street Walker, 452
String Leech, 453
Stroebel, Bob, 162, 244, 306, 328
Sullivan, Virgil, 364, 475
Sundowner (Series), 454–55
Sunglasses, 41–42
Suskeena Lodge, 355
Suskwa River, 248
Sustut Boss, 357
Sustut River, 279–89
Sustut Sunrise, 357
Sweet Loretta, 455
Sylbert, Dick, 424, 439

T

T.C.-3, 301
Tackle, 11–16
Tackle bags, 40
Taiwanese high seas netting, 4
Takahashi, George, 97, 101, 103, 114
Tan Estuary Shrimp, 313
Tarantino, John, 363
Tawny Port, 465
Teeny fly lines, 372–74
Teeny Leech, 373–74
Teeny Nymph, 372–74
Teeny Nymph Company, 372
Teeny, Donna, 373
Teeny, Jim, 366, 371–74, Plate 10
Telkwa Nymph, 433
Telkwa River, 248
Telkwa Stonefly, 337
Telkwa, British Columbia, 249–50
Tequila Sunrise, 421
Teresa's Tease, 300
Tetreau, Ron, 286
The .08, 404–05
The Stewart, 456
Thomas, Rai, 355–356
Thompson River, 51, 219–28, 311–12
Thompson River Caddis, 68, 330
Thompson River Caddis, (Stan Young), 472
Thompson River Rat, 227, 393
Thompson Special, 382
Thompson, David, 219
Thompson, Roy Angus, 387
Thor, 481
Thoresen, Walter, 184
Tiger's Paw, 456
Toutle River, 51
Tower, Ike, 478
Trask River, 353
Travel rods, 42
Trinity, 84
Trinity fly patterns, 299
Trinity River, 83
Trolitsch, Gerhardt, 244
Trueblood, Ted, 144, 152, 366
Tube Flies, 456–59

Tucker, Gary, 89
Tulalip Indians, 4
Turkey Tracker, 415

U

Ugly Bug, 459–62
Ultimate Leech, 358
Umpqua Feather Merchants, 411, 459, Plate 6
Umpqua Spade, 439
Umpqua Special, 116, 481

V

Van Demark, Dick, 463–65, Plate 9
Van Fleet, Clark C., 118
Van Iderstine, Ron, 401
Van Loan, Jim and Sharon, 121, 358
Van Luven, 481
Van Luven, Harry, 481
Variegated Ugly Bug, 462
Vests, 39
Veverka, Bob, 408, 466–68, Plates 4, 14
Vincent, Jim, 200–01

W

Waders, 37–38
Wagoner, Bob, 157, 402–03, 410, 447, 448–50, 454–55, Plates 6, 10
Wahl, Ralph, 84, 169, 190, 198–99, 269, 478
Waking flies, 68
Walbaum, Johann, 7
Walker, Olga, 9, 262, 379, 403
Wallace, Stew, 406, 436, Plate 11
Waller Waker, 69, 377
Waller, Lani, 269–74, 276, 375–78, 453, Plate 5
Ward's Wasp, 153
Ward, Ed, 152
Washington Fly Fishing Club, 175
Washougal Olive, 341

Washougal River, 179, 339, 452
Weasku Inn, 104–05
Weiler, Art, 316
Weitchpec Witch, 84
Wells Dam, 51
Wells, Henry P., 479
Wells, Jerry, 434
Wells, Sam, 384, 386
West, Howard, 372, 377
Wet Spider, 443, 481
Wet, suwet, en Indians, 250
Wharton, Joe, 94–95, 386
Whaka Blonde, 309
White Skagit Spey, 420
Whitlock, Dave, 426
Wiborn, Lone Angler, 97, 114
Wickwire, Bob, 273–74, 366
Wickwire, Jud, 271, 273, 436, Plate 5
Wild and Scenic Rivers Act of 1968, 94
Wilders, Dennis, 235, 236
Wiley, Warren, 357
Willamette River, 397
Winchester Dam, 111
Winter Orange, 469
Winter Red, 469
Winter Rose, 469
Winter Series (Trey Combs), 468–70, Plate 11
Winter's Hope, 207, 343–44
Winter's Hope (Combs), 470
Wintle, Jerry, 203–06, 437
Wolf, Mike, 217
Wood, Arthur, 57, 73
Wood, Bubba, 71
Woolridge, Glen, 103, 104–05
Wooly Worm, 481
Wulff, Lee, 39, 65, 316

Y

Yellow and Black Bomber, 390
Yellow Ant, 319
Yellow Dean River Lantern, 403
Yellow Guinea Spade, 309, 439
Yellow Skagit Spey, 420
York, Bob, 206, 379–83
Young, Paul, 316
Young, Stan, 439, 471–72, Plate 8